Harold Pinter

Harold Pinter was born in London in 1930. He is married to Antonia
Fraser. In 1995 he won the David Cohen British Literature Prize, awarded
for a lifetime's achievement in literature. In 1996 he was given the Laurence
Olivier Award for a lifetime's achievement in theatre. In 2002 he was made a
Companion of Honour for services to literature. In 2005 he received the
Wilfred Owen Award for Poetry, the Franz Kafka Award (Prague) and the
Nobel Prize for Literature. In 2006 he was awarded the Europe Theatre
Prize.

Michael Billington has been the *Guardian* theatre critic since 1971. He is a
regular broadcaster on radio and television arts programmes. His previous
books are on Peggy Ashcroft, Ken Dodd, Alan Ayckbourn and Tom
Stoppard. He has also published a collection of theatre criticism, *One Night
Stands*, and he edited *Directors on 'Twelfth Night'*. He is a Visiting Professor
at King's College London and an Honorary Fellow of St Catherine's
College, Oxford.

Harold Pinter

Michael Billington

faber and faber

First published in hardback 1996
by Faber and Faber Limited
3 Queen Square London WC1N 3AU

Previous editions published as *The Life and Work of Harold Pinter*

Paperback edition first published in 1997

This revised paperback edition first published 2007

The Nobel lecture was delivered by Harold Pinter on 7 December, 2005

Designed by Humphrey Stone
Photoset by RefineCatch Limited, Bungay, Suffolk
Printed in England by Mackays of Chatham plc, Chatham, Kent

Excerpts from *Conversations with Pinter* by Mel Gusson
reprinted by permission of Nick Hern Books Ltd,
14 Larden Road, London W3 7ST

Extract from 'I'm Explaining a Few Things' translated by Nathaniel Tarn,
from *Pablo Neruda: Selected Poems*, published by Jonathan Cape, London, 1970,
used by permission of The Random House Group

A CIP record for this book
is available from the British Library

ISBN 978–0–571–23476–9
ISBN 0–571–23476–3

10 9 8 7 6 5 4 3 2 1

Contents

Illustrations vii

Preface x

One Hackney Lad 1

Two Romantic Ireland 26

Three Baron Hardup 45

Four Early Stages 66

Five Playwright in Waiting 88

Six Power Play 114

Seven Sexual Politics 131

Eight Family Values 155

Nine Private Worlds 179

Ten Time Regained 203

Eleven Pinter's Way 221

Twelve States of Revolution 234

Thirteen Private Lives 257

Fourteen Voices from the Past 276

Fifteen Public Affairs 286

Sixteen Setting the Agenda 306

Seventeen Party Manners 321

Eighteen Moonlit Nights 339

Nineteen Festival Time 348

Twenty Onwards and Upwards 363

Twenty-One Memory Man 388

Afterword 'Let's Keep Fighting' 395

Appendix Art, Truth & Politics: The Nobel Lecture 431

Select Bibliography 443

Index 447

Illustrations

1 A Pinter Wedding, 9 June 1926: Harold Pinter's parents, Jack and Frances (née Moskowitz), flanked by his paternal and maternal grandparents

2 The evacuee: Harold Pinter at Caerhays, 1940

3 Harold Pinter with his father, 1946

4 Harold Pinter as Macbeth with Ron Percival as Lady Macbeth, Hackney Downs Grammar School, 1947 (© Lionel Fitzgerald)

5 Harold Pinter with Ron Percival, Henry Woolf, Morris Wernick and B. J. Law

6 On the road in Ireland with Anew McMaster, 1952

7 On tour in Galway: Barry Foster, Pauline Flanagan, Harold Pinter, 1952

8 Pinter as a saturnine Iago to McMaster's Othello and as a romantic Bassanio

9 The Anew McMaster Company after a performance of Wilde's *Lady Windermere's Fan*, 1951

10 Harold Pinter on tour in L. du Garde Peach's farce *A Horse! A Horse!* in 1954

11 Beatrix Lehmann as Meg and Richard Pearson as Stanley in *The Birthday Party* at the Lyric, Hammersmith, 1958

12 The week's receipts

13 Robert Shaw (Aston) and Donald Pleasence (Davies) in the New York production of *The Caretaker*, 1962 (British Arts Council)

14 A Japanese Davies in the Tokyo production of *The Caretaker* in 1967, and Sacha Pitoeff (Aston) and Jacques Dufilo (Davies) in the Paris revival of 1969 (© Nicolas Treatt, Paris)

15 Ian Holm (Lenny) and Vivien Merchant (Ruth) in Peter Hall's production of *The Homecoming*, Aldwych, 1965 (© Friedman-Abeles)

16 James Fox, Joseph Losey and Harold Pinter on the set of *The Servant*, 1962

17 Harold Pinter, John Fowles and Karel Reisz during the shooting of *The French Lieutenant's Woman*, 1980

18 Ralph Richardson (Hirst) and John Gielgud (Spooner) in Peter Hall's production of *No Man's Land* at the Old Vic, 1975

19 Paul Eddington (Spooner) and Harold Pinter (Hirst) in David Leveaux's revival of *No Man's Land* at the Almeida, 1993 (© Ivan Kyncl)

20 Michael Gambon (Jerry) and Penelope Wilton (Emma) in Peter Hall's production of *Betrayal* at the Lyttelton, 1978 (© Sally Fear)

21 Harold Pinter (Deeley) and Liv Ullmann (Anna) in David Jones's revival of *Old Times*, 1985–6

22 Harold Pinter and Peggy Ashcroft during the BBC Radio recording of *Family Voices*, 1981

23 Alan Bates (Nicholas) and Jenny Quayle (Gila) in *One for the Road* at the Lyric, Hammersmith, 1985 (© Ivan Kyncl)

24 Miranda Richardson as Young Woman in *Mountain Language* at the Lyttelton, 1988 (© Ivan Kyncl)

25 Gawn Grainger (Douglas), Dorothy Tutin (Melissa) and Barry Foster (Gavin) in *Party Time* at the Almeida, 1991 (© Ivan Kyncl)

26 Harold Pinter (Roote) and Tony Haygarth (Lush) in *The Hothouse*, revived at the Chichester Festival Theatre and the Comedy Theatre, 1995 (© Ivan Kyncl)

27 Harold Pinter with Vaclav Havel in Prague in 1988

28 Harold Pinter with the Nicaraguan poet Ernesto Cardenal, 1987

29 Harold Pinter and Antonia Fraser on their marriage day in 1980 (© *Daily Telegraph*)

30 Harold Pinter in his Holland Park studio, 2002 (© Eamonn McCabe 2005)

31 Harold Pinter and his step-granddaughter, Eliza Fraser, 2000

32 Harold Pinter and Antonia Fraser, Turin, 1996. 'Il Ritorno a Casa'

33 Antonia Fraser, with Harold Pinter, outside Buckingham Palace celebrating the award of her CBE, 1999

34 Corin Redgrave (Hirst) and Andy de la Tour (Briggs) in *No Man's Land*, National Theatre, London, 2001 (© Ivan Kyncl)

35 Keith Allen, Lia Williams, Lindsay Duncan, Andy de la Tour, Susan Wooldridge and Steven Pacey as the diners in *Celebration* at the Almeida Theatre, London, 2000 (© Ivan Kyncl)

36 Gina McKee (Kate), Jeremy Northam (Deeley), Helen McCrory (Anna) in *Old Times*, Donmar Warehouse, London, 2004 (© Ivan Kyncl)

37 Michael Gambon and Harold Pinter at the Gate Theatre, Dublin, 2005, on the occasion of Pinter's 75th birthday celebrations (© Shane McCarthy)

38 Harold Pinter in *Krapp's Last Tape*, Royal Court Theatre, London, 2006 (© John Haynes)

39 Harold Pinter on the steps of his house after the announcement of the award for the Nobel Prize for Literature, 2005 (© Martyn Hayhow/ AFP/Getty Images)

40 Harold Pinter, with his Italian translator Alessandra Serra, receiving the Europe Theatre prize, 2006 (© epa/Ansa)

41 Harold Pinter, 2005 (© REUTERS/Kieran Doherty)

All photographs not otherwise credited are by kind permission of Harold Pinter.

Preface

In the winter of 1992/93 I was asked by Faber and Faber if I would be interested in writing a short book about Harold Pinter: about his work, his political ideas and the way in which these relate to his life. The word 'short' now seems rather ironic. In the course of the research and writing, the book has grown into the current somewhat lengthy blend of analysis and biography.

There are several reasons for this. Even though there are numerous excellent critical studies of Pinter's work (not least, Martin Esslin's), there are hardly any that seek to place the work in the developing context of his life. It has always been assumed that the plays sprang more or less fully formed from his imagination and were largely divorced from private circumstance. The more I discovered about the plays, however, the more they seemed to be connected to Pinter's recollections of his own experience. Yet there is another, more crucial, reason why the book grew in scale and changed in format as it went along, which has to do with the attitude of Harold Pinter himself. He has always been a man who jealously guards his private life from journalistic intrusion, but he agreed to sit down with me on a number of occasions and talk about his past, not least his early days in Hackney. He also gave me access to his immaculately preserved cuttings books, and made it clear that I was at liberty to talk to his friends and colleagues. Antonia Fraser, his second wife, was also enormously helpful, both in exploring the Pinter family background and in providing insights into her husband's character and work.

I am extremely grateful to the Pinters for their help; but the book was not conceived as the definitive biography. It is, rather, a highly subjective interpretation of Pinter's work as seen in the context of his life. It is also an attempt to unlock some of the mysteries and answer some of the questions surrounding the two. Cyril Connolly once attacked the tendency of modern criticism to explain a writer in terms of his sexual experience or economic background: 'I still believe', he wrote, 'that this technique remains the soundest basis for a diagnosis, that it should be possible to learn as much about an author's income and sex life from one paragraph of his writing as from his cheque stubs and his love letters.' I have some sympathy with Connolly, which is why the bulk of my book focuses on Pinter's writing: his obsessive themes and dramatic method. But in many quarters Pinter is seen as an enigmatic writer, and accordingly I have tried to show how one key to the enigma is the way his major plays are all informed by some crucial life experience. In the end, nothing can explain how a work of art is achieved; biographical information can occasionally open one's eyes.

This book could not have been written without a good deal of help from various people who, either through interview or correspondence, supplied me with invaluable information. I happily acknowledge my debt to them all: Anthony Astbury, Joan Bakewell, Michael Bakewell, Melvyn Bragg, Barbara Bray, Adrian Brine, Michael Codron, Kenneth Cranham, Alan Curtis, Judy Daish, Eileen Diss, Paul Eddington, Susan Engel, Barry Foster, Donald Freed, Michael Goldstein, Gawn Grainger, Simon Gray, Kenneth Haigh, Peter Hall, Dilys Hamlett, Ronald Harwood, David Jones, Jill Johnson, Eric Kahane, B. J. Law, David Leveaux, Andrew Lovibond, Ian McEwan, Christopher Morahan, Arthur Miller, Jennifer Mortimer, Edna O'Brien, Roger Lloyd Pack, Donald Pleasence, Auriol Smith, Guy Vaesen, Morris Wernick, Henry Woolf.

Other people also deserve special mention for their extraordinary kindness and help: Sally Brown, curator of modern literary manuscripts at the British Library, who gave me valuable access to the Pinter Archive; Humphrey Carpenter, who generously sent me copies of BBC documents relating to Pinter's early years; Francis Gillen, who sent me every edition of the *Pinter Review*, an annual treasure-trove for all students of the work and which informed much of my thinking; Caroline Keely, who was Pinter's secretary during the period of the book's writing and who patiently answered any number of queries; and Fiona McLean, who produced for Radio 3 a sixtieth-birthday programme on Pinter which I presented and who, in a sense, set me off on the trail.

The book could not have been written without the help of many of Pinter's old friends and theatrical colleagues. They have provided me with information, offered critical insights and stimulated thought; but in the end, the opinions expressed both about Pinter's work and life are entirely and argumentatively my own.

One Hackney Lad

Evening. Winter. A room in Holland Park lined with books, manuscripts, family photographs. Two men talking. The occupant of the room is Harold Pinter, the visitor is myself. He is relaxed, hospitable, secure in his favourite chair; I am the inevitable invader of his territory. He pours a generous glass of white wine and jokingly recalls how a previous visitor mistook the tiny drinks-stool he placed in front of her for a seat on which she precariously perched. I make a mental note not to make the same mistake. But it's a measure of Pinter's hold on our imagination that even a professional encounter is shadowed by recollections of his plays: the notion that any conversation between two people conceals a tactical battle for advantage. What also comes across as we rake over his past is the imagistic nature of his memory. Key episodes of his youth are recalled with intense clarity, but he is often vague on precise dates. As his wife Antonia Fraser later tells me, 'Harold's memory is not linear at all. He's got a memory like a camera as if he's taking shots. Occasionally they are moving photographs: extraordinarily sharp and vivid, but not necessarily connected.' Memory is a theme that will recur throughout all my conversations with Pinter.

I am at the start of an attempt to crack the Pinter code. Who is he? What makes him tick? Why do his plays have such tenacity? And why is it that they have reached out far beyond the hermetic world of drama addicts to become part of the general culture? Even those who rarely set foot inside a theatre have heard of the Pinter pause, and the epithet 'Pinteresque' is now included in *The New Shorter Oxford English Dictionary*: 'of, pertaining to, or characteristic of the British playwright, Harold Pinter, or his works', it somewhat evasively says. It further defines the word through an example culled from the *Listener*: 'Everyone talked like overheard conversations . . . They invented a word for it – Pinteresque.' Who is this mysterious figure who has spawned his own adjective?

Harold Pinter was born on 10 October 1930 in Hackney, just beyond the borders of the traditional East End. He was the son of Jack Pinter, a hard-working ladies' tailor who eventually built up his own firm in Stoke

Newington, and his wife Frances (née Moskowitz). The family home was at 19 Thistlewaite Road: a solid, red-brick, three-storey villa just off the noisy, bustling, traffic-ridden thoroughfare of the Lower Clapton Road. Round the corner was the minuscule Clapton Pond, a token bit of *rus in urbe*. Down the road was the Lea River, a gloomy tributary of the Thames. Nearby were shops and factories. In *The Queen of all the Fairies*, an unpublished autobiographical memoir written in his early twenties, Pinter vividly evoked the Hackney of his youth:

> It brimmed over with milk bars, Italian cafés, Fifty Shilling tailors and barber shops. Prams and busy ramshackle stalls clogged up the main street – street violinists, trumpeters, matchsellers. Many Jews lived in the district, noisy but candid; mostly taxi drivers and pressers, machinists and cutters who steamed all day in their workshop ovens. Up the hill lived the richer, the 'better-class' Jews, strutting with their mink-coats and American suits and ties. Bookmakers, jewellers and furriers with gownshops in Great Portland Street.

The Pinter family, who were certainly not in that league, were part of the immigrant wave of Jews that arrived in the East End around the turn of the century and fanned out towards the North London boroughs of Hackney, Islington and Stoke Newington. According to the historian V. D. Lipman, North London Jewry was around 40,000-strong by 1930. A constant feature of the Pinter legend, repeated in all the books, is that the family were Sephardic Jews of Spanish or Portuguese origin and that the original family name was Pinto, da Pinto or da Pinta, but there seems no evidence for this whatsoever. Indeed Antonia Fraser, with a historian's passion for genealogy, sat down with Pinter's parents one afternoon after lunch in Holland Park and discovered the real story: three of Pinter's grandparents hail from Poland and one from Odessa, making them Ashkenazic rather than Sephardic Jews. They imported from East Europe a residual love of culture, a memory of suffering and an extraordinary resilience.

There were, however, marked differences between the two sides of Pinter's family: his father's relations were the cultivated ones, while his mother's were the more cheerful and fun loving. Both, however, had their share of domestic tragedy. Pinter's paternal grandfather Nathan was born in Poland in 1870 and came to England alone in 1900 in the wave of Russian pogroms. He later went back for his wife and family. Nathan, who settled first in Stepney and later in Amhurst Road, Stoke Newington, was a quiet man who worked in the garment trade specialising in ladies' wear. According to Pinter's parents, he always gave in to his dominating wife, born Fanny Baron, who was regarded as 'the real boss'. Fanny was a good-looking woman, small but powerful, who had trained as a ladies' hairdresser in Poland, ran her own business in Stepney and preferred listening to records by the great Beethoven and Mozart pianist Arthur Schnabel to doing housework. Her grandson Harold was deeply fond of her and, although he told Antonia Fraser in 1995 that he had forgotten his grandmother's maiden name was Baron, it can hardly be coincidence that he adopted it as his stage-name or, indeed, used it for the autobiographical character of Mark in the first draft of *The Dwarfs*.

The pacific Nathan and the indomitable Fanny were oddly matched but very happy – indeed, they had a large family of five children. The eldest, Rachel, was born in Poland in 1897 and died childless. The second, Sophie, was born in England in 1900 and was not only an excellent pianist but married a taxi driver, Isidor Lipstein, who was renowned in the family for his Communism, chess-playing and musical gifts. The love of music was inherited by their daughter Sue, whose son Steve eventually became a rock guitarist with an American band. The third child Jack, Harold Pinter's father, was born in the East End in 1902, to be followed by two more children, Mary and Dolly. The young Harold adored this musical and lively family, not least Aunt Sophie and cousin Sue, both of whom tragically committed suicide in the early 1960s. Yet what is clear is that the Pinters were a close-knit family in which the musical passions of the formidable Fanny were passed on from one generation to the next.

If one side of the family had artistic leanings, the other side was noted for its entrepreneurial flair and Cockney gaiety. Pinter's maternal grandfather Harry Moskowitz was born in Odessa and is remembered both for his handsome appearance ('he looked like Stalin') and business acumen. He arrived in London around 1900 via Paris and even though he was barely able to write his name and was lacking any skilled trade, he lived off his wits. He would pass pawn shops, see trousers in the window and then renovate them. Indeed, having bought a sewing machine he created his own clothing business, trading as Richard Mann, and employed six or seven commercial travellers. After the death of his first wife, whom he had met in South Africa, he married Polish-born Rose Franklin and they had four children. The eldest, Pinter's mother Frances, was born in 1904. It was she who as a young girl taught her father how to write and kept his account books for him. The second child, Ben, had a tragic life. After the death of his wife Fay from cancer, he took his own life and that of his baby daughter. (Pinter, as a boy, loved the tiny baby and was deeply distressed.) The third child, Judah, born in 1907 was an enormous ox of a man and became an East End boxer, fighting under the name of Joe Mann. He was the black sheep of the family. The last son, Lou, was born in 1918 and is still alive.

Although the family history was laced with tragedy, the Moskowitzes were a resilient, exuberant lot. When Jack Pinter and Frances Moskowitz got married on 9 June 1926, the East End wedding reception lasted from two in the afternoon until two the next morning. It proved so exhausting that they delayed their Bournemouth honeymoon and spent the night at Stamford Hill. Even when they got to Bournemouth, members of the Moskowitz clan came chasing after them to find out, somewhat superfluously, why they hadn't written. If he didn't realise it already, Jack Pinter soon found that he had married into a gregarious family that teemed with relations. Frances's mother Rose had three sisters who between them had five children who were all regular visitors at the big family gatherings. Pinter vividly remembers these cousins as 'real Cockney barrel organ as compared to the piano-playing and Schnabel records of Granny Pinter and Aunt Sophie.' But it was the black sheep Uncle Judah who left the most indelible impression on the young Pinter.

'This is a true story,' he says, 'and it happened about 1940 or '41. I never saw Uncle Judah fight, but he definitely was a boxer – whether professional or not, I don't know. But he fought in the East End and lived for a while round the corner from my parents' house in Thistlewaite Road. At that time, my grandmother Rose was living with us during the Blitz. We had the Morrison shelter and incendiaries in the back garden and all that. Anyway, one day Judah disappeared. He didn't die in a raid or anything. He simply moved out of his room. He'd gone. My grandmother and mother were absolutely appalled. He didn't say goodbye or anything. He didn't explain himself. About seven or eight months later, my grandmother, my mother and I were walking along the street by Clapton Pond. I was about eleven. Suddenly a great big dustbin-van passed and on it was Judah. He was just hanging off the back of this dustbin-van. My mother and grandmother looked up and I was agape. They cried out loudly, "JUDAH!", and he looked at the three of us and unequivocally raised two fingers and the van went on . . . and we never saw him again . . . I've been looking for him all my life and I've never found him.'

As a boy, Pinter grew up in a large extended family. There were constant get-togethers at the paternal grandparents' in Amhurst Road until Nathan's death in 1939. Passover – the Jewish festival commemorating the liberation of the Israelites from Egyptian bondage – was always a big event. The young Harold participated in the ritual of the symbolic descent of the Angel of Death which was always followed by a long, and significantly dramatic, pause. Grandma Fanny was also the life and soul of the party, though as in any family there were hidden tensions. Jack Pinter's branch of the family were Orthodox Jewish, while Frances's side – the Moskowitzes and the Franklins – were much more secular and sceptical. On one occasion, when Frances was asked if she was going to synagogue, she replied firmly, 'No, the synagogue is for those who feel they have a strong sense of sin.' There was also a strong suspicion that the house-proud Frances never approved of Grandma Fanny's slapdash attitude to domesticity. However, in general the family gatherings were cheerful, convivial affairs, with the cultivated, music-loving Pinters blending with the noisy, robustly extrovert Moskowitzes and Franklins.

The boy Harold clearly inherited qualities from both sides of the clan: the artistic instinct of the Pinters and the religious scepticism of the Moskowitzes. Equally important is that while being part of a large extended family, he was also the sole son of loving Jewish parents. He was the exclusive focus of their attention while possessing the only child's natural capacity for introversion. He was cherished by his parents and his adoring grandparents, aunts and uncles but, although from the age of six he attended an elementary school just by Clapton Pond, he had on his own admission few friends of his own age. One result was that from early on in life he developed a capacity for imaginative dialogue.

'I don't know,' he says, 'how it would have changed my life if I'd had brothers and sisters, but I can say one thing. I created a small body of imaginary friends in the back garden when I was about eight or nine. We had a lilac tree with an arch and beyond that arch was an untended piece of garden. I made that my home where I met these invisible friends who certainly weren't brothers and sisters but were definitely all boys. I had this total fantasy life in which we talked aloud and held conversations beyond the lilac tree. There was also – still is apparently – a laundry at the back of the garden so I was having this fantasy life with the laundry roaring away.' Out of solitude came the dramatic urge to create characters and exchange dialogue. The image of the back garden also took root in Pinter's mind, reappearing in his autobiographical novel *The Dwarfs* ('The sun was setting. Lilac hung heavy on the arched tree. The garden flickered'). This same garden – where in his late teens Pinter would sometimes sleep out under the stars with school friends – was the first in a whole series of private Edens that were to haunt Pinter's later work.

For all his tendency to reclusiveness, his home in Thistlewaite Road clearly represented for Pinter a haven of love, warmth and security. That childhood idyll was fractured by the outbreak of war in 1939 when he was summarily uprooted from his Hackney home as part of a nationwide evacuation process.

Along with twenty-four children from his elementary school – all of different ages – he was sent to stay in a John Nash, mock-Gothic castle, complete with fabricated battlements, at Caerhays about five miles along the Cornish coast from Mevagissey and owned by a Major Williams. It is hard to exaggerate the impact of this sudden expulsion on a solitary, sensitive nine-year-old used to being the spotlit focus of his parents' love. Ruth Inglis in *The Children's War* has charted the complex psychological effects of evacuation. For some children separation from a secure home and maternal affection was a traumatic and disturbing experience. For other working-class city kids it involved a first magical eye-opening encounter with rural life. For Pinter it seems to have had strong elements of both. It reinforced his tendency to introspection while at the same time opening him up to sounds and images that permeate his adult life and work.

His prime memories of evacuation today are of loneliness, bewilderment, separation and loss: themes that recur in all his works. The boys slept on uncomfortable wooden bunks in converted stables in the castle grounds. The teacher who accompanied them from Hackney, Mr Nelson, was an authoritarian figure who was known to the boys as 'big fat Nelly with the cast-iron belly' and who had 'a great habit of hitting you in the back with the knuckle of his middle finger extended'. The pain of being uprooted was intensified by the sudden news of distant death: one of Pinter's friends, Maurice, was thunderstruck to learn that his parents had been killed in a London air raid. But according to Pinter, separation from parents was hardly distinguishable from death. And even brief reunions were accompanied by the most heart-wrenching partings. Pinter's own parents, Jack and Frances, could ill afford the rail fare to Cornwall and when they did come down there were highly emotional and tearful farewells. 'On one visit,' Pinter recalls, 'when they left to get the bus it was a long way back to the lodge for me to walk. But I went all the way to the castle and looked back and could just see them as pinpoints waiting for the bus on the road; and I suddenly ran all the way back to them over the mounds of grass, racing towards them and of course they came towards me too.' The image is lodged in Pinter's memory.

Yet, along with the sense of exile and confusion, evacuation brought acute moments of self-realisation. Once when Pinter was having tea with his parents, his mother automatically gave him a cake from her own plate. The other boys spotted this and taunted him for weeks afterwards about being hopelessly spoilt. In these hothouse circumstances, the slightly sheltered Pinter also became aware for the first time of the low cunning and potential *Lord of the Flies*-like cruelty of boys in isolation: 'I think as a result of that loss and confusion one became, generally speaking, nastier; just horrid is the word. I think we were all a bunch of horrid little boys because of the loss of security.' Pinter was also deeply sensitive to the silence and sullen quietude of this remote part of Cornwall after the noise of Lower Clapton Road. But the image of the rhododendrons he passed on the mile-long morning walk from the stables to the village school, of the lake in the castle grounds, of the glades stumbled across when walking through the local woods, of the roaring Cornish sea with the bay and the cliffs all impressed themselves deeply on his imagination. They permeate his later work such as *A Slight Ache, Landscape, Old Times* and even *Moonlight*. But the most formative aspect of the whole evacuation experience was the loss of identity and the sense of living in some strange in-between world: an emotional no man's land. 'There was,' says Pinter, 'no fixed sense of being . . . of *being* . . . at all.'

Proof that evacuation to Cornwall − although it lasted only a year − had a profound influence on Pinter's childhood sensibility is confirmed by his constant, almost obsessive return visits as an adult. In his late teens he went hitch-hiking round Cornwall with one of his close Hackney friends, Morris Wernick. He took his first wife Vivien Merchant down to Mevagissey on their honeymoon, revisiting all his childhood haunts. And he later went back to Caerhays with his second wife, Antonia Fraser, where they found that the old converted stables, with their punitive memory of bunk beds, still existed. As the Austrian writer Thomas Bernhard points out in his memoir *Gathering Evidence*, we are drawn back in adult life to scenes of childhood unhappiness which, in his own extreme case, was a wartime home for maladjusted children in a Thuringian forest.

Like many people who grew up during the Second World War, Pinter remembers it through a series of graphic snapshots: as he talks of the past, people, places and incidents come to life in his imagination. A sense of disruption was also a crucial part of the wartime experience. Ironically, having been evacuated from London during the Phoney War in 1940, he was back for the most savage period of the Blitz. But in 1941 he was again evacuated, this time to Reading with his mother. Reading, where he and Frances were billeted with a factory worker's family, left behind several key memories. It was there that he took, and initially failed, his School Matriculation − the equivalent of the modern CSE − until his strong-minded father challenged the Local Education Authority and discovered that his son had just scraped through. 'Reading,' Pinter recalls, 'was also the place where I did my eyes in through devouring books every night by candlelight' − a fact of some significance to a writer later obsessed by sightlessness with its overtones of physical helplessness and spiritual impotence. The place also bred an affiliation, understandably short lived, with Reading Football Club, whose games Pinter used to go to every week. That was in total contrast to a later brief wartime stay in Yorkshire which bred a lifetime support of Yorkshire Cricket Club: something that, in view of its capacity for internecine warfare, argues considerable strength of character. Towards the end of the war, after Pinter had gained a place at Hackney Downs Grammar School, he found himself evacuated yet again, this time with his schoolmates to rural Norfolk. Once more the image of a country garden took root in his impressionable memory. 'That,' he says, 'was where the image of *A Slight Ache* came to me. When I started to write the play in 1959 – fifteen years later – I instantly recalled the image of the Norfolk house to which we were sent in 1944. There was a garden and lots of flowers – honeysuckle, convolvulus, and so on – the like of which I'd never seen before. There wasn't a matchseller . . . but that opening image came from Norfolk and, in a sense, triggered the play.'

For the bulk of the war, however, Pinter was in the East End which bore the brunt of the London bombing. The after-myth of war has bred a sense of folksy nostalgia and stoic good cheer of the kind sentimentally celebrated in Lionel Bart's *Blitz!* and savagely satirised in *Beyond the Fringe*, in which Peter Cook wittered on about the delights of popping out in the back garden to plant his carrots and putting on a nice cup of tea. But for those who were young at the time, there was nothing to get sentimental about. Bernard Kops, another embryonic playwright, was four years older than Pinter and living at nearby Bethnal Green. In his memoir *The World is a Wedding*, he explains how he feels not a shred of nostalgia for the communal spirit of the Blitz; his memory is of the fear and the horror. 'I stopped being a child', he wrote, 'and came face to face with the reality of the world.' For Pinter too the chief memory is of the life-and-death intensity of daily experience.

'For a young boy,' he says, 'there was a great sense of the dramatic. Sporadic but pretty intense bombardment. Air-raid warnings all the time. A real sense of an extreme and perilous life. The blackout also left a sharp memory. You lived in a world in which in winter after five o'clock it was totally black . . . with chinks of light flashing on the horizon. I remember when we filmed Elizabeth Bowen's *The Heat of the Day* the director Christopher Morahan and I were the only ones on the set who knew exactly what it was like. I loved the sense he got in the film of a world where even the traffic lights were dimmed and where you found your way about with torches. It was also a world that was highly sexual . . . there was a sexual desperation about the place. People really felt their lives could end tomorrow . . . Of course you tried to get on with whatever the hell you were doing, but fear was definitely about. You also became frightened on other people's behalf and you heard of people who bought it – that was the term, "bought it" – in the next street. There was this damned thing called a landmine. There were also incendiaries . . . at one point we were all evacuated from our house when there was a raid and we opened the door and that famous garden I told you about was alight all along the laundry wall including the lilac tree. We were evacuated straight away. Though not before I took my cricket bat.'

For Pinter the war left behind a set of ineradicable memories, images, sense-impressions. It also represented a speeded-up transition from boyhood to early manhood. Emotionally, he was a straightforward patriot: what else could he be at that time? But in matters of faith he quickly revealed his own stubborn independence. As a well-brought-up Jewish boy he went to classes at Lea Bridge Road *shul* in preparation for his bar mitzvah. 'I did it,' he says, 'because I knew I had to do it and I had very little control over it. But after the age of thirteen, that was it. I was finished with religion for good.' That argues peculiar intellectual certainty – influenced by the religious scepticism of the Moskowitz side of the family – in a young boy. Sexually, Pinter was also pretty precocious. One of his earliest sensuous memories is of huddling up to the girl next door – he was about twelve and she was in her twenties – in a Morrison shelter during a wartime air raid. And a year or so later he fell headily in love with a fourteen-year-old girl in Thistlewaite Road – an experience that brought out his inherent taste for the dramatic.

'I didn't know what to do about it,' he recalls. 'I kept seeing this girl pass up and down the street. I couldn't speak to her. So I phoned her pretending to be an American soldier and said how much I admired her. I put on an American accent and said I would be at the gates of Springfield Park, which was quite close by, at a certain time on a certain day. She said, "I've never heard of such a thing in all my life. How dare you? Who are you?" And so on. Anyway, I went to the gates of Springfield Park and she turned up. I remember it well because it was a drizzly day and she came to the gates and saw me standing there forlornly in a raincoat and cried out, "Harold Pinter! What on earth are you doing here?" I said I just wanted to see her, and we had a tortured relationship that lasted through the year.'

At the start of the war Pinter was a cosseted, protected, but emotionally solitary boy swathed in the affection of a large extended family. By the end of the war his paternal grandfather Nathan and his maternal grandmother Rose were both dead and he himself had experienced the pain of evacuation, the pangs of young love, the cruelty of his contemporaries, the fear of being bombed to oblivion and the daily drama of life in the East End. It is hardly surprising that he grew up with a sense of the precariousness and fragility of existence. But the war also seems to have heightened in him the power of what Proust called 'involuntary memory': the idea that a fragment of one's experience, suddenly overtaking one or conjured up from the depths of one's consciousness, can convey the full quality of the past. All writing, to some extent, is memory; but Pinter's particular gift is to seize on those visual or sensory flashbacks and invest them with dramatic significance. In the extremity of war every experience – Spitfires in the Cornish sky, the London Blitz and the V1s and V2s, the blackout, the musky aroma of sex, even the sights and sounds of nature – acquired a heightened urgency. Like many children who grew up in wartime, Pinter had a strong sense of life's drama and impermanence; and, like any incipient artist, he was alert to the significance of his own experience.

Books also forged and shaped Pinter's imagination. There were not that many around the house. His mother enjoyed reading the novels of Arnold Bennett and A. J. Cronin, but his father – who left the house at 7 a.m. each morning and returned twelve hours later – had little spare time for reading and not much money to buy books. Yet Pinter's own literary tastes were already taking shape. He started writing poetry at the age of twelve, and he soon discovered the joys of Hackney Public Library: 'a fountain of life', he calls it. Without any prompting from teachers, he started reading voraciously on his own initiative: Dostoevsky, Rimbaud, Woolf, Lawrence, Eliot, Hemingway – anything he could lay his hands on. What is revealing is that he seems to have quickly got through the Biggles-and-Just William stage, bypassed many of the standard classics – though he was given a *Collected Shakespeare* by his parents at the age of fourteen – and plunged straight into the whirlpool of Modernism : a reflection, not just of his own intellectual precocity but of the uncertain times in which he was brought up. And at fifteen he bought a copy of Joyce's *Ulysses*, somewhat to the dismay of his parents. 'That,' he says, 'wasn't taken very well for the simple reason that my parents had heard about it . . . they didn't look into it but they knew there was something fishy about it. My father, in fact, told me to take it off the living-room bookshelf. He said he wouldn't have a book like that in a room where my mother served dinner.'

If Hackney Public Library was an intellectual treasure-house, Hackney Downs Grammar School, where Pinter spent the formative years from 1944 to 1948, was an endless source of self-discovery. Most budding writers have a wretched time at school. But, although there were occasional clashes with bone-headed teachers, Pinter discovered his true potential at Hackney Downs. He encountered one of those enlightened English teachers who opens up new horizons, made a number of lifelong friends and explored his own intellectual and sporting potential. If there is a golden period in Pinter's young life, it was in his late teens; and if his work is full of the echoes and memories of some lost paradise, then the Grammar School years are his own personal touchstone.

The school itself has had an extraordinary history. It was founded in the 1870s by the Grocers' Company in exact imitation of a Prussian prototype. It was handed over to the then London County Council early in the century and, in the 1940s, by virtue of Hackney demographics, had an over 50 per cent Jewish intake and a high regard for learning. In its time it has produced two life peers, two university vice-chancellors and two famous actor-playwrights in Pinter and Steven Berkoff. Sadly, it was closed by the Secretary of State for Education and Employment in 1995 because of falling standards, but in Pinter's day it encouraged – at least among the staff – an eccentric individualism. The most influential figure on Pinter was an English teacher called Joe Brearley: a tall Yorkshireman who suffered from malaria, had been torpedoed at sea in the war and who was wont to march down corridors crying at the top of his voice, 'Othello's occupation's gone.' In fact, Brearley seemed to have found his *métier* in Hackney and passed on his passion for English poetry and drama to Pinter and other pupils. For Pinter, Brearley became counsellor, intellectual mentor and lifelong friend. 'We embarked,' Pinter remembers, 'on a series of long walks, which continued for years, starting from Hackney Downs, up to Springfield Park, along the River Lea, back up Lea Bridge Road, past Clapton Pond, through Mare Street to Bethnal Green.' On their walks they would declaim passages from Webster into the wind or at passing trolley-buses. Fifty years later, when receiving the David Cohen British Literature Prize, Pinter would recall: 'That language made me dizzy. Joe Brearley fired my imagination. I can never forget him.'

Inspired by Brearley, Pinter shone at English, wrote for the school magazine and discovered a gift for acting. But it was in those years, partly through the school and partly through the social life of Hackney Boys' Club, that Pinter – until then a natural loner – formed an almost sacerdotal belief in the power of male friendship. The friends he made in those days – most particularly Henry Woolf, Michael (Mick) Goldstein and Morris (Moishe) Wernick – have always been a vital part of the emotional texture of his life. Even fifty years later, though Woolf and Wernick live in Canada and Goldstein in Australia, they still correspond regularly and miss no opportunity for London reunions. If the notion of male loyalty, competitive rivalry and fear of betrayal forms a constant thread in Pinter's work from *The Dwarfs* onwards, its origins can be found in his teenage Hackney years. Pinter adores women, enjoys flirting with them, worships their resilience and strength. But, in his early work especially, they are often seen as disruptive influences on some pure, Platonic ideal of male friendship: one of the most crucial of all Pinter's lost Edens.

Talking and writing to members of the Hackney gang now, I sense that what united them was a love of intellectual adventure and a shared ironic sense of humour. Calling themselves, slightly self-consciously, 'The Boys', they were clannish, close-knit and both envied and resented by outsiders. Apart from Pinter, Woolf, Goldstein and Wernick, the key members of the gang were Ron Percival – blond, proud, demonic and the prototype of Pete in the novel and play of *The Dwarfs* – and B. J. (Jimmy) Law – a keen scholar and musician who fiercely contested Pinter's zealous admiration for Dylan Thomas and D. H. Lawrence. What bound them together was not precisely the school (since Goldstein went to nearby Raine's Foundation School), or Jewishness (since both Percival and Law were Gentiles), or even geography (though they were all avid table-tennis-playing members of Hackney Boys' Club), but a passion for intellectual discovery and argument about ideas. 'It was that,' says Pinter, 'and the sense of all being of independent mind. Not one of us adhered without question to any given, to any state of affairs or system of thought. Not one of us. That was what we all recognised in each other.'

That absolute refusal to accept handed-down truths – whether in religion, politics or art – remains the eternal constant in Pinter's character. Antonia Fraser says, 'I don't think Harold would accept anything, except the laws of cricket, without question.' But, although the Grammar School period was a golden age for Pinter and he was always a charismatic figure, he was in no way undisputed leader of the pack: each member of the group had his own area of expertise. Pinter knew a lot about literature and modern poetry, from Ezra Pound to George Barker, as well as about foreign films; he would take everyone off to see Buñuel's *Un Chien Andalou* at Imperial College Film Society or Jean Gabin in *Le Jour s'élève* or *L'Atalante* at the People's Palace in Mile End Road. Goldstein, like Jimmy Law, was highly knowledgeable about music and would talk animatedly about Beethoven's Late Quartets and would occasionally whisk Pinter off to Sunday concerts at the Conway Hall in Red Lion Square. Woolf was keen on fiction and, having discovered Joyce Cary's *The Horse's Mouth* – with its unforgettable portrait of the Bohemian artist Gully Jimson – made everyone read it. But talk and a passion for ideas were what fuelled and animated the group; they were more like a gang of European café intellectuals than the kind of residually philistine young men you find in most English public schools. They had very little money, but that didn't matter. As Woolf says, quoting Muriel Spark's *The Girls of Slender Means*, 'It was just after the war when all the nice people were poor.' Outside school hours, the gang would meet up in the Boys' Club, 'bowl about the streets of Hackney' in Woolf's phrase, or drop into each other's homes for intense discussions about life, literature and philosophy. 'At one of these late-night tea-tastings,' says Goldstein, 'I recall Harold quoting Cardinal Newman to me about the creation being a vast aboriginal calamity. I never forgot the phrase because it seemed to me beneath the surface of our talk lay the empty, gaping black hole which for me Schubert – and much later on, Beckett – knew all about.' If Goldstein never forgot the phrase, neither did Pinter. The notion that beneath the surface of daily existence lie desolation and emptiness permeates his work; and the idea that one has to carry on stoically in spite of the fact that 'everything's a calamity' is actually voiced by the young actor Mark who is Pinter's spokesman in *The Dwarfs*.

It was at this time that Pinter, already besotted by poetry and fiction, woke up to the power of drama. Joe Brearley – who was an adopted paternal member of the gang – dragged them all off to see Donald Wolfit playing Shakespeare at the People's Palace in the East End and at the Bedford, Camden Town. In 1947 he also took them up West to see Michael Benthall's production of *The White Devil* at the Duchess starring Margaret Rawlings and Robert Helpmann. 'It made ordinary life,' says Woolf, 'seem terribly boring. This was life to the power of twenty-three. It had a terrific impact on Harold and the rest of us.' Webster's poetry – 'tangy and bitter, full of warning and irrepressibly sombre' in the words of Kenneth Tynan writing about that same production – left its dark imprint on Pinter's imagination and on much of his early verse. Not only did he stroll through Hackney declaiming Webster with Brearley; even today I've heard him round off a supper party by quoting from memory Bosola's dirge in *The Duchess of Malfi*, relishing the lines 'Their life a general mist of error, Their death a hideous storm of terror' and playfully asking guests to identify the source. And when Andy in *Moonlight* declares 'The past is a mist' you can still hear the influence of Webster's chill compression on Pinter's language and thought.

Pinter's theatregoing was accompanied by a discovery of the joy of acting. One day in 1947 Brearley announced to the class that he would do a production of *Macbeth*, adding somewhat peremptorily, 'And you, Pinter, will play Macbeth.' And so he did, wearing the khaki uniform of a modern British soldier. 'I was so pleased with this uniform,' says Pinter, 'that I wore it on the 38 bus to go home to tea after the dress-rehearsal. Old ladies smiled at me. The bus conductor looked at me and said, "Well, I don't know what to charge you."' Even more surprising than Pinter's infatuation with uniform is that he earned his first recognition in print from Alan Dent, whom Brearley persuaded to come and review the production in the *News Chronicle*. 'All in all', wrote Dent, 'it was a clearly spoken, though dimly lit, production and Master Harold Pinter made a more eloquent, more obviously nerve-racked Macbeth than one or two professional grown-ups I have seen in the part of late years.' Heady praise for any boy-actor. That it meant a lot to Pinter was proved when he and Dent met in a TV studio in the mid-1960s during the recording of an arts programme. Dent was somewhat embarrassed because he'd been notice-ably cool about Pinter's early plays. According to the nervous critic, Pinter assured him, 'Don't you worry about that, Mr Dent. You gave me the most treasured notice I ever had as an actor and I still keep it at home tucked away in my Shakespeare.' Pinter's acclaimed thane was followed a year later by an equally admired Romeo who, according to the school magazine, 'flung him-self on the floor of the Friar's cell in passionate histrionic abandon'. All this fired Pinter's ambition to be an actor. It also – as often happens in the hothouse atmosphere of school plays – seems to have opened up unexpected feelings. Pinter's heterosexuality has never been much in doubt, but playing opposite him in the school play was the blondly beautiful Ron Percival who was both a close friend and an intellectual antagonist. Describing Percival as an extraordinary force, Pinter remarks, 'Don't forget that he was my Lady Macbeth. I'm not saying we fell in love with each other at that point.' Pinter never uses words lightly: he leaves behind the impression that there was a strong element of adolescent infatuation about his relationship with the mag-netic, Mephistophelean Percival.

If acting whetted Pinter's appetite for theatre, sport satisfied his fierce competitive instinct. Cricket – the perfect Pinter game in that it combines individual skill with team loyalty – was his prime passion. He was a goodish batsman, would listen to the early-morning radio commentaries from Aus-tralia in the winter of 1947 and nip off to Lord's with Michael Goldstein for the opening game of the season. Cricket even gave him a hero to worship, because of his wartime sojourn in Yorkshire, in Len Hutton. 'At school,' he says, 'I was also a fairly good soccer-player . . . Centre-forward . . . I was on occasion a bit of a cheat. On one immortal occasion in a house-match . . . I never forget it . . . I cried out in agony and collapsed. The whole game stopped . . . and I got up and continued and scored a goal. It was disgraceful . . . But my one real strength was sprinting. It's true I didn't really train but I was fast . . . I think this is why I lost contact with a friend I'd made around the age of twelve called Barry Supple. When I was sixteen I beat him in the 220 yards and broke the school record. He trained hard and was a beautiful stylist, whereas I had no style whatsoever. I beat him by brute force . . . and we haven't spoken for fifty years. He had a hell of a career and went on to become Master of a Cambridge college. But we never quite hit it off after that race and I don't think he's ever forgiven me.' Nor has Pinter, with his photographic memory for the crucial incidents in his life, ever forgotten it. But just as significant as Pinter's athletic skill is the fact that the school sports field was at Lower Edmonton: the place where Stanley in *The Birthday Party* gave the concert ('They were all there that night. Every single one of them') that was the crowning glory of his brief career as a concert pianist.

Pinter, who had been a somewhat solitary, introverted child, clearly blossomed at grammar school: Hackney Downs was his university. Like a college freshman testing his mettle, he loved late-night chat, showed a great flair for acting and sport, and took an active part in intellectual life. He wrote on James Joyce for the school magazine discussing 'the screen of the sub-conscious mind in *Ulysses*'; with the certainty of youth he wrote that 'This enormous work, which depicts a day in the life of a Dubliner, stands supreme among twentieth-century literature'. He opposed the motion in the Literary and Debating Society that 'A United States of Europe would be the only means of preventing war' and later supported the motion that 'War is inevitable', which suggests he was hardly indifferent to politics. He also showed his *cinéaste* tendencies by giving a talk on 'Realism and Post-Realism in the French cinema' and supported the motion that 'Film is more promising as an art form than Theatre'. And he was not shy of passing on his discoveries to others. He would often rush into class on a Monday morning urging everyone else to try *The Brothers Karamazov* or *The Trial* which he had just read. As B. J. Law – a close friend at the time – recalls: 'He had a certain cockiness. He had opinions on all manner of things and wasn't afraid to voice them. He was given to extraordinary sweeping generalisations about literature and life. But it has to be said that it was Harold who introduced us to many of the great writers, particularly Kafka and, later on, Beckett.'

That sense of certainty stemmed from being the apple of his parents' eye: the lovingly indulged only son. Jack and Frances were very emotional people and, according to Pinter himself, there were frequent rows. His father would snarl at him for days if he refused to get a haircut and fly into a rage if he were slow to clear the dinner things or clean his shoes. But all this was in the context of overwhelming love and sympathy. Pinter recalls with great affection a moment when his father found him, at the age of fourteen, sitting up very late one night in the kitchen tearfully writing some love poetry. Instead of packing him off to bed, his father simply encouraged him to go on writing. The house was also always open to Pinter's friends. One hot night several of them slept out in the garden, under the lilac tree, while Ron Percival sang 'Come Away, Death' and 'When that I was and a little tiny boy' from *Twelfth Night*.

Writing, in particular, was always treated with great respect. Pinter recalls a later episode that reveals a lot about the cultivation of East End Jewish life, about the sharpness of his emotional memory and about his ability to see his own experience in dramatic terms.

'It's really,' he says, 'a story about Henry [Woolf] and his parents. They lived in a little flat in Homerton. His mother was a tiny Jewish woman. A real *baleboosta*. She never stopped cleaning or polishing. Everything was immaculate. Henry's father regarded himself as a scholar or politician. Never did a day's work in his life, but sat and read the paper at home or in the Public Library . . . In those days you used to go to people's houses and knock at the door. There were no phones. We didn't have phones. That's a thing people don't recognise. People couldn't afford a phone. There was a phone next door in Thistlewaite Road but they were well off. But I knocked at the door one evening to see Henry. His father answered the door and I said, "Is Henry in?" He said, "No, but he might come back. Do you want to come in and wait?" I thought I'd wait a few minutes. I said, "You don't have a piece of paper or a pen?" A piece of paper, that was it. Mr Woolf said, "What for?" I said, "I just feel like writing something." He said, "You're thinking of writing something?" I said, "Yes." He said, "Don't worry – get him a piece of paper." He gave me the paper and I sat there for about ten or fifteen minutes writing a poem. Occasionally I'd be aware of them and look up. They were really pleased because they came from a Continental tradition in which writing was really good. Henry's father knew the Bible. He was a great Talmudic scholar too. The point of the story is that they delighted in the fact that their son's friend was actually engaged in the act of writing.' As Peter Hall always says, to understand a playwright's work you have to listen to the way he talks: the pauses, the repetitions, the speech-rhythms in this story are exactly those you find in Pinter's plays.

Apart from a shared delight in writing, art, movies, music and philosophy, the Hackney gang was also defined by its male exclusivity. Only one woman, Jennifer Mortimer, ever gained honorary admittance to the group. She became, in fact, the prototype of Virginia in *The Dwarfs* and was the subject of fierce sexual rivalry between Pinter and Ron Percival. According to Henry Woolf, members of the gang would have girlfriends and fall in love, but loyalty to the group supposedly superseded individual sexual relationships. One evening Pinter was bowling along the Lower Clapton Road with Woolf and Wernick, and there was talk about whether or not to go and have a cup of tea. Pinter, who'd already made a secret date for that night, confessed he had another appointment. 'The other two,' he says, 'just stared at me in mock-outrage as if to say, "Good luck, mate, if that's the way you understand life."

It was all a game, really.' In fact, Pinter's sexual adventurousness was the subject of much envious ribaldry. Morris Wernick used to say that all he had to do if he wanted to go to a fancy-dress ball was to hang his *youga* (Yiddish for penis) over his shoulder and go as a petrol pump. But even if it was all a game, it still concealed a strong communal ethic. Any violation of the unwritten code, as Pinter was one day to discover, was greeted with severe punishment, which helps to explain the psychological origins of his obsession with betrayal.

The group's defensive loyalty stemmed from intellectual kinship and shared poverty. It was also sharpened by the resurgence of Fascism in the post-war East End world; and it was very much a revival rather than a new phenomenon. Anyone growing up in the East End and aware of its history knew of the recurrent social and racial tensions. In the 1920s the *Hackney Gazette* fulminated against the presence in the borough of '30,000 Jewish and other aliens' turning the area into 'a sort of Middle East' and depriving locals of jobs and decent housing. Racial prejudice also found an outlet in support for Oswald Mosley's British Union of Fascists whose campaign against Anglo-Jewry became formal party policy in 1934. One should also remember that, although East Enders took to the streets in 1936 to prevent Mosley's blackshirts marching provocatively through a Jewish area, a year later in London County Council elections the Fascists polled 23 per cent of the votes in Bethnal Green, 19 per cent in Limehouse and 14 per cent in Shoreditch. The war, of course, had been fought to end all that, but anti-Semitism was as rife in the post-war East End as it had been before. Morris Beckman in his book *The 43 Group* – which takes its title from an organisation founded in March 1946 by forty-three ex-servicemen to fight against the new Mosleyites – paints a graphic picture of the ugliness of that period. Beckman points out that when the 43 Group was formed there were fourteen identifiable Fascist organisations operating on the streets and inside schools and halls in London. Fascist bookshops and debating societies were springing up everywhere. Newspapers and magazines with titles such as *Gothic Ripples*, *Britain Awake* and *Britain Defiant* were on sale outside tube stations. 'If', Beckman writes, 'one of the Sons of St George stood on a chair in Hackney and shouted, "The Nazis were right to have gassed the Jews," it would be terribly provocative and inexcusably vile but he had the right to say it. If a Jew in hearing protested, he could be arrested for causing a breach of the peace. Such was the law which the Home Secretary, Chuter Ede, never changed.'

Almost inevitably, Pinter and his friends were involved in confrontations with itinerant Fascist gangs. 'One typical incident,' recalls Goldstein, 'occurred in Ridley Road. We had decided to attend a meeting of the British

National Party (or whatever they were called at the time) and Jimmy Law was carrying a book under his arm (probably a volume of Baudelaire) when he was suddenly pointed at and accused of being a Commie. At which point Jimmy held his book aloft and called out, "Why – because I can read?" Of course, we thought this was very funny. We left the scene followed by a gang of thugs. Harold and I trailed the others – Henry, Moishe and Jimmy – by several yards. Those in front had already turned the corner into Dalston Lane when an enormous onion hit the wall of the bank Harold and I were just passing. I grabbed Harold by the arm to lead him quickly to catch up with the others but he shook me off and turned to face the thugs. I ran to the others and called out that Harold was in trouble. By the time we got back to him he was surrounded by about six of them. Some of them had bike chains, others carried broken milk bottles. Jimmy broke into the ring and took up a position next to Harold. It was a very brave thing to do. At that moment a trolleybus slowed down to take the corner and all of us managed to scramble on to it. But it was a nasty situation.'

Violence, even if it didn't always erupt, was sucked into the atmosphere; and Pinter acquired a gift for skilled verbal evasion useful to an embryonic playwright. He has often recalled how gangs would hang around under the local railway arches and there'd be exchanges such as: 'Are you all right?' 'Yes, I'm all right' 'Well, that's all right then, isn't it.' It's what Charles Marowitz once dubbed 'Nascent Pinterian dialogue in original settings of menace'. But although violence and menace were part of the social landscape of Pinter's late teens, it is facile to argue that he simply transferred that atmosphere, undiluted, into his early plays. It was clearly a factor, but by no means the only one, in his portrait of the precariousness of existence and of the abyss of terror lurking beneath all social relationships. That stemmed from many things including evacuation, the Blitz, childhood solitude and his wide reading, which included Dostoevsky and Kafka. In fact his contemporaries, while acknowledging the post-war Fascist threat, play down its long-term significance. Michael Goldstein claims, 'There was an undercurrent of anti-Semitism but by no stretch could you say it was felt more than skin-deep by any of us . . . Of course, it was mentioned now and again, but I can't personally see how it informs Pinter's work to any great extent. There is enough fear and menace in just being alive.' Henry Woolf agrees: 'The sense of violence was visible but, at the same time, it was unimportant. It was an annoyance and a threat and it was profoundly unjust that, after a war that had been fought against just this sort of thing, there were these guys beating up Jews. But it was principally a nuisance of an occasionally dangerous kind.'

Pinter was adept at taking care of himself either through verbal evasion or physical retaliation, but he stopped short of direct political involvement. One night a fellow ping-pong player at Hackney Boys' Club called Julie Konapinski ('I can see him now,' Pinter remarks, 'sallow, good-looking fellow') suggested joining the 43 Group, but Pinter politely demurred. The real significance to Pinter of the post-war anti-Semitic threat was not so much that it inculcated a sense of menace as that it developed his instinctual hatred of any form of injustice. Judging by his father's challenge to the authorities on his son's supposed failure of the School Matric, it was an hereditary quality, but it was already keenly developed in the young Pinter. When, at the age of fifteen, he was corporally punished by a grammar-school science master called Mr Gee, he marched out of the classroom demanding to see the head-master to complain that he had been unfairly treated. And what rankles, even today, about the Fascist menace in 1940s Hackney is not so much the physical threat as the manifest political injustice. 'It was all so odd and ironic,' says Pinter, 'because it was happening under a Labour Government which believed in freedom of speech . . . I mean we'd just fought for six bloody years to defeat, at the cost of millions of people, the Nazis and yet the Government allowed these groups of Fascists to congregate in the East End of London and beat people up . . . elderly Jewish people and so on. Extraordinary contradic-tions existed in that society.' It was the start for Pinter of a lifelong cynicism about politicians and the hypocrisy of Government.

The paradox is that – for all the undercurrents of violence and emotional fluctuations of youth – the immediate post-war years represent something of a golden age in Pinter's private development. He made lasting friends, learned to question existing credos, read widely and, through acting, writing, cricket, soccer and sprinting, explored both the introvert and extrovert sides of his nature. Pinter says that he was often morose, but everyone who knew him then testifies to his vitality, good looks and intellectual energy; and even today he keeps a photo of the Hackney gang, radiant with the promise of youth, propped up against his study wall. Like any child who had lived through the war, he had a keen sense of death. Yet he seems to have undergone a voyage of personal discovery in those austere post-war years; it is hard not to see that yearning for a secure past which permeates everything he writes, stemming from his memory of the iron-clad solidarity of his Hackney friend-ships. Though Pinter obviously changes and develops as an artist, these early years form the matrix of his creative imagination.

You would have thought, given his passion for the life of the mind and his love of sport, he would have gone straight from Hackney Downs Grammar School to university. But, rather like Peter Cook's park-bench philosopher who might have been a High Court judge, he didn't have the Latin. In fact he thought of Oxford or Cambridge when he left school in 1948 and took a week's cramming course in Latin but realised he was too impatient to master it. In terms of his development as a dramatist, it may have been just as well since – with obvious exceptions such as David Hare, Howard Brenton or John McGrath – an Oxbridge degree course often curbs and restricts a singular theatrical vision: it encourages the critical rather than the creative faculty. And B. J. Law, who later took naturally to schoolteaching, doubts that Pinter would have responded well to the disciplines of academic life. 'Apart from Joe Brearley,' he says, 'he wasn't that interested in what schoolmasters had to say. I remember we were given a personal essay to write at school and Harold came up with "The Value of a University Education": a sort of crazy impression of Oxford life which was all dreaming spires, sunlit quads and girls with milk-white thighs . . . I always remember those milk-white thighs.' Actually, it sounds quite an accurate picture of Oxford life.

Instead of pursuing that vision, Pinter – encouraged by Joe Brearley and with an admired schoolboy Macbeth and Romeo behind him – decided to study acting at the Royal Academy of Dramatic Art in Gower Street. In those far-off days, young people of proven talent but modest means could still get a local-authority grant to learn the craft of acting. On the recommendation of R. D. Smith, a BBC Radio Drama producer who was acting as an assessor for the London County Council, Pinter got a fee-paying grant to go to drama school. However, the year at RADA, starting in the autumn of 1948, turned out to be one of the unhappiest and seemingly most unproductive periods of his life. At that time RADA, under the benign supervision of Kenneth Barnes, still had the reputation of a glamorous finishing school; it was to be almost a decade before the eruption of a new working-class generation, led by Albert Finney, Peter O'Toole and Tom Courtenay, changed the character both of the institution and of British acting. Pinter, a chipper Hackney intellectual with a fertile mind and an iconoclastic temperament, was simply turned off by the class-consciousness, insular luvviedom and tramline disciplines of post-war RADA. His heart was still in the East End, as he makes clear in *The Queen of all the Fairies*:

When I went to Acting School I lost no contact with my friends. I couldn't bear the place anyway. Full of poofs and ponces, upstairs and downstairs, suspendered beauties, darlings and darlinged, 'shop' and flourish. The instructors were mostly crap too. The old hag that first produced us was like a witch, demonstrating actions, leaping, grimacing, her crabby face and straggled hair, causing all to be stricken, like medieval peasants at an evil magic fire dance. I hated her and she reported me as insolent, ill-mannered and turbulent. After a while I took days off till I was hardly there at all and eventually faked a nervous breakdown and attended no more. Then as Moishe [Morris Wernick] called it, my poncing days began; from café to library to pisshole [a marble palace behind Hackney Empire] and back.

For all his protestations about RADA's inbred theatricality, Pinter did in fact encounter a few like-minded spirits there: in particular James Grout, Rachel Roberts and Frances Hyland, with whom he helped to organise a short tour of London churches playing the choruses from T. S. Eliot's *The Rock*. But mostly he played hookey and led an extraordinary double-life. Every morning he'd leave home supposedly setting off for Gower Street. Instead he went to Hackney Library just up the road. Or he'd roam about the streets waiting for Henry Woolf and Morris Wernick, then still in the Upper Sixth, to come out of school. Or in the summer he would go off to watch cricket at Lord's. 'My parents never knew,' he says, 'because I'd come back in the evening and say, "My Horatio was pretty good," or whatever.' But what strikes one now is not so much the social insecurity as the self-assurance – or, at least, the strong inner conviction – needed to lead a life of such constant deception. And Pinter's intimate knowledge of London geography and sympathy with outcasts and dossers, which fed into his later plays, obviously owed something to his vagabond roamings during his 'year out'. Equally striking is the palpable reluctance to cut the umbilical cord tying him to Hackney with its deep-rooted friendships and life-giving Public Library. Hackney was not just home. It was a sanctuary, a retreat, an East End Eden from which Pinter was reluctant to be expelled. It was not, however, fear which tied Pinter to his birthplace so much as companionship and an inherent suspicion of any form of structured authority: academic, religious and, as it turned out, military. For in October 1948 – in common with every young male at the age of eighteen – Pinter received his call-up papers for National Service. And without a moment's hesitation he registered as a conscientious objector. It was the most momentous decision of Pinter's young life; one motivated by instinctive political conviction and presaging a lifelong belief in the right of the individual conscience to resist the demands of the State.

In the context of the time it was also a particularly courageous act. In the summer of 1948 the Cold War had reached a point of crisis. On 23 June the Soviets closed road and rail access to Berlin in an attempt to push the Western allies – the US, the UK and France – out of their three city zones. The Berlin blockade, which lasted until the spring of 1949, was countered by an

airlift of food and fuel to save the Western sectors from starvation and surrender. It looked for a time as if the Third World War was about to erupt
three years after the Second had ended. Nuclear retaliation against the Soviets was also regarded as more than an empty threat. In July 1948 the first
American B29s arrived in East Anglia, the start of an American nuclear
presence on British soil that was to last for over four decades. The US
Ambassador to Britain, Lew Douglas, sent a cable to Washington reporting
that Winston Churchill – then the Tory Opposition leader – 'believes that
now is the time, promptly, to tell the Soviets that if they do not retire from
Berlin and abandon Eastern Germany, withdrawing to the Polish frontier, we
will raze their cities'. Even Aneurin Bevan, the political conscience of the
Labour Party, urged that the Berlin airlift be backed by the dispatch of Allied
tanks through the eastern zone of Germany to relieve the Socialist administration of west Berlin.

That was the kind of fevered atmosphere in which Pinter found himself
appearing before two military tribunals and at two civil trials. It was a situation that, as he retells it now, combined high seriousness and low farce. But
conscientious objection was a landmark in Pinter's life for several reasons. It
led to his first serious rupture with his parents. It gave him his first decisive
experience of the conflict between individual determination and social conformity. It also bred a lifelong suspicion of the Kafkaesque workings of
bureaucracy. Put simply, it was his first conscious political act.

His parents were perplexed and appalled by his decision. They expected
him to go into the Army. They thought that was what one did. They even,
unfairly, blamed Henry Woolf for encouraging him. ('If that Henry Woolf
comes to the door,' said the normally hospitable Jack Pinter, 'I'll kill him.')
They also consulted Joe Brearley. 'You see, most conscientious objectors,' says
Pinter, 'had a priest or a rabbi to speak for them. I had none of that. I refused
to fall back under the shelter of a religious umbrella. The only person they
could call on was Joe. I never forget he came round one afternoon and my
father said, "Can you talk some sense into this boy? He's likely to go to
prison. He's crazy." I remember Joe Brearley saying, "No. If he wants to go to
prison, it's entirely up to him. I'm not saying one thing or the other. I
understand what he's doing even if I don't necessarily think it's a good
thing." It was remarkable that speech. I think it made a great impression on
them. What he was saying was that it was entirely my responsibility.'

Pinter's first action was to send back his call-up papers. He was then
summoned before a military tribunal in 1949 to explain the reasons for his
decision. Which were what exactly? 'I said something to the effect that the
recent war had killed millions of people. I made a big point of the fact that

there wasn't enough food in the world and that to cultivate another war meant that millions more people were going to starve. I was also questioning – since we'd just had this damn war – what the point was of preparing for another one. Who were we going to fight and why? I was quite resolute in all that. This was all at the first tribunal. But I was deeply disturbed by the statement I was sent afterwards. One of the judges had written that, in the event of war, I wouldn't defend my sister. I was on record as having said something which I never said and which I didn't believe. Because my view hasn't changed over the years: if I was in a position where I saw my putative sister being assaulted, I would do my best to defend her. It was a terrible distortion of the truth and an early example of the corruption of a certain kind of bureaucracy.'

After the first tribunal, there was an appeal in which Pinter was allowed to take a witness to testify to his integrity; a chance for a teacher, priest or figure in authority to explain the moral basis for his decision. With bare-faced chutzpah, Pinter took along his Hackney friend Morris Wernick who, like himself, was only eighteen. 'I remember it,' says Pinter, 'as if it were yesterday. I even remember where the tribunal was in Cumberland Place. Moishe got up and said to all these Colonels and Major-Generals, "Look, I know Harold a great deal better than you do. He means what he says. He's not a fake. He's not trying to get out of the Army. I'm conscripted and I'm going in in about a month's time. I've no objection to going in, but he has. I'm serious about going in and he's equally serious about not going in." And as he sat down I leaned over and said, "You've done me there, Wernick." And, of course, he had. They just said, "Appeal dismissed." When we got out into Cumberland Place that afternoon – and it was a lovely summer afternoon – I said, "Well, here we go, Wernick. You go into the Army and I go to prison." '

In that expectation, the two of them took off for a week's hitch-hiking holiday around Cornwall in the summer of 1949, rejoicing in the fact that not a soul in the world knew where they were. They toured the area around St Ives and Mevagissey where Wordsworthian shades of the prison-house had first begun to close upon the growing boy.

Once back in London Pinter received his call-up papers again and was asked to attend a medical. At which point – and the spectre of Kafka's Josef K more than once came into his mind – he was asked by the Medical Officer, 'Do you submit to a medical examination to come into the Army?' The answer – predictably – was no. Pinter was then placed under arrest, taken to a police court and kept in custody. Even here the gravity of the situation was offset by farce. 'I found myself,' recalls Pinter, 'with some chap in a cell. I said to him, "What are you in here for?" He said, "Oh, I just hit my old woman with a hammer. What about you?" I couldn't just say I was a conscientious objector so I found myself inventing some total cock-and-bull story.' After that, Pinter came up before a civil magistrate who asked whether he would accept the court's judgment or whether he wished his case to go to a jury. He opted for the former and was fined £50, a large sum then which his father, by now reconciled to his son's obduracy, promptly paid. A few months later the whole process was repeated with Pinter coming up a second time before the same magistrate and this time being fined £75, which his father again paid. The whole process might have been endlessly repeated had not the Board of Conscientious Objectors recently won a court agreement putting a stop to the Kafkaesque cycle in which you were tried, sent to prison, released, asked to attend a medical and sent to prison again. Pinter was lucky both in appearing before an unusually lenient magistrate and in the fact that it had now been decided to call it quits after two trials.

As Pinter himself says, becoming a conscientious objector was quite a lonely thing to do. The pressure to conform was enormous. And even though he had the total support of his old Hackney friends, they mostly succumbed to the organised pointlessness of National Service with Wernick going into the Royal Artillery and Woolf into the RAF. Pinter remained defiantly his own man following the dictates of conscience and refusing to hide under the convenient shelter of pacifist or religious principles. The whole episode also makes nonsense of the theory that Pinter belatedly woke up to political realities or suddenly acquired a questioning conscience in the 1980s. He was *always* an instinctive outsider; looking back, he sees conscientious objection as the first major political decision of his life. 'I was sort of smelling a rat,' he says, 'about the way these structures were conducted – these political structures. I wouldn't put it much higher than that. I really smelled a rat. A big one. And I felt I'm not having any of that. You know, we used to call an Army uniform a "shit-suit". I remember saying at the time, "I'm not going to put on a shit-suit for anybody after this war." There was a disease which I felt I wasn't going to succumb to.'

That obstinate nonconformity was to be stamped on Pinter's soul for life. In a sense, it was the culmination of all his experiences as a boy and as a teenager: the solitariness of his back-garden fantasies, the loneliness of evacuation, the early and decisive rejection of the Jewish religion, the creation of his own private literary pantheon, the sense of injustice at the post-war survival of Fascism, even the class-inspired loathing of the RADA ethos. Everything marked Pinter out, from his earliest years, as an independent spirit. He had found happiness with his soul-mates in Hackney but, with the diaspora of the old gang as they headed towards National Service or university, he faced a difficult problem. He knew he had a talent for acting and writing poetry; but, having dropped out of drama school, narrowly escaped prison and witnessed the break-up of his private Eden, what on earth was he going to do with his young life?

Two Romantic Ireland

While his old mates spread their wings, Pinter himself stayed on at home in Hackney for a couple more years – from 1949 to 1951 – before landing an acting job with Anew McMaster's touring company in Ireland. But there was no sense of domestic confinement. Self-consciously seeing himself as a bit of a Hackney Hamlet – he even favoured black apparel – Pinter wrote in *The Queen of all the Fairies* 'I, as a conchie, did not go to prison but counted myself a king of infinite space, while as an actor, I trod the boards'. It was a period in which he read and wrote copiously, saw friends, wrote endless letters to rep directors and BBC producers, went back to drama school, had a heartbreaking love affair. On the surface it seems a fitful, restless, impoverished time; one in which Pinter occupied a milieu not unlike that of Spooner in *No Man's Land* made up of small magazines, even smaller cheques and pub pipe dreams. But it was as if he was serving an unconscious apprenticeship to the craft of playwriting: partly by honing his gift for observation, partly by getting work as an actor, partly by testing his literary gifts in poetry, prose-poems and eventually an autobiographical novel. It looks like an in-between period. In fact, Pinter – like all young writers – was absorbing a welter of influences while finding his own distinctive voice.

G. K. Chesterton once wrote, 'There is at the back of every artist's mind something like a pattern or type of architecture. It is a thing like the landscape of his dreams; the sort of world he would wish to make or in which he would wish to wander; the strange flora and fauna of his own secret planet.' That makes it sound romantic–idealistic, but Pinter's own secret planet turned out to be a cratered paradise destroyed by the serpent of sexuality and the desire for domination. What is staggering is that that dream landscape makes such a sharply defined appearance in his earliest surviving piece – a prose-poem called *Kullus* written at home in 1949 – and continues, in some shape or form, in much of his succeeding work. *Kullus* immediately ushers us into a Pinter world that now seems eerily familiar: a room, a space, a territorial battle, a triangular encounter between two men and a woman, a reversal of power. Where on earth does this image come from? The easy answer is that

Pinter's acute sense of territory stems from the threat posed by the Fascist thugs in post-war Hackney. I suspect it has much more to do with the fact that Pinter and his friends all had rooms in their parents' houses which were simultaneously private sanctuaries, debating chambers and arenas of conflict; in particular, places where the claims of friendship came into head-on collision with external emotional ties. You don't live at home till your early twenties without developing an awareness of private space or a fear of unwanted invasion. One story Michael Goldstein told me illustrates just how territorially conscious they all were at that time. Goldstein was working at home one evening when Pinter, who had recently fallen in love, burst into his room and began to read a speech from *Troilus and Cressida* in which the hero moans on about his emotional inadequacy. Goldstein, who had himself just embarked on a love affair, felt he was being lectured about his own shortcomings, and was hurt and angry enough to ask Pinter to leave. A tiny incident; and the breach was quickly healed. But it reminds us of the way the occupant regards a room as a private bolt-hole, of how the new entrant often seeks to impose his or her will upon the space, and of how friendship is sometimes jeopardised by sexuality. All were to become classic Pinter themes.

These ideas hover around *Kullus*: a remarkably subtle, suggestive poetic dialogue which deals not just with territorial displacement but with control of a room and its owner expressed through images of cold and heat. It is written in three perfectly balanced sections. In the first, the narrator – secure in the dignity of solitude – admits a friend, Kullus, into his room. He invites him over to the fire. Instantly not just the room's chill, but by implication his whole life, is subjected to harsh criticism by Kullus: 'This can on no account be named a fire. It is merely another aspect of light and shade in this room. It is not committed to its ordained activity. It does not move from itself, for want of an attention and discernment necessary to its growth. You live an avoidance of both elements.' Having swiftly demolished the room's occupant, Kullus then seeks his permission to introduce a shawled girl with whom he proceeds to climb into his bed. The host is left as a passive and impotent voyeur: '*I placed a coat over the lamp, and watched the ceiling hustle to the floor. Then the room moved to the flame in the grate. I shifted my stool and sat by the flame in the grate.*'

By the second section, Kullus has taken over the room completely and exercises complete domination.

The window was closed, if it was warm, and open, if it was cold. The curtains were open, if it was night, and closed, if it was day. Why closed? Why open?

I have my night,

said Kullus.
I have my day.

Kullus controls not just the room and its owner but seeks to impose himself on the natural world: to determine day and night, heat and cold. At which point the girl-visitor starts to seize the initiative, presumptuously inviting the host to move into his own room and enlisting his help in closing the curtains in defiance of Kullus's orders. By the third section, Kullus 'has changed', the shawled host crouches far from the fire, the girl is in complete command of the room and the men in it, closing and opening the curtains at will. Everything has come full circle except that the power situation has been totally altered. Stripped of his identity and his cherished solitude, the host now surveys the girl close to the grate. '*The ceiling hustled to the floor.* You have not shifted the coat from the lamp, *I said.*'

You could place several interpretations on this. The action could, just possibly, be taking place in three different rooms: the narrator's, Kullus's, the girl's. It could also all be a dream in which a man fantasises about a nightmare occupation. But it makes most sense if read as a mini-drama about territorial displacement and psychological defeat. The amazing thing is that Pinter, at eighteen, thinks in such concrete dramatic and visual terms and maps out his own particular terrain. It's all there: the idea that we construct our own form of Edenic solitude, that we welcome over the threshold the agents of our own destruction and that women not only radically alter the balance of power between men but end up calling the shots. Formally, the piece is also astonishingly mature. I'm reminded of one of those circular Hitchcock camera shots – familiar from *Rope* – which take one on a 360-degree tour of a room by the end of which the furniture may look the same, but the relationships have acquired a totally new significance. Yet while being technically assured, the piece never seems far from Pinter's own world, particularly in Kullus's devastating critique of his host's failure, like his fire, to grow. That kind of thing was par for the course in Hackney. Pinter once told me that Henry Woolf, who had been invalided out of the forces, was walking past Hackney Hospital one day with Ron Percival when the latter turned to him and said, 'Now look here, Woolf, you haven't made any intellectual progress since you left the RAF,' to which the helpless Henry said, 'Haven't I?' Such abrasive directness underscores *Kullus.* And while Pinter was to develop both its structure and themes in his 1967 TV play *The Basement*, what is fascinating is that his first surviving work should reveal so much about his obsessive preoccupations.

If *Kullus* proves how Pinter's vision of reality was strongly defined from the start, much of the poetry he was writing at the time shows he was strongly under the influence of Dylan Thomas. When *Ten Early Poems* – work rediscovered by chance – was published by Greville Press Pamphlets in 1992, David Vilmure rightly pointed out that these early poems were not Pinter's plays in seed but 'fruit from a different vine altogether'. They are, in fact, mostly strenuous, word-drunk, alliterative stuff suggesting a writer passionately in love with language but not yet fully in control of it. Just occasionally, however, a line will leap out that arrests one by its resonant simplicity. In 'At the Palace of the Emperor at Dawn', for instance, a cluster of dense and often impenetrable images ('At Martinmas November stoat/ In nightmare claws a lover's thighs./ Eyes gnaw the hedge's coat) is followed by a last line ('And now we hear the distress of silence') that is both prophetic and eloquent. But mostly these early poems have a knotty verbal virtuosity as if designed to impress the reader rather than to include her or him in the experience.

A clear exception to this are the two poems with which Pinter first got into print in the August 1950 issue of *Poetry London*, the leading poetry magazine of the period founded in 1939 by Dylan Thomas, Anthony Dickins, Keirdric Rhys and, its first editor, the Ceylonese writer Tambimuttu. The poems were published under the name of Harold Pinta largely because one of his aunts was convinced – against all the evidence – that the family came from distinguished Portuguese ancestors, the da Pintas. Pinter's delight at recognition was mitigated only by the fact that, because of a printer's error, stanzas from the two published poems were interchanged: agony for any writer, but living hell for one of Pinter's innate fastidiousness. But the two poems show a great advance on the work of the previous year. 'New Year in the Midlands' – inspired by a brief Christmas engagement at Chesterfield rep in pantomime – is a vivid, racy evocation of a crushed camp pub at the height of festivities and filled with the phosphorescent lust of an Edward Burra painting. The alliterative exuberance is still there, but it is now controlled and used to create a series of memorable vignettes:

> The black little crab women with the long
> Eyes, lisp and claw in a can of chockfull stuff.

And in this gaudy, bawd-filled Midlands pub one even wonders if there is a glimpse of Pinter himself in 'the clamping/ Red shirted boy, ragefull, thudding his cage.' What is certain is that Pinter's literary début pleased his parents, who decided it should be made known to their most affluent relation.

'There was only one member of my family,' recalls Pinter, 'who appeared to be at all well-off, my great-uncle Uncle Coleman who was "in business". He always wore felt carpet slippers and skull-cap at home, and was a very courteous man. My father proposed that I show Uncle Coleman my poem in *Poetry London* when we next went to tea. I agreed, with some misgivings. My poem was called "New Year in the Midlands" and was to do with a young actor's vagabond life in rep. It was heavily influenced by Dylan Thomas. It contained the following lines:

> This is the shine, the powder and blood and here am I,
> Straddled, exile always in one Whitbread Ale town,
> Or such.

My father and I sat in the room in silence while Uncle Coleman read this poem. When he reached those lines he stopped, looked over the magazine at us and said, "Whitbread shares are doing very well at the moment. Take my tip."'

Also published in the same edition of *Poetry London* was 'Chandeliers and Shadows' that comes prefaced with a tag from *The Duchess of Malfi* ('I'le goe hunt the badger by owle-light: 'tis a deed of darknesse') and shows a pre-occupation with Jacobean decadence, a gift for pictorial compression and a delight in archaisms (words like 'deliverate' and 'stomacher'), which suggests Pinter has swallowed the plays of John Webster and the dictionary of Noah Webster. Still, the poem has an undeniable haunting, crepuscular power:

> Enwrapped in this crust, this crumpled mosaic,
> Camphor and rosefall stifle the years,
> Yet I, lunatic from lunatic spheres,
> Shall run crazy with lepers,
> And bring God down the chimney,
> A tardy locust,
> To plunder and verminate man's pastures, entirely.

These two published poems indicate a writer with, in the first example, a mercilessly observant eye and, in the second, a baroque imagination and in both cases a capacity for verbal mimicry; what they don't reveal, unlike the remarkable, as-yet-unseen *Kullus*, is someone who also has a distinctive voice of his own.

While still exploring his literary voice, Pinter was also trying to exploit his acting voice by writing endless letters – at the helpful suggestion of R. D. Smith – to all the top names in BBC Radio's features and drama depart-ments: Donald McWhinnie, Douglas Cleverdon, Terence Tiller, John Arlott, Frank Hauser. These men were not only legends in sound-radio, but often in their own lunchtimes as well; yet none had anything to offer either in the way of acting or poetry-reading work. Some were obviously secretarially handicapped. Arlott's reply is addressed 'Dear Miss Pinter' and Hauser's, 'Dear Mr Puiter'. When Pinter did eventually penetrate Broadcasting House it was in a series of productions for Smith himself late in 1950: in *Focus on Football Pools* and *Focus on Libraries*, both earning him three guineas with a £1 11s. 6d. repeat fee, and the minor role of Abergavenny in *Henry VIII*, for which the fee shot up to nine guineas with £4 14s. 6d. for the repeat. Which suggests that, however much life changes, BBC fees remain much the same. Like the well-brought-up boy he was, Pinter wrote a polite letter to Smith. ('I must thank you for the part in *Henry VIII* and hope you found my perform- ance satisfactory. I listened to the recording and, to me, my voice sounded unrecognisable.') On the strength of his track-record, he also got an audition for the features department. The audition report shows the BBC was still having trouble with his name, now given as Herbert Pinta, but is mildly favourable, ending up with the cryptic observation 'RADA. Cockney. Good quiet approach.' More casual work followed early in 1951 including the rare chance to narrate a radio feature *Mr Punch Passes By*, produced by Denis Mitchell – later a distinguished TV documentary producer – in Manchester.

By this time, Pinter was in a strange situation: seriously broke, living at home and making only minor headway as a poet and bit-part radio actor. Convinced he had some talent as an actor, he decided the best thing to do was to go back to drama school, this time at the Central School of Speech and Drama, where he spent two terms from January to July 1951. If the atmos- phere was infinitely more congenial than at RADA, it was partly because he met some inspirational teachers, in particular Cicely Berry, who later became the RSC's Head of Voice and something of an international guru, and Stephen Joseph, who went on to found pioneering Theatres in the Round in Stoke-on-Trent and Scarborough. At Central, Pinter also met fellow-student Barry Foster, who shared his appetite for life, love and poetry.

Foster recalls Central at that time as being full of callow youths and eighteen-year-old daughters of Home Counties admirals. In that context, Pinter inevitably shone out like a beacon. 'Harold,' says Foster, 'seemed far ahead of everyone else. He was writing a lot of poetry then. It was quite difficult stuff to grapple with until you got on his wavelength. Very knotted and intense imagery. He had a talent you could smell a mile off. He was also dashingly and saturninely handsome and blessed with a deep, dark, resonant voice quite unusual at the age of twenty. He was wonderful company and we'd drink the night through till the money ran out and then go to the Black and White Milk Bar in Fleet Street from which came a famous sketch. I've got a letter about that where he recalls sitting opposite a hair-twirler, bits of whose scalp and hair kept falling into Harold's soup. As a student, Harold was quite diligent. We'd do potted versions of plays at the end of term. I remember doing scenes from *A Midsummer Night's Dream* with Harold playing Bottom and myself Lysander. He plunged into that wholeheartedly, but that was very much to do with the inspirational direction of Stephen who was a highly intelligent, gifted man.' Indeed, Joseph became one of those influential father-figures who crop up throughout Pinter's early life. When the students were asked by Joseph to write an essay on dramatic history, Pinter suggested that he would like to do something on the crucial ulcer at the centre of the Jacobean world. Pinter gave it everything he'd got. 'You write then, do you?' said Joseph. 'Yes,' said Pinter. 'Well, hope you go on with that,' said Joseph, in a tone of warm encouragement that Pinter still remembers. It was also something that paid off in 1959 when Joseph got Pinter to direct the second professional production of *The Birthday Party* in Scarborough featuring another of his protégés, Alan Ayckbourn.

Pinter's character at this time was marked by a duality that has never quite gone away. He was, as Foster testifies, good company, a great drinker, a generous mate. Yet if you study his writing of this period it is full of almost apocalyptic angst. It was as if Pinter, even at twenty, was keenly attuned to life's suffering and harshness but was determined to rise above it with a mutinous stoicism. One of the most remarkable poems he wrote in 1951, 'I shall tear off my Terrible Cap', expresses something of this in that it is filled with a wild, antic despair and hints of possession by demons and devils. It begins:

> I in my strait-jacket swung in the sun,
> In a hostile pause in a no man's time.
> The spring his green anchor had flung.

The immediate impression is of madness, confinement, alienation; there's a lot of future Pinter locked into the idea of 'a hostile pause in a no man's time'. But the poem also sets up an instant contrast between its subject's constrained vitality and the indifferent world of nature. And it goes on to explore the idea of a wildly gabbling, almost insane hero subjected to social pressure, but finally striking a note of cock-a-hoop defiance:

> All spirits shall haunt me and all devils drink me;
> O despite their dark drugs and the digs that they rib me,
> I'll tear off my terrible cap.

An awareness of life's horrors and society's imprisoning tendencies countered by an absolute determination not to surrender to them: that same note, present in the poem, is also constantly sounded in *The Queen of all the*

Fairies which dates from 1951. It was not written as a personal credo or philosophical statement; taking its title from a bawdy song Pinter and his chums sang as boys, it is an autobiographical memoir full of Daumier-like sketches of places and people. But it does tell us more than anything about Pinter's early attitudes. He emerges as an impassioned outsider and obstinate nonconformist who, even if the world is going to hell in a hand-cart, is determined to cling on to his freedom and independence of thought. At this time, many of Pinter's Hackney contemporaries were sucked into existing society: Wernick was in the Army, Percival was something in the City, Law was studying to be a teacher. Pinter remained – and, to a large extent, has stayed to this day – a truculent non-joiner. The twenty-year-old Pinter of *The Queen of all the Fairies* is not so very different from the mature maverick who in 1993 told an interviewer from *Time Out*, 'I can't be sacked, you see, because I haven't got a job. Therefore, I'll continue to say whatever I like.'

It is in writing about others, however, that Pinter most clearly reveals himself in the memoir, and nowhere more so than in his portrait of Ron Percival:

Ron was slim and blond, crowned with a mass of curled fair hair. His face seemed carved, was pale and handsome. He was an explosive, singular person, convinced one could, and should, crack through everything, go through the dreariest and most unpleasant turge and sacrifice the nine-tenths of one's soul on the cross if the last tenth fulfilled that which it was compelled to. It was the nails that hurt though, said he. I could not agree, although I understood what he meant well enough. But I could not see the point in having showerbaths of shit for one's health. To a man fully alive each moment attempts asphyxiation. The sun ever makes the skin putty. The rain falls 'like showers of broken glass'. The awareness that comes in the flow of minutes, hours and days is akin sometimes to the lunatic, of insane possession and revelation, while beneath lies the stone depth of stillness. Suffering exists in far greater dimension than the suffering in-flicted by society, which begins as an imposition of a narrow realism: the Stock Exchange, the Fascists, the Ministry of Labour, General Elections; all it seemed to me, if placed in perspective, could be viewed from a Gulliver height. Jesus, I was told, it's real enough to be coshed by a Union thug or to be shot at but instead of cultivating suffering on this plane till I was in love with it, amorous with self-pity, always remaining within the limits of one world, one plane, I realised that in a life of unutterable dimensions, these phenomena were merely as marbles – which tend to topple the great. If my skull were sliced by a lout or a chimney-pot falling, then that would be so. 'The readiness is all. Let be.'

That's not only a vivid piece of prose. It also suggests that Pinter, at twenty, had an astonishingly clear vision both of himself and the world. He did not share Percival's masochistic belief that you had to endure endless pain for a glimpse of truth. Neither did he believe that one should be oppressed by daily reality or self-indulgently succumb to suffering. One had to acknowledge life's harshness: 'to a man fully alive each moment attempts asphyxiation' is pure Beckett, of whom Pinter had not yet even heard, let alone read. At the same time, one had to transcend life's calculated cruelties and accidental mishaps with stoicism and grace. It's an astonishingly mature philosophy: a mix of Buddhism, *Hamlet* and Marcus Aurelius, but – and this is the point – evolved by Pinter himself through a combination of life experience and reading. And even though it sounds apolitical, it is simply based on the belief that there is a higher truth than that expressed by the inbred power-jockeying of modern politicians (1951 was an Election year). There may be a touch of youthful attitudinising; but when Pinter talks of 'the stone depth of stillness' underneath the flow of time or of the 'unutterable dimensions' of human existence he is mapping out the dream landscape that forms the permanent background to his work.

In part, this memoir is a record of a lost Hackney Eden and of the diaspora that followed its break-up. One should also add that it's exuberantly funny – Henry Woolf 'had the greatest talent of anyone I know for appreciating a really good shit' – and often sharply self-critical. Pinter recalls the judgement of Ron Percival who 'accused me of operating on life while he operated in it'. That must have stung, since the phrase recurs in both *The Dwarfs* and *The Homecoming*. It implies that Pinter was a somewhat detached observer who imposed himself on existence rather than immersing himself fully in it. There may be some truth in that – isn't it the natural stance of any writer? – but Pinter was, and clearly is, as susceptible to wounds and hurts as the next man. Just how much so was shown one evening when he and I were talking about Jimmy Law, now a retired schoolmaster whom I had met recently and whom Pinter hadn't seen in over twenty years. Pinter's nostalgic affection for Law, his pinpoint reminiscence of a particular moment and his ability to invest the past with dramatic significance were all patently evident.

'By the summer of '51,' says Pinter, 'I'd had enough of drama school. I'd also met Dilys Hamlett who was a student at the Old Vic School and we'd had this desperate affair. I remember I was with Jimmy Law in his flat in Coleherne Mews in Earls Court. His parents were publicans and had a bob or two. Anyway, to have a flat in the Earls Court in the '50s was quite something. I went over to see him one day and he suddenly said, "About Dilys." I said, "Yes?" He said, "Well, you know that Swede or Finn she's been seeing." I said, "Yes, I've heard of him." He said, "Well, she's married him." I remember I dropped my coffee cup . . . And we just sat there. It must have been afternoon. We sat there for some time in silence . . . He finally said, "I'm thinking of walking over to Toynbee Hall." It was a hell of a long walk . . . There was a concert he wanted to go to . . . I said, "I'll come with you." We walked in absolute silence for two hours across London. We saw the concert. We heard the concert. We attended the concert. That's what I remember about Jimmy.' Life – even down to the dropped coffee cup – seems to take on the contours of a Pinter play.

In fact, the affair with Dilys Hamlett was both a crucial part of Pinter's early emotional life and, twenty years later, left its decisive imprint on one of his major works. Her own memory of the relationship is clear, precise and affectionate. 'At the time,' she says, 'and this was February 1950, I was sharing a room with a female friend in Walpole Street in Chelsea. My friend went off to Switzerland for a month. Meanwhile I'd been recommended by an actor, Roger Snowdon, to go to evening classes at the Unity Theatre in North London. In the class there was a Jewish girl from Hackney called Shirley who was unhappy at home and whom I invited to stay with me for a bit. After a week she said, "There's somebody you've got to meet." She then brought over Harold, Jimmy Law and the whole Hackney gang. I was a bit prissy, middle class and ladylike, and I'd simply never met people before with such intensity and extraordinary energy. I remember sitting on the gas meter absolutely mesmerised while they all talked. Eventually the boys all went off and Harold stayed on talking late into the night. He'd missed his last bus so he stayed over. It was all very innocent: he slept in one bed, and Shirley and I in the other. The next morning I caught the bus with him – he was getting the number 22 back to Hackney – and he was still talking nineteen to the dozen about Dylan Thomas and Joyce and Yeats. I'd never met anyone like this before. I always have an image of Harold striding down the street in his navy-blue coat with a rage against the world. But it was also a rage for life, a rage to do something, a rage to achieve something.'

Dilys Hamlett and Pinter started a passionate affair that lasted till October. He took her to see Buñuel's *Un Chien Andalou*, Wolfit's Lear at the Elephant and Castle, Anouilh's *Point of Departure* at the Lyric Hammersmith. He also gave her a copy of Rimbaud's *Une Saison en enfer* which she still treasures. They even went away for a weekend to the Cotswolds, signing the hotel register as 'Mr and Mrs Pinter' – still quite a daring thing to do in the unpermissive 1950s. But the affair, according to Hamlett, was also pretty tempestuous. She recalls that Pinter was furious when she danced with another actor at a Unity Theatre party. She also got a scholarship to the Old Vic School run by Michel St Denis, George Devine and Glen Byam Shaw. Pinter was persuaded to audition with her and didn't get in. 'I learned later,' she says, 'from Michel St Denis that the reason why was that the school was run very much on group principles and Harold was felt to be too much of an individual. I was also very stubborn and Harold had a strong possessive streak. At one point we were going to set up in a flat together and I just chickened out. I also remember asking him if I could go out with anyone else if I suddenly felt like it and he said very emphatically, "No." At that moment I felt it was finished. A few weeks later, at a Christmas Party, I met Caspar Wrede who was on the production course at the Old Vic School and within eight weeks we were married. I think, with the cruelty of youth, I gave Harold a great deal of pain – something you realise only later when you get some pain yourself. But he was a wonderfully loving person with a great deal of joy. I didn't see him after that for fifteen years, when my own marriage broke up, but even now we remain good friends. Whenever we meet it's always a joyous occasion.'

Pinter was deeply affected by the break-up with Dilys Hamlett and the memory lingered on: the pubs and parties they went to in 1950s London and even precise echoes of the relationship pervade *Old Times*. But in youth one survives heartbreak and, having taken the course at Central School, Pinter was faced with the business of earning a living. In July 1951 he wrote once again to his helpful BBC mentor R. D. Smith seeking advice and contacts. Smith replied suggesting that Pinter contact Douglas Seale at Birmingham Rep and an agent or two. Nothing came of that. But on 28 August a jubilant Pinter wrote back to say that, having answered an ad in *The Stage*, he had landed a good job. 'I'm going', he wrote, 'for a six-month tour in Shakespeare to Ireland next month. An Irish actor-manager called Anew McMaster. I'm playing, among others, Horatio, Bassanio and Cassio in *Othello*. I'll keep in touch.' It was to be the start of an engagement that stretched, on and off, over a two-year period and that was to affect radically Pinter's concept of theatre.

McMaster – by then sixty – was a rare survivor of the nineteenth-century actor-manager tradition. Though claiming in *Who's Who in the Theatre* to have been born in County Monaghan in 1895, he was, in fact, born in a suburb of Birkenhead in 1891; and even though he always said his Ulster Presbyterian father was in shipping, the old man was in reality a stevedore. But McMaster's whole life was steeped in romance. At the age of twenty he ran away from his Merseyside home to join the Fred and Julia Neilson Terry company at London's New Theatre. He fell under the theatrical spell of Beerbohm Tree, whose performances he eagerly attended at His Majesty's. Emotionally, he was also captivated by three young members of the *Peter Pan* company playing at the Duke of York's in 1913. One was 'a leggy boy with an alert, amusing face' who was Master Noël Coward. Another was a curly-haired boy with big brown eyes who was Master Alfred Willmore (who later changed his name to Micheal MacLiammoir). The third was Alfred's sister Marjorie who acted as her brother's keeper. Christopher Fitz-Simon, in his biography of MacLiammoir and Hilton Edwards, *The Boys*, speculates that it is likely McMaster fell in love with both Alfred and Marjorie. Happily, it was the latter whom he actually married and by whom he had a son and a daughter.

McMaster not only became a theatrical mentor to MacLiammoir but a superb classical actor. His Coriolanus at Stratford-upon-Avon in 1933 was said to be the greatest of his generation. But it was in Ireland that he became the undisputed monarch of the Shakespearean repertoire, touring towns large and small with his own company in the great barnstorming tradition of the previous century. According to the actor Christopher Casson, who saw a lot of his later work, he could play two-thirds of a performance indifferently and then suddenly give one a blinding revelation: almost literally so in the case of his Oedipus which, in the climactic stages, 'was so magnificent that you remember it as being better than Olivier's'. Mac was also the kind of charismatic figure around whom theatrical legends cluster. One story goes that, during one of his tours of what he used to call the Irish 'smalls', he stepped off the train at some obscure country town to enquire, in highly theatrical tones, 'What country, friends, is this?' – to which the Shakespeare-saturated local stationmaster replied, 'This is Illyria, lady.'

By the time Pinter came to work with Mac in 1951, the latter may no longer have been a blazing theatrical comet, but he was a living link with the great tradition and still capable of existing, in Pinter's eloquent phrase about his Othello, 'dead in the centre of the role'. For Pinter, whose professional theatrical experience was so far limited to *Dick Whittington* at Chesterfield Rep the previous winter, life in Mac's company was both an eye-opener and a theatrical education. After auditioning, somewhat to his surprise, in the grey area of Willesden Junction, Pinter was booked to play a batch of Shakespearean roles at six pounds a week: good money in Ireland in those days when you could get digs for 25 shillings. Six plays were rehearsed in Dublin in a fortnight and then it was off on the road to Skibereen, Tralee, Dundalk, Sligo, Ballina, Ballyshannon, Athlone and Mullingar, with occasional dates at bigger venues such as the Theatre Royal, Waterford, and the

Opera House, Cork, where Pinter remembers 'there was a backstage bar so that between cues you could pop in and have a quick one'.

What did Pinter learn from Mac? Judging from the affectionate and brilliantly precise memoir he wrote in 1966 – four years after Mac's death – he greatly admired his liberality of spirit, piss-taking humour, total lack of sentimentality and zealous anti-puritanism. It's the tribute of one natural outsider to another. But Pinter, although by inclination a poet rather than a playwright at this stage of his life, learned a vital theatrical lesson from Mac. He witnessed at first hand power, control, the actor's ability to seize the moment and impose himself on an audience. Playing Iago to the older man's Othello, Pinter saw how you could take an unruly collection of playgoers and bend them to your will. In his memoir, Pinter recalls one particular St Patrick's Night performance in Limerick where Mac gradually won over a drunken and noisy house. In the first half the actors could hardly hear themselves speak. Pinter writes

> I came offstage with Mac at the interval and gasped. Don't worry, Mac said, don't worry. After the interval he began to move. When we walked on to the stage for the 'Naked in bed, Iago, and not mean any harm' scene (his great body hunched, his voice low with grit), they silenced. He tore into the fit. He made the play his and the place his. By the time he had reached 'It is the very error of the moon; She comes more near the earth than she was wont, And makes men mad' (the word 'mad' suddenly cauterized, ugly, shocking) the audience was quite still. And sober. I congratulated Mac. Not bad, he said, was it? Not bad. Godfrey Tearle never did the fit, you know.

That's not only great criticism, it's also a testament to the transfixing theatrical power of language and personality. Pinter, as a dramatist, has never had to confront riotously drunk audiences – more often, in fact, dangerously reverent ones – but the primacy of the single moment and the capacity to instil silence through an isolated word must have sunk deep into his subconscious. Though he was, in many ways, to revolutionise playwriting, Pinter also learned from the past.

The paradox of Mac is that, while being a latter-day transplanted Tree who knew Irish audiences had come to see him, he could also be strangely unselfish. Barry Foster – who joined Mac's company direct from Central School in 1952 at Pinter's suggestion – recalls, 'Unlike Wolfit, Mac wanted us to be good. He wanted the ball fast and low over the net so that he could play his shots. He was also open to suggestion. Harold and I, for instance, persuaded him to put the England scene back into *Macbeth*. We were staggered that it wasn't there. Mac would say, "Well no, dear, they've come to see me." So we said, "There's a nice little rest there, you can put your feet up and it does make a bit more sense of the play if you think about it." So Mac said, "All right." Harold and I, who were playing Macduff and Malcolm, took mornings off before ordinary rehearsals and sometimes late afternoons as well and worked on the England scene, directed it ourselves and slotted it in. For all of us it was a wonderfully fermenting and fruitful time.'

Pinter concurs. 'Ireland', he writes in *Mac*, 'wasn't golden always but it was golden sometimes and in 1950 [actually 1951–53] it was, all in all, a golden age for me and for others.' For a start, he was learning his craft from a great actor and graduating from minor roles to ever bigger parts. In *Othello* he moved from Cassio to Iago ('Very good, but a bit flashy,' says Foster). He even got to play Hamlet at a Thursday matinée having mastered the text in a couple of days, although he'd been rehearsing the role in life for several years. Mac played the Gravedigger and kept a wary eye on him from the wings. 'How was it?' said Pinter afterwards. 'Very good,' said Mac, 'but next time be a bit nicer to your mother.' And, having turned his hand to Agatha Christie's *Ten Little Indians* and *Love from a Stranger* – significantly, in view of his later mastery of mystery – Pinter played lead roles in a trio of Wilde plays including *The Importance of Being Earnest*: 'Never', said one local critic, 'have we heard Wilde's unreasonable utterances spoken so reasonably as by Max Ettlinger (Algernon Moncrieff) and Harold Pinter (Jack Worthing, JP).' Commuting back and forth to London in the breaks, Pinter did five seasons with Mac in the years from 1951 to 1953. And if they were golden years, it was not just because he made new friends – including Patrick Magee and Kenneth Haigh – or because of the hectic excitement of the vagabond life, but because of the impact of Ireland on both his love life and literary development.

As the parts improved, so Pinter increasingly found himself cast opposite an actress called Pauline Flanagan, a young Irish beauty from a civically conscious background (both her parents had been Mayor of Sligo), with a magical voice and gentle manner. She was Portia to his Bassanio, Mrs Erlynne to his Lord Windermere, Gwendolen to his Jack Worthing. Photographs of the time show them either together or with a group – on a beach in County Clare, perched on a rock at Blarney Castle or posing beside a car in a snow-filled Kilkenny that looks like a small town in the Russian provinces. Pinter and Flanagan toured, line-studied, acted and read poetry together. 'He was mad about Yeats,' she remembers, 'and I think Yeats was highly influential. Harold introduced me to Yeats's more difficult late poems, the poems I wasn't familiar with like the one about the tin-can tied to a dog's tail. He also read Eliot and read *The Waste Land* aloud. You can imagine: "When Lil's husband got demobbed . . . – Good night, ladies, good night, sweet ladies . . . "'

Unsurprisingly, they fell headlong in love. But it seems to have been much more than the kind of passing theatrical fling that inevitably occurs when companies are on the road. (As the old theatrical joke goes: 'Did Hamlet sleep with Ophelia?' 'In my company, always.') In the break between seasons, Pinter brought Pauline over to London to meet his parents and friends. She remembers Moishe and Jimmy and Mick and how they all played cricket in the park one afternoon. She and Pinter also shared the delights of London life. 'Harold', she writes, 'loved London. He loved living there – the parks, the movies, the caffs . . . He introduced me to films that had never been seen in Ireland . . . We saw Buñuel's *Los Olvidados*. There was one scene, I recall, with a blind man – not your stereotypical blind man, but a nasty man flailing with a stick . . .' That's a particularly revealing memory since Buñuel's film, about three boys living on the outskirts of Mexico City, dealt not just with abandoned children but with blind beggars, sadistic underdogs, stick-wielding bullies – all images that recur in Pinter's later work. In fact, Buñuel, whose early surrealist classics such as *Un Chien Andalou* and *L'Age d'or* Pinter had seen as a teenager, is one of the most visible influences on his work. What both men share is an ability to make dreams concrete, a distrust of authority, a gift for recording low life without passing overt moral judgement and a blackly sardonic humour. Buñuel is more obviously an anarchist than Pinter, but both possess a deep-rooted concern with dramatic construction. Truffaut's comment on the great Spanish film-maker could be applied equally well to Pinter: 'Buñuel is a cheerful pessimist, not given to despair, but he has a sceptical mind . . . Buñuel's scepticism extends to all those whom he finds playing too neat a social game, those who live by accepted opinions.'

Aside from making trips to the Marx Brothers and Buñuel, Pauline also got to know Pinter's parents: 'they were very quiet, proud, very welcoming and modest'. She particularly remembers Frances Pinter's cooking and her concern to see there was always a chicken in the fridge for the hungry young couple. It is clear that Pinter and Pauline were very close. In fact they talked about marriage, but Pinter's mother, although hospitable, was deeply concerned about the idea of her son marrying an Irish-Catholic girl. Maybe also she was worried, understandably, about their economic prospects. Pinter asked one of his oldest Hackney friends, Michael Goldstein, what he should do and was advised to think very seriously about it. In post-war Hackney marriage between a Jewish boy and a *shiksa* was still the exception rather than the rule, and in the end Pinter and Pauline went their separate ways. But one of Pinter's rare qualities is that he always remains on friendly terms with former lovers – indeed in 1976 he directed Flanagan in *The Innocents* on Broadway. Even to this day, Ireland remains for both of them a golden memory.

Ireland, Yeats, the relationship with Pauline: all had a strong effect on Pinter's literary sensibility. They certainly changed his poetry. Just as Yeats's own work moves from the decorative, Pre-Raphaelite style of the early years towards an austere lyricism, so Pinter's own poetry undergoes a profound change. The poems of the late 1940s are ornate, overwrought, self-consciously Dylan Thomas-like. The poems written between 1951 and 1953 have not only greater directness and clarity, but also a sense of wounded emotion and an awareness of loss. What you hear at last is the true voice of feeling. Sometimes the poems are simply a response to Irish topography as in 'The Islands of Aran seen from the Moher Cliffs' (1951) which captures marvellously the bleakness and grandeur of these rocky isles seen from the stone of Connemara's head:

> The three whales of Aran
> Humped in the sun's teeth,
> Make tough bargain with the cuff
> And statement of the sea.

But one of the most remarkable discoveries in *Ten Early Poems* is a verse-dialogue called 'Episode' (1951): a deconstruction of a love-triangle that in some ways prefigures the world of *Landscape* and *Betrayal*. There is an un-named and unmistakably jilted speaker; an empowered rival given voice and identity as 'He'; a silent and shadowy woman who is the object of their struggle. Pinter captures marvellously both the fragility of possession and the obsessive nature of love ('I tread their shadow, Stranger and woman, Arranging the season In her curious dream'). But the most extraordinary feature of the poem is that it is the temporary winner of the struggle who launches a fierce litany of protest against his vanquished rival:

> HE:
> That you did barter
> And consort with her.
> That you did ash
> The fire at her departure.
> That you did enter
> Where I was unechoed.

That you did venture
Where I was a stranger.

From early on in his career, Pinter sees sexual relationships in terms of a male
battleground in which, in the end, there are no real winners and losers
because the desired object remains mysterious, enigmatic, unknowable. It's a
position Pinter would redefine in his later work as he gained a greater understanding of women; yet there is an archetypal pattern in 'Episode' that is
repeated, with variations, in many of Pinter's plays.

But the poems from Pinter's Irish period also show a greater liberation of
feeling than anything he had written before. They tend to be rural rather than
urban, lyrical rather than imagist, often using Celtic myth as a vehicle for
private emotion. A classic example is one called simply 'Poem' (1953) which
begins:

I walked one morning with my only wife,
Out of sandhills to the summer fair,
To buy a window and a white shawl,
Over the boulders and the sunlit hill.
But a stranger told us the fair had passed,
And I turned back with my only wife.

and which ends three stanzas later with:

The year turned to an early sunrise.
I walked one morning with my only wife,
Out of sandhills to the summer fair,
To sell a candle and a black shawl.
We parted ways on the sunlit hill,
She silent, I to the farther west.

We seem to be in the world of Yeats and Synge – a world of peasants,
shawls and summer fairs – and there is even a faint echo of 'The Lake Isle of
Innisfree' in the way the final stanza echoes the first. Yet the poem, which
deals with the loss of true love through the cycle of the seasons, also has an
aura of personal sadness as if Pinter is grafting his own feelings about the
transience of passion onto a standard Irish form.

'Romantic Ireland's dead and gone', wrote Yeats in 'September, 1913', 'It's
with O'Leary in the grave'. But, without being sentimental about it, Ireland
had a profound effect on Pinter in many ways. It became part of his imaginative landscape permeating his plays from *The Birthday Party* to *Betrayal*. As
Professor Harry White wrote, on the occasion of the Dublin Gate Theatre's

Pinter Festival in 1994, 'Pinter draws on his experience of Ireland or refers to Ireland in essentially two ways. Ireland symbolises the past and is an agent of romantic or nostalgic recollection or it embodies and encodes the threat of violence.' But Ireland was, above all, for Pinter in the early 1950s, a place of discovery. He delighted in the small towns, villages and constantly changing landscape of the country itself. As a poet, he gained new access to his own feelings: partly through the hammer-blow of love, partly through reading Yeats. And as an actor-writer, Pinter was exposed to a wide variety of influences: not only to Mac's magisterial control of an audience, but also to the practical techniques of individual playwrights. It was part of Mac's policy to interweave Shakespeare, Sophocles and Wilde with Agatha Christie who-dunnits and moral thrillers like Priestley's *An Inspector Calls*. One particular play on which Pinter worked in his last Irish season seems to have seized his imagination: Patrick Hamilton's *Rope*. In this psychological thriller about two Oxford undergraduates who murder a contemporary out of bravado and vanity, and hide the body in an on-stage chest, Pinter himself played the dominant, bullying Brandon and Patrick Magee the hysterical, jittery Granillo – prototypes, in a way, of Goldberg and McCann. Pinter wrote to his English friends that it was a work of great genius. A letter to Barry Foster declares 'What subtlety! What silence!'

Yet the biggest discovery of all was of a writer who was to become both a literary influence and a close personal friend. For Pinter it was a genuine *coup de foudre*: 'One day I came across, I stumbled across, a poetry magazine called *Poetry Ireland* edited by David Marcus in which I found a fragment of Beckett's *Watt*. I was stunned by it but I couldn't get hold of this David Marcus because the magazine telephone never answered so I never found out who this man Beckett was. I went back to London and no library or bookshop had ever heard of Beckett. Finally I went to the Westminster Library and asked them to burrow in their records and they came up with a book that had been in the Battersea Reserve Library since 1938 and that was *Murphy*. After a couple of weeks, I got it, pinched it and still have it . . . I suddenly felt that what his writing was doing was walking through a mirror into the other side of the world which was, in fact, the real world. What I seemed to be confronted with was a writer inhabiting his innermost self. The book was also very funny. I never forgot the laughs I immediately got from reading Beckett. But what impressed me was something about the quick of the world. It was Beckett's own world but had so many references to the world we actually share.'

It's fascinating that Pinter seizes on Beckett's ability to create his own unique yet universally recognisable world. For precisely what Pinter himself did in the four years between standing trial as a conscientious objector – something he has remained ever since – and leaving Mac's tours in Ireland was to map out his own universe. In *Kullus*, in 'Episode', in *The Queen of all the Fairies*, he writes of a world of territorial battle, of attritional sexual conflict, of profound social decay. In the memoir, while waiting one night for Henry Woolf he has an almost Blakean vision of the London streets with 'Carthorses lugging Etruscan crockery to the fire. Saucers and daffodils broken in the moon. Some vomit of A-bombs and H-bombs.' By his early twenties, Pinter had already created his own private landscape. He had even fashioned a style of jaunty stoicism with which to shield himself against the terrors of the world. At the same time he remained wide open to external influences. 'What was striking about Harold at the time,' says Barry Foster, 'was not just that the literary talent was there, but also an artistic sensibility. It was evident just in the way he talked about other writers.' Pinter's good taste is crucial to an understanding of him. For allied to his own dream landscape was an eclectic artistic pantheon that included Shakespeare, Yeats, Beckett, Patrick Hamilton and the films of Buñuel. Out of that collision would ultimately come a major body of work. But having decided to quit Mac's company in 1953 after five craft-improving seasons, he was once more a jobbing actor with a living to earn, as well as a writer with his own dark, mysterious portfolio.

Three Baron Hardup

Over the next three years from 1953 to 1956, Pinter led a curious double life. On the one hand there was the aspiring actor: in and out of work, slogging round the reps, dispatching endless letters to prospective employers. On the other hand there was the closet writer: penning poems and prose-sketches and, in every spare moment, writing an autobiographical novel in a series of exercise books. As an actor, Pinter frequently chafed against the drudgery of his craft. When his old mate Henry Woolf wrote to him in Ireland saying that he too intended to take up acting, Pinter replied, 'What do you want to go into this shit-house for? This shit-house of a profession. You'll meet very few people you want to have a drink with. Of course, it can be good. It can be gold and diamonds but there's also bags of the other stuff.' Despite that, Pinter – with characteristic generosity – helped Woolf get a job in Mac's company, and although Pinter's artistic soul was hardly satisfied by years of flogging round the reps playing CID inspectors, maniacal killers and family solicitors, he absorbed an enormous amount about the hidden techniques of stagecraft and the mechanics of suspense. Pinter may have lived two lives as actor and writer; but one constantly informed the other. Indeed, it's no accident that the two best English dramatists to have emerged in the late 1950s – Pinter and Osborne – were both products of the educative treadmill of weekly rep.

According to Barry Foster, what both he and Pinter dreamed of – over pints of Guinness in Irish tap-rooms – was being famous classical actors who would star at Stratford or the Old Vic; neither of them, he ruefully points out, did it. Ironically, if Pinter had made it to Stratford in 1953, he would have found the company contained two actors – Donald Pleasence and Robert Shaw – whose lives and careers were decisively to intersect with his own. In fact, he auditioned in December 1952 for Donald Wolfit's company which was planning a three-month eight-play season at the King's Theatre, Hammersmith, early in 1953. Ronald Harwood, then a young actor recently arrived from South Africa, remembers going to the same auditions at the Waldorf Hotel in London's Aldwych. 'I was sitting waiting for my audition or interview,' says Harwood, 'and I remember a young man came bounding down the stairs in a state of high excitement and saying to the beautiful red-headed girl who was waiting for him, "I've got it. I've got it." That was my first encounter with Harold. My initial impression was of how handsome he was; he also had a tough stage presence and a remarkably strong, resonant voice.' For Pinter, joining Wolfit's classical troupe straight after Mac's was like going from the Irish frying-pan into the English fire. Wolfit and McMaster were the last of the great actor-managers. Both had found fame at Stratford in the 1930s, both were nomadic figures touring at home and abroad with a portable Shakespearean repertory, and both ran their companies on patriarchal lines. But where Mac was a benevolent dominator who enjoyed the 'crack' with his company, Wolfit was an old-fashioned autocrat aggrieved at his treatment by the theatrical Establishment and not best known either for the quality of his supporting players or his generosity towards them. 'Every actor', James Agate once wrote of Wolfit, 'is known by the company he keeps', implying that his was not of the best. Within the pyramidal structure of Mac's company, there was a good deal of freedom and scope for development. Such was not the case with Wolfit and Pinter soon found his own unbending spirit clashing with his master's heavy-handed directorial style. In the first play of the season, *As You Like It*, Pinter was cast in the thankless role of Jaques de Boys and found it fell to him to come on at the end and deliver the deathless lines 'Let me have audience for a word or two, I am the second son of old Sir Rowland'. As Pinter, at the dress rehearsal, tentatively appeared from the wings, Wolfit thundered from his seat in the stalls, 'No, no, no, no. Nonsense. This is your moment. Give it some attack, panache. Get off and do it again.' A second appearance was greeted with an even greater volley of abuse. But the third and fourth times he appeared, Pinter cunningly pre-empted Wolfit by stopping in the middle of the second line and making an unscripted early exit. He paused in the wings again before entering for the fifth time to deliver the speech uninterrupted. Wolfit was reduced to speechless apoplexy while Pinter learned an important lesson in the strategy of survival.

Paternalism, as Ronald Harwood points out in his excellent biography of Wolfit, was at the heart of the actor-manager system: 'The supporting players were expected to conform to the rules of the family and the first rule was a proper deference to Father both on and off the stage.' But Pinter, whose symbol was the untugged forelock, refused to display unquestioning filial obedience. On one occasion, he objected to being summoned to a Sunday charity matinée performance at only a few days' notice and, to Wolfit's evident displeasure, was the only company member not to appear. 'The thing people don't understand about Harold,' says Harwood, 'is that he's always been the same. It's not fame that's made him vibrant, aggressive or anti-authoritarian. That's how he always was. He was very firm with Wolfit. I remember I was given a stutter as the tailor in *The Taming of the Shrew* and Harold complained to Wolfit about it because he thought it was making fun of a disability.'

Though unwilling to kowtow to Wolfit, Pinter does not deny that he was a great actor with an ability to take the moment and to invest even silence with maximum voltage. The young critic Kenneth Tynan picked out the self-same quality when reviewing Wolfit's Lear in the Hammersmith season. 'Best of all', he wrote, 'is the pause that follows his fit of rage at Cornwall's cruelty. "Tell the hot duke –" he begins and then stops in mid-eruption, veins knotted, fighting hideously to keep his foothold on the tiny ledge which stands between him and madness.' Pinter, on stage every night, was in an even better position to observe Wolfit's capacity to electrify silence and recalls one particular passage towards the end of *Oedipus at Colonus*. 'Wolfit,' he says, 'was standing high up on a rostrum with all the light on him ... he stood with his back to the audience with a cloak around him and there came the moment when the man downstage finished his speech and we all knew, the play demanded it, that Wolfit or Oedipus was going to turn and speak. He held the moment until one's stomach was truly trembling and the cloak came round; a tremendous swish that no one else has ever been able to achieve, I think. And the savagery and power that emerged from such a moment was extraordinary.' Pinter's own theatrical chamber style seems superficially different from that of these grand elemental titans – like Wolfit and McMaster – to whom he was apprenticed, but as a writer, what he learned from both was how to achieve moments of maximum intensity through silence or gesture. In a Pinter play, the movement of a glass from one side of a table to another or the simple crossing and uncrossing of a pair of legs becomes the equivalent of Wolfit's cloak.

Not surprisingly, given his questioning spirit, Pinter's contract with Wolfit was not renewed; there followed, from the spring of 1953 to the summer of 1954, the longest, bleakest, most out-of-work period of his life broken only by a brief return to the bosom of Mac's company, a play at the Embassy, Swiss Cottage, called *The Mother* and a single radio-play for Frederick Bradnum. Since he hadn't really made it as an actor as Harold Pinter, he decided to change his stage-name early in 1954 to David Baron, but even that decision didn't immediately change his luck or meet with universal approval. 'I think you must be mad to change your name from Harold Pinter to David Baron', said R. D. Smith in a letter. 'What a name to call yourself! I suppose you must feel there's some reason.' In truth, there seems to have been no deeper motive than a desire to make a fresh start, but even if the phone didn't ring much, the Baron year was not entirely a wasted year. Pinter was able to crack on with his novel of Hackney life.

Like most out-of-work actors, he also undertook a variety of odd jobs: doorman, dishwasher, door-to-door salesman, waiter at the National Liberal Club (where he got the push for discussing poetry with one of the members), Oxford Street hawker, snow-shoveller – which later inspired a famous passage in *The Homecoming* – and even bouncer at the Astoria dance hall in Charing Cross Road. Nothing for a writer is ever wasted; and, if Pinter's early plays and sketches show a deep familiarity with a raffish London subculture and a sympathy with dossers, down-and-outs and derelicts, much of that stems from his odd-job period. He wasn't exactly sleeping rough on the Embankment (in fact he was still in Thistlewaite Road), but he seemed to have had an instinctive bond with the outlawed. One afternoon, for instance, he was tearing tickets at the Astoria dance hall when a chap eagerly pressed a £5 note into his hand.

'Whereupon,' says Pinter, 'I looked up at him and he looked at me and I looked at the note and he looked at the note. And then he passed into the ballroom. I was mystified, but I put the note in my pocket. The next day the police arrived with a photo of the man asking whether anyone had seen him the afternoon before. They were coming to me and I really had no idea whether I should say yes or no. And I made a last-minute, split-second decision that logically it must be yes otherwise the man wouldn't have re-minded me of his presence. So I said to the police, "Oh absolutely, yes; he was here yesterday afternoon, I saw him." "How long did he stay?" "All afternoon," I said, "he was here till six o'clock," which was the time of the afternoon dance. They didn't like that at all – obviously the man came straight in and went out the back door – but there it was and it was a pretty sweaty experience.'

As in a Pinter play, the action is explicit but never explained since we don't know precisely what crime the man has committed: a Hitchcock movie with the last reel missing, as Alan Brien once said of *The Birthday Party*. But if the anecdote shows that life itself is full of unresolved endings, it also proves that Pinter, in any situation, instinctively sides with the underdog and against any form of authority. An even clearer example came when the work-drought finally ended and Pinter, as David Baron, got an engagement at the Whitby Spa Rep Company in June 1954 initially to play lead roles in Agatha Christie's *Murder at the Vicarage* and a stock farce *Here We Come Gathering*, co-authored by Philip King. It wasn't exactly Binkie Beaumont and the West

End but it was vital, much-needed work for a desperately hard-up young actor. But what happened? Pinter had a brief fling with a young ASM who was reported by her landlady to the theatre manager, a local butcher, for staying out late. The manager sacked the ASM and refused to reinstate her. Pinter, promptly and chivalrously, resigned in protest and returned from Whitby to London on the next train without even having the money for a ticket. As he was met by the police at King's Cross, he recalled the ringing words of his former employer: 'You'll never work in the theatre again!' One wonders if the man, a decade later, ever got to see *The Homecoming* with its portrait of a bullying, foul-mouthed and ultimately humiliated ex-butcher.

Even in the short term the Whitby meat-merchant proved a pretty lousy prophet, for that summer Pinter got a job in a touring version of a comedy by L. du Garde Peach called *A Horse! A Horse!* Admittedly, it was not much of a job: he had to manipulate the ears of a dummy-horse to make it look real and at one performance narrowly avoided dismissal for failing to make the horse 'speak'. It was, in fact, on this tour, while staying in grotesque, quasi-Dickensian digs in Eastbourne, that Pinter had an experience which he stored away in his memory and that later triggered *The Birthday Party*. But although Pinter was leading a weird double life in this period – of a poetic intellectual on the regional roundabout, rather as if Kafka had been obliged to appear in *Charley's Aunt* – he was learning every day about the practical mechanics of theatre: of what works and what doesn't, of how to pick up or lose a laugh, of how to create an effect through a surprise entrance or a well-timed 'curtain'.

David T. Thompson, in his invaluable book *Pinter – The Player's Playwright*, itemises all the performances Pinter gave in the Baron years. Pinter was at Huddersfield Rep for a winter season in 1954, did a long stint at Colchester Rep from February to December 1955, was with the Barry O'Brien Company at the Palace Court, Bournemouth, from March to September 1956 and later went on to the Pavilion, Torquay, from October 1956 to March 1957, the Alexandra Theatre in Birmingham, the Intimate, Palmer's Green, and the Connaught, Worthing. Pinter specialised in playing heavy villains and conventional leading-man roles, and, while it would be absurd to imagine that he sat there with a notebook storing up ideas for future use, the rep experience obviously bled subconsciously into his knowledge of the playwright's craft. Pinter was to become that rare creature: a revolutionary theatrical poet with an intimate knowledge of stage mechanics. And even if, by a nice irony, the kind of plays he appeared in were those he was ultimately destined to subvert, he retained an awareness of their theatrical clockwork. When the German director Peter Zadek staged *Moonlight* at the

Berliner Ensemble in 1995, he intriguingly remarked that it was like 'a mixture of Beckett and Agatha Christie'; it's worth recalling that, shortly after Pinter's discovery of *Murphy* and *Watt*, he was appearing in Christie's *Witness for the Prosecution* (Colchester, November 1955), *Peril at End House* (Bournemouth, April 1956) and *The Hollow* (Bournemouth, June 1956), as well as endless revivals of the Vosper-Christie thriller *Love from a Stranger* in which he played a maniacal killer. Thompson seeks to forge a direct link between the rep plays and Pinter's later work. He cites, for instance, how in Ronald Millar's *Waiting for Gillian* (Colchester, March 1955) a car's headlamps arc round a blacked-out room as if searching out a guilty party and how in Mary Hayley Bell's *The Uninvited Guest* (Colchester, April 1955) there is a crucial interrogation scene in which a runaway mental-patient, played by Pinter in rep, stands with his back to the audience while the other characters vehemently cross-question him. Similar devices recur in *The Birthday Party*. Yet what this proves is not so much conscious imitation as a retentive awareness of what works on a stage, and of the power of lighting and grouping to heighten theatrical effect. If, as David Edgar argues in *Pentecost*, a nation is the sum of all the people who've invaded it, an actor-writer is inevitably a portable memory-bank of all the plays in which he has appeared – but the memory itself would be valueless, or simply a repetition of hackneyed effects, without an original vision.

Those closest to Pinter in his rep years testify to his dual existence as conscientious actor and closet scribbler. Jill Johnson, who became an intimate friend during the Colchester year of 1955, reminds one of just how gruelling the schedule was. 'Your week,' she says, 'would start on a Tuesday when you'd move the play in the morning according to French's Acting Edition. Tuesday afternoon you'd learn Act One and in the evening perform the play before. Wednesday morning you'd rehearse Act One and in the afternoon learn Act Two. Thursday morning you'd rehearse Act Two and, between matinée and evening performances, learn Act Three. Friday morning you'd rehearse Act Three and in the afternoon run the whole play. Saturday morning you'd run the play again and then do matinée and evening performances. Sunday you'd be reading the next play. Monday afternoon you'd have a dress-rehearsal, open the play that night and then start the whole cycle again.'

It was a grinding system hardly conducive to psychological probing or intellectual agonising; which is why Pinter, however meticulous a director, has always been suspicious of too much theorising. It was also a system prevailing in the seventy-four weekly rep companies up and down the country. But whatever its obvious faults – such as the reproduction of stock performances and facile corner-cutting – it was a better training-ground for young actors than today's instant immersion in TV soaps which deploy the same quick turnaround without the vital contact with a live audience. What is astonishing is that David Baron the actor did not entirely submerge Harold Pinter the writer but, as Jill Johnson remembers, the two managed to coexist. 'At the time,' she says, 'he was writing poetry, the prose-pieces that became 'The Examination' and 'The Black and White', and his novel *The Dwarfs*. One knew he had this amazing talent but it never occurred to me he would be a playwright simply because he wasn't writing plays. I also wondered if he'd be a bit obscure. He'd produce a poem and I'd say, "Wonderful – but what does it mean?" Even then, you didn't say that to Harold. He'd say, "I don't know – you tell me what it means."'

Yet while Pinter was playing romantic or sinister saturnine parts in Colchester – a US slave-owner in *Georgia Story*, the villainous Petty Officer in *Seagulls over Sorrento*, a gentleman charmer in *The Moon is Blue* – the British theatre was on the brink of a seismic shock that would eventually reduce the comforting certainties of the penthouse comedy, the services farce or the Home Counties thriller to rubble. When the Colchester season ended in late June, the company decamped to Port Stewart in Co. Londonderry for a brief engagement at the Town Hall. Pinter and Jill, who were joined by Michael Goldstein, decided to turn the trip into a summer holiday when they got wind of impending excitements in London. 'I remember,' she says, 'we were in Ireland when we heard that Peter Hall was about to direct *Waiting for Godot* at the Arts Theatre. Harold wrote to Peter Hall saying how interested he was – I've got a feeling I typed the letter for him. We actually got hold of a copy of *Godot* in French and translated it as we went along. And as soon as we got back from Ireland, we dashed off to see it on its transfer to the Criterion. I never forget that, at the end, a man got up in the stalls – we were in the cheap seats in the gallery – and shouted out, "Before we leave, I just wanted to say that this is the greatest rubbish I've ever seen. I know you'll all agree with me." At which point everybody started either booing or cheering.' As one of the few Beckett buffs in Britain, Pinter was deeply shocked.

That summer in Port Stewart, where Pinter first heard about *Godot*, was idyllic for all concerned: golden weather, days on the beach, even a trip over the border to a pub where Pinter was chuffed to be remembered by the locals from his touring days with Mac. Shedding his David Baron persona, Pinter could also go back with Goldstein to the kind of conversations about art and literature they had long enjoyed in Hackney. One in particular sticks in Goldstein's mind. It took place as they were walking along the cliffs in Port Stewart one bright sunny morning. Goldstein mentioned to Pinter Janáček's attempt to capture the rhythms and intonations of his native Czech in his music – particularly in the string quartet Intimate Letters. 'I wondered,' recalls Goldstein, 'why no one had thought of doing the reverse. Of course, it was a silly idea but then it struck me that Beethoven used silence as a dramatic device in his symphonies. It was so powerful. His use of the rest in his music had an effect which Beethoven continued to use throughout his life. It was almost as if he'd invented it. No doubt other composers had used this device before him, but none with such effect. I don't know whether this sunk in on Harold because it was well before he started writing plays, but, in any case, we all had some effect on each other in this way by exploring our own thoughts out loud.' Given Pinter's retentive capacity, this conversation doubtless lodged in his memory. But who is to say exactly where Pinter's awareness of the theatrical power of silence stemmed from? From working with Mac and Wolfit? From playing in rep thrillers? From the odd conjunction of the conversation with Goldstein and the experience of seeing Godot? Probably from a mixture of all these. I once asked him point-blank when he first became aware of the dramatic power of the pause. He told me, with a slight twinkle, that it was from seeing Jack Benny, the master of suffering silence, at the London Palladium in 1952.

After which he lightly paused.

Once the idyllic Irish interlude was over, it was back to the slog of weekly rep in Colchester. Then in March 1956 Pinter moved to the Palace Court, Bournemouth, run by Barry O'Brien and Michael Hamilton, seaside entrepreneurs who had similar seasons in Shanklin and Ryde. The Director of Productions and Company Manager was a man called Guy Vaesen who took a shine to Pinter immediately and who was to remain a firm friend over the years. 'I always feel sorry for actors,' says Vaesen, 'when they join an existing company for the first time since they're just rehearsing in the daytime. So I took Harold to see that week's play and afterwards we went off and played canasta and got along famously. As an actor he had great integrity and intensity, but my chief memory of him is in those Agatha Christie Poirot thrillers where he'd play the dim, pipe-smoking Major Hastings who didn't always quite see the point. He was very funny. He wasn't always easy to cast and within the company he was very much a loner, but I only became aware of his hidden talent when he presented me with a story called The Examination with that strangely shy, sheepish grin he had then. I thought it was amazing, but it never occurred to me that he would later be writing for the theatre.'

Vaesen's other great friend in the company was a young actress called Vivien Merchant. She was fifteen months older than Pinter and a great deal more theatrically experienced. Born Ada Thomson to a Mancunian middle-class family in 1929 and educated at Bury Convent, Manchester, she too had adopted a stage-name. She called herself 'Vivien' because of her admiration for Vivien Leigh and 'Merchant' because she had a brother, of whom she was very fond, in the Merchant Navy. She had made her stage début in Peterborough at the age of fourteen as Adele in *Jane Eyre*, had worked in a couple of West End musicals and was in the same Wolfit season as Pinter at the King's Hammersmith. According to Ronald Harwood, no romantic sparks had been struck in Hammersmith: Pinter spent much of his free time carousing with fellow-actor Alun Owen. But Vivien, having done two years in rep at Nottingham with the Harry Hanson company and a season at Palmer's Green, was by the time she came to Bournemouth well established as a leading rep actress: darkly voluptuous, highly versatile, quick of study. The epitome, in short, of the theatrical pro. Vaesen had already directed her at Westcliff-on-Sea where at short notice he had to take over a production of *I am a Camera*, in which Vivien played Sally Bowles. He had been mightily impressed and booked her for Bournemouth where in the second production of the season she played Jane Eyre to Pinter's brooding Rochester. It would be nice to say that it was love at first sight – or even, on this occasion, second sight – but that is not exactly how Vaesen remembers it. 'After about six weeks of the season,' he recalls, 'Vivien knocked on my door and said, "Is *he* going to stay in the company?" – meaning Harold. I said, "Yes," because I took to him immediately. She said, "Well, if he doesn't go, I shall have to leave. I can't act with him." And so she left.' It is at this point, however, that the story gets somewhat murky. Vaesen's version is that she was persuaded to come back to appear in Coward's *South Sea Bubble* in which her heroine Vivien Leigh had scored a huge success and in which she would have only one brief scene with her less-than-admired colleague. The only problem is that I can find no record of the play in that Bournemouth season, although both the Pinters did appear in it at Torquay a year later. But Vaesen, a sweet-souled man and very loyal to both Pinter and Merchant, sticks by his version of events.

What is certain is that Pinter and Merchant did fall in love in the course of the Bournemouth season and that, as soon as their contract ended, they got married there on 14 September 1956. It was, ironically, where Jack and Frances Pinter had spent their honeymoon, but news of the marriage still came as a profound shock to Pinter's family. They had earlier welcomed Pauline Flanagan into their home but had advised against their son marrying an Irish-Catholic girl. Now, without any warning, he announced he was marrying the non-Jewish Vivien Merchant. Pinter himself simply says, 'I just married her and that was that, really. I made a booking at the Registry Office but what I'd forgotten, and which Vivien certainly didn't know, is that it was Yom Kippur [the Day of Atonement and the most solemn religious fast of the Jewish year]. I rang my parents to tell them I was getting married and there was quite a bit of perturbation and dismay: not only was I getting married out of the Jewish faith, but I had accidentally chosen Yom Kippur which seemed an insult to my parents. But that was it really . . . I had to live with that.' Pinter quickly scotches the idea that the introduction of a non-Jewish wife into the family eventually became the source for *The Homecoming*. At the same time he admits that the play had 'seeds of my own observation and, to a certain extent, experience of other people'. But the obvious tension within Pinter's family over marriage to a *shiksa* – and Jack and Frances certainly didn't attend the wedding – must have lodged within his creative memory. Equally significant, in the light of future events, is that Vivien Merchant's status within the company was superior to that of her husband. She was a leading rep actress; he, as David Baron, was a good journeyman actor adept at playing sinister heavies and CID inspectors. She was also the ultra-reliable, no-nonsense pro steeped in the business and, according to Vaesen, 'disdainful of anything intellectual'; he was decidedly equivocal about 'this shit-house of a profession', and poured much of his energy into writing slightly obscure poems and sketches as well as a discursive first novel. But, to adapt a phrase used by Henry Carr about Lenin in Tom Stoppard's *Travesties*, he wasn't Harold Pinter then. Having first known him as a struggling young rep actor, it is significant that Vivien always called him 'David' no matter how famous and internationally acclaimed he became in later life: a permanent and some-times wounding reminder of their differing status at the time of their marriage.

Pinter himself acknowledges the gap between them: 'When we met, she was the star. She really was. She was a star in rep.' He also points out that, as in any marriage, there were some extremely good times and many laughs, as well as conflict and strain. That dichotomy is well caught in two poems that significantly both date from 1956. 'Daylight' is ripe with sensual ecstasy and delight:

> I have thrown a handful of petals on your breasts.
> Scarred by this daylight you lie petalstruck.
> So your skin imitates the flush, your head
> Turning all ways, bearing a havoc of flowers over you.

In contrast, 'The Error of Alarm' is spoken by a woman and suggests that coition (and, by implication, marriage) is both a bargain and a contest in which the physical power is invested in men – hardly Pinter's definitive statement on the subject, but still personally revealing and implicitly feminist in its attitude:

> If my eyes cajole him
> That is the bargain made.
> If my mouth allays him
> I am his proper bride.
>
> If my hands forestall him
> He is deaf to my care.
> If I own to enjoy him
> The bargain's bare.

In professional terms, however, Vivien still had the better bargain. After a brief honeymoon in Cornwall, near the scene of Pinter's wartime evacuation, the pair of them set off for Torquay for another six-month stint in weekly rep. She played lead roles all season. Pinter mixed minor and supporting roles with leads in Christie's *Spider's Web*, Cargill and Beale's *Ring for Catty* (recently produced in the West End by Michael Codron and the ultimate source of the *Carry On* movies) and, intriguingly, Rattigan's *Separate Tables*. Unfashionably for the time, Pinter came to admire Rattigan and learned a good deal from him about the explosive power of theatrical understatement. But looking at Pinter's sustained period in weekly rep – from joining Colchester in February 1955 to leaving Torquay in March 1957 – what is striking is both its cryptic significance and its divorce from his ultimate concerns. As David Baron he learned a fantastic amount about the rhythm and structure of drama and the techniques of theatrical effect; at the same time, as the closet-writer Harold Pinter he was staking claim to private territory that would eventually overwhelm the mechanical resolutions of rep thrillers and the cosy banalities of French-window comedies. Just as Dickens used the cliff-hanging devices of popular serial fiction and allied them to a comic-surreal vision, so Pinter absorbed the disciplines of rep drama and applied them to his own peculiar landscape.

You can see him extending and defining that landscape by looking at the work he wrote in the odd hours stolen from playing suitors, villains and every possible rank of policeman. *The Black and White* (1954–55) is a bleakly brilliant monologue, later transformed into a revue-sketch, and based on the Fleet Street caff which Pinter and Foster used to frequent as students. We even get a glimpse of the man who pulled hairs out of his head which fell into other people's soup. But Pinter transforms observation into newly imagined reality. He creates a world that reeks of solitude, decay and a punishing fear of the dark that drives the woman speaker – an ageing bedsit denizen – to take the all-night bus from Marble Arch six times a week to seek out the temporary solace of the caff. Dickens, you feel, would have recognised this garrulous old party who turns self-address into a form of conversation. There's also something Beckettian about the idea of life reduced to a numbing nightly ritual. But what is peculiar to Pinter is the way he captures the rambling contradictions of the solitary: 'I never go down to the place near the Embankment. I did go down there once' or 'It's always warm in the Black and White, sometimes it's draughty.' The idea of the outside world as implacably hostile also reveals Pinter's distinctive signature. To the old woman, vans are mysterious, cops are suspect and visiting prostitutes evidence of unspeakable terrors: 'One got me sick. Came in a fur coat once. They give you injections, she said, it's all Whitehall, they got it all worked out, she said, they can tap your breath, they inject you in the ears.' This is a world that no one in English drama or fiction – save possibly John Wain in *Hurry on Down* – was recording at the time. Even more startling is the way Pinter neither sentimentalises nor despises this solitary night-owl: he simply presents her as she is.

If Pinter is fascinated by the paranoia of the lonely, he is equally intrigued by the power of the dominant intruder, particularly as embodied in the obsessive, mysterious figure of Kullus. He first cropped up in the dialogue-piece named after him. He appears again in the poem 'The Task' (1954) and the short story 'The Examination' (1955): both confirm Pinter's vision of human relationships as a quest for dominance and control in which the power-balance is capable of reversal. In the poem, Kullus is once more seen as the new arrival for whom the narrator 'closed the open night And tailormade the room'; in 'The Examination', we get a much more detailed account of the process by which power is achieved. Here the speaker summons a figure called Kullus into his room for a series of ritualised, closely structured talks or examinations. He allows Kullus precise intervals of silence in this formal disputation. Indeed, the exact timings of the talks and silences are registered in chalk on a blackboard. But the permitted silences are increasingly accompanied by unpredictable silences: 'where both allotment and duration had rested with me, and had become my imposition, they now proceeded according to his dictates, and became his imposition.' It is through not only the length but also 'the intensity of his silence' that Kullus achieves increasing authority over the speaker. Gradually Kullus starts to initiate intervals at his own inclination, and the physical properties of the room – originally intended to disconcert him – are now subject to his rule.

And when Kullus remarked the absence of a flame in the grate, I was bound to acknowledge this. And when he remarked the presence of the stool, I was equally bound. And when he removed the blackboard, I offered no criticism. And when he closed the curtains I did not object. For we were now in Kullus's room.

It's an archetypal Pinter situation, as he admitted in a 1966 interview in the *Paris Review*. Acknowledging that dominance and subservience was a repeated theme in his plays, he explained,

I wrote a short story a long time ago called 'The Examination' and my ideas of violence carried on from there. That short story dealt very explicitly with two people in one room having a battle of an unspecified nature, in which the question was one of who was dominant at what point and how they were going to be dominant and what tools they would use to achieve dominance and how they would try to undermine the other person's dominance. A threat is constantly there: it's got to do with this question of being in the uppermost position, or attempting to be. That's something of what attracted me to the screenplay of *The Servant*, which was someone else's story, you know. I wouldn't call this violence so much as a battle for positions, it's a very common, everyday thing.

Pinter describes the story as if it were a metaphor for private or domestic life, which in part it is, but it also has extraordinary political resonance. For a start, what separates it from *Kullus* or 'The Task' is that the speaker himself sets out to impose his own will on that of the new arrival. There is an element of coercion – 'Had Kullus not been obliged to attend this examination?' – not present in the previous versions. The speaker also uses his occupancy of the room to throw Kullus off-balance by, for instance, 'the absence of a flame in the grate'. And he deploys the cat-and-mouse tactics of the skilled interrogator: 'It was my aim to avoid the appearance of subjection; a common policy, I understand, in like examinations.' If Kullus eventually gains the upper hand, it is through the standard victim-tactic of silence and unpredictability. While I'm not suggesting that Pinter consciously sat down to write a political fable, it is one whose dynamic would be easily understood in any repressive society. Silence as a weapon of control is also a theme that recurs throughout Pinter's work; and I see an invisible thread linking Kullus's mutinous taciturnity with the subversive silence with which the prisoners in both *One for the Road* and *Mountain Language* challenge and even unnerve their interrogators. Kullus overturns the status quo in a way they never can; but, from the start, Pinter was alert to the political power, as well as the distress, of silence.

Pinter's early work, his later *oeuvre*, and indeed the personality and philosophy of the man himself only come into focus, however, when you read *The Dwarfs*: the patently autobiographical novel on which he worked throughout the early 1950s, dramatised rather tentatively in 1960 and finally published in 1990. It's dazzlingly well written and, rather like Tom Stoppard's sole venture into fiction, *Lord Malquist and Mr Moon*, it offers an invaluable guide to the author's later dramatic themes. But it's also something more than that. By offering a portrait of male friendship recklessly betrayed, it's an attempt to pin down the final break-up of the lost Eden of Pinter's Hackney youth. It clearly was a golden time, and – not unlike the characters in his plays – Pinter spends a lot of time trying to piece together memories of his past. He not only keeps in touch with old Hackney chums but, in his study, retains a picture of his former companions memorialised in a moment of youthful promise. As he once said to me, quoting Proust, '*Le vrai paradis c'est le paradis qu'on a perdu.*'

The novel is as close to actual characters and events as anything Pinter has ever written. Its setting is primarily Hackney with frequent references to Clapton Pond, the Swan café, the railway bridge, the bus routes, even the lilac arch that was a feature of the Pinter garden. And the four characters who dominate the story all have their prototypes in real life. Mark Gilbert, a slightly cocky young actor allegedly of Portuguese descent and just back from a stint in Huddersfield Rep (where Pinter played in November 1954) is a by no means uncritical self-portrait. Pete Cox, arrogantly intelligent and now working for a firm in the City, is closely based on Ron Percival, Pinter's adversarial friend, the most demonic member of the Hackney gang and someone who, in Henry Woolf's phrase, 'had a pride which made Lucifer look modest and shabby'. Len Weinstein, working as a porter at Euston Station and haunted in his imagination by hallucinatory dwarfs whom he finally banishes, is a variant on the music-loving Michael Goldstein. The three young men – close friends who debate art, religion and philosophy while veering from room to room – are all making a bumpy entry into the world of adult experience.

The catalyst who precipitates change in their relationship is an attractive schoolteacher Virginia, based on Jennifer Mortimer who was the only woman ever to be adopted permanently by the Hackney Gang. Virginia is Pete's girlfriend and, when he abandons her, Mark immediately jumps into bed with her. In the process he learns that Pete, with whom he has enjoyed an intellectual companionship of almost erotic intensity, in reality thinks him a fool: a revelation that leads to a blazing showdown between the two men and an irrevocable parting that also, obliquely, banishes the dwarfs that have plagued Len's imagination.

Jennifer Mortimer, now a freelance photographer with three grown-up children, certainly remembers that period as a golden time in her own life. 'I'd known Harold,' she says, 'since he was fourteen when I met him and the others at the Hackney Club. As a group they were terribly tight-knit, very loyal and extremely admired. There were people at the doors screaming to be let in . . . both women and men. Ron Percival was my boyfriend so I tailed along and listened. And if I was educated, it was by sitting around in cafés in Hackney listening to them all talking. They talked about and quoted Shakespeare all the time and *The Dwarfs* is absolutely how it was even to the moment when Ron flung a book at me for daring to quote from *Hamlet* . . . I might have been a catalyst in lots of ways, but the real fight was over the fact that Harold was that much more powerful as a person and Ron was fighting that because he wanted to be king. Harold wasn't fighting for supremacy. He was just floating to the top because of his genuine interest and love and talent. His parents must have been so wonderful to him because he has never, ever really doubted himself.'

The book works brilliantly on many levels, but its emotional drive comes from two things absolutely central to Pinter's work. One is the memory, which may be real or fanciful, of a time past when everything seemed secure, fixed, certain; and, for all Pinter's love of women, you feel the emotional bedrock of his early years was the idea of molten male friendship. But the other quality that drives the book, and much of the later work, is guilt: in particular the guilt that stems from betrayal. In that sense, *The Dwarfs* is far from being a work of self-exculpation. In the final showdown – written with the objectivity of a natural dramatist – Mark (Pinter) accuses Pete (Percival) of betraying the function of a true friend which is that 'of an ambassador to yourself from yourself'. Pete, for all his vainglorious pretensions to godliness, counters by hitting Mark where it hurts when he attacks his integrity: 'You made of your friendship a tool to bludgeon me with and you went off and slept with Virginia.' Hackney's version of the Arthurian Round Table, based on the Holy Grail of pure friendship, has been effectively shattered. Lest that seem a romantic exaggeration, it's worth quoting Pinter's own description on Radio 4's *Kaleidoscope* of an act of sexual betrayal that had extraordinary consequences:

I suddenly recalled a thing which happened to me, not to Mark in the book but to me in real life. I had a group of friends, of which these people in the book are actually included. And I . . . how can I put this? . . . I took one of my friend's girlfriends for a walk down to the River Lea one summer evening which I shouldn't have done, you know. This was found out, naturally, and I was invited one day by two men – I know this sounds like *The Birthday Party*, but I happened to know these people, they were very close friends – and they said, "We're going for a walk, Harold." We got on a bus . . . silence . . . dead silence . . . got to Victoria Park, which is a big park on the way to Bethnal Green in East London. They walked me in silence right into the middle of the park, turned and left me there. I saw them walk away and I felt absolutely desolated. I can't think of a more powerful chastisement really. They had no need to say anything and didn't. That was my humiliation and I realised I had betrayed the whole group of people . . . not only one friend, but the idea of friendship and that was not going to be tolerated by them. I don't think I've recovered since.

That last line was delivered on radio with an ironic laugh, but I was reminded of a remark by Pinter's friend of later years, Joan Bakewell: 'He's immaculate about the significance of his life. Which is why he doesn't need to do much more than walk to the tube – that is full of significance for him.' But this anecdote, as well as displaying Pinter's heightened self-awareness, is genuinely revealing. It shows the dramatic power of silence. It demonstrates the ambiguity and mystery of experience. To an outside onlooker, or someone passing through Victoria Park, the action of the two men – in fact, Henry Woolf and Jimmy Law – would have been inexplicable, whereas to the three participants it had deep personal meaning. Above all, it shows how the Hackney gang attached an almost sacred value to the principle of friendship. That belief is explicitly defined in *The Dwarfs* when Pete, having just described Mark and Len's faults to Virginia, underscores the group's devout sense of commitment: 'In fact he was not sure whether they might not be said to constitute a church, of a kind. They were hardly one in dogma or direction, but there was common ground and there was a framework. At their best they formed a unit and a unit which, in his terms, was entitled to be called a church; an alliance of the three of them for the common good, and a faith in that alliance.' Indeed, Pete goes even further: he tells Virginia somewhat patronisingly that insofar as she does him positive good, he will have more to offer this peculiar holy trinity.

Yet Pinter is a realist as well as an idealist. He knows that any triangular relationship is riddled with internal politics. Pete and Mark have a fierce, combative, intense friendship. The mystery figure is Len in whom each confides and to whom both give advice. Len seems detached, solitary, unworldly, directionless, but he is also more finely tuned than the others. The dwarfs that haunt his imagination – in a series of Joycean interior monologues – may be evidence of schizophrenia; or they may be a visible manifestation of the corruption within this private Eden. That seemed to be Pinter's own interpretation when he came to direct the stage version in 1960 and explained their function to the actors: 'The dwarfs have emerged out of Len's imagination as the truth of the relationship between himself, Pete and Mark. He sees a savage, predatory and disgusting world which is his truth. The fact that Pete and Mark's friendship ends so stupidly bears him out.' But what gives the novel its final glimmer of hope is that the burden of the dwarfs is lifted from Len: the severance of the friendship between Mark and Pete leaves him somehow cleansed, purified, stronger. Equally significant is the way Pinter's awareness of the politics of private relationships prefigures his later work. A point fully grasped by Henry Woolf: 'I once said to Harold it's fascinating how Len uses the two stronger people against each other for his own purposes. And I went on, "Just like in *Old Times*." Harold replied, "I was just going to say that." But, when you think about it, it's uncannily like the way Kate in that play uses Deeley and Anna against each other and emerges victorious.'

The Dwarfs is, in fact, the matrix of Pinter's dramatic imagination: it's full of ideas which echo through his later work. One is the importance of rooms. Not only does most of the action take place in basements, kitchens, bedrooms, but to each of the characters the spaces they inhabit mean something different. For Pete, a room is largely a static construct. For Mark, it is a token of possession and a place of self-definition. For Virginia, a room is a shifting environment depending on one's angle of vision. For Len, it is several things at once: a private sanctuary and retreat ('I have my cat, I have my carpet, I have my land, this is a kingdom, there is no betrayal, there is no trust') and also something that acquires a life of its own (rooms, he says at one point, 'change shape at their own will'). The novel's rooms may not have much of a view; but everyone seems to have views on rooms.

Jennifer Mortimer confirms the absolute accuracy of all this: 'Rooms were exactly the kind of thing the group would talk about. They could take something as ordinary as a cup on a table and by the end of the evening have transformed it. They brought all these new visions and thoughts to an everyday object or an everyday room. The great thing that I suddenly realised was that you didn't have to accept what you saw. That nothing really mattered except the way you saw it . . . But individually they could also be terribly prickly and sensitive so that one hardly dared say anything. Conversations would often run on the lines of "Would you like another tea?" "What do you mean?" "Would you like another tea?" "But I haven't had tea, have I?"' As she repeats this fictive dialogue, it takes on the natural rhythm of a Pinter play.

The Dwarfs is, in fact, very much a novel about language. Pete, Mark and Len talk to each other in a rapid private shorthand that is full of joke names, deft puns, Shakespearean quotations, bizarre *non sequiturs*, ironic clichés. The exchanges are often ritzy, funny and fast, betokening a born writer of dialogue. When Mark, for instance, proudly shows off a new suit to Len they indulge in the rat-a-tat dialogue of a Jewish music-hall double act:

– What's this, a suit? Where's your carnation?
– What do you think of it, Mark asked.
Len fingered the lapels, opened the jacket and looked inside.
– It's not a shmatta, he said.
– It's got a zip at the hips.
– A zip at the hips? What for?
– Instead of a buckle. It's neat.
– Neat? I should say it's neat.
– No turn-ups.
– I can see that. Why didn't you have turn-ups?
– It's smarter without turn-ups.
– Of course it's smarter without turn-ups.

Page after page also ripples with exchanges – sometimes even precise phrases – that would turn up in the later plays. Pete, echoing *The Queen of all the Fairies* and anticipating *The Homecoming*, accuses Mark of being a parasitical observer and implied ponce, 'of operating on life and not in it'. Pete, finding Virginia in a bath-robe and suspicious of her relationship with a friend who may be a scrubber, also asks with Deeleyesque fervour, 'Did she soap your armpits?' But the key point is that the zippy, idiosyncratic language used by the main characters is both proof of their camaraderie and a defence against appropriation by the outside world; against the kind of dead, sterile language used by an old school-chum whom Pete bumps into in Threadneedle Street or by his bureaucratic boss Mr Lynd. Francis Gillen even sees a throughline from *The Dwarfs* to *Mountain Language* where the state categorises everything by name, denies ambiguity, forbids the mountain people to use their own language. As Gillen points out, when individuals' faith in their private language is destroyed, they are already part of the organisation 'for they have nothing but the organisation's terms with which to express themselves'.

Yet the ultimate fascination of *The Dwarfs* is that it contains the seeds of Pinter's own aesthetic convictions. Len, Pete and Mark are forever talking about art: exactly like their counterparts in real life. And although the three men have wildly varying opinions on the function of art and the role of the artist, you feel Pinter draws what he needs from each of them.

In Chapter Six, for instance, Len and Pete engage in a wild, serio-comic discussion about Bach. Interestingly, it's the extract Pinter chose to read for a Platform Performance at the National Theatre in 1990. Who was Bach? asks Pete. What was he up to? Len, who's just been playing Bach's Sonata for Unaccompanied Violin to his cat, is incredulous. 'Bach?' says Len. 'It's simple. The only point about Bach is that he saw his music as emanating through him and not from him. From A via Bach to C. There's nothing else to say.' In fact, quite a lot more is said including the idea that Bach is not concerned with big things such as murder, massacre and earthquake: 'There is always room for him . . . You can put him in your back pocket.' To this day, Bach remains Pinter's favourite composer. It's not just because of his distilled purity of form, but because Pinter himself also seems drawn to the idea of the artist as intermediary to his own muse. His own later plays are nearly always triggered by some unbidden image. And someone who has directed two of them, David Leveaux, cannily remarks, 'I think when he's writing a play there's almost an unchecked open channel between his unconscious and the page. When he finishes that process, the door closes in some way and he is something of a stranger to the work itself.'

The novel also explores the relation between form and content. Pete may be a rum customer who thinks himself a god above the ordinary mortal cycle of love and despair, but his views on writing are full of witty intelligence. In Chapter Twelve, the characters are all sitting in a summer garden (clearly Pinter's own). Len says he's looking for an efficient idea: the way a nutcracker cracks a nut with no waste, but Pete points out that a nutcracker gives off an incidental friction. 'It's exactly the same', he goes on, 'with a work of art. Every particle of a work of art should crack a nut, or help form a pressure that'll crack the final nut. Do you know what I mean? Each idea must possess stringency and economy and the image, if you like, that expresses it must stand in exact correspondence and relation to the idea . . . If there's any excess heat or friction, if there's any waste, you've failed and you have to start again.' In fact, that is a variation on T. S. Eliot's idea of the 'objective correlative' as defined in his essay on *Hamlet*: the notion that you have to find a set of objects or a situation that is the precise formula for a particular emotion. But Pinter, through Pete, puts it more concretely and pithily than Eliot. Pete's observation is also Pinter's unspoken credo in that his whole career is a search for the perfect proportion between the original idea and its ultimate expression. It's what people mean when they call him a poet.

Eliot's ideas about the objective correlative recur in Chapter Twenty-three when Pete and Mark engage in a powerful pub debate – far better than you encounter in most academic tutorials – about Shakespeare and morality.

Pete's point about Othello, Macbeth and Lear, repeating what Eliot says about Hamlet, is that 'their feelings are in excess of the facts'. They seek to exist above and beyond conventional morality, which is simply a convenience suited to the needs of a given situation, and yet are inevitably judged by its criteria. 'Where these geezers slip up', says Pete, 'is that they try to overcome a machine of which they remain, whether they like it or not, a part. The machine, if you like, is morality, the standards of the majority. It seems to me that Shakespeare justifies both the man and the machine.'

Where Pete, who sees himself as superior to conventional morality, argues with tortured logic, Mark replies with a burst of poetic metaphor. To Mark, the Bard-loving actor, Shakespeare is simply too multidimensional, contradictory and audacious ever to be confined by conventional morality. 'How', he asks, 'can moral judgements be applied when you consider how many directions he travels at once? Hasn't he got enough troubles? Look at what he gets up to. He meets himself coming back, he sinks in at the knees, he forgets the drift, he runs away with himself, he falls back on geometry, he turns down blind alleys, he stews in his own juice, and he nearly always ends up by losing all hands. But the fabric, mate, never breaks. The tightrope is never less than at even stretch. He keeps in business, that's what, and if he started making moral judgements, he'd go bankrupt like the others.'

That's a brilliantly impressionistic bit of lit crit. What Mark responds to in Shakespeare is his ability to anatomise mankind without lapsing into easy moral judgements and to manipulate dramatic form without breaking the inherent structure. Everyone writes about the influence of Kafka, Joyce, Eliot and Beckett on Pinter – rightly so – but few people, with the exception of Francis Gillen, have written about the pervasive influence Shakespeare had on his thinking. Pinter prized his *Collected Shakespeare*, acted in the plays at school and also appeared in them with Mac and Wolfit. What he absorbed above all was Shakespeare's refusal to codify or categorise intransigent individuals and judge people according to abstract precepts – as Pete says in *The Dwarfs*, Shakespeare 'didn't measure the man up against the idea and give you hot tips on the outcome'. No more does Pinter. In his rare public pronouncements on drama, he always denies starting from 'any kind of abstract idea or theory' (Bristol, 1962) or setting out 'a blueprint for his characters' and keeping them rigidly to it (Hamburg, 1970). He is much too pragmatic and intuitive a writer for that. In private, too, he makes it clear that his characters are driven by primal needs rather than weighed in the moral balance. As he wrote to Guy Vaesen after the first night of *The Homecoming* in 1965, in a pregnant phrase that sums up a lot of his work, 'I don't feel myself more critical of any one character as opposed to another. I love and detest the lot of them.'

Yet the great thing about *The Dwarfs* is that it works on so many levels. It is a very precise record of the life led by Pinter and his intellectual chums in post-war Hackney. As Jennifer Mortimer says, 'It ought to be on a school syllabus. It captures exactly that feeling of London life in the late 1940s and early '50s. It was an embryo time for all of us.' It also outlines the aesthetic principles that were to govern Pinter's whole writing career. And it brings together many of the preoccupations that were to become part of Pinter's permanent theatrical landscape: friendship, betrayal, dominance, subservience, sexual rivalry, space invasion, the dream of a secure, paradisal past and the fear of an insecure, provisional present and future. By 1956, through a combination of his Hackney friendships, his odd-jobbing life experience, his years in rep and his absorption of varying external influences from Buñuel and Beckett to Shakespeare, Pinter's dream world had already taken shape. What he clearly needed was some event that would propel him towards his unavoidable destiny: the impossibly difficult business of writing plays.

Four Early Stages

It was, in fact, Quentin Crisp, a flamboyant, henna-haired sexual outsider immortalised in television's *The Naked Civil Servant*, who unwittingly inspired Pinter's first play, *The Room*. Everything – as so often in later years – began with an image that was secreted in the memory, acquired dramatic resonance and gradually evolved into a play. It was the very opposite of an instant Polaroid snap; the negative was stored away and slowly developed in the dark-room of Pinter's imagination. Pinter's memory is that while still in rep in Colchester in 1955, he had been taken by an actress in the company to a Sunday-night party in a big house in Chelsea. During the evening the actress invited him to meet the man upstairs. 'She knocked on the door and it was opened by a little man with the most extraordinary colour hair, bare feet and extremely fluid clothes . . . He welcomed us in, gave us a cup of tea, discussed philosophy and metaphysics, literature, the weather, crockery, fabrics. And all the while at a table sat an enormous man with a cap on reading a comic. The little chap was dancing about cutting bread and butter, pouring tea and making bacon and eggs for this man who remained quite silent throughout the whole encounter . . . We left after about half an hour and I asked the woman what the little chap's name was and she said Quentin Crisp.'

A silent giant and his attentive, chattering helpmate: the image stuck with Pinter. It may even have aroused faint memories of Lennie and George in one of his all-time-favourite American novels, Steinbeck's *Of Mice and Men*; a work that sees male friendship in specifically Arthurian terms with the journey towards the grail of a small-holding taking on the flavour of a knight's quest. But Pinter did not immediately rush home and set down his impressions. What happened was that over a year later in the autumn of 1956, Auriol Smith, who was President of the Green Room Society at Bristol University's recently founded Drama Department, was looking to put on an evening of one-act plays. She turned for advice to Henry Woolf who was doing a postgraduate year in Bristol after studying in the States. Woolf said he had a mate who was an actor in rep who might have something. Pinter had already spoken to him about an idea for a play based on the image of the two men in the room. Woolf wrote to Pinter, who was by now newly married and in the middle of a season at Torquay. He replied that he couldn't possibly deliver anything in under six months. In fact, the play arrived in the post very shortly. It was written over four afternoons and late nights while Pinter was playing in Rattigan's *Separate Tables* at the Pavilion Theatre, Torquay, in November 1956. *The Room*, as the play was called, was eventually staged by the Bristol Drama Department in May 1957 in a converted squash-court and in a production by Woolf himself in which every expense was spared. 'The first Pinter production,' claims Woolf, 'cost four and sixpence. It shouldn't even have been that much. I'd told the stage manager not to give the character of Bert real bacon and eggs except for one performance because we had no money. I'd budgeted the production, literally, at one and ninepence, and she went and spent four and sixpence. But it went down very well. It was menacing and very funny.'

Needless to say, the finished play is nothing to do with Quentin Crisp and his chum, but it capitalises on that same arresting image Pinter glimpsed in the Chelsea house and invests it with theatrical tension. We are in a bedsit dominated by a rocking-chair, gas stove and sink. An elderly woman, Rose, is making bacon and eggs, tea, and bread and butter for a man, Bert, who sits strangely, unnervingly silent at a table reading a magazine. Instantly, Pinter arouses one's curiosity. Why is Bert so silent? Why does Rose chatter incessantly? What is she frightened of? Why does she so frequently harp on the room's warmth and seclusion as against the dark and cold outside? And why is she so preoccupied by the dank and fearful basement? 'I don't know who lives down there now', she says. 'Whoever it is, they're taking a big chance. Maybe they're foreigners.' Within the first ten minutes of his dramatic début, Pinter has staked out his own peculiar territory.

The play's dynamic also springs from a subject Pinter was to make very much his own: the confrontation of an anxious recluse with the demands and pressures of the outside world. Rose's entombed withdrawal is, in fact, subject to endless interruption. First, it is Mr Kidd, the ostensible landlord who seems hilariously vague about his present, his past, his place of abode and even his origins. ('I think my mum was a Jewess. Yes, I wouldn't be surprised to learn that she was a Jewess. She didn't have many babies.') After Mr Kidd has left and Bert has gone off into the Arctic night to do an errand in his van, Rose's space is constantly invaded. A young married couple, Mr and Mrs Sands, suddenly appear at the door having penetrated the dark and mysterious basement where an unseen figure has told them that there is a room vacant: Rose's apprehension, and ours, is increased when the room turns out to be her own. Then Mr Kidd returns – having waited all weekend to catch Rose alone – to tell her that there is a man lurking in the basement desperate to see her. The wilting Rose agrees to see the earnest supplicant who turns out to be a blind black man called Riley. After being abused and insulted by Rose, he tells her he has a message for her. 'Your father wants you to come home', announces Riley. He then addresses her more directly. He repeatedly asks 'Come home, Sal': a name Rose initially denies and then tacitly acknowledges. But as Rose tenderly touches Riley's eyes, head and temples, the hitherto-silent Bert returns and the play builds to a violent climax. Bert draws the curtains, describes his van journey in aggressively sexual terms, upends Riley's chair and, with a cry of 'Lice', strikes him, knocks him down and kicks his head against the gas stove. Rose is left clutching her eyes crying: 'Can't see. I can't see. I can't see.' Blackout. Curtain.

What does all this signify? And what does all this tell us about the nature of Pinter's dramatic imagination? Although the play is now rarely performed, it has been subject to endless analysis. Woolf's original production emphasised the play's humour and saw Riley as a mythical magic man coming with a message of liberation. Others have seen Riley as a Christ-figure who dies for Rose or as a symbol of Death whom we reluctantly admit across the threshold. Patently Pinter, writing in haste over four days and simply opening a channel to his subconscious, did not set out to write an allegory. But as Jung once explained in a 1935 lecture at the Tavistock Clinic attended by Samuel Beckett, a writer inevitably dramatises his complexes or fragmentary personalities:

> When he creates a character on the stage, or in his poem or drama or novel, he thinks it is merely a product of his imagination; but that character in a certain secret way has made itself. Any novelist or writer will deny that these characters have a psychological meaning, but as a matter of fact you know as well as I do that they have one. Therefore you can read a writer's mind when you study the characters he creates.

So what can we read of Pinter's mind from *The Room*? Obviously the play was triggered by an observed image and expands on ideas present in his early prose-dialogues. But the piece's fascination lies in its unconscious mixture of biographical, literary and social themes: on one level, it deals with the clamorous demands made by family and, if you like, the traditional household gods upon someone seeking to evade their clutches. Six times Riley invokes the word 'home'. Five times he calls Rose 'Sal' (short for Sarah? asked Martin Esslin). All this implies Rose has shed her past and is living under an assumed name. And, when it looks as if she may succumb to Riley's urgent blandishments, Bert returns home and, in a mixture of sexual and racial fury, beats him to pulp.

My own initial assumption was that the play offers a metaphor for Pinter's experience. He wrote it only six weeks after his marriage to Vivien Merchant; also at the time when he was known as David Baron and was so addressed by his wife. By marrying outside the Jewish faith, Pinter, who was very close to his mother and father, had also caused a certain 'perturbation' (his words) within the family. And he had made an inevitable physical break with Thistlewaite Road where he had lived, on and off, for the first twenty-five years of his life. It seemed to me that *The Room* was a projection of his own guilt about the emotional dislocation caused by his marriage and his fear that the insistent claims of the family, of tradition and the past are never that easily put aside – a theme to which he constantly returns. But Pinter himself – in one of his rare discussions about interpretation – disputes that reading. 'I've always seen Riley,' he says, 'as a messenger, a potential saviour who is trying to release Rose from the imprisonment of the room and the restrictions of her life with Bert. He's inviting her to come back to her spiritual home; which is why he gets beaten up when Bert returns. But, to me, Riley has always been a redemptive figure and that was how I staged it when I later came to direct it with Vivien and a fine black actor called Thomas Baptiste.'

However you interpret it, *The Room* is a highly personal work in which Pinter is writing about the loss of identity that comes through the pincer-like claims of past and present. But he is also dealing with the perils of withdrawal from the outside world and the emotional hazard of turning a room into a fortress. Again, he is conceivably drawing on the memory of Len in *The Dwarfs* – closely based on his friend Michael Goldstein – whose partial breakdown is symbolised by his transformation of his room into a 'cell' and a 'compartment' where he is wedged 'between two strangers'. Convivial as the Hackney gang were, many of them lived close to the edge. Even Henry Woolf, who commissioned *The Room*, had been known to lock himself into his parents' house for a week and refuse to venture forth. Pinter knew all about the dangers of being bounded in a nutshell even though one counted oneself a king of infinite space.

Yet *The Room* is fascinating precisely because it unconsciously reflects so many of Pinter's deepest preoccupations. One of them was with Beckett's novel *Murphy*, which Pinter had so eagerly read three years before and pressed upon all his friends. Beckett's hero is an instinctive solitary who shares his creator's womb-fixation, who lives in a condemned building in London's West Brompton and who finds comfort only by stripping off his clothes, tying himself to a rocking-chair and going into a trance-like state.

Eventually he is forced by his girlfriend Celia into taking a job and winds up in a mental hospital where he comes to envy, and even emulate, the patients' withdrawal from the world. Indeed, the hospital's aim of restoring the inmates to the outer world is revolting to Murphy, 'whose experience as a rational being obliged him to call sanctuary what the psychiatrists called exile and to think of the patients not as banished from a system of benefits but as escaped from a colossal fiasco'.

Pinter does not swallow Murphy's philosophy whole (neither perhaps does Beckett), but the novel left its visible imprint on *The Room* and much of his early work. In the play, a key visual symbol is a rocking-chair in which Rose, not unlike Beckett's hero, achieves her few moments of immured content. ('If they ever ask you, Bert, I'm quite happy where I am. We're quiet, we're all right. You're happy up here. It's not far up either, when you come in from outside. And we're not bothered. And nobody bothers us.') And, although in this and other plays Pinter suggests that one can never escape the responsibilities that come from being a member of society, he nevertheless profoundly understands the impulse to withdraw; to say, like Beckett's Murphy, 'I am not of the big world, I am of the little world.' Indeed, much of his best work is an exploration of the tension between solitude and society.

One aspect of *The Room* which has been little noticed, however, is its social accuracy: in particular, its portrait of a walled-in isolationism and paranoid xenophobia that was to become a feature of English life in the late 1950s and that has grown to hideous proportions ever since. Rose takes pride in the fact that ' we keep ourselves to ourselves', fears there might be 'foreigners' in the basement and reacts with hysterical vindictiveness to the invasion of her sanctuary ('You're not only a nut', she tells Riley, 'you're a blind nut and you can get out the way you came'). Bert's instant reaction to finding a black stranger in his room is to beat him up. Pinter was not consciously making a political statement; but he was certainly picking up on something that was in the air at the time. He had lived through the racism of Hackney in the 1930s and 1940s. In the 1950s, as Kenneth O. Morgan has written regarding Sir Oswald Mosley's political re-emergence, 'blacks now replaced Jews as the threat to the Aryan master-race'. The decade saw a large increase in the number of Commonwealth immigrants not only from the West Indies but also from India, Pakistan and West Africa. In 1958 Lord Hailsham estimated the 'coloured' population at 180,000, and in the same year racial tension was to flare up in Notting Hill. Pinter is obviously not dealing explicitly with race relations, but he pins down with intuitive accuracy a localised prejudice that sees outsiders as inherently suspect. One easily forgets that, in the days before the Race Relations Act of 1965, it was not an offence to stick a card in a lodging-house window saying 'No blacks or Irish'.

Surrendering to his instinct, Pinter produced a remarkably assured first play in *The Room*, one that subconsciously interwove autobiographical, psychological and social themes. The dialogue also provides evidence of his uncannily accurate ear. Everyone who knew him in Hackney, Jennifer Mortimer especially, testifies to the fact that he was an extraordinarily good listener – in your company, he gave you his total concentration. He also, from the start, understood that conversation rarely proceeds according to question-and-answer logic, but is often more in the nature of an interrupted private monologue. It was a technique he was to refine and develop in the later plays, but already in *The Room* Pinter captures the comic inconsequentiality of everyday speech. At one point Rose asks the landlord Mr Kidd how many floors there are in the house. A pretty bizarre question, but first of all the landlord evades it: 'Floors. (*He laughs.*) Ah, we had a good few of them in the old days.' He then explains how he used to be on top of things, such as counting floors, when his sister was alive and that she took after their mum who may or may not have been a Jewess. But Rose obstinately persists in her single-minded interrogation:

ROSE: What about your sister, Mr Kidd?

MR KIDD: What about her?

ROSE: Did she have any babies?

MR KIDD: Yes, she had a resemblance to my old mum, I think. Taller, of course.

ROSE: When did she die then, your sister?

MR KIDD: Yes, that's right, it was after she died that I must have stopped counting. She used to keep things in very good trim. And I gave her a helping hand. She was very grateful, right until her last. She always used to tell me how much she appreciated all the – little things – that I used to do for her. Then she copped it. I was her senior. Yes, I was her senior. She had a lovely boudoir. A beautiful boudoir.

ROSE: What did she die of?

MR KIDD: Who?

ROSE: Your sister.

This is *echt* Pinter: the lapse into recollection of things past, the shock-tactic intrusion of demotic speech into golden memories ('Then she copped it') and, above all, the sense that conversation often proceeds along non-converging parallel lines.

However, when Pinter eventually saw *The Room* performed at Bristol in

May 1957 it was not the pleasure in hearing his own dialogue that first struck him; it was nerves and an overfull bladder. 'I wanted to piss very badly throughout the whole thing,' he recalls, 'and at the end I dashed out behind the bicycle shed.' But the more important discovery was that he could trust his own theatrical intuition. He had written *The Room* in a white heat of creative frenzy. 'I started at the top,' he remembers, 'and at a certain point there was a knock at the door and someone came in and I had absolutely no idea who he was, who he might be or what he might say. I let it run, let it happen and found he did have a voice and that he was the landlord. And then two visitors arrived and I didn't know what they were on about really, what they wanted but they were just part of the whole atmosphere.' But it worked. It made sense. And Pinter admits he became very excited 'by the way images could clearly be expressed on stage in theatrical form'. Not words, one notices, but images; which is significant in that nearly all Pinter's subsequent plays were to be triggered by a stored-up visual memory.

The play also impressed those who saw it and performed it. The critic of the *Bristol Evening Post* presciently remarked 'Throughout there runs a rare vitality and, with experience and greater conciseness, one feels Mr Pinter may well make some impact as a dramatist'. And Susan Engel (Rose), Henry Woolf (who played Mr Kidd, as well as directing) and Auriol Smith (Mrs Sands) all felt they had been involved in an exceptional play. 'We accepted its oddity,' says Smith, 'and the fact we weren't going to understand everything going on. But it gave us such rich dialogue to speak that we trusted the material. It was like going into someone's house for a day and picking up the strange vibrations going on. You don't have to know every detail of the relationships to pick up on the atmosphere. But the biggest surprise was when Harold himself arrived. I suppose I'd expected a slightly scruffy occupant of a bedsit. Instead I met a man in a smart pinstripe suit and – I swear – a hat.' The hat is hard to believe; but Pinter, even at his poorest, always prided himself on his sartorial fastidiousness.

At this stage of his life he was still desperately poor. Vivien got some work in 1957 with a travelling rep company; Pinter himself, after leaving Torquay, managed to get a job touring in a dim French-window farce, *Dear Charles*. But out of Pinter's poverty came a chance encounter that was to have a decisive effect on his professional future. One date on the dreaded tour was the Bristol Hippodrome. Because money was tight Pinter phoned Susan Engel – still a Drama Department student – who kindly offered him a spare bed in her flat. Pinter takes up the story: 'One night after the show I returned to the flat and went straight to bed. About midnight I was awoken by Susan. She told me that John Hall, the author of a play then playing at the Bristol

Old Vic, had popped in for a nightcap, bringing with him his literary agent from London. She thought it would be in my interests to meet this agent. I demurred, pleading exhaustion, but she insisted. I put on a dressing-gown and went into the kitchen. In the kitchen was Jimmy Wax. He told me he had heard about *The Room* and suggested that Susan and I read a scene from the play. So, at midnight in Susan's kitchen, in I think July of 1957, I, as it were, auditioned for Jimmy. He laughed a good deal during the reading and asked me to send him the play. The visitors left, Susan was delighted, I went back to bed.'

A week later Jimmy Wax – a First in Law at New College, Oxford, a former judge with the British Army of Occupation in Europe and a leading agent since 1946 – wrote to Pinter proposing that he represent him. Thus began a relationship, based on friendship and mutual respect, that was to last until Jimmy Wax's death in 1983. (Continuity was preserved, however, in that Pinter was then represented by Judy Daish who had trained with Wax for five years before setting up her own agency.) Wax also seems to have swung into action immediately on behalf of *The Room* which was then in the hands of BBC Radio's drama script unit. It had been sent to them in May 1957 by a Bristol-based producer, Patrick Dromgoole, but it seems to have aroused interest rather than enthusiasm. Barbara Bray, later to work closely with Pinter on a Proust film, was script editor for sound drama and wrote to Wax on 25 July 1957 saying that she didn't think it was 'a practical proposition' for radio, but expressing interest in Pinter's future work. She amplified the point in an internal memo to Dromgoole: 'I think the dialogue shows unusual skill but that the author has not taken enough pains to get his underlying intention across. This gives an air of pretentiousness which conflicts strongly with the assurance and comic sense which precede the resolution.' Pinter himself wrote to R. D. Smith in December enclosing a copy of the play and suggesting that, even if it was too visual to work on radio, it might work as a TV experiment.

Although rejected by the BBC, *The Room* rapidly became Pinter's calling-card. On 30 December 1957 it was revived at the National Student Drama Festival held that year at Bristol University. In fact, this was a new production jointly credited to the drama department and the Bristol Old Vic Theatre School, and directed – much to Henry Woolf's chagrin – by the school's principal, Ducan Ross. 'His version,' says Woolf, 'had no humour in it at all. It was the beginning of a Pinter tradition where the grim hand of reverence is laid on the work so that you don't laugh.' But the great advantage of the festival was that it was sponsored by the *Sunday Times* and in those more manageable days was attended by the paper's chief theatre critic,

Harold Hobson. Hobson was a hugely influential, idiosyncratic critic who relied – often to dazzling effect – on his own intuitions about drama. A devout Christian and a pugnacious moralist, he also had a keen sense of theatre's capacity to reverse expectations based, he often claimed, on his Oxford reading of Thucydides's account of the defeat of the Athenian expedition against Syracuse in the *History of the Peloponnesian War*. Hobson had already championed *Waiting for Godot* and *Look Back in Anger*. He seems to have had a similarly transforming experience on first encountering *The Room*. His *Sunday Times* review not only invoked Beckett, Ionesco and Henry James, but claimed that 'The play makes one stir uneasily in one's shoes and doubt, for a moment, the comforting solidity of the earth'. On a more practical note, his column also commended the play to the attention of the directors of the English Stage Company and London's Arts Theatre before they ate their Sunday lunch. For Pinter, living with a heavily pregnant Vivien in a flat in Notting Hill Gate and currently playing in R. F. Delderfield's *Worm's Eye View* for Fred Tripp's company at the Intimate Theatre, Palmer's Green, the notice was manna from heaven: the first major critical recognition of his talent. And, even if Hobson's clarion-call didn't seem to stir the directors of the Royal Court or the Arts, it did bring Pinter to the attention of a quiet-spoken twenty-seven-year-old commercial producer, Michael Codron, who had made his West End début in 1956 with *Ring for Catty*. Needlessly ashamed of his cramped office-quarters in Regent Street, Codron quickly arranged to meet Pinter and Wax in the slightly more sumptuous atmosphere of the cocktail bar of the Strand Palace Hotel in January 1958. He told them that in partnership with David Hall he had booked the Lyric Hammersmith for a season and was urgently looking for new plays. Did they have anything to show him? He was immediately sent a copy of a play called *The Party* – soon to be *The Birthday Party* – which Pinter had written in provincial dressing-rooms and theatrical digs in his spare moments during a tour in 1957 of *Doctor in the House*. 'I thought immediately,' said Codron, 'it was an excellent play. When it was later found to be obscure, I couldn't understand it: when you see it now, you're at a loss to understand why it should ever have been so bewildering.' Within three months, Codron had put the play into production with a first-rate cast and a fast-rising young director, Peter Wood. The result, of course, was to be one of the most famous flops in theatrical history.

The production of the play meant everything to Pinter. Throughout this period he was a hard-up, jobbing actor desperate to make ends meet. After the *Doctor in the House* tour, he'd had a four-play engagement with Derek Salberg's Alexandra Theatre Rep Company in Birmingham (July–October

1957), had moved on to the Intimate, Palmer's Green (December 1957–March 1958), where he'd ended up playing Cliff in *Look Back in Anger*. In April he got a job understudying in two N. F. Simpson plays and *Epitaph for George Dillon* at the Royal Court. Cash in hand was now an imperative since on 29 January 1958 Vivien had given birth to a son, Daniel. For her it had been a difficult and traumatic period of labour; one that eventually made her determine to have no more children. As if the painful childbirth were not enough, the Pinters at the time were living in a dismal basement in Notting Hill Gate. 'It was virtually a slum,' Pinter recalls. 'We were living rent-free in exchange for which Vivien was doing the laundry and I was stoking the boiler: in effect, we were the caretakers. I remember a terrible stone kitchen with water dripping down the walls. It would have been impossible to bring up a baby there and I recall having a drink with Henry Woolf in the Hoop in Notting Hill Gate and wondering how on earth Vivien and I were going to cope when she came out of hospital. In fact, I found a perfectly decent two-room, first-floor flat in Chiswick High Road, but I hadn't got the £100, or anything like it, for the deposit. So I wrote out of the blue to a producer, Rita Buchan, who was a great admirer of Vivien's work, and told her how desperate we were and she sent the money by return purely as a gift. It was an act of staggering generosity and really saved our lives.' Michael Codron also took out a £50 option on *The Birthday Party* which enabled them to turn down the offer of a double-job, at £17 per week each, in the spring season at the Alex, Birmingham. It was, in fact, Pinter who suggested to Vivien that they stay in London because of the upcoming production. 'But she,' he says, 'could not take it as a concrete thing, it was no more than a dream for her. However, I insisted and we did stay in London . . .We would, in fact, have done better to have gone to Birmingham, but we didn't and my life just changed.'

Rightly, Pinter perceived that his career was at a crossroads. In writing *The Room*, he had discovered his true vocation, which was for giving public form to private dreams: the essential occupation of the dramatist. In the summer of 1957 he had gone on to write, in fairly rapid succession, both his three-act play and a shorter piece called *The Dumb Waiter*. But from what recesses of the imagination did *The Birthday Party* spring? What was its source of inspiration? As so often with Pinter, the play derived from an image that took obstinate root in his memory. Just as Olivier would store up a mannerism or speech-pattern he had observed for future use, so Pinter allowed an initial image slowly to develop in his imagination. In this case it dated back to the summer of 1954 when he had been somewhat ingloriously operating the equine head in L. du Garde Peach's *A Horse! A Horse!* The tour had started in Eastbourne, Pinter had not fixed up anywhere to stay and on a rainy

Sunday evening was having a drink in a pub when he fell into conversation with a strange, laconic man:

'He said, "I can take you to some digs but I wouldn't recommend them exactly." I had nowhere else to go and I said, "I don't care what they are." I went to these digs and found, in short, a very big woman who was the landlady and a little man, the landlord. There was no one else there, apart from this solitary lodger, and the digs were really quite filthy, the house was quite filthy and I used to . . . I slept in the attic with this man I'd met in the pub . . . we shared the attic and there was a sofa over my bed . . . you know what I mean . . . propped up so I was looking at this sofa from which hairs and dust fell continuously. And I said to the man one day, "What are you doing here?" And he said, "Oh well I used to be . . . I'm a pianist. I used to play in the concert-party here and I gave that up." I said, "Where did you come from? Did you play the piano . . . " He said, "Oh I used to play in London, yes. But I gave that up." . . . The woman was really quite a voracious character, always tousled his head and tickled him and goosed him and wouldn't leave him alone at all. And when I asked why he stayed, he said, "There's nowhere else to go." That remark stayed with me and, three years later, the image was still there and I . . . this idea came to me about two men coming down to get him . . . '

The lonely lodger, the ravenous landlady, the quiescent husband: these figures, eventually to become Stanley, Meg and Petey, sound like figures in a Donald McGill seaside postcard. But the first key to unlocking *The Birthday Party* is to remember its roots in the popular culture of its day. It's vital to recall that, in the period between the Eastbourne experience and its transformation into drama, Pinter had appeared in over sixty plays, mostly potboilers, in provincial rep. Of all his works, this is the one that most obviously bears the stamp of the thrillers and comedies of its day; like a stick of seaside rock, it says 'rep' all the way through. The faintly maniacal fugitive, the interventionist authority figures, the cliché-toting working-class characters: these were the very stuff of 1950s theatre. The structure is also extremely traditional. There are three strong 'curtains' to each act: in the first, Stanley beats with savage ferocity the drum Meg has given him as a birthday present; in the second, the giggling Stanley is pinned against a wall in the darkness by the threatening Goldberg and McCann; in the third, everything reverts to apparent normality as Meg, after Stanley has been carted off by the mysterious visitors, lapses into girlish reverie. If the play had been tried out in seaside rep in Bournemouth or Torquay, I bet the audience would have loved it.

However, Pinter also picks up on other aspects of popular culture. The renegade hiding away from the mobsters he has betrayed was an archetypal Hollywood situation; it was there in Robert Siodmak's 1946 film, *The Killers*, which was a bastardised version of a 1926 Hemingway short story on which Pinter doted. Also, I can never sit through the quick-fire stichomythia of Goldberg and McCann's interrogation of Stanley without thinking of a 1950s quiz show in which a bullying Michael Miles forced contestants to answer as many questions as possible in sixty seconds without saying 'Yes' or 'No'. And Ronald Knowles articulated a thought that had been dogging me for years when he suggested that the comedy double act of Jewel and Warriss, famous in the 1950s on music-hall and radio, was the prototype of Goldberg and McCann. Ben Warriss, sleek and sharp-suited with patent-leather hair, was always the bullying straight man; Jimmy Jewel, nervously apprehensive, was the comic fall guy. Their double act was a classic study in domination and submission: the sketch that still haunts me is one where Warriss, as an over-enthusiastic salesman, inserted Jewel in a vertical tank to demonstrate the magical properties of a pen that wrote under water. Interestingly both of them – Jewel, more especially – turned into very good straight actors and would have been ideally cast in *The Birthday Party*.

The power of the play, however, resides precisely in the way Pinter takes stock ingredients of popular drama and invests them with political resonance. At its very simplest, the play shows an obstinately reclusive hero being ob-liged to conform to the external pressures of conventional society. Throughout the twentieth century, dramatists have been writing plays – Shaw's *St Joan*, Brecht's *Galileo*, Miller's *The Crucible* – that pit the indi-vidual conscience against the inflexible dogmas of religion and the state. And, around the time Pinter's play was being written, Osborne's *The Entertainer* was being staged at the Royal Court: a play that also shows the walls closing in on a failed artist who finally has to face emigration to the supposedly conformist hell of Canada. But although *The Birthday Party* is part of a long dramatic tradition and grows specifically out of *The Room* in its opposition of solitude and society, Pinter gives the issue infinitely greater political and philosophical complexity than in his earlier play.

In a letter written to the play's director, Peter Wood, on 30 March 1958, just before the start of rehearsals, Pinter rightly refused to add extra lines explain-ing or justifying Stanley's motives in withdrawing from the world into a dingy seaside boarding-house: 'Stanley *cannot* perceive his only valid justifi-cation – which is he is what he is – therefore he certainly can never be articulate about it.' But Pinter came much closer than he usually does to offering an explanation of the finished work:

We've agreed: the hierarchy, the Establishment, the arbiters, the socio-religious monsters arrive to affect censure and alteration upon a member of the club who has discarded responsibility (that word again) towards himself and others. (What is your opinion, by the way, of the act of suicide?) He does possess, however, for my money, a certain fibre – he fights for his life. It doesn't last long, this fight. His core being a quagmire of delusion, his mind a tenuous fuse box, he collapses under the weight of their accusation – an accusation compounded of the shit-stained strictures of centuries of 'tradition'.

This gets us right to the heart of the matter. It is not simply a play about a pathetic victim brainwashed into social conformity. It is a play about the need to resist, with the utmost vigour, dead ideas and the inherited weight of the past. And if you examine the text, you notice how Pinter has toughened up the original image of the man in the Eastbourne digs with 'nowhere to go'. Pinter's Stanley Webber – a palpably Jewish name, incidentally – is a man who shores up his precarious sense of self through fantasy, bluff, violence and his own manipulative form of power-play. His treatment of Meg initially is rough, playful, teasing: he's an ersatz, scapegrace Oedipus to her boarding-house Jocasta. But once she makes the fateful, mood-changing revelation – 'I've got to get things in for the two gentlemen' – he's as dangerous as a cornered animal. He affects a wanton grandeur with his talk of a European concert tour. He projects his own fear on to Meg by terrorising her with stories of nameless men coming to abduct her in a van. In his first solo encounter with McCann, he tries to win him over by appealing to a shared past (Maidenhead, Fuller's tea shop, Boots Library) and a borrowed patriotism ('I know Ireland very well. I've many friends there. I love that country and I admire and trust its people . . . I think their policemen are wonderful'). At the start of the interrogation he resists Goldberg's injunction to sit down and at the end of it he knees him in the stomach. And, in the panic of the party, he attempts to strangle Meg and rape Lulu. These are hardly the actions of a supine victim. Even though Stanley is finally carried off shaven, besuited, white-collared and ostensibly tamed, the spirit of resistance is never finally quelled. When asked how he regards the prospect of being able to 'make or break' in the integrated outer world, he does not stay limply silent, but produces the most terrifying noises:

> (*Stanley concentrates, his mouth opens, he attempts to speak, fails and emits sounds from his throat:*)
> STANLEY: Uh-gug . . . uh-gug . . . eeehhh-gag . . . (*On the breath*) Caah . . . caahh . . .

(They watch him. He draws a long breath which shudders down his body. He concentrates.)

GOLDBERG: Well, Stanny boy, what do you say, eh?

(They watch. He concentrates. His head lowers, his chin draws into his chest, he crouches.)

STANLEY: Ug-gughh . . . uh-gughhh . . .

You could argue that this is a man who, with his smashed glasses and maimed or ripped-out tongue, has been robbed of the power of sight and speech in the interests of social and political conformity. What I suspect Pinter is showing is that there is some grit in the human spirit that resists total submission.

On one level, it's a play about active resistance written by a born nay-sayer – a point Pinter confirmed in a public conversation with Mel Gussow in 1988. After noting that he himself had refused Peter Wood's request to spell out the play's message, Pinter continued:

Between you and me, the play showed how the bastards . . . how religious forces ruin our lives. But who's going to say that in the play? That would be impossible. I said to Peter Wood, did he want Petey, the old man, to act as a chorus? All Petey says is one of the most important lines I've ever written. As Stan is taken away, Petey says, 'Stan, don't let them tell you what to do.' I've lived that line all my damn life. Never more than now.

The play's autobiographical significance could hardly be more explicit: Pinter identifies with Stan and Petey's active and passive resistance to the 'religious forces' of Judaism and Catholicism represented by Goldberg and McCann. And Pinter knew what he was talking about: he himself had discarded the Jewish faith at thirteen and in Ireland had encountered the strictness of Catholic morality partly through his often sexually frustrating liaison with Pauline Flanagan. In one sense, Goldberg and McCann decisively represent the two great autocratic Western religions. In the interrogation scene, the questions are never merely random. Goldberg attacks Stanley for betraying wife, mother, origins ('Webber! Why did you change your name?') and religious faith. Indeed, he hammers away at the last point: 'You stink of sin' – 'Do you recognise an external force, responsible for you, suffering for you' – 'When did you last pray?' – 'When did you last pray?' McCann, meanwhile, goes for Stanley as a traitor both to Catholic morality and the linked cause of Irish nationalism: 'What about Ireland?' – 'You're a traitor to the cloth.' – 'What about the Albigensenist heresy?' – 'What about the blessed Oliver Plunkett?' Pinter subconsciously pours into that scene all his own detestation of the moral pressures of orthodox religion.

What, however, gives *The Birthday Party* its political and philosophical complexity is the sense that Goldberg and McCann are themselves victims. They represent not only the West's most autocratic religions, but its two most persecuted races. As the play proceeds, the two characters gradually fall apart making the climax much more equivocal than is generally recognised. Goldberg, who initially radiates *fausse bonhomie* and the weight of Jewish tradition, is eventually revealed as a weak-willed Organisation Man: 'Follow the line, the line, McCann, and you can't go wrong.' The man who at the start quelled his partner's nerves by announcing 'The secret is breathing. Take my tip' is forced to rely on his partner's injection of breath to continue. The man who promised that the mission would be accomplished 'with no excessive aggravation to you or myself' has been proved disastrously wrong. And the Goldberg who at first exuded philosophic certainty is unable to complete his final thought:

> And you'll find – that what I say is true.
> Because I believe that the world . . . (*Vacant.*) . . .
> Because I believe that the world . . . (*Desperate.*) . . .
> BECAUSE I BELIEVE THAT THE WORLD . . . (*Lost.*) . . .

If McCann's breakdown is less spectacular, it is because he has from the start shown nervous apprehension and a precarious stability symbolised by his obsessive tearing of a sheet of newspaper into five equal strips. But at the end, even the psychopathic McCann is reduced to a wreck announcing grimly, after the night-long bedroom subjugation of the mutinous Stanley: 'I'm not going up there again.' As Sam Mendes' 1994 production at the National Theatre brilliantly showed, Goldberg and McCann are even sweatily panic-stricken at the threat posed by the seemingly ineffectual Petey. *The Birthday Party* is not simply a play about a truculent recluse whose will is broken by two authority figures. It is a much more complex work about a defiant rebel who exposes the insecurity upon which adherence to orthodoxy and tradition actually rests: a theme Pinter was to pursue in the more overtly political plays of the 1980s.

Through the character of Goldberg, Pinter also reveals something of his own complicated attitude to the whole question of Jewish identity. He exposes the shakiness of a blind, unthinking obeisance to the past. Goldberg's cosy avuncularity is seen as essentially hollow and the 'respect' for one's forbears that he preaches to McCann shows how ancestor-worship can reach the point of dementia. But Pinter, while satirising Jewish tradition, also shows Goldberg as a terrified, even beleaguered figure. In a sense, that is an index of Pinter's own ambivalence. He rejects the Jewish religion, argues with his Zionist father over aspects of current Israeli policy and yet at the same time has always been profoundly conscious – how could he be anything else? – of the history of Jewish suffering. A story dating from the time of *The Birthday Party* illustrates this perfectly. Pinter had popped into a bar next to Sloane Square tube station for a quiet drink. A well-dressed man at the bar suddenly said to his neighbour 'Hitler didn't go far enough. That's the big problem.' Pinter, buying his half-pint, debated what he should do.

'Before I had the chance to come to any kind of conclusion, the other man, to whom he was talking, said, "Well, that's a load of rubbish." So I said spontaneously, "Yes, it's a load of balls." I remember these words very, very clearly. These images of the 1950s, in that bar in Sloane Square tube station have never left me. And this man turned to me and he said, "I suppose you're a filthy Yid yourself." So I said, "You know, you really mustn't say that kind of thing to me or to anybody else. You've got to stop saying it." He said, "No, answer the question." I said, "Say that again." He said, "You want me to say that again?" He said it again, "You're a filthy Yid." Whereupon I hit him. I remember there was a moment when he went absolutely white. He just went back against the bar and then there was blood spurting out of his cheek. Whereupon I turned away and he hit me. I suddenly went for him and it was really very ugly. I was actually pulled off him in the end. Then the police came and we all went to the station-master's office where the man said that he had been assaulted. The other man said that I had been insulted. The police officer told the first man to go home: "You go around saying things like that, you're bound to run into trouble." Then the man came up to me and said, "Are you a Jew?" and I said, "Yes," and he said, "Well, I can understand why you hit me but why did you hit me so hard?" . . . Why I hit him so hard is because he wasn't just insulting me, he was insulting lots of other people. He was insulting people who were dead, people who had suffered. I hadn't expected this to happen when I walked into that bar, but it did happen and my fury with him came from some part of my being which I didn't con- sciously analyse or think about.'

That story is relevant to *The Birthday Party* in any number of ways. It shows how prevalent anti-Semitism still was in the 1950s. It demonstrates how Pinter himself instinctively resisted any form of oppression. But above all it shows how Pinter was able to divorce his private identification with Jewish suffering from his public critique of Jewish tradition. He rejects every- thing Goldberg stands for; yet, insofar as the character is ultimately a prisoner of his own beliefs and riddled with insecurity, he portrays him sympathetically. Not the least astonishing thing about *The Birthday Party*, in fact, is Goldberg's multidimensionality: he is both villain and victim; a symbol of the knock at the door that has resounded throughout European history in the twentieth century and yet a member of the most persecuted of all racial groups. He also expresses the complexity of Pinter's attitude towards the Jewish inheritance and shows how a dramatist may like and detest a character at the same time.

The Birthday Party works as a populist thriller and as a deeply political play about the imperative need for resistance. But on yet another less noticed level it is a private, obsessive work about time past; about some vanished world, either real or idealised, into which all but one of the characters readily escapes. I doubt this was conscious on Pinter's part, but it is striking how in almost every interview he himself seizes on some moment of exemplary significance in his own life. It is equally noticeable how aspects of his own biography pepper the characters' reminiscences in the play. From the very outset, the defining quality of a Pinter play is not so much fear and menace – though they are undoubtedly present – as a yearning for some lost Eden as a refuge from the uncertain, miasmic present.

For Stanley, the golden moment is quite obviously the concert he gave at Lower Edmonton: subconsciously Pinter reaches for the scene of his own moment of athletic triumph on the grammar-school sports field. Goldberg, almost all of whose speeches are shot through with memories of idyllic 'golden days', also uncannily echoes some of Pinter's own experiences: 'When I was a youngster, of a Friday, I used to go for a walk down the canal with a girl who lived down my road. A beautiful girl. What a voice that bird had! A nightingale, my word of honour. Good? Pure? She wasn't a Sunday school teacher for nothing. Anyway, I'd leave her with a little kiss on the cheek – I never took liberties – we weren't like the young men these days in those days. We knew the meaning of respect. So I'd give her a peck and I'd bowl back home.' Goldberg's speech may be swathed in fake sentiment, but it also reminds one of Pinter's ill-fated canal-side courting and of how he and his mates would 'bowl' round the streets of Hackney.

Memory, for Pinter, is both personal and infectious. The strangest alliance of all comes during the birthday party itself when the infantile Meg and the brutal McCann sit drinking together. While she retreats into a cocooned imaginary world of happily families, he is enveloped in a Celtic mist that implies the male solidarity of an IRA gang.

MCCANN: I know a place. Roscrea. Mother Nolan's.

MEG: There was a night-light in my room, when I was a little girl.

MCCANN: One time I stayed there all night with the boys. Singing and drinking all night.

MEG: And my Nanny used to sit up with me, and sing songs to me.
MCCANN: And a plate of fry in the morning. Now where am I?

Roscrea has great emotional significance for Pinter himself. It was there while touring with Mac, as he later revealed to me, that he had a bizarre bar-room encounter with the company's business manager called Joe Nolan – an episode that found its way into *The Hothouse*. But here, Pinter's memory of Roscrea is subsumed into McCann's Irish romanticism as the character launches into a rendering of 'Oh, the Garden of Eden has vanished, they say, But I know the lie of it still'. McCann's bout of Irish Synge-song also triggers the memories of the pneumatic neighbour Lulu, who remarks to Goldberg 'You're the dead image of the first man I ever loved'. Significantly, the one character in the play who never looks back is Petey: the clear-eyed bystander who alone tries to help Stanley in his hour of need. Yet Pinter, whose Hackney adolescence constituted a golden time that was to stay with him for ever, understands how we all use a real or romanticised past to buttress the insecure present. That was to be his constant theme, and it is one that gives density and texture to a play that is otherwise a cry of defiance against the shit-stained strictures of tradition. The past in Pinter is both an historical curse and an emotional salve.

Believing passionately in the play, Michael Codron put it into rehearsal in April 1958. It was to have a short provincial tour to Cambridge, Wolverhampton and Oxford before opening at the Lyric Hammersmith in May. But, from Pinter's letter to Peter Wood in March resisting clarification of Stanley's motives, it is clear that from the start author and director were not in total sympathy. 'Temperamentally,' says Codron, 'Harold and Peter were completely at odds. Peter was very Oxbridge in his attitude. Harold would write studious notes and Peter would say things like, "This is the Preface to the published edition, is it?" This was very daunting for a man who had not been published and was a working actor. There was a kind of *froideur* between the two. Notwithstanding, we got a pretty good cast including Richard Pearson, Beatrix Lehmann and John Slater. We opened at Cambridge, but that again made the relationship difficult because Peter was on his home ground and went back to all his old cronies like Dadie Rylands and John Barton who were giving their views on the play and alienating Harold, I suspect.'

For all that, there was every reason to think they might be on to a winner. After the first night at the Arts Theatre, the *Cambridge Daily News* recorded that 'The great ovation given to this play at its première yesterday showed that the audience appreciated the venture even though they were puzzled by it'. Undergraduates in Cambridge who saw it included Bamber Gascoigne, John Tydeman (later head of BBC Radio drama) and John Drummond (subsequently head of Radio 3 and controller of the Proms), who all instantly recognised an important new voice in British theatre. To all of them the play was as much a landmark as Osborne's *Look Back in Anger*. In Wolverhampton – where the theatre manager was an old Variety pro who had booked the play on the strength of John Slater's name, assuming it to be a rollicking comedy – the response was equally enthusiastic. Sean Day-Lewis, then drama critic for the *Express and Star*, called it 'The most enthralling experience the Grand Theatre has given us in many months'. And on the third week of the tour, the Oxford critics got straight to the point. In the *Oxford Mail* Goldberg and McCann were compared to the gangsters in Hemingway's *The Killers* and to the guardians in Eliot's *The Cocktail Party*. The *Oxford Times* meanwhile said, 'It is brilliant, baffling and bizarre – Kafka, almost, spiced with humour'.

Pinter could hardly have asked for more perceptive notices or more re-sponsive audiences. When the play opened at the Lyric Hammersmith on 19 May, where the audience included a lot of old Hackney friends, there was every reason for optimism; but when Pinter opened his papers the next morning, he was greeted by the wails of incomprehension which London's overnight critics in the 1950s traditionally reserved for the arrival of a major talent. The cryptically signed M.W.W. in the *Manchester Guardian*, after summarising the plot, announced 'What all this means only Mr Pinter knows, for his characters speak in *non sequiturs*, half-gibberish and lunatic ravings'. W. A. Darlington in the *Daily Telegraph* reported that one of the characters was a depressed deckchair attendant, thoughtfully adding, 'Oh well, I can give him one word of cheer. He might have been a dramatic critic condemned to sit through plays like this.' In the *Financial Times* Derek Granger – later to become a successful TV producer – wearily began, 'Harold Pinter's first play comes in the school of random dottiness deriving from Beckett and Ionesco and before the flourishing continuance of which one quails in slack-jawed dismay'. And under a sub's headline in the *Evening Standard* which ran 'Sorry, Mr Pinter, you're just not funny enough', a perplexed Milton Shulman pointed out, 'Who the two strangers are, who Monty is, where they are all going are matters which may be lucidly clear to Mr Pinter but he has certainly not divulged them to me'.

The notices weren't just bad. They were catastrophic. And for forty-eight hours Pinter was plunged into a deep depression which was relieved only by Vivien's practical common sense in pointing out that, as an actor, he had had rotten notices before. In the theatre, however, all was gloom. The morning after the first night J. Baxter Somerville, who ran the Lyric along with the Theatre Royal, Brighton, said to Michael Codron and his partner David Hall, 'Look at these reviews! You're in the deepest shtuck and I've got this fabulous thriller waiting to come in.' Thinking he was baling out two young producers who would otherwise have been committed to paying costs and salaries for the whole month, he agreed with them that the play should come off on the Saturday night – a decision that Michael Codron to this day bitterly regrets. 'I really made a major mistake,' he says, 'and the reason was that Harold Hobson, who'd already championed Harold's work, didn't come to the first night which was a sign of his waywardness. Had he done so, the agent Peggy Ramsay, who acted as a kind of funnel between Hobson and the West End managers, could have rung him up and asked what he thought. In fact, Harold came to the Thursday matinée and the rest is history.'

On the following Sabbath, Hobson produced in the *Sunday Times* one of the great lyric paeans in modern criticism. In fact, while his notice is extremely perceptive, it set the tone for much subsequent Pinter criticism by ignoring the play's political resonances and seizing on its mastery of impalpable Jamesian terror:

> It breathes in the air. It cannot be seen but it enters the room every time the door is opened. There is something in your past – it does not matter what – which will catch up with you. Though you go to the uttermost parts of the earth, and hide yourself in the most obscure lodgings in the least popular of towns, one day there is a possibility that two men will appear. They will be looking for you and you cannot get away. And someone will be looking for *them* too. There is terror everywhere.

Hobson wasn't the only Harold in the house on that fateful Thursday matinée. Pinter himself had decided to pop in too and see how things were going. 'I was a few minutes late,' he recalls, 'and the curtain had gone up. I ran up the stairs to the dress circle. An usherette stopped me. "Where are you going?" she said. "To the dress circle," I said. "I'm the author." Her eyes, as I recall, misted over. "Oh, are you?" she said. "Oh, you poor chap. Listen, the dress circle's closed, but why don't you go in, go in and sit down, darling, if you like, go on." I went into the empty dress circle and looked down into the stalls. Six people were watching the performance which, I must say, didn't seem to be generating very much electricity. I still have the box-office return for the week. The Thursday matinée brought in two pounds six shillings.'

Why did *The Birthday Party* get such devastating notices? Was it the play? The production? Or some inherent myopia in the critics themselves? With hindsight, I suspect that the problem was that the majority of London critics, always excepting the intuitive Hobson, were still living in a world that expected drama to provide rational solutions to explicit problems. We fondly imagine that after the breakthrough achieved by *Look Back in Anger* at the Royal Court in May 1956, British theatre changed overnight and was wide open to new ideas and fresh forms. In fact, if you examine the playbills for early 1958 you find that the West End was still dominated by musicals, comedies, farces and deeply conventional plays by Terence Rattigan, Emlyn Williams and N. C. Hunter that depended on neatly resolved situations. Anything which attempted to break the mould, such as Ann Jellicoe's anarchic *The Sport of My Mad Mother* which opened at the Royal Court in February, got ritually slaughtered. Critics of the time also behaved as if they were the last bastions of logic in an increasingly irrational universe. *The Times* spoke of Pinter's 'puzzling surrealism' and Derek Granger of 'mad, wearying and inconsequential gabble', whereas *The Birthday Party* takes place in a real boarding-house and the only 'madness' on display is that of a man actively resisting confinement in the strait-jacket of conventional society.

The production itself, however, may have sent out the wrong signals. Looking back, without a trace of anger, Pinter now admits that the play posed all kinds of problems for a director. 'It was,' as he says, 'the first time the play had been done. It wasn't quite like anything else. It certainly wasn't like Beckett. It mixed what appeared to be naturalistic talk with highly stylised structures. The problem, I think, was that Peter fell back on the grotesque or pantomimic. The set [by Hutchinson Scott] was an absolute disaster. It was an enormous conservatory which never existed in anyone's mind or anyone's house. When I questioned the set, which I knew was wrong, Peter said, "They have conservatories like this all the way along the South Coast." I said, "Do they?" I'd certainly never seen one. I was the fellow who'd been in the digs! Anyway, the naturalistic base – which is extremely important – was not there, so the audience were in some kind of no man's land or fairy tale.'

Pinter's comment about the production is both practical and revealing. It suggests that *The Birthday Party* is a work whose larger metaphorical meaning grows out of an observed reality; or, as Irving Wardle once excellently put it, a banal living-room opens up to the horrors of modern history. But this mixture of the real and the imaginatively heightened was not easily grasped in 1958 when plays tended to be judged either by their social accuracy or nonsensical inventiveness. Pinter's play – a rep thriller with political resonance – was gloriously uncategorisable and, in a way, he had paid the price. But in retrospect, the fact that *The Birthday Party* was a resounding flop may not have been quite the disaster it first appeared. The very intemperateness of the reaction turned the play into a *cause célèbre*, bred a fierce critical backlash and stiffened Pinter's own spirit of resistance. Two days after the play opened, in fact, on 21 May he sent a revised copy of a radio play already commissioned by the BBC to Donald McWhinnie at Broadcasting House. Admittedly the letter ends on a somewhat wan, introspective note: 'The play has come a cropper, as you know. What else? The clouds. They are varied, very varied. And all sorts of birds. They come and perch on the windowsill, asking for food! It is touching.' But the letter, after saying Pinter is getting out of town for a couple of weeks, is full of concern about the rewrites and promises to keep in touch. It is the letter of a man who still has faith in the future. Stanley Webber may have been painfully 'adjusted' and 'integrated' into conventional society, but there was no way Harold Pinter was going to let them tell him what to do.

Five Playwright in Waiting

Pinter was obviously jolted by the party-pooping reviews for his first major play. He was not, however, going to be defeated. Shortly after the débâcle of *The Birthday Party*, he sent a postcard to the actress Susan Engel defiantly crying 'I ain't finished yet!' And in the two years between its début and the première of his next three-act work, *The Caretaker*, he was both creatively active and increasingly recognised as a writer of conspicuous promise. Pinter was often skint, but a lot happened to him in the period from May 1958 to April 1960. His cause was taken up by the hugely influential radical theatre magazine *Encore*, which treated him as a martyr to the critical Establishment. *The Birthday Party* was quickly revived. *The Dumb Waiter* was premièred in Germany. Pinter wrote a new political play, *The Hothouse*, adapted his skills to radio and television, and became a prolific sketch-writer for Codron revues. He also carried on acting as David Baron. Alan Curtis, who appeared with him at Richmond Theatre in September 1958 in *Any Other Business*, recalls, 'He was a meticulous pro and had great authority on stage. Look at the pictures of him in that production and you see a clean-cut figure with a decisive, thrusting jaw. But the actors in that company had great respect for him because he had actually written a play. He had done what, secretly, most of us wished we could do.'

Pinter's writing in this period shows him pursuing his private vision while experimenting with form. He worked in different media, but there is always an integrity of purpose; and it is very much to do with the conflict between the claims of a conformist society and the needs of the intransigent individual. In a sense, this was the pattern of English drama in the late 1950s. John Osborne created – in Jimmy Porter and Archie Rice –outsiderish heroes radically at odds with bourgeois convention. And Arnold Wesker wrote a famous trilogy – now chiefly remembered for *Roots* – that gloomily concluded that individual idealism was often wasted in a world irrevocably hostile to human brotherhood. But where Osborne was a Byronic romantic and Wesker a disillusioned socialist, Pinter wrote from a vantage-point of sceptical enquiry. He was a natural outsider who took nothing on trust; but he refused to see life in black-and-white terms, with society as automatically evil and the lone citizen as intrinsically heroic. It was a point he rammed home in a BBC World Service interview in 1960. 'In contemporary drama so often we have a villain society and the hero the individual. And a lot of people have said that about *The Birthday Party*. Well, it isn't like that. These two things – the man in relation to society – both exist and one makes the other. Society wouldn't be there without the man, but they're both dependent on one another and there's no question of hero and villain.' What Pinter obviously craves is a way of combining individual freedom with the humane structures that permit any society to function.

From the start, Pinter also demolishes the artificial distinctions we make between 'personal' and 'political' drama. Because his early characters mostly live immured in rooms and because Pinter himself was not initially drawn to rallies, causes and protest marches, he was wrongly assumed to be apolitical. But *The Room* and *The Birthday Party* are quite obviously concerned with the tension between individual need and the pressures of social conformity. And, as Pinter's career proceeds, he increasingly sees private life as a form of power-politics full of invasion, retreats, subjugations and deceptions. Conversely, when he later comes to deal quite overtly with the machinery of the state, he describes it in terms of individual power and powerlessness. To put it simply, marriage for Pinter is a highly political state, just as the relationship between torturer and victim often acquires a degree of marital intimacy. Eric Bentley in a classic essay pointed out that much drama that people loosely call 'political' might better be termed 'social'. 'It would be more sensible', wrote Bentley, 'to limit the term political to works in which the question of the power-structure arises'. Which it does throughout Pinter's entire *oeuvre*.

This seamless blend of the personal and political is evident in an early work like *The Dumb Waiter*, which Pinter wrote in 1957 but which only got its première in Frankfurt in 1959. Brief, bleak and funny, it deals with two hit-men, Ben and Gus, waiting in the basement of a Birmingham house to carry out a contract killing. The punning title carries several layers of meaning. It obviously refers to the antique serving-hatch that despatches ever more grotesque orders for food to these bickering gunmen. But it also applies to Gus who, troubled by the nature of the mission, fails to realise he is its chosen target; or indeed to Ben who, by his total obedience to a higher authority that forces him to eliminate his partner, exposes his own vulnerability. This being Pinter, the play has a metaphorical openness. You can interpret it as an absurdist comedy – a kind of *Godot* in Birmingham – about two men passing the time in a universe without meaning or purpose. You can see it as a cry of protest against a whimsically cruel God who treats man as His plaything – even the twelve matches that are mysteriously pushed under the door have been invested with religious significance. But it makes much more sense if seen as a play about the dynamics of power and the nature of partnership. Ben and Gus are both victims of some unseen authority *and* a surrogate married couple quarrelling, testing, talking past each other and raking over old times. Significantly, one of Pinter's old Hackney friends, B. J. Law, cottoned on very quickly to the significance of both *The Birthday Party* and *The Dumb Waiter*. He wrote to Pinter interpreting them as political plays about power and victimisation. Law remembers that Pinter wrote back instantly saying that his comments were spot-on.

What is intriguing about *The Dumb Waiter* is that Pinter conveys the idea of political terror through the staccato rhythms of music-hall cross-talk and the urban thriller: Hackney Empire cross-fertilises with Hemingway's *The Killers*. He also subtly suggests that we are watching a relationship on the point of disintegration. Ben, expressing disgust with the increasing level of public violence while delighting in woodwork and model boats, is the contract killer as good bourgeois citizen; Gus, forever complaining about the lavatory cistern, the windowless room, the pongy sheets, is nagging, nervous and questioning. Pinter also conveys a creeping sense of unease. First there is the revelation that Ben has suddenly stopped the car that morning, for no apparent reason, in the middle of the road. Then there is Ben's rejection of Gus's suggestion that they go to see a soccer match tomorrow – the Villa if they're still in Birmingham or the Spurs if they're back in London – with the unnervingly illogical answer that they can't go to a game because 'They're all playing away'. Most alarming of all is the sudden appearance of an envelope containing twelve matches pushed under the door. The religious interpretation seems far-fetched. What this tells us, since we already know that Gus's own matchbox is empty, is that the hitmen are under close surveillance and that wherever there are two people in a room, there is always a third unseen presence. It's a point with obvious political resonance; but it applies equally well to the sexual betrayals of the later plays.

Yet Pinter intensifies the unease through use of the semantic nit-picking that is a standard part of music-hall comedy. All the great stage and film double acts – Jewel and Warriss, Abbott and Costello – fall into this kind of verbal worrying in which the bullying 'male' straight man issues instructions which are questioned by the more literal-minded 'female' partner. At one point Ben tells Gus to go and light the kettle.

GUS: Light what?

BEN: The kettle.

GUS: You mean the gas.

BEN: Who does?

GUS: You do.

BEN (*his eyes narrowing*): What do you mean, I mean the gas?

GUS: Well, that's what you mean, don't you? The gas.

BEN (*powerfully*): If I say go and light the kettle I mean go and light the kettle.

GUS: How can you light a kettle?

BEN: It's a figure of speech! Light the kettle. It's a figure of speech!

This kind of comic pedantry has precise echoes of the great Sid Field – ironically a Birmingham comic – who had a famous sketch in which he played a virgin of the greens being hectored by Jerry Desmonde's golf pro who would cry, in exasperation, 'When I say "Slowly Back" I don't mean "Slowly Back", I mean "Slowly Back".' At another moment, the bullying pro would tell the hapless Sid to get behind the ball and he would vainly protest 'But it's behind all round it'. But, where in a music-hall sketch this kind of semantic by-play was its own justification, in Pinter it becomes a crucial part of the power-structure. Here the pay-off comes when Gus, having dogmatically insisted that the accurate phrase is 'put on the kettle', suddenly finds an irritated Ben adopting the right usage.

Everything in the play contributes towards a necessary end: the image, as Pete says in *The Dwarfs*, stands in exact correspondence and relation to the idea. The dumb waiter, despatching ever more unlikely orders, is both a visual gag and a metaphor for a manipulative authority. The speaking-tube transmits commands which Gus increasingly questions and Ben studiously obeys. Even the old double-act device of having one partner rehearse instructions which the other subtly misunderstands acquires a sinister edge. The victim, both agree, will come in. He'll shut the door. Gus will be behind it. The victim will see Ben. He won't see Gus.

BEN: He won't know you're there.

GUS: He won't know you're there.

BEN: He won't know *you're* there.

GUS: He won't know I'm there.

BEN: I take out my gun.

GUS: You take out your gun.

This could be Jewel and Warriss doing a Robbers in *Babes in the Wood* routine, except that Pinter gives this antiphonal exchange an equivocal edge by having Ben omit the line where he instructs Gus to take out *his* gun. The significance of this becomes apparent at the end when Gus enters through the door stage-right – the one marked out for the intended victim – stripped of his gun and holster, and clearly set up to be Ben's target.

It's a near-perfect play about the testiness of a collapsing partnership and the divide-and-rule tactics of authority. Gus is the man who questions the agreed system and who is ultimately destroyed by his quest for meaning. Ben is the man who blindly obeys orders and thereby places himself at risk. (If the system can arbitrarily dispose of his partner, why not of him?) This could not be further from the cul-de-sac of absurdism which presupposes that we live in an inexplicable universe. Neither is it simply a suspenseful *jeu d'esprit*. Pinter, who had already discarded the Jewish faith and defied the military authorities by refusing to wear a shit-suit, was writing a strongly political play about the way a hierarchical society, in pitting the rebel against the conformist, places both at its mercy. At the same time, it was a deeply personal play about the destructiveness of betrayal.

Looking back at early plays like *The Dumb Waiter* and *The Birthday Party*, Pinter now says 'they are doing something which can be described as political'. At the same time, he had – still has – an acute sense of the fragility of earthly happiness and of the terrors that haunt us even from infancy. By the summer of 1958, Pinter was recovering from his first flop, writing a play under commission from the BBC – that started its life as *Something in Common* and transmuted into *A Slight Ache* – and struggling to support his wife and six-month-old baby Daniel. They were living at the time in their tiny flat in Chiswick High Road. Money was short. Life was difficult. But a story Pinter told me, during a public interview at the Dublin International Writers' Festival in 1993, both relates to that time and illustrates his awareness of life's precariousness. I had suggested that the common factor in all Pinter's plays was a memory of, or a yearning for a secure past, even if it was no more than a fictional dream.

PINTER: What you're saying is that my work is to do with the memory of or reflection on a secure past. You know what Proust said, of course?

BILLINGTON: What did Proust say?

PINTER: He said, '*Le vrai paradis c'est le paradis qu'on a perdu.*' And I think there's a lot in that.

BILLINGTON: You stand by that?

PINTER: I don't stand by it entirely. The fact is that we're certainly not in paradise now. No one could describe the state of our lives as paradise, so if there was a paradise it's some time ago and in another association, another soil, another territory. I suppose, in a way, that must be child-hood, but I rather suspect it isn't that either as a matter of fact. Because childhood is undoubtedly full of fears and anxieties of the highest order ... One can't get that out of one's mind, really. I remember actually when I ... this is a true story ... I have a son, Daniel, who is now a grown-up man but when he was very, very young indeed I woke up one night – this is thirty-five years ago, but I can't forget it – and I found myself in tears. My first wife Vivien said to me, 'What in heaven's name is the matter?' Daniel, who was about six months old, was in a cot in the room. I didn't know what was the matter or how to explain what was happening to me. But I realised what was happening after half an hour or so. It was simply that I couldn't bear the life that was in front of him. I thought here he is having a good time, quietly asleep at this moment ... he was actually a very enthusiastic child too and I knew that at the time, but I actually looked ahead and thought, 'My God, what is in store for this infant?'

It was an extraordinarily moving and intimate confession; one made all the more so by the knowledge that Daniel, after showing outstanding academic promise at Oxford and early gifts as a poet, was to have a difficult life. He now lives as a recluse in the Cambridgeshire countryside, supported by his father but virtually estranged from him – a fact that helps to explain *Moonlight*. But the conclusion Pinter drew from the story is that the many moments of happiness in our existence need to be counter-balanced by an awareness of the pain and suffering that survive in the world around us. As Pinter went on to say, it is difficult 'to sustain and maintain an equilibrium', and he is suspi-cious of people who do. 'There is a kind of blandness which I simply don't understand. A resignation perhaps to certain states of affairs which I person-ally find infinitely painful and, to one degree or another, intolerable.'

Pinter was speaking both as an outraged citizen appalled at our indiffer-ence to global cruelty and as a concerned father remembering his fears for his son's future; the present and the past, the political and the personal seemed to merge even as he spoke. And that is crucial to any understanding of Pinter: the past is constantly alive within him and he has a rare capacity to invest private memory with a wider significance. It is this gift for seizing on the universal meaning embedded in a particular moment and this sensitivity to the mystery of memory that also explains his refusal, as a dramatist, to supply facile resolutions or to pre-empt the audience's experience – something we now take for granted but that was much less common in British drama in the late 1950s. In fact, while he was wrestling with *A Slight Ache* in the summer of 1958, he sat down for the first time ever to write an article explaining his dramatic credo. The piece appeared in the *Cambridge University Magazine* in October and it makes highly revealing reading.

It pays tribute to the student audiences – not least in Cambridge – who got *The Birthday Party* straight off. It totally denies the influence of Ionesco on his work; at that date, the only play of his Pinter had read or seen was *The New Tenant*. It acknowledges the dramatic tension and dynamic that comes from a man alone in a room receiving a caller. But the most significant aspect of the article is the way Pinter denies the possibility of philosophical certainty and discards the dramatist's historic obligation to provide a consoling resolution.

There are no hard distinctions between what is real and what is unreal, nor between what is true and what is false. A thing is not necessarily either true or false: it can be both true and false. The assumption that to verify what has happened or what is happening presents few problems I take to be inaccurate. A character on stage who can present no convincing argument or information as to his past experience, his present behaviour or his aspirations nor give a comprehensive analysis of his motives is as legitimate and as worthy of attention as one who alarmingly can do all these things. The more acute the experience, the less articulate the expression . . . To supply an explicit moral tag to an evolving and compulsive dramatic image seems to me facile, impertinent and dishonest. When this takes place it is not theatre but a crossword puzzle. The audience holds the paper. The play fills in the blanks. Everyone's happy. There has been no conflict between audience and play, no participation, nothing has been exposed. We walk out as we went in.

There is little in the first half of that credo, about the relativity of experience, with which Pirandello would have disagreed. But Pirandello evolved from it a defeatist metaphysic that eventually led him towards the nostalgia of Fascism. 'I am so impressed', he once wrote, 'with this sense of a changing life, so deeply distressed by my inability to seize upon anything that is certain, fixed, definite, true that almost in despair I cling to the sentiments that are most elemental and basic in me.' Pinter, in stark contrast, uses the impossibility of verification to explore the contradictions of human behaviour and to assert the need for active resistance to social orthodoxy. In a world of uncertainty, who has the right to tell us what to do?

However it is the latter part of Pinter's statement, about the need for conflict *between* the audience and the play, that is most revealing. Obviously throughout history dramatists have seen it as their job to challenge, disturb and unsettle audiences. Ibsen in *A Doll's House* questioned the notion that our paramount obligation was to social institutions, such as marriage, rather than to self-realisation. O'Casey constantly confronted the rhetorical sentimentality of Irish patriotism. Brecht in *Mother Courage* subverted the ideal of heroic survival. Many great plays are gauntlets thrown down at the audience's feet. But what makes Pinter radically different, even revolutionary, in his approach, is his belief that the meaning of a play should emerge from the evolving image and that the dramatist should leave some of the clues in the crossword puzzle open. The American writer Paul Auster in *The Art of Hunger* claims: 'The one thing I try to do in all my books is to leave enough room in the prose for the reader to inhabit it. Because I finally believe it's the reader who writes the book and not the writer.' In the same way, Pinter suggests that it's the audience that completes the play. In the light of structuralist criticism, which at its most extreme banishes the idea of the author, that may not seem especially heretical. But when you recall the extent to which drama has always traded in biographical specifics, fixed conclusions and consequential speech, you realise the revolutionary nature of Pinter's breakthrough. This does not preclude the dramatist having strong political convictions or charting his own private landscape. But in banishing the notion of the omniscient author and transferring moral responsibility to the audience, Pinter even in 1958 was starting to change the whole nature of the dramatic experience.

For a writer who questioned verifiable certainties and who believed in the audience's power to determine the 'meaning' of a work, radio drama was obviously the happiest of mediums; addressing an often solitary listener in conditions of domestic privacy, radio-plays positively demand creative participation. But Pinter was also lucky in coinciding with a golden age in radio drama when a BBC producer like Donald McWhinnie and a script editor like Barbara Bray – later a distinguished producer and translator – were actively encouraging innovation. 'Val Gielgud, then head of BBC drama,' recalls Barbara Bray, 'was a Somerset Maugham and Noël Coward merchant. Anything later than *The Vortex* was a closed book to him. But we had the power to commission and Donald included Harold among a group of young writers to whom we extended patronage and help. After the failure of *The Birthday Party*, we were able to help Harold keep body and soul together. He was also a natural radio dramatist. As with a lot of people who grew up during the war, that was their only theatre. People were extremely expert listeners.'

However, although Pinter took instantly to radio, not everyone in radio took instantly to Pinter. When he submitted a thirty-minute play, *Something*

in Common, in July 1958 there was a flurry of argumentative interdepart-
mental memos. Donald McWhinnie, backed up by Barbara Bray and a young
producer, Michael Bakewell, championed it as a natural piece for the Third
Programme. But the controller of the Third appended a dyspeptic handwritten note to McWhinnie's enthusiastic memo pouring scorn on its invocation
of Beckett ('he is a very considerable literary artist which Pinter is not') and
concluding 'Personally I am not at all convinced of Pinter's ability to construct a good play either for the stage or radio and I know H.D. [the head of
drama, Val Gielgud] has no great opinion of him'. The dispute was referred
upwards to the assistant director of sound broadcasting, R. D. A. Marriott,
who came down on the side of progress. In a long, well-reasoned memo he
referred to the fact that two plays by N. F. Simpson had lately been turned
down by the Third. He argued that listeners outside London should have the
chance to hear work by writers who were the source of current critical debate:

> Surely, when dealing with any kind of contemporary work, inclusion in
> our programmes does not indicate any faith in the discovery of a literary
> masterpiece but merely a belief that it is of sufficient interest for the
> audience to have the opportunity of making up their own minds. Because
> we have the monopoly in this medium it is obviously a particular responsi-
> bility on us to be catholic in our choice.

In the event, *Something in Common* was not put out. Pinter's own recollection is that it became the substance of a sixty-minute radio play he was
commissioned to write in July 1958 for a fee of 85 guineas: *A Slight Ache*.
Broadcast a year later, that too sparked off disagreements between the old
guard and the new inside Broadcasting House, but it remains a fascinating
piece: Pinter's first excursion into bourgeois territory and proof of his ability
to see marriage as a political battleground. It also exploits the ambiguous
possibilities of radio. One of its three characters, Barnabas, is a totally silent
old matchseller, jokingly billed in *Radio Times* as being played by David
Baron. In the course of the action Barnabas is invited into the house of
Edward, a nerve-racked countryman and writer of theological and philosophical essays, who seems strangely threatened by the presence beyond his
gate of this smelly old vagrant. By the end of the play, Barnabas and Edward
have switched places: the former is smothered in sexual affection by Edward's
wife Flora, and is given the run of the house and garden ('your garden', Flora
tells him), while the latter is reduced to grovelling impotence and is finally
handed the tray of matches by his wife. When the play was later televised and
staged – highly effectively – it became a more obvious study of territorial
takeover and psychological displacement. On radio, one was left with the

teasing possibility that the matchseller might simply be a fantasy-figure: an expression of Edward's subconscious fear, guilt and insecurity, and of Flora's overwhelming need for sexual and maternal fulfilment.

A Slight Ache – written during a hard-up Chiswick summer but inspired by Pinter's vivid memory of a flower-filled Norfolk garden during his years as an evacuee – works because the metaphorical meaning grows out of precise social observation. From the start, Pinter establishes that there is something rotten in the state of Edward and Flora's marriage. It makes a striking contrast with the openings of *The Room* and *The Birthday Party* which begin, in a lower-class milieu, with a largely passive or silent man being served breakfast by a suffocatingly loyal wife. Here we are in an elegant country garden where the day starts with strain and tension:

> *Flora and Edward are discovered sitting at the breakfast table. Edward is reading the paper.*
> FLORA: Have you noticed the honeysuckle this morning?
> EDWARD: The what?
> FLORA: The honeysuckle.
> EDWARD: Honeysuckle? Where?

As Barry Foster, who played Edward on stage at the Young Vic in 1987, points out, 'That can be a simple enquiry or it can express profound irritation at being interrupted while he is reading the newspaper. You've almost got the history of the marriage in the first exchanges. It isn't just vamping till ready while Harold thinks of another line to write. It's a revelation of the tension inside the marriage.' And that tension is marvellously sustained as Edward and Flora argue over the tactics to be employed on killing a wasp buzzing around the marmalade-pot. A seemingly trivial incident is used by Pinter to depict Edward's vindictive delight in trapping an alien creature and establishing bullying dominance over his wife. Edward first ensures the wasp is inside the marmalade-pot and then screws down the earthenware lid. He tells Flora to put the wasp in the sink and drown it; she objects that it will 'bite' and that it is trying to crawl out through the spoon-hole. Edward, the lord of the wasps, decides to go in for the kill.

> EDWARD: Bring it out on the spoon and squash it on a plate.
> FLORA: It'll fly away. It'll bite.
> EDWARD: If you don't stop saying that word I shall leave this table.
> FLORA: But wasps do bite.
> EDWARD: They don't bite. They sting. It's snakes . . . that bite.
> FLORA: What about horseflies?

(*Pause.*)

EDWARD (*to himself*): Horseflies suck.

Finally Edward dispatches the wasp by pouring scalding water down the spoon-hole, thereby blinding and killing it.

Pinter, with great precision, is establishing the dominant motifs of the play and preparing the psychological ground for everything that follows. Edward's response to the irritant wasp is to trap, dominate and neutralise it: exactly what he seeks to do with the matchseller as the play progresses. For Edward, killing the wasp also symbolises an attempt to exert total control over his environment. It is no accident that when his personality eventually disintegrates before the sweating, half-blind, half-dead matchseller, he harks back nostalgically to a time when 'I could pour hot water down the spoon-hole, yes, easily, no difficulty, my grasp firm, my command established, my life was accounted for . . .' The wasp-waste also exposes the crucial gulf between Edward, who is secure only when he can impose himself on his surroundings, and Flora, whose very name invokes the goddess of flowers and whose opening line implies a delighted curiosity about nature. Indeed, her reaction to the squashing of the wasp is 'What an awful experience' while Edward's is 'What a beautiful day it is'. Within the first ten minutes of the play, Pinter has established the governing themes: marital discord, domestic disharmony, male bluster masking fierce insecurity versus female compassion revealing a strong sense of self.

Everything that happens thereafter develops organically from the opening scene. You can argue, as Lois Gordon does, that the thrust of all Pinter's early plays is that the occupants of a room *project on to* an intrusive stranger their deepest fears. Riley, Goldberg and McCann, the blind matchseller, she suggests, 'all function as screens upon which the characters externalise their own irrationality' and that Pinter's intruders 'are, in a sense, his technique for leading the characters to expose their true identities'. But that irons out the subtle distinctions between the plays – in particular, the extent to which *A Slight Ache* works as a devastating critique of bourgeois marriage, and as an exploration of the differing male and female responses to the threat of the unknown.

That is very much the point. Pinter shows that Edward's reaction to the matchseller – who represents the world of poverty and degradation he has specifically denied – is one of colonial appropriation masking mortal terror. Inviting the vagrant into his study, Edward seeks to accommodate the matchseller to his own values with results that are both comic and creepy. Anyone familiar with the English class system will instantly recognise the tone of patronising absorption. 'I was in commerce too', Edward tells the pathetic vagrant and, exercising the rights of hospitality, enquires 'Well now, before the good lady sounds the gong for *petit déjeuner* will you join me in an aperitif?' That reminds me irresistibly of John Mortimer's story of the High Court judge who, confronted by a filthy, disgusting, alcoholic old tramp accused of petty larceny, put him on probation with the solemn warning never to drink again: 'Not even the smallest dry sherry before dinner.' But what gives the play its dramatic vitality is the way Edward's masculine inflexibility breaks down into panic and terror. At one point he associates the matchseller with a country-house cricketer called Cavendish who kept wicket and batted at number seven; but perhaps, Edward muses, you don't play cricket:

> Perhaps you never met Cavendish and never played cricket. You look less and less like a cricketer the more I see of you. Where did you live in those days? God damn it, I'm entitled to know something about you. You're in my blasted house, on my territory, drinking my wine, eating my duck. Now you've had your fill you sit like a hump, a mouldering heap. In my room. My den. I can rem . . . (*He stops abruptly.*)
> (*Pause.*)
> You find that funny? Are you grinning?

That's a graphic demonstration of the way bourgeois assimilation quickly degenerates into blustering rage. It also precipitates the play's final movement in which Edward retreats into a nostalgic vision of the past ('I was number one sprinter at Howells', he Pinterishly remarks) in which everything was fixed, stable and certain; and, in the end, almost envying the matchseller's surety of his place in the world, he voluntarily accepts his tray. There is no explicit moral tag; but Pinter clearly implies that the male bourgeois ideal of control and order is based on the flimsiest moral foundations.

In contrast, Flora – like so many of Pinter's women – has an instinctual warmth and sexual ardour that transcends the masculine preoccupation with status and power. Pinter's women, on the whole, are much nicer than his men. As his old Hackney girlfriend Jennifer Mortimer says, 'The wonderful thing about Harold is that he sees women as much stronger than they are. He gives them a power and generosity that most of them don't have. He may romanticise them. But I think there is a childlike joy in him that has never vanished. Women are included in it – there are no bad thoughts about them.' That is certainly true in this play. For Edward, the matchseller represents a threat; for Flora, he embodies the sexuality and motherhood she has been denied. It is clear that Flora is sexually aroused by the sight of the old tramp.

And in her private encounter with him she associates him with her fantasy memories of an encounter with a rapacious poacher and, while complaining of his smell, seductively urges him to 'Tell me all about love' and promises him 'little toys to play with' on his deathbed. Like Stanley for Meg in *The Birthday Party*, he becomes her surrogate lover and son. You could argue that she is appropriating him just as much as Edward, but Pinter is at pains to point up the contrast between Flora's willingness, literally, to embrace the unknown and Edward's urge to categorise, colonise and dominate it. Far from being 'the laziest of symbols', as Robert Cushman once suggested, the match-seller is the dramatic catalyst who exposes the difference between the male and female principles, and who highlights the psychic instability and un-expressed longings that lurk within bourgeois marriage and the pastoral ideal.

By September 1958 Pinter had finished the script and sent it to Barbara Bray at the BBC; after minor revisions and a flurry of internal memos, it was accepted for broadcasting on the Third Programme. But what is striking is how most of the senior producers seemed to have very dogmatic opinions about it: Pinter became a living issue within Broadcasting House. A senior producer, Archie Campbell, in a memo dated 25 March 1959 spoke for BH's conservative faction: 'By no standards could this work be judged a play but, even on the level of a conversation piece, the symbolism, if it exists at all, is obscure. If the script is merely intended as another essay on the "*Recherche du temps perdu*" theme, its implications are vaguely repellent.' Against that, Bryan Izzard (13 April 1959) recognised the play's roots in reality: 'People do talk like this at the breakfast table and people do discharge their worries on people once the initial barrier of recognition has been broken down.' Charles Lefeaux (23 March 1959) roundly declared: 'A claustrophobic and frighten-ing piece which develops its own inner tension and atmosphere, is shot through with sudden revelations of character and ends in terror.' And D. G. Bridson – assistant head of features – wrote a masterly page-long memo that invoked Ionesco, Ibsen and Melville, and that saw the matchseller as repre-senting to Edward all his own unrealised potential and to Flora everything her husband had failed to become for her. Praising its 'integrity as a piece of creative writing', he strenuously recommended its acceptance. It was eventu-ally broadcast on the Third Programme on 29 July 1959, with Maurice Denham and Vivien Merchant, though was somewhat grudgingly received in the *Listener* by Ian Rodger who claimed 'no amount of brilliance in dialogue makes up for the absence of a clear plot'.

By the time the play went out, Pinter could withstand critical pinpricks. He wasn't exactly in clover, but he had already completed two new plays (*The*

Hothouse and *A Night Out*), had written acclaimed sketches for two revues and had seen *The Birthday Party* revived at London's Tower Theatre. In fact, this is one of Pinter's most prolific periods. It was almost as if his first resounding failure had not only encouraged his iron determination to succeed, but had also released his creative energies. Yet he was extremely self-critical, as is shown by the fascinating saga of *The Hothouse*. This began its life as a possible sixty-minute BBC Radio play for which Pinter submitted a detailed synopsis in November 1958 to Barbara Bray. (He wrote in his accompanying letter: 'I'd certainly like to get down to it, but am much in need of a little money which would give me time to get down to it.') In his earlier work he had followed the promptings of his imagination; but the synopsis in the BBC archives offers a scene-by-scene breakdown of *The Hothouse* and an opening statement of its themes and purpose – a process that, for Pinter, often seems to cramp rather than liberate his imagination. He writes:

> The play is set in a psychological research centre. One department of this establishment is engaged in conducting tests to determine reactions of the nervous system to various stimuli. The subjects for these tests are drawn from volunteers who are paid an hourly rate for their services, in the interests of science. The play will demonstrate the indifference of this particular department (in the persons of the doctor and her assistant – also female) to the human material on which it bases its deductions. It will demonstrate the excesses to which scientific investigation can lead when practised by adherents dedicated to the point of fanaticism.

The scenic breakdown that follows offers an all-too-schematic treatment of the declared theme. In Scene 1, a woman doctor and her assistant greet a sceptical guinea pig. Scene 2 shows the man being placed in a soundproof room where electric clasps are attached to his wrists and earphones to his head. While he is subjected to nerve-racking tests, the two women casually discuss the clothes they are to wear at the institution's Annual Ball. Scene 3 cuts between the women lightly chatting in the canteen and the guinea-pig in the soundproof room responding to a series of taped questions. Scene 4 introduces a new volunteer: an old lady who regards these scientific experiments as a source of relaxation and who is bundled into a tiny room with the first guinea-pig and subjected to intense questioning. Finally, Scene 5 shows the old woman leaving refreshed by her afternoon's interrogation. The man meanwhile, by now broken down and inarticulate, is taken back to the original room to await further tests while the two doctors gaily go off to the ball. He is left in chill solitude with nothing but the echoing silence.

Some of these ideas bore fruit in the full-length stage version Pinter went on to write in the winter of 1958, but you can see from the synopsis why it wouldn't have worked as a sixty-minute radio play: it's too neat, too pat, too organised, as if Pinter is harnessing his baroque imagination to illustrate a predetermined thesis. And the idea that the institution has a wild, sinister, uncontrolled life of its own – which lies at the heart of the finished version – is here reduced to the rather tame symbol of the Annual Ball. In fact in its final version, *The Hothouse* is an eerily prophetic play about the secretive, bureaucratic insanity of a state institution apparently designed to 'cure' social dissidence. 'It *had* to be written,' says Pinter significantly; and the only reason that he eventually put it in a bottom drawer, leaving it unproduced till 1980, is that he felt it stood little chance after the brutal dismissal of *The Birthday Party*. 'Don't forget,' he says, 'that in the late '50s London was still dominated by a safe commercial theatre.'

Today the play survives as part of a political triptych, including *The Birthday Party* and *The Dumb Waiter*, all dealing in different ways with the oppression of the individual. And, as so often with Pinter, it has its origins in personal experience and inextinguishable memory.

'I went along in 1954 to the Maudsley Hospital in London,' Pinter now recalls, 'as a guinea-pig. They were offering ten bob or something for guinea-pigs and I needed the money desperately. I read a bona fide advertisement and went along. It was all above board, as it seemed. Nurses and doctors all in white. They tested my blood-pressure first. Perfectly all right. I was put in a room with electrodes. They said, "Just sit there for a while and relax." I'd no idea what was going to happen. Suddenly there was a most appalling noise through the earphones and I nearly jumped through the roof. I felt my heart go . . . BANG! The noise lasted a few seconds and then was switched off. The doctor came in grinning and said, "Well, that really gave you a start, didn't it?" I said, "It certainly did." And they said, "Thanks very much." There was no interrogation, as in the play, but it left a deep impression on me. I couldn't forget the experience. I was trembling all over. And I would have been in such a vulnerable position if they had started to ask me questions. Later I asked them what it was all about and they said they were testing levels of reaction. That mystified me. Who exactly were they going to give this kind of shock-treatment to? Anyway, *The Hothouse* was kicked off by that experience. I was well aware of being used for an experiment and feeling quite powerless.'

Pinter, yet again, is crucially aware of the significance of his own life: of the dramatic potential and political resonance lurking within a single defining moment. The finished play, of course, has nothing to do with the Maudsley itself. *The Hothouse* is in fact a black farce about the madness, paranoia, lust and suspicion that pervade a state-run 'rest home' in which the unseen in-mates are codified and abused, and the staff dehumanised, stripped of their identity and finally slaughtered. Intriguingly, it anticipates by a decade Joe Orton's *What the Butler Saw*, which is also set in a psychiatric institution and which suggests the divisions between sanity and madness, and even between male and female, are totally arbitrary. But Pinter's play is both subtler and more politically alert. Where Orton shows an indiscriminate scorn for human institutions and values, the whole point of Pinter's play is that there is a natural law which is being violated. Pinter is not just saying we are all mad; he implies, instead, that the state has a vested interest in producing contented model citizens who will conform exactly to programmed expectation. His hothouse is exactly the kind of place to which Stanley Webber might have been hauled off to be 'integrated' and 'adjusted'.

Pinter's prime focus, however, is on the staff. Isolated and immured, they have become victims of the bureaucratic machine they are supposedly operat-ing. The patients are identified by numbers rather than names, and the staff all have monosyllabic monikers, suggesting they too have sacrificed part of their identity to the institution. The show is run by Roote, a tetchy ex-colonel whose authority crumbles before our eyes. His subordinates include Gibbs, his hatchet-faced, piss-taking, ultimately treacherous lieutenant; Miss Cutts, their shared mistress who swivels between grey-suited masculinity and roguish femininity; Lush, an openly cynical staff member; and Lamb, the latest recruit who is relentlessly grilled for a security lapse in a nightmarish extension of the guinea-pig treatment Pinter himself briefly suffered. Even Tubb the gateman and Lobb, the Ministry desk-wallah we meet in the final scene, are part of the same world of single-syllable officialdom.

The mainspring of the plot is Roote's determination to root out who is responsible for the death of patient 6457 and the impregnation of patient 6459 who, on Christmas Day, has just given birth. It is immediately obvious that Roote is the father and at the end, after virtually all the staff have been slaughtered by the patients, he is accused by Gibbs of being the murderer as well. But this is not a Dürrenmatt-type thriller in which the investigator ironically uncovers his own guilt, but a moral and political farce about the way any watertight bureaucracy is corrupted from within by its own dis-regard of the natural laws.

Death – as we learn from the opening scene where Roote and Gibbs bicker over clashing dates in the former's desk diary – is seen, in this hothouse environment, not as an act of nature but as an administrative slip-up. It also runs counter to the 'curative' ethos of a place whose function is to adjust recalcitrant nonconformists to the demands of society. Hence the existence of 'the Halloween Feast, the May Dance, the October Revival, the Old Boys and Girls supper and social'. Hence also Roote's euphemistic language in describing the patients: 'After all, they're not criminals. They're only people in need of help, which we try to give, in one way or another, to the best of our discretion, to the best of our judgement, to help them regain their confidence, confidence in themselves, confidence in others, confidence in . . . the world.' It is precisely the soft-soap language with which authoritarian societies vindicate the use of psychiatric wards to reform dissidents.

In this world of inflexible order, birth is also, literally, a cock-up – a point Pinter makes with lethal irony. In his second encounter with Gibbs, Roote minutely identifies the physical characteristics of the patient who has given birth: 'Small?' 'Quite a sensual sort of face?' 'Wobbles when she walks?' 'Yes, she wobbles. She wobbles in her left buttock.' 'Likes eating toffees, too . . . when she can get any.' Having implicated himself with every question and statement, Roote ends up with the resounding *non sequitur*, 'No, I don't think I know her' – a classic music-hall technique. But Roote's heartlessness is shown when he says it's all right to copulate with the patients as long as you obey the rules: 'Never ride barebacked and always send in a report.' And any hint of a smile freezes on one's lips as Gibbs asks what he should do about the baby and Roote crisply retorts, 'Get rid of it'. I heard Pinter read this particular scene at the University of East Anglia in 1993 and I recall the frisson that ran through the hall at this particular point. Which is as it should be, since the play shows that any organisation that treats birth and death with casual contempt, as mere bureaucratic errors, is corroded from within.

The Hothouse deals with issues – such as the spiritual coarseness and whimsical arbitrariness of state power – that were to recur in *Mountain Language* thirty years later (so much for the myopic notion that Pinter discovered politics late in life), but the earlier play, written in more innocent times, has a careering energy and giddy momentum which you don't find in the later work. Pinter portrays a nightmare institution, but he also relishes harpooning its wicked absurdity. This reaches fever-pitch in the climactic first-act scene that Pinter extrapolates from his own experience. The hapless Lamb is led to the slaughter in the form of the soundproof control-room, guilelessly believing he is being considered for promotion. Even as electrodes are attached to his wrist and earphones to his head, he still doesn't twig. After a circuit has passed through his body, he is interrogated in a way that is brutally comic – indeed, it became the source of a revue sketch – and also indicative of his powerlessness:

CUTTS: Are you virgo intacta?

LAMB: What?

CUTTS: Are you virgo intacta?

LAMB: Oh, I say, that's rather embarrassing. I mean, in front of a lady.

CUTTS: Are you virgo intacta?

LAMB: Yes, I am actually. I'll make no secret of it.

CUTTS: Have you always been virgo intacta?

LAMB: Oh yes. Always.

CUTTS: From the word go?

LAMB: Go? Oh yes, from the word go.

This interrogation scene is comic, terrifying and structurally pivotal. It makes the point that conformity is the name of the game: at one moment Gibbs asks, 'Do you ever feel you would like to join a group of people in which group common assumptions are shared and common principles observed?' It also shows that both parties to an interrogation, questioner and victim, are contaminated by the process. Lamb begs for more questions, as if addicted to the drug of self-revelation, while Miss Cutts is sexually aroused by the control-room. In the second act, Pinter explicitly shows how the orgasmic fever of torture is transferred to her own private life. Employing Joycean verbal rhythms, she swooningly tells Gibbs 'your sense of timing is perfect, you know when the questions must stop, *those* questions, and you must start asking me questions, other questions, and I must start asking you questions, and it's question time, question time, question time, forever and forever and forever'. The final image of the play also echoes the interrogation scene. After the patients have made their murderous escape, as in some Jacobean tragedy to the sound of turning locks, rattling chains and clanging doors, and after Gibbs and the Ministerial Lobb, using the bland bromides of Whitehall, have swept the carnage under the carpet and determined that the work must go on, Pinter cuts back to the soundproof room and the image of Lamb staring ahead as in a catatonic trance: a forgotten figure like Firs in *The Cherry Orchard*, and a potent symbol of the negligent cruelty of arbitrary power.

The Hothouse is one of Pinter's best plays: one that deals with the worm-eaten corruption of bureaucracy, the secrecy of government, the disjunction between language and experience. It also reveals the acuteness of Pinter's political antennae. Written in the winter of 1958, it pre-empted by several years our awareness of the Soviet use of mental hospitals as repositories for social dissidents and it prefigured the American abuse of political prisoners in Central America, the stern methods of interrogation and detention used by the British authorities in the H-Block of Belfast's Maze Prison and the increasing number of deaths in Britain of prisoners held in official custody. Starting from a moment of private disquiet, Pinter sees its universal implications. The result is not political paranoia. It is a fable about what *can* happen when the rights of the individual are subordinated to the unaccountable power of the state. Had the play been produced when written, it would have established Pinter not as the master of the pause or the exponent of comedy of menace, but as a dramatist with an active political conscience.

As it was, the piece was stuck in a bottom drawer and Pinter occupied the position of playwright-in-waiting: someone whose first major work had been badly mauled but who was already undergoing critical reappraisal. In the September/October 1958 issue of the progressive playgoer's Bible, *Encore*, Irving Wardle had written a highly influential article that linked four promising new writers – Pinter, N. F. Simpson, Nigel Dennis and David Campton – and patented the phrase 'Comedy of Menace', which stuck to Pinter for years. That article struck a chord with Pinter's old mentor Stephen Joseph, who invited him to direct the first revival of *The Birthday Party* for the Scarborough Studio Theatre and a tour to Birmingham and Leicester in January 1959. Not only did the cast include the actor-writer David Campton and David Sutton, eventually to become Michael Codron's associate producer, but also a sharp-featured twenty-year-old actor called Alan Ayckbourn who was cast as Stanley. Ayckbourn has written of Pinter:

> When he arrived in Scarborough he was in a very defensive, not to say depressed state. We had probably three weeks to rehearse. I remember asking Pinter about my character. Where does he come from? Where is he going to? What can you tell me about him that will give me more understanding? And Harold just said, 'Mind your own fucking business. Concentrate on what's there.'

That was not brusqueness or rudeness – Ayckbourn testifies that Pinter was an extremely nice guy – but simply an absolute belief in the self-sufficiency of the text; a conviction that the clues are all inherent in the words spoken. It was also a reflection of Pinter's own writing process: in relying on what the Argentinian writer Borges calls the 'voluntary dream' of creative inspiration, he has no more notion than anyone else of where his characters come from. The rule doesn't apply to all Pinter's works but it certainly does to *The Birthday Party*, which is why he has always deflected questions about the characters' past and future. David Jones – later to become one of Pinter's best directorial interpreters – had the same experience when playing McCann in the first London revival of the play at the amateur Tower Theatre in Islington in May 1959. Like Ayckbourn, Jones found that his instinctive actor's questions about the character's origins came up against a brick wall. Jones recalls, 'I said to Harold, "Tell me about where McCann comes from before he arrives in the boarding-house." Harold said, "What do you mean?" I said, "What's McCann's background?" He said, "I have no fucking idea. I know everything about McCann after he walks through that door – I know nothing about him on the other side." I raised an eyebrow. He said, "That's the way it is in life. You meet people at parties. What do you know about what they did before they came in the door? Your only knowledge of them is in the room." I'd been brought up on Bradley's approach to Shakespeare which assumed that plays gave you deep insight into character. The idea that plays were more interesting if people were as mysterious or unexplained as they were in real life was quite a new idea to me.'

Pinter's radical refusal to supply cut-and-dried explanations was just as evident in the sketches he wrote for two revues that opened in London in the summer of 1959: *One to Another* at the Lyric Hammersmith in July and *Pieces of Eight* produced by Michael Codron at the Apollo in September. Revue, in those pre-*Beyond the Fringe* days, tended to come in two sorts: the glitzy kind, which invariably seemed to feature an Apache dance outside some ill-lit Parisian *boîte*, and the more intimate variety specialising in inbred, sophisticated camp. But the form was subtly changing under the influence of writers like Peter Cook, who scripted most of *Pieces of Eight*, and was leaning towards cryptic studies of the irrationality and inconsequentiality of human behaviour. Indeed, Cook, the Cambridge-educated product of a diplomatic family, and Pinter, the son of a Hackney tailor, have always struck me for all their differing backgrounds as artistic blood-brothers.

What is striking about Pinter's revue-sketches is the way they examine the same kinds of themes as his plays: the strangeness and solitude of the human animal, the subjectivity of memory, the use of language as a weapon of domination or a means of maintaining contact. They're not marginal little money-earners; they're extensions of Pinter's talent. As he himself told *The Times* in November 1959:

In both [revue-sketches and plays] I am primarily interested in people . . . In many British plays I find myself put off by the spectre of the author looming above his characters, telling them at every stage just what they are to think about them. I want as far as possible to leave comment to the audience; let them decide whether the characters and situations are funny or sad.

You see that in *The Black and White*, derived from his 1954 prose-piece and performed at the Lyric Hammersmith by Beryl Reid and Sheila Hancock, in which two female derelicts attempt to keep loneliness at bay by swapping inconsequential banalities about bread, soup, bus routes, menacing strangers and officious coppers. Or in *Request Stop*, in which a woman at a bus stop turns an assumed slight from the man standing next to her into a xenophobic tirade: a clear prefiguration of *The Caretaker* which was cooking in Pinter's imagination at the time. But the mini-masterpiece in this genre – originally seen in *Pieces of Eight* – is *Last to Go*. The setting is an all-night coffee stall. The barman, leaning on his counter, and an old newspaper-seller, standing with his cup of tea, engage in a desultory conversation that reveals a profound loneliness while also being very funny. David Lodge has treated the sketch to a brilliantly detailed structuralist reading in which he shows how what Malinowski called 'phatic communion' – speech whose primary function is to maintain contact between the interlocutors rather than convey information – becomes poetic in its echoes, symmetries and repetitions. There is nothing patronising, as is sometimes suggested, in Pinter's use of common speech rhythms. What you hear in the halting, pause-ridden dialogue between the two men is fear: fear of being the last to go home, fear of being the one to break the slender conversational thread, fear of death. The partiality of memory also intervenes when the newspaper-seller announces that around ten he went up to Victoria to see if he could get hold of George:

BARMAN: George who?

MAN: George . . . whatsisname.

BARMAN: Oh.

   (*Pause.*)

   Did you get hold of him?

MAN: No. No, I couldn't get hold of him. I couldn't locate him.

BARMAN: He's not much about now, is he?

   (*Pause.*)

MAN: When did you last see him then?

BARMAN: Oh, I haven't seen him for years.

MAN: No, nor me.

   (*Pause.*)

BARMAN: Used to suffer very bad from arthritis.

MAN: Arthritis?

BARMAN: Yes.

MAN: He never suffered from arthritis.

BARMAN: Suffered very bad.

   (*Pause.*)

MAN: Not when I knew him.

(*Pause.*)

BARMAN: I think he must have left the area.

This, to me, has the same fugal delicacy as Shallow and Silence discoursing on the price of livestock in *Henry IV Part Two*: both funny and sad, it shows two men using language not so much to communicate as to maintain the tenuous thread of human contact. They veer away from the subject of George (are they thinking of the same George or two different Georges?) precisely because it threatens to disrupt their precarious connection. Pinter also shows an uncanny ear for the rhythms of speech: yours, mine, his own. In the line 'No. No, I couldn't get hold of him. I couldn't locate him', the final verb is both a form of playing for time and an attempt to dignify the speaker: something we do all the time. The sketch is a masterly miniature that reveals Pinter's voracious interest in people, his flawless ear for the hidden poetry of everyday speech and his readiness to present the audience with the dramatic evidence rather than a foregone conclusion.

Pinter's skill in the popular form of revue raises an interesting paradox: his continuing ability to reach out to audiences over the heads of interpretative critics. At this period Pinter was gaining an increasing foothold in radio, television and theatre, yet audience appreciation was often accompanied by critical bafflement. In January 1960 Hampstead Theatre Club boldly paired *The Room*, directed by Pinter himself, with *The Dumb Waiter*, directed by James Roose-Evans. The word 'obscurity' was again promiscuously bandied about by the critics. The one really challenging review came from Alan Brien in the *Spectator*. Having perceptively seen the plays 'as warnings against being manipulated, as appeals in code smuggled out of semi-detached prisons', Brien went on: 'Now I want to know *why* we are trapped. Biologically? Socially? Theologically? I want to know how to fight back. It is the playwright's task to understand as well as to observe. Mr Pinter must now start to answer his own questions.' Once attacked for perpetuating mysteries, Pinter later came to be equally criticised for being overtly political. Anyway, the productions were a sufficiently popular draw to transfer to the Royal Court in March 1960, with Vivien Merchant repeating her performance as Rose and a young Michael Caine taking over as Mr Sands.

However, Pinter continued to attract prescriptive criticism. In February 1960 Arnold Wesker, writing about *The Birthday Party* in the *Jewish Chronicle*, claimed: 'The real weakness is that Pinter has used the right character in the wrong setting. It should all have taken place in a Jewish setting . . . It is not enough to say Goldberg is universal – people are only universal in their own setting.' Pinter, who was striving to show that oppression by shit-stained centuries of tradition was not an exclusively Jewish concern, reacted strongly to Wesker's point in an interview with Brian Glanville in the same paper: 'I do not at any point, in any way whatsoever, think of myself as a Jewish writer, except that I happen to be a Jew who writes.' He added that *The Birthday Party* was not intended as a specific criticism of Jewish society 'but if you're going to say anything about my attitude to society, then for God's sake don't leave *out* Jewish society'.

Debates about the play's Jewish provenance and supposed obscurity seem arcane when set beside its huge popular success when it went out on ITV on 22 March 1960. That broadcast stemmed from the total faith in Pinter's work of Peter Willes, a former Hollywood actor who became head of drama at Associated Rediffusion and a great champion of new writers including, later, Joe Orton. To this day, Pinter recalls his first extraordinary encounter with Willes. 'I was summoned to his office at Rediffusion. I knew he'd seen my sketches at the Lyric Hammersmith and been sent a copy of *The Birthday Party* but that was about all. I was ushered into his office by a secretary. Willes was standing by the window in a dark suit, turned to me and said, "How dare you?" I said I didn't understand what he meant. "How dare you?" he said again. "I've read your bloody play and I haven't had a wink of sleep for four nights. Well, I suppose we'd better do it. Who would you like to direct it?" As a newcomer to TV, I didn't know what to say but, after that, he became a great personal friend. In fact, by a strange irony, after Peter's death in the early 1990s his expensive suits were sold off to a theatrical costumier's, Carlo Manzi's, and when I went for a fitting for a production of *The Hothouse* in 1995, I looked inside the jacket of a particularly fine tweed suit I chose and there was Peter's name.'

It was Willes's faith that got *The Birthday Party* on to the screen; that historic 1960 production, brilliantly directed by Joan Kemp-Welch, was seen by 11 million viewers and gained glowing reviews. 'A play to scorch the nerve-ends', announced the *Daily Mirror* with metaphorical accuracy. 'A Stage Flop is Big Hit', trumpeted the *Daily Herald*. As one of those 11 million watchers, I recall the play as being like a hand-grenade thrown into one's sitting-room: a terrifying, gripping account of a nightmare invasion, with the director seeing the interrogative faces of Goldberg and McCann in looming close-up from Stanley's point of view. A play that had originally left Tynan, Shulman, Darlington and others bemused became a bus-stop talking-point the next day. It was the first of many occasions on which one of Pinter's plays, by tapping deep-seated fears, bypassed critical analysis to speak directly to the collective subconscious.

Something similar happened with *A Night Out*. Pinter had originally

developed it as a TV play in the summer of 1959. It was subsequently commissioned by BBC Radio as a sixty-minute play for the Third Programme
(for a fee of 95 guineas). Jimmy Wax then sold it to ABC TV's Armchair
Theatre on condition that they transmitted it after the radio broadcast. It's a
minor point but it's significant that the populist commercial channel was
much quicker to spot Pinter's potential than BBC Television's own hide-
bound drama department. In August 1959 Donald McWhinnie (assistant
head of drama, sound) had sent a copy of *The Dumb Waiter* to Michael Barry
(head of drama, television) with a note saying, 'This is a one-act stage play by
the provocative Harold Pinter. It seems to me to have strong visual possibilities for television but I think that you might feel it too obscure for your
audience. If you feel by any chance that you could accommodate it, it would
interest me very much as a production job.' Back came the cryptic reply from
the dismally unadventurous Michael Barry: 'Yes – too obscure, I feel.'

At this stage, BBC Radio and commercial television were Pinter's greatest
champions. *A Night Out* was broadcast on the Third on 1 March 1960 with
Barry Foster as the office-clerk hero who rebels violently against both his
nagging mother and a genteel tart. On 24 April it went out as part of ABC's
Armchair Theatre with Tom Bell in the lead. In both versions Pinter played
one of the hero's colleagues and Vivien the sedate whore – apart from anything else, they needed the money – but what is fascinating is the discrepancy
between the critical and popular reactions. Paul Ferris in the *Observer* was
sniffy about the radio version claiming that 'it lacked the final and only true
merit of somehow interfering with the listener' – a novel criterion for radio
drama – and in the same paper Maurice Richardson wrote of the TV production that 'You were left with the impression of a box of tricks, a scenario for a
ballet rather than a play'. Yet BBC Audience Research registered an
Appreciation index of 65 for the radio version which was considered decently
high. 'After hearing this play', commented one female listener, 'I made a vow
never to nag my husband or son again', which suggests drama can have an
unsuspected utilitarian function. On television it was number one in the
week's Top Ten ratings, outstripping even the massively popular *Sunday
Night at the London Palladium*. Ironic to think that a show whose prime
attraction was a grisly game called 'Beat the Clock' was pushed into second
place by a play in which the hero literally threatens to beat his mother to
death with a clock.

In all honesty, *A Night Out* is not a particularly difficult or mysterious play.
It is more realistic in tone than anything Pinter had written before. It deals in
narrative surprise. It is structured in three fairly conventional acts. In Act
One the twenty-eight-year-old Albert Stokes, setting out to meet his mates in

preparation for an office party, is almost persuaded to stay at home by his possessive mother. In Act Two he goes to the party, is falsely accused of touching up a young girl, gets into a fight with a bullying colleague and returns home where he apparently brains his waiting mum to death. In Act Three he gets picked up by a tart, is driven to violence when he hears in her voice an echo of his mother's nagging and returns home only to find his mother, whom he had left for dead, waiting for him with a mixture of baleful reproach and smothering solicitude.

Pinter clearly taps into a familiar masculine fear: of the repressive mother who threatens the ego-identity of her son and of the sexually available woman who challenges his potency. Equally obviously, there are strong echoes of *The Birthday Party* and of Stanley's eruptive hostility towards the mothering Meg whom he all but strangles, and of the sexually brash Lulu whom he vainly attempts to rape. It's a play about the way male inadequacy turns towards enraged, impotent violence. But there seems no personal pressure behind it: it's Freud for the mass-market, rather than something wrenched from the author's own psyche. (Pinter himself had a basically harmonious relationship with his own mum and rarely seems to have been weighed down by difficulties with girls.) Only in the third act does the play take wing. You feel Pinter's imagination is suddenly fired by an encounter between two lonely people – Albert and The Girl – who shield their profound solitude under a wall of pretence and who struggle to achieve a temporary ascendancy over each other. It's amazing how Pinter's writing takes off when power is at stake and he can explore the politics of the parlour.

Pinter also shows in this one gripping scene how words act as a camouflage for unexpressed needs and fears. Albert attempts to conceal his sexual panic and fear of impotence by pretending to be an assistant film director. The Girl tries to hide her loneliness and guilt at choice of profession by affecting a surface gentility: she protests at Albert's swearing, talks about taking a sherry before dinner and dwells on the photograph of her daughter at a Hereford boarding school which, pathetically, turns out to be a picture of her younger self. It's a classic piece of dramatic writing in which Pinter shows his compassion for both parties: the lonely prostitute and the mother-fixated male virgin. Even Albert's final attempt at domination – forcing The Girl to put on his shoes and tossing a half-crown in her direction with a cry of 'buy yourself a seat at a circus' – only serves to emphasise his sexual fear. And although Pinter denies that he consciously wrote female roles with Vivien in mind, it's hard to believe that he wasn't deploying aspects of her complex personality: in particular, her strange mixture of emotional fragility and physical poise. Those who knew her at this time paint a fascinatingly contradictory picture. Auriol Smith, who was in both the Hampstead production of *The Room* and the radio version of *A Night Out*, says, 'I felt she was a very insecure person. She seemed very vulnerable. I remember when she played the fifty-year-old Rose she complained about always having to play character roles and never being asked to do anything glamorous.' And Susan Engel, who was the original Rose at Bristol, always recalls her as 'very still, very erect as if she had consciously modelled herself on of those elegant 1950s *Vogue* models like Barbara Goalen'. That mixture of private insecurity and willed gentility is, of course, precisely what fuels the character in *A Night Out*.

What is extraordinary, however, is the journey Pinter himself had undergone in the two years since the resounding failure of *The Birthday Party*. In that time he had bounced back to write *A Slight Ache*, *The Hothouse*, *A Night Out* and a batch of admired revue-sketches. He had seen his first major play critically reappraised and revived first in the regions, then by London amateurs (at the Questors, Ealing, in 1959 Stanley was played by Peter Whelan, which suggests the role was a magnet for aspiring playwrights) and finally on television. He had – partly by continuing to act in rep until the late summer of 1959 – managed to earn enough money to put the groceries on the table. He had, by a mixture of hard work and resilience, shown that he damn well wasn't going to be silenced. He had also nurtured his obstinate belief in the rights of the individual when confronted by social conformity or state oppression. He had even managed to write a new play. What he didn't know, when *A Night Out* was transmitted on Sunday-night television on 24 April 1960, is that he was only three days away from being wrenched from the shadowy obscurity of the promising writer, and from finding his whole life and career totally transformed. Like Byron, he was about to wake up one morning and find himself famous.

Six Power Play

The work that catapulted Pinter into the heady arena of commercial success and national fame was, of course, *The Caretaker*. It opened at the Arts Theatre, London, on 27 April 1960 and transferred to the Duchess a month later, achieving a total run of 444 performances. But the play has had an after-life that has turned the itinerant Davies, the brain-damaged Aston, and the fly, entrepreneurial Mick into semi-mythic figures. It has been performed in every theatrical capital in the world, frequently revived in London, filmed, televised and subjected to every possible inter-pretation. It has been given with an all-black cast at Britain's National Theatre and all-female cast at the Sherman Theatre in Cardiff. I have even seen it played by Romania's National Theatre of Craiova as a piece of naked religious symbolism with a Christ-like Aston at the beginning washing Davies's feet to the sound of Bach's Mass in B Minor. Yet Pinter's most universally performed play had its origins in the specific circumstances of life in 373 Chiswick High Road. It is not a direct transcription of experience, but its three characters all had their antecedents in life and the play was sparked off by a flashpoint image – proof once again, as with *The Birthday Party* and *The Hothouse*, of Pinter's capacity to see the dramatic significance lurking within a single arrested moment.

Pinter has never talked in detail about the play's origins before, largely because they became a source of anguished conflict between himself and Vivien. 'We were living,' he explains, 'in this first-floor flat in Chiswick: a very clean couple of rooms with a bath and kitchen. There was a chap who owned the house: a builder, in fact, like Mick who had his own van and whom I hardly ever saw. The only image I had of him was of this swift mover up and down the stairs and of his van going . . . Vrooom . . . as he arrived and departed. His brother lived in the house. He was a handyman . . . he managed rather more successfully than Aston, but he was very introverted, very secret-ive, had been in a mental home some years before and had had some kind of electrical shock treatment . . . ECT, I think . . . Anyway, he did bring a tramp back one night. I call him a tramp, but he was just a homeless old man who stayed three or four weeks. I talked to the tramp only insofar as I bumped into him occasionally on the stairs . . . that was the only place you could ever meet. I never invited him in for a cup of tea, but I occasionally got glimpses of him in the other fellow's room . . . He wasn't anywhere near as eloquent as Davies but he was certainly . . . he didn't seem very content with his lot . . . The image that stayed with me for a long time was of the open door to this room with the two men standing in different parts of the room doing different things . . . the tramp rooting around in a bag and the other man looking out of the window and simply not speaking . . . A kind of moment frozen in time that left a very strong impression.'

Out of that momentary image came one of the most durable post-war plays; but as Pinter talks, what becomes clear is his intuitive sympathy with the prototypes of both Aston and Davies. Mick, as he says, was the most purely invented character of the three. For the tramp, however, he had a certain fellow-feeling. 'After he'd been thrown out of the house,' says Pinter, 'I met him one day on Chiswick roundabout. We had a chat and I asked him how he was getting on. I didn't mention the play, which I'd by then written, because he wouldn't have known what a play was . . . That sounds a little condescending, since I hardly knew what a play was myself. I'd like you to remember that my life at that time was writing on my old typewriter – with Daniel crawling about under my feet – and the round of the Labour Exchange and the odd half-pint at the Robin Hood and Little John down the road. It was a very threadbare existence . . . very . . . I was totally out of work. So I was very close to this old derelict's world, in a way.'

Allowing for a touch of poetic licence – by the autumn of 1959, when he wrote the play, Pinter had already had *A Slight Ache* done on the Third Programme and was starting to get regular commissions from radio drama – it was true that Pinter was extremely hard up and had a natural sympathy with vagrants. He had roamed around London during his truancy from RADA. He had done a wide variety of odd-jobs. And even before that, in his autobiographical essay *The Queen of all the Fairies*, he describes how he and his Hackney chums used to take up with old dossers.

During our walks we often met a beautiful old tramp called Charley. He slept in an Aldgate kiphouse and roamed aimlessly all day. He was slightly touched, weak with hardship. He seemed to have come to roost in Hackney and we often helped him. It was the least we could do in return for the gentle grace he bestowed on the district.

There's no 'gentle grace' in Davies, but at least that extract shows there's nothing fake about Pinter's constant fascination with hobos.

Even more significant is Pinter's affection for the prototype of Aston, whose real name, according to the actor Kenneth Cranham, was Austin. 'I remember,' says Pinter, 'that I managed to get a job out of London somewhere and had to go away for a month. When I got back home the Aston-figure met me on the stairs and said, "I've got a surprise for you." He showed me a new telephone directory which had just arrived and it said "H. Pinter – Scriptwriter". I'd told him earlier that, as actors, it would be very useful for Vivien and myself if we had a telephone – even if no one was likely to ring – so he'd gone out and had one specially installed on the stairs. He'd only done it because he also knew I was in the business of writing; and he was very proud of that . . . I'll tell you why I've never talked about this before and that is because Vivien was always very upset that I had written the play about this Aston-character. She felt that in some way I had betrayed him. But I didn't understand that. I said, "How could I betray him because I'm on his side? I like him very much. I feel very sympathetic to him." But she was intractable, if that's the right word, and could never see that. So I never discussed it publicly and never mentioned the play's source. I didn't want to compound the problem and upset her even further . . .'

Guy Vaesen, who remained a lifelong friend of Vivien's, confirms that 'she always detested *The Caretaker*': ironically, since it was the play that gave her and Pinter a longed-for financial security, but perhaps forgivably, in that it was a permanent reminder of the artist's need to plunder personal experience, her own included. It was both a source of material comfort and of marital conflict in that it fatally established her dependence on her now-famous husband. But Pinter's account of the play's origins is revealing in numerous ways. First, it shows that it was much closer to perceived reality than anything he had yet written: a point confirmed by Donald Pleasence who was the original, unforgettable Davies. 'I used to drive Harold home after rehearsals,' he told me, 'to his flat in the Chiswick High Road where the action really takes place. One night as I stopped outside the house I suddenly remembered something: that I had been there before. I'd had my photograph taken there by an Indian photographer who had a very beautiful wife. I suddenly realised these were the very same 'blacks' whom Davies rails against and who were living on the other side of the wall to the real-life original.'

Pinter's story of the play's genesis also goes some way towards explaining the mystery of his creative process. He starts with an image, a Proustian memory of a moment frozen in time; but he allows the image to evolve gradually and transforms it into something that conforms to his own continuing obsessions. You can see why Pinter has always resisted allegorical interpretations of this play, saying simply that it deals with 'a particular situation

1 A Pinter wedding: 9 June 1926. Harold Pinter's parents, Jack and Frances (née Moskowitz), flanked by his paternal grandparents, Nathan and Fanny (left), and his maternal grandparents, Harry and Rose (right).

2 The evacuee: Pinter at Caerhays, 1940.

3 Harold Pinter with his father, 1946.

4 Harold Pinter as Macbeth with Ron Percival as Lady Macbeth in Joseph Brearley's Hackney Downs Grammar School production, 1947.

5 Harold Pinter (extreme left) with a group of friends including Ron Percival (third from left), Henry Woolf (foreground), Morris Wernick (third from right), B. J. Law (extreme right).

6 On the road in Ireland with Anew McMaster. Harold Pinter (extreme left) with Pauline Flanagan and members of the company, 1952.

7 On tour in Galway: Barry Foster, Pauline Flanagan, Harold Pinter, 1952.

8 Pinter in contrasting modes as actor, 1952: (a) as a saturnine Iago to McMaster's Othello, and (b) as a romantic Bassanio played, according to the *Waterford Reporter*, with 'fine impetuousness'.

9 The Anew McMaster Company after a performance of Wilde's *Lady Windermere's Fan*, 1951. Harold Pinter (second row right) standing in front of Joe Nolan, business-manager and actor, and Kenneth Haigh. Pauline Flanagan is seated down left.

10 Harold Pinter on tour in L. du Garde Peach's farce *A Horse! A Horse!* in 1954. It was while staying in digs in Eastbourne that Pinter had a strange encounter that later triggered *The Birthday Party*.

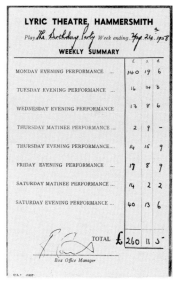

11 Beatrix Lehmann (Meg) and Richard Pearson (Stanley) in the ill-fated production of *The Birthday Party* at the Lyric, Hammersmith, 1958.

12 The week's receipts.

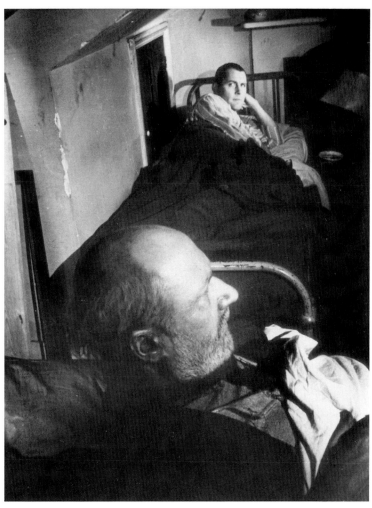

13 Robert Shaw (Aston) and Donald Pleasence (Davies) in the New York production of *The Caretaker*, 1962.

14 Alternative visions of *The Caretaker*: (a) a Japanese Davies in the Tokyo production of 1967, and (b) Sacha Pitoeff (Aston) and Jacques Dufilho (Davies) in the acclaimed Paris revival of 1969.

15 Ian Holm (Lenny) and Vivien Merchant (Ruth) in Peter Hall's original production of *The Homecoming*, Aldwych, 1965.

concerning three particular people'. But any play, if it has any quality, expands beyond the original impulse that created it. Goethe once said of drama, 'A play should be symbolic, that is to say: each bit of action must be significant in itself and point to something still more important behind it. Molière's *Tartuffe* is a great example of this.' So too *The Caretaker*. It is obviously a specific play about three individuals and about the idea of a room as a temporary sanctuary from the outside world. But it is also a play about the domestic nature of power and about the shifting alliances we form as part of our survival tactic; about the pipe dreams and protective illusions that sustain us from one day to the next; and about the way we use language as a weapon of domination, evasion or tactical negotiation. Obviously, we bring to any work of art our own preconceptions and I would not seek to exclude other people's religious, metaphysical or Freudian interpretations. However, *The Caretaker* for me is above all a play that conclusively blitzes the artificial distinctions people make between the private and the public Pinter: it is simultaneously a highly domestic play about the unyielding strength of fraternal ties when confronted by an intruder, and in the excellent words of John Gross 'a deeply political play in that its basic image of life is one of ceaseless struggle'. Ultimately, the two ideas become inseparable.

Strip away one's received ideas about the play and what does one find? For a start, as so often with Pinter, an arresting opening image; one that communicates much of the play's meaning. Our first sight of the junk-filled room – with its lawnmower, shopping trolley, suitcases, boxes, old newspapers, statue of Buddha and endless bric-à-brac – tells us that whoever lives there must be solitary, anally retentive, disorganised, even a little *distrait*. We then see a leather-jacketed character (Mick) surveying each object in turn, staring at the bucket hanging from the ceiling, sitting silently for thirty seconds, slipping out quietly when he hears voices on the stairs. At this stage, we have no clue as to who he is. We have no idea that he is the owner of the property or the brother of its chief tenant. But his silence, his cool assessment of the room's contents, his occupancy of the bed implies that he has a proprietorial attitude to the space. His quick exit at the sound of voices also suggests furtiveness and secrecy. And the first sight of Aston, with his shabby dark-blue pinstripe suit plus pullover, and of Davies, with his worn brown overcoat, waistcoat, vest, no shirt and sandals, also signifies something about their relative status.

Pinter instantly establishes Davies's querulous dependence on Aston's generous hospitality: the old man, evidently some kind of vagrant, craves warmth and shelter but knows this places him in a subordinate position. 'Sit down' are Aston's first words; it sounds a perfectly innocuous opening to a play. Yet although it's a kindly gesture, it puts Davies in an inferior position and he knows it. His instant reaction is a mixture of aggression and defence: 'Sit down? Huh . . . I haven't had a good sit down . . . I haven't had a proper sit down . . . well, I couldn't tell you . . .' Twice more Aston offers him a seat. Davies refuses it. Instead he roams around the room splenetically raging against the Poles, Greeks and blacks who pinched his seat at the caff where he's been working, and at the 'Scotch git' who ordered him to take out a bucket of rubbish. Who sits and who stands may seem a trivial question. In Pinter, it is all a crucial part of the jockeying for power. In *The Room*, the marital tension between the new arrivals is signified by Mrs Sands's accusation to her husband 'You're sitting down!' which is countered by a defensive 'Who is?' And, more famously, Goldberg's injunction to Stanley in *The Birthday Party* to sit down and the latter's mutinous refusal are part of a crucial manoeuvring for position. Here, the fact that Aston sits rolling a cigarette and fiddling with the plug on an electric toaster – an action that absorbs him throughout the entire play – while Davies shambles vituperatively about the room tells us that the host's territorial rights are already under threat.

Power is the theme: dominate or be dominated. And Pinter realises that it is nothing to do with epic scale but with what is at stake for the contestants. Marlowe's *Tamburlaine the Great* deals with the conquest of vast kingdoms; *The Caretaker* is about three men in a West London room, but there is a much greater apprehension of power in the latter than in the whole of Marlowe's glitteringly monotonous saga about world domination. For what Pinter grasps is that life is a series of negotiations for advantage in which everything comes into play: even a pair of shoes, which here acquire talismanic significance. It is Davies who first brings up the subject with Aston: 'I'll tell you what, mate, you haven't got a spare pair of shoes?' Even that phrase, with its sudden illogical switch from statement to question, from aggressive assertion to earnest plea, shows the confusion in Davies's mind: the constant tug-of-war between domination and dependence. And his long account of the trip to the Luton monastery in search of free footwear, where he is told by the monk to 'Piss off', shows that his natural condition is one of truculent ingratiation. Even when Aston offers him a perfectly decent pair of leather shoes, Davies turns the situation, with the rat-like cunning of the dispossessed, to his own advantage:

> DAVIES: Not a bad pair of shoes (*He trudges round the room.*) They're strong all right. Yes. Not a bad shape of shoe. This leather's hardy, en't? Very hardy. Some bloke tried to flog me some suede the other day. I wouldn't

wear them. Can't beat leather, for wear. Suede goes off, it creases, it stains for life in five minutes. You can't beat leather. Yes. Good shoe this.

ASTON: Good.

(*Davies waggles his feet.*)

DAVIES: Don't fit though.

ASTON: Oh?

DAVIES: No. I got a very broad foot.

ASTON: Mmnn.

DAVIES: These are too pointed, you see.

ASTON: Ah.

DAVIES: They'd cripple me in a week. I mean these ones I got on, they're no good but at least they're comfortable. Not much cop, but I mean they don't hurt. (*He takes them off and gives them back.*) Thanks anyway, mister.

ASTON: I'll see what I can look out for you.

DAVIES: Good luck. I can't go on like this. Can't get from one place to another. And I'll have to be moving about, you see, try to get fixed up.

ASTON: Where are you going to go?

DAVIES: Oh, I got one or two things in mind. I'm waiting for the weather to break.

(*Pause.*)

ASTON (attending to the toaster): Would ... would you like to sleep here?

Anyone who wants to know why Pinter is a first-rate writer need only study the subtle manoeuvrings in this harmless-looking exchange. First Davies establishes his expertise in the matter of footwear. He then throws the burden of moral guilt on to Aston as if he is to blame for offering him a potentially crippling pair of shoes. Having put him at a disadvantage, Davies exploits Aston's charitable good nature to place him in a position of placatory servitude – there's something wonderfully patronising about his cry of 'Good luck'. By establishing that the fulfilment of his plans depends on being solidly shod, Davies also negotiates a position where Aston has virtually no alternative but to offer him a bed. Obviously there is something comic about a sandalled toe-rag quibbling, like a dowager-duchess in Jermyn Street, about a precise and perfect fit, but Davies consciously uses the rejection of the shoes to gain a tactical advantage. The point is clinched later on when Davies, left to his own devices, fishes the self-same shoes out from under Aston's bed and appreciatively murmurs: 'Not a bad pair of shoes. Bit pointed.' Pinter shows, with consummate dramatic skill, how the battle for supremacy is dependent not on a cosmic scale but on what is at stake for the individual: in fact, there's no business like shoe business.

The action of the play also underlines that Davies is good on short-term tactics, but weak on overall strategy. His immediate aim is clear: to get a free doss and milk Aston for all he can. His long-term goal – to get down to Sidcup and retrieve his papers – is no more than a delusion, but in the course of the play he is undone by a succession of factors: by the offer of the job of caretaker which exposes his panic at any form of commitment, by his fatal shift of allegiance from Aston to Mick, and by his grave underestimation of the bonds of fraternal kinship. Excluded from the network of family relationships, he is totally unable to comprehend the idea of sibling protection; which is partly why the whole balance of power changes with the return of Mick at the end of Act One. From then on, it is clear that Mick is testing Davies, laying traps for him and seeking to expose his real character so that Aston will be driven to expel him on his own initiative. Mick is playing his own long-term political power-game in that he is trying to shield his brother from exploitation without seeming to cut his balls off.

Mick, in fact, is fly, devious and clever. He dominates Davies in several ways: by brute force, by sheer linguistic expertise, by terrifying him with the Electrolux, by offering him all kinds of bait which he naïvely swallows. Davies has an animal instinct for survival; Mick has a master-plan dictated by fraternal love:

MICK: If you got an older brother you want to push him on, you want to see him make his way. Can't have him idle, he's only doing himself harm. That's what I say.

DAVIES: Yes.

MICK: But he won't buckle down to the job.

DAVIES: He don't like work.

MICK: Work shy.

DAVIES: Sounds like it to me.

MICK: You've met the type have you?

DAVIES: Me? I know that sort.

Mick clearly eggs Davies on with his man-to-man tone, offers him a cruel mirror-image of himself, sets the trap by getting him to suggest that Aston is a bit funny ('You don't want to start getting hypercritical') and slams it shut by offering Davies the job of caretaker. Aston – who, in a sense, takes care of Davies just as Mick takes care of Aston – has made the same offer apparently out of compassion and the need for company: Mick does it as part of a strategic plan to expose Davies's shifting treachery. From this moment on,

Davies's fate is sealed. He throws in his lot with Mick. He disowns his saviour Aston ('He's no friend of mine'). He threatens Aston with a return to the mental hospital where he was once incarcerated and pulls a knife on him. By allying himself with the stronger-seeming brother, he overplays his feeble hand and is finally exposed as a conniving parasite whose punishment is to be banished from this temporary Eden. Mick's triumph is to use devious political tactics to lead Davies into revealing his malevolence and contempt so that it is Aston who takes the initiative in asking him to leave.

Pinter combines a realistic study of family ties with a microcosmic study of power, but Aston's role in all this needs to be clearly defined. He is, as Pinter told Kenneth Cranham when he played the role in 1980, 'a gent'. Pinter also did not dissent from Cranham's conviction that Aston may have had some past religious insight: initially, in his treatment of Davies, he is the soul of charitable goodness. But it is misleading to treat him purely as a milk-and-water Christian symbol. Listen closely to his long speech at the end of Act Two about his incarceration and what you notice is that Aston was also an active resister. Locked away in a mental hospital, he frequently tried to escape. Told that shock-treatment would enable him to 'live like the others' – always the cardinal fear in a Pinter play – he spent five hours sawing through the bars of his window. And rather than passively waiting for the pincers to be placed round his head, he stood against a wall and laid out one of the doctors and seized another by the throat. Aston, however gentle, is still possessed by the memory of a violent injustice: 'I've often thought of going back and trying to find the man who did that to me.' And, even though he needs his brother's protection, he is still capable of positive action. After Davies's fatal political miscalculation of siding with Mick and his invocation of Aston's greatest terror ('They can put the pincers on your head again, man!'), it is Aston who precipitates the tramp's expulsion, a process confirmed and completed by Mick. Indeed, one of the key moments of the play is when Aston returns after Davies has been decisively ordered out: '*Aston comes in. He closes the door, moves into the room and faces Mick. They look at each other. Both are smiling, faintly.*' Pinter signifies that they understand not only each other but the nature of Davies's character who is left at the end supplicatory and powerless. As Davies is left pleading for another chance, Aston remains still, his back towards him, at the window: almost a replica of the potent image Pinter glimpsed through an open door in Chiswick High Road.

Like all first-rate realistic plays, *The Caretaker* is obviously open to metaphorical interpretation. Kenneth Tynan in the *Observer* floated the possibility that the two brothers may be bifurcated halves of a schizoid personality, or that Mick may stand for the super-ego, Aston for the ego and the tramp for the id. Martin Esslin, while acknowledging the play's solid foundations in reality, intriguingly suggests that Davies may be the father-figure whom the two sons are forced to expel and reject. Terence Rattigan, on first seeing the play, suggested to Pinter that the three characters represented God the Father, God the Son and God the Holy Ghost: Pinter, as always, listened politely. Others have seen Davies as Dionysus, the Wandering Jew, the tempter in an Everyman play. But the more elaborate the hypotheses become, the more they de-nature the play by refusing to see what is actually there: an acute study in domestic politics in which an arch-manipulator is outmanoeuvred by a smarter, wittier rival; an exploration of the unyielding bond of fraternal kinship; and an attic tragedy in which our sympathy finally swings back towards Davies who transmutes into a North Circular Road Lear.

Yet it is also a play that deals with one of the great themes of modern drama, one that haunted Ibsen, Chekhov, Pirandello, Williams and, most specifically, O'Neill in *The Iceman Cometh*: the attempt to shield ourselves against diurnal reality through protective illusions. Davies, without a fixed abode, identity, verifiable name or even precious belongings, is a tragicomic figure who reinvents himself according to the needs of the moment. 'I've eaten dinner off the best of plates' is an unlikely assertion dictated by the pungent memory of his wife's alleged squalor. When Aston recalls how a woman in a café put her hand on his and asked whether he would like her to have a look at his body, Davies caps it with 'They've said the same thing to me'. And when Mick suggests that Davies might have been in the services – and even the colonies – Davies retorts: 'I was over there. I was one of the first over there.' He defines himself according to momentary imperatives and other people's suggestions. The idea that he can affirm his identity and recover his papers by journeying to Sidcup is perhaps the greatest delusion of all, though one with its source in reality. Pinter's old Hackney friend Morris Wernick recalls, 'It is undoubtedly true that Harold, with a writer's ear, picked up words and phrases from each of us. He also picked up locales. The Sidcup in *The Caretaker* comes from the fact that the Royal Artillery HQ was there when I was a National Serviceman and its almost mythical quality as the fount of all permission and record was a source.' To English ears, Sidcup has faintly comic overtones of suburban respectability. For Davies it is a Kentish Eldorado: the place that can solve all the problems about his unresolved identity and uncertain past, present and future.

Aston, the ineffectual handyman who spends much of the play trying to mend the same electric plug, is also sustained by an illusion: that he can transform the wilderness of a garden and build a shed before decorating the upper part of his brother's house. As he patiently explains to Davies:

Once I get that shed up outside . . . I'll be able to give a bit more thought to the flat, you see. Perhaps I can knock up one or two things for it. (*He walks to the window.*) I can work with my hands, you see. That's one thing I can do. I never knew I could. But I can do all sorts of things now, with my hands. You know, manual things. When I get that shed up out there . . . I'll have a workshop, you see. I. . . . could do a bit of wood-work. Simple woodwork, to start. Working with . . . good wood.

This has the same note of wistful delusion you find in O'Neill's waterfront bums, but without the consolation of drink. What makes it all the sadder is Aston's inability to mend a toaster, let alone erect a shed or decorate a flat.

Mick, too, though manipulative and sharp-witted is also sustained by the unrealisable dream of turning this junk-filled attic into a *House and Garden*-style penthouse with teal-blue, copper and parchment linoleum squares in the kitchen, and mahogany and rosewood furniture in the bedroom. It's pure Mittyesque illusion. And when he finally hurls the Buddha against the gas stove, it seems to me less a symbolic destruction of the Davies father-figure than an expression of pent-up fury at the knowledge that his dreams are incapable of fulfilment. Just as Mick knows that Davies is a battening tramp who stinks from arsehole to breakfast time, so he realises that he himself will always be a West London cowboy and small-time builder with a brain-damaged brother.

What adds piquancy to these pipe dreams, however, is that each character can see through the other's pretensions while still clinging desperately to his own. When Aston talks dreamily of clearing the overgrown garden to build a shed, it is Davies who points out, with savage realism, 'You'd need a tractor, man'. Davies's own particular life-lie is itself harshly punctured by Mick: 'You make a long speech about all the references you've got down in Sidcup and what happens? I haven't noticed you go down to Sidcup to obtain them.' And even Aston is shrewd enough to quash Davies's final, pathetic dream of staying on and helping with the garden shed by bluntly saying 'You make too much noise'. This is the play's supreme irony: that while clinging desperately to our own private illusions we hack through other people's with a verbal machete.

The most radical feature of the play, however, is Pinter's dramatic lan-guage. It is not something one can divorce from character or situation as if it were a mere virtuosic feat or a piece of ostentatious verbal trickery. Even the more obvious solo flights – Davies's account of his Luton pilgrimage in search of shoes, Aston's pained recall of his incarceration, Mick's detailed description of his Conranesque penthouse – have a different rhythm and tone that reflects the speaker's thought processes and the dramatic situation. But far more than in his previous plays Pinter shows how language is a continuous battle-tactic: a potential weapon of domination, a defensive posture to secure one's position, a source of evasion to hide truth. Ibsen said 'to be a poet is chiefly to see'; what Pinter sees is that the language we use is rarely innocent of hidden intention, that it is part of an endless negotiation for advantage or a source of emotional camouflage. It is nothing to do with 'failure of communication', the tired critical cant-phrase of the period. As Pinter himself said in a BBC Radio interview with Kenneth Tynan in 1960, 'I feel that instead of any inability to communicate there is a deliberate evasion of communication. Communication between people is so frightening that rather than do that there is a continual cross-talk, a continual talking about other things, rather than what is at the root of their relationship.'

Yet Pinter's specific advance in *The Caretaker* is to show that we respond less to what is actually said than to the motive behind it; that we constantly second-guess other people's intentions. One exchange between Aston and Davies demonstrates this perfectly:

ASTON: What did you say your name was?

DAVIES: Bernard Jenkins is my assumed name.

ASTON: No, your other one?

DAVIES: Davies. Mac Davies.

ASTON: Welsh, are you?

DAVIES: Eh?

ASTON: You Welsh?

  (*Pause.*)

DAVIES: Well, I been around, you know ... what I mean ... I been about ...

ASTON: Where were you born then?

DAVIES (*darkly*): What do you mean?

ASTON: Where were you born?

DAVIES: I was ... uh ... oh, it's a bit hard, like, to set your mind back ... see what I mean ... going back ... a good way ... lose a bit of track, like ... you know ...

It's a wonderful passage: richly funny and deeply disturbing. Aston's questions are innocent enough on the surface; but they spring from a desire for human contact – 'At the beginning of the play,' Pinter told Kenneth Cranham, 'Aston hasn't spoken to anyone for ten years' – and a need to get some purchase on this mysterious, irascible guest who has just spent a night under his roof. Davies, an outlaw from society and doubtless harassed and bothered by everyone from coppers to café owners, sees every question as a potential threat. He ducks and bobs and weaves under each enquiry as if unable to distinguish any longer between prying officialdom and simple human curiosity. At the same time he reveals that a lifetime on the road has so eroded his identity that he is reduced to babbling incoherence when asked about his place of birth. It's not that Aston and Davies fail to communicate. What Pinter shows is that they proceed on different tracks: one is nakedly hungry for contact; the other seeks to avoid it through verbal feints and defensive withdrawals. The only critic to grasp the revolutionary nature of this kind of tactical inconsequentiality was Penelope Gilliatt when she came to write about the 1964 film version of *The Caretaker*. Perhaps because she was married to a dramatist, John Osborne, and was a film and short-story writer herself, she saw precisely what Pinter was doing:

> The fact that people often talk like this, replying not to the meaning of the speech but to what they can guess about motives, is such a simple and compassionate observation that it is hard to think how so many writers of dialogue have managed without it for so long. For unless your characters are Jesuits, to follow a question by an answer that makes logical sense is actually a very stylised way to write lines. It is one of the things that gives Shaw's plays, for instance, their rather inhuman surface. But this is the way most dramatists have written, even when they intend to be realistic. It is as though for thousands of years we have been drawing profiles of people with two eyes and just this moment noticed that only one eye actually shows. To most people in the past to have followed a line like 'Where were you born?' by 'What do you mean?' would have been pure gibberish. The stinking, obsequious old man replies like this because he thinks the brother, who has given him a bed in his lumber room, is trying obscurely to get at him. If he could get down to his papers in Sidcup, everything would be all right.

'Compassionate' is a perceptive word to describe this discovery. It's the direct opposite of Kenneth Tynan's reaction to the original production where he qualified his enthusiasm for the play by remarking: 'Time and again, without the least departure from authenticity, Mr Pinter exposes the vague, repetitive silliness of lower-class conversation. One laughs in recognition; but one's laughter is tinged with snobbism.' Maybe that was true in 1960, but with hindsight what strikes one is that only a dramatist with a profound awareness of human insecurity would have seen that dialogue is often a form of evasion or self-protection as well as a means of achieving tactical advantage. Pinter is often thought of as a detached, ironic observer; in fact, his plays reveal an extraordinary fellow-feeling for the dispossessed. He also leaves you with an abiding image of man's eternal aloneness. In *The Caretaker* that is palpably true of Davies and Aston. Of Mick also who at one point takes Davies on by dazzling him with a litany of London boroughs: 'You know, believe it or not, you've got a funny kind of resemblance to a bloke I once knew in Shoreditch. Actually he lived in Aldgate. I was staying with a cousin in Camden Town. This chap, he used to have a pitch in Finsbury Park, just by the bus depot . . . ' This is not simply a virtuosic riff. Mick is trumping Davies's sole ace by showing that, however well this scrofulous old vagrant knows the London streets and suburbs, he himself knows them even better. In its circuitous tour of the city, the speech strikes at the heart of Davies's dilemma which is that he is a man of no fixed identity or abode. But it also leaves you feeling that Mick, in his preoccupation with the minutiae of London Transport, is swathed in eccentric solitude. Even the language of power in Pinter often reveals the speaker's vulnerability.

The Caretaker is an austere masterpiece: a universally recognisable play about political manoeuvring, fraternal love, spiritual isolation, language as a negotiating weapon or a form of cover-up. What no one could have foreseen in 1960 was that the play would eventually become a worldwide hit and a contemporary classic. Michael Codron agreed to put it on, but had no extravagant hopes of its commercial success: 'I remember saying to Harold, after *The Birthday Party*, that I was going to do his next play in the West End and not mess about with try-outs. Then *The Caretaker* arrived and I went back on my word and told Harold I could only do it at the Arts which was a small 330-seater. To my surprise, he agreed. But he did say that he wanted it to be directed by the man who'd done his radio plays, Donald McWhinnie. I put the play on as well as I could because I owed it to Harold, but all my hopes at that time were pinned on a musical called *The Golden Touch* by Julian More and James Gilbert, directed by Minos Volonakis and designed by Hugh Casson, which opened a week later at the Piccadilly. That turned out to be a complete disaster losing me around £20,000. If I hadn't had *The Caretaker*, which cost precisely £1,166 to mount at the Arts, I would have gone bankrupt.'

Yet although *The Caretaker* saved Codron's skin, he did not own the rights to the play. After the collapse of *The Birthday Party*, Pinter's agent Jimmy Wax had approached the American producer and gentleman-philanthropist Roger L. Stevens and done a deal whereby Stevens paid Pinter £1,000 in exchange for his next three plays; which is why, even though *The Homecoming* and *Old Times* were eventually mounted by the Royal Shakespeare Company, they were Stevens's property. Codron, however, was still the producer of *The*

Caretaker and, as always, cast it with loving care – with Donald Pleasence, Alan Bates, Peter Woodthorpe – and then left the director and actors to get on with it. Rehearsals lasted three weeks and seem to have been conducted as much through osmosis as analysis. 'The first run I saw of it,' says Codron, 'was the technical rehearsal. McWhinnie was very taciturn. I was famous for my long pauses. And Harold was pretty reticent. For everyone it was a journey into the unknown. Alan Bates complained that McWhinnie hadn't given him any notes during rehearsals, but he promised to change that after the "technical" because the management were in. The run-through happened. Alan came down to the edge of the stage and said, somewhat anxiously, "How was it?" and Donald just gave him a thumbs-up. That was the note.'

Pleasence was luckier in that, since he was a fellow-Chiswickian, he drove Pinter home after rehearsals each night and used to fire questions at him about the play and the character. In later years Pleasence claimed that Pinter had said one should feel relief at Davies's ultimate expulsion. Pinter now strongly denies that, understanding, since one's attitude to Davies subtly shifts in the course of the evening: the manipulative exploiter of the first two acts invariably comes to seem, by the end, a pathetic outcast who engineers his own destruction. Pleasence, in fact, brought to the role his own intuitive sympathy with the character. 'I loved playing Davies,' he told me, 'because I've always been very interested in tramps. They seem to have a limited attitude to any kind of responsibility which is either deliberate or because, as in Davies's case, they're obsessed with other things. On the whole, they're very self-centred. Life somehow owes them. I'm not talking of homeless people – that's not a condition, but a scandal. Davies, however, is sharp and clever, but it's a sharpness that is born of his hatred of other people's ideas. Also the feeling that other people are always trying to deceive him.'

The first night of *The Caretaker* took place on 27 April 1960 in the same week as Orson Welles's production of Ionesco's *Rhinoceros*, starring Laurence Olivier, at the Royal Court. In the event, the Pinter première dwarfed the supposedly more prestigious offering at the Court and the press – with a few exceptions – showed a perceptive appreciation that had been denied to *The Birthday Party*. Codron feels there may have been a collective awareness of the injustice done to the earlier work. Intriguingly, the popular papers uttered the loudest huzzahs. The *Daily Herald* recorded the next morning: 'Tumultuous cheers. Twelve curtain calls. And then, when the lights went up, the whole audience rose to applaud the author who sat beaming in the circle.' The *News Chronicle* roundly declared: 'This is the best play in London.' Bernard Levin in the *Daily Express* – a play too late – invoked 'the terrifying world of Kafka in which the enemy is all-powerful, invisible, implacable and above all capricious'. T. C. Worsley in the *Financial Times*, after comparing Pinter to Beckett, remarked, with great acuity: 'Mr Pinter's vision begins with the dispossessed and the disconnected. The characters who set him off are those whose connection to the world hangs by a thread.'

The play was an instant hit and transferred to the Duchess on 30 May. Inevitably it also prompted a display of multiple critical backlash, the phenomenon whereby a play hailed in the dailies and Sundays is viewed more sceptically in the monthlies and the specialist magazines. Irving Wardle in the June issue of *Encore*, while generally appreciative, objected to Aston's aria on the grounds that it gave the character a biography while 'elsewhere the play of language creates its own world, incidentally flowering into biographical detail'. Aston's long speech was also a sticking-point for fellow-playwright John Arden in a highly intelligent analysis in the July edition of *New Theatre Magazine*. He said the play's story might have been heard in a pub or turned into a TV play by Willis Hall or Ted Willis.

> The interesting thing is the closeness with which Mr Pinter's writing, in fact, does approach such a treatment. But he leaves his corners never quite joined up. There is a deliberate haze about the past, and indeed the present, of all his characters which never quite becomes so opaque that we are entirely bewildered. Their inconsistencies are never quite contradictory. We can never quite catch a complete view of them. They are seen in vivid glimpses for moments and then seem to disappear. Thus the elder brother's account of his brain operation is highly detailed and circumstantial. But is it true? If it is true, why isn't Mr Pinter writing that serious social play to denounce the cruelty prevalent in mental hospitals? And if it is not true, why does it take the crucial place in the text – the climax of Act Two?

What Arden didn't know was that Pinter had already written that serious social play in *The Hothouse*. What he perhaps didn't appreciate is that for Pinter the provisional nature of truth and the unverifiability of experience is part of his view of society. Nigel Dennis was much harsher in *Encounter*, seeing the play as imitation *Godot* without the particular quality – 'the vision that lay around the corner, the unseen hope' – that animated the original.

In fact, it was the Shaftesbury Avenue generation of dramatists who appreciated the play more than Pinter's own immediate contemporaries. Terence Rattigan – a close friend of T. C. Worsley's – adored it, discovering in it all kinds of religious symbolism. Noël Coward confessed to his diary that he approached it with fear and dread: '*The Caretaker*, on the face of it, is everything I hate most in the theatre – squalor, repetition, lack of action etc. – but somehow it seizes hold of you . . . *Nothing* happens except that somehow it does. The writing is at moments brilliant and quite unlike anyone else's.' What Rattigan and Coward presumably responded to was Pinter's innate theatrical timing and immaculate sense of form – something that paradoxically made him seem closer to his historical forbears than to his own contemporaries who often subordinated structure to the annexation of new thematic territory. But although the play received the imprimatur of the ruling deities of the well-made play, there was also a grave danger of its being absorbed by the commercial theatre on its own terms; in other words, turned into a fashionable comedy about a group of amusing derelicts. Leonard Russell, literary editor of the *Sunday Times*, wrote an open letter in his own paper in July 1960 calling attention to the insensitivity of audiences and to the gales of 'happy, persistent and, it seemed to me, totally indiscriminate laughter which greeted the play'. Pinter replied a week later, arguing that audiences use laughter to rationalise the tragic fact of existence: 'As far as I am concerned *The Caretaker* is funny, up to a point. Beyond that point, it ceases to be funny and it is because of that point that I wrote it.' The real problem is that the long-run system inevitably has a coarsening effect on both performers and audiences. By the time I got to see that production, at a Thursday matinée in mid-December, I can only report that it looked like a technically correct but somewhat faint carbon-copy of a great original.

Recasting, or doing it in repertoire, is the only way to keep a play fresh, and *The Caretaker* got a shot in the arm when, a year after its opening, Pinter himself took over the role of Mick for a four-week period. 'Alan,' Donald Pleasence recalled, 'went off to do *Whistle Down the Wind* and somehow it came about that Harold said, "I'll play it." He was dying to, actually. He was very good. Of all the Micks I've played it with – about five – he was the most frightening . . . By far the most frightening. He used to terrify me every night and I liked that. Alan was not so frightening, but it was a much more subtle performance with Alan's own brand of malign understatement.' Indeed, the *Guardian* reported of Pinter's performance: 'He has a fine presence and, with faultless timing, forces us to endure to the limit those ominous silences that punctuate the action with the impact of explosions.' But Pinter has always been particularly good at playing those of his characters – such as Lenny in *The Homecoming* – who have a sharp, slightly spivvy, intimidatory quality.

By now *The Caretaker* was a runaway success. It was being produced all over Europe (Amsterdam, Düsseldorf, Hanover, Essen, Bielefeld), was particularly popular in South Africa (in Cape Town, Nigel Hawthorne was a distinguished Aston) and Broadway was inevitably beckoning. Back home it picked up the *Evening Standard* Award for Best Play of 1960, despite a few routine grumbles from Milton Shulman. Only in Paris was it a flop the first time round: the play, claimed *Le Figaro* in January 1961, 'erects *misérabilisme* into a dogma, promotes starvation to the level of heroism, and glorifies the sordid and petty in boredom'. But elsewhere, Davies, Aston and Mick were becoming part of the mythology of modern drama. Pinter had started with a play about three particular people and seen it grow into a resonant drama about power, pipe dreams and the politics of relationships. The German playwright Friedrich Hebbel once said, with a degree of overstatement, 'In drama no character should ever utter a thought: from the thought in a play come the speeches of *all* the characters.' In other words, drama should start with an image of experience rather than a set of preordained ideas or an analysis of society; ideas should flow from the interplay of character, rather than the characters being a vehicle for the ideas. It is not a rule you can apply to every writer in history, but it certainly applies to Pinter. *The Caretaker* had started with him pausing on the stairs one day at 373 Chiswick High Road and glimpsing a spatial relationship pregnant with meaning. Out of that came a play that triumphantly showed how an intimate personal drama can explore the dynamics of power and how a work rooted in the local and specific can achieve universal application.

Seven Sexual Politics

The success of *The Caretaker* changed Pinter's life. It brought him popular acclaim, put money in the bank and gave him creative freedom. It was, in fact, to be five years before the première of his next work written specifically for the theatre, *The Homecoming*, but during that period from 1960 to 1965 he was hardly idle. He wrote prolifically for television, film and radio, saw his work for other media transferred to the stage, made his début as a writer on Broadway, took to directing his own work and was showered with awards. After years of hardship and penury, he acquired the comforting patina of success. The first sign of that was his move with the family, in the summer of 1960, from Chiswick High Road to Fairmead Court in Kew. 'It almost echoed Mick's dream,' Donald Pleasence recalls, 'in that it was a quite new suburban maisonette with brand-new furniture. Harold also bought a car although he couldn't drive. [In fact, Vivien did.] He acquired all the trappings of a successful bank manager while at the same time being an extraordinary brilliant playwright.' In 1963 he and the family moved again, this time to a bow-fronted Regency house at 14 Ambrose Place, Worthing: 'a ten-minute ... no, a seven-minute walk from the sea', Pinter recalls with characteristic precision. Yet money in the bank could not conceal a certain social insecurity. Donald Pleasence, shortly before his death in 1994, rather touchingly remembered that just after *The Caretaker* opened Pinter took Vivien and Daniel to stay at a posh hotel in Eastbourne. 'He called me up one night,' said Pleasence, 'and asked me how much he should tip the head waiter. You think of Harold now and that's very interesting.'

Fame also brought with it countless requests for interviews. In the aftermath of *The Caretaker* he appeared on a wide variety of BBC Radio programmes, both for the domestic and external services: *Today*, *In Town Tonight*, *Dateline London*, *People Today*, *London Echo: An Interview with John Wain*, *Critic at Large*, *Talking of Theatre*. The idea of Pinter as a grumpily reclusive, ivory-tower artist unwilling to talk about his work is something of a myth. He rarely, if ever, discusses the meaning of his plays, but he has often been surprisingly willing to discuss the circumstances surrounding its creation or the principles behind it. Indeed, in 1962 he went down to the National Student Drama Festival in Bristol – only four years after *The Room* had played there – and gave a talk which has acquired the status of Holy Writ for all Pinter analysts. It is a very good talk, typically candid and forthright, much of it based on the article Pinter had written in 1958 for the *Cambridge University Magazine*. However, because Pinter warns in the opening paragraph against the danger of categorical statements, it is unwise to treat it as an unchanging aesthetic credo.

Pinter talks about his own methods: about the importance of starting with characters in a particular context, of not beginning with an abstract theory or allegorical meaning, of the impossibility of verifying the past, of the dangers of exhortation or prophecy. The most revealing section, however, concerns the delicate balance to be struck between allowing characters their own inner momentum and giving a play a strong overall structure. 'I think a double thing happens,' says Pinter. 'You arrange *and* you listen, following the clues you leave for yourself through the characters. And sometimes a balance is found, where image can freely engender image and where at the same time you are able to keep your sights on the place where the characters are silent and in hiding. It is in the silence that they are most evident to me.'

Some of the views expressed in this talk have been modified over the years, particularly Pinter's distrust of plays that engage with contemporary issues or that offer 'warnings, sermons, admonitions, ideological exhortations, moral judgements, defined problems with built-in solutions'. Although Pinter has never written drama that offered comfortable, gift-wrapped solutions, he was to go on to write plays that dealt with explicit political issues and clearly attacked the moral hypocrisy of the Western democracies. Talking to me in Dublin in 1993, he also lamented the marginalisation of Bond and Brenton. And he became a keen admirer of Sarah Kane's explosive *Blasted*. Yet his vision of playwriting as a dual process seems to have a perennial truth. On the one hand, the dramatist has to allow the characters sufficient elbow-room to develop in their own idiosyncratic and unforeseen way; on the other hand, he or she has to have an instinctive sense of dramatic rhythm and structure. When characters arrive at a destination dictated by plot necessity rather than their own impulses you always get strained dramatic writing. When the characters head the dramatist off at the pass and dictate their own journey you get good writing: witness *The Caretaker*. Indeed, Pinter himself revealed in an article in *New Theatre Magazine* in 1961:

At the end of *The Caretaker*, there are two people alone in a room, and one of them must go in such a way as to produce a sense of complete separation and finality. I thought originally that the play must end with the violent death of one at the hands of the other. But then I realised, when I got to the point, that the characters as they had grown could never act in this way.

Pinter says quite clearly in his Bristol talk that a play is not an essay or a demonstration of an abstract theory. In his case, it often stems from a pregnant image, an overheard remark, an experience in life. His plays are much more related to his own biography than commentators have allowed, which raises the fascinating question as to why in the early 1960s he wrote a succession of plays – including *Night School*, *The Collection*, *The Lover* and climaxing in *The Homecoming* – that dealt with the duality and the strength of the female psyche, as against the sexual and emotional insecurity of the average male. Pinter doesn't work to a preconceived programme; but the same themes recur in play after play, particularly the notion that women are more easily able than men to reconcile their sexual and social selves. Equally obvious is the fact that all Pinter's major roles at this time were played by his wife Vivien. By the spring of 1960 she had already played Rose in *The Room*, Flora in *A Slight Ache* and The Girl in *A Night Out*. After *The Caretaker* – which she so cordially loathed – she went on to play Sally in *Night School*, Stella in *The Collection*, Sarah in *The Lover*, Wendy in *Tea Party* and Ruth in *The Homecoming*. Since the roles have so much in common – in particular, a mixture of external gentility with inner passion – you inevitably wonder how much Pinter is trying to appease Vivien, how much his vision of women is determined by her qualities as an actress and a person, and how much he is subconsciously exploring his own marital tensions through drama. For the supreme irony is that the period when Pinter was creating some of his juiciest roles for Vivien also saw the beginning of the long, slow, painful disintegration of his marriage. It was never quite the same after the transformation of his life through *The Caretaker* and, in fact, in 1962 Pinter began a serious extramarital relationship that was to last for seven years and ultimately to bear creative fruit in *Betrayal*. It was a time of intense marital strain for the Pinters, yet it was also one in which he moved from his initial protest at the suffocating power of tradition and conformity towards an exploration of the politics of sexuality; even, in *The Collection* and the film of *The Servant*, to the nature of triangular desire in which two men reveal a latent homosexual impulse through their wish to possess the same woman.

Pinter himself denies that he sat down at his desk to write parts tailored to

Vivien's personality. 'I wasn't consciously doing that,' he says, 'but I suppose I was doing a good deal of that nevertheless, consciously or not. Certainly with *The Collection*, *The Lover*, *Tea Party* and *The Homecoming*, she seemed to walk into the roles. It was always on the cards that she would play them. It was unquestioned. But – it's curious this – I never thought of her when I was writing the plays. I am convinced this is true. At the time they were produced, they seemed to have been written for her, but while I was writing the plays, I never thought of her. The character of Ruth was not Vivien. It was Ruth.'

One accepts Pinter's point: that he was not sitting down – unlike, say, John Osborne in *Time Present* – with the uxorious intention of writing a whacking good part for his wife. But is it conceivable that Pinter's imagination was not, in some way, sparked by the woman to whom he'd been married since 1956? Edna O'Brien is an old friend of Pinter's and a novelist who understands the interaction of fiction and life. Does she believe Pinter's women are shadowed by the image of Vivien? 'I'd use the word "illuminated" and not "shadowed",' she says. 'Illuminated, because it would be impossible not to interconnect Vivien the person – as wife, lover, mistress – with the stage presence who had flesh, blood and very good legs. I'm thinking especially of *The Collection*, *The Lover*, *Tea Party*, those plays. It would be impossible not to think of Vivien because he's the creator and the writer, but the inspiration must have come from her. There's a wonderful line in one of Keats's poems about Fanny Brawne, whom he was in love with: he saw her going over Vauxhall Bridge in a carriage and he wrote of being "snared by the ungloving of thy hand". And it would be the same thing with Harold: snared, for better or worse, by the image of a woman who happened to be his and who happened to act – sublimely – in his plays. So I think her place in the galaxy is assured and is rightly there.'

Vivien clearly had something of the duality Pinter put into his plays: she was the homespun Manchester girl who modelled herself on Vivien Leigh; a woman with a stunning figure who cultivated an old-fashioned style and decorum; the wife of a fashionable playwright who showed an active disdain for intellectual pursuits. What is intriguing is that everyone you talk to has a different 'take' on Vivien Merchant. Shy and vulnerable, according to some; high-handed and manipulative, according to others. 'I always thought Harold's success went to *her* head,' one of the playwright's oldest friends observes. But Guy Vaesen, who stuck loyally to Vivien through thick and thin, recalls, 'Harold was passionately fond of her and wanted very much for her to be established in her own right. But it was very difficult for her to escape from being Harold's wife . . . She was disdainful of anything intellectual and made a great show of this. She disliked practically everything Harold was interested in, even cricket. I remember on one occasion Harold asked me down to Surbiton to do a painting of a cricket match he was involved in. Vivien took me down to the game so that I could sketch and then sat, rather ostentatiously, with the Sunday papers in front of her so she didn't have to watch.'

Joan Bakewell confirms the dichotomy within Vivien. 'When they first met she was the star actress of the company and Harold was the adoring lover. Then, of course, the plays made him the hero. Vivien thought, "I'm not entering that field and being part of all that intellectual claptrap." She was certainly intelligent. At the same time, she'd make a point of reading *Titbits* in the dressing-room. I think she flourished her ignorance as a dare within the marriage as if to say, "You can impress all the others, but don't think you can pull that one on me."' Yet Joan Bakewell also shrewdly suggests that the characters Vivien played were, to some extent, an embodiment of Pinter's own private sexual fantasies. 'Vivien,' she says, 'always played the parts and played them as Harold wanted them to be. Which was very '60s sexiness – the stockinged legs and the high heels – but covered with a veneer of gentility as if the external behaviour will shield the sexuality underneath. Harold's very good at that, not least in *Old Times* where Deeley and Anna talk about the dressing-gown and the bath and the bubbles on Kate's body. It's the knowledge that people sitting around fully dressed in rooms are actually sexual animals. I think Harold, because of those antennae which are so acute, sees that as a great turn-on.'

Pinter's fascination with female duality, to be fair, goes back a long way. The heroine of *Kullus* combines a shawled reticence with a mysterious availability, and Virginia in *The Dwarfs* is both a respectable schoolmistress and a highly sexed woman who knocks about Soho with alleged prostitutes. Yet in the 1960s plays, Pinter seems increasingly haunted by the contradictory nature of women and their capacity to exist in two dimensions at once. One of the clearest examples is *Night School*, a TV play transmitted by Associated Rediffusion on 27 July 1960 and originally excluded by Pinter from the collected edition of his plays on the grounds that it was too mechanically 'Pinteresque'. But even though it's minor Pinter, it's a highly revealing work in that the heroine Sally is a respectable games mistress who moonlights as a nightclub hostess. We learn this because she haunts the mind and loins of a habitual criminal and petty forger aptly named Wally. Emerging from prison, he finds that schoolteacher Sally has taken over his old room in his aunts' house. At the same time, he is obsessed by the image of a girl he has seen in a nightclub photograph. Cocooned in his own world of naïve romanticism,

Wally either cannot – or will not – recognise that the adored teacher and the idealised nightbird are one and the same person. It is, in fact, left to the aunts' goatish landlord Mr Solto to discover Sally's double life, after which she vanishes for ever into the night.

Pinter deals with Sally's bifurcated life without being censorious, moralistic or chauvinist. His tone is more one of intrigued curiosity at the way women achieve an equilibrium palpably denied to men. Solto is a lying old lech and Wally is a pathetic fantasist who sees women as either dream figures or sex objects; but through Sally, Pinter suggests that women achieve a balance between outward decorousness and inner fire. It is that quality which often makes his female characters, in Edna O'Brien's phrase, seem 'slippery' or 'diffuse', but which also enables them to exercise control over men. Schoolteacher Sally runs rings round Wally, first apologising profusely for taking his room, then firmly resisting transfer to a downstairs put-you-up ('Oh, I don't trust those things, do you? I mean, this is such a lovely bed') and eventually offering to share the room on a Box-and-Cox basis. Even when the enslaved Wally asks Sally to cross and uncross her legs – echoing a scene in *The Dwarfs* where Mark gets Virginia to lift her skirt above her knees – you feel it is she who is in charge of events. Equally the night-school Sally is not some pliant bimbo but a woman who maintains a cool contempt for both the club clients and the pimping proprietor. Pinter's point, as his title clearly implies, is that the day and night-time Sally are not signs of a Jekyll-and-Hyde division, but overlapping aspects of a complex personality used to achieving effortless domination over helpless males.

Martin Esslin claims that 'this sense of the duality of the female psyche has been one of Pinter's least productive preoccupations'. On the contrary, it strikes me as one of the unifying themes of his 1960s plays and part of a continuing obsession with the politics of sex. It is as if Pinter is exploring, through the public medium of drama, aspects of his private life with Vivien. Esslin also argues that a work like *Night School*, while being highly amusing and proficient, is part of a larger Oedipal battle which rages through the early plays and achieves its fulfilment in *The Homecoming*. 'In *Night School*', writes Esslin, 'a son (Walter) is fighting a father-figure (Solto) for the possession of a girl who is half schoolteacher (mother) and half nightclub hostess (whore).' Well, possibly. However, the real point of the play is not some archetypal male battle, but Sally's absolute refusal to be possessed or pigeon-holed by Wally, Solto, her night-time clients or the club proprietor ('I'll kick him in his paraphernalia one of these days'). If it anticipates *The Homecoming* – and later plays like *Old Times* and *Betrayal* – it is in the way in which it deals with women's desire for unclaimed independence and the power of choice over how they live. It is not so much a Freudian battle as a mixture of sexual fantasy and feminist statement.

The price of independence may, of course, be emotional solitude: that is one of the key themes of *The Collection*, Pinter's next original work for television. It was broadcast by Associated Rediffusion on 11 May 1961 in the halcyon days when commercial television regularly presented one-off plays by major writers. Can you imagine the total panic into which such a seemingly 'difficult' script, with never a policeman or car-chase in sight, would throw the network controllers today? But despite its elusiveness, *The Collection* is genuinely fascinating. It is also one of Pinter's most misunderstood works. It is always thought to be about the unverifiable nature of truth: did Bill sleep with Stella in a hotel room in Leeds? In fact it is about a whole raft of other things: about the way people manipulate 'truth' to their own advantage; about the latent homosexuality within triangular desire; about the triumphant unknowability of women. Sally in *Night School* disappears in order to maintain her double life; Stella in *The Collection* is left coolly victorious and maintaining her Sphinx-like secret to the last.

Pinter presents us with two couples linked by sexual desire and a professional involvement in the rag trade. On the one hand we have middle-aged gay Harry and his working-class protégé Bill, who occupy a comfortable Belgravia house; on the other hand we have James and his wife and business partner Stella, who live in a nearby Chelsea flat. James, as the outraged husband, forces his way into the Belgravia ménage and accuses Bill of seducing Stella the previous week in a Leeds hotel room. He cites chapter and verse provided, he claims, by his wife. While James receives variant versions of what happened in Leeds from the devious Bill, the possessive Harry puts the situation into reverse and goes to visit Stella who claims that her husband has dreamed up the whole fantastic story. Which is not what Harry says when he returns home to find his lover suffering a minor hand-wound after James has thrown a knife at him: Harry claims that Stella confessed that it was *she* who made the whole thing up. Bill's public version, designed to placate all parties, is that he and Stella *did* meet in Leeds, but only sat in the hotel lounge talking about what they would do if they went to her room. The final moments show James returning home and relaying this version to Stella and pathetically asking 'That's the truth . . . isn't it?' Pinter's stage directions in the published version tell us '*Stella looks at him, neither confirming nor denying. Her face is friendly, sympathetic.*'

So what did happen in Leeds? Adulterous sex? A speculative flirtation? Or is the whole thing a manipulative fantasy cooked up by Stella and endorsed by Bill for their own domestic purposes? Obviously, part of the pleasure is that we never know the precise truth. And this has led several critics to compare the play to Pirandello's 1916 masterpiece *Right You Are (if you think so!)* which also hinges on an unresolvable conundrum: the identity of a mysterious veiled lady Signora Ponza. Is she her husband's first wife, as her mother still believes? Or is she his second wife as the husband himself claims? But there is a crucial difference between Pirandello and Pinter. Pirandello's point is that privacy is what matters: that the truth of the story is no more the audience's concern than it is that of the prying townspeople; or, in the words of a Connecticut housemaid Eric Bentley once came across when he was directing the play, 'I guess it just says keep your nose out of other folks' business.' Pinter's play, however, is not about privacy or even the subjectivity of truth. Stella and Bill clearly *know* exactly what happened – or didn't happen – in Leeds. Both, however, manipulate the truth for tactical reasons: in Stella's case, to exercise control over her husband; in Bill's, to get revenge on the possessive, patronising Harry.

It is also a play about the equivocal nature of sexuality, in particular the way two men are drawn together by their desire for the same woman. Pinter had always been fascinated by the thin dividing line between male bonding and homoerotic instincts. In *The Dwarfs* there is a fascinating passage where Pete and Mark return from a party in a drunken stupor. Pete helps Mark to undress and Mark crawls into bed in his shirt. The chapter fades out on a cryptic exchange:

- Pete!
- Yes.
- There's no doubt.
- None at all, Pete said.

You can interpret that exchange in many ways; but what is undeniable is that Pete and Mark share an intellectual and social intimacy which is later re-inforced by the fact that they both sleep with Virginia. And Michael Goldstein, musing on a friendship with Pinter that has lasted fifty years and that consists of numerous exchanges of letters, once wondered aloud whether there was some subconscious homosexual impulse behind it. He doubted it. But any intelligent men with a passionate commitment to male friendship, such as Pinter has, is bound to ask himself at some point whether male bonding carries with it implications of homosexuality. It is also intriguing how often Pinter returns to the subject of what René Girard calls 'triangular desire', in which two men are drawn together by their urge to possess the same woman. It is there in *The Dwarfs*, in *The Collection*, in *Betrayal* and in the film of *The Servant*: a work of which Pinter completed the first draft (in July 1961) shortly after he had finished *The Collection*. The parallels between the two are fascinating. In the film, both the master (Tony) and the servant (Barrett) sleep with the same woman (Vera), and partly through that action acquire a molten intimacy that leads to an ersatz male marriage. In the TV play it could be argued that James (the husband) and Bill (the lover) have also slept with the same woman (Stella), and that much of the dramatic tension springs from the husband's attraction to the seducer. Everything in the text points to the fact that James is more than an injured husband: he is totally obsessed by Bill.

In the early scenes James importunately phones Bill and is seen off the doorstep by Harry, clearly scenting a sexual rival. And when James and Bill finally come face to face, there is much more to the encounter than a simple desire for information as to what happened in Leeds. 'You're not a bad-looking bloke', remarks James to Bill; he goes on to recreate, with suspicious exactness, every detail of his wife's alleged seduction and makes a move towards Bill that causes him to fall over a pouffe and establishes his own physical dominance. Returning home, James taunts Stella with his assumed intimacy with her lover, compares him to his old chum Hawkins – a *fidus Achates* of the kind you constantly find in Pinter – and ends by saying: 'No, really, I think I should thank you rather than anything else. After two years of marriage it looks as though, by accident, you've opened up a whole new world for me.' That could be a tactical move; or it could imply James's willing entry into a homosexual milieu.

The second encounter between James and Bill strongly suggests the latter. At one point the two men stand in front of a mirror, ostensibly comparing heights. James moves to the left of the mirror to look at Bill's reflection ('I don't think mirrors are deceptive'): it's an image eerily echoed in *The Servant* where we see master and servant, locked together in intimacy, staring at each other's reflection. James later challenges Bill to a mock duel with fruit and cheese knives that ends with a knife being thrown at Bill's face: that, too, has its parallel in *The Servant* where Tony and Barrett play a ball game on the central stairs that is an embodiment of their own private power-battle and that ends with Barrett being viciously hit on the nose. One could push the resemblances further and say that the growing intimacy between James and Bill threatens Harry's possession, just as the closeness between Tony and Barrett excludes both the former's fiancée and the promiscuous Vera. Even the title of the play – as so often in Pinter – is shot through with ambiguity. It could refer to a dress collection; or to Harry's penchant for collecting people as if they were social specimens; or to a collection of men who have more in common with each other than with Stella, who spends much of the play alone listening to a Charlie Parker record or playing with her kitten.

In one way, Stella is victorious. It is, after all, she who has initiated the whole business, who has told James of her sexual encounter in room 165 of a Leeds hotel, who has disrupted Harry and Bill's relationship, who has exposed her husband's sexual insecurity and who finally reels him in like a fish. She knows the truth; he doesn't. At the same time, Stella's victory has a pyrrhic ring to it. She has opened James up to 'a whole new world': that of male intimacy. And in testing her husband's sexuality, she discovers that the price of power is solitude. It's a point that doesn't easily emerge on television, simply because the camera inevitably cuts to where the action is. But when the play was first staged – by Peter Hall and Pinter himself – at the Aldwych in 1962, one was constantly aware of Stella's presence: enigmatic, solitary, ambiguously in control, while the men engaged in their own private war games. A lot of Pinter's meaning always emerges from the physical choreography of the action: he thinks visually as well as verbally. On stage, the dominant image was of Stella's cool, manipulative independence.

That production of *The Collection* at the Aldwych was a turning point for Pinter in many ways. It not only brought him into the embrace of a big subsidised company, the RSC; it also saw the start of a working relationship with Peter Hall that was to last uninterrupted for twenty-one years, be broken off by Pinter amid accusations of betrayal after the publication of *Peter Hall's Diaries* in 1983, and be resumed only in 1990 with Hall's revival of *The Homecoming*. For both men it was an absolutely crucial partnership. Pinter found a director who brought to his work a high-definition quality, a precise musicality of speech, an awareness of the passion and personal melodrama that exists beneath the controlled social mask. Hall, for his part, found a living writer who could fulfil and justify the RSC's declared aim of bringing the same degree of textual rigour to the classics and contemporary work.

Looking back over the relationship now, Hall says, 'I have to say, rightly or wrongly, that I've never worked with any dramatist in my life where I knew so instinctively what he was driving at and what it was he wanted. In the best years of our relationship, it was a complete empathy. I found a great deal from him as a writer and I think he found a great deal from me as a director . . . We're the same age. I'm a country boy and he's a Londoner. But we come out of the same moment in history. We both went through that Richard Hoggart time of windows being opened in our adolescence. I went to university and he went to drama school. But we were both stage-struck. We were both literature-struck. We were both only children. There are many similarities.

We're very different people, but the nurture we had has parallels. I felt from the beginning with his work: this is it.'

In fact, they knew each other before they co-directed *The Collection*; Hall had been approached to direct both *The Birthday Party* and *The Caretaker*, but on each occasion had been heavily committed elsewhere. He had also, from the very inception of the RSC in 1960, sought to engage Pinter in the company's work: something which produces a fascinating revelation.

'It's a central belief of mine,' says Hall, 'that the most important thing about doing a living dramatist is to hear him talk: his tone of voice, his rhythm of speech. I've learned how to do Beckett, Pinter, Ayckbourn by listening to them talk. Harold's precision of speech is absolute. He is also the most compassionate, warm-hearted, generous, funny man and also has the most violent, irrational temper. But Harold's precision goes beyond language. The cut of a coat, the fit of a collar, the temperature of a room, the mix of a Martini are all important. I think the reason is that there is an awareness of the anarchy and chaos and violence and disorder of life that are pressing in and have to be controlled. I remember something from years ago. It must have been around 1960, I'd just taken over at Stratford and I was trying to get Harold to write something for us. It was a very hot day. I remember Harold arriving at Stratford by train – via Leamington Spa – and needing to wash and change his shirt before we talked. I remember thinking, "What's wrong here?" But it was just that Harold had had a grubby, sweaty journey on British Rail and needed to be in good order, so we had to run around and find him a place where he could wash and change. Then he was crisp and clean and OK and we could start talking about plays. It's all part and parcel of the same thing: the concern with precision. It's why it's not at all absurd for Harold to ring up and say, "Page 37 – cut the pause."'

That concern with precision was evident in the stage version of *The Collection*. Kenneth Haigh, who played James, remembers Pinter giving Michael Hordern, who was Harry, a note which has since become the stuff of legend. 'Michael,' said Pinter at one point, 'I wrote dot, dot, dot, and you're giving me dot, dot.' It sounds absurd. But Hordern, far from being bemused, instinctively grasped Pinter's point: that there is all the difference in the world between a long and a short pause, and that much of the meaning of Pinter lies in the musical rhythm as well as the stage picture. Take an obvious instance. After Harry has returned from his encounter with Stella, the length of the pause in a line like 'What she confessed was . . . that she'd made the whole thing up' is absolutely crucial. A two-dot pause implies that Harry is thinking on his feet and uttering an almost impromptu evasion of truth; a three-dot pause suggests a premeditated lie designed to ensnare Bill, banish James and incidentally prove that this is just the sort of thing a woman would do.

The Collection was well received when shown on television in 1961 and when it opened at the Aldwych – in tandem with Strindberg's *Playing with Fire* – in June 1962. It was even more intelligently analysed when it was shown off-Broadway at the Cherry Lane Theatre in November 1962, just a year after *The Caretaker* had bowed on Broadway where it had enjoyed the five-month run of a *succès d'estime*. By this time, however, Pinter was in demand on all fronts. Peter Hall wanted him to become an integral part of the RSC. He was working with Joseph Losey on the film of *The Servant* for which shooting began in January 1963. Another film – that of *The Caretaker* – had begun shooting on location in Hackney in December 1962, with financial backing from an impressive group of showbiz names including Noël Coward, Richard Burton, Elizabeth Taylor, Peter Sellers, Peter Hall and Leslie Caron. Pinter was also still working for BBC Radio and had a new TV play, *The Lover*, ready for Joan Kemp-Welch at Associated Rediffusion. Within a short space of time Pinter had moved from struggling actor-writer to public property, courted by every medium and mogul. He had not, however, shed all his insecurities. During London rehearsals of *The Collection*, John Gale wrote a perceptive piece in the *Observer*:

> Pinter, strong black hair, gleaming spectacles, dark suit, well-polished shoes was, superficially, more solid than one might have expected from his work. At first glance, you might have taken him for a person who enjoyed discussing fast cars in pubs . . . It was when he took off his dark glasses and twirled them round that you noticed the dark eyes and sensitive face that looked as though it had its worries.

Around the same time Ronald Searle did a witty drawing of him in *Punch*. It imagined him as a bespectacled, furry animal curled up on the floor with one ear cocked. Uncannily, he was listening to the ramblings of a paunchy pipe-smoking figure in a cloth cap and string vest: someone who looked prophetically like Max in *The Homecoming*.

Pinter was, in contemporary jargon, 'hot'. And the peculiar excitement generated by a Pinter play – not least on the box – was precisely caught by Maurice Richardson in the *Observer* after the first broadcast of *The Lover* in March 1963. Richardson imagined the frenzied Home Counties reactions to Pinter's latest exploration of the mysteries of sex.

> A Pinter first night is carpet-biter's night in subtopia. You can hear the wires humming with nervous controversy. 'Absolute rubbish.' 'Joan. You

old trog! How can you! We all loved it!' 'You're so terribly with it in the Drive, aren't you? We had to stop Uncle Wally from ringing up to say Pinter should be horse-whipped.' 'Straight propaganda for schizophrenia, that's what it was. Trying to send us all round the bend.'

One can imagine just such conversations taking place in that *The Lover*, an absolute gem, is one of the most candid and revealing plays about sex in the English language. It is also a potent reminder of the libertarian mood of the 1960s that allowed one to dramatise intimate details of private sexuality. 'Sexual intercourse', as Philip Larkin ironically reminds us, 'began in 1963'. But even before then, new freedoms were being exploited. In 1962, John Osborne's *Under Plain Cover* at the Royal Court showed a close-knit couple deriving sexual pleasure from clothes-fetishism and sadomasochistic games. But where Osborne never reveals anything of his characters' lives beyond their sex-play and complicates the issue with incest, Pinter in *The Lover* gives his characters an implicit social background and stresses the normality – rather than the aberrant nature – of their fantasy games. Even more significantly, the play picks up ideas from *Night School* and *The Collection* in suggesting that women, in sexual matters, cope with their duality far better than men, and possess a much greater sense of equilibrium and balance. Pinter is not just dramatising the erotic games-playing and sexual fantasy that is a vital part of any marriage. He also shows himself to be an instinctive feminist *avant la lettre*.

The Lover is a very deceptive play. It starts as social comedy, moves into an exploration of the fetishistic illusions that can both sustain a marriage and induce nervous breakdown, and finally achieves a reconciliation of reality and fantasy. But at first it is the contrast between manner and matter that is so engaging. The setting is precise. Summer. A detached house near Windsor. Sarah wears a crisp, demure dress. Richard, her husband, is departing for a day in the City. He kisses his wife on the cheek. She smiles.

RICHARD (*amiably*): Is your lover coming today?
SARAH: Mmnn.
RICHARD: What time?
SARAH: Three.
RICHARD: Will you be going out . . . or staying in?
SARAH: Oh . . . I think we'll stay in.
RICHARD: I thought you wanted to go to that exhibition.
SARAH: I did, yes . . . but I think I'd prefer to stay in with him today.
RICHARD: Mmn-hmmn. Well, I think I must be off.

Pinter's openings are always good; this one is no exception. Behind the exchange of civilities there is a charged politesse. We instantly learn that the arrival of the lover is an habitual event, that Richard is suspiciously curious and that Sarah is not to be budged from her plans. For all we know, at this stage, the lover is a third party and we are witnessing an unusually sophisticated marital accommodation. Anxiety surfaces, however, when Richard, on returning home, exposes the pain of his cuckoldry, Sarah is caught out still wearing her afternoon high-heels and Richard, challenged about his own sexual dalliance, replies that he hasn't got a mistress but a whore. Even before he springs his main surprise, Pinter pins down one of the play's key themes: the male distinction between the dignity of marriage and the brutality of casual sex, and the female need to find some emotional continuum between husband and lover. Richard describes his own woman as if she were a sexual pit-stop – 'A quick cup of cocoa while they're checking the oil and water' – and is obviously gnawed by guilt and anxiety; Sarah, on the other hand, speaks warmly of her afternoon man and wishes to preserve the status quo, 'Because I think things are beautifully balanced, Richard'.

By now, most people will have guessed that Richard himself is the *post meridiem* lover, but Pinter achieves his shock-effect very artfully. A cheapskate writer would have had Richard turn up disguised as a Spanish gaucho or put Sarah into Soho-fladge uniform; here, the eroticism derives from the interplay of the partners' fingers on a bongo drum. The role-playing is also lightly done. She (who, significantly, retains the name of Sarah) moves from teasing enchantress to coy victim while he (now rechristened Max) shifts from solicitous protector to rapacious seducer. The fantasy game even reaches its climax under the tea-table: the solid symbol of English middle-class life.

But Pinter's point is that Richard – a man on the verge of a nervous breakdown – is being driven into a state of schizophrenic guilt by his dual existence. In the final movement, he returns home from a day in the City and announces that his wife's life of depravity has to stop and that the lover is henceforward banished; but Sarah saves the situation by the admission of shock-therapy and the declaration that she receives a host of afternoon lovers. Without adopting the Max-persona, Richard glides into one of their regular seducer-victim games to which Sarah readily responds. This time she – not he – crawls under the table, drags him down to the floor and offers to change her clothes. Three times he urges her to change, finally addressing her as 'You lovely whore'.

With great finesse, Pinter shows how Englishmen of a certain class and type have a psychological need to divide women into elegant partners and marketable whores. I am reminded, oddly, of Goldsmith's *She Stoops to Conquer*, in which Marlow is stammeringly apprehensive with women of his own class and sexually liberated with the woman he takes to be an innkeeper's daughter. But Pinter's concluding point is the triumph of female sanity over male guilt. Pinter's Sarah also stoops to conquer and rescues Richard from his middle-class angst and nervous crisis: by the end, a perfect accommodation has been reached in which the fantasy life of the afternoons invades the respectable bourgeois existence of the evenings. It is a humane, optimistic play; one in which Pinter offers a critique of male hang-ups while celebrating the accomplished duality of the English female who recognises that lust and love are compatible, and that fantasy and illusion have a vital place in a well-regulated sex life.

That is clearly Pinter's own interpretation. We know because when *The Lover* was staged in a double bill with *The Dwarfs* at the Arts Theatre in September 1963, Guy Vaesen not only worked as assistant director but also kept a detailed rehearsal diary. It's a crucial document that gives us greater insight into Pinter's directorial methods than anything we possess: it reveals his surprising willingness to discuss the biographical backgrounds of his characters, his occasional speculation as to what the author may have meant, his sympathy with actors and impatience with interruption. It also gives us a vivid picture of the Pinter marriage which, by then, was already beginning to fall apart. Marital tension was heightened by the very way the whole project had developed. In January 1963, Pinter had asked Vaesen – an old friend of himself and Vivien from Bournemouth Rep – to direct *The Lover* on the London stage, but in July Michael Codron – who had come in as producer and decided to pair this TV one-acter with the version of *The Dwarfs* which had already been heard on radio – wrote to Vaesen asking him to consider Pinter as co-director. Pinter, who sets great store by loyalty to old friends, was mortified about reneging on a promise; Vivien, meanwhile, was absolutely furious about the treatment of Vaesen. With great tact, Vaesen himself resolved the difficulty by volunteering to act as assistant director on both halves of the double bill. 'Harold's reaction', his diary records, 'is immediate and joyous but Vivien is too disapproving of the whole unfortunate business to see a way out for her.' She wanted to withdraw, but eventually agreed to play Sarah as she had – quite superbly – on television. However, from the first morning her manner was mildly subversive of her director-husband. Pinter gave the two casts a pep-talk about the need for punctuality and the banishment of time-wasting and egoism. He then gave out cuts and rewrites. 'I am intrigued', writes Vaesen, 'that these have been gone into so minutely – even to the odd pause being removed. Occasionally I glance at Vivien who is calm – the faintest hint of a scornful smile at an occasional amendment which would have automatically righted itself at rehearsal.'

Rehearsals began in earnest on 19 August 1963 at the Portcullis Theatre in Monck Street. For the first week, Pinter and Vaesen worked together concentrating on *The Lover* in the mornings, *The Dwarfs* in the afternoons. In Week Two, Vaesen worked exclusively on the former, Pinter on the latter. In Week Three, they swapped around. For the final week, running up to the first night, they came together again. It was all very methodical and practical, but what strikes one about Vaesen's diary is Pinter's readiness, in contrast to his stonewalling refusal to answer Alan Ayckbourn's and David Jones's questions about Stanley, to explore the biographical past of Richard and Sarah in *The Lover* without trespassing on the rights of the author.

On the first morning, he gives a short talk about the characters:

They attend the Hunt Ball, play golf. Both of them are sophisticated in the fullest sense of the word. They are socially admired – a thoroughly nice couple. Their obsessional private life is what gives the kick to the routine of their lives. Sarah is on village committees and all that sort of thing – but not a member of the dramatic society. Before she married she was probably a private secretary. Whilst it is doubtful if either of them were virgins before marriage, there was no great sexual indulgence . . . The fantasy-life started as a joke. One day, perhaps, he came home, saw some old clothes in the garage so he changed into them – he thought he would play a joke on the old lady. 'Is your husband at home?' he says when she answers the door-bell. 'No,' she says, amused. 'Can I come in? I've been wanting to make your acquaintance for some time.' She lets him in, blazed with a great sexual excitement that's never occurred to her. They probably had sex on the carpet . . . Children? This is a subject only mentioned when on the warpath. Either they were not able to have them or it was not acceptable to the pattern of their lives to have them. The playwright hasn't told us this.

Pinter does not direct as the omniscient author; more as the objective explorer trying to illuminate a relationship from the hints in the text. But, like any good director, he offers valuable guidelines:

When the play starts, Richard is becoming jaded. He is finding the games-playing exhausting physically – I mean two or three times a week. And he is fearful of losing his identity as a husband. Her enjoyment of the lover idea is extending into the evenings and this is telling on him. He has made his own life but where is he as far as marriage is concerned? Sarah, from her point of view, perceives a balance in all this. Her husband exists to her and she can't understand what is causing him to change. It's the story of a man who is trying to break out of a pattern, to put it simply. He comes round so many corners at her. And the point is that she is proved the stronger. She turns the tables at the end by the simple means of sexual compulsion. What looks as though it's going to be his success suddenly turns into hers. The lover comes in the evenings.

Pinter explains the play clearly and logically, but even on the first day, Vivien's defensive anti-intellectualism becomes apparent. She interjects: 'All this talk about a play makes me feel bogged down. Surely there is lots of comedy in the play? Yet all this analysis indicates we shouldn't be playing for comedy.' To which Pinter carefully replies: 'If played with truth, the comedy is there. There is no need to elaborate the lines too much.' But the marital strains surface two days later when they come to discuss the tapping and scratching on the bongos. Vaesen records:

> For some reason Vivien seems reluctant to tell what happened at the television performance. Later on she says she didn't think he would want to stage it in the same way. Pinter says, 'But, of course, why not? I don't understand you.' And so, embarrassed, she takes us through the routine – her fingers making their spiders' approach. They make individual scratches on his knuckles. That makes me laugh. I try to ease a situation that has suddenly become a little tense.

With *The Lover*, there was the problem that Vivien had played the role before and was now being directed by her husband. *The Dwarfs* posed different difficulties: the autobiographical origins of the piece, the riddling symbolism, the weird omission from the play of Virginia whose presence in the novel sharpens the sense of rivalry between Pete and Mark. But reading Vaesen's diary, one is struck by Pinter's sympathy with the slightly bemused actors: John Hurt as Len, Philip Bond as Pete and Michael Forrest as Mark. Pinter talks – as someone who has the ear of the author – about friendship as the theme of the play. He explains, in very masculine terms, the nature of the mutual wariness between Pete and Mark, and indicates the precise symbolism of the dwarfs: they represent, to Len, a savage and predatory world that he sees as the truth of the relationship between himself, Pete and Mark. But Pinter is also very practical when he gets down to daily rehearsals. When John Hurt is worried at one point that the audience will find the shifts in Len's character obscure, Pinter simply says, 'Fuck the audience and let him go straight through. The play should go sharply from there to there.' Later,

when Hurt is concerned about making Len too introverted, Pinter tells him
that he wants to get a sense of the character's aloneness – 'though not a dark
Raskolnikov aloneness.' Hurt immediately understands. But perhaps the
most practical advice, which should be taken to heart by Pinter directors the
world over and set down in letters of fire, comes when he talks to the actors of
the musical elements in the text:

> It isn't a question frequently of this doesn't mean this – it means that – but
> of emphasising the word and the meaning will become clear. If you hit a
> line with particular emphasis – within the rhythm – its meaning will
> become apparent. Listen to the sound first and the meaning will become
> clear through that. A half-hour debate can be more confusing than one
> clearly put sentence. Music and rhythm: they must be your guides.

Rehearsals proceeded smoothly except for the underlying tension with
Vivien: working together seemed to exacerbate the difficulties of their married life. After a run-through of *The Lover* at the end of week two, Pinter and
Vaesen went for a stroll in the August sunshine in Millbank Gardens. Pinter
said he had enjoyed the performance. Vaesen's diary continues:

> And then on to the jagged state of their relationship since rehearsals
> began. And for the first time I began to get alarmed because I hadn't
> appreciated how deeply angry they both were. Back to the flat for a cup of
> tea and a continuation of the subject – I try to explain how I think she feels
> about his fame and her career. It has all been so sudden – if her success had
> been parallel with his, I am sure this situation would never have occurred.

Vaesen, who was sympathetic to both parties, articulates an uncomfortable
truth: the growing disparity between Pinter's sudden world-fame and
Vivien's more localised reputation as a highly accomplished actress. She was,
in many ways, his muse; but the more he wrote roles that exhibited her
genteel sexuality, the more her reputation came to depend on his creative
talent. It was a paradox from which there seemed no escape.

Michael Codron, whose working relationship with Pinter declined for several years after this double bill, also feels it was largely because of Vivien. 'She
was,' he says, 'rather suspicious of me. A tiny incident always sticks in my
mind. Harold bought a very grand house in Worthing not far from the
Connaught Theatre where he had acted as David Baron. I happened to be in
Worthing one day with Kenneth Williams. We'd gone over to see a play and
we suddenly saw Vivien coming towards us. We were actually standing outside the house and she could easily have said, "Would you like to come in and
see it? After all, you had some small hand in our being here." But she didn't.

That was the moment I thought, "Maybe I haven't got an ally there." Anyway, she was at her most high-handed during *The Lover*.' Vaesen, for his part, records in his diary that the stage-crew were persistently difficult. He also recalls an incident in the final week when Pinter – who has a lifetime's hatred of extraneous noise – was disturbed by the racket emanating from the restaurant kitchens above the Arts Theatre. Pinter threatened to cancel rehearsals, dress-rehearsals and even the first night unless something was done about it. It took a call from Codron's office to the Arts Theatre's catering manager to calm all parties.

Yet in the event, the double bill, which opened on 18 September, went off extremely well. *The Lover* was highly praised for its formal elegance: Philip Hope-Wallace in the *Guardian* compared it to Henri Becque's *La Parisienne*, Molnar's *The Guardsman* and Mozart's *Così*. And even if *The Dwarfs* mystified some, Bamber Gascoigne in the *Observer* perceptively saw that it contained the seeds of Pinter's successful plays. The venture had come safely home. Reading Vaesen's diary, the lasting impression is of Pinter as a highly organised, meticulous and tactful director: tactful in that he used his specialised knowledge of the texts wherever it was helpful without making it seem as if he had come down from Mount Sinai bearing the tablets. The only sadness is that *The Lover*, while celebrating female poise and the fun and flexibility of marriage, was accompanied by private disharmony and that the double bill marked the end, for a time, of Pinter's working relationship with Codron. 'One day,' Codron recalls, 'Harold said, "I want you to come and have lunch" – which is never a good sign. We went and had lunch at a restaurant in Knightsbridge near Harrods. Harold insisted on paying for the lunch and said, "Look, I think I've found the director of my dreams. He happens to be Peter Hall and he happens not to work in the commercial theatre." It was a blow but what could one say? Peter did a superb job on Harold's plays. And Harold and I later started a new relationship as producer–director.'

Professionally these were rich times for Pinter. He was in hot demand from all the media. His work was being more intelligently analysed. The autumn issue of the Cambridge magazine *Granta* contained a fine piece by an undergraduate, Michael Pennington, which pursued parallels with Chekhov ('Central to Pinter's work, as to Chekhov's, is the fluctuating relationship between the form of expression and the thing expressed – a source of comedy and at the same time of great emotional implication'). Also in 1963, Pinter's work was showered with awards. The TV version of *The Lover* won the Prix Italia for Television Drama and a clutch of prizes from the Guild of British Television Producers and Directors – whose award ceremony coincided with the night of Kennedy's assassination. The film version of *The Caretaker* won awards at the Berlin and Edinburgh Film Festivals. And in November, Joseph Losey's film of *The Servant* opened to ecstatic reviews.

The Servant was a project with which Pinter had been involved, on and off, over a long period dating back to 27 April 1960 when Losey had sent him an admiring note after seeing *A Night Out* on television: 'It has an intensity and inner truth both horrifying and purgative', he wrote. At the time, Losey was nursing the idea of transferring *The Servant*, a slim sixty-eight-page novella by Robin Maugham, to the screen and felt Pinter would be the ideal writer. In fact, director Michael Anderson jumped in ahead of Losey to acquire the film rights to the book and himself commissioned a script from Pinter in 1961. Anderson was unable to get financial backing, Losey snapped up the rights and worked closely with Pinter on a new script that went into production early in 1963. The partnership between Losey and Pinter was to prove a perfect creative marriage based on mutual sympathy: as important to the cinema as the Hall–Pinter partnership was to the theatre. Like Pinter, Losey – an exiled and formerly blacklisted American director – had a contained rage against the injustice of society. Also like Pinter, Losey was gifted with an overpowering sense of place and of the effect of rooms and possessions on their inhabitants. But *The Servant* also occupies a vital place in Pinter's own *oeuvre*. Screenwriting for Pinter has never been a hack task undertaken simply to earn money. Though his screen work largely consists of adaptations of novels, it always springs from a fierce sense of commitment and often pursues themes inherent in his plays. *The Servant* is a classic example. Written shortly after *The Collection*, it is an extension of that work's pre-occupation with the politics of domestic power and the equivocal nature of sexuality.

When you read Robin Maugham's lurid Wildean novella, you realise how subtly Pinter has extracted its central theme – the possession of a master by his servant – and refined it into something peculiarly his own. Obviously, there are major differences between the book and the screenplay. Maugham's story is set in London just after the war, and the action is narrated by Richard Merton who records his private guilt and class revulsion at seeing his old Desert War chum Tony being manipulated and eventually destroyed by his oily, diabolical manservant Barrett. Pinter updates the action to the 1960s and instantly removes the censorious authorial voice: in virtually all his screenplays he banishes, as a matter of principle, the first-person narrator. But the crucial difference is that, where Maugham makes everything melodramatically explicit, Pinter works in more delicate shades and half-tones. In the book, for instance, Tony's girlfriend Sally Grant spells out the problem unequivocally to the horrified narrator:

'I'm losing Tony.'
'Another woman?'
'No, another man.'
I stared at her. She took a sip of cocktail.
'I'm losing him to Barrett,' she said.

Maugham's dialogue is crisply dramatic; but it presents the situation almost too bluntly. Maugham also treats Barrett as a figure of Mephistophelean evil who attracts adjectives like 'slimy' and 'snake-like'. Typically, when the narrator turns up unexpectedly at Tony's house and finds Barrett and his presumed niece Vera making love in the master's bedroom, the servant is described in the extravagant terms of Grand Guignol: 'His long, thin body was green and horrible in the moonlight.' And in the climax, after the narrator has threaded his way through a pea-souper to make one last effort to rescue Tony from Barrett's clutches, he confronts his old chum with the hideous truth:

'Don't you see that in each case he destroys his victims from within? He helps them destroy themselves by serving their particular weakness. In Vera's case it was lust. In her father's case it was avarice. In your case it began by being plain love of comfort. I don't think it's much more than that even now, is it? Is it, Tony?'
His eyes were haggard as he stared at me.
'It's more than that now,' he said. 'You know it is.'

Maugham's novel is undeniably powerful and dramatic: indeed, he himself turned it into a stage play in 1958 which he then revised in 1966 and was seen at Birmingham Rep in 1995. Yet it seems almost Victorian in its sensibility: it is filled with moral revulsion at the idea of a rich toff being dominated and corrupted by his proletarian servant.

Like the book, Pinter's screenplay is about a predatory servant who brings about his master's downfall by exploiting both his infantile dependence and sexual ambivalence. It is rather as if Barrie's Admirable Crichton were transformed from omniscient helpmeet into bloodsucking parasite. But where Maugham is explicit, Pinter is elliptical. Maugham treats the story as a modern-day morality play with Tony's 'good' angels – his girlfriend Sally and his oldest chum Richard – battling with the 'evil' Barrett for possession of his soul; Pinter is much more fascinated by the growing intimacy between two men locked together in a state of shared degradation. Even the contest between Tony's apprehensive fiancée (now called Susan) and Barrett is done with a nuanced economy. In the film, there's a classic dinner-party scene where Susan seeks to belittle Barrett by pointing out the camp chichi of his white cotton gloves. 'It's Italian, miss. They're used in Italy', observes Barrett. 'Who by?' Susan tartly enquires.

The Pinter–Losey film is partly about sexuality as an instrument of power: a theme that constantly recurs in Pinter's plays of this period. And although the homoerotic element in the film is very strong, it is handled with none of the flushed excitability you find in the book. Indeed, it is established almost subliminally. There's a revealing scene in a phone box where Barrett phones his pseudo-sister Vera. Outside a group of giggling girls, impatient to use the phone, gathers and the skirt of one of them blows up in the wind. In Pinter's script we are told 'Barrett observes this blankly'; Losey goes further by having Dirk Bogarde press his palm against the window to blot out this displeasing sight. Later, in a Soho restaurant scene, Pinter counterpoints Susan's attempt to reclaim Tony with snatches of overheard conversation between a jealous lesbian and her younger partner. And the Chelsea pub-scene, where the sacked Barrett is naïvely rehired by Tony, has the slightly furtive, sidelong quality of a gay pick-up.

Maugham's novel is full of shocked horror at the destruction of a master by his prole servant: it can even be seen as a political fable about the effect of Attlee's post-war socialism on the British class-system. Pinter's screenplay is much more fascinated by the insidious process of takeover and by the way Tony and Barrett feed off each other's weaknesses. Pinter's Tony is a Mittyesque fantasist vaguely involved in a pipe-dream project to develop the Brazilian jungle; and his Barrett is no working-class demon, but a prissy, lower-middle-class figure swathed in fakery and pretence. In the second half of the film, Pinter shows how their domestic intimacy leads to a gradual erosion of their previous roles. Over a candlelit dinner they achieve a male bonding that in both of them invokes nostalgic memories of the Army. And Barrett's gradual assumption of the combined roles of master/servant, wife/mistress is underlined when, having briskly seen Vera off the premises and fed Tony his laudanum, he cries, 'You won't get any better than me, you know. What do you want? An old hag running round the house, getting you up in the morning at crack of dawn telling you what to do?' In Pinter's hands it becomes much more than a story about a servant who displaces his master; it's a study in mutual degradation and the boomerang nature of sexual power. Even in the final orgy scene, when Barrett seems to be pimping for Tony, you get the feeling that the glazed tarts adorning the room are no more than a form of wall-decoration: 'Make it tomorrow night and bring John', is Barrett's significant parting shot to one of the women. The atmosphere is one of sadness, satiety and inertia. But Barrett is not simply an evil temptation-figure or a gutter Mephistopheles like Auden's Nick Shadow in *The Rake's Progress*. He, too, has declined from the prim, dapper figure of the opening scenes, as tightly furled as his own umbrella, into a slightly scruffy slut. Barrett is both the instrument of his master's decline and at the same time the 'female' partner in a wan, cocooned, desperately insulated homosexual marriage.

That reading is underlined by Richard Macdonald's superlative design which, in Penelope Gilliatt's phrase, 'makes the house itself seem almost malignant': the pristine whiteness of the early scenes contrasts with the tumbled disorder of the later ones evoked by vases of dead twigs and pussy-willow. And if James Fox captures all of Tony's negligent vapidity, Dirk Bogarde as Barrett gives one of his finest screen performances. His achievement is to elicit a measure of sympathy for this ambivalent intruder, nowhere more so than in the scenes where he maintains an impassive mask while Wendy Craig as Susan blows smoke-rings in his face or impertinently asks 'Do you use a deodorant?' One of Bogarde's chief memories of the shooting, however, is of Pinter's absolute concern with textual precision. 'I remember,' says Bogarde, 'Harold came on the set one day and I extended a speech because I had to go up a staircase rather quickly and it left me with three stairs to go at the top without any dialogue. So I had to invent a litany of "Who looks after you? Who does the cooking? Who washes your pants?" It got me to the top of the stairs but obviously the lines weren't Harold's. Anyway, he heard what I'd said, considered it, chewed it over like a cow with cud and then said, "All right, you can use it." But that kind of addition was a very rare event because you just don't find writers of his calibre in cinema. You just don't find people who write that kind of dialogue.'

Yet the final triumph of *The Servant* derives from the seamless conjunction of Pinter's and Losey's talents. Every shot in the film registers, from the silhouette of Barrett emerging defiantly naked from his master's bedroom – contrast the lurid green glow of the Maugham novel – to the final image of the slumped Tony caged and imprisoned behind the barrier of the staircase-slats. Pinter's script also offers the first proof of his ability to absorb another writer's narrative idea and turn it into an extension of his own world. Critics were not slow to realise this at the time. David Robinson in the *Financial Times* related the film to *A Slight Ache* in that 'a manservant takes possession of his master'. John Russell Taylor in *The Times* noted that 'the balance of power in the triangle made up of Barrett, Tony and his fiancée is not so different from that of *The Caretaker* and again the business of the plot is the elimination of the odd man out (whoever that may prove to be) in order that the other two shall be able to live in peace'. But the film is also part of Pinter's obsessive fascination in the 1960s – evidenced by *Night School*, *The Collection* and *The Lover* – with the multiple conjugations of sexuality. Having explored the resilience of women and the accommodation between reality and fantasy in marriage, he here shows us a subtle power-play which ends with two lost, mutually dependent men locked together, apparently forever, in an echoing solitude.

Eight Family Values

Rooms and houses, as *The Servant* shows, take on a character of their own in Pinter's work. In his life too, in that he always has a precise recollection of where he wrote particular works. He associates *The Birthday Party* with tatty Midlands dressing-rooms. It was in a cramped room in Chiswick, with a young child in noisy attendance, that he wrote *A Slight Ache*, *The Hothouse*, *The Caretaker* and the first draft of *The Servant*. It was in the modern flat in Kew ('Which, at least, had two decent rooms and a little garden,' he says) that he wrote more spacious plays such as *The Collection* and *The Lover*. He then moved to the Regency house in Worthing in 1963, where he wrote the film script of *The Pumpkin Eater* for Columbia Pictures and *The Homecoming* for the RSC. And it was after he and the family, late in 1964, had moved to Hanover Terrace in Regent's Park ('An enormous house,' says Pinter. 'The biggest house you've ever seen in your life. It was on six floors. The kitchen was all right. We used to hang around in the kitchen') that he wrote *Tea Party* for the European Broadcasting Union. It is tempting to see some correlation between Pinter's growing acquisition of space and status and his characters' gradual move upmarket. Except, of course, that the point Pinter constantly makes is that affluence affords no protection against one's private demons. It is also an ironic fact that *The Homecoming*, which offers a love-hate vision of the Hackney family jungle, was written in the sedate, cosily geriatric environment of Worthing. Odd to think that only seventy years before it was where Wilde, on a family holiday, wrote *The Importance of Being Earnest* which, in Richard Ellmann's phrase, 'constructs its wonderful parapet over the abyss of the author's disquietude and apprehension'.

For Pinter, *The Homecoming* is forever associated with memories of Worthing and of his old Hackney Downs English teacher. 'I have,' he says, 'a very strong image of my old schoolmaster Joe Brearley sitting in my big room in Worthing . . . it was a rather lovely house, bow-fronted, in the only part of Worthing that is really attractive . . . a street called Ambrose Place very close to the Connaught Theatre. It's a Regency street with its own front garden the other side of the road. Anyway, Joe Brearley came to Worthing and read *The Homecoming* and I was at the other end of the room reading something else. I had only one copy of the play. I'll never forget he finished it, slammed it down and walked out of the front door. I didn't see him for about forty-five minutes as he went striding down towards the sea. He then came back and we talked. But he'd been so affected by the play that he had to get a blow of sea air.' Brearley's violent reaction keenly anticipated the visceral impact the play was to have on theatre audiences in London and elsewhere.

For Pinter, the mid-1960s was a highly productive period; but although he was shuttling between stage and screen and the three main works produced were variable in quality, there was still an extraordinary imaginative cohesion to his output. Like a stick of seaside rock, it said Pinter all the way through in that in different ways it dealt with patriarchal bluster, male vanity and female obduracy. *The Pumpkin Eater*, for all its flaws, is filled with dismay at men's abysmal failure to understand women's needs and desires. *Tea Party*, written after *The Homecoming* but produced before it, shows how a masculine pre-occupation with power, money and status affords no protection against private dread. And *The Homecoming* itself is partly about the disruptive effect of a female intruder on a misogynist, oppressively male household. Pinter's works are not essays – they don't make statements or advance theses – but as these three pieces show, he has a built-in bullshit-detector when it comes to male crassness and hypocrisy, and an endless fascination with female resilience.

Even during a busy period of writing, Pinter remained active in the world outside. In March 1964 Michael Bakewell directed nine of his sketches for the Third Programme, with Pinter himself playing the Barman and Geoffrey Bayldon the newspaper vendor in *Last to Go*: a version, with silences ranging in duration from three to seven seconds, that has an eerie music of its own. Pinter was also heavily involved with the RSC. In July 1964 he directed the first major London revival of *The Birthday Party* at the Aldwych, though, by his own admission, it was not a great success. Peter Wood's original production had veered towards the grotesque. 'My production,' says Pinter, 'pushed it back, probably too far, towards naturalism. But I had to do the play with resident RSC actors – apart from Pat Magee who, as McCann, was the strongest member of the cast and whom I introduced to the company.' Bamber Gascoigne, a Cambridge apostle of the original *Birthday Party* and now drama critic of the *Observer*, agreed with Pinter's own verdict on his production: 'Six years ago *The Birthday Party* was by Hieronymous Bosch. This time it was Holman Hunt.' But Pinter's loyalty to Peter Hall and the RSC remained absolute. When the company was ludicrously accused, by members of its own executive council, of putting on Dirty Plays such as the *Marat/Sade* and *Afore Night Come*, Pinter wrote a supportive letter to Hall claiming that 'the RSC bestrides the world – I must say it – like a colossus'.

In the same month as *The Birthday Party* was revived at the Aldwych, Pinter's screen adaptation of Penelope Mortimer's *The Pumpkin Eater*, directed by Jack Clayton, opened in London cinemas. It has never achieved the classic status or long shelf-life of *The Servant* and it is not hard to see why. Mrs Mortimer's original first-person 1962 novel is about the existential despair of a woman with six children whose marriage to a successful but compulsively unfaithful screenwriter is falling apart. It is a book written out of pain and anger. At the time, it was widely assumed to be autobiographical: just how much so became startlingly apparent thirty years later with the publication of Mrs Mortimer's personal memoir *About Time Too*. In both books, the heroine's writer-husband has copious affairs, encourages her to be sterilised while impregnating his latest mistress and even – in the heat of a blazing marital row – asks her, 'Why don't you die?' Truth is said to be stranger than fiction; in this case, it's almost identical. But when you take the novel's narrator and translate her to the screen, you are caught uneasily between the subjective and objective viewpoints. The story is still shaped by her vision even though there is a pretence at neutrality.

It is a recurrent technical problem: how to put first-person novels on to the screen. Pinter's instinct is always to dispense with narration. 'I see a lot of it in other films,' he says. 'French films particularly, where they never stop talking away and illustrating exactly what you're looking at through language. They say, "I felt very hot that day," and there you see someone looking very hot. I find a good deal of that redundant.' Yet the problem with *The Pumpkin Eater* is that the heroine's conviction that she has no identity outside her children is so embedded in the texture of the novel that it is difficult to view her situation dispassionately. It is hard to turn such a subjective book into an objective film.

Against that, one has to say that *The Pumpkin Eater* was one of the first post-war British movies to treat a specifically feminine problem with any degree of seriousness. The process of adaptation was also valuable for Pinter – whose intuitive feminism often seemed the by-product of a certain romanticism about women – in that it forced him to explore the female psyche. He's far too good a writer to moralise or to suggest that all the problems of the heroine Jo stem from her husband Jake, but he heightens the story's central irony: that Jo is surrounded by women who gush about her husband's creative sensitivity while she has to live with the reality of his moral indifference. To that end, Pinter sets up all kinds of internal verbal echoes. A supine house-guest called Philpot (a superb Maggie Smith) oozes praise of Jake Armitage, telling Jo 'but, of course, his understanding is so extraordinary'. An adulterous actress, Beth Conway, later tells Jo that 'he's got such extraordinary understanding, such ... swift ... you know kind of illumination of people'. Both women have, of course, slept with Jake; but Pinter's point is that Jake's bruited compassion scarcely extends to his wife, of whom he insensitively remarks to a doctor 'all she wants to do is sit in a corner and give birth'.

It's a flawed film. Even Anne Bancroft's famed breakdown in Harrods' Food Hall carries overtones of privileged despair, as if it were inherently more tragic than a nervous collapse in the Birkenhead Safeway's. But Pinter's screenplay captures very well both Jake's utter incomprehension of his wife's compulsive childbearing and the twisted anger of Beth Conway's cuckolded husband when he learns that his wife is carrying Jake's child. In a remarkable scene full of rancid vituperation, Conway tells Jo over the phone: 'I'm going to grind the slime out of her. I'm going to see her own oozing in her own slime. Until she's dead. She's going to hate that kid almost as much as I will. I'm going to see that she bleeds to death in Jake Armitage's dirt.' That is pure Pinter: language given a tactile, poetic force to convey the knotted rage of the wounded male. The film also shows Pinter experimenting with time, as the action shuttles freely between past and present. In many ways, it's a strange film for Pinter to have written, not only because his talent was for cool objectivity, but also because his own predicament was the exact opposite of Jake Armitage's in that he yearned for his wife to have more children and was delighted, in later years, to find himself presiding over a large inherited family. Yet by the very act of writing what was traditionally seen as a 'woman's picture', Pinter was forced to extend his imaginative range. After creating a whole series of conspicuously childless heroines, he was at last obliged to confront the joys and miseries of motherhood.

Tea Party, which was the next Pinter work to be seen, is somewhat closer to home. It was Pinter's first direct commission from BBC TV where a buoyant Canadian, Sydney Newman, had just arrived from commercial television to energise the sedate, old-boyish drama department: I worked there briefly in the spring of 1965 and remember well Newman's brash check-jackets, belief in 'agitational contemporaneity' and missionary enthusiasm for the Wednesday Play. But the BBC was also part of the European Broadcasting Union, one of whose aims was the simultaneous transmission of prestigious single plays. Pinter, following in the wake of Terence Rattigan and Fritz Hochwalder, was asked to fill the slot of what was somewhat portentously known as 'The Largest Theatre in the World'. Not someone who works easily to commission, he came up with *Tea Party* which was an extension of a short story he had written in 1963 and read on the Third Programme in 1964. The play was transmitted in Britain on 25 March 1965 and within the course of a week was seen in twelve different European countries. Pinter himself says that, 'In my view, the story is the more successful.' But while that is true, the TV play is not without significance in that it is both a projection of some of Pinter's own subjective fears and a critique of contemporary capitalism.

The virtue of the short story is that it is tight, crisp, poetic: a chilling first-person account of a collapse into paranoid fantasy symbolised by the narrator's deteriorating eyesight (metaphors of failing sight and blindness haunt Pinter's work from *The Room* onwards). It begins with the phrase 'My eyes are worse'. It goes on to tell the story of a man who has all the external trappings of success and security – wife, sons, hobbies, good job, vivacious secretary – but who is plagued by his own dark imaginings. He sees double images, is haunted by his sons' reserve, believes that his brother-in-law business partner and his secretary are furtively copulating. It's a fear rendered in a wonderfully staccato, impressionistic, Freudian prose-poetry:

> With my eye at the keyhole I hear goosing, the squeak of them. The slit is black, only the sliding gussle on my drum, the hiss and flap of their bliss. The room sits on my head, my skull creased on the brass and loathsome handle I dare not twist, for fear of seeing black screech and scrape of my secretary writhing blind in my partner's paunch and jungle.

Gradually the hero descends into a madness in which a tightly knotted bandage around his eyes gives him physical comfort, but also releases nightmare images of an orgiastic office tea party that climaxes with his partner stripping his wife and secretary under the eyes of his children. The power of the story resides in the compact energy of the language and the way Pinter takes you inside the man's skull to convey the sense of total breakdown.

Turning the story into a TV play was not easy; that much one can deduce from the existence of two radically different drafts in the Pinter Archive. Draft One starts with the hero, a sanitary engineer called Sisson, in a state of impending breakdown and having his eyes tested by a physician. It then flashes back in time to show Sisson at the peak of his success before the onset of ocular strain and nervous collapse. Pinter, on a separate sheet, even numbers the scenes precisely and gives a rough indication of their content. This rather tricksy time-bending Draft One is succeeded by a much more successful Draft Two – very close to the finished version – which preserves strict chronological time and shows the hero, now called Disson, undergoing a gradual process of disintegration.

As a short story, *Tea Party* was an intimate study of breakdown. As a TV play, it becomes a much more explicit account of a man who has hauled himself out of his own class by denying his former self which now exacts its revenge. Disson is a rich self-made man – whose office boasts a showcase full of washbasins, lavatory bowls and bidets – obsessed by the differences in status and class between himself and his second wife Diana, and her brother Willy. Disson exudes capitalist arrogance but is insecure, isolated, friendless, full of contradictions. On taking his brother-in-law into the business, he one moment stresses his own impersonal grandeur: 'Our only contact is by inter-com, unless I need to see someone personally which is rare.' The next minute he is all paternalist bonhomie: 'I've always made it my business to be on the most direct possible terms with the members of my staff and my business associates.' It is a play about a man whose loss of specific identity takes the symbolic form of rapidly deteriorating eyesight and uncontrollable, lubri-cious fantasies.

It would be ludicrous to argue that Disson is Pinter. At the same time, Pinter's plays are invariably triggered by personal experience and memory; and it is worth recalling the context in which he wrote the play. He was not only flush with money, but had just moved into a grand house in Regent's Park and was conscious of his own – and Vivien's – increasing isolation. Thinking back to those times, he told me: 'I think she was uneasy about the life in which we finally found ourselves. She wasn't really cut out – nor was I, for that matter – for a big social life. We weren't brought up to it. We had an odd life in Hanover Terrace. We lived an incredibly reclusive life apart from our work in the theatre. We gave one enormous party at the time of *The Homecoming* for about 200 people, but normally we saw very few people indeed . . . People never knocked at the door. We never answered the bloody door. Nobody came, except by appointment.' Donald Pleasence, one of the few people who did call, also had one particularly pertinent memory of the house: 'It was a very beautiful Nash house that had gold taps in all the baths and a footpedal to flush the toilet so that you didn't have to touch a chain or plug with your hand.' Disson boasts of just such a property in *Tea Party*, to his secretary's surprise:

WENDY: Footpedals?
DISSON: Instead of a chain or plug. A footpedal.
WENDY: Oh. How marvellous.
DISSON: They're growing more popular every day and rightly so.

One footpedal doesn't automatically make Pinter an autobiographical plumber, but as a writer he is far too aware of the significance of his own life not to be conscious of the perils of upward mobility or the cocooning effect of wealth. Indeed, it was a theme he later explored in *No Man's Land* where Hirst is a writer increasingly cut off from reality by the bland routine of affluence. And in *Tea Party* Pinter, always an acute self-analyst, seems to tap into some private dread that material wealth may be a source of spiritual corruption.

Yet *Tea Party* is also a sharp satire on contemporary capitalism: a point understood better by viewers than by many critics. The latter seemed blind to the visual irony of Charles Jarrott's production with its sweeping Wellesian tracking shots around the vast expanses of the bidet-maker's barony; and one has to turn to the Communist *Daily Worker* for any dialectical discussion of the play's themes. Its TV critic gave it an initial morning-after thumbs-up. Stuart Douglass, a freelance writer, then weighed in, accusing Pinter of endorsing the status quo: 'The task of the capitalist class is to preserve its way of life as long as possible. Anyone who will convince vast numbers of people that the pattern is set and that they are incapable of changing it is a welcome recruit to the existing ranks of intellectual cynics.' But this, in turn, provoked a contradictory letter from a reader on 9 April who saw the play as unequivocally political:

> What a picture of class division! No need for pages of theoretical dialogue. The worker I talked to in the train the following morning saw the lesson in that one flash. "What a life," he said. "He [Disson] couldn't enjoy a game of table-tennis for fear of losing. He had nothing to say to his old mum and dad. He couldn't look at a smashing figure for fear of what he was thinking." Living with the profit-motive does this for everyone.

Pinter is not a writer to peddle simple Marxist messages, but the chap on the train – who takes one back to a lost era when a major TV play was part of common culture – was far closer to the truth than many of the critics with their talk of 'titillatory, fetishistic capers' and 'preening self-sufficiency'. *Tea Party* is partly a play about the barrenness of the business ethic and the danger of denying your class roots; indeed, everything in the action confirms the ironic truth of Disson's remark that 'Nothing is more sterile or lamentable than the man content to live within himself'. But Pinter also – as the original story shows – empathises with Disson, and sees that power and money afford no protection against private phantoms and wracking guilt. *Tea Party* may not be Pinter's most profound or complex play, but it is one in which personal obsession and political comment achieve a stylish synthesis.

It was, of course, seen by millions on television throughout Europe, but it was ten weeks later, with the opening of *The Homecoming* at the Aldwych on 3 June 1965, that Pinter advanced his claim to be seen as Britain's foremost living dramatist. It was a heady year for new drama in which a number of leading writers pushed the frontiers outwards: Osborne's *A Patriot for Me* scandalised the Lord Chamberlain by presenting a drag-ball in the declining days of the Austro-Hungarian Empire; Edward Bond's *Saved*, in examining the roots of social violence, put a baby-stoning on stage; and Peter Shaffer's *Black Comedy* dazzlingly reversed the possibilities of light and dark. All those plays entered the modern repertory, but none so securely as *The Homecoming*: in its image of the naked violence of family life and of the primal, atavistic power of the female, it shocked, disturbed and seemed to establish a direct line to the collective subconscious. Even today, it has lost none of its power to astonish. I heard a young Paris audience at the Théâtre de l'Atelier in 1994 – in a less than perfect revival – gasp with amazement at Ruth's decision to abandon Teddy and her children and join the domestic jungle of his Hackney family. *The Homecoming* has its roots in a specific locality, but it still seems to speak to audiences everywhere.

It has been interpreted from every possible standpoint: the social, the psychological, the ethological, the linguistic. Ever since 1965, there has also been a determined attempt to see it as a particularly Jewish family drama. But what does it stem from: real life, or the dark recesses of Pinter's imagination? The answer seems to be a combination of the two. Pinter took aspects of character and the domestic context from personal knowledge of the East End, but in tracing the play's development through the Pinter Archive, you can also see how it grows organically from an image of sexual disharmony.

Peter Hall gave me an unexpected clue to one of the characters when I asked him if he thought Pinter's work was haunted by an obsession with the past. 'There's a very interesting quality in Harold,' said Hall, 'both as a man and a writer. He will say, "That's a poem I wrote when I was fifteen," or, "That man taught me at school," or, "This is a friend from the past and we used to run around Hackney Recreation Ground together." There's an almost mystic quality about things and people from his past. I remember when we were filming *The Homecoming* he took me to a street in Hackney because I wanted an exterior shot of Teddy and Ruth arriving in a taxi. He took me to a street full of huge Victorian houses and he said, "We'll just go and call on someone." He rang this doorbell and an old man appeared – I swear to you – in plimsolls and cloth cap. And he said, "Harold, my boy, how are you? Come in." We went in and Harold said, "How's Moishe?" The man said he was doing very well and it emerged that Moishe was a Professor of

English at Montreal University and was a friend of Harold's from his Hackney youth. I thought I was in some strange time-warp. I thought to myself: how did Paul Rogers on stage come to be costumed in plimsolls and cloth cap? I have no memory of Harold suggesting it.'

Pinter himself recalls the incident well and admits that Max had his origins in real life. At the same time, he is anxious to point out that *The Homecoming* is not intended to be a localised Jewish family drama. He says, 'The image of the old man – who was Moishe Wernick's father – may have been a kind of source. I didn't know him well. We didn't discuss our parents in those days. But the image of Moishe's father in cap and plimsolls was one I carried with me. I knew him to be a pretty authoritarian figure. A really tough old bugger. That was the image I had of him. But there was nothing else to it. *The Homecoming* did not take place in that house. Nor was there any one source. There was the image of the old man and of the street itself: if you look at the shot in the film, that's how I see it. That's where it takes place. In that district. After all, the play was embedded in the East End. But although I was once attacked in the *Jewish Chronicle* for not admitting the play was about a Jewish family, I don't subscribe to that. I do see there's a seed there. For a Jewish man to bring back a *shiksa* was in those days a dread thing to do. I heard later that one or two people I knew at school had done it. Their families considered them to be dead. I'm not denying that there's a spring somewhere of that kind. Why deny it? But I've always felt it wasn't a play about Jewish society. The fact that it makes sense in all sorts of languages and communities not remotely Jewish bears that out. The narrative continues.'

In fact, the play is much closer to real life than Pinter, out of consideration for a friend and a long-preserved pact of mutual silence, admits. When I wrote to Morris (Moishe) Wernick in Canada asking if it were true that Max was based on his father, he sent a very revealing reply explaining the whole situation:

I married in 1956 and left immediately to start life in Canada. I never told my father that I was married and for the next ten years continued to keep up this "pretence" even on my infrequent visits to England. Harold thought this action on my part unwise, as did Henry, Joe Brearley, my wife and, come to think of it, everyone except me. They all went along with it out of respect for my wishes. I came, in time, to join the ranks of those who felt that it was ridiculous and in 1964 I brought my whole family to England where my father met his daughter-in-law and grandchildren. I do not need to tell you that it was one of the memorable moments in my life. Why did I take what I now regard as a mistaken course? For the simple reason that I believed it would spare him being hurt. Forty years ago marrying "out" was still not regarded lightly. My father was in no sense a bigot and I certainly did not live in fear of his displeasure. Harold would get a laugh out of this idea, as would anyone who knew him.

Morris Wernick goes on to say that he had an uncle who was a cabbie – not a chauffeur – and 'something of a free spirit, with a small reputation for violent reaction' and a fund of colourful stories; also that Pinter knew both his father and uncle. But he adds that his father never wore plimsolls in his life: 'so much for the Peter Hall memory.'

What seems clear is that Morris Wernick's situation – that of a Jewish East Ender who married a Gentile girl, emigrated to Canada and kept his marriage secret from his family – acted as a springboard for Pinter's dramatic imagination. Wernick's 'homecoming' in 1964 coincided with the writing of the play and indeed Pinter sent his old friend a first draft, freely acknowledging that he had expanded on the idea. Michael Goldstein, in conversation, also claims that Max was 'a dead ringer' for Morris Wernick's father and recalls that Morris was one of three sons and that their relationships were not unlike those depicted in the play. But Goldstein adds that he himself had a brother who, like Joey in the play, was training to become a boxer. And one can't forget that there was a boxer, Uncle Judah, in Pinter's own family. Yet none of this makes the play a specifically Jewish drama. What it does suggest is that *The Homecoming* was triggered, in part, by a particular domestic situation and is much closer to observed reality than has ever been acknowledged.

At the same time, it also grows out of Pinter's imagination, as you can see from studying his Archive. The play doesn't start with the image of Max or a fractious household. It begins with a fragment of conversation, written in pencil on a few sheets of lined paper, between two characters simply called A (a man) and B (a woman). We don't know who they are. We don't know if they are married. We know nothing of their setting. All we deduce is that he is anxious and overbearing, she is restless and independent-minded. Their rhythms certainly seem to be out of sync:

A: Why are you yawning?
B: I'm not.
   (*Pause.*)
A: Are you tired?
B: No.

It transpires that B (the woman) is anxious to go out for a breath of fresh air,

A (the man) isn't. Their dialogue, clipped and laconic, even has a faint touch of *Private Lives*:

B: What's the weather like?
A: It's a bright night. Venus is in the ascendant.
B: Venus?
A: It's in the ascendant.
B: How do you know?
A: I looked.

What is significant is that the play stems from a male–female relationship steeped in discord and that the woman seems anxious to assert her freedom: the Ruth–Teddy situation in embryo.

This cryptic scrap then develops into a typed six-page sketch in which A has become even more heavy-handedly patronising ('Who's my little sweetheart?' he asks) and B still more fretful and restless. But an element of sexual tension and verbal menace is now added through the presence of a third character, C. The context is not precise, but we deduce from the dialogue that A is a policeman who has brought his new bride (B) back to a house where a criminal who is on the run (C) also lives. There is no hint that the two men are brothers. Otherwise, what we have in outline is the first encounter in the finished play between Teddy, Ruth and Lenny. What is astonishing is that the character of Lenny seems to have arrived fully formed in Pinter's imagination. C is lewd, aggressive, posturing; a cocksure prattler who makes two long speeches: one about a dockside encounter with a poxy whore and the other about a snow-clearing experience leading to the duffing up of an old woman. These appear only slightly revised in the final version, but the differences are fascinating. For instance, C's aria about his encounter with a waterfront whore ends with this exchange:

B: How did you know she was diseased?
C: Well, that's quite an acute question. Well, you can tell.

Contrast the final version:

RUTH: How did you know she was diseased?
LENNY: How did I know?
  (*Pause.*)
  I decided she was.

In the early sketch, C's response is weak and equivocal. In the play, Lenny's answer both points up his attempt to reconstruct reality through language and Ruth's ability to expose the fact. But the real dramatic shock in the six-page sketch comes when C, having learned that A and B have just returned from a honeymoon in Venice, suddenly asks 'Would you mind sleeping three in a bed?' There is a suggestion that C has already enjoyed an intimate relationship with A and would now be happy to extend his favours to his wife (B) as well. There is even a remarkable passage in which A accuses C of using up the whole contents of a tin of face-powder and then goes on to assure B (his wife) 'There's nothing homosexual in this'. Pinter is clearly working out various imaginative possibilities. But what is clear from the very start is that he is haunted by the idea of a marriage that is under threat both from its own internal tensions and the external manoeuvres of a third party.

Out of this sketch Pinter evolves a recognisable first draft of *The Homecoming*. At this stage it is a black, bilious one-act comedy about a bruising patriarch (Wally), his brother (Sam) and his three sons (Lenny, Joey and Teddy), the last of whom is married to a woman called Susan. Everything is short, sharp, shocking and violent. At the beginning of the play, Joey is upstairs in the family house clearly having it off – or trying to – with Susan. When they emerge we get some idea of the tensions within the group. Wally is rude to Sam. Lenny is jealous of Teddy. Teddy is deeply patronising to Susan. And Susan gets her revenge by driving a tough sexual bargain with her husband's family and agreeing to stay with them and work as an upmarket prostitute. The bones of Act Two of the finished play are all there, but at this stage everything is very blunt and direct. There is no explanation as to Teddy and Susan's homecoming, no mention of their American campus life, no hint as to what Teddy will do next. The most significant aspect of this version is that Pinter locates the action in the East End and that Wally, judging by his opening speech on the first page, seems to be Jewish:

> I used to knock about with a man called Berkowitz. I called him Berki. Come on Berki, where are you going tonight? Coming up West tonight? We'd go round the back doubles, turn over a couple of tarts. I still got the scars. We used to walk back to back, Berki and me. The terrible twins they used to call us. He was six feet tall. But even his family called him Berki. Of course the old man was a Berkowitz too. They were all Berkowitzes. But he was the only one they called Berki.

Even though Pinter in the margin writes in the name 'MacGregor' alongside that of Berkowitz, it is revealing that his initial instinct was to give the action a Jewish context.

It is only with the second typescript draft that Pinter fits all the ideas together: the apprehensive homecoming and the rocky marriage that we find in the early sketches, with the ruthless sexual bargain that is at the heart of

Draft One. Suddenly the finished play begins to take shape. But what is fascinating as you study Pinter's endless changes and crossings-out is that he alters anything that pre-empts the audience's judgement. Teddy's patronising tone towards Susan (or Sue, as he often calls her) as they arrive at the house is initially much more explicit:

TED: You'd be better off in bed, my sweetheart. Who's my sweetheart? My little sweetheart. You're not worried about anything, are you?
SUSAN: No.
TED: Leave it all to me.

Wally's crudeness is also much more signalled than it is when he becomes Max. At one point, he asks Susan if her three children are hogs or sows. When she replies 'Hogs', he responds 'You're a sow with three hogs'. Lenny, who in Draft Two is a milkman rather than a professional pimp, makes obvious fun of his Uncle Sam announcing 'The man's an automatic bachelor'. And Susan, having rolled around the floor with Joey, tells him to 'put that record off' and smacks him around the face. But what is extraordinary is the journey Pinter's imagination has already undergone in the process of rewriting. He starts with a few scraps of paper exploring a relationship between a protective, overbearing man and an independent-minded woman. As each version develops, Pinter gives the action a social context, builds up a detailed picture of the family background and makes the woman herself progressively tougher and more determined. You not only see how Pinter's mind works; you also get a strong clue as to the central theme of the play.

Yet any discussion of *The Homecoming* has to acknowledge one easily overlooked fact: Pinter's imaginative delight in the world he had created. It comes across in a letter Pinter wrote to Guy Vaesen in 1965 after his old friend had had a sighting of the script. Vaesen was appreciative but invoked O'Neill which, judging by the tone of Pinter's letter, touched a raw nerve.

You say, have you been reading any O'Neill lately? I haven't but surely you wouldn't suggest I have to read other playwrights before writing my own work? There might indeed be an O'Neillish bell rung since I deal with a family in the play but I didn't have to do any homework on any of his work first. In fact, I haven't thought about him for years.

Pinter goes on chattily to point out that Paul Rogers is due to play Max and that the Lord Chamberlain, the official theatrical censor, has hung on to the manuscript three times longer than usual. He then adds, as a postscript: 'By the way, after thought, I don't feel myself more critical of any one character than another. *I love and detest the lot of them.*' The italics are mine, not

Pinter's; but the remark is highly significant. Unless one understands the creative pleasure Pinter gets out of recording the family's ferocious amorality and his refusal to sit in judgement, one will never get to grips with the play.

The Homecoming still shocks because of the absence of a conventional moral framework. It also reflects Pinter's love-hate attitude towards his characters, but it inevitably expresses certain values. The plot itself is clear enough. Bernard Dukore, putting it as neutrally as possible, says 'several members of a male family struggle for power over each other and manoeuvre to win the favours of the sole woman in their midst'. But what does the action signify? You can see it in terms of Frazer's *Golden Bough*-type ritual: 'Pinter dramatises the ancient archaic rite of the sacrifice of the ritual king and the mating of the fertility goddess with the new conqueror' (Vera M. Jiji). You can interpret it in terms of ethological battles of the kind Robert Ardrey explored in *The Territorial Imperative*: 'What we see is a ritualised tournament in which the two instincts of sexual desire and territorial aspiration fight it out under the scrutiny of an emasculated observer on the sidelines' (Irving Wardle). Or you can see it as a play that exists on the dual levels of observable reality and Freudian dream: 'From the sons' point of view *The Homecoming* is a dream-image of the fulfilment of all Oedipal wishes, the sexual conquest of the mother, the utter humiliation of the father' (Martin Esslin).

All these interpretations are valid, and I share Esslin's belief that the play works simultaneously – like most good drama – on two levels. On the realistic level, it is a socially accurate study of the tribal behaviour of a group of desperate Hackney predators. But where, on the metaphorical level, Esslin sees it as a fulfilment of the sons' Oedipal fantasies, I interpret it as a feminist challenge to male despotism and to the classification of women as either mothers or whores. From that standpoint, the play shows the elusive Ruth escaping from an arid marriage and a sterile academic environment into one where she exercises social, sexual and economic control. Esslin's reading depends on a view of Ruth as an essentially passive creature: in fact, for much of the play, as both Peter Hall's 1965 and 1990 productions showed, she radiates an amused, manipulative superiority. In that sense, *The Homecoming* seems to me not just an extension of but also a radical advance upon all those plays – *A Slight Ache*, *Night School*, *The Collection*, *The Lover* – where women challenge patriarchal assumptions and expose male vulnerability. It also fulfils a pattern not uncommon in explicitly feminist drama: the pattern, for instance, of Githa Sowerby's *Rutherford and Son* (1912) in which a domestic tyrant is undermined and a wife, having sent her husband packing, strikes a hard-headed practical bargain based on sound economic principles.

Sowerby's heroine may be motivated by the need to guarantee her son's future rather than sexual power; but the basic dynamic is the same. All first-rate plays offer the satisfaction of myth; and the one that *The Homecoming* appeals to is less that of Oedipal wish-fulfilment than of female triumph over a male power-structure. Pinter himself could hardly have spelt it out more clearly than in an interview he gave to the American critic Henry Hewes in 1967:

> If this had been a happy marriage it wouldn't have happened. But [Ruth] didn't want to go back to America with her husband, so what the hell's she going to do? She's misinterpreted deliberately and used by this family. But eventually she comes back at them with a whip. She says, "If you want to play this game I can play it as well as you." She does not become a harlot. At the end of the play she's in possession of a certain kind of freedom. She can do what she wants, and it is not at all certain she will go off to Greek Street. But even if she did, she would not be a harlot in her own mind.

Ruth, in short, is the agent of change in a household obsessed with power, status, position; also one filled from the start with a strange, edgy ambivalence towards women. In his opening address to the cast in 1965, Peter Hall talked of this peculiar all-male atmosphere: of 'the jungle and destructiveness and the unfeminine society, the hatred of women that informs this society'. But it's less pure misogynistic hatred than the simmering preoccupation that comes of deprivation. Max constantly harks back to his dead wife Jessie: 'Even though it made me sick just to look at her rotten stinking face, she wasn't such a bad bitch.' He also recalls his days on the racetrack where he appraised horses much as he does women. Fillies were more unreliable than colts, but he always knew how to tell a good one: 'I'd stand in front of her and look her straight in the eye, it was a kind of hypnotism, and by the look deep down in her eye I could tell whether she was a stayer or not.' Easy to dismiss this as an old man's fantasy; except that Max later looks Ruth directly in the eye, instantly appraises her and, at the end, is the only one to realise that she is not a 'stayer' and may be using them rather than they her. Max is a magnificent character because of his contradictions: his crudeness and shrewdness, his vulgarity and sense of loss. He attempts to demean the men around him by feminising them – calling both Lenny and Teddy a 'bitch', and Sam a 'tit' – and spurns the maternal role his sons inflict upon him (in Draft Two, Pinter changes 'Find yourself a skivvy' to 'Find yourself a mother'). Yet he also lives off memories of Jessie, who is idealised saint one minute and 'slutbitch' the next.

Pinter shows all the men in the play, in fact, as sexually screwed up. Lenny exploits women as a pimp, as if exacting some permanent adolescent revenge against his own mother. The extraordinary fact about his brutal aria describing the booting and clumping of the pox-ridden whore who dared to accost him down at the docks is that the memory – whether true or false – is replete with filial rage. Lenny talks of the chauffeur who located the woman, the insistent liberties she took, his desire to kill her. 'Don't worry about the chauffeur' he tells Ruth. 'The chauffeur would never have spoken. He was an old friend of the family': impossible not to think of the professional chauffeur Uncle Sam escorting Jessie round town in the back of his car – the same car in which MacGregor allegedly had her – and hard not to conclude that Lenny is seeking vindictive triumph over his faithless mother. Even Lenny's story about the old lady who asks her to help him with the iron mangle ends with an act of gratuitous violence. And soon after he has recounted these stories, Ruth provocatively calls him Leonard:

LENNY: Don't call me that, please.
RUTH: Why not?
LENNY: That's the name my mother gave me.

Driven by filial hatred – and presumably the loss of his mother's love – Lenny has turned all relationships with women into the commercially exploitative or the sentimentally violent.

For Joey, the beef-witted demolition expert and failed boxer, life is simpler in that women seem to be there simply as a source of sexual gratification: 'he's had more dolly', Lenny informs Teddy, 'than you've had cream cakes.' Even the returning Teddy, for all his academic sophistication, treats his wife largely as the lucky receptacle of his enlightened patronage. One son's a ponce, another a mindless lech, the third a condescending campus Torvald Helmer out of *A Doll's House*. All of which lends a mordant irony to Max's observation of his sons that 'Every single bit of the moral code they live by – was taught to them by their mother'. As for Max's brother Sam, he displays the old-fashioned gallantry of the totally asexual. But the portrait Pinter offers is of a household that, in the total absence of women, is torn between idealisation and vilification of the sex, and can see them only as saints or sinners, Madonnas or tarts, mothers or whores.

Pinter, consciously or not, exposes the arbitrariness and sentimentality of the whole mother–whore dichotomy. Running through the play is the male ideal of the perfect wife as expressed by Max to Ruth: 'I've been begging my two youngsters for years to find a nice feminine girl with proper credentials — it makes life worth living.' On the other hand, there is the constant categorisation of women as sex objects and whores. But what, Pinter asks, if these categories coexist in the same woman? Does it not explode all the traditional male assumptions and at the same time give women a new power and authority? What makes *The Homecoming* a more radical play than its Pinter predecessors is that the two women at its centre – the dead Jessie and the living Ruth – transcend male definitions: they are both mothers *and* sexual icons. Flora in *A Slight Ache*, Stella in *The Collection*, Sarah in *The Lover* all in different ways represent sexual freedom and power, but all are conspicuously childless. Both Jessie and Ruth, however, have given birth to three children, all boys. Both, judging by what we learn of Jessie and what we see of Ruth, have a strong libido. Which is what makes the play subversive: the idea that the supposedly fixed identities of mother and whore are flexible, shifting and perfectly compatible.

One's first reaction to *The Homecoming* is almost inevitably one of shock. How can Ruth be persuaded into abandoning home and family, and allowing her predatory in-laws to set her up as surrogate mum and Soho prostitute? And how can husband Teddy stand by and simply let it happen? But the more you see or read the play, the clearer it becomes that Ruth is no hapless victim but a shrewd manipulator, and that Teddy is no tragic cuckold but a hard-hearted bystander. The play is the story of Ruth's triumph and ultimate empowerment.

Even from Ruth and Teddy's arrival it is clear that there is something askew in their relationship: there is a lack of both physical and emotional synchronicity – the very point from which Pinter began in his original jottings. Ruth is tired after the journey; Teddy seems alert. But although Teddy is the academic philosopher, it is she who shows a niggling semantic precision:

TEDDY: . . . Shall I go and see if my room's still there.
RUTH: It can't have moved.
TEDDY: No, I mean if my bed's still there.

And although Teddy is coming home, it is Ruth who seems to be staking claim to the territory. She takes in the father's chair: in the film version, Vivien Merchant gives it a long, lingering, almost voluptuously possessive look. She refuses to sit – always a sign of independence in Pinter – and slowly paces the room. And she wants to go out for a breath of air. Small gestures, but all signs of a shifting power-balance in the relationship. Penelope Gilliatt made a sharp point when reviewing the Aldwych production in the *Observer*. The drama, she said, is not in the plot.

It consists in the swaying of violent people as they gain minute advantages.

A man who does the washing-up has the advantage over a man sitting in an armchair who thinks he can hear resentment in every swilling tea-leaf. The member of a married couple who stays up late has the advantage over the one who goes to bed first. A father has the advantage over his children as long as he can make them think of their birth and not let them remind him of his own death.

The key point is that Ruth, in every single encounter, gains the tactical advantage – not only over Teddy, but just as importantly over Lenny in their first bruising meeting when she returns from her nocturnal walk:

LENNY: Good evening.
RUTH: Morning, I think.
LENNY: You're right there.

Deflating Lenny's ironic greeting, Ruth goes on to take the scene game, set and match. Her laconic replies to Lenny's questions, her refusal to rise to his sparring insults or be provoked by his sexual manoeuvres ('Do you mind if I hold your hand?') goads him into self-revelation. His speech about the dock-side whore, with its phallic references to booms and yardarms and its coiled violence, is obviously meant to impress; what it actually does is to expose his macho posturing and mother-fixation. Even the crucial moment when Ruth asks Lenny how he knew the prostitute he encountered was diseased – 'I decided she was' – reveals his attempt to pass off arbitrary classifications as proven fact (something common to all the men in the play). That Ruth forces him to admit this confirms a point made by the feminist critic Deborah A. Sarbin: that she functions in the play as a disruptive force.

The scene reaches its climax in the famous moment when Lenny tries to relieve Ruth of the glass of water on the side table next to her chair:

LENNY: Just give me the glass.
RUTH: No.
   (*Pause.*)
LENNY: I'll take it then.
RUTH: If you take the glass . . . I'll take you.
   (*Pause.*)
LENNY: How about me taking the glass without you taking me?
RUTH: Why don't I just take you?

This is not just a battle of wills which Ruth obviously wins. It shows Pinter's ability to invest a theatrical moment with weight and resonance: it is, in its own terms, the exact equivalent of Wolfit's slow turn with the cloak in

Oedipus Rex. What Ruth is doing is stripping Lenny of his potency and exposing the bluster of his purported violence towards women. Up to that point, we have taken Lenny pretty much at face value as a dominant petty thug. The ruthless Ruth, however, exposes his terror of female sexuality. When she invites him to sit on her lap and put his head back while she pours the contents of the glass down his throat, she challenges him on two fronts: as a sexy woman and surrogate mother. The scene ends with her draining the glass and him shouting up the stairs after her retreating figure 'What was that supposed to be? Some kind of proposal?' Ruth has not only chopped Lenny's balls off. She has also ensured that we now view his cocksure arrogance in a different light.

Ruth almost throughout is cool, poised, unruffled. Sometimes she dominates through silence; even when Max, the morning after her arrival, calls her 'a whore', 'a smelly scrubber', 'a stinking pox-ridden slut' she says nothing as if in amused contempt at the accusation's hyperbolic excess. When she does speak, it is often to disruptive effect. Witness the way in Act Two, as Lenny tries to draw Teddy into a bit of post-prandial philosophy, she instantly shifts the enquiry from the metaphysical to the material:

> Look at me. I . . . move my leg. That's all it is. But I wear . . . underwear . . . which moves with me . . . it captures your attention. Perhaps you misinterpret. The action is simple. It's a leg . . . moving. My lips move. Why don't you restrict . . . your observations to that?

Ruth both insinuates herself into the male-dominated discussion and exposes its absurdity. And although Pinter explicitly says Ruth is not Vivien, one can't help wondering how much he was subconsciously using his wife's proven physical magnetism and defiant anti-intellectualism.

What Pinter does do – consciously, it seems to me – is carefully to prepare the ground for Ruth's apparently shocking decision to junk her life as a campus wife and mother. Pinter does it partly through the use of antithetical imagery. For Teddy, life in America represents 'the pool', 'swimming,' 'sun'; for Ruth, it is 'rock', 'sand', 'insects', which conveys an Eliotesque dryness and aridity. But the American life implied by Teddy is also one that slots Ruth into a subordinate, supportive, little-wife role. 'You can help me with my lectures when we get back. I'd love that', he tells her, which shows Teddy is totally oblivious to the fact that a few minutes earlier Ruth had cut like a knife through the vanities of male philosophical discourse. Teddy's tone of benign paternalism is also pure *Doll's House*. 'You liked Venice, didn't you? It was lovely, wasn't it? You had a good week. I mean . . . I took you there. I can speak Italian.' To which suffocating patronage Ruth responds: 'But if I'd been a nurse in the Italian campaign I would have been there before.' That's both a declaration of independence and a conscious echo of an earlier remark by Lenny suggesting the extent to which Ruth's emotional allegiances have shifted.

But was Max right? Is Ruth a whore? What, for instance, of her bout of snogging on the sofa with Joey? Pinter in the interview with Henry Hewes explicitly denies it means she's a harlot ('The most respectable women do this'). In the dramatic context, it is quite obviously a means to an end: total domination. It is Ruth who abruptly terminates the clinch and announces 'I'd like something to eat'; who peremptorily demands a tumbler for her whisky; who gives the orders. Ruth deploys her sexuality to gain power and territory; the stage direction reads '*Ruth walks round the room*', as if she's laying claim to her new-found space. Even when after a couple of hours in the upstairs bedroom with Joey she denies him sexual climax, it's proof not just that she's a tease but that she's skilled at using her sexuality as a weapon of control.

This seems to me the whole point of the last movement of the play: the one in which Ruth agrees to stay with her adopted family and apparently earn her keep as a prostitute. Among themselves the men discuss the idea in the crudest possible terms – talking to Teddy of visiting professors who need to have 'a nice quiet poke' and telling him he'd be in a position to give them 'inside information' – whereas to Ruth's face they are all evasive euphemism. But it is she who cuts through the male bullshit and dictates terms: she demands three rooms and a bathroom, a personal maid, a handsome wardrobe. She talks like a practised lawyer: 'All aspects of the agreement and conditions of employment would have to be clarified to our mutual satisfaction before we finalised the contract.' She gets everything she wants. Only Max, so used to appraising fillies, smells a rat: 'She'll use us, she'll make use of us, I can tell you! I can smell it! You want to bet?'

Even a sympathetic critic like Deborah Sarbin says that we have to resist 'the smug conclusion that Ruth wields the power in the family now'. But why smug? Surely, that is precisely what happens. Sarbin says that the final tableau suggests a passing on of the role of dominant male from Teddy to Lenny, but is that really how it plays? At the end, Ruth is enthroned in Max's chair; the chair she eyed enviously at the start and that is clearly the seat of domestic power. She has Joey kneeling at her feet, still clamouring for, and denied, sexual satisfaction. Max, having suffered a mild stroke in the final moments, is left as an impotent supplicant begging a kiss. It is true that the final stage direction reads '*Lenny stands, watching*'. That could be taken to mean that he is still the master-manipulator. More plausibly, it could also mean that he is forever the permanent outsider. We have seen Lenny outsmarted by Ruth in sexual challenge and totally outmanoeuvred over her commercial future. His physical isolation at the end implies that he is doomed to the role of helpless voyeur. That seems to be Pinter's view, judging by his reaction to the 1994 Paris production at the Théâtre de l'Atelier. 'I was really quite upset at the end. We all had a drink on stage afterwards. The only thing I said was that I didn't understand the end when Lenny came up to Ruth and put his hands on her while she was sitting there. If you put your hands on someone's shoulders, it means you possess them, that you have power over them. But Lenny does not have any power over her. The actress said, "Is he not my *macrou*, my pimp?" I said, "He'd love to be, but he is not at this moment." I thought that was really a bad mistake.' That's straight from the author's mouth. Which is why I quibble with Martin Esslin's view that the play is a form of Oedipal wish-fulfilment and that Lenny's desire to kill the father and find a mother-substitute has been gratified now that he has Ruth in his power. It is Ruth who has come home, who has rid herself of a suffocating husband, who has *chosen* the relative squalor of Hackney life over the sterile cleanliness of American academia, and it is she who has reconciled the supposedly incompatible roles of mother and whore. No Pinter play is ever a statement; but the inference to be drawn from the dramatic action and from the concluding image is that by the end Ruth has acquired a new freedom and that women – through strength of will and sexual authority – can achieve their own form of empowerment. As Penelope Gilliatt wrote: 'Ruth looks on her body rather as a landlord would look on a corner-site. As soon as she has apparently been exploited sexually she really has the advantage because she owns the property.'

I see *The Homecoming* as an implicitly feminist play. It is not the only solution. It is, however, one that accords with the developing role of women in Pinter's plays, with the work's physical imagery and with my memory of successive interpretations. Yet even though for many of us it is Pinter's masterpiece, what is amazing is that it was only Peter Hall's passionate advocacy that secured the play for the RSC; Peter Brook, John Barton, Michel St Denis, Clifford Williams and Trevor Nunn all thought it wasn't right for the Aldwych. David Jones, who had just joined the RSC as an associate director, recalls: 'We had a think-tank session where we keelhauled the whole theory of doing modern plays in harness with classical plays. We sat down for a weekend and said, "What sort of modern plays do we really want?" In a quite logical way, everyone said because we've got a large company and because we're a classical troupe we want Brechtian plays or Elizabethan-scale plays. *The Homecoming* had just come in and was seen as a very tight East End domestic drama. There was a majority vote at the end of the meeting that said we admired the play enormously, but it was not the kind of thing we should be doing. Peter Hall registered the vote and said, "I'm still going to do it," which was all credit to him.' Which makes one grateful not only for Peter Hall but for the fact that, in those pre-studio days, the RSC were committed to doing new plays in the large public space of the Aldwych.

Rehearsals, as with any new Pinter, were dangerous, exploratory, exciting. The most vivid account of them has been given by Paul Rogers (Max) in an interview with John Lahr, and by Peter Hall in his autobiography. Rogers catalogues a whole series of discoveries he made: that Joey is not Max's son but MacGregor's and Jessie's, that it is partly a play about love, that one of the family rules is that nobody ever shows a blow actually register, that the whole power of the play is that nobody must be defeated until the end. Hall also confirms that he once held a dot-and-pause rehearsal to mark the precise musical notations in Pinter's text. Hall writes:

> The longest break is marked *silence*: the character comes out of it in a different state to when he or she began it; the next is marked *pause*, which is a crisis point, filled with the unsaid; and the shortest is marked with three dots, which is a plain hesitation. The actors had to understand why there were these differences. They chafed a little but finally accepted that what was not said often spoke as forcefully as the words themselves. The breaks represented a journey in the actor's emotions, sometimes a surprising transition.

Yet there were few indications, on the play's short provincial tour before its Aldwych opening, that it was going to be a runaway success. In Cardiff, many of the audience stomped out in fury. Benedict Nightingale has recalled trying to write an overnight review in a local hotel lounge full of spluttering and expostulating theatregoers. In Brighton, which has one of the most conservative audiences in Britain, the reaction was just as bad. Even when the play opened at the Aldwych on 3 June, there was little instant recognition of its classic status – Pinter's plays nearly always take time to gain critical acceptance. Irving Wardle in *The Times* qualified his admiration by saying the play fell away badly in the second act partly because of Pinter's mixture of 'real and imaginary biography'. Philip Hope-Wallace in the *Guardian* argued – not for the first time – that Pinter reversed the normal pleasure of theatre in that the audience sat in total ignorance while the actors exchanged 'wreathed smiles and knowing nods of complicity'. Even Harold Hobson in the *Sunday Times* was disturbed 'by the complete absence from the play of any moral comment whatsoever'. Only Penelope Gilliatt in the *Observer* grasped the historic nature of the event: 'The opening of Harold Pinter's *The*

Homecoming was an exultant night. Quite apart from the experience of seeing a modern play produced in a style as achieved as the best we do for Shakespeare, it offered the stirring spectacle of a man in total command of his talent.'

What is significant, however, is how many people claimed the play as part of their world. A thirty-one-year-old stockbroker, replying to a questionnaire in the RSC's house magazine, wrote: 'The play was about the problems of education in an upwardly mobile society.' Joe Orton later confided to his diary that *The Homecoming* couldn't have been written without *Entertaining Mr Sloane*, which ends with a brother and sister agreeing to share the hero's sexual favours. Orton concluded that while *Sloane* sprang from the way he thought, the second act of Pinter's play wasn't true. ('Harold, I'm sure, would never share anyone sexually. I would.') But the most obvious appropriation of the play was by Jewish critics. Montague Haltrecht in the *Scotsman* saw the play explicitly as a ghetto–allegory in which characters 'hopeless of any outside help bear down on one another destructively'. And Barry Supple, a former Hackney schoolmate, wrote a review in the *Jewish Chronicle* that even today sets Pinter's teeth on edge. To Supple, the play was unequivocally a picture of East End Jewish life; one that exposed the hypocrisy of a community which attacks men who marry *shiksas*, while at the same time coveting the objects of their affection. Supple also argued that Pinter's points of reference are autobiographical:

A Pinter play is indeed a great echo–chamber in which the only sources of sound are the prosaic data of the dramatist's life-story but in which nearly all the sounds are magnified and distorted into bizarre and sometimes shocking combinations. And, as with his other works but to a greatly heightened degree, *The Homecoming* is really Harold Pinter's own homecoming.

Supple is both right and wrong. I take Pinter's point that it narrows *The Homecoming* down to see it as a specifically Jewish play; that it makes total sense in non-Jewish societies. Yet there is some truth in Supple's general observation that Pinter's reference points are autobiographical and are then invested with larger significance. All his early major plays – *The Birthday Party*, *The Hothouse*, *The Caretaker*, *The Homecoming* – were triggered, to a greater or lesser degree, by personal experience; but Pinter's genius is to apprehend the universal meaning that lies within the particular moment. This is what distinguishes the true artist from the mere recorder of events: the ability to incorporate her or his experience and at the same time transcend it. The sixty-one-year-old Ibsen, to take an obvious example, was totally infatuated by an eighteen-year-old Viennese girl Emilie Bardach, whom he met at Gossensass in the summer of 1889. Three years later Ibsen sat down to write *The Master Builder*, calling up his memory of that experience but transforming it into a much larger study of the dangerous magnetism of youth, and the hollowness and despair that often accompanies fame and success. All art has to start somewhere; as often as not, it is with individual recollection. Yet it is the moment when imagination outstrips memory that produces a universal metaphor; and so it is with Pinter, who has both the retentive memory of the true artist and the gift for allowing the inventiveness of fancy to take over. As he himself said when speaking to students in Bristol in 1962, it is a case of achieving a position where 'image can freely engender image'.

Not everyone – even among Pinter's closest friends – agrees that that does happen in *The Homecoming*. Joan Bakewell finds herself repelled by the play's cruelty and viciousness. 'How,' she asks, 'is this woman being deployed? Even if she is running rings round the men, I find that equally disgusting. She achieves independence – but at what price?' Simon Gray also told me that he thought the appropriation of the girl by the family (or is it the other way round?) was simply a way out of a theatrical impasse. 'The life of the play,' he claimed, 'is in Max and the chaos of the family. I think Harold suddenly felt: I've got to end this. Ruth is simply a convenience. She brings the work into focus for us. But sometimes an enigma is something that the writer can't resolve. Ruth isn't a sexual fantasy; she's a dramatist's fantasy. She got Harold out of a pickle. You don't know enough about her and you don't believe she'd marry a British academic.' But don't British academics ever marry whores? 'Not unless they're very lucky,' he replied.

Against this, I remember the great German director Peter Stein telling me how he happened to be in London in the summer of 1965 and that seeing *The Homecoming* had been one of the great formative influences on his career. 'I suddenly saw,' he said, 'the possibilities of witty, intellectual dialogue, of highly calculated and perfect actors, of a play-machine at work.' I agree: it was then, and it still remains, Pinter's masterpiece. It quite obviously starts with Pinter's memories of Hackney life and a fragmentary dialogue about marital disharmony, but it transforms those memories into a spectacle that recreates the cruel intimacies and daily manoeuvrings of family life with an abhorrent fascination. In Ruth, Pinter gives us not an empty cipher or a blank theatrical device, but a positive, strong-willed woman who both exposes phallocentric vanity and achieves the necessary dramatic feat of disrupting the power-structure and changing the situation.

Nine Private Worlds

How to follow up *The Homecoming*? Pinter is not the kind of writer who feels he has to capitalise on success by rushing into another play. Anyway, he didn't need to. *The Homecoming* was quickly picked up around the world with productions in Paris (with Pierre Brasseur), Berlin (with Bernhard Minetti), Geneva, Gothenburg, Munich, Bremerhaven, Amsterdam, Copenhagen, Helsinki, Stockholm and Sydney. Peter Hall's production, after running for eighteen months in the Aldwych repertory, also moved to Broadway in January 1967 where it triumphed over managerial jitters and a chilly notice from Walter Kerr in the *New York Times*. There was a legendary moment on the out-of-town tour to Boston when, after a number of customers had stomped out angrily, the producer Alexander Cohen asked Pinter 'to fix the second act'. He had chosen the wrong man. As Peter Hall recalls, 'Harold took his glasses off, his eyes glinting. "What exactly did you have in mind?" he said. It was one of the few times I have seen a Broadway producer at a loss for words. Cohen never returned to the subject.'

Aside from Kerr, a staunch Catholic who seemed perturbed by the lack of an obvious moral framework, the play was more intelligently analysed in New York than it had been in London. Richard Gilman in *Newsweek* intriguingly invoked *The Brothers Karamazov*, and Harold Clurman in the *Nation* tackled head-on Pinter's presumed iciness of tone:

> At first, one is inclined to think that he must be either wickedly unfeeling or perhaps that he has no convictions. But no. Only a prophet or a fanatic, fiercely moral, can be so damning. But Pinter is wholly of our moment: we refuse to be hortatory, to cry out, plead, condemn or call to account. Since we don't permit ourselves to 'take sides' overtly, we grin or keep our jaws so tightly clamped that it becomes hard to tell whether we are kidding or repressing pain. The mask is one of horror subdued in glacial irony.

That pins down brilliantly Pinter's ability to conceal turbulent emotion under a facade of brutal comedy.

In the years immediately following *The Homecoming*, Pinter was, as ever, busy in the world. He wrote movies, worked in television, directed and acted in the theatre (playing Lenny at Watford in 1969), and wrote *Silence* and *Landscape*, only to fall foul of the Lord Chamberlain who struck like a wounded snake in the death-throes of his role as theatrical censor. But it is clear that *The Homecoming* marks a vital turning point in Pinter's career. After 1965, the stage plays become smaller in scale if not in impact. They also turn increasingly to themes of solitude, separation, the distances which isolate human beings from each other, the subjectivity of memory. Why should this be? I suspect the reasons are both technical and personal. In a remarkably intense creative period from 1957 to 1965 Pinter had written four major plays, nine shorter works and two film scripts. He had defined his own particular world: one to do with power, territory, dominance and subservience, resistance to authority, the politics of private relationships, the magic and mystery of women. He had also exhaustively mined his own background. Having delved deeply into memories of his Hackney youth, the vagabond theatrical life, seaside digs, West London flats, the abrasiveness of East End families, he had inevitably reached some kind of watershed. Pinter had not only plundered his own past; he had also become increasingly impatient with the paraphernalia of naturalism – all those exits and entrances – and wanted to pare the dramatic situation down to its absolute essence. As Beckett once observed, 'The only possible development for the artist is in the sense of depth. The artistic tendency is not expansion but a contraction.'

Pinter's growing preoccupation with solitude and separation reflects the change in his own circumstances. After the success of *The Caretaker* he had moved, with astonishing rapidity, from desperate poverty to comfortable affluence. And although he never forgot his old friends, the move to Hanover Terrace in Regent's Park in 1964 seems to have had an extraordinarily insulating effect. As Pinter himself says, neither he nor Vivien was born to a life of much social entertaining; and no one who visited them in their new house remembers it as a place overflowing with communal warmth. The abiding impression, in fact, is one of claustrophobic grandeur. Antonia Fraser recalls, 'It was the grandest house I've ever been in. I went there once and it was absolutely, totally silent. I don't think I'd have understood *No Man's Land* if I hadn't seen it. Every room was immaculate with this terrible silence.' Another visitor remembers that the house was so structured that Pinter had to ring down on the intercom to communicate from his sixth-floor study. He recalls a professional chat with Pinter being interrupted by Daniel coming up the stairs clutching a bottle of white wine and announcing, with sharp irony, 'I'm the dumb waiter.' And Pinter himself, in a rare personal interview with Kathleen Tynan in the *Evening Standard* in 1968, confirmed this image of opulent solitude:

I was a morbid youth. But I had a remarkably enjoyable association with five other boys. It was a great relief, I remember, that they knew what I was about. Ruthless mutual confrontations. Out of that group two have remained my closest friends. Other friends are theatre people like Robert Shaw and Donald Pleasence. But I live a pretty closed life. I sit and talk to my wife a great deal in the kitchen. We're pretty tight as a family. People don't come round except by specific invitation. Nobody just rings the door and comes in.

It is clear that Pinter's domestic life in the post-*Homecoming* period was increasingly strained and reclusive. In the monastic splendour of Hanover Terrace, his marriage to Vivien had deteriorated even further. It reached a crisis point in 1968 when he offered the female role in *Landscape* to Peggy Ashcroft. Pinter, a loving father, was also worried about Daniel who by then was at St Paul's School for Boys, but who showed a disposition towards solitude. Pinter had wanted his son to go to Bedales as a boarder simply to acquire some friends, but Daniel refused to go. Given all these factors, the change in tone and style that overtakes Pinter's work after 1965 becomes easier to understand. For one thing, there was the knowledge that with *The Homecoming* he had reached some kind of aesthetic terminus: that, as he said, he 'couldn't any longer stay in the room with this bunch of people who opened doors and came in and went out'. But, given Pinter's heightened self-awareness, he could hardly be indifferent to the growing gulf between himself and Vivien or the bizarre, reclusive strangeness of family life in Regent's Park.

Pinter did, in fact, go through a low period after the success of *The Homecoming*. He found himself jotting odds and ends down on scraps of paper: nothing happened, nothing flowed. He was kept busy, however, by a commission from producer Ivan Foxwell to write the film script of *The Quiller Memorandum*, Elleston Trevor's first novel to be written under the pseudonym of 'Adam Hall' and originally entitled *The Berlin Memorandum*. The film was part of the espionage-cinema vogue of the 1960s that included the screen versions of Ian Fleming's *From Russia with Love*, John Le Carré's *The Spy Who Came in from the Cold* and Len Deighton's *Funeral in Berlin*. In anyone else's hands it might have been a routine piece of work: the story of an agent dispatched to Berlin to uncover the base of a neo-Nazi movement and using a local schoolteacher, Inge, as his point of entry, thereby confirming her involvement with the group. But while sticking closely to the conventions of the genre, it also becomes a classic Pinter film: one concerned with the ambiguity of action, female resilience and mystery, and the need for resistance to authoritarianism of whatever kind. In adapting other people's work, Pinter constantly reveals his own obsessions.

Pinter makes many crucial changes in transferring the book to the screen. As always, the first-person narrative goes. Adam Hall's Quiller is a veteran undercover British agent who sought to free concentration-camp inmates in Nazi Germany and who is now mopping up Nazi remnants in Berlin. In the film he is an American (the admirable George Segal) with no detailed past or visible future, and with an attitude of sceptical hostility towards his current British spymasters. Even more significantly, in the book he is described as 'bold, brave, quick-witted, and ruthless, impervious to torture and sodium-amytal interrogation'; in Pinter's version he is much less of a Bond-style superman and more of an obdurate professional determined to do things his own way.

Pinter makes the hero more human and at the same time excises much of the book's heavy-handed symbolism. In one of the key sections of the story, Quiller allows himself to fall into the hands of the neo-Nazis, led by the aristocratic 'Oktober' (Max von Sydow), by whom he is interrogated under drugs. Far from being impervious to the numbing influence of sodium-amytal, Pinter's Quiller initially deflects his torturers' questions through sardonic humour. When they demand to know his identity, he is mischievously defiant, claiming his surname is Canetti – a Bulgarian writer famous for his anti-authoritarianism – and that his mother's maiden name was O'Reilly. And when the truth-drug is administered, Quiller steadies himself by fixed concentration on a nude painting on the wall. In the book, the painting is a vulgarly explicit symbol of Nazi hypocrisy. Pinter typically strips away such needless italicising and simply tells us in the camera script that Quiller focuses on 'an oil-painting of a nude blonde, leaning across a chair, on the far wall'. As Pauline Kael once wrote 'Pinter's art is the art of taking away'.

In fact, the skill of Pinter's script lies in the way it shows Quiller caught in a no man's land between the insidious ordinariness of the neo-Nazis and the manipulative coldness of the British spymasters: both sides use masks to conceal their real feelings. On the German side, the pivotal figure is the schoolteacher Inge, who represents not just the conventional love-interest but the smiling, duplicitous face of neo-Nazism. Throughout the film we are never quite sure whether Inge (the darkly mysterious Senta Berger) leads Quiller towards the secret Nazi hideaway out of mutual sexual attraction or because she wants to neutralise him. Even when Oktober has both Quiller and Inge within his clutches and tries to blackmail the former by saying that he will release the girl in exchange for information about the site of Berlin Control, we are still unsure of her precise status. Is she with Quiller or against him? Only after Quiller has escaped and the Nazi base has been raided without the supposedly captive Inge being found do we realise the truth: that she is part of the movement. In a superb final scene – *echt* Pinter, in that every line is loaded with meaning – Quiller revisits Inge in her classroom. She knows that he knows and he knows that she knows that he knows. At one point Quiller advises Inge to take things a little easier to which she replies, 'Oh no. I have my work to do. I must do it. I want to do it.' By that time, it is clear that her mission is the indoctrination of future generations of German children and in the telling final shot she calls to her pupils who collect lovingly around her. Pinter's direction tells us: '*They talk eagerly to her. She listens to them, smiling.*' The process goes on.

The film uses a genre-plot to make a political point: that the post-war German return to normality conceals unassuaged dreams of domination. But Pinter – much more than Hall – also highlights the masked indifference to human feeling of the Western democracies. In particular, Pinter uses the consumption of food as a constant metaphor for a kind of moral blankness. He shows two Whitehall spymasters coolly setting up the dangerous Berlin mission over a club lunch. Pol (Alec Guinness), who is the head of Berlin Control, gives Quiller his orders while blithely munching sandwiches in the 1936 Olympic Stadium. And their next meeting takes place in a café where Quiller describes his initial penetration of the neo-Nazi base while Pol enjoys coffee and cakes. Their dialogue also has a characteristic Pinter obliqueness:

QUILLER: Met a man called Oktober.
POL: Oh yes.
QUILLER: Know him?
POL: We've never actually met.
QUILLER: At the end of our conversation he ordered them to kill me.
POL: And did they?
  (*Pause.*)
QUILLER: No.
POL: Odd.

Typically, the scene ends with Pol taking a currant from a cake and using it as a symbol of Quiller's position in the gap between two opposing forces; he then pops the currant into his mouth and eats it. And in view of Pinter's savage denunciations of American foreign policy in the 1980s and 1990s, there is a strangely prophetic exchange when Inge describes the neo-Nazis' dreams of domination. Quiller, with deceptive irony, replies: 'Well listen, I don't think there's anything basically wrong with that is there? I mean we believe the same in the States. We believe our country should be strong. I wouldn't say dominant – I mean we don't want to dominate anybody – but I would say strong. Yes, I'd say that.' Pinter wrote that in 1965; in 1994, he was to take the argument several stages further in a letter to the *New York Review of Books* drawing parallels between the mass murder inspired by Hitler, Stalin and Mao, and the practical consequences of American foreign policy. But although written in the context of the 1960s, what is impressive about *The Quiller Memorandum* is Pinter's ability to see that the Western democracies in countering the evil of neo-Nazism operate with the same veiled coldness and indifference to the individual. Michael Anderson was the film's director; Pinter is the real *auteur*.

Pinter's film script is a great improvement on the original novel. Indeed, Mark Auburn has argued in the *Pinter Review* that Adam Hall's subsequent Quiller books were tightened and sharpened as a result of the screenplay. In one of them, *Quiller KGB* (1989), the author even pays conscious tribute to his adapter by characterising a conversation as 'Pinteresque, loaded with all the things that couldn't be said'. But it is a general truth that Pinter's work for the cinema is much more than a way of filling in time between plays or simply exploiting his talent. His film scripts are works of art in their own right. They are models of verbal economy. Although invariably adaptations of existing novels, they express a strong personal vision. And in the process of rethinking a story in filmic terms, they often correct some weakness in the original characterisation or structure.

After completing *The Quiller Memorandum*, Pinter quickly got to work in the summer of 1965 on his next film script, an adaptation of Nicholas Mosley's novel *Accident* which was to be directed by Joe Losey. Originally, Sam Spiegel had bought the rights to Mosley's book, but sensing that the American mogul would want to leave his visible thumbprints all over the finished film, Losey and Pinter persuaded him to relinquish the rights for $30,000 and a percentage of the profits. Eventually the film was produced by Sidney Box's London Independent Productions who put up £150,000 with a matching investment from the National Film Finance Corporation. It is a measure of Pinter's growing prestige as a film-writer that in 1963 he had received a modest £3,000 for *The Servant* as against the £11,500 paid to the original author Robin Maugham; for *Accident* he was paid a total of £20,000 while Nicholas Mosley was paid £2,700 for the rights.

Like the book, the film is about a complex network of erotic relationships seen against the background of an Oxford summer. But without destroying the fabric of Mosley's novel, Pinter makes several radical alterations. The movie starts with a skidding car crash near the home of an Oxford philosophy don, Stephen Jervis. One of the car's occupants – an aristocratic student

William, who was on his way to see Stephen – is dead. The driver – a magnetically beautiful Austrian princess called Anna – is rescued by Stephen from the crash. He takes her home, calms her down, deliberately omits to tell the police that she was in the car at the time. We then flash back in time to discover how the film's three principal male characters have all been disastrously embroiled with Anna. Stephen himself – married with two children and conscious of his advancing years – has not only been her tutor, but also ineffectually in love with her. He finds out that Charley – a worldly TV don who is both his best friend and dark rival – has been having a clandestine affair with the enigmatic Anna. Meanwhile William, who has good looks and the heroic innocence of youth, has secretly become engaged to her only days before the crash. Towards the end of the film we revert to present time and see Stephen, in the aftermath of the accident, making love to the traumatised Anna before smuggling her back into college. The next morning he and Charley – unaware of the full story of the night's preceding events – go to see her in her rooms and find she is leaving Oxford for good. Charley is mystified and deflated. Stephen, having attained his sexual dream, is left morally guilty. In the final shot, which completes the film's circular structure, we see Stephen in his drive playing the role of family man, but over the soundtrack we hear the reverberant sound of the car crash which will forever haunt his life.

Pinter's most basic alteration to Mosley's novel is to dispense with Stephen's first-person narration: to turn the self-conscious observer into the objectified protagonist. Evidently Pinter and Losey discussed the idea of telling the whole story from Stephen's point-of-view through a series of mental flashes; that notion was quickly discarded. 'Almost every possible mental flash', Pinter wrote to Losey in July 1965, 'seemed to me, while working, unnecessary, too explicit, even crude. I couldn't see room for them, I don't know. Eventually I decided to go the whole hog and tell the whole thing without them. . . In principle I've tried to concentrate on a hard appraisal of the happenings and keep it objective.'

'Hard appraisal' is exactly right. In the book, we inevitably sympathise with Stephen. In the film, where he is expertly played by Dirk Bogarde, he becomes an archetypally Pinterish example of male insecurity. As a philosopher, he asks questions rather than provides answers. As a careerist don, he is outpointed at every turn by Charley; hilariously so in a scene where he goes for an interview with Charley's TV producer only to be fobbed off by a brutal sidekick played, with vindictive relish, by Pinter himself. And, as a man, there is something slightly wan about his adulteries – in a phone booth his finger indecisively dithers before he rings an old mistress – and furtive about his lust: Pinter plots beautifully a scene in a punt where Stephen is aroused by the curve of Anna's reclining body and even the fuzz of her armpit. Mosley's subjective Stephen is a man who falls apart as he confronts the human mess created by academic games-playing: Pinter's objectively seen hero is an Oxford nearly-man who retreats behind the ambiguities of philosophy and who is forced – by accident, as it were – to engage with the real world.

Pinter's most controversial change is to have Stephen sleep with Anna after the accident and to exclude Charley from his moral calculations. In the book there is no physical contact between Stephen and Anna, but Pinter's drastic change to the original follows logically from the decision to objectify Stephen. Stephen's virtual rape of the traumatised Anna – while his wife is in hospital giving birth – is further proof of his weakness, not his strength. And his exclusion of Charley from any of the deliberations about perjury means that he alone has to bear the future burden of moral guilt. In a sense, Pinter distorts the original; at the same time, he makes it dramatically stronger.

What is significant is that Pinter's own moral conscience was aroused by the need to make radical changes. He and Mosley had a very friendly lunch where they discussed certain basic questions about the story ('Was the girl Anna a victim or a bitch?' Both, they agreed). After he had finished the screenplay, Pinter sent it to Mosley with an accompanying letter which he asked him to read only after he had gone through the script. David Caute in his biography of Losey describes it as a *mea culpa* letter. In fact, it seems to me to reveal Pinter's scrupulous concern for a fellow-writer's feelings and his need to explain the precise motives for his changes:

I must tell you that I worked very hard to follow your ending at all points to begin with and in fact finished a complete first draft following that course. But there was something *wrong*. This of course could have been entirely my fault, my inadequacy, probably was, but the long debate between Stephen and Charley simply did not work, convince, sustain itself in dramatic terms. A novel is so different. You have so much more room. A dramatic structure makes its own unique demands. They're unavoidable. Anyway, the more the whole thing grew in me, the more one fact sank in and finally clarified itself – that is, that Stephen, ultimately, must be alone in his final complicity with Anna, or so it seemed to me. And, in many long discussions, to Losey. It seemed to follow; it seemed to be logical. Dramatically, it economised and compressed, and by narrowing the focus achieved a greater intensity. Or so we felt. So that Charley finds himself staring at a blank wall. And Stephen has to, will have to, carry his own can, alone, with whatever the can holds . . . Clearly there has been a certain switch of viewpoint in the passing of your work to me. Not too much, I very much hope, but one inevitable in that we're two very different men, two different writers. I have willingly 'distorted' nothing – couldn't do that since I admire the book so much – but yes, there's been a change. But has there??!! We spoke once about the notion of 'correct' or 'incorrect' moral attitudes in Stephen at the end. But these are terms. I haven't attempted to work in these terms or stand as a judge. I have, I think, seen it as something that happens, that has happened, something that has taken place. But where possibly there is a shift of interpretation between us is that your view at the end is optimistic and I haven't felt it as such. But if I do not feel the end as optimistic, neither do I feel it as pessimistic. Something had taken place, something that will always live, on all levels.

That's an honest, revealing letter: one that shows Pinter's tortured concern to do the right thing; also his crucial belief that characters should be defined by their actions rather than judged by their author. (As Chekhov wrote in a letter in 1888: 'The artist ought not to judge his characters or what they say but be only an unbiased witness.') But in a sense, the greatest change Pinter makes to Mosley's book is in the quality of the dialogue. In Mosley's original, the dialogue is swift, sharp and staccato; it's also frequently accompanied by Stephen's slightly tiresome, free-associating internal reflections. But in Pinter's version, as in his best plays, every line has a tactical purpose, wins or yields an inch of ground. Nothing is innocent of intention. The clearest example comes late in the story. Stephen, having just had sex in London with the provost's daughter, returns home to discover Charley sleeping with Anna. He then goes to visit his pregnant wife at his mother-in-law's house. In the book, the scene takes place in a bedroom and is filled with subliminal, guilt-ridden images flashing through Stephen's mind: precipices, horses, the wind in fir trees. On screen, the scene is visually idyllic – a nice house, a manicured lawn, two chairs by the side of lapping water – but the dialogue is pared-down, ruthless and economic as Stephen tells the truth about Charley while lying about his own reasons for returning home drunk:

STEPHEN: Oh, I had dinner with Francesca. You remember. You remember Francesca?

ROSALIND: Yes.

STEPHEN: Just gave her a ring, you know. It was quite pleasant.

(*Pause*.)

ROSALIND: He's sleeping with her, is he?

STEPHEN: Who?

ROSALIND: Charley. With Anna.
STEPHEN: Of course.
ROSALIND: How pathetic.
STEPHEN: What do you mean?
ROSALIND: Poor stupid old man.
STEPHEN: He's not old.
ROSALIND: Stupid bastard.

Classic Pinter: every line is fraught with a sense of battle-advantage, especially as played on screen by Bogarde and Vivien Merchant. Bogarde's statement that he simply rang Francesca is full of hollow evasiveness. The pause that follows is just long enough to register Rosalind's sense of insult to her intelligence. Rosalind's next line ('He's sleeping with her, is he?') is a calculated ploy: it applies to Charley and Anna, but could just as well refer back to Stephen and Francesca, as Bogarde shows by a tiny start and turn of his head. Every subsequent line of Rosalind's is an overt reference to Charley, but a covert demolition of her husband. 'Poor stupid old man' is especially wounding. Throughout the film, Stephen is haunted by the idea of age: his own and Charley's. After he has fallen into the Cherwell from a punt in front of Anna he snarls at William: 'I'm getting old. Don't you understand? Old.' And when he discovers that Charley has got into his house through a lavatory window he bluntly tells him: 'You're a bit old for that.' Rosalind's harping on Charley's age becomes an oblique assault on himself; and her 'Stupid bastard' is a succinct put-down of the folly of middle-aged lust. As in any Pinter duologue, there is agent and victim: often the roles switch in mid-stream, but here Rosalind conclusively skewers her husband. The same scene in the book focuses on Stephen's internal remorse; here, he is quietly demolished.

The strategic battle of conversation is echoed in *Accident* in the constant emphasis on sport and games. Punting may be recreation rather than sport, but it ends in Stephen's watery humiliation. A game of weekend tennis exposes Charley's childish crudity and possessive intimacy as he serves a ball into Anna's backside, as well as William's youthful power. But sport-as-metaphor really takes off in two crucially juxtaposed scenes late in the film. In the first, Stephen is coerced by William ('You must play. Only the old men watch') during a country-house weekend into playing a primitive mix of indoor rugger and Eton Wall Game. The background – actually Syon House, with its heraldic crests, tiled floor and life-size copy of the Apollo Belvedere — expresses the aristocratic ideal: the game itself is a thuggish ritual ('a communal buggery . . . a bowel with a gut gone', is Pinter's vivid description) that ends with Stephen savagely kneeing William in the face and the latter losing possession of the cushion-ball. The scene (not in the book) works brilliantly on all levels: as a symbol of the revenge of age on youth, and of the adolescent brutality of the upper classes. Pinter cuts straight from that to an Oxford cricket field in the shadow of Magdalen Tower. The tonal contrast is explicit: we move from the vicious shambles of rugger-buggery to the contained and ordered violence of cricket. And the personal roles are now reversed: William is a stylish stroke-player and Stephen, with his gown and brolly, an afternoon bystander – a sexual bystander too, since it is on the shadowed boundary that Anna first tells Stephen she is going to marry William: a blunt conclusion to his romantic dreams and Charley's affair. Pinter – as in all his films with Losey – uses games not just to give the action a specific context. Sport becomes an objective way of expressing character and of exploring shifting power-relationships. You only have to watch Pinter patrolling the boundary when his own cricket team is up against it ('Go for the jugular, Gaieties!' I once heard him cry) to realise that for him sport is no laughing matter.

Accident is, by any standards, a wondrous film. Not a line is wasted. Every encounter is freighted with meaning. And the circular structure means that the noise of the car crash not only dangles in the imagination throughout the story, but lends the characters' sexual games-playing a crucifying irony. My only cavil is that professional obligation all too rarely impinges on emotional crisis. Oxford, like any university, is a place where lectures, tutorials (in the book, Stephen has eighteen pupils whom he sees for an hour a week) and admin overlap with private passions. That aspect goes uncovered. And Losey's direction, for all its finesse, offers a rather romantic, dreaming-spires, *Zuleika Dobson* view of the place. I certainly can't remember ever being offered a glass of dry sherry in the midst of a tutorial.

What is dismaying, however, is that a film of this calibre never got far beyond the art-house circuit. John Russell Taylor in *The Times* spoke for the majority of London critics when he wrote: 'Harold Pinter has recreated, rather than adapted, substituting for Mr Mosley's empurpled passages of Dylan Thomasy free association a scrupulously trim and spare dialogue and an action pared down to barest essentials.' The only dissenting voice was Robert Robinson in the *Sunday Telegraph* who wrote: 'Losey works with film and Pinter with words and, though Pinter's dialogue is frugal, it attracts an immense amount of attention to itself. It is a sophisticated, highly wrought, *literary* idiom and in *Accident* it seemed to displace far more than its own weight in the film.' It's an odd objection on two counts. Scrutiny of the script shows that, although Pinter obviously works in words, he also thinks in terms of filmic images. Witness the almost wordless scene on the punt. And from Robinson's description you might think Pinter was writing in some high-mandarin style. In fact, what counts is the subtextual undertow to surface banalities, so that a line like Stephen's invitation to Anna – 'Would you like to come to my house for lunch on Sunday?' – is charged with meaning.

If any critic understood one of the key points Pinter was getting at in the film – the seductively destructive power women exercise over men – it was Penelope Gilliatt writing in *Life* magazine. As played by the blankly beautiful Jacqueline Sassard, Anna is part doe-eyed innocent, part upmarket Lulu: a point Gilliatt eloquently grasped. She wrote: 'The mute women in Pinter's works who look like men's suffering objects are often the most powerful combatants of all.' Pinter, significantly, has ringed this phrase in coloured pen in his cuttings-book as if it carried special weight. Gilliatt continues:

> *Accident* revolves around one of them, a girl of unbeatable negligence. She is a numb-spirited Austrian university undergraduate who characteristically crawls out of a car crash that kills her fiancé and who sustains no emotional scar at all from having caused a pile-up in the lives of five other people. She will obviously cause and endure catastrophes all her life, protected by a pristine lack of imagination and a drowsy greed. These allow her to interpret the fact that three men are simultaneously in love with her as less of a responsibility than a due.

Gilliatt is much more censorious and judgemental than Pinter is in the film; but her argument about the silent strength of his female characters is spot on. Yet despite glowing reviews and a clutch of film-festival prizes – including the Grand Prix Spécial du Jury at Cannes in 1967 – the film was a financial disaster, thanks partly to lousy distribution both in and out of London. I remember seeing it at the Odeon Kensington where it was presented as one half of a double bill. David Caute records a royalty statement from London Independent Producers to 31 May 1968 showing gross UK receipts of £43,010 and gross overseas receipts of £95,153; and that against a budget of £272,811. *Accident* may have been a financial flop; but it confirmed Pinter's absolute mastery of screen storytelling and his ability to turn the adaptation of other people's work into both a creative and critical act.

As *Accident* proves, Pinter's work for the cinema uses skills honed and perfected in the theatre: in particular, an awareness of the importance of subtext, of the dreams and desires that lie hidden under the camouflage of everyday conversational exchange. But Pinter's work for the screen also feeds back into his stage plays. His increasing involvement with film and television in the 1960s made him aware of the camera's ability to handle fantasy, memory, rapid shifts in time and the subjectiveness of perception: in particular, the contrast between a character's individual perspective and external reality. Up to and even including *The Homecoming*, his stage plays are still formally derived from his work in rep; the works after 1965 – including *Landscape*, *Silence*, *Old Times*, *No Man's Land* and *Betrayal* – are more clearly influenced by his experience of film and television. He attempts in dramatic form something very close to what James Joyce and Virginia Woolf accomplished in the novel: the theatrical equivalent of the interior monologue.

A work that stems from this transitional period is *The Basement* which was shown on BBC TV in February 1967, the same month that *Accident* was released for the cinema. In fact, the chronology is a little misleading. *The Basement* was conceived in 1963 when the American publishers Grove Press had one of those ideas that sound seductive in theory but rarely work in practice: a three-part film project – a kind of Cinema of the Absurd – comprising new work from Beckett, Ionesco and Pinter. But the idea never really got off the ground. Beckett's contribution *Film* was in fact made and provided Buster Keaton with one of his last roles. For all that, it was booed when shown at the New York Film Festival in 1965 and was not much better received in London ('personally I think *Film* is a load of old bosh' wrote Dilys Powell in the *Sunday Times*). Ionesco's script *The Hard-Boiled Egg* to this day remains uncracked. And Pinter's contribution *The Compartment* lay dormant until he rewrote it for television as *The Basement*. It is not one of his major works, but it is significant from three points of view. It reveals an obsessive reworking of his earliest theme involving the control of a room. It shows him switching, with great ease, between internal fantasy and external reality. And it demonstrates, very amusingly, how Pinter transforms an experience from life into art: nothing is ever wasted.

The Basement takes us back to the world of *Kullus* and *The Examination*. The owner of a room, who bases his identity on his furnishings, his accessories, his safe retreat, finds his space occupied and invaded by an old friend whose female partner has a disruptive effect on their relationship. This time the owner is called Law (the name of one of Pinter's old Hackney friends), who sits in his basement reading Persian love manuals; the new arrival (played by Pinter in the TV production) is Stott, who brings with him a young girl called Jane whom initially he keeps waiting outside in the rain. Law welcomes them both in: they proceed to undress and make love, unembarrassed by Law's presence. What follows is a mixture of reality and fantasy, revealing Law's deep envy of and hostility towards Stott, and profound wish to possess Jane. The tension between the two men builds up to a sequence – taking place in Law's mind – in which they square up to each other with broken, jagged milk bottles while Jane calmly prepares *two* cups of coffee, implying that she, along with the coffee, goes to the victor. Pinter then cuts to a record on a turntable and a replay of the opening scene, except that this time Law, looking menacing and potent, is the one outside in the rain with Jane waiting to be admitted by the weak, almost wimpish Stott.

Thematically it seems to me a retreat to the early Pinter of rooms, territory, rival males, female catalysts: a bit old hat, in fact; almost 'Pinteresque'. If the work is an advance, it is mainly on the technical level in that it shows Pinter using the freedom of the camera to explore the violent contrast between objective reality and Law's burgeoning fantasies. His room is transmogrified first into a place filled with light Scandinavian furniture, then into a dream of neo-Renaissance opulence, and finally into a stripped, bare-walled battle-ground. For the specialist, Christopher C. Hudgins has provided the definitive analysis of the play, precisely denoting Law's increasing recourse to a Mittyesque fantasy world:

Paradoxically, Law's fantasy of himself as Stott indicates his complete defeat, his loss of his room. We know, from the previous action, that Law would never be brave enough to face that harsh rain. In R. D. Laing's terms, like Stanley in *The Birthday Party*, Law is a victim of what he has feared in the first place, 'engulfment' by another, stronger personality. But he has conditioned that engulfment himself, almost encouraged it. Courage to confront one's dangerous experience more fully is the television play's implied alternative or 'answer' to such a horrifying surrender.

I think that's right – the play is about the need to embrace life and resist takeover – but it also shows once again Pinter's ability to seize on a moment from his own experience and invest it with dramatic significance. One of the early realistic scenes from the play gives proof of Stott's gamesmanship as he and Law race across a cow-pasture at night:

> *Exterior. Field. Evening. Winter.*
> STOTT *and* LAW. JANE *one hundred yards across the field. She holds a scarf.*
> LAW (*shouting*): Hold the scarf up. When you drop it, we run.
> (*She holds the scarf up.*
> LAW *rubs his hands.* STOTT *looks at him.*)
> STOTT: Are you quite sure you want to do this?
> LAW: Of course I'm sure.
> JANE: On your marks!
> (STOTT *and* LAW *get on their marks.*)
> Get set!
> (*They get set.*
> JANE *drops scarf.*)

Go!

(LAW *runs.* STOTT *stays still.*

LAW, *going fast, turns to look for* STOTT*; off balance, stumbles, falls, hits his chin on the ground.*

Lying flat, he looks back at STOTT.)

LAW: Why didn't you run?

Donald Pleasence recalled the exact origins of this scene with great clarity. 'It all took place in New Haven in 1961 on the pre-Broadway tour of *The Caretaker*. It was late August. Ninety-five degrees. Harold, myself and Robert Shaw – who had by then taken over the role of Aston – used to go out every night after the show. We'd go to a bar and then have ham and eggs in a diner. We made this particular one into a replica of the Hemingway diner in *The Killers* – a favourite story of Harold's and of all of us. We could even repeat the dialogue line for line. Anyway, we went out one night and Robert suddenly challenged Harold to a 100-yard sprint. Robert was always very serious about sport, but Harold of course was a champion runner at school. I don't think Robert knew this. He was quite sure he was going to win. I was the guy with the handkerchief starting them off. Anyway, Harold went off from the starting place like an electrified rabbit and Robert just stood stock-still in amazement. When I asked him why, he just said, "Oh, fuck it – I just didn't want to show him up."' Pinter verifies the truth of the story: 'Shaw didn't run. I ran. Halfway along I fell over because I was off balance. I said, "Where is my opponent?" Shaw said, "I didn't want to beat you, you bas-tard." I took the opposite view which was that he knew he was going to lose. We'll never know.'

It may seem a trivial incident triggered by late-night booze in New Haven, but it offers further proof of Pinter's retentive memory and ability to see the significance of his own life. It also feeds into the world of *The Basement* in that it demonstrates how the man who refuses to participate – Shaw in life, Stott in the play – gains a tactical advantage through untested superiority. Indeed, it's the pivotal scene in the play in that it leads to Law's unavailing attempts to evict Stott and his conflation of fantasy and reality. And although Pinter and Shaw remained close friends – and even formed a production company called Glasshouse Productions with Donald Pleasence to stage *The Man in the Glass Booth* in 1967 – one senses it was a friendship shaded by competitive rivalry. As Pinter says, life is an endless battle for positions.

Pinter's own life in the late 1960s was one of strange dislocation: of con-stant activity in the public arena of theatre, film, television and radio, but also of growing awareness that his marriage was inexorably falling apart. His only consolation lay in an ongoing affair with a prominent TV journalist, but even that concluded in an amicable parting towards the end of decade and was replaced, in Pinter's own words, by a series of 'intermittent sexual relationships'.

Pinter immersed himself in work as a protection against his domestic solitude and private unhappiness. His diary for 1967, for instance, was exceptionally busy, involving a good deal of transatlantic commuting. In January he was in New York for the Broadway opening of *The Homecoming*. February saw the screening of both *Accident* and *The Basement*. In May he was back on Broadway when *The Homecoming* won a Tony Award for Best Play. July saw the London opening of his production of *The Man in the Glass Booth* at the St Martin's. He then joined Vivien in Stratford-upon-Avon where she was playing Lady Macbeth for Peter Hall in an ill-starred production of the Scottish play. Indeed, it was in the depths of the Warwickshire countryside that he sat down to write *Landscape*. By October, he was back on Broadway for the opening of *The Birthday Party* at the Booth Theater.

Pinter was in increasing demand. At the same time, writing was becoming more and more difficult: a fact that may explain a growing testiness at the process of examination-by-interview and at critical imperceptiveness. My own bizarre first encounter with Pinter took place, in fact, the night after the opening of *The Man in the Glass Booth* when I interviewed him and Robert Shaw on live TV. Shaw's play was a tough moral thriller which raised the question, through the trial of a New York tycoon who poses as a concentration-camp guard, as to whether the Germans should be absolved for the killing of the Jews. The play raised big issues, but was patronisingly put down by the overnight critics. Although I had not written about the play, as the deputy to *The Times* drama critic Irving Wardle I was deemed guilty by association, and I recall being trapped in a hostile pincer-movement from the two heavyweights Shaw and Pinter, with which I was ill-equipped to cope. After a pretty disastrous interview, Shaw and Pinter wrung from me Wardle's telephone number so that they could give him a severe bollocking. I thanked my lucky stars that the mild-mannered Irving was not at home.

In October that same year *The Birthday Party* was well received by the Broadway critics, not least by the supremely intelligent Jack Kroll on *Newsweek* who saw the influence on Pinter of Eliot's *Sweeney Agonistes*, with its ritualised dialogue and evocation of mortal terror. But the play left the matinée-ladies bothered and bewildered ('What's with this Pinter? Why?') as hilariously recorded by William Goldman in his book *The Season*. Goldman went on to check out Pinter's reaction:

It's a bloody big bore when they can't accept a thing for what happens on stage. On the whole, the what's-it-all-about business is more pronounced over here. It's about what the people do on the stage. Otherwise, you could just put a poster up on stage, couldn't you? This scene is about . . . the next scene is about . . . I'm not a sociologist; I'm just a writer. And I don't conceptualise very much. Never before and very little after . . . This what's-it-about business – one regrets it. I'm doing a play now [*Landscape*]; it's my first in three years and it means a great deal to me. I've done less and less writing for the stage. Writing becomes more difficult the older you get, at least it does for me. I found some 1950 poems of mine recently; I was astonished by the freedom I had, the energy, a complete uncaringness about form. I can't write that way any more. I'm thirty-seven now. I feel as if I'm eighty.

Pinter's creative anxiety comes across in that interview. So too does his equivocal relationship with America and its audiences. He obviously enjoys the recognition his work receives in the States. Indeed, it's a measure of his New York fame that in Stephen Sondheim's musical *Company* (1970), the Ladies Who Lunch include 'a matinée, a Pinter play' high on their list of pretensions to chic. But since the late 1970s, Pinter has also grown increasingly critical of American foreign policy and domestic hypocrisy. His ambivalent attitude to the States was already detectable, however, as early as October 1968 in a highly revealing interview he gave to the *New York Times* while directing the Broadway production of *The Man in the Glass Booth*. In 1968 the notorious Democratic Convention in Chicago took place when Mayor Daley called in the National Guard to suppress – with the utmost ruthlessness – the protests of students, pacifists and New Left intellectuals. At the same time, it was a period of aesthetic revolution in which the sanctity of text and the stability of the actor–audience relationship was being challenged by groups such as the Living Theatre, the Open Theatre and La Mama. What is fascinating is Pinter's mixture of artistic rigour and political libertarianism; to put it crudely, you could say he was on the right aesthetically and on the left politically. Proudly displaying a black-leather case that contained a portable bar with tiny ice bucket, glasses and liquor, Pinter launched a serious attack on New York avant-garde theatre: 'Last year,' he said,' I went to the American Place Theatre to see Sam Shepard's play *La Turista*. Right in the middle of the performance one of the actors suddenly left the stage and charged up the aisle inviting members of the audience to feel his muscle. I was furious. I watched this actor moving about the theatre and suddenly my spine chilled because I knew eventually he was going to come over to me.

Sure enough, he did. All I could do was give him a look of utter devastation; he ultimately cast down his eyes and moved on. This kind of theatre produces propagandists who spout love and freedom and openness. But that's empty phraseology. They love themselves so terribly. I don't,' he murmured and drank deeply, 'love myself.'

What Pinter clearly detested was the rank hypocrisy of these aesthetic bullies. It was the same quality of double-think that coloured his reaction to the infamous Chicago Convention where, as Norman Mailer memorably wrote, 'it was as if the Democratic Party had broken in two before the eyes of a nation like Melville's whale charging right out to sea'. As an outsider, Pinter's reaction was one of appalled horror: 'I did watch a bit of the Democratic Convention on television,' he said, 'and I couldn't believe it. If this is the American democratic process, I thought . . . Do you recall the keynote speech that was made by the delegate from Hawaii? He ended it with something like, "To some of you aloha means hello, to some of you aloha means goodbye, to me it means I love you." Everyone began cheering him because he loved them and outside there was violence and tear-gas on the streets and he was saying, "Aloha means I love you." We have an old saying in London – Then what does that make me? Shamus to the pope of China.' It is possible to date Pinter's disillusion with the double standards of American politics from that vicarious experience of the Democratic Convention.

Back home, Pinter had also been having his own troubles with a peculiarly British form of hypocrisy: the powers of censorship exercised over the theatre by the Lord Chamberlain. In the autumn of 1967 Pinter had completed a new play *Landscape*. The intention was for Peter Hall to direct it at the Aldwych, but the Lord Chamberlain, Lord Cobbold, whose arbitrary power of censorship was due to be terminated under the Theatres Act which became law in September 1968, was digging in his heels over the use of the phrases 'fuck all' and 'bugger'. He refused to grant *Landscape* a licence. Pinter was equally obdurate and refused to alter the text. He'd just have to wait till after the Lord Chamberlain's demise and in February 1968 wrote to Peter Hall: 'All things being equal, including that cunt the Lord Chamberlain, do I take it you still see December as a practical date?' A week later he wrote to Sir George Farmer, the RSC's chairman, thanking him for his personal intervention with Lord Cobbold, but adamantly sticking by the word bugger: 'How childish the whole thing is and what a pity one word is now between us and public performance.' In the event, *Landscape* had its première on the uncensorious BBC Third Programme on 25 April 1968 in a production directed by Guy Vaesen, with Eric Porter and Peggy Ashcroft. Eventually Pinter wrote an accompanying play, *Silence*, and the double bill was staged at the Aldwych in July 1969. Pinter had, you might say, been badly buggered about.

Silence and *Landscape* represent a change of direction for Pinter. They offer cross-cut monologues rather than genuine verbal exchange, dispense with exits and entrances, are distilled poetic evocations of separation and solitude. Pinter seems to be reaching out for a simpler, more direct form of theatre. Technically, he was influenced by Beckett's *Play*, with three characters in identical funeral urns, and by his own discovery of the camera's capacity to convey interior monologue. Emotionally, he was affected by the circumstances of his own life: the knowledge that marital happiness was increasingly becoming a distant memory. The idea that couples, as they grow apart, even start to create alternate pasts surfaces in a short, strangely neglected dialogue, *Night*, that was first staged at the Comedy Theatre in April 1969 as part of an eight-play anthology called *Mixed Doubles*. It overlapped, both chronologically and thematically, with the Aldwych double bill and, significantly, was played by Vivien Merchant in partnership with Nigel Stock.

In outline, it recalls that old Lerner and Loewe song from *Gigi* – 'I remember it well' – in which Hermione Gingold and Maurice Chevalier trade competing memories of their past erotic encounters. But where that is schmaltz, Pinter introduces the acid tang of vermouth: he implies that couples not only have different recollections of the past, but that there is a fundamental difference between male and female memory. He presents us with a married duo in their forties sitting over coffee. The man recalls their first walk together on a bridge; the woman remembers an encounter by some railings in an open field. In his version, he stood behind her fondling her breasts; in her version, her back was to the railings and she was gazing into his eyes. He claims to have undone her coat; she says it was closed against the cold. What they can agree on is that they are married, have children and are swathed in past memories. It is just conceivable that they are remembering different partners. But to me the play's twilit poignancy rests on the idea of a long-married couple who reconstruct the past in different ways: the man's memories are of waists, breasts, undone brassieres, the practical tactics of seduction, whereas hers are of eyes, soft enquiries, the gentle declarations of love. The play echoes Pinter's lifelong fascination with the tenacity of memory, but it also relates to *Landscape* – in particular, to the differing nature of male and female sensibilities and to the discovery, after prolonged cohabitation, that two people's lives can be built on foundations that have nothing in common. *Night* deals in a minor key with major themes that were to preoccupy Pinter for years.

What is startling, however, about the Pinter double bill that opened at the Aldwych three months later is the qualitative gap between the two plays. Both deal with similar themes: loneliness, isolation, the fleeting nature of love, the partiality of memory. But where *Silence* – the only Pinter play without a laugh – seems opaque, cerebral and confusing in its non-linear structure, *Landscape*, for all its ambiguity, has the visual simplicity of a Grant Wood painting, the echoing resonance of a Wordsworth poem. *Silence* has not been revived in Britain since its première: *Landscape* has been glowingly rediscovered.

A play, however rich or dense, has to make an immediate impact. The problem with *Silence* is that it takes repeated readings or viewings to grasp its structure and its themes. Everything seems to be built around the rule of three. The stage directions say starkly: '*Three areas. A chair in each area.*' The characters are also three. Rumsey is a philosophical gentleman-farmer; Bates, slightly younger, is a blustering farmhand; Ellen, who sits between them, was apparently loved by both men in her younger days. The play also seems to inhabit three different periods of time: the brooding present, the recent past and a period long ago when the two men enjoyed a relationship with Ellen. The abiding impression is of people locked into their memories and recalling, with a mixture of poignancy and stoicism, the loss of love.

The play is structured like a poem. It works through verbal echoes, conscious repetitions, rhyming memories. Rumsey begins and ends with the phrase: 'I walk with my girl who wears a grey blouse.' Bates starts and finishes with the phrases: 'Caught a bus to the town. Crowds. Lights around the market.' Ellen, plagued by a drinking companion to recall her early experiences, first tells her that 'my youth was somewhere else, far away' and eventually capitulates and says that she was married: 'Certainly. I can remember the wedding.' And it is that phrase which she repeats at the end. But it takes time – and patience – to piece together what may have happened to the characters. Rumsey – a good fifteen years older than Ellen – has known her as a girl, has had a brief affair with her, but has encouraged her to find a younger lover. Bates, presumably Rumsey's employee, also fell in love with her, took her to live in town, seemingly married her but the relationship broke up. Ellen, we deduce, was passionately in love with Rumsey, but, rejected by him, succumbed to Bates's pleadings and now lives off her memories – as do they all.

Yet even though there is an inevitable pathos about characters marinated in past memories, there is nothing inherently dramatic about the structure. The time-scheme is difficult to work out. The social gap between the characters is not marked by sufficiently distinct diction. And there is a lack of circumstantial detail about the characters' lives. David Jones remembers that as an RSC associate director he was dispatched by Peter Hall, who was tied up elsewhere, to get Pinter's first thoughts on casting. 'I was sent by Peter to find out what Harold's requirements were. I asked what age the woman was. Harold said, "The script doesn't seem to be very clear. It's very hard to reach a definite conclusion about what age this woman is. She could be twenty-five or thirty-five." I asked whether he had any views about whether she was attractive, whether she was blonde or brunette. Harold said, "The script doesn't tell us much about this." In the end, Harold wouldn't say what age or type he wanted. It was difficult trying to find what chemistry he had in mind for those three characters. He was very Sphinx-like and refused to come up with a glib, easy formula for cracking those two plays.' In the end, the casting for *Silence* was perfectly good: Anthony Bate, Norman Rodway, Frances Cuka. But my chief memory is of John Bury's beautiful design: a mirrored floor with tilted back wall mazily reflecting the actors as in moving water.

Landscape also presents us with a potent image; but, like the play itself, it is sharper, clearer, more defined. We are in the kitchen of a country house. There are two characters. Beth sits in an armchair slightly away from the left of the table: Duff sits in a chair at the right corner of the table. According to the stage directions: '*Duff refers normally to Beth but does not appear to hear her voice. Beth never looks at Duff and does not appear to hear his voice. Both characters are relaxed, in no sense rigid.*' You could watch the play in a foreign language and instantly grasp much of its meaning: a woman locked in impenetrable memory and a man trying, with increasing urgency, to communicate with her. The intimacy and separation of the two characters – 'Alone together so much shared', as Beckett says in *Ohio Impromptu* – would instantly be apparent.

But what is the play about? We learn that Duff and Beth have worked as chauffeur-handyman and housekeeper to a long-gone employer Sykes. They now inhabit his old derelict house. Beth, who once studied drawing, has now retreated into composition of her own private, internal landscape: she is entirely preoccupied by her memory of a golden day on the beach where she asked her infinitely tender lover for a child. Duff tries to engage her attention and pierce her (to him unheard) erotic reverie with stories of his own: he talks of walks with the dog, of odd encounters in a pub, of the techniques of the professional cellarman, of his own betrayal of Beth during a trip north with Sykes and of a subsequent occasion when he raped Beth on the stone hall floor. Ronald Harwood, as a fellow-playwright, picks out Duff's speech about the techniques of letting beer breathe ('Spile the bung. Hammer the spile through the centre of the bung') as a classic example of Pinter's gift for taking something apparently tangential 'and making it feel as if it's part of the centre'. Pinter, he points out, researched the subject and then transformed it.

Yet in *Landscape*, Pinter is writing, beautifully and graphically, about physical nearness and emotional separation: it is a play about a man desperately trying to get through to a wife who has calculatedly, and even vengefully, retreated into a private world. The physical closeness is established by the stage picture; which is why, I think, John Bury was wrong in the Aldwych production to separate Duff and Beth by a fault-line running through the stage surface as if there had been a minor earthquake. The distance between them is suggested by the way they appear not to hear each other; even more crucially, by the language they use. Duff is rough and tough in his diction. On a walk he encounters 'Dogshit, duckshit . . . all kinds of shit'. In the pub he meets a truculent drinker: 'Someone's made a mistake, this fellow said, someone's used this pintpot instead of the boghole.' And his rape of his wife is evoked through hard, clangorous, resonant monosyllables: 'I would have had you in front of the dog, like a man, in the hall on the stone, banging the gong, mind you don't get the scissors up your arse . . .' The key phrase is 'like a man': an indication of Duff's roughneck notion of male assertiveness. But the magic of the play lies in the constant aural counterpoint between Duff's coarseness and Beth's lyricism. While Duff talks of piss, pintpots and bogholes, Beth is all soft consonants and flowing verbal lines: 'Suddenly I stood. I walked to the shore and into the water. I didn't swim. I don't swim. I let the water billow me. I rested in the water. The waves were very light, delicate. They touched the back of my neck.' But there is more than simple verbal contrast. It is as if Beth, half-hearing Duff, deliberately counters his crudity with the provocative language of ecstasy. His description of the rape, full of words like 'bang', 'slam', 'gong', 'hook', is followed by a silence and then by Beth's climactic recollection of her beach encounter:

> He lay above me and looked down at me. He supported my shoulder.
> (*Pause.*)
> So tender his touch on my neck. So softly his kiss on my cheek.
> (*Pause.*)
> My hand on his rib.
> (*Pause.*)
> So sweetly the sand over me. Tiny the sand on my skin.
> (*Pause.*)
> So silent the sky in my eyes. Gently the sound of the tide.
> (*Pause.*)
> Oh my true love I said.

It's beautiful to read, but the true meaning of the play becomes apparent only in performance. In Peter Hall's Aldwych production – with Peggy Ashcroft and David Waller – you felt that Beth could be describing a remembered, transcendent experience with Sykes, or possibly recapturing her idyllic early life with Duff. What one recalls is the exquisite contrast between Ashcroft's lyric rapture and Waller's bluff bluntness. But when Pinter himself revived the play at the Gate Theatre Dublin in May 1994 – and later at the National Theatre and on BBC Television – it became instantly apparent that Beth was speaking of her husband in an earlier time and had cocooned herself in reverie in retaliation for his professed adultery. As played by a real-life married couple – Penelope Wilton and Ian Holm – it became a harder, tougher play about the open wound of betrayal, about memory as a form of revenge and about the painful transitions of time. Wilton – still, cool, focused and implacable – made Beth into a woman who had *chosen*, almost vindictively, to retreat into the past. And Holm's Duff became a tragic figure who had coarsened with time and who, with hands tightly clenched around a coffee mug that he finally banged on the table, craved absolution and forgiveness from his voluntarily walled-off wife. The final image of Pinter's production, with the couple apparently doomed for eternity to petrified non-communication, was as chilling as anything in Beckett.

Landscape is one of Pinter's best-written and most deeply felt plays; and, without limiting its universal meaning, it is impossible not to see it as being triggered by the circumstances of his own life. He wrote the bulk of it in the Stratford-upon-Avon countryside in 1967 when Vivien was playing in Peter Hall's production of *Macbeth*; which may account for the odd fact that the names of the two characters, Beth and Duff, imply the invisible prefix 'Mac'. Even more to the point is that the Pinter marriage had now declined into a state of shared resentful solitude. It is a play that could have been written only by someone with a knowledge of the guilt, desperation, non-communication and paradoxical memory of times past that are inseparable from a failing marriage. The sad irony, however, is that the production of *Landscape* itself contributed to the marriage's decline. Up to this point, Vivien had automatically assumed that she would play the female lead in her husband's work. On this occasion, however, both Pinter and Peter Hall wanted Peggy Ashcroft to play Beth. The news came as a bombshell to Vivien. Pinter himself painfully recalls: 'I think that had a great deal to do with the way our life together began to fall away. When I wrote *Landscape* and offered it to Peggy Ashcroft, Vivien was deeply upset. But I resisted that. As far as I was concerned, I was extremely happy that Peggy wanted to do it. So Vivien was upset and I was equally upset that she could never bring herself to see the play on stage. It's a sign of the way our life had become a very thin thing by that time.' *Landscape* is a deeply moving poetic play that transcends the particular circumstances of Pinter's own life, yet it seems to have been written out of an ungovernable emotional impulse. It is possible to see it both as a reflection of a marriage sustained by weary habit and fitful memories of past happiness, and as a contribution to its inevitable dissolution. Pinter is often thought of as an icy, impersonal dramatist. In fact, his public art is constantly informed by private experience. As *Landscape* definitively shows, he has a Keatsian sense of life's heartache and melancholy.

Ten Time Regained

Landscape and *Silence* both cemented Pinter's relationship with Peter Hall and were reasonably successful at the Aldwych box office. But what to write next? By 1970, this was becoming a problem confronting not only Pinter but the whole generation of dramatists of which he was a part. The historical fact is that most twentieth-century playwrights — with certain obvious exceptions, such as Shaw and Ayckbourn – have enjoyed a vital ten-to-fifteen-year creative span in which they have done their best work. But by the early 1970s it was beginning to look as if the new movement, made up of violently heterogeneous individuals, that had redefined post-war British drama was beginning to run out of steam. In *West of Suez* (1971), John Osborne's flame-throwing anger turned towards an elegiac despair at the state of Western civilisation. In *The Friends* (1970) – in which a character attacks the working-class for 'their cowardly acquiescence, their rotten ordinariness' – Arnold Wesker seemed to have lost much of his impassioned idealism. And John Arden – with his wife Margaretta D'Arcy – was gradually moving away from engagement with mainstream theatre to populist community work. The fact is that the British theatre was rapidly changing. On the one hand, there was a new generation of emerging dramatists spearheaded by David Hare, David Edgar, Howard Brenton and Trevor Griffiths, with their own radical political agenda. On the other hand, there was a move, influenced equally by Artaud and American companies such as the Living Theatre, towards an anti-textual, anarchic experimentalism. The writers who had sprung up in the late 1950s, after opening all kinds of doors to the future, suddenly began to look rather isolated.

Pinter was not immune to the problem. He was temperamentally out of sympathy with group experiment. And although he had a built-in suspicion of authority, he was not the kind of writer suddenly to start dealing in ideological certainties or offering blueprints for change. In many respects, his social attitudes were not so far removed from those of the new generation of political dramatists. In 1969, five of his sketches were enjoyably animated by a Montreal-based TV producer, Gerald Potterton. They were framed by an interview with Pinter in which, while claiming, 'I'm not interested in ideolo-gies,' he said some harsh things about the British police for their failure to combat Fascist violence in post-war London and expressed strong concern about global suffering and death. 'You can't,' he said, 'expect this to be in any way a just world . . . I have no expectation of the world getting better in any way.' But Joan Bakewell recalls that while Pinter had close social ties with radical writers of his own generation, he was also determined to keep his creative distance. 'David Mercer, in particular,' she says, 'was very important to Harold. I introduced the two of them in the 1960s. At that time, David was running a hotbed of neo-Marxism down in Maida Vale and I used to go round a good deal on my way home from presenting *Late Night Line-Up*. I'd arrive about midnight and the joint would be jumping and everyone would be full of plans: Ken Tynan, for instance, would be talking about taking over Covent Garden. I was very close to Harold at that time and dared to ask him why he didn't write about politics. He'd say, "Hold on a minute. I write what I write. I write about what I know. I can't just write about politics to order." In the 1960s Mercer and Wesker and all the others were hammering at the system and Harold simply said, "That's not what I do." And although his work of course has changed in recent years, he was writing then about the psychic politics of people. Harold didn't write about world politics. He wrote about personal violence.'

His main problem, at one stage, was writing anything at all: a dilemma he movingly addressed in a speech he made in Hamburg in June 1970 when he was awarded the prestigious German Shakespeare Prize. His acceptance speech is one of his most revealing public statements about the hazards and rewards of the dramatist's life. He disowns a famous impromptu remark he had once made when asked what his plays were about: 'The weasel under the cocktail cabinet.' He talks about his sense of alienation from the endlessly analysed public playwright: 'Praise and insult refer to someone called Pinter. I don't know the man they're talking about.' He dwells on his distrust of theory and his belief in pragmatic solutions to the problems any play poses: 'A rehearsal period which consists of philosophical discourse or political treatise does not get the curtain up at eight o'clock.' He defines his work not through the statements it makes but through the characters it creates and the pain that goes into bringing them into existence: 'I have witnessed *their* pain when I am in the act of distorting them, of falsifying them and I have witnessed their contempt. I have suffered pain when I have been unable to get to the quick of them, when they wilfully elude me, when they withdraw into the shadows. And there's a third and rarer pain. That is when the right word or the right act jolts them or stills them into their proper life.' Pinter emerges as a writer who doesn't set out with a conscious agenda, but who finds that the content of his work is compelled, not chosen: 'I am aware, sometimes, of an insistence in my mind. Images, characters, insisting upon being written.' It is an acute piece of self-analysis in which Pinter comes across as a writer who has a direct channel to his own subconscious and who is very much at the mercy of his own imaginative impulses: what in another era might have been airily described as his Muse, or what Coleridge meant when he wrote in *Biographia Literaria*: 'The Fancy is indeed no other than a mode of memory emancipated from the order of time and space.' It is this which gives a certain pathos to Pinter's Hamburg peroration in which he admits that currently nothing is haunting his imagination:

> I find it ironic that I have come here to receive this distinguished award as a writer and that at the moment I am writing nothing and can write nothing. I don't know why. It's a very bad feeling, I know that, but I must say I want more than anything else to fill up a blank page again, to feel that strange thing happen, birth through fingertips. When you can't write you feel you've been banished from yourself.

In this speech Pinter comes clean. He lays bare the obsessive nature of his craft, the ambivalent relationship he has to characters whom he has brought into being yet who achieve their own truculent autonomy, and the sense of self-exile that comes from periods of creative impotence.

Pinter makes it clear in the Hamburg speech that he has no set agenda. All the same, it is fascinating to note the imaginative coherence of his work in the post-1968 period. While other British dramatists were haunted first by the possibilities and then by the failure of the revolutionary dream, Pinter became increasingly preoccupied with time, memory, the indivisibility of past and present. For him, these were hardly new themes; but whereas in early work, such as *The Birthday Party* and *A Slight Ache*, he had shown how we create an idealised past – almost a nostalgic paradise – to compensate for jangling present discontents, in the post-1968 period he becomes much more interested in the coexistence of past and present. Partly it was a result of the commissions he undertook for the different media, but, even so, one notices how themes from one work bleed surreptitiously into the next. His work on *The Go-Between*, which experiments with the structural possibilities of story-telling, leads almost inevitably to *The Proust Screenplay* – still sadly unfilmed – in which he confronts the greatest of all twentieth-century works about the power of involuntary memory and the notion of time past as something always within us. And having directed James Joyce's *Exiles* at the Mermaid Theatre in 1970, a play which deals with the omnipresence of past moral conventions, he went on to write *Old Times* which unforgettably shows how we create the past as a weapon of psychological domination. You could argue there is a strong element of accident and chance in all this, but there is also a consistent pattern to Pinter's work in this period as he himself acknowledged in a *New York Times* interview with Mel Gussow in 1971: 'I think I'm more conscious of a kind of ever-present quality in life . . . I certainly feel more and more that the past is not past, that it never was past. It's present.'

That certainly is the theme that runs through Pinter's radical screen adaptation of L. P. Hartley's novel *The Go-Between*, which may seem odd given that the novel's famous opening sentence is: 'The past is a foreign country; they do things differently there.' But Pinter's screenplay exposes the irony and ambiguity hidden within that statement: while it is palpably true that social and class attitudes have drastically changed since 1900, the fact is that in our emotional lives the present is constantly shaped and informed by the past. By his vital structural changes, Pinter forces us to rethink what the novel is in fact about. Not that he started with anything less than devout admiration for Hartley's work. Pinter was first asked by Joe Losey as early as October 1963 whether he had read the book and replied, '*The Go-Between* is superb . . . It's wonderful. But I can't write a film script of it. I can't touch it. It's too painful, too perfect, if you know what I mean.' Yet he did write a first-draft screenplay that was completed by the spring of 1964, but was put aside because of legal difficulties. He completed a second revised screenplay in 1969 that not only rethought the book's whole structure, but that gave him a chance to explore the coded hypocrisies of English life and to explore the contradiction between appearance and reality.

Hartley's novel is constructed like a triptych: prologue, main story, epilogue. It starts with the first-person narrator uncovering a schoolboy diary for the year 1900 which joltingly awakes his own sense of disappointment and defeat, and of the vanquish of the century's millennial hopes (the novel appeared in 1955). The bulk of the book is then taken up with the recollection by the narrator Leo Colston of a Norfolk summer in boyhood. Having been invited to spend part of the holidays at the grand country house of a snobbish school friend, Marcus Maudsley, he finds himself used as a Mercury-like messenger by Marcus's sister, Marian, who is carrying on a clandestine affair with a local tenant-farmer, Ted Burgess. Ultimately, the affair and Leo's part in it are uncovered; his pubertal confusion, emotional jealousy and sense of betrayal induce a temporary breakdown and destroy his adult capacity for love. In the Epilogue, he is drawn back to the Norfolk village, meets the aged Marian and is induced by her to visit her grandson – indirectly descended from Ted Burgess – and to tell him of the beauty of her past liaison. Once more, Leo is cast in the role of go-between.

It's a fine book: both the story of an unhealed emotional wound, and a metaphor for the innocence and experience of twentieth-century man. ('In my eyes', says Leo, 'the actors in my drama had been immortals, inheritors of the summer and of the coming glory of the twentieth century.') However, it set hellish problems for the adapter – not only the first-person narration, but the slow-burn irony of its revelations. Pinter's solution was both brilliant and daring: to eliminate any hard-and-fast distinction between past and present, and to make the time-planes coexistent. He gives us an increasingly lengthy, and at first slightly mysterious, series of flash-forwards showing the return of the aged Leo Colston to the Norfolk village; and it is through the deepening perspective of those sequences that we begin to understand the havoc wrought by the events of that sunlit childhood summer. Yet Pinter goes much further than that by including a deliberate temporal disjunction between sound and image. The present constantly invades the past so that over an idyllic shot of Marian and the young Leo riding in a pony and carriage, we hear the aged narrator murmuring: 'You flew too near the sun and were scorched.' Conversely, the past always exists in the present. Over a shot of the aged, desiccated Leo being shepherded into his car by a chauffeur, we hear Mrs Maudsley telling his younger self at a summer swimming party that he can watch the others bathe: a potent reminder that Leo has always been shielded and protected from life. Pinter's dual time-scheme is not only an audacious cinematic device; it makes us rethink what the novel is about. It reminds us that while in some ways the past *is* a foreign country, in that the Edwardian England on display seems wreathed in whaleboned snobberies and rigid class distinctions, in other ways it leaves its inescapable imprint on the present.

According to Losey's biographer David Caute, Pinter's flash-forwards were subject to a good deal of internal criticism, particularly from the movie's editor, Reginald Beck. On 28 October 1970 Beck wrote to Losey from the Elstree cutting-rooms: 'Regarding the present-day scenes my concern is that they are at present so much out of continuity that it is quite impossible to get any dramatic value from them.' John Heyman, the film's executive producer, wanted the flash-forwards removed. And James Aubrey, head of MGM who shared the production costs with EMI, rudely described *The Go-Between* as 'the greatest still picture ever made'. But although the final cut did modify Pinter's flash-forward sequences, they still seem to me to give the film its point and purpose. Nothing in the story is quite what it seems. Just as we penetrate beneath the charming exterior of the Maudsley household to explore what Pauline Kael called its 'sunny rot and corruption', so we gradually discover through the deadened features and sloping shoulders of Michael Redgrave's Colston what the effect of Leo's adolescent humiliation has been. Had Pinter followed Hartley's chronology – with its prologue and epilogue forming a pair of bookends to the main story – it would have been a highly literary film. By making past and present coexistent, Pinter both exploits the possibilities of cinema and opens up the story's meaning. The device also left its imprint on Pinter's future work. Caute suggests that *Old Times* was conceived in the Norfolk countryside during the shooting of *The Go-Between* in the summer of 1970. There is no hard evidence to support that. What is true is that the film's interaction between past and present decisively permeated Pinter's next play.

Whatever doubts were expressed about Pinter's narrative structure for the film, Losey was staunch and unwavering in his support. By now, after *The Servant* and *Accident*, the two men had reached a perfect creative understanding that reflected both their similarities and differences. Both were natural outsiders, both were steeped in theatre, and both viewed the British class system, a constant factor in all their work, with a mixture of moral disapproval and grudging fascination. One of the strongest threads running through *The Go-Between* is the conflict between sexual desire and upper-class propriety as expressed in the guarded looks, raised eyebrows and running battle of wills between Julie Christie as Marian and Margaret Leighton as her mother. But Pinter and Losey were also sufficiently dissimilar to make a perfect team. Pinter's verbal economy checks and balances Losey's baroque tendencies, while Losey's visual stylishness amplifies Pinter's exactness and precision – in the film a series of plunging vertical camera shots reminds us of Leo's Icarus-like descent after flying too close to the sun. This film, which was to be the climax of the Pinter–Losey collaboration though not their final project, rewarded them well in terms of prizes and profits. It won the Grand Prix (Palme D'Or) at the Cannes Film Festival in May 1971, beating off fierce competition from Visconti's *Death in Venice*, to the disappointment of Dirk Bogarde who starred in the latter and to the undisguised chagrin of Visconti himself who was eventually to become engaged in a noisy controversy over Pinter's next play. Later that year, the film also won glowing reviews from the British critics and shoals of awards from the Society of Film and Television Arts, including Best Film and Best Screenplay. Unlike *Accident*, it was also a great success at both the European and American box office: good news for Pinter, who was paid the dollar equivalent of £75,000 for his script plus 5 per cent of the profits. But the really heartening news was that Pinter, in his exploration of social detail, sexual confusion and temporal fluidity, had not only brought out the Proustian qualities in L. P. Hartley's novel, but had also opened up a rich seam for future development. The experiments in time he conducted in *The Go-Between* were to influence his future work in theatre and cinema.

Pinter had completed the screenplay for the film in 1969. By May 1970, he was complaining in Hamburg of the sense of banishment from self that came from being unable to write anything new. But in a strange way the choices he made in the way of alternative work were all leading him inexorably towards a new play. Pinter was certainly not out of the public eye in 1970. In February, William Friedkin's rather literal-minded film version of *The Birthday Party* opened in London. In April, Peter Gill directed new productions of *Landscape* and *Silence* at New York's Lincoln Center. And in September, James Hammerstein directed the first London stage productions of *Tea Party* and *The Basement* at the Duchess (better suited to television, was the general view). Yet one of the most formative ventures for Pinter that year was his partnership in a new company called Shield Productions. His colleagues were David Mercer, Christopher Morahan, Jimmy Wax and Terence Baker, and the aim was to present new plays in the West End. The team kicked off with David Mercer's *Flint*, dealing with a seventy-year-old ton-up Communist vicar, which was directed by Morahan at the Criterion in May and was a moderate success, thanks largely to a louchely eccentric performance by Michael Hordern. But the second venture – Pinter's production of James Joyce's little-known *Exiles* at the Mermaid in December – was acclaimed as a major theatrical discovery; so much so that the production was absorbed into the RSC's Aldwych repertory nine months later. If Joyce owed a post-humous debt to Pinter, it was equally clear that Pinter was a living beneficiary of Joyce, not least in his preoccupation with the unverifiable nature of truth and the unpossessability of the female soul. The confluences of style and theme between the two writers were extraordinary; and working on Joyce's unclaimed masterpiece seemed to have a liberating effect on Pinter himself as a writer.

Before Pinter rediscovered it, *Exiles* had a very chequered history. Joyce wrote it in 1914–15, a decade after he had started *Dubliners* and *A Portrait of the Artist as a Young Man*, and around the same time he was beginning work on *Ulysses*. It was performed briefly in Munich in 1919, was turned down by Yeats for Dublin's Abbey Theatre and, after an initial wartime rejection by the Stage Society in London, was eventually given its British première by them at the Regent Theatre in 1926. Joyce himself came to believe that Shaw had originally vetoed a London production on grounds of obscenity. Michael Holroyd scotches that myth by showing that although Shaw advocated the excision of a few 'unmentionable passages', he thought it was just the kind of thing the Stage Society – which was dedicated to plays unlikely to be performed by the commercial theatre – ought to be doing. But one member of the Society's Reading Committee had originally scrawled on his ballot paper: 'Reminiscent of Strindberg at his worst. Putrid.'

In fact the real influence on Joyce was not Strindberg but Ibsen, since *Exiles* is about characters seeking to escape dead moral conventions and the stranglehold of the past. The hero Richard Rowan (a self-portrait of the author) returns to Dublin after nine years' exile with his common-law wife Bertha and their child. Rowan and Bertha aim to live a life of total sexual freedom; but all the old obsessions, doubts and fears remain. In the first act, Robert Hand – a Dublin journalist and Rowan's oldest friend – turns up and propositions Bertha, inviting her to visit him at his secret cottage that night; but Rowan, while subscribing to the idea of total freedom, demands to know every detail of his wife's encounter with Hand. In the second act, Rowan himself turns up first at Hand's secret hideaway, informing the potential seducer that he knows all about the intrigue; when Bertha arrives he tells her once again that she is free to do as she sees fit. In the third act, which takes place at Rowan's house the next morning, the air is heavy with suspicion. We are left unsure whether the affair between Bertha and Hand has been consummated. But Hand turns up announcing that after writing an overnight article proclaiming Rowan's genius, he is himself preparing to go into exile – though only, as it turns out, for two weeks in Surrey. Rowan, having given his wife her freedom, is tormented by 'a deep wound of doubt which can never be healed'. It is left to Bertha, without revealing her Hand or disclosing what happened the night before, to reclaim Rowan as her 'strange, wild lover'.

The debt to Ibsen, both thematically and structurally, is explicable given Joyce's admiration for the sage of Skien. What is almost uncanny are the pre-echoes of Pinter. The scene where Rowan demands to know every detail of his wife's first encounter with Hand (and I can still hear the sound of John Wood's tight, hammer-tap voice insistently repeating, 'And then . . .') reminds one of Richard in *The Lover* self-torturingly exploring his wife's afternoon 'adultery'. *The Collection* also constantly comes to mind: first, in the calculated uncertainty about what actually happened in Hand's cottage, but even more in the latent homosexuality of imitative desire whereby two men wish to possess the same woman. Hand in fact spells it out quite clearly when he says to Rowan of Bertha: 'You love this woman. I remember all you told me long ago. She is yours, your work. And that is why I, too, was drawn to her. You are so strong that you attract me through her.' But although Pinter himself strenuously denies any direct cause and effect, the experience of working on *Exiles* also seems to have permeated his artistic imagination. He sat down to write *Old Times* in the winter of 1970 while saturated in Joyce's play; and while the two works are obviously very different, both deal with the contest between two figures for the soul and body of a third, and with the ultimate unpossessability of the triumphant heroine. *Exiles* also planted seeds which were to germinate many years later in *Betrayal*, in that it is the 'lover' Robert Hand who feels that it is he who has been deceived by the complicity between husband and wife about his advances. None of this is a matter of conscious imitation; it is simply proof of the extraordinary creative affinity between Joyce and Pinter.

That affinity was also borne out by Pinter's production of *Exiles*: a masterly affair played *sotto voce* with every phrase and every pause microscopically gauged and without a single superfluous gesture, so that even the removal of a pair of gloves was invested with emotional significance. As Irving Wardle wrote in *The Times*, the production offered 'the kind of insight which only one creative artist can perform in the service of another'. Pinter also showed himself to be a very good director of actors. Just as his casting of Patrick Magee in *The Birthday Party* in 1964 had introduced a remarkable Irish actor to the RSC, so now the performance he helped to elicit from John Wood as Rowan ultimately ensured that he too became one of the company's stars of the 1970s. Whether withdrawing distastefully at the sight of a whisky decanter, or smiling sardonically at the moral dilemma of his friend, Wood's Rowan suggested a man harbouring demons under a blanched mask of impassivity. Pinter's production was rightly lauded to the skies, and one of its many admirers was Michael Codron, who ended a period of mild estrangement by asking him to direct Simon Gray's new play, *Butley*, due to open in the West End in the summer of 1971.

Exiles was a landmark production for Pinter in many ways; not least because, while working on it, the sense of self-exile he had experienced from being unable to write suddenly came to an end. David Caute claims that the idea for *Old Times* came to Pinter during the shooting of *The Go-Between* in the summer of 1970. Pinter himself told Mel Gussow that the play was conceived on a sofa in his house in Regent's Park one afternoon that winter while he was reading the paper. 'I rushed upstairs to my room. I live in a very tall house. I usually find some difficulty getting to the top. But, like lightning, I was up.' What, asked Gussow, was the thought that got him going? 'I think it was the first couple of lines in the play. I don't know if they were actually the *first* lines. Two people talking about someone else. But then I really went at it.' So much so that within three days he had completed a rough first draft which he then reworked over the next few months. And although the final version is very tight and contained, it has a lyrical fluency and imaginative consistency that suggests it was written in a great creative burst. Like most good plays, the action has the seeming inevitability of a guided dream; but also a dream that, as I discovered, has its roots in Pinter's own memory.

There is certainly something mysterious about the structure of *Old Times*. It starts in a dim light with three figures discerned:

> DEELEY *slumped in armchair, still.*
> KATE *curled on a sofa, still.*
> ANNA *standing at the window, looking out.*
> *Silence.*
> *Lights up on* DEELEY *and* KATE, *smoking cigarettes.*
> ANNA'*s figure remains still in dim light at the window.*

It is as if the characters are being plucked out of time. Indeed, the opening conversation between Deeley and his wife Kate about the latter's old friend Anna, whose arrival is clearly expected at any moment, starts *in medias res.* And the play ends some 100 minutes later in a blaze of bright light with Deeley slumped once more in the armchair, Anna lying on one divan and Kate sitting on another. The hallucinatory framework, the contradictory statements the characters make about each other, the oddly varying descriptions of past encounters have led to endless speculation among commentators. Is Anna really present or is she simply a figment of Deeley's and Kate's imaginations? Are Kate and Anna – who worked as secretaries and shared a London flat together twenty years ago – separate characters or dual aspects of the same woman? Are all three characters dead and simply re-experiencing some past meeting? You can understand why the questions arise. At the same time, the moment you see the play on stage you realise their sublime irrelevance: the whole impetus of this haunting work depends upon the vitality of the contest between Deeley and Anna for superior knowledge and ultimate possession of Kate; and also upon Kate's final triumph over the disintegrating Deeley and the vanquished Anna. Whatever larger meaning arises from the action about the provisional nature of memory or the essential solitude of human existence, the dramatic action proves the point made by Robert Hand in *Exiles* that 'All life's a conquest'. When Mel Gussow suggested to Pinter that New York audiences would inevitably argue about the reality of the events, Pinter succinctly replied, 'I'll tell you one thing about *Old Times*. It happens. It all happens.'

Yes, but what happens exactly? Is the whole play – like all Pinter's work, according to Nigel Dennis in a devastating critique in the *New York Review of Books* in 1971 – simply an exercise for actors? Or is there something serious going on? It seems to me there are two main movements in the play, subtly intertwined. On one level, Deeley and Anna are clearly engaged in a verbal, musical and physical battle over Kate, who emerges victorious partly through her chilling incuriosity. But the play is also a sustained meditation on time and memory in which Pinter suggests the past is no more fixed or certain than the present or the future. *All three characters create the past according to the psychological or tactical needs of the moment and, as they do so, it acquires a tangible reality.* I am reminded of an exchange in *The Importance of Being Earnest* in which Miss Prism announces 'Memory, my dear Cecily, is the diary that we all carry about with us', to which Cecily replies 'Yes, but it usually chronicles the things that have never happened, and couldn't possibly have happened'. Pinter takes the argument a stage further. He's not just suggesting that the memory lies, but that through the very act of remembering, the past acquires an imaginative truth. It may seem obvious, but who else has dramatised the idea so effectively? I think one has to go back to the early scenes of *Peer Gynt* where as Ibsen's hero describes plunging from a steep clifftop into a lake astride a reindeer, the event becomes real to him; or even to *Henry IV Part One* where as Falstaff graphically conjures up the eleven men in buckram who assailed him at Gadshill, they come alive in his imagination. The difference in Pinter is that we are never quite sure at what point vivid memory shades into spontaneous creation.

Pinter sets out the basic motifs very clearly in the opening exchange where Kate and Deeley discuss Anna even as she stands upstage in semi-darkness. She is clearly present in their imaginations even before she appears:

KATE (*reflectively*): Dark.
    (*Pause.*)
DEELEY: Fat or thin?
KATE: Fuller than me. I think.
    (*Pause.*)
DEELEY: She was then?
KATE: I think so.
DEELEY: She may not be now.
    (*Pause.*)
    Was she your best friend?
KATE: Oh, what does that mean?
DEELEY: What?
KATE: The word friend . . . when you look back . . . all that time.
DEELEY: Can't you remember what you felt?

(*Pause.*)
KATE: It is a very long time.

Instantly you get a sense of Deeley's fretful insecurity, of Kate's deceptive passivity, of their joint preoccupation with Anna, of the obsession with semantics that runs through the play, and of the idea that one's memories of the past are always provisional, subject to the inaudible process of time and therefore capable of being reinvented. Even the seeming facts established in the opening scene are subsequently shown to be capable of contradiction. Kate observes that she herself had no friends; later, she and Anna launch into a communal riff about their male chums. Kate also says of Anna that 'She was a thief. She used to steal things', including her underwear; later, Anna specifically says that Kate lent her her underwear. In a world where memory is hazy or subjective, the past can be used to gain leverage over other people: one of the key points of the play. Pinter also gives you a strong sense of male exclusion from female intimacy with Deeley's shocked discovery that Kate and Anna once lived together. And when he concludes 'Anyway, none of this matters', it could mean one of several things: that *he* now has possession of Kate, that these hazy memories are irrelevant when set against the fact of Anna's imminent arrival, or that any attempt to recover the past is ultimately futile.

What is clear is that the opening scene defines the territory Pinter is going to explore. Two academic commentators, Alan Hughes and Robert Conklin, both describe the scene in terms of a scientific experiment: one in which Deeley and Kate are 'creating the suitable laboratory environment whereby a bride of Frankenstein, namely Anna, may be resurrected' (Conklin), and one in which 'Deeley leads the reluctant Kate in the fabrication of her imaginary old friend' (Hughes). But that makes it sound like a calculated conspiracy and is not, I suspect, how a theatre audience sees it. Indeed, when Pinter himself took over the role of Deeley from Michael Gambon in David Jones's 1985 London production for the tour to St Louis and Los Angeles, he gave it a very different spin. Jones recalls, 'It's hard to get the right tone. What is the scene about? How anxious is Deeley? Harold played it very fast and light and inconsequential and what I heard was Noël Coward: he played it with a Coward insouciance. You were intrigued and laughed, and weren't too disturbed, and then when he fell into the black pit later, you hadn't seen it coming. I think Harold understood that character very well: in particular, the frustrated aggression and the way in which life doesn't live up to his expectations.'

The opening scene is packed with information, yet if played too portentously, as Pinter realised, it kills the dynamic of the play which is to show the veneer of civilisation being stripped away. That process starts from the very moment of Anna's eruption into the lives of Deeley and Kate by a simple move downstage: no messing with doors and entrances. Anna immediately launches into a long, detailed stream-of-consciousness account of London life with Kate twenty years ago: 'Queuing all night, the rain, do you remember? my goodness, the Albert Hall, Covent Garden, what did we eat? to look back, half the night, to do things we loved, we were young then of course, but what stamina, and to work in the morning, and to a concert, or the opera, or the ballet, that night, you haven't forgotten?' Two things, at least, are happening in that speech. Anna is appropriating the past and laying claim to a prior superior knowledge of Kate; but she is also – as Steven H. Gale has pointed out – describing a London life that exists in her mind either as a vivid memory, or as a spontaneous creation, or as a combination of the two. As she describes that life, so it becomes real to her: a recurrent theme of the play. But the idea that it may have nothing to with reality was neatly caught in Lindy Davies's 1995 West End revival: as Anna (Harriet Walter) described how she and Kate used to sit up half the night reading Yeats, Kate (Julie Christie) and Deeley (Leigh Lawson) exchanged a furtive smile suggesting stark disbelief.

Pinter uses a variety of techniques in the play both to depict the battle between Deeley and Anna, and to denote the subjectivity of memory: songs and movies, for instance, enrich the texture of the play. At one point, Anna and Deeley engage in a competitive recollection of popular standards from the 1930s and '40s. On one level, it's a lightly nostalgic riff; on another, an acquisitive contest in which Deeley constantly caps each of Anna's quotations. But the songs themselves are also calculatedly chosen to reinforce the play's basic theme of remembrance. One of them is Eric Maschwitz's 'These Foolish Things', which first appeared in a 1936 revue, *Spread It Abroad*, and of which Maschwitz said he was inspired by Cole Porter's 'You're the Top' to write a catalogue-type lyric made up 'of small fleeting memories of young love'. The song, in fact, is pop-Proust in that it shows how a smell, a sound or an image from the past ('The smile of Garbo and the scent of roses') unlocks a whole set of emotional experiences.

Carol Reed's *Odd Man Out* is also very exactly chosen as the occasion for Deeley's alleged first meeting with Kate. The title could refer to Deeley himself: he is the odd man out in this peculiar triangle. And the film, in which an Irish revolutionary is hunted down after a raid on a Belfast factory, is not only one of the supreme poetic tragedies of post-war cinema, but also a reminder of how Pinter throughout his work uses Ireland, in Harry White's phrase, as 'a vital trope for the past'. Like Anna's earlier description of

London life, Deeley's account of his cinematic encounter with Kate is circumstantially detailed. But does that make it true? Or is it simply an invention dictated by the needs of the moment? In dramatic terms, it is undercut by Anna in two ways. First, Deeley's paean to Robert Newton's performance is punctured by Anna's 'F. J. McCormick was good too': one of those classic undercutting Pinter lines on which Vivien Merchant got a big laugh in Peter Hall's original production. Anna also extrapolates from Deeley's story a statement that seems to stand as an epigraph for the whole play: 'There are some things one remembers even though they may never have happened. There are things I remember which may never have happened but as I recall them so they take place.' Everyone quotes the first sentence to pin down the play, but Anna's second statement is just as crucial: the idea that the recreation, even of a fictive past, can be so vivid as to seem to be taking place. As Pinter himself said to Mel Gussow: 'So much is imagined and that imagining is as true as real.' Or, as Shakespeare's Theseus put it to Hippolyta: 'Imagination bodies forth The form of things unknown.'

Memory, Pinter shows, can operate on a variety of levels. It can offer a fiction that takes on the reality of a fact, as when Anna describes the improbably artsy London life she led with the deeply incurious Kate. In the process of recollecting the past, one can also create the future: witness Anna's description of a man crying in the room she once shared with Kate which exactly anticipates the final moments of the play. In a world where nothing is verifiable, memory can also be a weapon of psychological domination: in her description of rushing off with Kate to some obscure, unfamiliar district to see *Odd Man Out*, Anna strikes a blow at Deeley and reinvents the past to suit her own purposes.

The lingering silence that follows Anna's recollection of the Reed film shifts the play on to another level: one where Deeley, seeing his proprietary claim to Kate under threat, battles to re-establish his identity. He does this by vainglorious boasts about his movie-making career, by assuming a knowledge of Anna's home territory in Sicily, and by presenting himself as a genuine artist in a world of commercial prostitutes (not unlike Newton's painter in *Odd Man Out*). 'I had a great crew in Sicily', he brags: 'A marvellous cameraman. Irving Shultz. Best in the business. We took a pretty austere look at the women in black. The little old women in black. I wrote the film and directed it. My name is Orson Welles.' In his very astute essay, Steven H. Gale seizes on this last line as a turning point. Its palpable untruth leads us to regard every other statement on the past as suspect. I think the line bears a wholly different weight. Its parodic braggadocio is a sign of Deeley's mounting panic and knowledge that the game is slipping away from him. And when

– after another profound silence – Anna and Kate shift into a re-enactment of their old London life, it is proof not just of the Eliotesque argument in *Burnt Norton* that 'all time is eternally present', but of Deeley's exclusion from conspiratorial female intimacy.

In Act Two, set in the bedroom, the battle lines are clearly drawn: Deeley and Anna are now engaged in an eyeball-to-eyeball confrontation. The gloves are off and the pretence at cool insouciance is gradually dropped. While Kate bathes, Deeley brings in the coffee and launches into a precise reminiscence of meeting Anna twenty years ago in a pub called the Wayfarer, and later at a party in Westbourne Grove where he stared up her skirt at her white thighs. True or false? It's unprovable, either way, but there are plenty of hints to suggest that Deeley is creating the past to suit his own needs. There is a conscious irony about his evocation of the Wayfarer's clientele: 'poets, stunt-men, jockeys, stand-up comedians, that kind of set up.' He says of his up-skirt-peering that 'You didn't object, you found my gaze perfectly accept-able', mockingly deploying the very noun Anna earlier used to describe her rhapsodic attention to Kate. Deeley is also deflating Anna's pretension to have been a metropolitan culture-vulture by reducing her to the level, quite literally, of a bit of skirt. The contest becomes even more blatant when Deeley, in a gesture of provocative deference, suggests Anna might like to dry Kate in her bath towel. And when Deeley and Anna reiterate their song-snatch of the first act, it is now with an audible undercurrent of malice, brought out superbly in Bill Alexander's 1993 production at Birmingham Rep where Tim Pigott-Smith on the final line cried 'No, no, they *can't* take that away from me' with a naked desperation.

The play now moves into its last phase: what David Jones accurately calls 'the final shoot-out between the two women'. Increasingly, in fact, Kate stirs herself from her exquisite sloth. In her first long speech, she expresses her preference for the country over London – so much for Anna's hymns to the metropolis. It is Kate who now initiates the switch into time-past which Anna obediently has to follow. And it is she who cuts Deeley short when, visibly agitated by evidence of the women's past friendship, he is about to accuse them of being lovers. As Peter Hall says, 'It is not a play about lesbians. Categorically no.' If it were a play about two women using their sexual intimacy to drive a man to distraction, it would simply be coarse melodrama. Pinter is much subtler than that. In effect, he shows Kate preserving her mask of silence as Anna undermines Deeley's superior claims of possession; and once Deeley is floored, she moves in to demolish Anna's own propri-etorial arrogance. Kate's long final speech is, in fact, a ruthless demolition of Anna: of her supposedly inviolate memories, of her sexual sophistication, of her possessive claim to have 'found' Kate. The Sphinx-like Kate goes for the jugular: she picks out Anna's conscious imitation of her own smile, of the skull beneath the skin, of the suffocating effect of close female companionship. But she saves the *coup de grâce* for the end of the speech, describing how she and Deeley violated Anna's bed, and how she plastered Deeley's face with dirt from her window box:

> ... He was bemused aghast, resisted, resisted with force. He would not let me dirty his face or smudge it, he wouldn't let me. He suggested a wedding instead and a change of environment.
>
> (*Slight pause.*)
>
> Neither mattered.
>
> (*Pause.*)
>
> He asked me once, at about that time, who had slept in that bed before him. I told him no one. No one at all.

These are the last chilling words spoken (words that demolish both Anna's friendship and the whole history of Kate's marriage to Deeley) before the final graphic image which contains a re-enactment of the bedroom scene described in Act One: the sobbing Deeley goes to Anna's divan and looks down at her, moves to the door and returns, goes towards Kate's divan and lies on her lap, and walks to the armchair where he sits slumped. The final tableau in 'very bright' light is of Deeley in armchair, Anna lying on divan, Kate sitting on divan. Some critics take this to symbolise a return to reality and enlightenment; others to mean that the characters are all dead. I take it to signify that although Kate has triumphed on the temporal level and proved her own ultimate unpossessability, all three characters are locked, like the rest of humanity, into a condition of frozen, permanent solitude.

However, like a great poem, the play has multiple layers of meaning. The least noticed aspect of it is Pinter's delighted evocation of the London – his London – of the late 1940s and early 1950s: the pubs, the parties, the caffs, the cinemas, the Bohemian variety of the city before it turned into a hard-nosed tourist toytown. We have it on the authority of early girlfriends like Jennifer Mortimer and Pauline Flanagan that Pinter 'loved London' and, in part, *Old Times* is a recreation of his own old times. Very much so, according to Dilys Hamlett, with whom Pinter had a tempestuous affair in 1950 that ended abruptly in her throwing him over. She recalls that Pinter sent her a copy of the original script in 1971 with a note saying: 'This will ring bells.' Indeed it did. Very loud ones. 'When I read it,' says Hamlett, 'it seemed to me to be about our whole milieu in the London of 1950: the Queen's Elm pub in Fulham Road where we used to drink, the flat in Chelsea I shared with another girl, even the window boxes on the ledge outside the flat. But there is something else as well. I started the affair with Harold while my flatmate was away in Switzerland. She was very possessive of me – though there was nothing sexual about it – and she deeply resented Harold. She didn't like it and it was partly because of her influence that Harold and I didn't go and live together . . . I remember another occasion when a group of us, including Harold, went to a dance at Hampstead Town Hall and then came back to the Chelsea flat. I had a French female friend with me, who actually was bisexual, and we had to sleep in the same bed, which meant nothing but I always remember Harold raging in the corner . . . Ironically, I ended up playing Kate at York Rep in 1976 and I remember the director Gerald Chapman suggesting we improvise. I said, "I've no need to – I know quite a lot about it actually!" I don't think any of this is just my imagination, otherwise Harold wouldn't have sent me that card.'

Once again, Pinter's life feeds directly into his plays. *Old Times* may not be a literal transcription of reality, but clearly the memory of the Walpole Street flat in Chelsea shared by Dilys Hamlett and her friend, with Pinter as the intruding third party resented by the female companion, provides the emotional context for much of the action. Through the character of Deeley, who gradually disintegrates from a suave inquisitor into someone who is coarse, brutal and terrified, it also becomes a play about the pathos of male insecurity and the fragility of the concept of bourgeois ownership. It would be stretching it to describe it as a 'political' play, but there is a sense in which the cool, Cowardly façade is stripped away to reveal the naked ugliness of the battle for possession. It also moves effortlessly from the particular to the universal by suggesting, in contrast to John Donne, that each man *is* an island, and that while we make necessary gestures towards each other of love and friendship, we are all in the end trapped inside our own skins and live in a state of inviolable loneliness. That seems to me the meaning of the final image with the characters all occupying their own space: what Octavio Paz, describing the miniaturist collages of the artist Joseph Cornell, once called 'cages for infinity'. And running through it all is the idea that linear time is an artificial construct, and that we create the past in response to the needs of the present and in order to shape the future. Many people consider it Pinter's best play. It is certainly his most elusive and mysterious; one that yields up new meanings on each viewing depending on the inflexion it is given by particular performers and directors.

Peter Hall's première production – which opened at the Aldwych on 1 July 1971 and got Pinter the best reviews he has ever had first time round – was a game of skill played to the death and was remarkable for its visual control, its musicianly ear for word and silence, and for its balance of sympathy between Colin Blakeley's Deeley, Vivien Merchant's Anna and Dorothy Tutin's Kate. (As Blakeley remarked, '*Old Times* is a play about a certain time of life – the forties. Practically everyone concerned with the play was roughly the same age. It's a time when you do begin to re-evaluate – when you stand still for a moment and think about old times.') David Jones's 1985 revival was earthier and sexier. The most inspired idea was the casting of Liv Ullmann as Anna in that her perceptible Scandinavian accent explained both the character's verbal precision and faint outsiderishness. Bill Alexander's brilliant production at Birmingham Rep in 1993 brought out both the physical complicity between the two women – Estelle Kohler as a smiling predatory Anna, Carol Royle as a frighteningly incurious Kate – and the savagery lurking behind the smooth veneer of Tim Pigott-Smith's Deeley. Kevin Billington's 1994 Dublin production – part of the Gate Theatre's Pinter Festival – pitted an English Deeley (Michael Pennington) against an Irish Anna and Kate (Olwen Fouéré and Catherine Byrne), thereby highlighting his sense of emotional isolation. And Lindy Davies's 1995 production – which started at Theatr Clwyd before moving into Wyndham's – was chiefly memorable for the radiant beauty and impermeable serenity of Julie Christie's Kate: only when she revealed her hand in the final scene did you realise the tragic loneliness behind her silent withdrawal from a disastrous marriage.

Old Times is a play that constantly renews itself, partly because of the extraordinary tension between what is said and what is felt, partly because of its mixture of exact social observation and emblematic imagery, and partly because so much depends on the chemistry of the casting. It is a work of beautiful elegiac obliquity and one that touches some chord in all of us. But its personal significance for Pinter in 1971 was that, after a prolonged period of self-doubt and creative uncertainty, he was once more in command of his talent. And his preoccupation with time and memory, which had been present since his first stirrings as a dramatist, was also leading him inexorably towards one of the most satisfying, if ultimately unfulfilled, projects of his whole career.

Eleven Pinter's Way

Before Pinter immersed himself in the giant project of adapting Proust to the screen, which was to occupy the whole of 1972, he had another commitment to fulfil: directing Simon Gray's *Butley* in the West End. It was the start of a professional relationship that was to extend over six plays and one film; also of a strong friendship that survives today, despite Gray's lightly disguised portrait of Pinter in his TV film *Unnatural Pursuits*. At first sight, they seem an unlikely pair. Pinter is precise, meticulous, well organised. Gray, with his mass of unruly hair, his shoulder bag stuffed with books and papers, and his permanently lit cigarette, still retains the air of a faintly *distrait* junior lecturer late for a tutorial – not altogether surprising, since Gray taught English Literature for twenty years at Queen Mary's College, London. But the two men are united by their passion for literature, cricket and drink. And their creative dissimilarity – if Pinter's plays are poetic metaphors, Gray's are acerbically witty reports from the front line of academia and publishing – seems to strike sparks.

Gray's first memory of Pinter, recorded in *An Unnatural Pursuit and Other Pieces*, is of going to his house in Regent's Park where 'Harold was lying on a *chaise-longue* in a black silk shirt (and other garments like boots and trousers, etc), a dandy at first glimpse, or something worse, even'. It sounds an un-characteristically Wildean posture for the normally upright Pinter, and it is a portrait he emphatically rejects. But the two men hit it off and Pinter readily agreed to direct *Butley*: a well-written study in personal disintegration in which a university lecturer – distantly related, one feels, to John Osborne's Bill Maitland in *Inadmissible Evidence* – in the course of a single day is abandoned both by his wife and his live-in male partner, and suffers the routine disappointments of academic life. Pinter had no problem in under-standing Gray's world.

'This whole "world" thing,' says Gray, 'is rubbish. It's a play about people, not about worlds. As far as the "world" was concerned, Harold simply came down the Mile End Road and looked at my office. That didn't take long. He quickly saw the dingy, uninteresting, lifeless place an academic office is. I remember we then had a meeting in a pub and he said, "We're very different kinds of writer, you and I, and I like that." I sat in on his rehearsals which were conducted with clarity, precision and ease. I think what I learned from him is that directing is simply a matter of the application of common sense. Anybody should be able to do it who is capable of thinking practically and specifically about the meaning of this or that line. What Harold and I used to do was go to a pub every evening and have long discussions about that day's work. What do you say about *Butley*? There it is. It doesn't involve metaphysical speculation. It was really a matter of whether there might be one line too many. As Harold would wonder about lines, I would wonder about moves. It was a perfect collaboration.' And although the play itself got mixed notices when it opened at the Criterion in the summer of 1971, there was universal praise for Alan Bates's performance as the chaotic, despairing, vituperative hero, and for Pinter's production, which enjoyed a year's West End run: a propitious start to the enduring Pinter–Gray partnership.

After the success of *Butley*, Pinter had a number of other projects to keep him busy. He spent the autumn of 1971 writing a film adaptation of an Irish novel by Aidan Higgins, *Langrishe Go Down*. It was a script he was anxious to direct himself, though in fact it was to be another seven years before it was turned into a remarkable TV film by David Jones. In November 1971, Pinter was back in New York fine-tuning the script of *Old Times* for its Broadway production. ('I did change a silence to a pause. It was a rewrite. This silence was a pretty long silence. Now it's a short pause.') By that time, he was also about to embark on what he described to Mel Gussow as 'a film that is going to be the most difficult task I've ever had in my life – and one which is almost impossible'. It was to be the adaptation of *A la recherche du temps perdu*: what Aldous Huxley called 'Proust's horrible great book', or Middleton Murry the record of 'a new sensibility'.

The notion of turning Proust's mammoth 3,300-page novel – or, at least, parts of it – into a film had long been the obsession of a French producer, Nicole Stéphane. She had discussed with François Truffaut, René Clément and Luchino Visconti the idea of filming limited sections of the book; Visconti's regular screenwriter had even done a version of Sodom and Gomorrah. Nothing came to fruition. After the triumph of *The Go-Between* at Cannes in 1971, it was almost inevitable that Stéphane would turn to Losey and Pinter; indeed, the adaptation of Hartley's novel, with its fluctuations of time and memory, seemed almost like a preparation for tackling Proust. They had conquered the lower slopes; why not go for the peak itself?

The problems the book presented were obvious. The length. The style. The symphonic structure. The filtering of events through the first-person narrator. The vast number of themes the work contains: childhood, memory, time, love, music, art, sleep, society, the historic France. Also there was what Martin Turnell – one of its profoundest admirers – calls the appearance of considerable confusion it presents to first-time readers. Turnell summarises its structure as well as anyone:

> It opens with the narrator's recollections of his childhood at Combray, switches towards the close of the first volume to a long account of Swann's love affair with Odette de Crécy which took place before the narrator was born; returns in volume three to his childhood memories and his first love affair with Swann's daughter Gilberte, and describes a seaside holiday at Baalbec where he meets Albertine Simonet and the *jeunes filles en fleurs*. Two volumes are devoted to the Guermantes family and to Marcel's infatuation for the Duchess, three more to the world of the homosexuals and the love affair with Albertine. At the end of *Sodome et Gomorrhe* his attention is largely concentrated on Albertine. Her death and his jealousy occupy four more volumes. *Le Temps retrouvé* deals with the changes that have taken place in society since the war and with the theory of art which underlines the whole work. All through the sixteen volumes there are elaborate accounts of dinner parties, receptions and the life of the worldlings. The principal difficulty is to discover the connection between the brilliant social life and the private love affairs of the individuals which are described with an even greater wealth of detail.

How to start work on the huge task of adapting Proust? Where to begin? Pinter had previously read only the first volume, *Du Côté de chez Swann*. His first task was to sit down and master the intricate complexity of the novel and see if a cinematic structure could be found. At an early stage he suggested calling in as an adviser Barbara Bray, whom he had known in the late 1950s as a BBC script editor and who was both a French scholar and a Proustian authority. She met Losey, they got on fine, and so the three of them formed an artistic triumvirate with the aim of cracking the seemingly insoluble problem of filming Proust. Pinter himself sat down for three months early in 1972 to immerse himself in the work, in the C. K. Scott-Moncrieff translation, making hundreds of notes as he went. But there were regular meetings with Losey and Bray, and gradually a plan began to emerge.

'Nicole,' Barbara Bray recalls, 'initially wanted us to limit ourselves to one section of the first volume, *Un Amour de Swann*, as she had with Truffaut. But I, as a pedant, said, "I don't think we can possibly do that." It was that, I suppose, which made it a bit of a white elephant because it was bound to be long and bound to be ambitious. Actually, the basic structural idea came from

Sam Beckett. I was talking to him about it and he said that you really ought to start at the end with *Le Temps retrouvé* and so that's what we did. As you know, Proust wrote the first part – *Du Côté de chez Swann* – and then the last part – *Le Temps retrouvé* – and then what he called the bit between. So we worked out a structure that starts with the party at the Prince de Guermantes' house in 1921, from the very end of the novel, and then goes back to Marcel as a boy of eight at Combray in 1888, which is the beginning of the book.'

For Pinter, the experience of total immersion in Proust was a kind of homecoming: he was dealing with a writer whose ideas about time, memory and the importance of art in many ways coincided with his own. He himself says, 'I think that's right: a sense of homecoming. I became totally absorbed by it, swallowed by it, I went in and in and in. I was swallowed up by it. It was an enormous bloody magnet. I felt a great kinship with it, but I also had to maintain an objective relationship with it. It was a very interesting tension between those two things.' Pinter also acknowledges, with great pleasure, the collaborative nature of the enterprise. 'I'm not up to reading the whole of Proust in French, but I had many questions about what the French was doing and Barbara was enormously helpful on questions of style and overall struc-ture. The opening montage [a sequence of thirty-five shots before a word is spoken] was my idea. But I remember Joe being absolutely clear about the *View of Delft* being a visual entry point. Barbara followed it by saying that Swann's exchange with Marcel about the painting, just before Swann's death, was absolutely crucial. Barbara kept us on our toes. The great thing about the venture was that the three of us all kept each other on his or her toes. It was a damned good enterprise.'

That sense of homecoming felt by Pinter is most evident when you read *Le Temps retrouvé*: whole sections of it might almost be a statement of his own artistic beliefs. In one remarkable passage, Proust concludes that 'in fashion-ing a work of art we are by no means free', suggesting that it pre-exists us and that, since it is both necessary and hidden, it lies waiting to be discovered. That is uncannily like Pinter's reference, in his speech to the Bristol students in 1962, to the self-propelling nature of drama and the need to keep one's sights on 'the place where the characters are silent and in hiding'. Proust goes on to attack the idea that art should be used as a vehicle for literary or aesthetic theory: 'Authentic art has no use for proclamations of this kind, it accomplishes its work in silence . . . A work in which there are theories is like an object which still has its price-tag on it.' Again, one is reminded of Pinter telling his Hamburg audience in 1970 that he distrusted theory and was not concerned with making general statements. Proust goes on to speak of the importance, for the writer, of involuntary memory as against the so-called 'realities' of the present age:

> The reality that he has to express resides, as I now began to understand, not in the superficial appearance of his subject but at a depth at which that appearance matters little; this truth had been symbolised for me by that clink of a spoon against a plate, that starched stiffness of a napkin, which had been of more value to me for my spiritual renewal than innumerable conversations of a humanitarian or patriotic or internationalist or meta-physical kind.

Even if Pinter was less disdainful than Proust of the world of external reality, he would have understood precisely what Proust meant when he referred to those who lack the artistic sense, which is to say, 'the faculty of submitting to the reality within themselves'. Proust is often misleadingly characterised as an élitist snob; but what he is driving at in this passage is the need for the artist to think of nothing 'but the truth which is before him'. So Pinter had also declared in 1962: 'What I write has no obligation to anything other than to itself.'

Proust completes that paragraph with a fascinating parenthesis, prompted by speculations about the death of literature, upon the nature of cinema itself. 'Some critics now liked to regard the novel as a sort of procession of things upon the screen of a cinematograph. This comparison was absurd. Nothing is further from what we have really perceived than the vision that the cine-matograph presents.' Writing at a time when cinema was still in its infancy, Proust implies that its sequential progression of literal images was in direct antithesis to the chance happenings of authentic memory. Yet there is a paradox here. Proust's own prolonged essay in memory was, in Eric Rhode's words, 'woven with numerous tropes picked from the field of physiological optics, from stereoscopy and from a study of the magic lantern and the kaleidoscope'. And Proust's exploration of the random nature of involuntary memory was to have its own effect on a whole generation of film-makers including Resnais (particularly in *Hiroshima Mon Amour*), Bergman, Visconti and Losey himself. Proust may have distrusted cinema; yet he himself was to shape its attitude to human consciousness and to the discontinuity of time.

Pinter's *The Proust Screenplay*, in its published form, goes a long way towards confronting Proust's own scepticism about cinema. In fact, it seems to me one of Pinter's most extraordinary achievements: an act of homage by one artist to another. For a start, it has many negative virtues. It takes the most famous of all first-person novels and, until the very last line, makes absolutely no use of external narration. One can imagine how, in the hands of a lesser writer, there would be acres of intrusive voice-over with Marcel telling us everything he was thinking and feeling; Pinter, true to past form, allows nothing to come between the viewer and the event (voice-over is essentially a radio device to compensate for the lack of visual information). Pinter also makes no attempt to cram in every aspect of the novel or every character and yet manages to distil its essence. He even, with a reckless bravura, omits the one episode that even those who have never read the novel instantly associate with Proust: that of *la petite madeleine* dipped in coffee which Aunt Leonie used to offer the young Marcel and whose flavour subsequently brought Combray and his whole childhood involuntarily flooding back from the past. But its loss is never felt (anyway, how can you do 'taste' in the cinema?) because Pinter uses other sights and sounds to convey the pervasive nature of memory.

On the positive side, Pinter's total understanding of Proust is evident from his introduction to the screenplay which, in a few crisp sentences, shows a masterly grasp of how the novel works: 'We decided that the architecture of the film should be based on two main and contrasting principles: one a movement, chiefly narrative, towards disillusion, and the other, more intermittent, towards revelation, rising to where time that was lost is found, and fixed forever in art.' That exactly captures the dual momentum of the novel: the sense that, on the one hand, it is recording the disintegration of French society from 1880 to 1919 and Marcel's private disenchantment; on the other, it is the pursuit of an absolute, an experience that would be untouched by the devouring action of time. As Pinter says in the introduction: 'The whole book is, as it were, contained in the last volume. When Marcel, in *Le Temps retrouvé*, says that he is now able to start his work he has already written it. We have just read it. Somehow this remarkable conception had to be found again in another form. We knew that we could in no sense *rival* the work. But could we be true to it?' Having discovered a form that made cinematic sense, Pinter explains how he and his colleagues isolated a central theme:

> We evolved a working plan and I plunged in the deep end on the basis of it. The subject was Time. In *Le Temps retrouvé*, Marcel, in his forties, hears the bell of his childhood. His childhood, long forgotten, is suddenly present within him but his consciousness of himself as a child, his memory of the experience, is more real, more acute than the experience itself.

That again pins down Proust with unerring precision. As Beckett wrote, the book is very much about 'that double-headed monster of damnation and salvation – Time'.

Pinter's cinematic intelligence – his ability to render Proust's ideas in visual terms – is evident from the opening montage of thirty-five shots. What Pinter does is to conjure up impressionistically the various aspects of Marcel's life to be recalled, explored and ordered in the body of the film. The first shot is: '*Yellow screen. Sound of garden-gate bell*.' We then get glimpses of a line of trees seen from a railway carriage, of the sea from a high window, of a window in a Venetian *palazzo*, of the dining room at Baalbec, before we see the middle-aged Marcel arriving at the Prince de Guermantes' house for a party in 1921. Temporally, we start at the end of the novel, but Pinter instantly introduces the aural and visual motifs – the sound of a spoon hitting a plate, the crackle of a stiff napkin, the unlaced boots conveying Marcel's grief at his grandmother's death – that will recur throughout the film. In Shot 22, the camera also pulls back to discover that the yellow screen – already seen in four earlier shots – is part of a yellow wall in Vermeer's *View of Delft*. The significance of the painting in the book is that Swann, who is writing a study of it, creates Odette in the mould of his imagination just as Vermeer created his work of art; this is paralleled by Marcel's love for Albertine and his creation of an imaginative picture of a social Sodom and Gomorrah that reflects the reality of his desires. Before a word has even been spoken, Pinter has established the punctuating sounds and images that will dominate the film.

The circular structure of Pinter's screenplay also cunningly echoes that within the book itself. Pinter starts with a shot of the yellow screen and of Marcel arriving at the Prince de Guermantes' party. The climax of the film, over 400 shots later, takes us back to the self-same party where the people Marcel has encountered throughout his life are transfigured by age and where he is introduced to the daughter of Gilberte, the girl whom he first silently adored in his Combray childhood. This triggers a memory of the sights and sounds of his youth: the church steeples, the river, the roofs of Combray, the sound of the garden-gate bell. Finally, the camera moves in on the patch of yellow wall in the Vermeer painting and we hear Marcel announcing, in the solitary line of voice-over: 'It was time to begin.' This is not, of course, a literal reproduction of Proust's beginning and end. But what Pinter does, with consummate skill, is to find a precise visual equivalent for the verbal music of the novel. It was Edmund Wilson who described the opening sentence of the book – '*Longtemps, je me suis couché de bonne heure*' – as the opening chord in a vast symphony; and the echoes of that chord are heard over 3,000 pages later as the book closes with the phrase '*dans le temps*'. Pinter not only concludes with an act of revelation, Marcel's awareness that art alone can triumph over cormorant time; he also gives the film a harmonious sense of completion matching Proust's use of verbal rhythms.

Pinter also grasps the point that the novel works on an infinite number of levels. Marcel himself describes it as 'the story of an invisible vocation': the quest for time regained and *la vraie vie* involving the repudiation of social life, love and friendship. But Marcel also calls it 'the memoirs of Saint-Simon of another period', and on that level the book records the disintegration of an aristocratic élite and its absorption by the bourgeoisie: an event symbolised by the marriage of the Prince de Guermantes to the rich and inalienably middle-class Mme Verdurin. Argument still rages over Proust's class attitudes. There are those who see him as an arrant snob, complicit in nostalgia for a lost aristocratic world and retreating from history into the private epiphanies of the 'aesthetic'. On the other hand, Walter Benjamin saw Proust as a prophet of a cataclysmic class conflict:

> Proust describes a class which is everywhere pledged to camouflage its material basis . . . He did not mean to do it a service. Here speaks Marcel Proust, the hardness of his work, the intransigence of a man who is ahead of his class. And much of the greatness of his work will remain inaccessible or undiscovered until this class has revealed its most pronounced features in the final struggle.

Even if that final struggle has been indefinitely postponed, Benjamin is surely right. There is in Proust a much tougher, harder attitude to the world he describes than is commonly allowed: 'I had seen enough of fashionable society', he writes at one point, 'to know that it is there that one finds real illiteracy and not, let us say, among electricians.' And Pinter's screenplay brings out the brutal social comedy that is a vital part of the book: for instance, in the superb scene where the Duc de Guermantes brushes aside the news of Swann's impending death to deplore his wife's breach of style in setting out for a fashionable dinner party wearing a red dress with black shoes.

On yet another level, Proust's novel is about the mystery and ambiguity of love and the discovery that behind the innumerable illusions which it creates there is nothing but a void. In a crucial sentence, Proust writes of '*L'acte de possession physique – où d'ailleurs l'on ne possède rien*' (The act of physical possession in which, paradoxically, the possessor possesses nothing). That idea of the ultimate unknowability of the desired must have struck a chord with Pinter, even though his attitude to women is vastly different from Proust's. But in the screenplay, he faithfully captures the tremulous uncertainty that surrounds Marcel's relationship with Albertine. Marcel first sees her on the promenade at Baalbec in 1898 walking with a group of girls against the background of the glittering sea. The camera direction reads: '*a*

16 James Fox, Joseph Losey and Harold Pinter on the set of *The Servant*, 1962.

17 Harold Pinter, John Fowles and Karel Reisz during the shooting of *The French Lieutenant's Woman*, 1980.

18 Ralph Richardson (Hirst) and John Gielgud (Spooner) in Peter Hall's original production of *No Man's Land* at the Old Vic, 1975.

19 Paul Eddington (Spooner) and Harold Pinter (Hirst) in David Leveaux's revival of *No Man's Land* at the Almeida, 1993.

20 Michael Gambon (Jerry) and Penelope Wilton (Emma) in Peter Hall's production of *Betrayal* at the Lyttelton, 1978.

21 Harold Pinter (Deeley) and Liv Ullmann (Anna) in David Jones's revival of *Old Times* that toured to St Louis and Los Angeles, 1985–6.

22 Harold Pinter and Peggy Ashcroft during the BBC Radio recording of *Family Voices*, 1981.

23 Alan Bates (Nicolas) and Jenny Quayle (Gila) in *One for the Road* at the Lyric, Hammersmith, 1985.

24 Miranda Richardson as Young Woman in *Mountain Language* at the Lyttelton, 1988.

25 Gawn Grainger (Douglas), Dorothy Tutin (Melissa) and Barry Foster (Gavin) in *Party Time* at the Almeida, 1991.

26 Harold Pinter (Roote) and Tony Haygarth (Lush) in *The Hothouse*, revived at the Chichester Festival Theatre and the Comedy Theatre, 1995.

27 Harold Pinter with Vaclav Havel, lately released from prison, in Prague in 1988, a year before the Velvet Revolution.

28 Harold Pinter and the Nicaraguan poet Ernesto Cardenal launch the Arts for Nicaragua Fund at the Royal Court, 1987.

29 Harold Pinter and Antonia Fraser on their marriage day in 1980.

confusion of faces, eyes, colours, hair, moving together, as parts of one unit', from which Albertine suddenly emerges in precise focus. Even on the page, it is a heart-stopping moment. Yet although Marcel is obsessed by Albertine, he is also plagued and tormented – most especially when she shares his Paris flat two years after their Baalbec encounter – by the suspicion that she constantly betrays him with her friend Andrée, and that a notorious lesbian actress, Lea, and the young Mlle Vinteuil have both been her lovers. Pinter, like Proust, leaves us in a state of fretful, ambiguous uncertainty about Albertine's trust-worthiness, not least in the famous scene where she keeps Marcel at bay supposedly because he is drenched in the scent of syringa which she detests. Yet over and above the point about Albertine's equivocal lesbianism, Pinter scrupulously follows Proust in suggesting the impossibility of really knowing the person that we imagine we love.

Pinter's skill in both condensing and heightening Proust is vividly dis-played in the scenes following Albertine's death in a riding accident. As in the book, Marcel feverishly interrogates her friend Andrée about the nature of their relationship. As in the book, he gets two versions of the truth: in one, Andrée protests that her friendship with Albertine was totally innocent; in the other, she confirms that they were lovers. But whereas in the book these conversations are separated by a long period of time, in the film Pinter rapidly intercuts between them. One conversation takes place by day, the other at night. Marcel and Andrée sit in different positions in the night scenes and Andrée wears a different dress. But the effect of the intercutting is to sharpen the sense of contradiction. In one scene Andrée says 'I never did anything with Albertine'. In the next, she provides circumstantial evidence that she did: 'She was so passionate. Remember that day you lost your key, when you brought home syringa? You nearly caught us. It was so dangerous, we knew you would be home any minute, but she needed it, she had to have it. I pretended she hated the scent of syringa, do you remember? She was behind the door. She said the same thing, to keep you away from her, so that you wouldn't smell me on her.' Pinter's cross-cutting is not only cinematic-ally effective; it also clarifies Proust's point that the distinction between lies and truth is arbitrary, that Marcel is happier to have Andrée in his company than he would be to have Albertine restored to life, and that the memory of Albertine has become a transition to fresh desires. It is also a classic case of Proust and Pinter meeting on common ground: you hear unmistakable echoes of Deeley's puzzled curiosity about the relationship between Anna and Kate in *Old Times* and of the pervasive insecurity of Pinter man when confronted by the enigma of woman.

Brilliant as Pinter's screenplay is, it obviously cannot capture the multiplicity of meaning with which Proust can invest a single moment. There is an instance early on when the eight-year-old Marcel is denied his mother's kiss because of Swann's presence at dinner, sends a secret note to her via the maid and is unexpectedly rewarded by his mother's agreeing to spend the night in his room. The episode is all there in the screenplay. It makes a touching and poignant scene. What no adapter could possibly convey is its endless rever-berations. In the novel, it's a sign of Marcel's desperation since he knows that by staying up late he risks banishment to boarding school. It's a symbol of Marcel's shame that Swann has witnessed his abject craving for love, though Swann's later servile dependence on Odette matches his own feelings about his mother. It shows his mother's reluctant, but dutiful, cruelty (in the novel, on receiving Marcel's note at the dinner table, she tells the maid 'there is no answer'). Above all, the incident proves to Marcel that personalities are not predictable and principles are not absolute, since his father unexpectedly gives Marcel's mother permission to sleep in the boy's room. For Marcel, the experience becomes part of what he calls the vast structure of recollection:

> Never again will such moments become possible for me. But of late I have been able increasingly to catch, if I listen attentively, the sound of the sobs which I had the strength to control in my father's presence, and which broke out only when I found myself alone with Mamma. In reality their echo has never ceased; and it is only because life is now growing more and more quiet round about me that I hear them anew, like those convent bells which are so effectively drowned during the day by the noise of the street that one would suppose them to have stopped, until they ring out again through the silent evening air.

As Pinter says, you cannot rival the book; but *The Proust Screenplay* still strikes me as a masterpiece. It captures Proust's merciless social comedy. It brings the characters richly to life, not least the glamorously decadent Baron de Charlus who at one point wickedly asks Marcel: 'I mean, how on earth can a man be a lesbian? In other words, what do they *do*?' It shows, rather than describes, how involuntary memory works. For instance, as Marcel makes his way to the Guermantes Hotel towards the end of the film he stumbles on the cobbles and suddenly his surroundings are forgotten in a memory of Venice in earlier days. The screenplay also confirms Beckett's point: 'Proust is com-pletely detached from all moral considerations. There is no right or wrong in Proust nor in his world.' Above all, Pinter captures both the novel's progress towards disillusionment and revelation; the sense that life is a succession of losses devoid of reality and yet the thrilling intensity of Proust's discovery of 'This notion of Time embodied, of years past but not separated from us' —

which, of course, is what enables him to write the monumental novel we have just read.

At first, there was a genuine hope that the film might be made. After Pinter had digested the book and sketched out a possible structure, he, Joe Losey and Barbara Bray made a number of exploratory trips to France in the summer of 1972. They went to Illiers, Cabourg and Paris, steeping themselves in Proust's world and scouting for possible locations. 'We weren't going to do anything in the studio,' recalls Barbara Bray. 'It was all going to be done in real locations. We also looked at grand houses around Paris where Proust used very snobbishly to go and spend the weekend. Because Nicole Stéphane was a Rothschild, we had an *entrée* to all the Rothschild houses.' Dream-casting was also discussed: Olivier or Boyer for the Baron de Charlus, Garbo for the Queen of Sweden, new faces for Marcel and Albertine. By November of 1972, Pinter, having got a total command of the book and its atmosphere, had produced a first-draft screenplay – one eventually reduced from 468 shots to 455. What followed was more than two years of agonising wheeling and dealing in which Losey turned for backing to all the major Hollywood movie moguls, to his old Dartmouth College classmate Governor Nelson Rockefeller, even to the President of France Valéry Giscard d'Estaing. All to no avail. At one stage, there was even talk of doing a television deal whereby the original script would be sliced up into five fifty-minute episodes: something to which Pinter was vehemently opposed since his screenplay was based on a chain of visual and aural motifs, and interlocking images. Barbara Bray recalls that there were moves by Nicole Stéphane to ditch Losey from the project since he was regarded as box-office poison in the United States. When I put that to Pinter, he said, 'Nobody ever suggested that to me. It would have been quite pointless to say that to me. They may have suggested it to Barbara. Nobody did to me because I wouldn't have given it house-room.' Eventually in 1982, Nicole Stéphane, who still owned the rights to the novel, produced a single section of it, *Un Amour de Swann*, directed by Volker Schlondorff and starring Jeremy Irons and Alain Delon. It was an artistic and box-office failure; but with unflinching optimism Barbara Bray says of the Pinter version, 'It'll be made one day and it'll be made properly.' Somewhat ironically, in view of its complex visual subtlety, it has, to date, surfaced only as a drama-production broadcast in December 1995 by BBC Radio 3. It was skilfully adapted by Michael Bakewell, with Pinter himself doing the linking narration and John Wood making an outstanding Charlus: drawling, dandified and yet dismissing Marcel as a 'microbe' with a volcanic anger. Yet the more closely one listened to the radio version, the more one ached to see the finished work on screen.

The screenplay was, however, published in 1978. Pinter was apprehensive, fully expecting to be roasted alive by protective Proust authorities in the *TLS* and elsewhere. In the event, his adaptation was greeted with almost universal acclaim. The sourest review came in the film magazine *Sight and Sound*, where Tom Milne claimed Proust had melted away and described the script as no more than 'an exquisitely aromatic concordance to the original text'. But the response that really gratified Pinter came in 1983 from the Proust scholar George Painter, who had not only written a classic two-volume biography of the writer, but who knew as much about the work itself as any man alive. After reading the screenplay, he wrote Pinter a letter which speaks eloquently for itself:

> I expected it to be very fine, but in fact it is a masterwork. All Proust is in it (not only people and plot, but metaphysics of time, emotion, music, speed and stillness, grandeur and tension of structure), nothing is not Proust; but somehow it's more important that everything is created new as an independent work of art, every sentence and phrase is the real thing and so is the whole. I wouldn't have wanted a word different, or anything left out, or anything put in. The reader is horrified, enchanted, moved to tears and laughs like mad, and yet it is the writer's feeling in and under the words that makes the words true . . . I can't think of anything except Cocteau's *Orphée* fit to match it and no other work which really illuminates the causes and effects of *A la recherche*. Certainly none of the billions of Proustian critics has so impressed me; but one doubts whether criticism as such has any valid function at all.

The Proust Screenplay may not have achieved cinematic life (indeed, in a medium that seems increasingly aimed at backward adolescents and is dominated by the sense-bombarding editing techniques of rock videos and commercials, it is unlikely ever to do so) but the process of writing the script was anything but time lost for Pinter himself. As he says in the introduction: 'Working on *A la recherche du temps perdu* was the best working year of my life.' For a start, there was the sheer intellectual pleasure of undistracted immersion in a literary masterpiece: as Edmund Wilson once wrote, 'every genuine work of art enriches the reader's knowledge of life and heightens his artistic sensibility and his emotional culture'. But working on Proust was for Pinter both a homecoming and a journey of discovery. It was a homecoming in that it confirmed or clarified many ideas that had long been part of Pinter's consciousness: about the multiplicity of selves contained within any one individual, about the ultimate unpossessability of women, about the sharpness of the sensory impressions experienced in childhood, about the ability of memory to operate on different levels. Pinter's work is both inspired by and saturated in past memories, but Proust's fiction constantly exemplifies and illustrates the difference between voluntary and involuntary memory. It is a distinction Proust himself explained in an interview in *Le Temps* in 1913, just before the publication of *Du Côté de chez Swann*:

> To my way of thinking, voluntary memory, which belongs above all to the intelligence and the eyes, offers us only untruthful aspects of the past; but if an odour or a taste, re-encountered in totally different circumstances, unexpectedly reawakens the past in us, then we can sense how different this past was from what we thought we could remember, from what voluntary memory offered us, like a painter working with false colours.

Pinter's own memory, incredibly strong on visual and sensory impressions, operates in a very Proustian way. One recalls how the recollection of honeysuckle and convolvulus from a Norfolk garden sparked off the writing of *A Slight Ache*.

However, the year spent working on Proust affected Pinter at a profound level. When I asked Barbara Bray how she measured the work's impact on its adapter, she intriguingly replied, 'The message of *A la recherche du temps perdu* is the categorical imperative of art to the artist, and I think that probably reinforced Harold's own convictions about art. As you get older, you get more and more like yourself and different things help you to do that.' The immediate practical effect of working on Proust was to stimulate and encourage Pinter's experiments with time and memory, and to drive him further away from a narrow representational realism. It also confirmed his belief in the absolute integrity of art. Yet Pinter did not read Proust uncritically. While he shared Proust's belief that authentic art has no place for proclamations or dogma, at some deeper level he must have questioned whether it can also be detached from a social and political purpose. Working on Proust was a deeply enriching experience for Pinter and his screenplay is simultaneously an adaptation, a recreation and an act of loving scholarship: a masterpiece. But as he himself said, he also had to retain his objectivity. As Pinter's future development was dramatically to prove, he was aware of the limitations as well as the strengths of Proust's sensibility.

Twelve States of Revolution

The rigorous, contemplative year Pinter spent working on Proust was something of a watershed in both his public and private life: once he emerged from his own version of the cork-lined room, nothing was ever quite the same again. For a start, he was invited by Peter Hall in 1973 to become an associate director of the National Theatre. This not only involved him in the company's turbulent transfer from the Old Vic to the South Bank, but proved to be a ten-year-long commitment. Pinter, who had been a life-long opponent of apartheid and champion of unilateral nuclear disarmament, also started at this time to give public voice to his political opinions: initially, at least, at the prompting of his close friend Peggy Ashcroft. In 1973, he voiced his opposition to the American government's involvement in the over-throw of President Allende in Chile. It was a military coup which, in the words of Eric Hobsbawm, 'introduced Chile to the characteristic features of 1970s military regimes – executions or massacres, official and para-official, systematic torture of prisoners and the mass-exile of political opponents'. For Pinter this was a turning point in his role as a political activist, but he was opposed to any violation of human rights from whatever source. In 1974 he wrote to *The Times* strongly attacking the incarceration of the Soviet internee Vladimir Bukovsky. He also became embroiled in theatrical politics; in particular, in a bitter public row about Luchino Visconti's production of *Old Times* – something of a Roman scandal – which involved fundamental questions about the sanctity of text and directorial freedom. And at the very moment when the National Theatre was staging one of his most formally perfect, linguistically funny and philosophically bleak works *No Man's Land*, he found his private life in total turmoil. His marriage to Vivien Merchant had for a long time been in crisis. Early in 1975 he met and fell in love with the biographer Antonia Fraser, who was the wife of a Tory MP and the mother of six children. Their affair led to a tabloid frenzy in which the pair of them were relentlessly pursued from pillar to post. For Pinter, with his loath-ing of personal publicity, it made a normal working routine impossible. But even though the break-up of Pinter's marriage became a messily public affair that inevitably left its residue of guilt, it also led him towards an extremely fulfilled and happy relationship; one, moreover, that was to have a decisive effect on his writing.

In all the upsets and *bouleversements* of the early 1970s, one thing remained constant: Pinter's belief in loyalty and friendship. That was proved by both the provenance and production of a strangely neglected twenty-minute piece *Monologue*. Written in the aftermath of *The Proust Screenplay*, it was offered immediately to Henry Woolf to perform and was directed by Christopher Morahan on BBC Television in April 1973. Yet even here, there is a certain irony. It was almost like a present to one of Pinter's oldest chums. At the same time, it deals with an archetypal Pinter situation: the way the intimate bonds between men are eroded by sexual rivalry. The factors are constant. A room. An occupant. A visitor. A woman who transfers her affection from one to the other. Sometimes, as in *Kullus* and *The Basement*, the two men simply exchange roles. In an elaborate variation on the theme, such as *The Homecoming*, the woman assumes complete power. But the pattern is strangely familiar: the disruption of some platonic ideal of male solidarity.

What gives *Monologue* its poignancy is that the speaker seems to be making a special effort to summon up some past paradise and to bid time return. He is simply 'Man'. He has no name. No fixed identity. All we see is him conversing with an empty chair as if seeking to recapture his past in order to validate his solitary, vacant present. 'I think I'll nip down to the games room', he begins. 'Stretch my legs. Have a game of ping-pong. What about you?' The choice of words is significant. It implies an institution: a home, an asylum, even a prison. Or the speaker could simply be the occupant of a lonely bedsit fantasising about his past (ping-pong, one recalls, was a vital part of the Hackney Boys' Club which Pinter, Woolf and the rest of the gang used to frequent). The speaker then spins off into verbal free-association: a metaphorical reference to a flinging down of gauntlets leads to memories of real gauntlets, helmets, motoring jackets and motorbikes. 'Of course', the man says of his absent friend, 'you weren't cut out to be a motorbikist, it went against your nature, I never understood what you were getting at.' Motorbikist? The word has an odd ring implying something awry about the character.

The pathos of *Monologue* stems from the fact that the speaker, trapped in a static present, feeds off a vividly imagined past. In that sense, it seems a halfway house between the earlier Pinter and *No Man's Land*. Linda Ben-Zvi, one of the few critics to have analysed the play in depth, sums it up neatly: 'With economy Pinter describes a world with no future, only the past linguistically replayed over and over in the present. Even a count of the verb tenses in *Monologue* illustrates the situation: 48 are past tense, 18 present and only six future.' What is more, Pinter uses the cultural signposts of his own past to give the situation concrete dramatic life. The speaker was introduced by his old friend to Webster and Tourneur. In turn, he got his old mate going on Tristan Tzara, Breton, Giacometti, Celine and Dos Passos. All artists and writers who were part of the Hackney gang's cultural trade and mart. But sex, as so often in Pinter, is the wedge driven between two male friends. In this case, the source of division is a black girl from their past. The speaker loved her body; she, he claims, loved his soul. He took her to see his old mate in his Notting Hill Gate flat; she temporarily switched her affections to his sly, aquiline, more ethereal friend: 'It was your detachment that was danger-ous. I knew it of course like the back of my hand. That was the web my black darling hovered in, wavered in, my black *moth*. She stuttered in that light, your slightly sullen, non-committal, deadly dangerous light.'

It's a familiar pattern; but, claims the speaker, it's all in the past: he enjoys his freedom, his mind is sparking, the crap is cut. Every line in the play, however, shows that the speaker is totally obsessed by times past. Pinter underlines the point by a final, crucial shift of tense in which the speaker imagines what would have happened if his friend had had two black kids:

> I'd have died for them.
> (*Pause.*)
> I'd have been their uncle.
> (*Pause.*)
> I am their uncle.
> (*Pause.*)
> I'm your children's uncle
> (*Pause.*)
> I'll take them out, tell them jokes.
> (*Pause.*)
> I love your children.

The shift between the past-conditional, the future and the present indicates the desperation of the speaker's desire for a literal brotherhood with his best friend. (The change of tense to achieve dramatic impact was a device which Pinter was later to use, with even more devastating effect, at the end of *One for the Road*.) It gives *Monologue* great emotional impact and underlines its expression of, in Ben-Zvi's words: 'not just a wish for love but for the return to some Edenic state, before maturity and childhood reared their fractious, male heads.' It is one more expression of Pinter's obsession with a paradise lost; but he also makes unsentimentally clear that the attempt to talk the past into being is either shadowed with ambiguity or destined to become what Beckett once called the 'churn of stale words in the heart again'.

When it went out on television in 1973, the piece was little noticed or understood. The device employed by Christopher Morahan of cutting between Woolf's right-facing profile to the reverse image led people to infer that the character was simply talking to his other self. Henry Woolf recalls, 'I wasn't very good on TV. We had a lovely meal after the recording and Harold said it was marvellous, but we all went our separate ways knowing it hadn't quite worked. A few months later I did it at the Orange Tree and it played much better. With the television version, Harold knew the camera script wasn't going to work and there was a question of either going along with it or scrapping it. But Christopher's first wife had just been taken into hospital and was gravely ill. In those circumstances, Harold knew that he couldn't ask him to rethink the whole shooting script. He allowed his whole play to be sacrificed because of a human consideration. It redounds greatly to his credit.'

Pinter was prepared to see *Monologue* misfire out of compassion for his director; he was not, however, in a mood to see one of his major plays sacrificed to interpretative ego. In May 1973 he became embroiled in an extraordinary public row with one of the great gods of Italian film, theatre and opera Luchino Visconti, an aristocrat with a whim of iron, over his Teatro di Roma production of *Old Times*. Initially, the row was provoked by the theatre's use of a translation that took liberties with the text and that Pinter's Italian agent Laura del Bono considered 'unactable'. But the real problem lay with Visconti's violently unorthodox production. He mounted the play on a boxing ring in the centre of the theatre's stalls. Pinter's famous silences were punctuated by beats on a gong. Anna and Deeley's lyrical contest of memories became an after-supper sing-song accompanied by a pianist who carried on playing while Deeley described going to see *Odd Man Out*. Worst of all, from Pinter's viewpoint, the relationship between Anna and Kate became explicitly lesbian.

Pinter's agent unavailingly tried to get the production stopped after the first night. And when Pinter himself flew to Rome to view the production, he was horrified by what he saw. On 11 May he held a press conference in Rome in which he itemised his objections:

I have never heard of or witnessed a production such as this which is totally indifferent to the intentions of the author or which introduces such grave and shocking distortions and which I consider a travesty. I did not write a play about two lesbians who caress each other continually. I did not write a scene in which a woman exposes herself to a man on the stage. There is nothing in the text to indicate that the man and the woman powder the naked breasts of the wife on stage. I did not write a scene about a man masturbating his wife. Nor did I write a musical. The characters sing songs but I did not state that a piano should accompany them in the most wildly improbable places. All the sexual acts I have referred to are not only inexpressibly vulgar in themselves but are totally against the spirit and intention.

The Rome press, possibly influenced by the fact that Visconti had recently suffered a stroke, sided with their own revered cultural icon. The leading daily, *Il Messagero*, reported Pinter's press conference under the banner headline 'No Sex Please, I'm English'. But Richard Roud, the *Guardian*'s roving cultural correspondent who had seen Peter Hall's original production, described Visconti's version as 'a travesty' and was particularly harsh on Valentina Cortese's performance as Anna: 'It was as if, Visconti having told her there was supposed to be a lesbian undertow in her relationship with the wife, she had taken this as *carte blanche* for the most grotesque display of pawing, fawning and slobbering.' The production continued until the end of the season, but the whole rumpus left, on the one hand, a bitter after-taste with Visconti, and on the other, Pinter feeling equally aggrieved. John Francis Lane, however, put his finger on the real problem when he wrote in *Plays and Players* that, in its desperate need for writers, the Italian theatre had transformed its directors into authors in the filmic sense of the word: 'The idea of the *metteur en scene* who puts another author's work on the stage is almost foreign to their natures.'

Pinter clearly felt his play had been butchered to make a Roman holiday. But behind the specifics of the row lay a much larger issue: how much creative freedom should a director be allowed? In Pinter's case, it would be wrong to claim that he hovers hawk-eyed over every production, making sure that three dots are not wantonly converted into two. In later years, for instance, he sanctioned an all-female version of *The Caretaker* at the Sherman Theatre in Cardiff and approved a Roger Planchon production of *No Man's Land* that ended with empty whisky and champagne bottles cannoning down towards the footlights. But when a writer sees his play being virtually re-invented, he is entitled to protest. As a broad generalisation, it also seems to me there are different rules for the living and the dead. Once a play has become a canonical classic, it achieves a kind of after-life and is bound to be subject to all manner of re-evaluation. While a writer is still alive – and available for consultation – it is incumbent on the director to respect the author's known intentions. On the evidence available, it would seem that Pinter was well within his rights to lam into Visconti's attempt to turn the subtle, delicately shaded *Old Times* into a soft-porn version of *The Well of Loneliness*.

The irony is that Pinter's own view of the director's role is as a faithful interpreter of the text. A few years earlier he had been approached by Trevor Nunn and asked if he would be interested in directing a Shakespeare play for the RSC and, if so, which one. Pinter instinctively replied, '*Othello*.' What, Nunn enquired, was his angle on the play or his visual concept? Pinter replied that he had none: he simply wanted to realise the text. The idea was never taken any further. But Pinter's principle of fidelity to the writer became an article of faith when, in February 1973, he accepted Peter Hall's invitation to join the National Theatre. He was part of a team that included Michael Blakemore, John Bury, John Dexter, Jonathan Miller and John Schlesinger, as well as the retiring – though not excessively so – NT boss Laurence Olivier. The transition period from Olivier to Hall and from the Old Vic to the new building on the South Bank was – as Peter Hall's *Diaries* record – one filled with trauma, treachery, back-stage venom and press hostility. Through all this, Pinter remained unwavering in his support of Peter Hall, and in his belief in the sanctity of the text and the supremacy of the writer.

One acid test of Pinter's view came with Jonathan Miller's proposal, in the first full season of the new regime, to mount an all-male version of *The Importance of Being Earnest*. Hall records the resulting contretemps in his *Diaries*.

> There was a sharp division between Jonathan and Harold Pinter. Pinter's position is clear: an author has certain clear intentions and Wilde's intentions were not that women should be played by men. Jonathan asserted repeatedly that it was a director's right to interpret a play in any way that seemed significant to him, once the play was no longer new. He was making a fool of nobody but himself and the play was still there at the end of the day. Harold feels one has a greater responsibility to a dead dramatist than to a living one.

In the end it became a non-issue because of Miller's public, and highly publicised, departure from the National Theatre. But in this particular instance, I see Miller's point. Once a play has acquired classic status and had as many productions as *The Importance* has had over the years, it is open to reinterpretation; indeed, that becomes proof of its multidimensionality. And how can we be sure, nearly a century after an author's death, we know his or her intentions? Might not Wilde have been teased and tickled by the idea of a baritone Bracknell or a dragged-up Gwendolen and Cicely? Would an all-male version have released the homosexual subtext of a play that, even in its title, plays on the fact that 'Earnest' was a Victorian code word for 'gay'? Pinter was right to protest about Visconti's Sapphic *Old Times*, and possibly overprotective in his objections to Miller's revamped Wilde.

Miller and Pinter were, however, very different animals. Peter Hall remembers that Pinter would cut through some of Miller's more baroque conversational flights by asking, 'What do you mean?' Gawn Grainger, who was in Miller's production of Beaumarchais' *The Marriage of Figaro* and Pinter's production of John Hopkins's *Next of Kin* at the National, also recalls their totally different directorial techniques: 'Jonathan's productions were like big sweeping paintings in which the wall would be painted in a variety of different colours. Harold was exactly the opposite: meticulous, detailed, and with the ability to focus something right down like a pinpoint.'

Pinter's production of Hopkins's domestic drama, which opened at the Old Vic in May 1974, was his first for the Peter Hall regime and was rightly praised for its scrupulous realism. The play was about a Sabbath family-gathering in desolate suburbia in which the host suddenly walked out on wife, children, brothers and sisters, and widowed mother. His defection brought the skeletons tumbling out of the family closet, but no reason was offered for his departure and no hint as to whether he might ever return. Harold Hobson in the *Sunday Times* astutely related the play to Pinter's own belief in the author's freedom to leave unresolved mysteries in a work of art. 'One immediate sign of that freedom', wrote Hobson, 'was the unexplained disappearance of the girl in Antonioni's *L'Avventura*; another is the vanishing of Brian Lloyd from his suburban home in *Next of Kin*.' The crucial difference was that Hopkins's play was almost engulfed by its realistic dialogue and that the family emerged as a set of bizarre case-histories. Even then it struck me as ironic that such a wordy piece was directed by a master of verbal economy. On this occasion, Pinter's principled respect for a fellow-author's text seemed somewhat exaggerated.

Pinter was deeply committed to the National, but he also found time to work in film. In 1973 he directed his first movie: a screen version of Simon Gray's *Butley* made for the short-lived American Film Theater series for which Peter Hall also shot a masterly version of *The Homecoming*. Pinter's directorial screen début was highly impressive: faithful to Gray's play, but also opening it out sufficiently to show the hero's incapacity to handle daily life. There was a marvellous prefatory sequence which showed Butley hacking away over his first cigarette of the day, staring bleakly at a can of empty shaving-cream, cutting himself on the chin with an old razor blade, moodily travelling to work on a jolting tube train. Even before a word had been spoken, we knew this was a man who made heavy weather of the simplest daily rituals.

Pinter also spent much of 1974 wrestling with a screenplay of *The Last Tycoon*, commissioned by Sam Spiegel and based on the novel about the Hollywood power-game that Scott Fitzgerald left uncompleted and un-revised at the time of his death in 1940. Technically, Pinter did a good job in fleshing out the novel and charting the obsession of the producer-hero Monroe Stahr (based on Irving Thalberg) for an Anglo-Irish girl who resembles his dead wife. There's one marvellous sequence in which Pinter juxtaposes the tinsel falsity of Hollywood's idea of the parting of two lovers with the monosyllabic awkwardness of the real thing. The latter makes a splendidly cryptic scene, all Rattiganesque subtext, where Stahr suddenly stops the car in which he and the girl are driving. ('STAHR: Listen. KATH-LEEN: What? (*Pause.*) STAHR: Nothing. (*They drive on in silence approaching Kathleen's house.*) KATHLEEN: Can you drop me here at this corner?'). But the star-laden finished film, released in 1977, was something of a disaster. Elia Kazan directed it with laborious, reverential heaviness. And a kind of noth-ingness hovered in the air in the big scenes between Robert De Niro as the falling Stahr and Ingrid Boulting as Kathleen. It was like watching Jimmy Connors have a knock-up with a ball-boy on an outside court at Wimbledon. Donald Pleasence who played a boozy British writer rebelling against Stahr's paternalism recalls, 'Kazan was after a sexually very explicit film and Harold would never go for that. He didn't want people writhing about the floor with no clothes on. The film wasn't a success, but I enjoyed doing it.'

The Last Tycoon presented Pinter with problems that were vastly different compared to earlier screenplays: how to finish Fitzgerald's uncompleted novel, how to convey Stahr's mixture of old-fashioned anti-union autocracy and artistic integrity in the face of the Hollywood barracudas. But it was while brooding on the technical problems of adaptation that Pinter was sud-denly seized with an idea for a play; or, if not an idea, an image that de-manded instant exploration. It is a classic example of how Pinter's creative imagination works at some intuitive, supra-rational level. One evening he'd gone out to dinner alone to mull over the problems of the screenplay. On the taxi-ride home something suddenly clicked into place. 'I remember,' he says, 'I was sitting in this taxi and I actually saw two people sitting in a room and one of them was about to pour a drink and he said, "As it is?" and the other character said, "As it is, yes please, absolutely as it is." I didn't know who they were, but I knew that the fellow pouring the drink was going to give the other man his drink and pour himself another drink and that things would go on from there. I pursued that. I had the image of two people standing up in a room and one offering the drink. It's a very simple thing. It can hardly be called complicated. But I was thrust into a situation where they knew more about it than I did. So I had to find out, I had to pursue it . . . It's easy to sound pretentious about this, but in fact it's the way I think writing – in my case, dramatic fiction – works. You have to follow the clue of what you're given, but the crucial thing is to get a clue in the first place, to have a *donnée*, a given fact. If I don't have that, I'm in the desert.'

The play in question is *No Man's Land*, and it is possible, through the Pinter Archive housed in the British Museum, to see how quickly the play took shape in his imagination. But the key point is that, although the finished work can be – and indeed has been – analysed to death, it starts from a phrase or an image rather than an intellectual concept. Pinter's description of the invasion of the imagination and of relentless pursuit brings to mind – appropriately for a play saturated in echoes of T. S. Eliot – Helen Gardner's words about the shaping of *The Four Quartets*: 'Mr Eliot has not at the back of his mind an idea or argument which could have been expressed quite simply, and which he is purposely disguising. These poems do not begin from an intellectual position or a truth. They begin with a place, a point in time, and the meaning or the truth is discovered in the process of writing and in the process of reading.' Substitute Pinter's name for Eliot's, and the words seem equally apt.

Delve into the Pinter Archive and you also discover several things. One is that Pinter is obviously trying to explore a mood rather than articulate a ready-made idea. For a start, there are more alternative titles than for any other Pinter play and they make a fascinating list: *The Morning After*, *Faces in Shadow*, *A Sidelong Glance*, *A Tomb of Honour*, *Long Ghosts*, *Drowning*, *The Drinking Party*, *The Photograph Album*, *The Bull's Head*, *The Last Toast*, *After Hours*, *Closing Time*, *Night Quartet*, *The Previous Subject*. Some of them are clearly phrases extracted from the completed draft. The majority of them have a terminal, faintly doom-laden quality. Like *The Waste Land* or *Endgame*, they reek of desolation or mortality: there is an air of finality about them which doesn't exactly suggest we are in for a robustly optimistic view of the human condition.

Yet one of the paradoxes of the finished play is its combination of global despair and localised activity: it offers a tragic vision filled with mercurial humour. That contradiction is evident from the scraps of paper on which Pinter jotted down initial fragments of dialogue. He was clearly fascinated by the prospect of a confrontation between two topers: one rather silent and withdrawn, the other a periphrastic interloper. Consider this:

A: Have I met your wife?

B: Of course.

A: Not the one with the blazing hazel eyes, hangs about north of the river, never ventures south, sometimes seen floating on a barge off Battersea?

B: I don't think so . . . no.

A: I wonder to be quite frank whether I can trust that denial or whether I can comply with that doubt. I wonder, to approach it from another approach, whether you know your wife, whether you can report her fairly, whether accurate and therefore essentially poetic definition means anything to you at all, whether you truly remember her, truly did caress her, truly did know her, truly did dream or truly did adore. But because of these doubts and because I too am human I'll drink another without . . . further ado.

Already Spooner's tone of voice is there: the questing, probing, cawing circumlocution. So, too, the idea that the past is unverifiable, mysterious, uncertain. Also the comic notion that Spooner knows more about Hirst's wife than he does himself, though it is noticeable that in the finished version Pinter cuts the more obvious jokes about her floating on a barge off Battersea.

Many of the scraps of dialogue are incorporated into the first draft which is unusually close to the finished play. As so often, Pinter starts out by calling the characters A, B, C and D, finding names for them only in the process of writing, though the character who later becomes Foster is here 'Jack Lee' and Briggs at this stage is 'Mr Bolshaw'. Other differences are very revealing. In this version it is A (the Spooner figure) rather than B (Hirst) who introduces early on the key poetic motif: 'Experience is a paltry thing. The crucial fact to understand is the essential and thank goodness irresistible damnation of no man's land which never moves, which never grows older and which remains forever icy and silent (*pause*). Have I gone too far do you think? You find that too palpably rhetorical?' At this stage, the idea of no man's land is introduced by Spooner as a literary conceit to be held up to the light and examined; only later does it become the play's controlling metaphor. Also Pinter has yet to finalise the physical action. In this first draft, Hirst staggers to the door on his first exit rather than ignominiously crawling on hands and knees. And Act Two is prefaced by a large handwritten note saying CLOSE CURTAINS SOME-WHERE; in the final version it becomes a definite action signalling a decisive tonal shift into a world of arrested motion. But compared to, say, early drafts of *The Homecoming*, the world of the finished play is remarkably complete in Pinter's imagination.

The key question is how we interpret the work itself. Whatever the

ultimate meaning, the events of the play are perfectly clear. Hirst, an immured and wealthy man of letters, has met Spooner, a minor poet and Chalk
Farm potman, in a Hampstead pub and invited him back to his sterile, if
drink-filled, home. The dynamic of the play consists of Spooner's attempt to
penetrate Hirst's booze-cocooned defences, to outflank his sleekly sinister
servants, Foster and Briggs, and to find a way of establishing himself permanently in this carpeted mausoleum. As the play draws to a close, it would
seem that Spooner is failing and that the other three characters are closing
ranks against him; that Hirst is finally retreating into a form of living death, a
spiritual and physical no man's land, from which Spooner has, out of a
complex mixture of self-interest and compassion, tried to rescue him. At the
very end, Spooner acknowledges that Hirst is now in that solitary, icy waste-
land which gives the play its title: a fact underlined by Hirst's final cry of 'I'll
drink to that'.

Old Pinter hands can, of course, spot plenty of echoes of previous plays.
Spooner – 'the opportunist with territorial ambitions, the intruder on the
hunt for space to steal', as Benedict Nightingale once dubbed him – is not
unlike a better-educated version of Davies in *The Caretaker*, and he is harassed and abused by Foster and Briggs in the same odd, oblique way as Mick
flusters the invading tramp. And just as in *Old Times* Anna and Deeley swap
competitive recollections of the past to achieve psychological dominance, so
Spooner enters Hirst's memories of his Oxford youth to try to increase his
sway over the old boozer. Yet *No Man's Land* is infinitely more than a summation of past Pinter themes. There is a radically new tone of voice and
philosophical stance: under the surface comedy lies a bleak recognition of the
fact that we are all trapped inside our own skins and that we all occupy some
undefined space between past and future, birth and mortality, security and
fear. The comedy is still there. So, too, the sense of brutality lurking under a
sophisticated veneer. But it is, by some way, Pinter's harshest vision of the
human predicament.

First impressions are very important, and my own initial reaction to *No
Man's Land* on seeing it at the Old Vic in April 1975 was that it was a
profoundly personal play. I took Hirst and Spooner to be projections of
Pinter's own darkest fears. Hirst – wealthy, immured, isolated and increasingly cut off from the source of his original inspiration – seemed to me
Pinter's nightmare vision of the kind of artist he might, unless he were
careful, become. Spooner – the pub poetaster haunted by memories of other
men's lines – was a distant memory of the marginalised versifier he might
once have been. It was no more than an intuition; and when I mentioned it to
Pinter over a lunch table twenty years later, he grinned rather wryly and said

there had never been a Briggs and Foster in his life, dutifully protecting him from the outside world. But without wishing to narrow *No Man's Land* down, it still seems to me to reflect Pinter's own anxieties. As Peter Hall said, it is inescapably about 'the nature of the artist'. And twice, in conversation with me, Antonia Fraser has related it to Pinter's personal circumstances. As she says, she would never have understood the play unless she had visited the Pinter house in Hanover Terrace, 'immaculate with this terrible silence'. On another occasion, she pointed out that it stemmed from a very unhappy period in Pinter's personal life when his first marriage was in terminal decline and when many of his natural political instincts were repressed. As she says, '*No Man's Land* was a very bleak play – not the work of someone who was going to take a banner and protest about the state of the world.'

Like all Pinter's best plays, *No Man's Land* addresses universal issues while stemming from some deeply personal core of anxiety: Pinter's nightmares and fears become ours. When the play was revived at the Almeida in 1992, with Pinter himself playing Hirst, John Peter in the *Sunday Times* pinned down better than anyone the play's hallucinatory quality:

> It is haunting because it speaks of, and speaks to, the unconscious. Spooner is not only a down-at-heel poet; he is also Hirst's alter ego, his conscience, his nagging reminder, the painful debit on his spiritual balance-sheet. This is why each man keeps recognising features of his life in the other. Hirst is the king of the mind, arrogant but crumbling: Spooner is the exile of that mind, anxious but tenacious. *No Man's Land* is an anatomy of the creative life in which smug success is forever haunted by shabby failure, the public posture by the private anguish.

That sense of umbilical connection between Hirst and Spooner is reinforced by the very choice of names. It is a well-known fact that all four characters in Pinter's play were named after famous cricketers from the pre-1914 era. What has been less noticed is that George Hirst, the aggressive Yorkshire bowler, and R. H. Spooner, the stylish Lancashire batsman, were both Roses-match opponents and figures whose names were inextricably linked. Neville Cardus in his *Autobiography* recalls sitting in the sixpenny seats at Old Trafford as a boy and watching his Lancashire heroes assailed by the 'barbarians' from Yorkshire. He leaves us with a powerful image: 'George Hirst rolling up the sleeve on his great ham of a left arm, ready to swing it and hurl a new red ball at the wicket of Reggie Spooner, hurl it like a live coal; and Spooner seemed frail and his bat scarcely a solid, while the other Yorkshire men swarmed all around him.' Spooner, Cardus explains, was, for all his apparent vulnerability, a lyrical batsman: 'Herrick to the Gibbon prose of a MacLaren innings.' Hirst, for all his danger and menace, was 'endowed with the gusto of humorous genius'. Though from opposite sides of the Pennines, their names were forever conjoined. There is even a strange, oblique connection between the original Foster and Briggs. Frank Foster was a dashing Warwickshire batsman whose sporting career was finished when he was crippled by a First World War motorcycle accident in 1915. Johnny Briggs was a versatile Lancashire all-rounder who suffered from epilepsy and who died prematurely at the age of thirty. As Pinter says, the characters in his play are not meant literally to resemble their cricketing counterparts ('My Briggs is a tough bugger if ever there was one'), but their names are not randomly chosen. They both evoke memories of a Golden Age terminated by the 1914–18 war, with its ineradicable image of a literal no man's land, and underline the hidden connection between Hirst and Spooner.

This image of Hirst and Spooner – antithetical, yet interdependent – provides a crucial clue to the play's meaning and structure. As Peter Hall confessed to his *Diaries* when directing the original production: 'A feeling that I really know what it is about – opposites. Genius against lack of talent, success against failure, drunk against sobriety, elegance against uncouthness, smoothness against roughness, politeness against violence.' One could easily add to Hall's list: fixity against flux, past against present, memory against reality, town against country. But these opposites constantly feed off each other as if Pinter is saying that the gradual withdrawal into death that we witness is accompanied by a keen apprehension of what life was and could be. John Bush Jones in an essay in *Modern Drama* has argued that the whole play is about stasis in the sense of 'total, final immobility': that Spooner effects no change, that there is no development of character or situation, that the chief linguistic device is one of repetition. But if that were true, it would make for deadly drama. What gives the play its tension and energy is the constant switch between the opposite magnetic poles of paralysis and activity, resignation and resistance. It is this conflict between Spooner's attempt to re-engage Hirst's creative imagination in the last hours of his life and the knowledge that we inhabit a no man's land ringed by outer darkness that gives the play its dynamism. It is also what makes the play superior to its obvious ancestor, Beckett's *Endgame*, in which the sense of four characters passing the time until death and engaging in desultory exchanges comes to seem enervatingly hermetic.

Opposites and parallels: that is the key to Pinter's play. You see it in the opening exchanges. Hirst is smart, oracular, immobile; Spooner is shabby, talkative, restless. Yet there are similarities under the contrast. 'Do you often hang about Hampstead Heath?' Spooner asks Hirst. 'Tell me ... do you often hang about Jack Straw's Castle?' Hirst later enquires of Spooner. Inside Hirst, who is keenly aware of his terminal state, lurks some obstinate need for the solace of companionship: two mugs are kept ready on the shelf and it is he who has invited Spooner home. Meanwhile Spooner, while critical of Hirst's drinking, impotence and unpersuasive memories of a wife, a country cottage, a village church where male and female virgins are ceremonially honoured, reveals an equally desperate need for friendship. He is at once Hirst's alter ego and potential salvation. 'Let me perhaps be your boatman', says Spooner. 'For if and when we talk of a river we talk of a dank and deep architecture. In other words, never disdain a helping hand, especially one of such rare quality.' The classical reference is clearly to the Virgilian ferryman Charon, who in the *Aeneid* steered great heroes, boys and unmarried girls, 'as numerous as the leaves that fall at autumn', across the black river Cocytus. Spooner is knowingly picking up on Hirst's reference to the village maidens. At the same time he is clearly offering to be Charon to Hirst's Aeneas and transport him towards the Elysian fields. It is a gesture born simultaneously out of shared classical knowledge, self-interest and charity.

Antitheses and parallels: the whole play is based on them. With the arrival of Foster and Briggs, Pinter clearly establishes a sense of conflict between their world and Spooner's. Spooner speaks in the consciously Prufrockian phrases of some ageing belletrist. 'I have known this before', Spooner says witnessing Hirst's drunken, crawling departure on all fours. 'The exit through the door, by way of belly and floor.' That pastiches the melancholy cadence of Prufrock's 'I know the voices dying with a dying fall/ Beneath the music from a farther room'. Foster, on entry, instantly establishes a different, direct, down-to-earth tone: 'What are you drinking? Christ I'm thirsty. How are you? I'm parched.' Spooner is the shabby sham-artist carrying about him the faint aura of the London literary quarter, at its heyday in the 1940s and '50s, known as Fitzrovia; the two servants evoke power, clarity, the brute sophistication of the arriviste delighting in a world of inherited taste. ('It's a world of silk. It's a world of organdie. It's a world of flower arrangements. It's a world of eighteenth-century cookery books. It's nothing to do with toffee apples and a packet of crisps. It's milk in the bath. It's the cloth bellpull. It's organisation.' So says Foster in one of the play's funniest, most beautifully written speeches.) In fact, the battle between Spooner and the two servants is territorial, emotional and linguistic. Spooner wants to be part of Hirst's world, to re-engage his imagination, to challenge his sense of paralysis; they simply want to be his amanuenses on the silent journey to oblivion.

Obviously there is a desperate power-battle going on throughout the play between Spooner and the two servants; but whereas in early Pinter that battle would have been brutal and clear cut, it is now more shaded and subtle. There are even parallels between the opponents. Spooner describes an experience in Amsterdam when he was sitting outside a café by a canal and decided to paint a picture of what he saw: 'of the canal, the waiter, the child, the fisherman, the lovers, the fish, and in background, in shadow, the man at the other table, and to call it The Whistler.' Spooner uses the experience as proof of his European cultural sophistication; as a weapon with which to dominate the servants. But Foster shortly after describes an experience out East when 'a kind of old stinking tramp, bollock naked' threw back a coin which Foster had tossed towards him and made it disappear into thin air. Spooner instantly dismisses the event as 'a typical Eastern con trick', but like his own description of the Amsterdam canal-scene, it has a sense of arrested motion: a feeling, which runs throughout the play, that the past is pinned down through a series of snapshot images, moments frozen in time. Hirst himself, when told that Spooner claims to be a friend of his replies:

> My true friends look out at me from my album. I had my world. I have it. Don't think now that it's gone I'll choose to sneer at it, to cast doubt on it, to wonder if it properly existed. No. We're talking of my youth, which can never leave me. No. It existed. It was solid, the people in it were solid, while . . . transformed by light, while being sensitive . . . to all the changing light.

Spooner and Foster pin down the past through arrested moments in time; Hirst through faces and actions recorded by the camera (what Eliot in 'East Coker' calls 'The evening with the photograph-album'). But for all their differences of language, style and outlook, all three characters are haunted by the hunger for a secure and certain past as a form of protection against the fragmented, discontinuous present. Again, opposites and parallels.

Part of what makes *No Man's Land* so beautifully tantalising is its own sense of contradiction. Its bleakness and humour. Its lyricism and laughter. Its meditation on age, death, memory, time, art, and its often parodic tone and use of traditional effects. At the end of Act One, after Briggs has led the legless Hirst out of the door, Foster shows his cool sadism by plunging the room and Spooner into total darkness: a simple effect that both reminds you of the old rep thrillers Pinter acted in in the 1950s and demonstrates where the power lies. Act Two, again as in one of those old rep plays, takes place the morning after. It opens with a cat-and-mouse contest between Spooner and Briggs. The former affects a lofty insouciance ('Food? I never touch it') while tucking into a breakfast of champagne and scrambled eggs. Briggs, after announcing that the financial adviser has not turned up because he finds himself 'in the centre of a vast aboriginal financial calamity' (Pinter's favourite Cardinal Newman phrase), launches into his now-celebrated speech about the impenetrable one-way intricacies of Bolsover Street. Harold Hobson once took the trouble to drive round the area to prove the speech was a fabrication; but that surely is beside the point. As with Mick's geographical *tour de force* to Davies in *The Caretaker*, it is largely designed to cow and impress the recipient; to prove to Spooner that Briggs, for all his crudeness, is a man who understands the Byzantine mysteries of life. It also, from a purely practical point of view, occupies the stage-time while Spooner devours his breakfast.

Pinter's ability to mix parody and serious purpose is shown in the brilliantly funny scene when Hirst bursts in bright and sparkling the morning after, greets Spooner with a cry of 'Charles. How nice of you to drop in' and proceeds to launch into a competitive memory-game about long-ago love affairs in a raffish Brideshead Oxford. It's a scene that operates on any number of levels. It's an exhilarating piece of cod-Coward banter in which proper names are used as a card-trumping device: 'May I further remind you', says Spooner itemising Hirst's imagined sexual betrayals, 'that Muriel Blackwood and Doreen Busby have never recovered from your insane and corrosive sexual absolutism?' It also shows Spooner wittily seizing the moment. By entering into a competitive memory-game about a fantasy-past, he tries both to secure a foothold in Hirst's present and quicken him into life. But on the larger global level it suggests yet again that we deploy our recollections of the past, even absurd and fantastical ones, as a means of warding off our fears and insecurities: keep talking, keep changing the subject, keep playing games and you postpone your terror of extinction, death and eternal silence.

That comic canter through an imagined past is abruptly shattered as the play moves towards its final desolate stages. Pinter marks the transition in several ways. One is by Hirst's offer to show Spooner his photograph album. To Hirst's poetic imagination the ghostly figures in the photographs can be quickened into existence by the sympathy of the living ('Deeply, deeply, they wish to respond to your touch, to your look, and when you smile, their joy . . . is unbounded'); to the pragmatic, ruthlessly undercutting Briggs they are simply the empty past ('They're blank, mate, blank. The blank dead'). But Pinter also registers the play's final transition through physical action: the fading of the light, the return to the drinks cabinet, the decisive closing of the curtains.

This symbolises the final shift towards a living death, an entombed stillness from which all memory is excluded. Spooner at first fights desperately against this by pleading with Hirst for a job as secretary, by admitting his own fluidity, by seeking to reclaim Hirst for the active present by offering him a poetry reading in the upstairs room of a pub. But the silence that follows that request is greeted by the following exchange:

HIRST: Let us change the subject.
(*Pause.*)
For the last time.
(*Pause.*)
What have I said?
FOSTER: You said you're changing the subject for the last time.
HIRST: But what does that mean?
FOSTER: It means that you'll never change the subject again.

What Hirst has done is to deny the possibility of change, to acknowledge that he and his companions have reached a terminal point, and that he is trapped in the unyielding fixity of no man's land which, as Spooner reiterates, 'remains forever icy and silent'.

The ending is one of stasis. Yet the remarkable feature of this play, which like a great poem almost transcends rational analysis, is its tension between death and life, between resignation and resistance; between the desiccated order, sterile affluence and conspicuous consumption of Hirst's home and the remembered world of country cottages, sunlit lawns, bucolic gaiety. What we see on the literal level is a titanic struggle going on in the last few hours of man's life to re-engage his imagination and creative power, and stir his memories. Only with the closing of the curtains and the fading of the light does the attempt fail as Hirst starts to crawl unburdened towards death. But the play works through a series of interlocking oppositions and, as Austin E. Quigley astutely wrote: 'where there is putative stasis in the action it is the enforced stasis of arrested motion not the tensionless stasis of absent motion.' I dislike the word 'Pinteresque'. It's become a vague and sloppy critical term implying anything from shadowy menace to subtextual anxiety. But to me this play does capture a sensation that is very peculiar to Pinter the man and the artist: a simultaneous rage and appetite for life combined with a sense that we pass our days singing in the void and awaiting the inevitable fact of mortality.

Pinter finished the play early in September 1974. What is extraordinary is the speed of events thereafter. On Friday the 13th – in a brief pause between filming commitments in Hamburg – Peter Hall read and instantly admired it. A slot was found for it in the National Theatre's spring programme. Casting was also quickly and painlessly achieved. 'Everyone,' says Hall, 'can always cast a play in ideal terms. The problem is that people aren't always available or don't want to do it. Then you start the real casting. With this play, I read it, gave it instantly to John [Gielgud] and Ralph [Richardson], and within a few days they had accepted. It was one of the most extraordinary experiences I've ever had. They fully entered into it. But they found it extremely hard to learn because of the long sentences. In fact we rehearsed early in February 1975 for a fortnight and roughed it out, stopped for a fortnight while they went away and learned their lines. That was one of the luxuries of the National Theatre: a long rehearsal period. I think they were both a bit naughty about it subsequently – making jokes in interviews about not knowing what it meant. Absolutely untrue.'

As Hall's *Diaries* show, rehearsals were also based on his own confidence that he too knew what it was all about. On 11 February he records: 'The play is hard complex chamber-music but I've got it . . . a very satisfying feeling.' His main worry was with Gielgud's Spooner. On 7 April he writes: 'John was hesitant and humble. At the moment he is inclined to play what the audience should conclude about the character rather than the character himself.' A day later – two weeks before the opening – Hall's worries about Gielgud intensify: 'He's over-experimenting: playing it humble, playing it conceited, playing it creepy, playing it arrogant. It is a search for the simple key. Whereas the truth is that Spooner is many things and changes his posture from second to second. So there isn't a simple key.'

In fact when the play opened on 23 April 1975, Gielgud's Spooner stole the notices. The play itself was greeted with a mixture of admiration, respect and bewilderment – not surprisingly, when you consider the absurdity of daily critics having to describe, analyse and assess a new Pinter play within an hour after curtain-fall. The echoes of Eliot and Beckett were duly noted, and Irving Wardle in *The Times*, having expressed reservations about the work's knowingness, ended unequivocally: '*No Man's Land* remains palpably the work of our best living playwright in its command of language and its power to erect a coherent structure in a twilight zone of confusion and dismay.' Everyone agreed that Richardson's Hirst, Michael Feast's Foster, Terence Rigby's Briggs, Peter Hall's production were fine; but it was Gielgud's transformation as Spooner that astonished the critics. He had long been regarded as the high priest of English acting, but also as someone who, as Max Beerbohm said of Bernhardt, 'rarely stooped to impersonation'. That was what made his Spooner – based on a mixture of Auden, his own brother Lewis and the Bohemian semi-failures who ran ballet bookshops off the Charing Cross Road – such a shock. The baggy, grey-pinstriped demob suit, the untidy sandy hair, the beer-belly, the sandals implying slightly odorous socks evoked the ageing relic you might meet in a BBC pub like the George.

To Benedict Nightingale, Gielgud suggested the kind of figure 'one can still sometimes see padding about Hampstead or Highgate, head full of little magazines and the Spanish Civil War'. Gielgud also caught the contradictions in Spooner's behaviour: the slyness, the ingratiation, the furtive filching of cigarettes when left alone, the superciliousness towards servants. But Hall felt, with some justice, that the general astonishment at Gielgud's character-acting led to Richardson being undervalued. 'John's performance', he recorded on 24 April, 'is magnificent but there are other actors who could do it, whereas I do not think any other actor could fill Hirst with such a sense of loneliness and creativity as Ralph does.'

No Man's Land was a great popular success, transferring to Wyndham's in July. What is extraordinary is that the whole period of its preparation and rehearsal coincided with the most profound upheaval in Pinter's private life: the start of an affair with Antonia Fraser leading to the final and long-inevitable disintegration of his marriage. For all concerned, it was a traumatic period made infinitely worse by the zealous voyeurism of the popular press. Pinter suddenly found his private life was becoming public property and it left permanent scars in his relationships with journalists. But out of the agony of a marital break-up conducted in the public gaze came a prolonged period of domestic security that was to have a big effect on his work. Pinter himself is still understandably reluctant to relive that period of painful transition in his life but Antonia Fraser recalls it with total candour.

'Harold and I,' she says, 'first met, briefly, through a recital programme that John Carroll organised at the National Gallery in 1969 about Mary Queen of Scots. I did the narration, and Vivien and John Westbrook were the readers. But I certainly remember that first meeting with Harold. The National Gallery recital was being recorded for the BBC, but the recording was totally spoilt by someone at the back shouting at a noisy attendant, "Will you kindly shut up." That was Harold. I said to him afterwards, "I hear that was you." He said, "Yes, I do that kind of thing all the time." I can't say I wasn't warned. We then met again round about 1970 at a Biafra benefit concert hosted by Sam Spiegel and then in January 1975 at a revival of *The Birthday Party* at the Shaw which was directed by my brother-in-law Kevin Billington. And that was how it all started.' As Pinter himself says, 'We fell in love instantly and have remained just as strongly in love over all the years that have passed.'

For six weeks in early 1975 the affair was conducted in clandestine secrecy. Vivien at the time was playing Linda in *Death of a Salesman* at Guildford in a production which went on to the Hong Kong Festival. She fell ill in Hong Kong, had to come out of the play and convalesce at home. It became impossible for Pinter to tell Vivien about his state of emotional turmoil, though he did confide in Peggy Ashcroft, to whom he was very close at the time, as well as to Peter Hall and Guy Vaesen. 'When he does tell Vivien,' wrote Peter Hall in his *Diaries* on 14 March, 'I should think the explosion will be heard the other side of Regent's Park.' Eventually, in late March, Pinter confessed to Vivien that he was having a serious affair. According to Guy Vaesen, Vivien initially took it very well: 'She said she liked Antonia, having worked with her on the National Gallery recital, and that she was a very nice woman.' But Vaesen's recollection is that a female friend of Vivien's trotted round to her house and poisoned her mind against Antonia. Life in Hanover Terrace gradually became impossible and, five days after the first night of *No Man's Land*, Pinter finally left home. Peter Hall, in fact, records the precise day in his diary entry for 28 April. 'Spoke to Harold. He was, at that very moment, packed and about to leave home: "The point is, I am at this moment leaving my home. I am leaving my house." It is a tough business for him. He told me that whatever happened he thought that Vivien and he were now through.' Having packed his bags, Pinter initially went to stay at Sam Spiegel's apartment in Grosvenor House. Later he moved in with his old friend Donald Pleasence and his family in their riverside house in Chiswick, where Daniel quickly joined him. According to Pinter, Vivien couldn't cope with bringing up Daniel alone – a point confirmed by Guy Vaesen who stayed at Hanover Terrace throughout the spring and summer, at Pinter's suggestion, to look after Vivien. Even the mild-mannered Vaesen, however, stomped out angrily when he came down to breakfast one morning and picked up a copy of the *Daily Mail* and saw a big headline saying 'Actress Tells All'. As Vaesen recalls, 'I spoke to Vivien on the phone later in the day and she simply said, "Oh, that rubbish. I don't know who can have put that in the paper."'

In fact, press fascination with the break-up of the Pinter marriage had started in April at the time of *No Man's Land*. On the first night, Pinter asked Peter Hall to stick close to him in case he was accosted by reporters. Pinter himself, Antonia and her husband Hugh Fraser studiously said nothing in the vain hope that the fuss would eventually die down. Vivien, however, had been threatening all summer to sue Pinter for divorce, publicly citing Antonia if he did not return to her. She finally did so, via her lawyers, on 27 July, though later on she was to drop her petition. But she certainly chose her moment in order to cause maximum publicity and embarrassment: it was just before the first night of Pinter's production of Simon Gray's *Otherwise Engaged* at the Queen's. It was not the ideal time for Pinter to be putting on a play about a man attempting to preserve his sang-froid and listen to a recording of *Parsifal* while his domestic life slowly disintegrated. Pinter made a good job of it despite the voracious attentions of the Fleet Street pack. Simon Gray recalls how absurd it all became: 'I went into the theatre one day and found that Harold had had to do a bunk because he was being pursued by journalists. So I had to take over the production – which was fortunately in very good shape – for the last three previews. I remember coming into rehearsal one morning and seeing bulging shapes behind the seats who turned out to be photographers from the tabloids crouching with their cameras. God knows what they thought they were going to photograph – possibly the character of Davina in my play taking her top off with Harold in the foreground. But sadly Harold couldn't make it to the first night and it took a long time for the dust to settle.'

What gave spice to the whole story was Vivien's threat to cite Antonia, the wife of a Tory MP and a well-known public figure, in the divorce petition and her ability to use the popular press as her court of appeal. On 29 July she talked to William Hickey in the *Daily Express*. 'Antonia is Accused by Harold Pinter's Wife', screamed the huge banner headline. In the interview Vivien went on to paint a ludicrously glowing picture of the Pinter marriage and to put the stiletto heel into her rival. 'At her home in Regent's Park', ran the Hickey column, 'Mrs Pinter said, "I'm still numb with all that has happened. Ours has always been a legendary marriage in show-business circles. We were the happy couple that other actors used to talk about." . . . Curled up on a sofa, Vivien said, "I promise you he is a wonderful man . . . But it seems he is possessed by Lady Antonia – she has cast a spell on him. How she can do it with six children to look after I don't know."' Hickey followed up the story on 30 July with an 'exclusive' about a 'distraught' Pinter saying that his wife had given an undertaking not to talk about the matter. In the end, however, there was no stopping her. Hickey went on: 'In an unrecognisably husky voice, the actress – a much-acclaimed Lady Macbeth for her Stratford-upon-Avon role – said, "This is all too dreadful. For 19 years we were very happily married, at least I was." While Vivien talked ceaselessly to the papers, Pinter and Antonia decided the only way to escape their clamorous attentions was to leave town and go into hiding at a village near Burford in the Cotswolds, staying in a converted barn belonging to Diana Phipps, a friend of Antonia's who was away on her summer holidays. There they bought the papers every day only to find themselves confronted by Vivien's vindictive bulletins from the marital front line.

For all concerned, it was a traumatic summer: one of separation, confrontation, pursuit and flight. What kept the story alive were Vivien's indiscretions and her refusal to accept the role of the mutely suffering wife. Everyone else, to their credit, maintained a stoical silence. Eventually the press fever abated a bit and in late August Pinter and Antonia returned to London, setting up residence in a house in Launceston Place in South Kensington. 'Logistically,' Antonia recalls, 'it was very difficult. Harold couldn't do anything in the house. There wasn't much space and he didn't have his books there. It was also very difficult for me as all my books were in Holland Park. I should add that Daniel came to live with us in the house and was always very easy with us. He was very nice to me at a time when it would have been only too easy for him to have turned on me . . . simply because he had been the sole focus of his father's love and now manifestly wasn't.' Significantly, Daniel at this time changed his name from Pinter to Brand, his maternal grandmother's maiden name. Pinter, however, does not see this as a symbolic rejection of himself; it was, he claims, a largely pragmatic move on Daniel's part designed to keep the press, who had been relentlessly hounding him also, at bay.

The break-up with Vivien and the new life with Antonia was to have a profound effect on Pinter's personality and his work. In the short term, it made it impossible for him to write. Not until he and Antonia moved back into her Holland Park family home in August 1977 was he able even to contemplate a new play. For two years his time professionally was taken up with directing and acting: he did a fine production of *Blithe Spirit* at the National in 1976 (one that underlined his strange affinity with Coward), went on to direct *The Innocents* (with his old friend Pauline Flanagan) and *Otherwise Engaged* in New York, and appeared on radio in plays by Beckett and Havel. But in the long-term his new life deeply affected his writing and his engagement with the public world. Antonia Fraser is quick to qualify the idea that she had any direct input into his plays and points out that other people had a shaping influence on his politics. In particular, she feels Peggy Ashcroft encouraged him to believe that protest over American action in Chile might have some practical effect. Yet while Vivien was ostentatiously indifferent to politics, Antonia was the daughter of Labour peer Lord Longford, the ex-wife of a Conservative MP, a practising member of PEN and someone who grew up in a world where politics permeated daily life. Presumably that must have had some impact? 'It would be gratifying,' says Antonia, 'to claim that I had some influence over Harold, but I think what happened was that he had an unhappy, complicated personal life which gave way to a happy, uncomplicated personal life, and a side of Harold which had always been there was somehow released. I think you can see that in his work after *No Man's Land* which was a very bleak play. But I've always felt that the outburst of activity that followed came about partly because of the drastic change in Harold's personal life.'

The disintegration of his marriage and the formation of a new and infinitely happier life with Antonia was a decisive moment for Pinter that produced an inevitable mixture of security, guilt, self-torment and renewal. It also led to significant changes in his work. In the 1980s, Pinter took an increasingly public stand on major issues and wrote a number of plays reflecting his lifelong hatred of oppression. Whether that would have happened without the dramatic transformation in his private life is extremely doubtful, but the work of any major artist does not fall into neat, critically satisfying patterns. It is much too simple to say that Pinter's work started by dealing with external menace, moved on to a period obsessed with time and memory, and then became militantly political. The truth is that Pinter's obsessions constantly fold into each other and overlap. He had always been fascinated by the politics of private relationships and alert to world affairs, and he was still very much preoccupied by time, male friendship and the intricacies of sexual deception. His life had undergone a major upheaval; but after existing for two years in a creative no man's land where writing was out of the question, he was to delve once more into his past in a much-attacked play that was as nakedly and recklessly personal as anything he had ever written.

Thirteen Private Lives

What is the link between a writer's life and art? Auden once claimed that 'A writer is a maker not a man of action', but even he went on to admit that all works are, in a sense, transmutations of personal experience. In the case of drama, one might add, very much so. Hedda Gabler may be the bored, repressed daughter of a Norwegian general, but she is also Ibsen in skirts. Oscar Wilde said of *The Importance of Being Earnest* that 'it is quite nonsensical and has no serious interest', but it is also a deeply revealing portrait of its author's double life. And plays like *Long Day's Journey into Night* and *The Glass Menagerie* are thinly veiled accounts of the circumstances of O'Neill's and Tennessee Williams's private lives.

The case of Pinter is particularly fascinating. His stage plays are commonly triggered by a sharp memory of some personal experience which then develops according to its own internal logic. You cannot say the plays are literally autobiographical; yet they inevitably reflect his own fears, anxieties and preoccupations, and in one specific case – *The Caretaker* – are closely based on living people. With *Betrayal* – the first play Pinter wrote after the break-up of his marriage – both the external events and many of the internal details derive directly from his own life. Given the play's title and theme, it was inevitably assumed when it was first produced in 1978 that it had something to do with his own marital crack-up. When Mel Gussow raised that very question, Pinter quickly kiboshed the assumption: 'I'm very glad you asked me that question because I can tell you that it's totally irrelevant. One thing has absolutely nothing to do with another.' In fact, *Betrayal* is based – even down to the general chronology and specific incidents – on an affair between Pinter and the greatly admired TV presenter and journalist Joan Bakewell that long predated his meeting with Antonia Fraser and lasted from 1962 to 1969.

Pinter now openly acknowledges the affair and Joan Bakewell talked to me about it with great candour, but it raises an important question. In the past, both in *The Dwarfs* and *The Caretaker*, Pinter had utilised not just his own experience but also that of friends and acquaintances. He was to do the same in *Betrayal*. Does that present him with any kind of moral dilemma?

'I think,' he told me, 'every writer does that one way or another. Otherwise, what are we writing about? We're writing about something to do with ourselves and observable reality about us. We're not writing about the moon. But I think, as long as the work is written with understanding, it is legitimate. I'm not using words like "compassion", because that is not what drama has to do . . . I don't think compassion registers as a relevant virtue in relation to the writing of plays . . . I'd go so far as to say that a hard, clear understanding which throws a light on a state of affairs is what you're aiming at. If you're true to that, then you're not doing any harm . . . I'm hesitant to defend what one does as a dramatist in creating characters which are loosely or glancingly or obliquely based on others . . . But, for example, in *Betrayal* I think the situation that the wife finds herself in is one which a lot of people will associate with . . . It's a situation you find yourself in and what do you do about it? You live it and you find your ways out . . . this is life . . . What can I say about *Betrayal*? . . . I did that.'

Betrayal is a good opportunity, generally, for coming clean. When the play opened at the National's Lyttelton Theatre in November 1978 it got a guarded, even downright hostile, critical reception. And no one was ruder than myself about Pinter's depiction of the emotional entanglements of the north London literati. The play was technically original in its arrangement of the scenes in reverse chronological order; but after the meaty familial politics of *The Homecoming* and the poetic profundity of *No Man's Land*, Pinter seemed to be taking drama back to the days of smart-set adultery. In a notice written on the night – a condition that tends to produce either flushed excitement or intemperate dislike – I announced: 'What distresses me is the pitifully thin strip of human experience it [the play] explores and its obsession with the tiny ripples on the stagnant pond of bourgeois-affluent life.' I even went on to declare: 'Harold Pinter has betrayed his immense talent by serving up this kind of high-class soap-opera (laced with suitable brand-names like Venice, Torcello and Yeats) instead of a real play.'

Since then I have seen and read the play many times and drastically revised my opinion, but why was I – along with many others – so initially hostile? A number of possible reasons. One was my belief that British theatre should engage, wherever possible, with momentous public events. The year 1978 gave us David Hare's *Plenty* dealing with the failures of post-war Britain, Howard Barker's *The Hang of the Gaol* which was a wide-ranging assault on cosy English liberalism, and the multi-authored *Deeds*, directed by Richard Eyre at Nottingham Playhouse, which examined the ethical standards of hospitals, the police, MPs and giant corporations. Without reneging on my commitment to political drama, it is possible that I was less than fair to any play that dealt with private experience.

Also, the circumstances of the original production were not ideal. Not only did *Betrayal* open at a time when the National was beset by industrial problems. It was also unsuited to the large Lyttelton Theatre which demands expansive action and large statements. In retrospect even Peter Hall, who directed the production, admits it might have been more successful in the smaller Cottesloe. But Hall has his own theory about why the play was so dustily received: 'I think Harold was coming out of a slightly different box. He was dealing with male–female extra-marital relationships and if you just receive the play without digging underneath it, it's a rather trite story. The obvious question is, "Who is being betrayed?" and, with respect, most of you missed the point. You took it like a Mills and Boon story. But the sleight of hand that Harold has performed is that, while dealing with a triangular relationship, he's talking about something else. He seems to be saying that if you start with self-betrayal, it gradually infects everything like a dreadful, destructive virus.'

Hall is right. In the course of nine symmetrically arranged scenes we witness a whole series of interlinked betrayals: of marital fidelity, lovers' trust, male friendship and literary idealism. Pinter explores this through a reverse replay of a seven-year-long affair between Jerry, a literary agent, and Emma, who is the wife of his best friend since undergraduate days, a publisher called Robert. Pinter leaves no aspect of betrayal untouched. Jerry has betrayed both Robert and his own unseen wife Judith, who herself may be having an affair with a doctor. Emma has betrayed not only Robert, but also Jerry by not disclosing to him that her husband found out about the affair five years into its duration. And Robert has betrayed both Emma through his own serial adultery and Jerry by not letting on that he knows about the affair. Yet Pinter is not writing a moral tract endorsing Arthur Hugh Clough's point: 'Do not adultery commit, advantage rarely comes of it.' Behind the play's action lies an aching awareness of the way the high ideals of youth are betrayed by the compromises of daily life. Jerry and Robert were, as undergraduates, both editors of poetry magazines. Jerry also used to write long letters about Ford Madox Ford, Robert about Yeats (the ultimate poet of loss and decline). Now Jerry is an agent hawking around a writer called Casey who is a useful money-spinner but little more; Robert, a successful publisher, drunkenly confesses that he hates the whole business of pushing, promoting and selling modern prose literature. They are not only parasitic literary middlemen, but, by extension, symbols of all those who betray their youthful commitment for the sake of bland, middle-aged affluence.

Hall's point about the destructiveness of betrayal, however, is worth quali-
fying. Repeated viewing of the play has convinced me that Emma survives
this network of deceit with great style, while the two men are spiritually
annihilated by it. As so often in the past, Pinter, while prizing male companionship in almost Hemingwayesque fashion, seems awed by women's infinite
capacity to adapt and survive. That is certainly what comes across in the first
scene: a pub reunion between Emma and Jerry two years after the end of the
affair (it was this unbudgeable image of two people talking about the past that
kick-started Pinter's imagination). Emma's self-control, emotional poise and
professional success contrast with Jerry's tentativeness, uncertainty and en-
slavement to past memories. She runs a thriving gallery, is having an affair
with Jerry's client and her husband's author Casey, and has the past in perspective. 'I thought of you the other day', she tells Jerry, revealing that a
chance trip to Kilburn, where they had an adulterous love-nest, has stirred
up happy recollections of old times. Contrast Jerry's later line 'I don't need to
think of you', implying that his whole being is still permeated by her presence. Emma's memory is also very sharp. It is she who introduces one of the
key motifs of the play: a recurring image of a moment at a party when Jerry
threw her baby daughter Charlotte up in the air and caught her. Throughout
the play it becomes a symbol of pure irrecoverable happiness: another of
Pinter's lost Edens and an episode of almost Proustian power in its ability to
unlock the past. The one production I've seen fully to grasp its significance
was Matthew Warchus's at the West Yorkshire Playhouse in 1994 when it was
constantly replayed between scenes on an overhanging screen. But while
Jerry remembers the emotion that moment engendered, it is Emma who
recalls the precise circumstances:

> JERRY: Yes, everyone was there that day, standing around, your husband,
>   my wife, all the kids, I remember.
> EMMA: What day?
> JERRY: When I threw her up. It was in your kitchen.
> EMMA: It was in your kitchen.

Emma's recollection is clearer and her character more resilient than that of
Jerry, but Pinter does not suggest she is emotionally impervious – she is still
shocked and hurt after learning the previous evening of her husband's persistent infidelity. But crucially Jerry seems even more wounded than Emma
by the news of Robert's clandestine affairs ('I never suspected . . . that there
was anyone else . . . in his life but you'). Jerry also naïvely and hopelessly
swallows Emma's lie – another nuanced betrayal – that she told Robert of
their own affair only the previous evening. It is a perfectly pitched scene that

catches the halting poignancy of an ex-lovers' reunion, the Rattiganesque inequality of passion, the toughness and fortitude of women and, most of all, the labyrinthine nature of betrayal which continues even after an affair is long over.

Pinter scores the scene beautifully for two voices, but this counterpoint between form and content is a vital part of the play's appeal. The theme is the corrosive complexity of betrayal and the mess of our emotional lives; the structure, however, is harmonious, shapely and clear. Peter Hall intuitively grasped the point in a way we salaried hacks didn't. In his *Diaries* (20 October 1978) he first of all describes Emma as 'the best woman's part Harold has ever written' and attributes it to the influence of Antonia. He goes on to say: 'It is an advance for Harold, this play. The tension builds up at an enormous rate. It is not fanciful to think of Mozart. From my point of view, there's the same precision of means, the same beauty, the same lyricism and the same sudden descents into pain which are quickly over because of a healthy sense of the ridiculous. A strange comparison I know. But it's there.' The play's strict musical sense of form has been noted by others – not least Austin Quigley and Ruby Cohn – who have pointed out the symmetrical balance of the scenes and the way the action pivots on Robert and Emma's Venetian holiday. Lay the scenes out in columns, as Cohn does, and you get the point:

1. 1977: Emma and Jerry in a pub.
2. 1977 (later): Jerry and Robert at Jerry's house.
3. 1975: Emma and Jerry in a flat.
4. 1974: Emma, Jerry and Robert in Robert's house.

6. 1973: Emma and Jerry in a flat.
7. 1973 (later): Jerry and Robert in a restaurant.
8. 1971: Emma and Jerry in a flat.
9. 1968: Emma, Jerry and Robert in Robert's house.

5. 1973: Emma and Robert in Venice.

Everything leads either to or from the Venetian hotel scene in which Robert reveals his discovery of Emma's affair; the musical structure is enhanced by the way, at mid-point in the play, Emma and Robert are discussing a novel, the theme of which he takes to be 'betrayal' though Emma disputes the fact. ('I haven't finished it yet', she says. 'I'll let you know': the sense of being in a Borgesian hall of mirrors is intensified by the fact that we too haven't yet 'finished' the play). But what gives the scene dramatic tension is Pinter's ability to convey both Emma's guilt and Robert's pain through circuitous banter. I heard Pinter read the scene at the University of East Anglia in 1994 and he caught superbly Robert's tone of insouciant lightness concealing inner mortification: a classic demonstration of the masked nature of Pinter dialogue.

The scene starts with Emma on the bed reading, Robert gazing out of the window. They talk casually about tomorrow's trip to Torcello, about the new novel by Spinks that Emma is reading. Robert circles around like a plane waiting to land before lightly remarking that he dropped into the American Express office in Venice where he found a letter addressed to Emma. The more Robert spins out his mock-indignation at the way a letter intended for Emma was offered to him ('whom they laughingly assume to be your husband'), the more we understand his emotional devastation. And the more he talks fondly about Jerry, having recognised his handwriting on the letter, the more we understand his sense of betrayal of their past friendship. It is a classic Rattigan technique most persuasively used in *The Deep Blue Sea*, in which what is said is in direct opposition to what is felt. Even Emma's enforced confession that 'We're lovers' is followed by Robert's 'Ah. Yes. I thought it might be something like that, something along those lines.' But what is fascinating is the way Pinter gradually allows Robert's pain to seep through the defensive irony like acid eating into metal. Emma's revelation that the affair has been going on for five years is followed by Robert's italicised '*Five years?*' which suggests a mixture of emotions: incredulity, indignation, real anguish. It is instantly followed by Robert's very Strindbergian question about the paternity of their one-year-old son Ned. Emma's assurance that Ned was conceived while Jerry was in America leads to an extraordinary exchange:

ROBERT: Did he write to you from America?
EMMA: Of course. And I wrote to him.
ROBERT: Did you tell him that Ned had been conceived?
EMMA: Not by letter.
ROBERT: But when you did tell him, was he happy to know I was to be a father?
(*Pause.*)
I've always liked Jerry. To be honest, I've always liked him rather more than I've liked you. Maybe I should have had an affair with him myself.
(*Silence.*)
Tell me, are you looking forward to our trip to Torcello?

Pinter crams a wealth of meaning into a short passage. For a start, we are confronted by one more form of betrayal: Robert twists the knife in Emma's side by reminding her that she calculatedly deceived her lover by conceiving a child in his absence. His confession to his preference for Jerry also works on multiple levels. It is partly an ironic joke in keeping with his earlier mood of studied indifference. It is partly an open expression of the way two men who sleep with the same woman are linked by imitative desire: a theme that runs through *The Dwarfs*, *The Collection*, *The Basement* and *Monologue*. It also touches lightly on a very English kind of masculine intimacy that occupies a grey hinterland between friendship and sex. In the end, this is what gives the work its emotional impetus. In a play littered with manifold forms of betrayal, the most profound is that of some Edenic notion of male friendship based on shared intellectual passions and youthful idealism. Emma is a strong and powerful character; but as Pinter once publicly and succinctly said, *Betrayal* is 'about a nine-year relationship between two men who are best friends'.

That yearning for a lost paradise informs the remainder of the play in several subtle ways. It is not strictly true that the play goes in reverse chronology: the two scenes immediately after the Venetian episode pursue its reverberations. Scene 6, back in the Kilburn flat, shows precisely how Jerry is kept in the dark by Emma over the revelation of their affair and how she returns from Venice with both a tablecloth and a heightened capacity for dissimulation. And Scene 7, when Jerry and Robert lunch together, is sustained by a keen sense of dramatic irony: we and Robert both know something which Jerry doesn't. But the scene is also full of nostalgia for a lost world of unadulterated friendship and undiluted love of literature. Contrasting his loathing of the world of London publishing with his morning alone on Torcello reading Yeats, Robert expresses a hunger for an almost pre-sexual world where friendship was free from taint, and the love of poetry was uncontaminated by notions of commerce. Even the final scene, which takes us back to 1968, shows us the point of deviation when Jerry in gaining one paradise discarded another. As Jerry makes his first move towards Emma, Pinter captures the heightened self-awareness of love. He also pins down the precise moment at which the serpent enters the garden. Discovered alone with Emma in the bedroom by Robert, Jerry skilfully masks the intensity of his desire in phrases of actorish adoration:

JERRY: As you are my best and oldest friend and, in the present instance, my host, I decided to take this opportunity to tell your wife how beautiful she was.

ROBERT: Quite right.

JERRY: It is quite right, to . . . to face up to the facts . . . and to offer a token, without blush, a token of one's unalloyed appreciation, no holds barred.

ROBERT: Absolutely.

JERRY: And how wonderful for you that this is so, that this is the case, that her beauty is the case.

ROBERT: Quite right.

(JERRY *moves to* ROBERT *and takes hold of his elbow.*)

JERRY: I speak as your oldest friend. Your best man.

ROBERT: You are, actually.

(*He clasps* JERRY's *shoulder, briefly, turns, leaves the room.*
EMMA *moves towards the door.* JERRY *grasps her arm.*
She stops still. They stand still, looking at each other.)

The final image underlines the point of the play: it is a moment frozen in time and the start of a process that will eventually unravel the close ties of male friendship; that will leave both Jerry and Robert feeling weakened and mutually betrayed, but that will also signal Emma's liberation and acquisition of independence. It is not a moralistic play, as Harold Hobson once rather Victorianly suggested, showing that adultery is not a profitable investment. It is a play partly about the way betrayal of oneself and others spreads like a bacillus through the whole system of human relationships, and partly about the ability of women to transcend the destruction of male bonds. It is a work of resonant complexity: a perfectly balanced trio about emotional havoc; a poisoned comedy of manners that changes its meaning depending on the prism through which it is viewed.

It also shows Pinter, more than in any of his previous plays, feeding directly off the circumstances of his own life. That doesn't mean it should be read purely as an essay in autobiography or that it lacks universality; but it depends very heavily on Pinter's seven-year-long affair with Joan Bakewell, then married to the radio and TV drama director and producer Michael Bakewell, who was one of Pinter's early champions. It all happened long ago, and all three parties are now very happily remarried. If one rakes over the embers, it is partly because it helps to illuminate *Betrayal* and partly because it shows how even the participants have a slightly different 'take' on past events.

Joan Bakewell talks very perceptively about Pinter, and when I asked her how autobiographical a writer he was, she was characteristically candid in her reply. 'I think,' she said, 'he mines exhaustively what is happening to him. It's very difficult to talk about this without talking about *Betrayal* which is about my relationship with Harold; and which is all true. It's accurate in its chronology and in its events. Often quite tiny events like that in which Jerry talks about picking up this little girl – called Charlotte in the play – and throwing her in the air. Harold actually did that with my three-year-old daughter at a party for Daniel's birthday. He used that moment and the way she was caught. It was a magical moment; and he mines that right through the play. The story about the poste restante at the American Express office in Venice is also literally true. Though there are some alterations. One of the things that Emma does is to bring back a gift from Venice which is a tablecloth: an emblem of the domesticity she wishes to preserve. I brought back something much wittier: an hour-glass. So sometimes the detail of life is better. But it's like a diary and so I was upset when I first read it. Harold kept saying, "It's a play – it's a play." I was upset, however, because it was called *Betrayal*. It's such a judgemental word. But we go on betraying, don't we? Here am I telling you about it. The irony is that the process never ends.'

Whatever distress Joan Bakewell felt about the transposition of her life into drama has long since faded. Now she sees the play much more as part of Pinter's ungovernable preoccupation with the past and with memory. 'Harold and I are very fond of each other,' she says, 'and have terrific lunches. The nature of memory is also very important to him. We were talking about something recently and he moved over to his shelf and pulled out a copy of *Old Times* and quoted that line about "There are some things one remembers even though they may never have happened." He said, "Isn't it interesting that one tries to remember something and one isn't sure that it happened exactly like that?" He's just fascinated by memory and its influence on daily life, on the choices that are made and how memories come up. Of course, his shrewd intelligence can control his daily life: his appearance, his friendships, his lifestyle. But he can't control the flood and the flow and the flux of memory or his subconscious. *Betrayal* is part of that process. Except that the affair described in the play was so intense that one can't ever forget how fraught it was and how riddled with moral underpinning. As we lived through the events, there really was a moral imperative to do the right thing. It was a serious matter and I think it took Harold a long time to decide to come to terms with it by writing about it. He also knew that if he had mentioned it to me in advance, I would have just blown up. Now when I see the play I feel it's a brilliant convoluted piece of writing, even if it lacks the real character of the people involved: maybe it's just too close to actual events. But Harold also universalises the situation so that people who see the play come out saying, "Oh, it's the story of my life."'

What is clear is that Pinter took what he needed from actual experience and invested it with dramatic significance. The throwing of the baby in the air is a classic example of how a momentary incident can be turned into a

dramatic metaphor. The episode of the Venetian letter is likewise both fact-
ually true and a pivotal part of a theatrical construct. Pinter also mined his
own sense of shock at discovering that Michael Bakewell had known for two
years about the affair and turned it into a symbol of personal betrayal. But
Pinter's imagination also transforms reality. The two male characters in the
play are literary middlemen rather than a playwright and director. Unlike
Jerry and Robert, neither Pinter nor Michael Bakewell could ever be accused
of betraying their youthful idealism; nor, indeed, have they ever felt a molten
sense of kinship. In other words, the play is both true to events and a piece of
dramatic fiction; much closer to reality than any of Pinter's previous plays yet
also a work of art.

Again, the perspective changes depending on the vantage point. For Joan
Bakewell, the play is understandably like an intimate diary of a private affair.
For Pinter, it is a piece of drama with an objective life of its own. And when I
asked him whether the cannibalisation of his own – and other people's –
experience ever gives him pause before he writes, his answer was extremely
revealing: 'No . . . it gives me pause *after* I've written it. At the time the
compulsion to write is such that it overrides all else. The whole point about
Betrayal is that it struck me from the start as an extremely exciting concept
. . . I got this original image of the pub and I thought, I know where I am in
this . . . I knew I was going to go into something related to my own past, but
not literally my own past . . . because that was not the case. The experience
was transmuted into something else . . . The fact is that Michael Bakewell
and I were never close friends and I wasn't best man at his wedding. We had
simply worked together and got on perfectly well . . . The play just happened
. . . The kind of questions you refer to only start to arise when you send the
play to the person involved.'

Pinter is referring to Joan Bakewell; but her then husband Michael was
also intimately involved for, while Robert is not a direct portrait of him, the
character's situation in many ways coincides with his own. Sitting in his
sunlit Essex garden talking about his relationship with Pinter, Michael
Bakewell looks back with rueful fondness to happier times past. 'I first met
Harold,' he says, 'just after the fiasco of *The Birthday Party* when he came to
see me in Broadcasting House with two possible ideas for plays. One was
about a man who wakes up to find that he has been sleeping next to a corpse;
the other was the work that eventually became *A Slight Ache*. Most writers
when they outline ideas for plays are tentative and inarticulate. I always
remember Harold looking at me with that fierce gaze of his and giving me an
absolutely clear and precise synopsis of both plays. He was highly impressive.
And though I went with *A Slight Ache*, there was a tremendous battle within

the BBC drama department to get it on the air. Barbara Bray, Donald McWhinnie and myself fought passionately for Harold against Val Gielgud and all the old-guard producers who were still very much in the ascendant. It was recorded on spec, was highly successful when it went out, and started a professional and personal association that covered many years. I did several of his works on radio including the *Kullus* monologues, which I think are seminal in that they show how the interrogator loses his power because of his inability to control the pauses, thereby turning himself into the victim. We also worked together in television when I was a producer on what was rather grandly called *The Largest Theatre in the World*. But obviously our friendship was ended by the writing of *Betrayal*. It's not something I really want to talk about; but I remember vividly Harold's indignation at the fact that I had known for a long time about the affair without saying anything. I think he personally felt betrayed.' Pinter himself comments: 'I felt nothing like indignation. I simply felt deeply distressed.' Yet even though Michael Bakewell is saddened by what happened, it is one of life's nicer ironies that in 1995 he adapted Pinter's *Proust Screenplay* into a very successful two-hour radio play. Some wounds time does heal.

Everyone, however, has a different perspective on *Betrayal*: on its approximation to reality and on its ultimate meaning. David Jones, when he came to make the film version with Jeremy Irons, Patricia Hodge and Ben Kingsley that was released in 1983, discovered its tantalising elusiveness. 'I found while making the film,' he says, 'that I was constantly taking different sides. Sometimes you think how extraordinary Emma is to accommodate both men. At other times you think, "How dare she? How could she conceivably continue the affair after her husband has discovered it?" But the story is a totally human emotional triangle about male and female insecurities. On the whole, because Harold is a man he's writing about male insecurity faced by this great enigma, this exciting enigma, this maybe destructive enigma called woman. What's so good about Harold is that he doesn't write fluffy little ladies; he's only interested in women prepared to take you on.' That's as shrewd an observation as any; and one of the many reasons why *Betrayal* has been shown to be as durable as steel.

Two months before *Betrayal* had its theatrical première, Pinter's screen adaptation of Aidan Higgins's novel *Langrishe, Go Down* was also shown as a BBC2 Play of the Week, superbly directed by David Jones. Pinter had written it as a movie in 1971 and hoping to direct it himself had included highly detailed camera shots. Sadly, the money for the film was never found. As Pinter laughingly remarked to Mel Gussow: 'It's on a subject which doesn't seem to be very appealing. It's about three middle-aged spinsters living in a house in Ireland in the 1930s. At the lodge-gate there's a cottage and a German philosophy student in his thirties working on a thesis. Now they don't seem to feel this is the brightest subject.' But on TV it was turned into a deeply moving, neo-Chekhovian film with unforgettable performances from Judi Dench, Annette Crosbie and Jeremy Irons.

As Jones astutely says, *Langrishe* was in part 'a love poem to Harold's own time in Ireland'; a reminder also of the clandestine nature of passion in that often puritanical country. But it is of significance in Pinter's *oeuvre* in that it shows his preoccupation (particularly in the early 1970s) with time and memory, while also reflecting his fascination with the duality of the German character. Cutting between a run-down Irish country estate in 1937–8 and 1932, it recaptures an intense summer-long affair between the sexually ardent, if inexperienced, Imogen Langrishe and a mature Bavarian student Otto Beck, who is studying seventeenth-century Ireland and its customs. It is also about the memory of that affair and its profound emotional repercussions. Imogen's unposted love letters to the exploitative Otto, written after she has thrown him out, are stolen by her sister Helen and secreted in a drawer. For Imogen, the letters are a tangible reminder of her momentary release from a life of gentrified repression; for Helen, they are a symbol of the physical passion she herself has never enjoyed.

Pinter thinks visually – not least in a dazzling montage of opening shots that, as in his work on Proust, shifts rapidly between past and present. He also explores the intricacies of time through character. Otto, in his early encounter with Imogen, plays lavish tribute to the 'essential purity' of Irish women; a speech that acquires a boomerang irony after he has introduced her to all manner of sexual humiliation, reduced her to the status of a skivvying whore and betrayed her with a village tart. Yet Pinter is clearly haunted by the ambiguity of the German character – a subject he dealt with in *The Quiller Memorandum* and explored in a later film *Reunion*. On one level, Otto represents the meticulous, precise, academic German mind: he explains to Imogen, with pedagogic accuracy, the etymology of Irish place names and when he takes her to Dublin to see a production of Strindberg's *Miss Julie* – another work in which a member of the gentry is dragged down by her passion for a social inferior – he learnedly compares it to a rival version in Düsseldorf. But Otto's academic scrupulousness is accompanied by an appetite for physical torment. It is no accident that the two features of his native land he misses most are the Munich whores and the teaching of Heidegger, a philosopher who displayed an initial enthusiasm for the Nazi regime and who was repelled more by the vulgarity than the cruelty of Nazism. On one level, Otto could be said to liberate Imogen's unclaimed sexuality; on another, he is a moral monster whom you could easily imagine joining the SS. As well as a love letter to Ireland, the film is also an exploration of Pinter's complex feelings about the German psyche.

It's a work about passion, politics and class; in particular, the emotional reticence of the Anglo-Irish near-gentry that is part of the historic reason for their downfall. *Three Sisters* also constantly comes to mind. As with Masha's passion for Vershinin in Chekhov's play, nothing is overtly said by the sisters about Imogen's relationship with Otto. Even the theft of the love letters is referred to only obliquely. One scene on a landing between Imogen and Helen after the letters have gone missing is in fact a model of economical screenwriting in that everything lies just beneath the surface:

HELEN: What is it?
(*Pause.*)
IMOGEN: I was just wondering . . . why you . . . I mean . . . if you . . .
(*Pause.*)
HELEN: If what?
(*Pause.*)
IMOGEN: Well, I just wondered . . .
HELEN: You wondered what?
(*Pause.*)
IMOGEN: Have you been in my room?
(*Pause.*)
HELEN: For what purpose?
(*Pause.*)
IMOGEN: Well, it's of no importance, really. It's really of little importance.
(*Pause.*)
So.
(IMOGEN *turns out of shot.* HELEN *turns, in opposite direction. The camera remains looking down the empty staircase.*)

The half-sentences, the fragmented rhythms, the pauses conjure up the whole history of a relationship: of the younger sister's deference to the older, of Imogen's shy reluctance to confront and break apart Helen's sad, emotionally vicarious existence, and of the twilit world of a decaying class where nothing is ever said and where decisions are somehow vulgar.

The film is by no means all pastel shades. Pinter underscores beautifully the contrast between rural reticence and urban vulgarity in a riotous scene in Dublin where Imogen and Otto encounter an intoxicated drama critic Shannon and his actress-doxy Maureen, who seethe with the bilious energy of city Catholics. Pinter himself played Shannon and, as David Jones recalls, displayed both his customary vigour and extreme sensitivity to noise: 'Harold came out for two days and he was still on a very urgent, impatient London rhythm. It took him a day to get into it. He was playing this drunken critic and we were shooting in very claustrophobic surroundings. He was very exercised by the fact that there were flies buzzing about on two occasions. He said, "I can't work if there's a fly in the room," and so the fly had to be eradicated. I don't think he had a good time for those two days in a hot, sweaty attic room, but the sweatiness and the belligerence got into the performance in a very good way.'

For Pinter, acting was always a form of release. So too was poetry: not only writing it, but also active promotion of the form itself. In 1975 Pinter had accepted an invitation from Anthony Astbury, a poetry-loving teacher at a private school in Warwick, to give a reading of his own work at the Warwick Gallery. The evening was not only a big success. The two men discovered they shared similar tastes in poetry, and when Astbury and another friend, Geoffrey Godbert, decided to set up a small publishing imprint called the Greville Press, Pinter gave it his enthusiastic support. Indeed, the Press was launched with an event at the Purcell Room in September 1979 when George Barker, William Empson, David Gascoyne, W. S. Graham, John Heath-Stubbs and John Wain all read from their work. Pinter chaired and compered the evening; and over the years he has devoted a good deal of time, energy and money to the Greville Press. He co-edited two anthologies – *100 Poems by 100 Poets* and *99 Poems in Translation* – formally joined the board in 1987 and privately financed some twenty volumes of poetry, as well as paying for sundry launch parties. Pinter's the last person to seek publicity for his efforts, but it's a good example of how he frequently does good by stealth.

Poetry was always one of his main loves, but in the period from 1978 to 1981, when he was adjusting to a new house and a new life as well as wrestling with the legal entanglements of divorce, he turned increasingly to the disciplines of directing and screenwriting. It was work that imposed a definite structure on daily life and, although intensely demanding, was less hazardous than the surrender to the subconscious required of playwriting. He was also able to work regularly with old friends. He directed three new Simon Gray plays in this period: *The Rear Column* at the Globe (1978), *Close of Play* at the Lyttelton (1979) and *Quartermaine's Terms* at the Queen's (1981). He also worked twice at Hampstead Theatre: in 1980 he gave *The Hothouse* its first ever production (it later moved into the Ambassadors), and in 1981 directed *Incident at Tulse Hill*, written by a cricketing colleague and old chum Robert East. Pinter was the ultimate writer's director: someone in whom an author could place absolute trust, knowing that he would never bugger up the text. However, the Gray plays, in particular, were attended by off-stage traumas.

Despite a good cast, including Jeremy Irons and Barry Foster, and an interesting subject – the fate of five men left behind in a Congo encampment after Stanley's march to the relief of Emin Pasha in 1887 – *The Rear Column* never took off: no metaphor, frosty notices, short run. *Close of Play*, a powerful domestic tragedy, seemed dogged with problems from the start. Rehearsals coincided with a period of intimidatory picketing by National stagehands. At one point Michael Redgrave, suffering from Parkinson's disease, was forced to get out of his cab and shuffle a hundred yards to the stage door. Peggy Ashcroft, after rehearsing for a week in agonising pain with a cartilage problem, had to leave the cast. And in September 1979, three months into the run, there was a fierce debate about whether the show should go to Dublin in the wake of the murder by the IRA of Lord Mountbatten and members of his family. Initially, Pinter sided with those members of the cast and crew who refused to go; eventually, however, the tour went ahead. Even *Quartermaine's Terms* – arguably Gray's best play – had its problems. Gray remembers the odd explosive argument with Pinter, always resolved the next morning, over practical matters like Pru Scales's costume in the last act. And Michael Codron, as producer, looks back on the show somewhat lugubriously. 'It wasn't,' he says, 'the happiest experience. Everything went at Harold's pace in that we had to wait till he had fulfilled other commitments and then we were obliged to go into the Queen's which was too big. Harold also became overprotective of his position as director. I remember that on the pre-London tour I went into Jenny Quayle's dressing-room and she asked me if her performance was getting across. I said, "Yes, but you were rather soft." She said, "Yes, I was." I then got a blast from Harold saying, "Would you please remember that in future all notes are to be given via the director." That was quite shaking. After all, it wasn't as if Harold was someone I'd just started to work with.'

Pinter's new-found domestic happiness with Antonia was often accompanied by a short fuse in public. In mitigation, one can only say that he had just gone through an extremely trying time with the divorce from Vivien. She had done everything to make life difficult right up to the last moment. Finally, it looked as if everything was legally settled and a marriage party was arranged for October 1980 to coincide with Pinter's fiftieth birthday. The scene was set. The guests were invited. A marquee was erected on the lawn of the house in Campden Hill Square where Pinter and Antonia had lived for three years. But at the very last moment Vivien refused to sign the relevant divorce papers so the marriage took place two weeks after the reception: a small vindictive triumph for the disgruntled Vivien.

While wrestling with the agonies of divorce, Pinter had also been struggling with the seemingly intractable problem of turning John Fowles's *The French Lieutenant's Woman* into a film. Anyone familiar with the book will appreciate the difficulties: the trickiest task Pinter had faced since tackling Proust. On one level, Fowles's modern classic is a pastiche Victorian romance. It is the story of Charles Smithson, a wealthy amateur palaeontologist, who falls under the magnetic spell of Sarah Woodruff, a mysterious woman who haunts the Cobb at Lyme Regis wistfully remembering the French soldier who abandoned her. On another level, the book is a playful post-modernist work in which the characters' quest for spiritual freedom is echoed by the reader's ability to choose between alternative versions. Three-quarters of the way through the book, Fowles shows his hero doing the decent Victorian thing and abandoning his obsession with Sarah for the sake of marriage to his conventional fiancée. But what, Fowles asks, if Charles had chosen to pursue his passion for Sarah? Charles searches endlessly for her and discovers years later that she has blossomed into a Victorian New Woman and is working as an amanuensis to the painter Dante Gabriel Rossetti. In one ending, Sarah reveals that she has borne Charles's illegitimate child and the couple begin a new life based on sexual equality; in the other ending, Charles leaves the house unreconciled to lead a life of brooding solitude. To complicate matters further, Fowles is also present in the book meditating on the nature of fiction and the author's relationship with his characters. In one speculative chapter he writes: 'It is only when our characters and events begin to disobey us that they begin to live.' It is an extraordinary and inventive work in which Thackeray meets the world of the *nouveau roman*: high-class romance (a kind of corn on the Cobb) mates with Robbe-Grillet and Sarraute.

How to put all that on the screen? How to achieve a filmic equivalent of Fowles's peculiar form of literary alienation effect? How to cope with the shifts of perspective and the alternative endings? The solution was to draw a constant parallel between the fictive lives of Charles and Sarah and the emotional experience of the actors – Mike and Anna – playing them. But Pinter modestly takes none of the credit. 'It wasn't,' he says, 'my invention at all. It was that of the director Karel Reisz. When we sat down to discuss it I had no idea at all . . . I knew what I *didn't* want to do . . . Can you imagine a narrator sitting in his room and saying, "I am the author of this book." . . . We thrashed around a bit and then Karel suddenly said, "What about having the two actors acting it?" That immediately set me alight because I thought that was a kind of perspective that was really interesting. It could do something similar to the book . . . It was Karel's idea. But the fact is I immediately said, "I'd like to have a go at that."'

Pinter's juxtaposition of two worlds – 1867 and the present – is done with great dexterity and wit: fiction and 'fact' constantly interweave in a way that both points up the parallels and exposes the sexual, moral and ethical differences between then and now. Mike, who's married, and Anna, who has an American boyfriend, are having a location affair that both echoes and anticipates the dilemmas faced by the fictive Charles and Sarah. In Shot 27, Mike and Anna are in bed in her hotel room. Mike answers a call from the unit to say that Anna is late on set. She mockingly protests at his taking the call in her room: 'They'll fire me for immorality. They'll think I'm a whore.' To her, as a liberated modern woman, it is an ironic joke, but it anticipates the very real Victorian dilemma which Sarah later (Shot 103) articulates to Charles on the Undercliff at Lyme Regis. Because of her liaison with the foreign stranger who abandoned her, she has become a social outcast: 'I have set myself beyond the pale. I am nothing. I am hardly human any more. I am the French Lieutenant's Whore.'

However, Pinter doesn't just set up ironic echoes between past and present. Taking a strong feminist line, he contrasts Anna's growing identification with Sarah, with Mike's concern with the purely technical aspects of performance. In Shot 49 they are in their hotel room. Anna is researching the Victorian background; Mike is reading the sports page of the paper. Anna works out that if Sarah left Lyme Regis for London, she would be in a city where the prostitutes were receiving clients at the rate of two million per week while the male population was one and a quarter million. For Anna, this is a way of exploring the character's limited options and the exploitation of Victorian women; for Mike, whipping out his pocket calculator, it proves that outside marriage and making adjustments for boys and old men, 'a Victorian gentleman had about two point four fucks a week'.

Pinter is not only contrasting American Methodism and English flippancy. He constantly shows how Anna is 'inhabited' by the character of Sarah and even uses the affair to explore her freedom as a woman. Mike is imbued with something of Charles's dilettantism while at the same time being as sexually and emotionally enslaved as the character he is portraying. Pinter is not simply saying that life imitates art or that actors are inevitably shadowed by the characters they depict. His larger historical point is that our sexual identities and our present attitudes are shaped and moulded by an accumulation of past experience. Anna's feminist freedom – and it is she who, after the unit party, drives off in a white sports car to pursue her own existence – is the result of the painful struggles endured by her Victorian predecessors. Mike's helpless infatuation so closely resembles Charles's, however, that we are led to conclude that men remain locked in unyielding attitudes. Women progress and profit from the past; men remain insecure and exploitative. That seems the inescapable conclusion, reinforced by Mike's last despairing cry of 'Sarah' as his mistress zooms off into the distance.

Pinter not only finds a filmic parallel to Fowles's literary alienation device. He takes the argument a stage further. He contrasts the wracking passions of the Victorian past with the ability of modern woman to make moral choices. He also makes Sarah's transmogrification from the standard mystery woman of Victorian fiction into a free, independent spirit much clearer: her development as an artist becomes a symbol of her personal growth. Inevitably Pinter's screenplay is forced to omit whole sections of the book – we lose, for instance, the episode in which Charles squanders his expectations of a title and a fortune – but the movie, on its release in 1981, was glowingly received both in Britain and the States, where it got an Academy Award nomination for Best Film. Joe Losey, when he saw it, called it superb and noted, a touch ruefully, the parallels with *The Servant*, *Accident* and *The Go-Between*. The film's severest critic, as so often with Pinter's screen work, was the highly influential Pauline Kael in the *New Yorker*. For a start, she lammed into its female star: 'We never really get into the movie because, as Sarah, Meryl Streep gives an immaculate, technically accomplished performance but she isn't mysterious. She's pallid and rather glacial.' Kael also disliked the refined, calibrated tone of the movie: 'Harold Pinter, the famed compressor who did the adaptation, has emptied out the story and the director, Karel Reisz, has scrupulously filled in the space with "art" . . . the result is overblown spareness.' But Kael, who always preferred funky American roadmovies to stylish British ones, was something of a lone voice. She also failed to recognise Pinter's achievement in finding a cinematic equivalent to Fowles's literary device. Even the book's alternative ending is matched in the screenplay in that we are offered the prospect of reconciliation between Charles and Sarah and of unyielding separation between Mike and Anna. And that in itself is one of Pinter's subtlest effects. In fiction, he implies, we seek resolution and harmony. In life, events move differently: one partner's new maturity is achieved at the expense of the other's pained solitude. Pinter has rethought and restructured Fowles's novel without betraying its quintessential feminism or self-referential playfulness.

As Alice Rayner has perceptively pointed out, Pinter in much of his work for stage and screen from *The Proust Screenplay* onwards becomes, in fact, a meta-dramatist 'who illustrates the fact of intervention and the act of

PRIVATE LIVES 275

making'. Rayner seizes on the symbolic aspect of the second shot in *The French Lieutenant's Woman* which shows Charles examining a fossil under a microscope:

He is scraping at it and gradually the shape of a chambered nautilus appears. What is impossible to determine visually, however, is whether he is sculpting it or simply uncovering it. I like to think of this image as Pinter's own self-consciousness, particularly when he is adapting the work of other authors to the screen. For he is doing both: making for the first time and uncovering something that is already there. The ambiguity of the image contains the ambiguity of the process of making art.

One can see how this fascination with the process of 'making' informs Pinter's work through the 1970s and early 1980s. *The Proust Screenplay* ends with Marcel ready to start work ('It was time to begin') on the story we have just witnessed. *The Last Tycoon* is not only about the process of film-making, but also about Monroe Stahr's desire to recreate the image of his dead wife both on celluloid and in reality. *The French Lieutenant's Woman* is obviously about the interplay between reality and fiction. Equally, *No Man's Land* is about the nature of writing itself and *Betrayal*, through the conspicuous artifice of a narrative that proceeds backwards in time as the play develops forwards, cannot help reminding you of the author's presence. Pinter does not set out with a conscious agenda, and obviously the structural solution in all these varied works was a response to specific problems. But what is un-deniable is the way Pinter, post-Proust, seems fascinated by the process of making and the mysterious ambiguous relationship between art and life. In his screenplays he constantly counterpoints 'fiction' and 'reality', just as in *No Man's Land* he turns the fearful dreams and in *Betrayal* the actual events of his own life into a form of resonant fiction. Through the alchemy of the imagination, autobiography is transmuted into art.

Fourteen Voices from the Past

Art may be a form of memory – a distillation of the key experiences of one's life – but there are some events that are too tragic and painful to be sublimated into dramatic fiction. There is no doubt that Pinter was deeply and permanently affected when he learned in 1982 of the death of Vivien, through chronic alcoholism, at the age of fifty-three. Her life and career, after the separation and divorce from Pinter, were undeniably fraught. She worked occasionally, playing in Coward's *The Vortex* and Strindberg's *The Father* at Greenwich Theatre, doing a tour of Albee's *All Over*, and providing memorable cameos in films and television. Eventually, however, the work thinned out as she acquired a reputation for unreliability. But according to Andrew Lovibond, who acted as her legal adviser during her final years, she cultivated the impression that she had been totally abandoned, while the reality was slightly different. 'She lived in a comfortable flat,' says Lovibond, 'which was part of a house called Cator Manor in Blackheath. This had been bought from the sale of the house in Hanover Terrace which had not fetched as much as hoped because it was on a Crown Lease. But she drew a regular salary as director of a company which she and Harold Pinter had set up. She had a very caring secretary Roberta Harris, who drove over from Willesden every day to answer letters and look after her affairs. And there was a group of minders looking after her, including a very nice chap called Ant Peters who was a general factotum at Greenwich Theatre and who often came to stay with her. That said, none of us could stop her drinking herself to death. I think she could never quite accept, despite the divorce, that she wasn't Harold Pinter's wife; it was as if she still expected him every day to come through the door. He, on his part, did everything possible to support her and, in a strange way, he held her very dearly. She was a very sad person, but despite the impression she liked to give, she didn't lack for moral and financial support.'

It is easy to moralise about other people's misfortunes: pop-press pundits and hardline feminists, especially in America, have not been slow to put Pinter in the dock and blame him for his wife's gradual disintegration after their separation and divorce. But the truth is infinitely more complicated than that. The marriage had begun to dissolve, despite the public façade, soon after Pinter's first big success with *The Caretaker*. And Vivien's own natural insecurity was obviously compounded by the knowledge that much of her fame and reputation depended on her husband's work. What she seemed unable to do, even after the final break-up and divorce, was to accept the reality of the situation. However much people tried to help her, and they obviously did, she was still engaged in what Andrew Lovibond calls 'a mental war' with her former husband.

Pinter now speaks of his first marriage reluctantly and with an obvious sense of pain. 'The trouble is,' he says, 'one is speaking here of eighteen years of married life and it can't simply be referred to under a couple of headings. What I'm trying to say is that we had some extremely good times and many laughs. It wasn't all doom and gloom, clash and conflict and strain. Vivien had the most wonderful attributes as a person. She had a great sense of humour. I remember she wrote me a wonderful note once about the time we were trying to do Proust. She said Joe Losey phoned and was short of an eleventh man for *A la recherche* . . . The message mixed Proust and cricket in a very sparky way. She could see that cricket meant as much to me as Proust. She also read a lot of poetry. We did a number of poetry readings together. And in the early days, she and I and Daniel had some marvellous holidays together . . . I always remember one in Scotland when Daniel was about six. All that was smashing. But life, for any amount of complicated reasons, became more difficult. We had an odd life in Hanover Terrace before we finally split up in that we saw very few people except old friends. People never knocked at the door. We never answered the bloody door. Nobody came, except by appointment. I had other sexual relationships during this period. The whole question of Vivien's relationship with me professionally was also soured by the business over *Landscape*. Life became gloomier and violenter . . . But the violence was never physical . . . it was just explosions, really . . . The pity of it was that her reputation as an actress became tied up with my work, but it didn't need to. After all, she went to the RSC. She played Lady Macbeth. She could have done a lot of other things . . . Particularly after Antonia and I lived together, she could have had a tremendously rich career. But part of the problem was that she was a pretty solitary person. She had very few women friends . . . She also no longer really had the desire to act. She had become very possessive and dependent. It was all very sad. But it is not something one can sum up in a few sentences . . .'

It was not the first theatrical marriage to have been destroyed by sudden

success or by the growing gulf in public recognition between the two partners, and it is pointless to apportion retrospective blame. The fact is that,
after the break-up, Pinter did everything possible to ensure that Vivien had
no financial worries. He even went out of his way to see that she had a
permanent companion. That she had a rooted place in his heart and his
memory, and that he was deeply affected by her death goes without saying: I
remember on the day I wrote a glowing tribute to Vivien's work in the
Guardian, a grateful letter of thanks from Pinter, with whom I had previously
been on distinctly cool terms, suddenly arrived at my door. What is harder to
assess is the long-term effect of the separation, divorce and Vivien's early
death on Pinter's psyche and professional career. In earlier, happier days
Vivien was, consciously or not, his muse and there seems little doubt that his
portrayal of women was, in Edna O'Brien's phrase, 'illuminated' by her
physical presence. It is also no accident that as the marriage declined, so his
depiction of male–female relationships became bleaker and harsher to the
point where, in *No Man's Land*, they exist only in the form of competitive
memory-games. Pinter's new life with Antonia also obviously released something that had long been dormant: a preoccupation with the injustices and
hypocrisies of the public world. What one can only guess at is the extent to
which sorrow, and even residual guilt, over Vivien's death explains Pinter's
creative blankness over a three-year period in the early 1980s. My surmise,
based on Pinter's palpable sensitivity when discussing personal matters, is
that Vivien's death was a contributing factor to a period filled with 'the
distress of silence'. Pinter has the reputation of being a somewhat forbidding
figure. In fact, he is an intensely emotional man who often masks his powerful
feelings under a peremptory façade and dark glasses.

Death seemed to stalk Pinter in 1982. That August he also lost Patrick
Magee, a cherished friend from his early days as a touring actor in Ireland.
But private pain was partially camouflaged by the outstanding success of a
triple bill collectively entitled *Other Places* which Peter Hall directed at the
Cottesloe in October. One of the three plays, *Family Voices*, had been written
for radio in 1980 and already presented as a Platform Performance at the
National. Of the other two, *Victoria Station* harked back to Pinter's early
success at exploring serious themes in a revue format. But it was the third
play, *A Kind of Alaska*, that represented a new departure. Although it was
Pinter's first stage play to be inspired by an existing work – Oliver Sacks's
Awakenings – it also contained a naked emotionalism that was to bear even
greater fruit eleven years later in *Moonlight*. It was a fascinating triple bill that
explored familiar terrain – such as loss, loneliness, failure of communication
and the no man's land between life and death – while also offering a signpost

to the future. That is why Pinter's work resists easy pigeon-holing: themes, ideas, moods constantly reappear like symphonic motifs.

Of the three works that make up the triple bill, *Family Voices* is in some ways the strangest. It is a work for three voices: son, mother, father. It consists mainly of an apparent exchange of letters between the first two, with a final spectral intervention from the third. But it subtly shifts its meaning depending on the medium in which it is played. On radio, it all seems to take place within the young man's consciousness as he imagines the letters he might have sent and the replies he might have received. On stage, with the mother and son sitting alongside each other and the father's ghostly voice issuing from the grave, it becomes much more obviously a play about the deep longings that transcend the chasm between kith and kin.

What is also striking is the contrast between matter and manner. The issues are deadly serious: guilt at leaving home, at separation from parents, at replacing the family we are born into for the ones we inherit. Yet the tone is blithely comic and the characters in the eccentric lodging-house, which the son describes in his letters home to his mother, seem positively Dickensian. The women are all called Withers and are inconclusively related. The landlady Mrs Withers is a roguish seventy-year-old ex-WAF who treats the hero as a surrogate son and who has a choice turn of phrase, such as 'Don't drop a bollock, Charlie', inherited from her rackety service-life. 'You'd really like her, mother', the son somewhat unpersuasively suggests. There is also a Lady Withers who acts as procuress for the Lolita-ish fifteen-year-old Jane Withers who provocatively rests her black-stockinged legs on the hero's thighs and who has a gift for catching buns between her toes. And even the male occupants of the house are pretty bizarre: the old, evidently deranged Benjamin Withers who offers cryptic religious warnings, and an Ortonesque gay cop called Riley who unnervingly equates death with love. At the very moment when the son decides to abandon his surrogate family and return home, he imagines himself rejected by his mother and forever cut off from his dead father.

It is interesting to speculate on why Pinter, at the age of fifty, should have suddenly chosen to write a play about what is by and large the experience of youth. Hersh Zeifman has an intriguing theory that the play is Pinter's *Portrait of the Artist as a Young Man*; that it is about the artist who creates, through his work, an alternative family as real and substantial as his own; that Pinter, like Joyce's hero, has chosen 'silence, exile and cunning'. And it is certainly true that it is a deeply self-referential work: it is full of thematic and verbal echoes from the Pinter *oeuvre* ranging from the smothering motherhood of Mrs Withers through to the idea of buns as a symbol of sexuality. It is also true that the play touches on the unspoken love between fathers and sons – something of which Pinter, with a father in his late seventies and a son in his early twenties, must have been acutely aware. But the most plausible explanation for the play is that Pinter, shortly to marry into the Longford family, was subconsciously motivated by something else: a feeling of guilt about the happiness that a new-found family casts upon the duties that one owes to the old. Shortly after his marriage to Vivien, Pinter wrote *The Room* (also, coincidentally, featuring a character called Riley) which is about the implacable demands of family and the past. Now, as he was about to acquire a new set of in-laws, Pinter returns to the same theme. *Family Voices* seems prompted by personal circumstance while expressing a universal fear that, whether as parents or children, we never truly express the depth of our love.

Victoria Station, the middle item on the bill, in one sense seems a throwback to the earlier Pinter of the 1950s revue sketches. We see a foul-mouthed controller of a radio-cab firm wrestling with both the incomprehension of a hapless driver who seems never to have heard of Victoria Station, and his own raging loneliness. It is funny, bleak, and yet connects very strongly with the plays that precede and follow it. Like *Family Voices*, it shows us two people in different worlds vainly trying to communicate. Where in the earlier play solitude and separation are engendered by family life, here they stem from the work process itself. But the play also anticipates *A Kind of Alaska* in that the driver, although a professional cabbie, has 'gone missing' and exists in a state of suspended consciousness:

> CONTROLLER: You've never heard of Victoria Station?
> DRIVER: Never. No.
> CONTROLLER: It's a famous station.
> DRIVER: Well, I honestly don't know what I've been doing all these years.
> CONTROLLER: What have you been doing all these years?
> DRIVER: Well, I honestly don't know.

That sense of living in a state of dubious suspension between sleeping and waking is exactly what informs *A Kind of Alaska* – a play that, even on first acquaintance, struck me as a masterpiece. It is, of course, radically different from all Pinter's other stage plays in that it stems from Oliver Sacks's *Awakenings*: a compassionate, medically detailed account of a group of twenty patients who were victims of an epidemic illness – *encephalitis lethargica*, or sleeping sickness – which spread through Europe and the rest of the world in the winter of 1916/17. In the next decade almost 5 million people fell victim to the disease; more than a third died from it. As Pinter says in his introduction to the play:

> Of the survivors some escaped almost unscathed but the majority moved into states of deepening illness. The worst-affected sank into singular states of 'sleep' – conscious of their surroundings but motionless, sleepless, and without hope or will, confined to asylums or other institutions. Fifty years later, with the development of the remarkable drug L-DOPA, they erupted into life once more.

Pinter's play was triggered by the book, but the creative process was astonishingly similar to that with works drawn directly from life: an image, an idea took root in his consciousness before finding dramatic expression. And when it came to the actual writing, the image developed according to its own internal logic. In the 1990 revised edition of *Awakenings*, Sacks summarises the various attempts to film and stage his work and, in so doing, graphically describes Pinter's method:

> Early in 1982 I received a packet from London, containing a letter from Harold Pinter and the manuscript of a new play, *A Kind of Alaska*, which he said had been inspired by *Awakenings*. In his letter Pinter said that he had read *Awakenings* when it had originally come out in 1973 and had been deeply moved; but that he had then 'forgotten' it and that it had stayed 'forgotten' until it suddenly came back to him years later. (I was reminded here of the genesis of Rilke's *Duino Elegies* which had submerged for so long and then re-emerged, explosively, ten years later.) Pinter had awoken, he said, one morning the previous summer, with the first image of the play – the patient awakening – and the first words of the play ('Something is happening') clear and pressing in his mind; and the play had then 'written itself' in the days and weeks that followed.

In a curious way, the language used to express the creative process parallels the theme of the play: the memory of the book is secreted in Pinter's consciousness and exists in a frozen state until released almost a decade later. No one would claim for a moment that artists suffer in the same way as the tragic victims of sleeping sickness, but maybe one reason why Pinter empathises so strongly with Deborah in the play – who awakes at the age of forty-five after a twenty-nine-year 'sleep' – is that as a writer he understands what it is like to live in a half-world between furious bursts of activity. There are other obvious reasons why Pinter's imagination should have been sparked by the subject: it triggers all kinds of reflections on the strange no man's land between the conscious and the unconscious worlds, and the peculiar nature of human memory in which past events retain their morning freshness. But what makes the play so moving is that Pinter both subordinates himself to the material and yet allows it to express his own preoccupations. Sacks, as acute a literary critic as he is a neurologist, seized on that very point when he first read Pinter's manuscript. Margie Kohl, a colleague at New York's Mount Carmel Hospital to whom he showed the play, remarked, 'It's not like Pinter. It's just like the truth.' But Pinter, Sacks replied, *is* just like the truth. He writes:

> I felt Pinter had somehow perceived more than I had written, had penetrated, divined, inexplicably into the heart of the matter, the inmost truth. Despite what Margie said, it was a very Pinterish play: his mind, his language were everywhere apparent – no one but Pinter could have written the play. And then again, paradoxically, it was in another sense not really Pinterish, for the play was utterly transparent and transcendent; the author was there, invisibly, behind it, above it but (to paraphrase Joyce) he had refined himself out of existence.

The play is clearly inspired by the particular case recorded by Sacks of Rose R, the youngest child of a large, wealthy, talented New York family, and endowed with a passion for parties, social life and aeroplanes. She was struck down by *encephalitis lethargica* in 1926 ('the last year in which Miss R really lived') and for forty-three years had existed in a permanent trance or stupor. In 1969 Sacks started her on a course of L-DOPA and recorded her astonishing awakening: her songs, her jokes, her references to figures current in the mid-1920s, her obsolete mannerisms and turns of speech, her incontinent nostalgia. She seemed, in fact, never to have moved on from the 'past'. But although de-blocked for a few days, she eventually returned to something like her former state of entrancement. The drug, suggests Sacks, produced some reduction of her rigidity but she regressed to the state of a Sleeping Beauty whose awakening was unbearable to her and 'who will never be woken again'.

Pinter is writing drama, not case history. He changes the specific circumstances of Miss R's case. His heroine Deborah is English well-to-do, not American. The process of awakening, spread over the course of a month in Sacks's diary, is condensed into a fifty-minute play. And the heroine's relapse into trance-like torpor is not reproduced. But Pinter seizes on a crucial point in Sacks's record which is that Miss R feels her 'past' as present and that it has never felt 'past' for her. Pinter makes this the fulcrum of his play, contrasting the inner subjective reality of Deborah's remembered world with the outer objective reality of the doctor Hornby who has lovingly tended her for years and that of her sister Pauline who is Hornby's wife. Both worlds, Pinter implies, are equally valid; the tragedy is that they can never connect. He also suggests, with tact and quiet sympathy, that in a case of this kind the watchers suffer more than the watched. But Pinter's achievement is to turn Deborah's awakening into a metaphor for a sensation most of us experience at some time, when even those closest to us – family, friends, lovers – become like figures in a dream.

It is the subtlety and economy of the play that strikes one. The contrast between Deborah's world and that of Hornby and Pauline is established partly through language: her slightly dated, breathless upper-class slang ('Have you had your way with me?') has a totally different ring to their cool, spare, unadorned tone. Even a change of tense – as so often in Pinter – conveys an impression of seismic emotional shock. Deborah chatters brightly about the future, and in particular about the marital prospects of her other sister. At one point she asks: 'Is Estelle going to marry that boy from Townley Street? The ginger boy? Pauline says he's got nothing between his ears.' The response is quietly devastating:

HORNBY: She didn't marry him.
DEBORAH: Didn't?
　(*Pause.*)
　It would be a great mistake. It would ruin her life.
HORNBY: She didn't marry him
　(*Silence.*)

In that short exchange and in the decisive shift from Deborah's future-conditional tense to Hornby's emphatic past, you sense her bewilderment and disorientation. It's as if she is still trying to get her mind round Hornby's denial of a possibility that, to her, remains unresolved. Every word of Pinter's dialogue is exactly chosen and contributes to both the pathos and the oblique humour of the situation. Deborah's confrontation, for instance, with her younger sister Pauline is shot through with awkwardness and comic confusion, not least because the 'younger' sister is now a middle-aged woman. 'Well, you've changed', says Deborah. 'A great deal. You've aged . . . substantially. What happened to you?' The perfect word there is 'substantially'. It implies that this saddened grey-haired woman who claims to be her sister has altered not only in form but also in substance: she is a different *kind* of person to the lively romping sister Deborah remembers.

We are moved by the situation, by the sense of two different realities coming into collision. We are moved by the tactful spareness of Pinter's language. But we are also moved by the waste of Deborah's youthful vitality and love of life and by the emotional cost to those who have tended her. 'Your sister Pauline', says Hornby, 'was twelve when you were left for dead. When she was twenty I married her. She is a widow. I have lived with you.' In those few simple phrases, you sense that three lives have been destroyed; not just Deborah's, but also Hornby's through his monastic devotion, and Pauline's through her wounded neglect. But the final tragedy is that even though Deborah experiences this brief awakening, she retreats into a confused state in which she accepts Pauline's falsified version of their parents' fate rather than Hornby's revelation of the exact truth. Her last words, as she looks first at Pauline and then at Hornby, are:

> She is a widow. She doesn't go to ballet classes any more. Mummy and Daddy are on a world cruise. They've stopped off in Bangkok. It'll be my birthday soon. I think I have the matter in proportion.
> (*Pause.*)
> Thank you.

But the words acquire a subversive irony because proportion is one thing Deborah can never possess: by the very nature of things, she can never distinguish between the no man's land in which she has lived for so long and the empirical reality of Hornby's world.

Yet the paradox of the play is that, in performance, one is uplifted more by the spectacle of Deborah's resurrection than downcast by thoughts of her future presumed incarceration. That at least was the impression left by Judi Dench in Peter Hall's original National Theatre production. As I wrote of Dench at the time:

> Her great, sad eyes roam the strange room seeking comfort. She struggles to walk, arms extended like a condor's wings, as if motion were a human miracle. Yet through her performance comes a sense of recollected gaiety. Face glistening, she cries, 'Of course I laughed. I have a laughing nature,' and Ms Dench, an actress to her fingertips, gives one a sense of deep, buried happiness. To convey a feeling of being reborn is a rare achievement; and it is reinforced by the amazed, compassionate stillness of Paul Rogers and Anna Massey as the unrecognised relations.

Other critics were equally impressed. Michael Coveney in the *Financial Times* called Dench's performance 'a superb display'. Robert Cushman in the *Observer* said 'she really is total theatre'. And Oliver Sacks, when he saw the performance, could scarcely contain his wonder at its intuitive understanding. 'Dench', he writes in *Awakenings*, 'like Pinter, had never met a post-encephalitic patient; indeed, she said, she was not sure whether she wanted to . . . She felt she could imagine the patient sufficiently from Pinter's portrayal. This struck me as extraordinary but her performance was gripping and what she said, I had to admit, seemed to be so.' Sacks also says that Pinter's play was for him a turning point. It convinced him that there is no necessary dilution of reality in representation: 'quite the opposite if the representation has power.' Pinter many years later was to return the compliment. Meeting Peter Brook at a birthday party for John Gielgud, he recommended that he read Oliver Sacks's work. A chance remark that led in 1991 to Brook's famous Paris production of *L'Homme Qui*, based on Sacks's *The Man who Mistook his Wife for a Hat*, which was eventually translated into English and traversed the globe. It was a production that was rooted in a mixture of curiosity, compassion and a sense of the strange processes of the human mind. And exactly the same could be said for Pinter's play. Through its aesthetic skill, intuitive understanding and human compassion, it hauntingly conveyed what Lear called 'the mystery of things'.

Fifteen Public Affairs

After the success of *Other Places*, there was undeniably what Pinter calls a 'down time' in his work for the theatre. As he told Mel Gussow:

> There was a period of roughly three years when I did not write a play. Something gnaws away – the desire to write something and the inability to do so. But you have to accept it. I'm not the kind of writer who can force anything. It's impossible. I cannot force a word out if it's not there to come out. I think I was getting more and more imbedded in international issues.

It is perfectly true that Pinter's sense of creative impotence was accompanied by a growing and ungovernable concern with injustice, official mendacity and the denial of human rights. Yet it is crass and vulgar to assume, as many commentators do, that Pinter's growing preoccupation with politics and international affairs in the 1980s was the result of writer's block. If anything, it was the *cause* rather than the consequence: he was struggling to find a way to express in dramatic terms his powerful political instincts. But what was it precisely that transformed Pinter, the supposed trader in mystery and ambiguity, into a political animal?

There are many answers to the question. The most obvious is that Pinter's work in the 1980s, far from being a sudden Damascene conversion, was a logical development of everything that had gone before. Both his character and his work had long been imbued with a profound suspicion of authority and of handed-down judgements: this was a man who had rejected Jewish Orthodox religion at the age of twelve, who had been part of a teenage group none of whom 'adhered without question to any given, to any state of affairs or system of thought', who had risked imprisonment as a conscientious objector at eighteen, who had taken a swing at a man in a Chelsea pub for anti-Semitic remarks. This was also a man whose early work had been dominated by the conflict between the individual conscience and the arbitrary nature of authority. 'I must repeat,' he told me in 1995, 'that *The Dumb Waiter*, *The Birthday Party* and *The Hothouse* are doing something which can only be described as political.'

Pinter's political awareness was also fuelled in the late 1960s and early 1970s by a mixture of personal relationships and public experience. His close friends included Joan Bakewell, a highly committed TV journalist; Peggy Ashcroft, a great actress and lifelong political campaigner; Joe Losey, a director who had been forced to leave the United States because of his left-wing connections; and not least David Mercer, a prolific playwright and rumbustious Yorkshire Marxist. 'I was much closer to David Mercer than is generally known,' says Pinter. 'We were really close friends.' Joan Bakewell goes further and suggests that since Mercer's untimely death in 1980, Pinter has in a way become his political heir. 'I think Harold has a great sense that there is a mantle of moral obligation and rage which consumed David and made him both glorious and monstrous. Harold is as passionate now as David was then. Harold really loved David and the anarchic violence in him that covered his political anger. And I think, unwittingly, he has taken on something of that rage. David would be pleased to know that.'

Pinter's politics were shaped by a mixture of his questioning conscience, his network of friends and the immediate pressure of public events. 'It came to a crux,' he told me, 'with the military coup in Chile in 1973. One of the few socialist governments in the world to be democratically elected attained power in 1970: pretty precariously and by a small majority, but nonetheless it was a democratically elected government and it was destroyed by a coup in 1973. Mr Pinochet took over and, as I speak [this was 1993], is still there as Commander-in-Chief of the Army. One's attention is drawn to a state of affairs like that in very particular and distinct ways. While I knew what was going on and was appalled by it – terribly concerned and enraged by what was going on – I was appalled, on the personal level, by the fate of an Argentinian director who had done one or two of my plays. He came to see me in London around 1970 and said that he was going to Chile. I never heard from him again and I knew that he had ended up in that stadium for the "disappeared" in Santiago. So I suppose my political conscience – which had always been around – was refined and distilled by experience.'

Everything in the 1970s conspired to activate that conscience, not least the break-up of Pinter's marriage to Vivien Merchant and his new relationship with Antonia Fraser. The contrast between the two women, in that regard, was total. For Antonia, by virtue of her parentage, her first marriage and her own profession as a historian, politics was part of the air she breathed. And she and Pinter have been discussing, and even disagreeing about, public issues for the whole of their life together – something that could never conceivably have happened with Vivien.

'In my previous life with Vivien,' says Pinter, 'we had absolutely no discussion about politics. She didn't even know what politics was. She refused to have anything to do with it. She did drop one or two wonderful clangers in her life. She was certainly a card. I remember in November 1963 we went to the Writers' Guild Ball at the Dorchester when I'd won the TV and Film Awards for *The Lover* and *The Servant*. As we walked into the lobby, the news came through that Kennedy had been shot. So the dinner was off and everyone was walking about in a bit of a daze and Vivien said, "It serves him right for thinking so much of himself." Nobody could quite believe that she'd said it, but she had. She just thought politicians were self-aggrandisers . . . being in an open car was showing off. She was hardly aware who Kennedy was. It reminds me of the story of Tom Stoppard going for a job at the *Evening Standard* having declared on the application form that he was interested in politics. When they asked him the name of the Education Secretary or something, he replied, "I said I was interested in politics – I didn't say I was obsessed by them." Well, Vivien was totally un-obsessed by politics.'

Antonia Fraser doesn't claim directly to have influenced Pinter's politics; she simply suggests that her husband's new-found domestic security released a moral and political animus that had always been there. She also doesn't see Pinter's politics as being driven by a specific ideological or party commitment. 'I would say,' she argues, 'it's more a rage against social injustice; against any injustice or unfairness. Why does he not protest about China, for example, when he does against the United States? I think it's because he sees that China is rightly perceived as a cruel tyranny whereas we turn a blind eye to US foreign policy; and I think it's the unfairness of that which angers Harold. We don't necessarily agree on everything. We argue about Cuba, for instance. We both think the American economic blockade should be lifted, but we differ about Cuban society, though Harold did join with me in protesting about the imprisonment of Cuban writers. Harold wouldn't deny Cuba's cruelty towards homosexuals or writers. But I think it's the injustice of the American blockade that angers him. Likewise his feelings about Turkey stem from the fact that we try to pretend it's a nice holiday spot and a member of NATO and so overlook its internal oppressiveness . . . I think Harold would argue that it's wonderful to be a playwright who can have your plays done all over the world, but the other side of that is that it carries a responsibility to question the nature of particular regimes.'

Pinter's political instinct was always there. It simply matured in the 1970s in response to friendship, a new life and the imperative of public events. In the 1980s, it manifested itself in greater activism and the writing of political plays. But that in itself raises crucial questions. Are burning moral convictions inherently dramatic? If you start from a position of certainty, do you deny drama's hunger for dialectic? Do you inevitably have to sacrifice human complexity to make a political point? My own answer would be that, if you exclude from drama the expression of strong political convictions, then you rob it if one of its ancient sources of energy. It is part of the liberal fallacy that *all* drama must at *all* times express multiple viewpoints. From Aristophanes to Brecht, there is a long and honourable tradition of instructive – even propagandist – drama. In Pinter's case, it seems to me that he has been consistently successful in creating dramatic images and situations that jolt our moral complacency and bourgeois blindness. It is futile to complain that his openly political plays of the 1980s don't have the polyphonic richness of a work like *The Homecoming*; they serve a different purpose. Shaw once said that *A Doll's House* may not be as durable a work of art as *A Midsummer Night's Dream* – though even that is debatable – but that it will have 'done more work in the world'. Pinter's late political plays are to be judged by similar criteria. They are public acts designed to draw attention to the bureaucratic euphemisms surrounding nuclear war (*Precisely*), the abuse of human rights (*One for the Road*), the oppression of minorities (*Mountain Language*), bourgeois complicity in governmental cruelty (*Party Time*). Far from signalling a diminution of Pinter's creative flair, they represent an extension of his human sympathies and theatrical range.

Pinter struggled for a long time to find the right form to express his political feelings, but although he kept himself busy with other projects, they often, obliquely or directly, hint at the new direction his work was to take. In 1982, for instance, at a time when he was bereft of ideas for a new play, he sat down to write a film script based on Joseph Conrad's *Victory* – not in any overt sense a political story, except that it deals with the dangers of human isolation and detachment from society. It's a beautiful script that never reached the screen. So what happened? 'The film company behind it,' Pinter explains, 'was Universal and they simply said they didn't want to do a period film set in the Far East. It was too expensive and who cared anyway? They probably hadn't even read the book. It was Richard Lester, who had a lot of muscle in those days, who set the whole thing up, but when Universal read the script they thought, "What the hell is all this?"'

What it is, in fact, is a classic adaptation of Conrad's last great work, written between 1912 and 1914, and set in the Dutch East Indies. The novel is a compelling mixture of adventure and allegory; the story of a doomed Swedish solitary Axel Heyst who seeks to remain 'the most detached of creatures in this earthy captivity', but who is destroyed by his own altruism. He lives alone on the remote island of Samburan – until, that is, he rescues Lena, a young violinist with a seedy travelling orchestra, from a savage Surabaya hotelier and allows her to share his idyllic solitude. But three bandits turn up in search of the non-existent profits from a disused mine and terrorise Heyst and Lena. In the final disaster the villains perish, but Heyst sets fire to his house while holding the dead Lena in his arms. If there is any victory, it belongs to the malign fates and the implacable cosmos.

Pinter's great achievement is to clarify Conrad's story and strip it of romantic rhetoric to expose its real themes: the impossibility of escape, the danger of rejecting life, the failure of unheroic kindness in a predatory world. But, as always in adapting another writer's work, Pinter reveals his own obsessions. The invasion of Heyst's sanctuary by Jones (representing evil intelligence), Ricardo (instinctive savagery) and their manservant Pedro (brute force) inevitably recalls the eruption of Goldberg and McCann into Stanley's seaside retreat in *The Birthday Party*: snickering menace hides under a façade of formality without being able to conceal its own internal divisions. Like many of Pinter's women, Lena also combines eroticism and mystery in a way that presents the male characters with a moral test; one that Heyst signally fails in that he realises too late the extent of her love. Yet the Conradian idea that crucial values are being tested runs through the whole script. Heyst himself seems aware that his Utopian dream is being placed under scrutiny. After he has rescued the invading bandits from death by thirst and they have regrouped, he tells Lena: 'Something is being worked out. Perhaps they don't know what it is either.' (Compare Deborah's 'Something is happening' at the opening of *A Kind of Alaska*.) It is dismaying that a script which combines a thundering good story with such a vibrant sense of fate was so casually rejected by Universal. Pinter is not only faithful to the nihilism in Conrad's book. In showing the collapse of isolationist dreams in the face of human evil, he extends his own vision of the world: retreat into one's own private Eden is, he implies, no longer a possibility.

For Pinter himself, detachment from public affairs was clearly no longer an option: he became increasingly ready to campaign, demonstrate, protest about injustice or the abuse of human rights. Even the work he undertook to direct often had a strong political theme. In May 1983, for instance, he directed Jean Giraudoux's *The Trojan War Will Not Take Place* at the Lyttelton. In truth, he was asked to do it by Peter Hall to fill a gap in the National's repertory, but Giraudoux's heavily ironic play about the peace-seeking Hector's unavailing attempt to forestall war had a certain fortuitous topicality. Britain at that time was still recovering from the bellicose jingoism induced by the Falklands War the previous year. The government's invest-ment – at an initial cost of £10 billion – in Trident as a replacement for ageing Polaris submarine-based nuclear missiles also guaranteed the survival of the so-called 'British independent deterrent'. In theory, it was a good moment to revive a basically pacifist play; in reality, Pinter's production turned out to be leaden and heavy-footed. It also led to a decisive break with Peter Hall and the National Theatre. Pinter was angry that during a difficult rehearsal period Hall was in Bayreuth starting work on his own production of *The Ring*. As Pinter told Stephen Fay, 'I thought "fuck it", he's the artistic director and I want his help. We'd both become very selfish at the same point but I wasn't just thinking of myself. I was thinking of a production at the National Theatre for which he was, finally, responsible.' Pinter, in fact, re-signed forthwith as an associate director of the National. The final rupture came with the publication in the autumn of Peter Hall's *Diaries* which, from Pinter's point of view, contained unforgivable revelations about his private life and broke the essential vow of trust between colleagues. To this day, Hall protests his innocence and says he cannot see why Pinter was so offended. 'What I wrote in the *Diaries*,' he says, 'was written out of love and compas-sion. Certainly nothing I said about him and Antonia had not been said – and much worse – in the public prints.' That is undeniably true. But for Pinter, friendship carries with it an almost sacred moral obligation, including a mutual discretion about private conversations. It was a sad, albeit temporary, conclusion to a relationship that had lasted twenty years and had vastly enriched the British theatre.

Pinter's production of the Giraudoux was one of his rare directorial duds, but two of the actors from that production – Barry Foster who played Ulysses and Martin Jarvis who played Hector – turned up to much greater effect in a short sketch, *Precisely*, which Pinter wrote for an anti-nuclear show, *The Big One*, at the Apollo Victoria Theatre in December 1983. The piece is propa-ganda, but it is propaganda for life and it does its business – which is to expose the thinking behind the notion of 'acceptable' levels of nuclear death – with brutal economy. It is vital to remember that at the time Britain was not only investing heavily in Trident, but was also allowing US cruise missiles to be sited on British soil and that the Campaign for Nuclear Disarmament had acquired a stimulus unknown since the early 1960s. What Pinter does is to shock us into recognition that the once unthinkable – the idea of nuclear devastation – was back on the agenda: as Eric Hobsbawm has recalled, state-ments by US Cold War warriors in 1983 convinced the Soviets that a pre-emptive attack by the West on the USSR was not merely possible, but even impending.

In Pinter's sketch, two men called Stephen and Roger, who could be Ministry of Defence officials or members of a government think-tank, are meeting for an out-of-office-hours drink. They never once mention the subject of nuclear war, but the implication is clear:

> STEPHEN: I mean, we've said it time and time again, haven't we?
> ROGER: Of course we have.
> STEPHEN: Time and time again. Twenty million. That's what we've said. Time and time again. It's a figure supported by the facts. We've done our homework. Twenty million is a fact. When these people say thirty I'll tell you exactly what they're doing – they're distorting the facts.
> ROGER: Scandalous.

Stephen is outraged that his carefully calculated figures about the consequences of nuclear devastation are being challenged. And when Roger reveals that some people are even putting the figure as high as 70 million, Stephen hits the roof:

> STEPHEN: You see what makes this whole business doubly disgusting is that the citizens of this country are behind us. They're ready to go with us on the twenty million basis. They're perfectly happy. And what are they faced with from these bastards? A deliberate attempt to subvert and undermine their security. And their faith.

After this intemperate outburst, Roger tries to persuade Stephen to up the figure of 20 million by another two in exchange for one more drink. He is finally frozen out by Stephen, who refuses to budge from his original figure:

> ROGER: Twenty million dead, precisely?
> STEPHEN: Precisely.

Over thirty years before in, *Beyond the Fringe*, there was a sketch satirising the conscienceless ease with which defence experts tossed around the idea of 'mega-deaths'. But Pinter's sketch, while in some ways echoing that, achieves dramatic bite through its inversion of conventional values. In any anti-nuclear piece, you expect the outrage to come from protesting campaigners. Instead, Pinter transfers the moral indignation to the desk-wallahs when they find their mathematical calculations scrutinised and attacked. It's an idea he pursues in all his political plays dating back to *The Birthday Party* and *The Hothouse*: it is those invested with power and authority who are the most rattled and insecure. Here he shows how Stephen's fury at finding his figures challenged leads to a manic desire to eliminate the sceptics: 'I'm going to recommend that they be hung, drawn and quartered. I want to see the colour of their entrails.' And Pinter implies that even in Whitehall there is division between inflexible die-hards like Stephen, and more malleable, and therefore suspect, people like Roger, prepared to acknowledge that no death-calculation can be exact. Pinter is shocking us into an awareness that there are people who rationally accept the idea of a nuclear strike, inevitable retaliation and unprecedented annihilation; he uses the techniques of irony and inversion to give it dramatic punch.

Pinter does something similar in *One for the Road*, a play which balances moral conviction with latent irony in that it shows that even those backed by the awesome power of the state have an unresolved craving for respect, admiration, even love. It's a short play, but it is also the one which proved to Pinter himself that his three-year creative crisis was coming to an end; that he could find a way of matching his politics to his art. It was first played at the Lyric Studio in Hammersmith in March 1984 as part of a lunchtime double bill with *Victoria Station*. It was also written in response to a very particular situation: Pinter's growing awareness of the systematic use of torture by the Turkish state and its oppression of writers, intellectuals, peace campaigners and racial minorities. Whereas in the past there had been a long gestation period between the image and its expression, in this case Pinter was driven to write the play in a state of controlled fury; though he had, as he explained in a prefatory interview to the published edition, been absorbing the facts about Turkey for a long time.

I then found myself at a party where I came across two Turkish girls, extremely attractive and intelligent young women, and I asked them what they thought about this trial which had recently taken place, the sentences . . . and they said, 'Oh well, it was probably deserved.' 'What do you mean by that, why was it probably deserved?' They said, 'Well, they were probably communists. We have to protect ourselves against communism.' I said, 'When you say probably, what kind of facts do you have?' They of course had no facts at all at their fingertips. They were ignorant, in fact. I then asked them whether they knew what Turkish military prisons were like and about torture in Turkey and they shrugged and said, 'Well, communists are communists, you know.' 'But what do they have to say about torture?' I asked. They looked at me and one of them said, 'Oh, you're a man of such imagination.' I said, 'Do you mean it's worse for me than the victims?' They gave yet another shrug and said, 'Yes, possibly.' Whereupon instead of strangling them, I came back immediately, sat down and, it's true, out of rage started to write *One for the Road*. It was a very immediate thing, yes. But it wasn't only that that caused me to write the play. The subject was on my mind.'

The resulting play deals, in four short scenes, with the relationship be-tween Nicolas, a high-ranking government official in an unnamed state, and three imprisoned members of a single family: Victor, his wife Gila and their son Nicky. Nicolas embodies the power vested in the state; and in the course of the interviews, we learn that Victor has been tortured and mutilated, Gila raped and sexually abused, and in the last moments that Nicky has been killed. But how do you translate political anger into effective drama? Pinter himself is alert to all the aesthetic problems involved. 'It's difficult,' he told me, 'to write about something to which you know the answer. If you know that a brutal dictatorship is a bad thing, what are you going to do? Are you simply going to say "A brutal dictatorship is a bad thing"? I think that what I was finally able to do in *One for the Road* was to examine the psychology of a man who was an interrogator, a torturer, the head of an organisation, but was also a convinced passionate man of considerable faith; in other words, who believed in a number of things and fought for those . . . was able to subject his victims to any amount of horror and humiliation for a just cause as he saw it. I believe that reflects, as you know, situations all over the world, under one hat or another, now, as then, or at all times. The question of a just cause.'

That is one reason why the play works so well. Nicolas acts not out of pure sadism, like the interrogator in a bad spy movie, but out of a righteous belief in family, state and religion. In fact, the play's horrific irony is that Nicolas tears asunder an individual family in the name of patriarchal values. But what makes the play *dramatically* effective is that Nicolas, who wields all the power, seems less secure than his victims and craves validation for his actions. A parallel comes to mind. Peggy Ashcroft once told me that the key to the famous scene in *The Wars of the Roses* where Queen Margaret daubs the face of the captive Duke of York with a napkin wreathed in his children's blood lay in the fact that *he* was the stronger character. In a similar way, Nicolas, who has the authority of the state behind him, seems to yearn for acceptance from the disempowered.

It is perfectly true that, in the first scene, Nicolas seeks to assault every aspect of Victor's masculinity: power, possession of women and property, sexual potency. Nicolas waves first his big finger and then his little finger in front of Victor's eyes: 'Do you think waving fingers in front of people's eyes is silly? I can see your point. You're a man of the highest intelligence. But would you take the same view if it was my boot – or my penis?' American critic Judith Roof has argued that the transition from finger to boot to penis implies an ideological complicity between authority and masculinity. To me, it also suggests something else: the strange sexual attraction the victim possesses for his interrogator. Indeed, in John Crowley's 1994 production at Dublin's Gate Theatre, Michael Pennington as Nicolas at one point buried his face in Victor's blood-spattered hair. Even more strongly, it implies that Nicolas, who seems to have no life outside his official function and who is sustained by the ersatz family of the state, is magnetically drawn to the very people he is bound to destroy.

Nicolas's tone in that first scene constantly wavers between assertion and question. He claims that God speaks through him. At the same time, he craves reassurance. 'You do respect me, I take it?' he asks. 'I would be right in assuming that?' And again, 'Would you like to know me better?' and later, 'What do you say? Are we friends?' and 'Tell me . . . truly . . . are you beginning to love me?' This is the voice not of strength but of a weak and insecure man who goes on to brag, somewhat pathetically, of his intimacy with the head of state and who finds in the idea of a common patriotic heritage the emotional dynamic missing in his nature: 'I feel a link, you see, a bond. I share a commonwealth of interest. I am not alone. I am not alone!' That is the cry of a born solitary who finds consolation in the embrace of the state. One recalls other Pinter interrogators – such as Goldberg and McCann in *The Birthday Party*, and Oktober in the film of *The Quiller Memorandum* – who are made aware, by the intransigence of their victims, of the provisional nature of their power.

Omnipotent torturer meets helpless victim would make for pathos, not drama. But scene by scene, Pinter establishes the psychological complexity of his protagonist: a flawed, uncertain man who has to destroy Victor's potency to reclaim his own, an unloved son who cannot understand the natural bonds between parent and child, a man who looks to the state to provide strong, patriarchal father-figures. In the encounter with the boy Nicky, he tries to forge a link through the coincidental similarity of their name, and his probing question 'You don't like your mummy and daddy?' harks back to his own revelation in the first scene: 'Do you think I'm mad? My mother did.' Rejected or even hated by his mother, we deduce, Nicolas has developed an obsessive worship of fathers which in Freudian terms is an index of an authoritarian nature. Significantly, Nicolas is at his cruellest with Gila whom he abuses precisely because of her disloyalty towards her own father who was a soldier of the state. 'To spawn such a daughter', cries Nicolas. 'What a fate. O, poor, perturbed spirit, to be haunted forever by such scum and spittle. How dare you speak of your father to me? I loved him, as if he were my own father.' The echo of *Hamlet* ('Rest, rest, perturbed spirit') is obviously quite intentional on Pinter's part. It implies that Nicolas seeks both to romanticise and appropriate the dead patriot whose values Gila has decisively rejected.

Pinter is charting a process at the same time as painting a portrait. And the final scene, in which Victor appears before Nicolas tidily dressed but with his tongue maimed or removed (compare Stanley at the end of *The Birthday Party*), both confirms and extends our knowledge of the protagonist. We see once again his yearning for acceptance ('We'll meet again', Nicolas tells Victor. 'I trust we will always remains friends') and his belief in his own mission 'to keep the world clean for God'. But we also see that his strength conceals desperate weakness: above all, a destructive envy of the things Victor possesses or perhaps possessed. The cutting out of Victor's tongue can be seen as a clear castration symbol. And the killing of Nicky, revealed through Pinter's most devastating change of tense, is proof of a vindictive jealousy. The final words and image are unremittingly powerful as Nicolas's *fausse bonhomie* is savagely exposed:

> (VICTOR *mutters*.)
> NICOLAS: What?
> (VICTOR *mutters*.)
> NICOLAS: What?
> VICTOR: My son.
> NICOLAS: Your son? Oh, don't worry about him. He was a little prick.
> (VICTOR *straightens and stares at* NICOLAS.
> *Silence.*
> *Blackout.*)

Where does the power lie in that final moment? With Nicolas? Or with Victor? The former still has the machinery of the state behind him. But if, as Nicolas earlier suggests to Victor, 'your soul shines out of your eyes', then that final stare implies an unyielding and resilient hatred.

What might have been a simple play about police-state brutality becomes a psychologically complex work about the tortured nature of the torturer. It also establishes something crucial about Pinter's art: while his supposedly private, personal plays are invested with political tension, so his political plays start from the personal and work outwards. He does not – like Hare, Edgar or Brenton – operate on a huge canvas. The dynamic of *One for the Road* springs from Nicolas's worm-eaten envy of a family life he does not possess and from his faith in the apparatus of the state as an emotional substitute. My initial doubt about the play was that it was too unspecific; that we never quite knew where it was happening. But that calculated ambiguity now seems to me part of the point. Pinter is dealing not merely with a universal process – as he pointed out at the time, at least ninety countries now practise torture quite commonly – but with a separation between language and reality that is eating into our culture.

In fact, Pinter's direct engagement with politics was very well received and his disquieting lunchtime production at the Lyric – featuring Alan Bates, Jenny Quayle and Roger Lloyd Pack – received glowing reviews. Michael Coveney in the *Financial Times* described the play as 'violent, disturbing, enthralling'. Giles Gordon in the *Spectator*, having invoked *King Lear*, wrote that Pinter's play is 'as necessary and inevitable a work of art as Koestler's *Darkness at Noon*'. But it was a fellow-playwright Simon Gray – whose *The Common Pursuit* Pinter directed at the Lyric in June 1984 – who opened up a different perspective on *One for the Road*. 'I like it,' he told me, 'because in one way Harold is on the side of the torturer. His creative juices are with the torturer, not with the victims. I think the lead is a wonderful creation; he obviously had a ball with him. The fact that Harold is making a moral point is irrelevant to the creative drive. The torturer is a Dickensian character – this is something I've always felt about Harold. People talk about Kafka and Beckett, but Harold's real strength is a sense of the grotesque. His family characters in *The Homecoming* or the group in *The Caretaker* have a mad life that is straight out of those peripheral chapters you find in Dickens.' In fact, the line dividing Dickens and Kafka is very thin, but I see Gray's point. And one of the many reasons why *One for the Road* works is that Pinter, while detesting everything Nicolas stands for, is able to enter into his consciousness and understand both his fanaticism and fear – in short, to turn what might have been a didactic tract into drama.

As an artist, Pinter sought to comprehend; as a citizen, he was much more prepared to engage in outright condemnation. A year after the London première of *One for the Road*, in March 1985, Pinter and Arthur Miller, as vice-presidents of English and American PEN respectively, spent five days in Turkey with the initial aim of expressing solidarity with dissident writers. It was a visit that was to have endless repercussions inside and outside the country. While they were in Turkey, Pinter and Miller talked with over a hundred intellectuals, former prison inmates, politicians and diplomats. They appeared before the Istanbul Journalists' Association with a petition signed by 2,330 writers, scientists and churchmen demanding international respect for human rights. They held a joint news conference in Istanbul to protest Turkish human rights abuses. It was both a fact-finding and morally supportive mission. But at the very end of their stay, they attended a dinner given by the US Ambassador at which Pinter could no longer contain his fury, as Arthur Miller vividly recalled in a Radio 3 interview:

Turkey has always had a problem trying to decide what to do with prisoners: instead of making a decision they simply beat them up. We went in the hope of drawing some attention to it and Harold was quite a revolution: a one-man revolution in Turkey. What it came down to was that since the United States is basically the paymaster of the country – Turkey is one of the two or three largest recipients of American aid since they have a long border with the Soviet Union – we had a dinner with the American ambassador which in Turkey turned out to be historic. What happened was that I was sitting next to the ambassador's wife and the whole thing was quite formal and civil when I heard Harold growling down at the other end of the table. He was shouting across the table at a lady editor of the largest newspaper in Turkey who, it turned out, had said that we were there simply to get publicity. Harold blew his stack and said, 'I throw that back in your face': I was glad he just did it figuratively. But anyway, I then had to make a small speech to the ambassador explaining what a catastrophe Turkey was in our eyes, and Harold and I . . . we weren't exactly thrown out . . . we slid out at the end of the dinner. And, as we got on the plane at the end of the trip, I learned that we had been banished . . . I'd never have done what Harold did because I'm too polite but he was terrific. As it worked out, we were a good pair because he exploded and I imploded. We were the bad guy and the good guy. The FBI and the police usually send out a couple like that: one of them threatens you and the other one becomes your friend. I was the friendly fellow. But I thought Harold behaved marvellously as he always does. I just wouldn't want to be at the other end of his anger, that was all.

Pinter and Miller's visit was widely reported in the British and American press. Amnesty International later included their findings in a report which contained the devastating statement that 'more than a quarter of a million people have been arrested on political grounds in Turkey since the 1980 military coup and almost all have been tortured'. Pinter also became President of the Friends of Turkey in the UK and kept up the campaign to expose the political reality within the country. In a letter to the *Guardian* in January 1987 he protested at the torture during five-year custody of trade unionists for engaging in 'basic trade union activities'. As he became increasingly aware of the plight of Turkey's 15 million Kurds, he was also propelled into writing *Mountain Language*.

What did Pinter's political anger achieve? Cynics would argue that it did nothing to stop Turkey's systematic torture of political prisoners or suppression of basic liberties. Ten years after Pinter's visit, one of the country's most famous writers, Yasher Kemal, was on trial for 'threatening the unity and integrity of the Turkish state' by writing an article for a German magazine criticising the country's Kurdish policy. But Pinter's vehement behaviour at the American Embassy and his subsequent reporting of what he saw in Turkey did something to rattle Western complacency. And plays like *One for the Road* and *Mountain Language*, while not exclusively about Turkey, have provided ineradicable images of torture and brutality that have been seen around the world. Representation, at the very least, has a jolting effect on the lazy liberal conscience. Artists are not, of course, under any explicit obligation to take a political stand in either their work or their life; but it strikes me as foolish and myopic to deride those who do. And Pinter's belief since the 1980s in the need to explore issues of conscience seems to me infinitely preferable to the traditional acceptance of artistic impotence expressed by Auden in 1939 in *The Prolific and The Devourer*: 'Artists and politicians would get along better in a time of crisis like the present, if the latter would only realise that the political history of the world would have been the same if not a poem had been written, not a picture painted nor a bar of music composed.' Auden's philosophy that no line of poetry ever stopped a Jew going to the gas chambers is often invoked to justify the artist's detachment from society. Pinter's growing conviction that the writer has dual responsibilities, as both a private citizen and a public figure, strikes me as more positive and productive. But in Pinter's own case, the need to engage with politics was less a matter of conscious choice than of internal compulsion.

Pinter's political convictions also to a large extent informed his whole output during the 1980s and 1990s – not just the plays he wrote, but also his film scripts, his poetry and the work he undertook to direct. He was still concerned with time, memory, loss, separation and solitude, but increasingly one becomes aware of a political subtext to his work. It may seem like straining at a gnat to include a screenplay like *Turtle Diary*, which went into production in 1985, in this category, but Pinter's adaptation of Russell Hoban's 1975 novel avoided the twin pitfalls of Ealingesque whimsy or sentimental romance. It is the story of two lonely, introverted people who join forces to free three large sea-turtles from their captivity in London Zoo and return them to the sea. But it is also a work about people who achieve personal liberation through joint action. It is not 'political' in the sense of being a piece of noisy ecological breast-beating; only in the degree to which it implies that the individuals concerned, by freeing the turtles, liberate themselves.

Even in terms of the structure of the film industry, the movie had a broadly political aim. In 1983 Richard Johnson formed a consortium called UBA (United British Artists) with the aim of making films and producing plays that would be determined by the participants themselves. Pinter joined a board that included such household names as Albert Finney, Maggie Smith, Glenda Jackson, John Hurt and Diana Rigg. The model was clearly the American film company United Artists, which was founded in 1919 by Mary Pickford, Douglas Fairbanks, Charlie Chaplin and D. W. Griffith, and which produced the famous quip from a studio executive that 'the lunatics are taking over the asylum'. The British aim was more modest: simply to tap into the expertise of workers in the film and theatre industry to get some worthwhile projects off the ground. *Turtle Diary* was one of its first and most successful ventures.

The striking quality of Pinter's screenplay is the subtlety with which he suggests that the leading characters, William (Ben Kingsley) and Neaera (Glenda Jackson), are two people shyly drawn together by a sense of captivity: their own and the turtles'. The point emerges beautifully in two brief pub encounters. In the first, William, having already discussed his plan with the head keeper at the zoo, warily shares it with Neaera. Cautiously, he asks her if she likes turtles. When she says 'They're in prison', he replies 'They're not alone in that', which is as close as the film ever gets to a general statement.

In a matching later pub scene, Pinter shows the characters edging nervously towards action in language often at odds with their real thoughts:

(WILLIAM *and* NEAERA *at the table.*
Silence.)
WILLIAM: So you . . . you want to do it.
NEAERA: Yes.
    (*Pause.*)
WILLIAM: How do you know I'm competent?
NEAERA: I don't.
WILLIAM: And what about you?
NEAERA: I don't know.
    (*Pause.*)
WILLIAM: I think it's crazy. We could end up in prison. Or worse.
NEAERA: Well, don't do it.
WILLIAM: No. All right. We'll do it.
    (*They sit.*)

Brief as it is, it's a perfect bit of screenwriting. William tries to throw the moral burden of decision on to Neaera first by a challenge, then by self-denigration and finally by outlining the consequences. Each time she concedes his point rather than contradicting it, but all William's arguments for inaction conceal a desperate desire to do something. All the time the text is saying 'Let's forget about the whole plan', but the subtext is arguing the reverse: 'Let's go for it.' A lesser writer would either turn it into a 'message' scene or a piece of knockdown dialectic. Pinter instead shows two nervous solitaries moving towards a form of commitment; and by a nice irony, William, having been given three opportunities to back down, ends up by saying in effect 'OK, you talked me into it'. Good psychology; good writing. But all the way through, Pinter defines the characters by their actions and implies, through their resolution to meet again in twenty years' time to release the next generation of turtles, their potential for continuing growth. It may seem an unlikely film for Pinter to have scripted. In fact, he gives a humanist message a political dimension.

The plays Pinter chose to direct at this time also had a strong political element: sometimes overt, sometimes oblique. The Theatre Royal, Haymarket, may not seem the likeliest address for an assault on contemporary values, and I suspect most playgoers were drawn to Pinter's revival there of Tennessee Williams's *Sweet Bird of Youth* in July 1985 by the mouth-watering prospect of seeing Lauren Bacall as a decaying movie-queen living it up on the Gulf Coast with a local one-time golden boy. But Pinter's work on the Williams play was dictated partly by an awareness of the socio-political element, always ignored by British critics, in the American playwright's work, and partly by strong mutual affection. Way back in 1961, Williams had described Pinter as the writer of the future, adding that 'he drives me crazy with jealousy'. In 1981, the two playwrights were also joint recipients of the third annual Common Wealth award 'for excellence and outstanding achievements in various fields of human endeavour'. Pinter, in his acceptance speech at New York's Shubert Theatre, called Williams 'the greatest American playwright'. And backstage Williams, by now a desperately sick man, told Pinter, 'Harold, take care of your health – I could have done a lot more if I'd taken care of my health.' Shrewd advice, since there is an obvious connection between physical fitness and creative stamina – something which Pinter, still then regularly playing cricket and tennis, well understood.

Pinter also got right to the heart of *Sweet Bird of Youth*, which had last been seen in Britain in 1968 at the Palace Theatre, Watford, in a production starring, coincidentally, Vivien Merchant. The casting of Lauren Bacall – wry, dry and throaty – as the square-shouldered movie-queen highlighted Williams's vein of Gothic comedy. But Pinter also realised that the ultimate castration of the gigolo-hero by a Southern redneck's bully boys was not just a piece of overheated melodrama; it was a symbol of Williams's hatred of the Fascist instinct in American life. In fact, Williams explicitly shows that the sexual vindictiveness of the patriarchal Boss Finley, who controls the town where the action takes place, is accompanied, in a speech relayed on a giant TV screen, by racist bigotry. In Britain we tend to ignore or downplay this aspect of Williams's work, but the great American director-critic Harold Clurman long ago recognised that Stanley Kowalski in *A Streetcar Named Desire* is not just the embodiment of animal force, but 'the unwitting anti-christ of our time' and that 'his mentality provides the soil for fascism'. Williams's whole career can be seen as an attack on a society that elevates crude energy and muscular materialism above delicacy of feeling. Pinter's fine production of *Sweet Bird of Youth*, in which his old RADA colleague James Grout played the monstrous Boss Finley, brought out Williams's tough political fibre.

After directing the Williams, Pinter came back to the boards as an actor to play Deeley for an American tour of *Old Times* to St Louis and Los Angeles. David Jones's revival of Pinter's play had preceded *Sweet Bird of Youth* into the Haymarket in April 1985 with Michael Gambon as Deeley, the odd man out. Gambon was unavailable for the tour, so Pinter jumped at the chance of joining the original cast of Nicola Pagett and Liv Ullmann. Pinter encouraged David Jones to treat him simply as an actor and, not for the first time, proved himself eminently capable of taking direction even if rehearsal-discussions were slightly bizarre. 'About halfway through the first morning,' Jones recalls, 'because Harold was over-fast and tended to jump over things, I said to him, "I know the pauses aren't sacred, but I think the author has an intention here – I think he means that you have to pause here because so and so is happening." Harold said, "Oh, you don't think he'd like the way I'm doing it?" I said, "Dislike might be rather strong, but I don't think you're playing what he intended." He said, "You don't think I'm doing what he wanted?" and I said, "No." He said, "We'll change that then." From then on that became the formula. Liv Ullmann couldn't quite believe this conversation and looked on in bog-eyed amazement, but in the end it worked very well. I thought Harold would have no trouble with the dark side of the character, but wouldn't have Mike's sense of comedy. Curiously, Harold was lighter, more Noël Cowardish than Mike, but Gambon opened up the desperation at the end more than Harold did.'

After this brief excursion into acting, Pinter returned to directing and here his choice of play was unequivocally political: Donald Freed's two-hander *Circe and Bravo*, which he staged at Hampstead Theatre in June 1986, and later at Wyndham's, with Faye Dunaway in the lead. Sheridan Morley suggested in *Punch* that after directing Bacall in *Sweet Bird of Youth*, Pinter was fast becoming the George Cukor of the 1980s, 'drawing immensely strong performances from hugely starry ladies in often shaky scripts'. But Pinter was drawn to Freed's play by something much more potent: its moral outrage at American foreign policy and at the growing belief in strategic victory in a protracted nuclear war. Freed's modern Circe was an American First Lady vilified as a dipso nympho and kept under strict surveillance at Camp David because of her failure to share her husband's enthusiasm for the idea of nuclear devastation. Freed's attack on the idea of a winnable nuclear war, America's use of torture in Vietnam and illegal attempts to undermine the Nicaraguan revolution coincided precisely with Pinter's own passionate views. But Freed, who has written a play about Nixon called *Secret Honour* and a book about the Socialist Chilean Defence Minister Orlando Letelier who was killed in Washington in 1976, was thrilled by something more than Pinter's fidelity to his text. 'There is,' he says, 'something very old about Harold's work which is the ravishing beauty of it. At the end of *Circe and Bravo*, for instance, there is a litany of horror as all the bombs dropped on mankind are individually named. Harold created a perfect dialectic between terror and beauty.' Indeed Freed, who admires what he calls 'the persistence of style' in Pinter's work from first to last, sees him as being in the line of Shakespeare and Molière: the writer-actor-director who is the perfect man of the theatre.

Yet Pinter's choice of *Circe and Bravo*, which had a savage indignation that overweighed its lack of debate, and the whole impetus of his career in the 1980s can be understood only in the context of a decisive shift in his consciousness. It was not that he had 'suddenly' discovered politics or that he overnight swapped mystery and ambiguity for direct statement. Power relationships had always been his prime concern and anti-authoritarianism had long been part of his make-up. What I believe happened is that Pinter increasingly questioned the Proustian belief that 'the supreme truth of life resides in art'. The more he immersed himself in the public world and the more his moral sensibility was outraged both by arbitrary cruelty and the hypocrisy of Western democracies, the more he began to see art not as something self-sufficient but as a way of expressing his justified anger. There was a telling exchange with Mel Gussow in a New York interview in 1988 when Pinter deflected questions about the themes of his plays: 'I understand your interest in me as a playwright. But I'm more interested in myself as a citizen. We still say we live in free countries, but we damn well better be able to speak freely. And it's our responsibility to say precisely what we think.' In other words, activism was now as important for Pinter as art; his abilities as a stage and screenwriter were his means of telling uncomfortable truths and registering his protest at the state of society. He had moved a long way from the position he had adopted in 1962 when he told a Bristol student audience that 'what I write has no obligation to anything other than to itself'. By the 1980s, he acknowledged that he did have another obligation which was to expose the lies by which we live and the reality beneath the rhetoric of politicians. As he once concretely put it, behind the fact of torture and repression so blandly accepted by Western governments lies 'mess, pain, humiliation, vomit, excrement, blood'.

Pinter's choice of work in this period is consistently a keen reflection of his politics. In 1987, for instance, at Karel Reisz's instigation he began work on a screenplay of Margaret Atwood's novel *The Handmaid's Tale*: a powerful dystopian work set towards the end of the twentieth century and positing the idea of an authoritarian America in which the moral tone is set by telly-evangelists and behaviour is regulated by a highly visible paramilitary. Over the next three years the project itself turned into something of a living nightmare. 'It became,' says Pinter, 'a hotchpotch. The whole thing fell between several stools. I worked with Karel Reisz on it for about a year. There are big public scenes in the story and Karel wanted to do them with thousands of people. The film company wouldn't sanction that so he withdrew. At which point Volker Schlondorff came into it as director. He wanted to work with me on the script, but I said I was absolutely exhausted. I more or less said, "Do what you like. There's the script. Why not go back to the original author if you want to fiddle about?" He did go to her. And then the actors came into it. I left my name on the film because there was enough there to warrant it – just about. But it's not mine and to this day I've never published it.'

While Pinter was wrestling with a script based on a nightmare vision of America, he was actively engaged in attacking American foreign policy in the real world. The two activities were not separate but entirely complementary: expressions of an ungovernable moral concern. From the mid-1980s onwards, Pinter became increasingly involved in the defence of human rights in Nicaragua. In 1979 the Somoza family, who had been kingpins of US control of the various small republics of the region, had finally been overthrown by popular revolution. Free elections in Nicaragua had been held in 1984, witnessed by seventy-nine observers from all over the world. The Sandinistas had been put in power. The US, however, gave military and financial support – without the official approval of Congress – to Contra terrorist organisations dedicated to the overthrow of the elected government. Pinter protested about this flagrant abuse of power by every means at his disposal. He formally objected to invitations to members of Contra organisations to speak at the Barbican Centre and the Royal Institute of International Affairs. In February 1987 he took part – along with Antonia Fraser, Ken Follett and MP George Galloway – in a dramatic protest outside the American Embassy in London where 1,800 black balloons were released, symbolising Nicaragua's Contra war deaths. Later that year he launched an Arts for Nicaragua Fund at the Royal Court. And he wrote a reasoned but impassioned article in the *Guardian* in December 1987 drawing attention to the judgment of the International Court of Justice at the Hague in June 1986. It had found, in Pinter's words, that 'the US by training, arming, equipping, financing and supplying the Contra force or otherwise encouraging, supporting and aiding military activities in and against Nicaragua, had breached its obligations under international law not to intervene in the affairs of another state'. Pinter went on to attack the United States for helping to bring down the legally elected democracies of Guatemala in 1954 and Chile in 1973. He ended by expressing his fears for the country in which the US-backed Contras, compared by Reagan to the founding fathers, 'have murdered and mutilated . . . thousands of Nicaraguan men, women and children . . . They have been raped, skinned, beheaded and castrated.'

Pinter's outrage at the hypocrisy of Western governments – claiming moral superiority, while sanctioning the most extreme cruelties – was not something separable from his concerns as an artist: the conscience of the citizen and the preoccupations of the writer went hand in glove. In fact, Pinter's achievement in 1980s was to challenge the British idea of the artist – sanctioned by Auden's view that 'poetry makes nothing happen' – as an impotent, detached observer of world affairs. He was not thanked for his pains in the British press, but Pinter's willingness to enter the public arena and take a stand on specific issues was proof of neither political naïvety nor creative bankruptcy. It was evidence of his realisation that the artist can use his claim on public attention to expose the injustices carried out in the name of a supposedly civilised society. It also yielded a series of pithy, powerful political plays that, far from being a symptom of Pinter's artistic decline, confirmed the unity of his life and art.

Sixteen Setting the Agenda

Throughout the late 1980s, Pinter was understandably exercised by internal repression in Turkey and American intervention in Nicaragua, as well as a host of other foreign-policy issues. But he was also deeply concerned about the radical changes that had taken place in Britain since the election of the first Thatcher government in 1979. Ironically Pinter, like Peter Hall, had voted Tory in that election, inspired partly by his disgust with the National Theatre's wave of wildcat strikes. Pinter now says, 'I look back on that vote with disbelief. I in fact realised within weeks that it was a stupid, totally irresponsible and shameful act.' One can easily see why. On her election to power, Mrs Thatcher abandoned one-nation Toryism, unstitched the post-war consensus on a whole range of issues from the Welfare State to education, introduced anti-union legislation, set about the privatisation of national utilities and turned a belief in the free market into a form of secular religion. Her admirers felt she had modernised Britain; her detractors believed she had changed the country for the worse.

The area that particularly concerned Pinter was her undermining of what he saw as fundamental liberties. He was far from being alone. *Index on Censorship* in September 1988, in the first ever issue devoted to a Western democracy, examined the state of freedom in Britain. In the introduction Ronald Dworkin, the American legal philosopher and Oxford Professor of Jurisprudence, warned: 'liberty is ill in Britain . . . The sad truth is that the very concept of liberty is being challenged and corroded by the Thatcher government.' He argued that freedom of speech, conviction and information were among fundamental human rights and that the protection of those rights was essential to 'the culture of liberty' which had been part of Britain's national heritage as handed down from Milton through John Stuart Mill.

Peter Jenkins, a political commentator with a passion for social democracy, took up Dworkin's argument in the December 1988 issue of the *New York Review of Books*. He itemised a whole series of measures which he thought had led to a diminution of freedom of speech in Britain. These included the tightening of the Official Secrets Act of 1911; the restriction of press reporting on Peter Wright's allegations of wrongdoings by MI5 in the book *Spy-catcher*; the attempt to suppress or censure BBC programmes touching on matters of national security; the banning of broadcast interviews with members of the IRA, Sinn Fein and extreme Loyalist groups; the restrictions on the right to silence when citizens were arrested and questioned by the police; and Clause 28 of a proposed government bill which would forbid local authorities 'to promote homosexuality' or allow schools to teach 'the acceptance of homosexuality as a pretended family relationship'. Jenkins concluded that liberty, while not yet dead in Britain, was certainly under attack on a series of fronts.

Concern at growing intolerance, at the tendency towards intellectual conformism and at the low level of political debate was not exclusively a left-wing concern; it was widely felt in Britain in the late 1980s. It was in this context that Pinter and Antonia Fraser offered to play host to a private discussion group made up largely of writers opposed in principle to Thatcherism. The idea arose at a dinner party at which the Pinters were talking to the congenitally liberal dramatist and former QC John Mortimer and his wife Penny. Mortimer was lamenting the absence of good left-wing journalists and the poor quality of political argument even in such prestigious weeklies as the *New Statesman* and the *Spectator*. 'All we had believed in,' says Mortimer, 'was dismissed as dangerous or absurd or both. After I had gone on in this vein for a while, Harold had me rattled by exclaiming, "Do you realise what you've been saying? What are we going to do about it then?"' A decision was taken to get a group of friends together to explore the situation. Antonia Fraser, as the ex-wife of an MP, had experience of hosting discussion groups and suggested someone be invited to read a paper. So on 20 June 1988 the political journalist Anthony Howard came round to the Pinter house in Holland Park and gave a talk on the decline of the Left in Britain and the inconceivability of Labour ever winning another election: hardly the stuff of revolutionary uprising. A lively debate ensued from a gathering that included Salman Rushdie, Germaine Greer, Melvyn Bragg, Margaret Jay, Margaret Drabble and Michael Holroyd, Peter and Thelma Nichols, and David Hare, who went on to tackle a similar theme himself in his 1993 play *The Absence of War*. The intention was never to form a protest group; it was primarily to debate the state of society. As Hare later put it, 'The meetings were our evening classes.'

Salman Rushdie confirms that the June 20th Society, as it came to be known, was not exactly a revolutionary cell. 'I never saw it as more than a place to go to have interesting discussions with intelligent people; given the kind of people who were in the room, it seemed to me more fun to be there than not. It was never designed as any kind of ginger group, but simply as a place in which we might be able to thrash out ideas about what was happening in the country. If something were to come out of that in terms of public statements, then well and good. But if not, not. It was never meant to be a pressure group or an intellectual support system for the Labour Party.'

Meetings were certainly never dull. Ian McEwan recalls papers on education, the environment, the state of the Left, always followed by supper and a vigorous debate in which punches were never pulled. In London literary life, however, there are few well-kept secrets and news of the June 20th Society quickly spread on the bush telegraph. The Pinter house was staked out by reporters and photographers on the nights of meetings. Not only right-wing columnists such as Frank Johnson and Peregrine Worsthorne, but even, sadly, more liberal figures such as novelist Paul Bailey and Peter Jenkins (whose own Clapham dinner table was a centre of political debate) poured scorn and ridicule on the idea of a leftish discussion group. The participants were airily dismissed as 'champagne socialists', as if high thinking should automatically be accompanied by low living and as if a comfortable lifestyle precluded political passion. In any other European country a private talking shop of this kind would have been regarded as a healthy part of the nation's intellectual life. But it is a measure of just how intolerant and conformist Britain had become in the 1980s that it was treated as vain and presumptuous. Antonia Fraser remembers the meetings now only with wan regret. 'The only thing they really instructed us about,' she says, 'was the media. Between the preliminary meeting, which was quite jolly and nice, and the first meeting proper, the press got hold of it and effectively wrecked it. The idea of an intelligent, exploratory discussion group was destroyed by the publicity – with the press installed outside the house – and so became self-conscious. In fact, we only had two meetings in this house and then we went to the River Café in Hammersmith, but that was too chic by half, and finally to the Groucho Club in Soho. The idea of the group wasn't helped, indeed was damaged, by the presence of Harold and myself. What happened was that we wrote a letter withdrawing from the management of the group and handed all the organisational work over to Penny Mortimer. But we carried on as rank-and-file members of the group. I still attended every meeting and Harold was there at the last one, shortly before the 1992 General Election, when we were addressed by John Smith. After that, it was dissolved. There was a feeling in 1988 and the years following that you couldn't have left-wing intellectuals getting together, but that it was OK for people of the Right like Roger Scruton to air their views whenever they wished.'

Pinter himself was deeply hurt by the derision with which the group was treated and, in consequence, over-reacted. On one famous occasion, when they were meeting at the River Café to discuss the fatwa imposed on Salman Rushdie, Pinter supervised the ejection from the restaurant of a BBC journalist who had gone there simply to have dinner with his girlfriend. And he later reacted angrily to press attacks by saying, 'We have a precise agenda and we are going to meet again and again until they break the windows and drag us out.' That much-quoted remark was obviously a dramatic metaphor rather than a statement of reality. It also brings to mind Edgar Allan Poe's observation: 'A wrong – an injustice – done to a poet who is really a poet excites him to a degree which to ordinary apprehension appears disproportionate with the wrong.' The sad truth, in retrospect, is that the June 20th Society was sabotaged not by any co-ordinated conspiracy but by the media triviality and intellectual intolerance of British society in the 1980s – ironically enough, the very things that had led to the group's formation in the first place.

Pinter's anger at that intolerance found permanent expression in *Mountain Language*, which had its première as an early-evening Platform Performance at the National's Lyttelton Theatre in October 1988. Pinter had started writing the play in 1985, inspired by his visit to Turkey and his experience of the suppression of the Kurdish language. He put the four or five pages he had written aside and only completed the play in 1988 when he became alarmed at developments in Britain. As he told Mel Gussow:

> From my point of view, the play is about suppression of language and the loss of freedom of expression. I feel therefore it is as relevant in England as it is in Turkey. A number of Kurds have said that the play touches them and their lives. But I believe it also reflects what's happening in England today – the suppression of ideas, speech and thought.

For all his protestations, I don't think Pinter is literally equating England – or Britain – with Turkey. What he is trying to do in *Mountain Language* is shock us into a realisation that there is no longer an automatic division between Them and Us; between morally bankrupt tyrannies and supposedly superior Western democracies. The play offers a bleak vision of the tendency towards the suppression of any views that contradict the prevailing orthodoxy. It also implies that there is an instinct inside all of us to banish, negate or deny what we cannot comprehend. Pinter expressed the point forcefully to me in a conversation in 1995. 'I recently read,' he said 'a very good essay by Margaret Atwood on Salman Rushdie when she pointed out something I fervently believe: that it isn't the them, it's the us. We can all behave in exactly the same way. There isn't a good and a bad – it's preposterous. The complacencies that we inherit are based on nothing, really, except power. I've seen the police here and, by God, they can behave like any other police. I think we should look at what's happening in our own societies and at the wider idea of democracy. It's used more and more as a fake word and a sham word and it doesn't mean anything.' Pinter is not denying that there are different degrees of oppression in different societies. What he is trying to puncture, through shock images, is the isolationist smugness which assumes that the Western democracies are, by definition, guiltless. Intriguingly, we cut short our discussion that evening because of a Channel Four documentary about British companies that manufacture and export electro-shock weapons, for the electrocution of genitals, to countries such as Saudi Arabia and China.

Mountain Language is not documentary drama; it is an imaginative projection of Pinter's private fears about British society. Almost a 'what if' play. What if, it asks, we go down the road towards oppression already indicated in the late 1980s by a number of factors: the restrictions on the suspect's right to silence, the extension of the Official Secrets Act, the anti-homosexual Clause 28, the banning of trade unions at Government Communications Headquarters, the raid on a reporter's home and the offices of the BBC in Glasgow to remove everything relating to the TV series *Secret Society*. How far, the play asks, do we have to go before we become the kind of anti-democratic society we so readily condemn? The springboard for the play was the Kurds, but the few specific references in the text are British, and when Carey Perloff gave the play its New York première at CSC Rep in 1989 and tried to Americanise those references, she quickly found she had to revert to the original text. But the play works as much through images as through statements: it seeks to open up a direct line of communication between Pinter's subconscious and our own.

There are four scenes all taking place in and around a gruesomely functional camp. The first shows a line of women outside a prison wall and hinges on names, definitions, the power of verbal assignation. A young woman protests to an officer that a dog has bitten an older woman's hand. It is established that it was a Dobermann pinscher. The Officer in charge repeatedly asks 'What was his name?' This absurd insistence on classification is a prelude to the Officer's key statement of intent:

> Now hear this. You are mountain people. You hear me? Your language is dead. It is forbidden. It is not permitted to speak your mountain language in this place. You cannot speak your language to your men. It is not permitted. Do you understand? You may not speak it. It is outlawed. You may only speak the language of the capital. That is the only language permitted in this place. This is a military decree. It is the law.

Your language is forbidden. It is dead. No one is allowed to speak your language. Your language no longer exists. Any questions?

As Jeanne Colleran has pointed out, the curious logic of this speech recalls Lenny's explanation in *The Homecoming* of how he determined the woman he met in the docks was diseased: 'I decided she was.' The speech is also full of contradictions. The mountain language exists; it is dead. It is banished by military decree; it is banished by law. You may not speak it; you cannot speak it. Through these contradictions, Pinter points up the arbitrary nature of classification. A woman – Sara Johnson – who is in the wrong batch and has simply come to see her husband is immediately singled out and classified by the Sergeant as 'a fucking intellectual'. But, objects the Officer, you said her arse wobbled. 'Intellectual arses', retorts the Sergeant, 'wobble the best.'

Some women object to this line. Amanda Sebastyen, who among the London critics was almost alone in understanding the play's relevance to Britain, wrote in *Tribune*: 'Pinter really must clean up his act on women.' But Edna O'Brien made a much sharper point: 'I remember coming across that line about intellectual arses when I read the play and I thought, "Wait a minute – what's this?" A line like that comes from the author's unconscious. Every word is that word and, no matter how you think they talk in that country or how the torturers talk, finally the writer is the creator of how they talk. A writer reveals himself in every single word he uses.' O'Brien was not trying to censor the line. Her point was that it both reveals the Sergeant's crudity of thinking and something of Pinter's own equivocal response to women. Pinter's response to the criticism is very direct. 'The ladies,' he says, 'seem to me to have omitted one thing. It is the Sergeant talking. As a dramatist, I create characters. A female writer who was creating this Sergeant could equally well have written the same line.'

The second scene takes place in the Visitors' Room. The Elderly Woman who was bitten by the dog has brought provisions for her son. She is rebuked by the guard for speaking the supposedly dead mountain language. Her son is also reported by the guard for insolence ('I've got a wife and three kids' is all he says). But the most significant moment comes when the lights go down to half and we hear the recorded voices of the woman and her son as they sit in stillness. Pinter's point is that while language is the tool of the oppressor, it is also the salvation of the victim. The voice-overs are, in Carey Perloff's touching phrase, 'a small bud pushing through the muck'. The guards, hearing nothing, assume they have absolute control; in the language of the mind, people still reach out to each other.

The third scene takes place in a corridor and is entitled 'Voice in the

Darkness'. It refers partly to the Sergeant's voice railing in the dark about the bureaucratic cock-up that has let Sara Johnson into the inner sanctum where her husband is kept. It also refers to the imaginary exchange between the hooded husband and Sara herself. 'We are out on a lake.' 'It is spring. I hold you. I warm you.' Simple, direct, poignant: a possibly unconscious echo of *Krapp's Last Tape* in which the hero's memory of youthful romance contrasts with his tormented present. But the scene also shows how we are all degraded by the structure of power. The Sergeant admits a mistake has been made – Sara has come in the wrong door – but when he tells her that if she wants any information on this place there's a bloke comes in every Tuesday week, she asks 'Can I fuck him? If I fuck him, will everything be all right?' Sara has been classified as a whore and so adopts the language of a whore. In short, we take on the role society assigns us.

The final scene is the most harrowing. We are back in the Visitors' Room. The prisoner has blood on his face; his mother sits opposite him. The guard announces that the rules have now been changed: 'She can speak. She can speak in her own language. Until further notice.' Arbitrary decisions can be arbitrarily reversed, but, as Jeanne Colleran points out, 'lives lived on the margins of these kinds of arbitrariness are not so flexible'. The elderly woman cannot speak; even as her son begs her to, she remains silent. The prisoner then falls from his chair to his knees and begins to gasp and shake violently. The Sergeant enters and studies the shaking prisoner: 'Look at this. You go out of your way to give them a helping hand and they fuck it up.' Pinter brings the story back to base: the Sergeant's phrase is exactly the kind used by petty power-merchants and jobsworths the world over. Which is precisely why *Mountain Language* is so powerful. This is not the satanic autocracy of the cheap thriller. This is an extension of a world we already inhabit: the hooded man in the third scene reminds us that the Security Forces in Northern Ireland used just such practices. Pinter is not offering us the consolation that we are witnessing something hopelessly alien and remote. He is saying it could happen here; maybe some of it even does. But even more importantly he implies that we cannot shove the moral responsibility for such actions on to others. The terror is within us, not without.

On stage at the National Theatre, what struck one about this short twenty-minute play was Pinter's ability to distil the daily barbarism of an oppressive society with painterly precision. The scenes between Tony Haygarth as the tortured son and Eileen Atkins as a mother full of sadness, desperation and love were tremendous. Pinter also implied a whole world beyond the confines of the action in a play that was economical, impassioned, chilling: a masterly portrait of compressed suffering. Yet the critical reaction ran the gamut from wholehearted admiration to lofty derision. Paul Taylor in the *Independent* invoked Milan Kundera's point that the final barbarity of totalitarian regimes is that they deprive their victims of the tragic dignity which their sufferings merit. In stark contrast, Milton Shulman in the *Evening Standard* cynically announced that 'at the price of about 20p a minute, the National has established Pinter as Britain's most expensive playwright'. In retrospect, I suspect Pinter's production may have sent out a few misleading signals. Michael Gambon's Sergeant in tinted pebble-specs was, for instance, too like a figure from standard dystopian nightmare. The more we sense that the military are ordinary men doing a routine job, the more shocking the play becomes. This is precisely what happened when Pinter re-directed it at the Almeida in 1991: it became a deeply British play about the suppression of local differences in favour of a centralised culture and an image of a society that sees any brand of nonconformity as a threat. In the later production, Peter Howitt's Officer had a clipped Sandhurst accent and Barry Foster's Sergeant was a rough, recognisable regimental type: all too clearly us and not them.

Life, however, sometimes mirrors art in the strangest of ways. In June 1996 a group of London-based Kurdish actors from the Yeni Yasam (New Life) Company, London, decided to revive *Mountain Language*. They hired a community centre in Haringey, north London, in which to rehearse. They also obtained military uniforms and plastic guns from the National Theatre. But when a local resident, unaware they were actors, spotted a group of armed men entering the Kurdish community centre he contacted the police. Suspecting a shoot-out between local Turks and Kurds, the police despatched a helicopter, stationed marksmen with automatic rifles on an adjoining roof and besieged the building. The actors emerging from the hall were handcuffed, interrogated and manhandled by the fifty or more police. *Above all, they were forbidden to communicate with one another in their native Kurdish language.* Eventually, the police, who had actually been given advance notice of the rehearsal, grasped the situation and allowed the production to go ahead. On one level, it was all a ludicrous comedy of errors: on another, a graphic rebuke to those who insist that Pinter's astonishing play is totally alien to British experience.

Pinter's fascination with politics extended in the 1980s to his work for film and television. It wasn't always that he chose the material; but even when it chose him, it seemed allied to his principal concerns. In 1988, for instance, he was commissioned to write a television adaptation for Granada of Elizabeth Bowen's *The Heat of the Day*, a wartime novel dealing with sexual and political betrayal, the masks we wear in our private lives and the threat of Fascism. All classic Pinter territory; which is why June Wyndham-Davies, who had produced an earlier Bowen novel, *The Death of the Heart*, for television approached Pinter to write the script and Christopher Morahan to direct. 'My main discussions with Harold,' says Morahan, 'were about how to make it visually exciting and how to give it the texture of *film noir*. It mostly takes place at night in the middle of war and I found myself having to be an expert on the blackout: how people moved about, what they ate, how the traffic lights were partially blacked out and so forth. It was a very amicable partnership and the only sadness was that it was broadcast late in December 1989 at the height of the festive season. As a result, virtually nobody watched it.'

You can easily see why Pinter responded so warmly to the material. Bowen, in her own words, is dealing with 'a subsidence of the under soil' which alters the characters' lives 'without the surface having been visibly broken'. And exactly as in Pinter's *Betrayal* (in which both Patricia Hodge and Michael Gambon, who appeared in *The Heat of the Day*, had also played) there is a sense of deceit and disloyalty spreading like a poison through the system. Set mainly in 1942, the story shows the divorced Stella Rodney learning, through an espionage agent called Harrison, that her lover Robert who works at the War Office is passing secret information to the enemy. Stella, by keeping her knowledge of Robert's treachery to herself for so long, betrays their mutual intimacy. Harrison, by using the information to try to blackmail Stella into sleeping with him, betrays his professional trust. And Robert betrays his country *tout court*. It is as if Pinter finds in Bowen's story an astonishingly exact echo of his own preoccupations: the changes he makes are chiefly shifts of tone and emphasis which draw the narrative even closer to his own concerns. Where in the book, for instance, Harrison's desire for Stella is uncomplicated by what he calls 'fine feelings' and is no more than straightforward lust, in the screenplay it is more in the nature of a romantic fixation. We also see Pinter's fascination, comparable to Antonioni's in *Blow Up*, with arrested time: Stella's actions are constantly frozen as we hear the click of a recording camera. As Ronald Knowles points out: 'Photographs are literal and symbolic in the film, both part of Harrison's surveillance work and icons of his obsession.'

However, Pinter is also fascinated by the politics of the story and by what it is that drives a British officer to work for the Germans. He implies that Robert, lacking a strong father-figure and intimidated by his domineering mother and doting sister, craves not only order and discipline but the patriarchal values of Fascism. Like Nicolas in *One for the Road*, he finds in a political system a remedy for his own private deficiencies and believes in the idea of a just cause. 'You may not like it', he says to Stella of what he sees as the ultimate triumph of Nazism, 'but it's the beginning of a new world.' Pinter also highlights the strange complicity induced by betrayal. In the final scene, when Harrison revisits Stella's flat two years after Robert's death, Pinter makes a minor but significant change to the book. In the novel, after an air raid has taken place, Harrison gently enquires 'Would you rather I stayed till the All Clear?' In Pinter's screenplay, that becomes a statement followed by the directions: '*They sit in silence. After a time the All Clear sounds. They do not move.*' The inference is that Harrison and Stella are irrevocably bound together by the process of betrayal and that, in the distorting circumstances of war, people are united more by their own labyrinthine deceptions than by noble idealism.

Pinter pursued his fascination with masks, betrayals and the corrosive effect of Fascism on human relationships in *Reunion*, another screenplay he wrote shortly afterwards based on a novella by a German painter Fred Uhlman and directed for the cinema by Jerry Schatzberg. As Pinter himself said, the film, which was released in 1990, seemed to pass as if nothing had happened. Which is curious, since it is one of Pinter's very best screenplays and deals with a subject of enormous resonance: not only the rise of National Socialism in Germany in the 1930s, but also with the schizophrenia in the German soul that allowed one of the most historically cultured nations on earth to descend into barbarism. Pinter explores how and why that happened with great delicacy. Yet he is not just handling a Big Theme. His screenplay works as well as it does because it is permeated by the memory of one of his own youthful relationships.

In outline the film takes the form of a quest: a search by a rich Manhattan lawyer Henry Strauss for his own past in the Stuttgart of the 1930s. Then he was Hans Strauss, the son of a Jewish doctor; his greatest friend was Konradin Von Lohenburg, a scion of the German aristocracy. In the film the hero rakes over his memories of how this passionate intellectual friendship was destroyed by the virus of anti-Semitism. But Pinter makes dualism the key to the story. The dualism within individuals and within the German psyche. As a sixteen-year-old, Hans gives a classic classroom analysis of the character of Hamlet, explaining him in terms of split personality. Hans's own father declares himself proud to be a Jew and equally proud to be a German (he argues, in the early 1930s, that the country of Goethe, Schiller and Beethoven will not stand for Hitler). But the greatest dualism of all lies within the divided soul of Konradin, who rejects his schoolboy peers to befriend the young Hans and yet later, as Hans leaves Stuttgart for America, tells him that the Führer will come to distinguish between 'the good Jewish elements . . . and the undesirable Jewish elements'. Only on his return journey does the hero discover that his former friend was executed for his role in the von Stauffenberg bomb plot against Hitler.

Pinter knits all these separate ingredients together with his usual expertise: youth and age, experience and memory, friendship and separation. The ground is also prepared for the final revelation of Konradin's fate by opening shots of an execution room filled with butcher's hooks and by Henry's sudden glimpse on German television of the ranting Judge Freisler who in 1944 sentenced to death the German officers involved in the Hitler assassination attempt. But the film is pervaded by the mystery of the German character and by the sense that the country has both eradicated its past and is still haunted by it.

If, however, Pinter's script moves one deeply, it is because of the sense of his personal investment in the story. Pinter evokes the lost Eden of schoolboy friendship in the relationship of Hans and Konradin: their mutual affection, their intellectual excitement, their earnestness about sex touch profound chords. It is all the more moving because we know that this adolescent paradise will shortly be invaded by historical reality. Yet Pinter, perhaps subconsciously, is also playing on memories of a ruptured friendship of his own. One of Pinter's closest friends and intellectual opponents in his Hackney youth was Ron Percival, the Pete of *The Dwarfs*. In the end, their relationship was destroyed by sexual rivalry rather than by the pressures of history. Yet everyone who knew Ron Percival comments on his Aryan blond good looks: something that shines out of group photographs of the period. And in later life he sent strange letters to members of the Hackney gang boasting of his connections with the French government and questioning the fact of the death of 6 million Jews in the war. He specifically wrote to Pinter warning him, for his own sake, against too great an involvement in the Salman Rushdie affair. *Reunion* is a deeply political film about the enigmatic dualism within the German psyche and about the pressures that led the country to elect Hitler democratically to power. But it is also informed by grief at the betrayal of a close adolescent relationship. While not directly autobiographical, it is clearly permeated by Pinter's own conviction that the loss of a friend is always a gash to the soul.

For many dramatists, writing film scripts is largely a way of commercially exploiting their talent. If the film gets made, well and good; if not, at least they have burnished their bank balance. Yet Pinter not only takes fierce pride in the unusually high percentage of his scripts to have reached the screen. He also, through the medium of film, explores his governing obsessions. While *The Heat of the Day* was about the infinity of betrayal and *Reunion* was about dualism and loss of friendship, *The Comfort of Strangers*, also released in 1990, was about the close connection between sexual and political authoritarianism. The film was an adaptation of an Ian McEwan novel about a pair of young holidaymakers in Venice destroyed by an older married couple into whose orbit they are fatally drawn. Pinter was extremely well rewarded for his labours – he was paid £250,000 for his screenplay – but you feel that what fired him up was the chance to turn McEwan's loosely dated allegorical novel into a very specific attack on the curtailment of freedom in Britain in the 1980s.

Any film set in Venice is inevitably haunted by a whole host of cinematic, literary and theatrical echoes. In more innocent days it was the city where, in David Lean's movie *Summer Madness*, Katharine Hepburn's mid-Western schoolteacher was swept off her feet by a romantic merchant. In Visconti's adaptation of Thomas Mann's *Death in Venice* it was the setting for Aschenbach's fatal infatuation with a beautiful sailor-suited young boy. In Nicolas Roeg's version of Daphne du Maurier's *Don't Look Now* it was the wintry backdrop for a Gothic thriller about a young British couple trying to make contact with their dead daughter. And Pinter himself, of course, used it for the pivotal scene in *Betrayal* in which Robert first learns of Emma's infidelity. What all these works have in common is the notion that Venice forces outsiders to confront the reality of their lives and that this Borgesian labyrinth of a city is an agent of change and transformation.

So it is in *The Comfort of Strangers* where a visiting English couple, Colin and Mary (played by Rupert Everett and Natasha Richardson), fall into the sinister clutches of the Venetian Robert (Christopher Walken) and his Canadian wife Caroline (Helen Mirren). Yet what is clear from the very beginning is that Pinter is fascinated – as in *One for the Road* and *The Heat of the Day* – by the influence of fathers on sons and the connection between patriarchy and political absolutism. Pinter's opening shots always establish the key motifs of the film. Here there is a long tracking-shot through Robert's Venetian apartment full of dark mahogany furniture, stuffed birds and glass domes, a Nikon camera with a zoom lens and a tray full of men's clothes brushes and cut-throat razors all inherited by Robert from his father. As the camera glides through the apartment, Robert's voice-over tells us:

> My father was a very big man. All his life he wore a black moustache. When it turned grey he used a little brush to keep it black, such as ladies use for their eyes. Mascara.
> (*Pause.*)
> Everyone was afraid of him. My mother, my four sisters. At the dining table you could not speak unless spoken to first by my father.
> (*Pause.*)
> But he loved me. I was his favourite.

These words recur at two key points in the film. First, when Robert finds Colin and Mary lost in the labyrinth of Venetian alleys and takes them to a backstreet gay bar that he runs. Second, at the very end of the film when Robert is being interrogated by a detective after he and his wife have first seduced and then murdered Colin. Their significance becomes evident as the story unfolds. They establish not only the dominance of the father, but also the Freudian connection between Robert's filial worship and his own authoritarian, neo-Thatcherite political views. (Mrs Thatcher famously worshipped her own father Alderman Roberts, while making scant reference to her mother in interviews or her own memoirs.) Robert's lines also reveal that his bullying father was imbued with a vanity that led him to apply ladies' make-up to his moustache. The idea that patriarchal masculinity conceals a sexual ambiguity – which its owner then guiltily seeks to punish in others – is one that recurs throughout this strange, compelling film.

In adapting McEwan's novel to the screen, Pinter stays faithful to its story-line and central scenes while heightening its social and political relevance. It remains, as in the novel, a story about a young couple self-destructively drawn into a world of mirrored decadence; but where McEwan focuses on the sexual strangeness of the story, Pinter builds up all kinds of contrasts, not least between Mary's feminist independence and Caroline's intellectual and sexual passivity. He makes Mary, for instance, a much more clearly defined figure than she is in the novel. Pinter lays great stress on her two children, especially her daughter who has joined the school soccer team. He allows her to send up Colin's emotional dither and sexual vanity, not least in a restaurant scene where the men at an adjacent table seem to be eyeing him as much as her. He also gives more focus to Mary's involvement in a women's theatre group which once presented an all-female *Hamlet*. Pinter does not suggest Mary is a hardline ideologue, but he pointedly contrasts her independence with Caroline's sexual subjugation and domestic imprisonment.

Yet Pinter's most dramatic innovation is to change the whole tone and nature of a dinner-party scene in which Robert and Caroline abrasively entertain the visiting English couple. In McEwan's novel, the conversation centres on Robert's new manager at his bar and is riddled with sexual innuendo. In the film, it becomes a headlong contretemps about British politics and about the decay of basic freedoms:

ROBERT: So how is England? Lovely dear old England? Hampshire. Wiltshire. Cumberland. Yorkshire. Harrods. Such a beautiful country. Such beautiful traditions.
MARY: It's not quite so beautiful now. Is it Colin?

(COLIN *does not respond.*)

Colin? Are you feeling all right?

COLIN: (*quietly*) Sure.

ROBERT: In what way? In what way not beautiful?

MARY: Oh, I don't know – freedom . . . you know . . .

ROBERT: Freedom? What kind of freedom? Freedom to do what?

MARY: Freedom to be free.

ROBERT: You want to be free? (*He laughs.*) Free to do what?

MARY: You don't believe in it?

ROBERT: Sure I believe in it. But sometimes a few rules – you know – they're not a bad thing. First and foremost society has to be protected from perverts. Everybody knows that. My philosophical position is simple – put them all up against a wall and shoot them. What society needs to do is purify itself. The English government is going in the right direction. In Italy we could learn a lot of lessons from the English government.

COLIN: Well I'm an Englishman and I disagree violently with what you've just said. I think it's shit.

ROBERT: I respect you as an Englishman but not if you're a communist poof. You're not a poof are you? That's the right word, no? Or is it 'fruit'? Talking about fruit, it's time for coffee.

Pinter is not simply shoe-horning a debate about Clause 28 and the consequences of Thatcherism into a Venetian dinner party. The scene extends our knowledge of the characters and contains its own built-in ironies. Robert's privileged, romantic, essentially pastoral view of England, based on his experience as a son of a member of the diplomatic corps, is contrasted with present-day reality. Robert's venomous hatred of 'poofs' masks his own profound sexual ambiguity, indicated by his voyeuristic preoccupation with Colin, and implies that sexual intolerance invariably shields an uncertainty about one's own identity. And Mary's stumbling, inarticulate defence of freedom suggests that even the most intelligent, liberally inclined people are aware that something is wrong without being able to identify it. Pinter is exploring his own concerns, but without violating the integrity of the characters.

McEwan is perfectly happy with Pinter's political interpolation. 'It's not there,' he says, 'in the novel, but it fits perfectly well with the general nature of the tension between Robert and Colin. And I could well imagine that it's the kind of conversation that could crop up in Harold's life in London where one can be at a very pleasant dinner table and suddenly be confronted with the most appalling political views. Many of us would swallow hard on the soufflé and change the subject, but Harold will not. He's very courageous. He has a great wish to air a difference if he thinks it's going to lead somewhere fruitful; and I think there's just a touch of that in this exchange in the movie.'

Pinter's notes on the screenplay, preserved in the British Library's Archive, make it clear how central this scene was to his concept of the film. The Archive also reveals significant changes between the first draft and the final screenplay in the ending of the story. In both versions, Colin and Mary find themselves powerless in the face of attack from the crazed Robert and his accomplice wife. Mary, in fact, is forced to watch through a narcotic haze as Colin is seduced by Caroline and then has his throat cut by Robert. But Pinter, between the first and second versions, tones down the specific sexual violence to lend more weight to the coda of the murder.

In fact, Pinter adds a crucial final scene in the police station in which Robert is asked by puzzled detectives how he could have planned everything in advance while still leaving incriminating evidence and making no effort to avoid arrest. He returns to the opening statement of the film ('My father was a very big man . . .') as if he feels himself protected by – even exculpated by – the weight of the past and the arrogance of patriarchal values. And the final word of the film, 'Mascara', is a reminder of the ambiguity that underlies sexual absolutism. Pinter's original ending offered an ironic counterpoint to the violence with Mary sitting in a drugged haze while gondoliers played concertinas in the distance. In the final version, Pinter returns to the complex connection between political and sexual power. It is a perfect ending to one of Pinter's most intriguing and under-rated screenplays; one that harks back to *The Servant* in both its perverse eroticism and its study of the invasion of one personality by another. But where *The Servant* is primarily about the mutual disintegration of an upper-class wimp and a smooth predator, *The Comfort of Strangers* implies that the whole concept of freedom is at risk from a resurgent crypto-Fascism. It is not only one of Pinter's best films; it is also one of his most acutely political. While exploiting Venice's melancholy and sinister aura, it is imbued with an irrepressible concern for the sickness of liberty in Britain itself.

Seventeen Party Manners

Pinter was sixty on 10 October 1990 – a fact that did not go unremarked in the media. The British papers were full of profiles focusing less on his achievements than on all the usual issues: his supposed irascibility at dinner parties, his relative theatrical unproductiveness during the 1980s, the quirks and quiddities of his character. Christopher Silvester in the now-defunct *Sunday Correspondent* wrote a piece headed 'Angry Old Man', itemising anecdotes about Pinter's apparent social brusqueness. At Lord Weidenfeld's seventieth birthday party he had been approached by a journalist who explained that he was from the Londoner's Diary on the *Evening Standard* and asked if he had a message for it. Pinter's recollection is different from Silvester's. He did not bellow, as alleged, at his questioner. According to Pinter, he whispered quietly, 'Yes I do have a message for Londoner's Diary. Tell it to go fuck itself and you go with it.' A not unreasonable response, given the Diary's endless tittle-tattle about Pinter's private life and its preoccupation with the June 20th Group. Silvester's piece decided that the problem with Pinter was that he wanted the world to march to his rhythm – hardly a unique failing.

Not even his closest friends would deny that, along with a sense of generosity and good humour, there *is* a strong vein of anger in Pinter which is often impatient with the social niceties. But by a peculiarly British trick, discussion of its source – the hypocrisy and injustice of the world around us – was increasingly deflected by the media into a caricature of the man. He became part of a 'celebrity' world, largely created by the British press, in which everyone is assigned a one-dimensional role and fixed persona like characters in a minor Restoration Comedy: Pinter became the Angry Playwright who made good knocking-copy for journalists who saw something inherently comic about the idea of a wealthy writer with passionate convictions. Fellow-artists, however, took a somewhat larger view. The Mexican novelist Carlos Fuentes wrote a piece for the 1990 *Pinter Review* built on an intriguing paradox: while Pinter created a literature of stark nakedness out of a society of relative abundance, Latin American writers offered baroque abundance in a world of stark nakedness: 'In the European world, Harold Pinter places absence at the centre of opulence, discovers want in the heart of abundance, gnaws at the garish baroque of post-industrial society and reveals a chasm as great as that between Pampa and ocean, Utopia and conquest.' But Fuentes went on to suggest that, for all their apparent differences, Pinter's vision had a lot in common with that of Latin American writers.

> Are not these realities radically fraternal, supporting each other, in sympathy with their humanity – *our* abundance of poverty, *his* poverty of abundance? And are not the answers the same: his punished English language revealing the immensity of want, our Spanish language seeking what we think he has, and he telling us that his abundance is as barren as our poverty; but language, imagination and desire are still there, giving us the eyes and lips and ears of a possible survival?

A moving birthday tribute ended with the words: 'Pinter is truly ours, in Mexico, Nicaragua or Argentina.'

The contrast between the global vision of Pinter on the one hand and the parochial belittlement on the other is very striking. His plays are constantly produced around the world where they are admired not just for their verbal precision, but also for their political resonance. In Britain we seem obsessed by Pinter's party manners and the supposed irreconcilability of fame and comfort with moral passion. But none of this – though it undeniably irked him – had a deterrent effect on Pinter himself. In fact, 1990 was for him a typically active year. In February, he delivered the Herbert Read Memorial Lecture at the ICA on behalf of Salman Rushdie. In May, he gave a talk on Channel Four about the misuse of language and launched a swingeing attack on American policy in Nicaragua in the *Independent on Sunday* ('Yanquis Go Home') which was strong enough to elicit a reply from the US Ambassador in Britain. In the same month he directed Jane Stanton Hitchcock's *Vanilla* at the Lyric, Shaftesbury Avenue – a clumsy satire on the American super-rich and their grovelling sycophancy towards foreign dictatorships, in this case that of Imelda Marcos and the Philippines. One can only assume that Pinter's subscription to the play's attack on authoritarian cruelty blinded him to its technical gaucheness. But it was his Channel Four talk that was the most revealing in that he returned to one of his favourite themes: the idea of language as 'a permanent masquerade' that conceals substantive reality. One of the sources of Pinter's anger is that we frequently use language, both on the social and political level, to camouflage truth – an issue he addressed directly in his radio broadcast:

Do the structures of language and the structures of reality (by which I mean what actually *happens*) move along parallel lines? Does reality essentially remain outside language, separate, obdurate, alien, not susceptible to description? Is an accurate and vital correspondence between what *is* and our perception of it impossible? Or is it that we are obliged to use language only in order to obscure and distort reality – to distort what *is* – to distort what *happens* – because we fear it? We can't face the dead. But we must face the dead, because they die in our name. We must pay attention to what is being done in our name. I believe it's because of the way we use language that we have got ourselves into this terrible trap.

This anguished talk, with its insistent questions, is as close as Pinter comes to a statement of his credo in later years; in particular, his despair over the growing gulf between the rhetoric and euphemisms of political discourse and brutal reality. It is the theme that lies behind *Precisely*, *One for the Road* and *Mountain Language* and that makes them, for all their brevity, not just marginal footnotes to his dramatic *oeuvre* but important extensions of it. Pinter has always been obsessed with the way we use language to mask primal urges. The difference in his later plays is not simply that they move into the political arena, but that they counterpoint the smokescreen of language with shocking and disturbing images of torture, punishment and death.

Pinter's sixtieth year proved, if nothing else, his tenacity. The press was filled with profiles ranging from the equivocal to downright hatchet-jobs. But the novel of *The Dwarfs* was finally published in October to modest acclaim, though few critics saw in it the seeds of all his later work. And BBC Radio, which had done so much to rescue the young Pinter after the failure of *The Birthday Party*, made amends for the peevish tone of so much print-journalism. On 3 October, Radio 3 put out a new recording of *Betrayal* directed by Ned Chaillet in which Pinter himself played Robert, bringing out the acute sense of pain behind the polite mask of formality. And to coincide with the actual birthday on 10 October, they cleared the decks for a four-hour Sunday-evening programme which I had the luck to present. It consisted of interviews, broadcasts of the work (several of the sketches and the whole of *Family Voices*), readings (with Pinter delivering the close of Beckett's *The Unnameable*), favourite music (including the Bach Violin Concerto in A Minor) and reflections on Pinter's involvement with politics, film and cricket. It captured, I hope, something of the breadth and range of Pinter's output. My chief memory is of the producer Fiona McLean and myself both trying to get through the four-hour evening while struggling with severe flu. But the programme proved that the BBC – under attack at the time from the Tory

Right and with talk of privatisation in the air – was still capable of paying proper attention to a living writer.

If there was any major disappointment as Pinter took his score into the sixties, it was that his screenplay of Kazuo Ishiguro's masterly Booker Prize-winning novel *The Remains of the Day* fell foul of the Byzantine politics of the movie industry. Pinter was the ideal writer to translate Ishiguro's book to the screen in that it deals with masked affections and hidden beliefs. It's the story of an immaculate English butler who faces up to his repressed passion for a former housekeeper and his denial of his moral obligations in deferring to his aristocratic master's Fascist sympathies. Classic Pinter material. In fact he bought an option on the book which he eventually sold to Mike Nichols: Pinter wrote a screenplay which Nichols looked forward to directing. However Columbia, who finally acquired the rights, turned the project over to the production team of Ismail Merchant and James Ivory, who brought in their own regular writer, Ruth Prawer Jhabvala, to do a new version. 'There are still seven or eight scenes in the finished film that I wrote,' says Pinter. 'Indeed, James Fox who played Lord Darlington was furious with me for not taking a credit, since he thought they were the scenes that worked best. But you can't get too worked up about this. Up to now [this was said in 1995] I've written twenty-two film scripts of which seventeen have been made exactly as written: that's not too bad a statistic, given the nature of the movie industry.'

Even if the screenplay he worked on throughout 1990 was revamped, at least Pinter's sixtieth birthday triggered a series of major theatrical revivals the following year. It was a healthy start to a decade that witnessed both a critical re-evaluation of his work and a resurgence of Pinter's own creative energy. Appropriately, it was Peter Hall who started the process with a revival of *The Homecoming* at the Comedy Theatre in January 1991. Pinter had famously broken with Hall in 1983, but typically it was he who took the initiative in restoring the bruised relationship. He wrote to Hall, after a gap of six years, congratulating him on one of his productions. The two men then met socially at an Edna O'Brien dinner party. Finally, Pinter wrote Hall another letter saying: 'Life's too short – let's make it up.' Though sudden and quick in quarrel, Pinter is also a great believer in reconciliation.

Hall's initial instinct was to remake *The Homecoming* from top to bottom. But the more he talked to his designer John Bury, and the more he looked at the film of his 1965 production, the more he felt there was no point in being different for its own sake. So he and Bury went back to the original image of a cavernous, grey-walled, barrack-like room ('even the lampshade', wrote Benedict Nightingale in *The Times* 'might have been rescued from the ashes of Hiroshima'), in which the only colour came from the acid-green apples.

Time and recasting, however, wrought their own inevitable changes. The most drastic revision lay in the character of Teddy who, as Irving Wardle noted, was converted 'from the plot's apparent victim into its disdainful instigator'. Greg Hicks played him as a smooth, isolated, passionless figure who had achieved intellectual equilibrium at the expense of his humanity and who treated Ruth as if she were a convenient appendage to his American academic life. Lines like 'You can help me with my lectures when we get back' suddenly seemed far more chillingly patronising than anything Ibsen's Torvald might have said to his doll-wife. Given the choice between the sterile dependence offered by Teddy and the noisy turbulence of his native household, Ruth's homecoming seemed more comprehensible than in 1965. Moreover, Cherie Lunghi as Ruth, constantly smiling with upturned, peach-coloured lips at all the bull-swagger and bravado around her, seemed like a woman discovering her identity in a world that would enable her to operate as a manipulative queen bee.

Peter Hall confirms that this is what he was after. 'In 1965,' he says, 'there was some slight sense that Ruth was a victim. In the second version there was no question that the men had been destroyed and rightly so. I also don't think we got Teddy right before. He's the most difficult and complex character. We had three Teddys in the '6os: Michael Bryant, Michael Craig and Michael Jayston. They were all good. But what we didn't get is that Teddy is the biggest bastard in the play – he's absolutely fireproof. He has no intention of letting any human feeling get to him or alter him. This time we played him much more unsympathetically and the play made much more sense.' The most debatable performance came from Warren Mitchell as Max. I thought he was tremendous: full of Cockney-Jewish speech rhythms, paternally vituperative one moment, maternally sentimental the next, and at the end strangely moving as, in craven capitulation, he begged Ruth for a kiss. Pinter, too, thought he was very good, but, ever anxious for *The Homecoming* not to be defined as a Jewish play, questioned the accent: 'It doesn't,' he says, 'make sense for Max to be Jewish if the rest of the family isn't.'

The Homecoming was a huge popular and critical success: an 'imperishably funny and disturbing classic', wrote Michael Coveney in the *Observer*. It was as good, if not better, than everyone remembered it to be. But two weeks later, when *Betrayal* was revived by David Leveaux at the Almeida, the Islington air was filled with the sound of self-flagellating critics – myself not least – upwardly revising their notions of a play they had largely trashed thirteen years before at the Lyttelton. The physical context made a huge difference: a simple drop-curtain between scenes, an intimate space in which the slightest movement of a face or body made itself felt, a chaste white-box set by Mark

Thompson, the accompanying sound of the Goldberg Variations. Where once the content had seemed old-fashioned and the form futuristic, the two now harmonised perfectly. John Peter in the *Sunday Times* intriguingly suggested that the reverse chronology indicated the way experience can devalue feeling and impoverish language: 'The final effect is nightmarish: as if you realised with a shudder that what you have just been through were only about to begin. It reminds me of something Freud has written: that when a dream tells events in reverse order it wants to deny something.' What struck me even more was Pinter's moral ambivalence. Cheryl Campbell played the opening scene on a note of cool self-determination denoting Emma's survival instinct. At the same time, you felt you had been witnessing a dizzying vortex of corruption. As David Leveaux said, 'As usual, Harold's title is more than it appears to be. It's fascinating that he didn't call the play *Infidelity*. He called it *Betrayal*. The idea runs very deep: betrayal of self, betrayal of others, betrayal of art. It's a study of what happens when truth itself becomes poisoned and of the way, once poison enters the system, there are huge spiritual consequences. A word like "betrayal" is a Biblical word, though Harold wouldn't consciously have thought of that. The play has a limited social milieu; but I felt there was a deeper dimension suggesting a humanist catastrophe which is around in other plays as well.'

The third major revival in London's unofficial Pinter retrospective was the author's own production of *The Caretaker* which opened at the Comedy on 20 June with Donald Pleasence, now seventy-one, returning to the role of Davies after thirty-one years. The old haunting mannerisms were still there: the jabbing, air-punching right hand, the defensive hunch, the mongrel voice wavering between rage and subservience. Age had certainly not withered Pleasence, but it had mellowed him a bit: there was now a twilit pathos about this homeless hobo that left you at the end, as he hugged his bag to him like a security blanket, almost pitying his plight. But the great gain was the casting of Peter Howitt and Colin Firth as Mick and Aston: the one a flashy, leather-jacketed bruiser who you could imagine, as Benedict Nightingale said, 'leaving the pub for a game at Highbury'; the other a gentle, slow-moving, lobotomised giant. Originally, Gary Oldman and Alfred Molina, who had played Joe Orton and Kenneth Halliwell in the film of *Prick Up Your Ears*, had been sounded out as possible casting. But it is hard to imagine them bettering Howitt and Firth: two looming six-footers with similar strong-jawed faces and quite plausibly brothers. It became not just a play about the politics of possession, but, reminding one of its origins in Chiswick life, a study of the tensile strength of family ties.

While obviously gratified by this *ad hoc* London celebration of his work,

Pinter remained as deeply involved with politics as ever. He could hardly be otherwise in a year that began in January with the momentous Gulf War. It was a war that was relayed to us all in graphic detail on television and that seemed to be prompted less by the US government's desire to protect Kuwait's independence against Saddam Hussein's invasion than by what Eric Hobsbawm called 'a belated compensation for the awful moments in 1973 and 1979 when the greatest power on earth could find no response to a consortium of feeble Third World states which threatened to strangle its oil supplies'. No amount of protest could affect American policy, but something could be done about the monstrous inequity of the British government's decision to round up and deport a number of Iraqi and Palestinian nationals resident in Britain on the grounds that they constituted a security risk. They were instantly classified as prisoners of war and were not allowed to hear the evidence against them. One such arrested on 17 January was Abbas Cheblak, a Palestinian who had been resident in Britain for sixteen years, who was a lifelong campaigner for Arab rights, who had spoken out against Saddam Hussein, and who was an advocate of the peaceful settlement of the Arab—Israeli dispute. Pinter, along with Martin Amis, David Edgar and Ian McEwan, protested about Cheblak's arrest in a letter to the *Independent* on 29 January and about the whole policy of proposed indiscriminate deportation. Pinter and his fellow-writers were way ahead of the British press in realising the enormity of what was happening. By their swift action, they not only secured Cheblak's release but exposed the whole issue and helped to ensure that none of those arrested, many of whom were Iraqi dissidents, were tried or deported. So much for the idea that protest is pointless or that writers have no business interfering in state affairs.

Pinter continued to be exercised by injustice and hypocrisy from whatever source. In June 1991, he and other members of the Nicaragua Solidarity Campaign urged the United States to recognise the verdict of the World Court in the Hague of an 'illegal war against Nicaragua and to respond to that country's claim for reparations'. In July, he spoke at the launch at the House of Commons of the '500 Years of Resistance Campaign': a counter-protest, organised by more than twenty Latin American groups, to America's celebration of Christopher Columbus's mercantile adventurism. In September, Pinter was to be found protesting at the Israeli government's illegal abduction of Mordechai Vanunu and his sentence to eighteen years of solitary confinement for exposing Israel's nuclear capacity. And in the same month he read on Radio 3 a selection of work by the much-imprisoned Turkish poet Nazim Hikmet, including the title poem from the broadcast 'A Sad State of Freedom'.

His particular loathing of the sanctimoniousness of Western democracies found expression that year in a polemical sketch and poem. The sketch was *The New World Order* which was played in July at the Royal Court – first in the Theatre Upstairs and then in the main house – as a curtain-raiser to Ariel Dorfman's ethical thriller *Death and the Maiden*. Pinter's play was inevitably mocked for its brevity – it ran a mere eight minutes – but in that time Pinter packs in a lot. He shows two sharp-suited interrogators – the warrant officer Des and the gentlemanly Lionel – preparing to go to work on a silent blindfolded figure. They talk ominously of what they 'might' and 'will' do to him. They threateningly invoke the torture they will inflict on his wife. They engage in semantic quibbles as to whether he is 'a cunt' or 'a prick'; in fact, Des tells Lionel that by employing such mutually contradictory terms he would lose face in any linguistic discussion group. They delight in the enforced silence and humiliation of their victim. 'Before he came in here', says Des, 'he was a big shot, he never stopped shooting his mouth off, he never stopped questioning received ideas' (a phrase that Pinter has used about himself and his friends from Hackney days). Warming to his appointed task, Lionel begins to cry with delight at feeling so pure – a phrase that leads to the cryptic denouement:

> DES: Well, you're right. You're right to feel pure. You know why?
> LIONEL: Why?
> DES: Because you're keeping the world clean for democracy.
> (*They look into each other's eyes.*)
> DES: I'm going to shake you by the hand.
> (DES *shakes* LIONEL's *hand. He then gestures to the man in the chair with his thumb.*)
> And so will he . . . (*he looks at his watch*) . . . in about thirty-five minutes.

That last line, with its calculated precision, has a powerful dramatic impact. But the whole sketch, with its tone of cool irony, is intended to shock and stir; to remind us that there is little room for dissent in the promised new world order, that torture is not invariably carried out by some mysterious 'other' but by recognisable figures in snappy suits, and that the abuse of power is constantly legitimised by the invocation of lofty principles. One is reminded of Nicolas in *One for the Road* telling his victim that 'he was keeping the world clean for God'. The whole thrust of Pinter's late political plays, in fact, is to try to jolt our complacency about the self-righteous superiority of Western democracies. *The New World Order* may be a summation rather than a development of Pinter's ideas, but Robert Cushman in the *Independent on Sunday* announced that 'it gets closer to the nerve of torture than any play I know'. It also attempts to pierce the insulated Western conscience which casually accepts the death of 150,000 Iraqis in the Gulf War, or the use of torture in Central America or Turkey, provided it is done in the holy name of 'freedom' or 'democracy'.

It is significant that on the death of Graham Greene in April 1991, Pinter praised him for his ability to look beyond political rhetoric at the reality of 'a tortured naked body'. Pinter's own obsession with the gulf between language and fact prompted him in August that same year to write a poem called 'American Football – A Reflection on the Gulf War'. It was rejected for publication by the *Independent*, the *Observer*, the *Guardian* (on the grounds it was 'a family newspaper'), the *New York Review of Books* and the *London Review of Books*. The last named, in particular, aroused Pinter's ire by accompanying rejection with the assurance that the poem had 'considerable force' and that it shared the author's views on the United States. Since the poem has been so little read and circulated, it is worth reproducing in full:

Hallelullah!
It works
We blew the shit out of them.

We blew the shit right back up their own ass
And out their fucking ears.

It works.
   We blew the shit out of them,
They suffocated in their own shit!

Hallelullah.
Praise the Lord for all good things.

We blew them into fucking shit.
They are eating it.

Praise the Lord for all good things.

We blew their balls into shards of dust,
Into shards of fucking dust.

We did it.

Now I want you to come over here and kiss me on the mouth.

What Pinter is clearly doing in *American Football* is satirising, through language that is deliberately violent, obscene, sexual and celebratory, the military triumphalism that followed the Gulf War and, at the same time, counteracting the stage-managed euphemisms through which it was projected on television. General Schwarzkopf talked of 'surgical bombing' and 'collateral damage'. Perry Smith, a retired general and CNN analyst, claimed that the Gulf War would 'set a new standard' in avoiding civilian casualties. When an Iraqi air-raid shelter was hit, American officials quickly went on television and claimed that it was 'a command-and-control facility'. Death was smothered in the language of technology and bureaucracy. But as the *New Yorker* reported on 25 March 1991, Operation Desert Storm not only involved massive civilian casualties but 'battle carnage on a scale and at a pace equal to some of this century's most horrifying military engagements'. Pinter's poem, by its exaggerated tone of jingoistic, anally obsessed bravado, reminds us of the weasel-words used to describe the war on television and of the fact that the clean, pure conflict which the majority of the American people backed at the time was one that existed only in their imagination. Behind the poem lies a controlled rage: that it was rejected, even by those who sympathised with its sentiments, offers melancholy proof that hypocrisy is not confined to governments and politicians.

Pinter has always been concerned with the divorce between language and reality. At this time, he also became concerned by our culpable indifference to the sins being committed in the name of social order and 'good' government: the theme of a new forty-minute play, *Party Time*, which had its première at the Almeida in October 1991. I first got a sighting of it in March of that year when it struck me as a powerful Buñuel-like parable about a vacuum-sealed, high-bourgeois world cut off from the surrounding harshness. It was also given a highly appreciated public reading at a gathering in Ohio in April of 250 scholars and artists convened to celebrate Pinter's sixtieth birthday. Many of the papers that were read are published in *Pinter at Sixty*. The response of the London critics, when the play opened at the Almeida in conjunction with a revival of *Mountain Language*, was much less enthusiastic than it had been in Ohio. Mark Lawson in the *Independent* referred to the ceremony that comes late in the career of major writers, 'The Veneration of the Nail-Clippings'. Malcolm Rutherford in the *Financial Times* told us that nobody laughed much at the Pinter style any more 'because the audience has seen through it'. Charles Spencer in the *Daily Telegraph* told us that 'it is all so glibly and glumly predictable that you feel like screaming'. What was depressing was how few critics stopped to ask whether there might be some truth in Pinter's central point that bourgeois privilege increasingly coexists with greater investment of power in the state and that our lives are more and more governed by a narcissistic materialism in which it is uncool to get het up about injustice and corruption. Maybe the play doesn't have the multivalent richness of *The Homecoming* or *Old Times*; what it does do is offer a deadly assault on our own moral myopia.

The location of the party that Pinter depicts is unspecified, but from all the internal evidence it seems to be happening in London. The host Gavin (played by Barry Foster in a smart brocade waistcoat) is a high-ranking government official clearly responsible for the 'round-up' that is going on in the streets outside and that has made access difficult for many of the super-rich guests. The majority of them are members of an exclusive, elegant new health club and join in praising its 'fantastic' hot towels, its 'brilliant' cannelloni and 'wonderful' lighting. They gossip about sexual affairs and the rapacious activities of a 'nymphomaniac slut'. They brag of their summer island retreats and the pleasure of fucking on boats. And a survivor from the *ancien régime*, Dame Melissa, talks of the tennis and swimming clubs of her youth which have died because they had no moral foundation. 'But our club', she says, 'our club – is a club which is activated, which is inspired by a moral sense, a moral awareness, a set of moral values which is – I have to say – unshakeable, rigorous, fundamental, constant.' If anything disrupts this atmosphere of smug, self-satisfied harmony, it is the running battle between Terry, an Essex-man bruiser employed to carry out his social superiors' dirty work, and his wife Dusty, who naggingly enquires after the fate of her missing brother. All, literally, becomes clear at the end when a bright light that has burned into the room at intervals reveals the thinly dressed figure of the brother Jimmy, a victim of the state oppression to which the partygoers have turned the blindest of eyes.

Where is the play actually happening? In one sense, it could be Paris, Berlin, Washington, Istanbul, Buenos Aires or Santiago; but watching the play in the Almeida, it seemed very much about present-day England. Irving Wardle – one of the few critics to understand the play fully – hit the mark when he said in the *Independent on Sunday* that 'the play reflects the reported iniquities of Africa and Latin America in the perspective of a London Pinter knows inside out'. Pinter is not literally suggesting that roadblocks are being set up in Holland Park or round-ups are taking place in Belgravia. What he does imply is that one of the preconditions of Fascism – a myopic and self-preoccupied wealthy élite, totally indifferent to the decisions taken in its name – is becoming dangerously apparent in Britain. But he goes much further and suggests that under the drawing-room elegance, private relationships echo public brutality and that language itself is corrupted. In this context, for instance, the word 'agenda' acquires sinister connotations. As Dusty repeatedly asks after her brother, the abrasive Terry tells her that the subject of Jimmy is 'not on anyone's agenda'. When Dusty twice defiantly says that it's on her agenda, Terry brutally replies: 'No, no, you've got it wrong there, old darling. What you've got wrong there, old darling, what you've got totally wrong, is that you don't have any agenda. Got it? You have no agenda.' Once the word neutrally applied to items of business to be considered at a meeting; now it has become a euphemistic prescription for political action.

Likewise, Pinter endows the word 'regime' with a double-edged potency in the climax to a clenched exchange between two of the guests: the widowed, beautiful Charlotte and her saturnine ex-lover Fred. This is some of Pinter's best writing in years in that the formal, staccato, almost Cowardesque dialogue contains a wealth of buried emotion:

FRED: You said your husband died.
CHARLOTTE: My what?
FRED: Your husband.
CHARLOTTE: Oh my husband. Oh yes. That's right. He died.
FRED: Was it a long illness?
CHARLOTTE: Short.
FRED: Ah.
  (*Pause.*)
FRED: Quick then.
CHARLOTTE: Quick, yes. Short and quick.
  (*Pause.*)
FRED: Better that way.
CHARLOTTE: Really?
FRED: I would have thought.
CHARLOTTE: Ah. I see. Yes.
  (*Pause.*)
  Better for who?
FRED: What?
CHARLOTTE: You said it would be better. Better for who?
FRED: For you.
  (CHARLOTTE *laughs.*)
CHARLOTTE: Yes! I'm glad you didn't say him.
FRED: Well, I could say him. A quick death must be better than a slow one. It stands to reason.
CHARLOTTE: No it doesn't.
  (*Pause.*)
  Anyway, I'll bet it can be quick and slow at the same time. I bet it can. I

bet death can be both things at the same time. Oh by the way, he wasn't
ill.

Nothing is directly stated, but we infer from this loaded exchange that
Charlotte's husband, whose death was both quick and slow, was the victim of
state torture; and when Fred goes on to warn her to 'leave the street to us',
she realises that her ex-lover is implicated in the process. Staring hard at him,
she comments on his looks and asks 'How do you do it? What's your diet?
What's your regime? What *is* your regime by the way?' By careful dramatic
placing, the word 'regime' – like 'agenda' – suddenly acquires a terrifying
resonance.

Roger Lloyd Pack, who had played the tortured Victor in *One for the Road*
and was now the menacing Fred in *Party Time*, suggests that Pinter's direction of the latter was much more socially precise. 'With *One for the Road* no
one ever raised publicly the question of where it was set. But with *Party Time*
we all assumed it was set in England and that the club referred to was a
particularly trendy place, with a gym and swimming pool, in west London.
Harold was also much more explicit both in terms of character detail and in
how he wanted the play done. He gave everybody a background saying,
"You're probably someone in the City," or, 'You're someone high up in the
Civil Service." He knew how he wanted everything to be, even down to line-
readings.' Gawn Grainger, who played the slick chauvinist Douglas, concurs,
adding that Pinter constantly related both *Party Time* and *Mountain
Language* to the outside world. 'Most days,' says Grainger, 'he would come in
with the newspaper saying, "Have you read this in *The Times* or the
Guardian?"' It is also significant that when Pinter wrote in extra dialogue for
the TV version in 1992, he made the location even more specifically English
with references to Oxford and county horse trials.

Party Time offers a powerful, developing image of an hermetic, heedless
society so preoccupied with its own conspicuous consumption and health
Fascism that it is blithely indifferent to the erosion of civil liberties. The most
interesting criticisms of the play, however, came not from journalists but from
Pinter's fellow-playwrights. In a live discussion on BBC TV's *The Late
Show* after the first night, Edward Bond complained about the lack of explicit
identifiable commitment, and John McGrath talked of the play being 'uncon-
cretised' and the action 'taken out of context'. I met a similar objection from
John Arden after the play had been screened on Channel Four on 17
November 1992, a version to which I supplied an explanatory postscript.
Arden's point was that he wanted to know who was conducting the revolution
in the streets: if, for example, it was a socialist overthrow of a corrupt, Fascist

regime, then it would alter his judgement of the play. I countered that there was ample internal evidence to prove this was an act of repression from the Right: the elitist delight in the 'club', the brutal contempt for people who break its rules ('And if they do', says Terry, 'we kick them in the balls and chuck them down the stairs with no trouble at all'), the sanctimonious appropriation of moral values. But supposing – by some perverse twist – you saw the play as being about a set of champagne socialists delighting in a successful left-wing coup, Pinter's point would still be the same: that the myopic acceptance of suffering and repression in the name of order and stability is morally unforgivable.

What is dismaying, in the larger framework, is the way Pinter is constantly patronised in the media for expressing political opinions. The same treatment is frequently meted out to actors – always dismissively referred to as 'luvvies' – who campaign on public issues. Yet in my experience, writers and actors often have a more acute social conscience than journalists and media-folk who, most particularly in the 1990s, have become obsessed by their own goldfish-bowl world. Pinter's views on politics – most particularly, the perversion of words like 'freedom' and 'democracy' – are consistent, impassioned and well informed. Shortly after the première of *Party Time*, for instance, he sat down to write an article for *World*, an excellent magazine published by BBC Enterprises. His piece, published in March 1992, was written to accompany a documentary film made by the photographer Susan Meiselas about Nicaragua. Meiselas's pictures of Nicaragua during the overthrow of the Somoza dictatorship had been published worldwide in 1979; ten years later, she returned to record the country's fight for survival. Pinter's accompanying article is worth quoting in detail, since it combines passion, irony and first-hand knowledge:

The vicious Somoza dictatorship held power in Nicaragua for over 40 years, created by the US and fully supported by it. When the Sandinistas overthrew this regime in 1979 – a breathtaking popular revolution – it inherited a country with no health service, very high levels of infant mortality and malnutrition, widespread illiteracy, appalling poverty. The Sandinistas set out to correct this, to change people's lives. The death penalty was abolished. Two thousand schools were built. Over one hundred thousand peasant families were given title to land. Illiteracy was cut to less than one seventh. Malaria, measles and tetanus were dramatically reduced. Infant mortality was reduced by a third. Polio was eradicated.

The US denounced these achievements as Marxist-Leninist subversion.

The Sandinistas were of course setting a very bad example to the region.

They had dared to assert their country's independence from US influence and had had the impertinence to implement a concept of something called "social justice". The US Administration, the big banks and the multination-als were, quite understandably, aghast. The powerless millions in neighbour-ing Guatemala, El Salvador and Honduras might derive encouragement from these endeavours and get ideas above their station. The Sandinistas had to be destroyed at all costs, to preserve – as President Reagan never tired of saying –"freedom" and "democracy" in the area.

Wonderful words, freedom and democracy.

Writing after the 1990 elections in which the Sandinistas were defeated, Pinter freely acknowledges the imperfections of their period in office, but he also pinpoints their respect for human dignity and the 'quite clinical cam-paign of lies, intimidation, embargo, manipulation, blockade, bribery, black-mail, sabotage and terror' waged by the USA which led to the death of 30,000 people and the maiming for life of 6,000 others. Pinter writes in knowledgeable anger. But his real fury is directed against the cloak of self-righteousness with which the USA surrounds itself. Better for him the pragmatic honesty of a George Kennan (who in 1948 as head of the US State Department said that 'we should cease to talk about vague and unreal object-ives such as human rights, the raising of living standards and democratisa-tion' and focus on immediate national objectives) than the pious platitudes of a Reagan or a Bush. What Pinter hates, above all, is hypocrisy; what he values is truth. I am reminded of an occasion in 1995 when Pinter was describing to me a TV encounter between John Pilger, who was describing the massacres in East Timor, and Alan Clark. Pilger said to Clark that he cared a great deal about the death of animals. 'Yes, I do indeed,' said Clark. 'You don't seem to care quite so much about the deaths of humans,' countered Pilger. 'Curiously not,' Clark coolly replied. While deploring Clark's attitude, Pinter was pre-pared to acknowledge its candour.

Pinter's concern with politics is constant. You can see that from his Holland Park work-room which is always filled with documents from Amnesty International, Human Rights Watch Helsinki and particular protest groups from around the world – not only documents, but also a poem by John Berger commemorating the Socialist Chilean Defence Minister Orlando Letelier, who was tortured, exiled and killed by a car bomb in Washington, DC, in 1976. Pinter's own involvement with that country was recognised in April 1992 when he received the insignia of Grand Officer, the Chilean Order of Merit for his 'support for the Chilean people in their fight to recover democracy'. The idea fostered in sections of the British press of Pinter as a political dilettante forever pontificating about situations of which he knows little is absolute rubbish. Indeed, he took great pleasure that summer in nailing a lie, perpetrated by several newspapers, that when Tory MP Tristan Garel-Jones challenged him to name two Nicaraguan poets he was unable to do so. At the time he was, in fact, involved in arranging readings in the UK of the work of Ernesto Cardenal and Gioconda Belli. As a partner in the Greville Press, he had also privately subsidised the publication of a pamphlet, *Nicaragua Water Fire*, containing two long poems by the latter.

Yet Pinter is a theatre animal as well as an impassioned citizen, and when Ian McDiarmid and Jonathan Kent, joint directors of the Almeida, decided to follow up the success of *Betrayal* and the double bill of *Party Time* and *Mountain Language* by reviving *No Man's Land*, unseen in London since 1975, Pinter was, in Lenny's inimitable phrase, 'chuffed to his bollocks'. The catch was that they wanted him to play Hirst. Not only had Pinter not done any stage acting since the 1985 revival of *Old Times* (and that was for an American tour), but he would also find himself competing with the memory of Ralph Richardson. He agreed to do it. But, to add to his own natural apprehensions, just as rehearsals were getting under way in October 1992, he learned that his mother Frances was dying of cancer in a Brighton hospital. Both Pinter and Antonia were with her during her last hours and at the moment of death. Having to cope both with the emotional shock of bereavement and the practical arrangements for his mother's funeral, it would have been understandable if he had pulled out of the production of a play haunted by death. But work is an antidote to grief and Pinter continued, conscientiously immersing himself in the rehearsal process. Only later was he able to relieve his pent-up emotion; and then in creative form.

For David Leveaux, who was half Pinter's age and who had never seen the original *No Man's Land*, directing the author in his own play posed few problems. Pinter told him early on in rehearsals, 'You must be yourself in this situation. You will direct and I will be the actor.' Pinter's tact extended to his fellow-actors: he allowed them to work out their own solutions to the play via the director. The late Paul Eddington, who admits that he was baffled when he first saw *No Man's Land*, came to his own conclusions about Spooner. 'I was puzzled,' he told me, 'as to who he was. I thought to myself, "What is his function?" Then a light dawned on me during a speech in the first act when I offer Hirst the hand of friendship. "Let me perhaps be your boatman. For if and when we talk of a river we talk of a deep and dank architecture." The picture that came into my mind was of Doré's illustration of Dante's Inferno. Caverns of ice and the Styx. I thought perhaps that I'm Charon and my purpose is to convey him from this world to the next. When I make that long speech at the end and appear to be asking to be taken on as Hirst's companion and secretary, I thought that it wasn't so much a plea for a job. Perhaps it was a last opportunity for Hirst to be guided by Spooner towards death. I was interested to find that Salman Rushdie thought exactly the same thing, though I discussed it with Harold and he was non-committal.'

Eddington, however, came up with a solution that was both right for him and true to the text. The end result was a performance that challenged – and often overtook – memories of Gielgud. Eddington, his fine chiselled features ravaged by a wasting cancer, was both prey and predator: 'a hunched stork', according to Paul Taylor in the *Independent*, 'a moulting eagle' in my own review in the *Guardian*, 'a marsh-bird past its prime yet capable of banging open a shell and sucking out the flesh if a plump snail should insist on being eaten' in Benedict Nightingale's phrase in *The Times*. Eddington, torn be-tween deference and defiance, was particularly fine in the parodic Brideshead games when he invoked the name of 'Doreen Busby' with triumphant cocki-ness as if to confirm Hirst's unspeakable sexual iniquity. Pinter himself, stocky, jaw-jutting and fruity-voiced, also showed that his technique had not grown rusty with the years. The moment I'll always remember from his Hirst is when, after being reduced to befuddled leglessness by a night of epic boozing, he breezed into the room the morning after exuding dangerous authority. But the great virtue of Leveaux's production was that it reminded you the play was a string quartet rather than a duo and that Briggs and Foster were central to the action. Gawn Grainger and Douglas Hodge, who played those roles superbly, even found themselves inventing character biographies in true Stanislavsky fashion.

'Duggie and I,' says Grainger, 'used to talk about it a lot between ourselves. I remember a note from David to the effect that once you walked through that door, that was it. Everything happened in that space. I disagreed with that, but I decided not to open that one up. My idea of Briggs was that he'd fucked them all. I saw him as a bit like that guy in *The Innocents*, Peter Quint. There's nothing gay about him. But when Foster says at the end "I came, I was summoned", I think that's what really happened: that Foster was a seaman and that Briggs picked him up at the corner of Bolsover Street and brought him in. Duggie, on the other hand, saw Foster as a would-be poet and that every time he tried to write, Briggs would fuck it up. It's what happens at the end of Act One when Foster comes out with this rich speech about the Siamese girls and the happiness he's lost and Briggs undercuts it with "We're out of bread". We invented this other world for ourselves, as to some extent did Paul, who saw Spooner as Charon taking Hirst across the Styx with Duggie and myself as the Furies.'

Grainger also recollects how much Pinter relished the camaraderie of the dressing-room and all the back-chat that went with it – so much so, that all four actors frequently dined together even after the production was over. 'I remember,' says Grainger, 'remarking to Harold one day that poetry is like a cat: it'll come to you when it's ready. Harold said, "That's it – that's absolutely true." I think sometimes his plays are like that . . . they just arrive. I can remember quite clearly the day when *Moonlight* started. We were sitting one night in the communal dressing-room and Harold said, "I've written three-and-a-half minutes today." Duggie said, "It's not long enough." Harold loved all that: simply being one of the boys again and being with guys who sent him up. I said to him one night, "Here you are in this tatty dressing-room in Islington – one of the great writers of the twentieth century." He looked at me with mock-fierceness and said, "What do you mean, *one of*?" I think all those little jibes and jokes and jigs got him going again as a writer.'

There is no doubt that the Almeida run of *No Man's Land* had a galvanising effect on Pinter. The suspended grief over his mother's death, which he was forced to keep in check through the rehearsal period, inevitably triggered thoughts of mortality. The nightly discipline of turning up at the theatre (which meant fiercely restricted daytime drinking), of confronting an audience head-on and sharing the bantering company of actors in a grubby dressing-room, also seems to have liberated Pinter's creative urge. *Moonlight* is a play with many complex sources, but the fact is that Pinter started work on it during the Almeida run. Between the closure of *No Man's Land* in mid-December and its transfer to the Comedy in February 1993, Pinter and Antonia took a holiday in Mauritius during which he completed the writing of it on the plane and in the hotel suite, sitting in a black dressing-gown with a large yellow lawyer's writing pad balanced on his knees. Running eighty minutes, it was dubbed – somewhat arbitrarily – Pinter's first full-length play in fourteen years. More significantly, it showed Pinter temporarily forsaking politics to explore his own private griefs and anguish in the most nakedly and unashamedly emotional of all his plays.

Eighteen Moonlit Nights

*M*oonlight, which had its première at the Almeida in September 1993, represents both a homecoming and a major departure for Pinter. A homecoming in the sense that it picks up on many of the themes that have haunted him over the years: the subjectivity of memory, the unknowability of one's lifelong partner, the hunger for an ascertainable past, the idea of family life as a brutal battleground. But there is also something new here in Pinter: a total emotional openness. Andy, the play's hero, is a dying, foul-mouthed, irascible ex-civil servant. He is anything but a self-portrait or a mouthpiece for the author. But there is a tangible sense of mortality, a yearning for contact between the living and the dead and a grief over the alienation of one's children that seems to come from the heart. What John Lahr in the *New Yorker* excellently called the play's 'litany of loss' expresses something deep inside Pinter himself.

Antonia Fraser confirms that the play has its origins in Pinter's own experience. When, during rehearsals for *No Man's Land*, Pinter had received a message that his mother was dying, he and Antonia sped down to Brighton to offer what comfort they could and, after Frances's death, to attend to all the funeral arrangements. It was a hectic, traumatic period for Pinter, but with a production in rehearsal he had no choice but to go back to work after his mother's death. As Antonia Fraser says, 'Because of the pressure of events, Harold never had time to mourn his mother fully and *Moonlight* is, in part, an expression of that. But it also has many other sources such as the fact that Daniel for many years never had anything to do with his grandparents. It's also a play about Harold's own mortality. All that fed into it. Some people assumed that because Harold lived in a house with teenage children it was somehow a reflection of his own inherited family, but that is totally untrue. Others thought that one of Andy's sons, Fred, was dying of Aids, but again there is no evidence for that whatsoever.'

In a sense, *Moonlight* is tone-poem as well as play: a single-movement piece full of interwoven themes. Dying is obviously one. But so too is separation. Separation within marriage. Separation between a father and his sons.

Separation between the living and the dead who still ache to make contact. The first speech belongs to Bridget, Andy's daughter, whom we see 'in faint light' and who exists in a world of her own. 'I have a feeling that Bridget is dead,' said Pinter to his director David Leveaux the day after giving him the script. And the initial staging, with Bridget seen in a gauze-covered chamber above stage-level, confirmed that. Although in her first speech she talks of her parents in the present tense, it is with a ghostly solicitude: 'They have given so much of their life for me and my brothers. All their life in fact. All their energies and all their love. They need to sleep in peace and wake up rested. I must see that this is my task.' Instantly, Pinter introduces one of the main motifs: that the dead show concern for the living.

After this tender prologue, we are introduced to the bedridden Andy and his wife Bel sitting alongside doing embroidery. An image of domestic closeness, except that Andy's first question to Bel is an angry 'Where are the boys? Have you found them?' Pinter establishes that this is Andy's driving concern: to make contact with his lost boys. And Bel, through her failure to find them, becomes the object of his scorn and derision: 'What a wonderful woman you were', he says, calculatedly using the past tense. But behind Andy's immediate rage and panic lies something much larger: an awareness that the twin props that have traditionally supported human existence, faith and reason, have both been eroded. He tells Bel:

> Rationality went down the drain donkey's years ago and hasn't been seen since. All that famous rationality of yours is swimming about in waste disposal turdology. It's burping and farting away in the cesspit for ever and ever. That's destiny speaking, sweetheart. That was always the destiny of your famous rational intelligence, to choke to death in sour cream and pigswill.

The language is scatological, reminiscent of Max in *The Homecoming*, but maybe it also echoes Pinter's own sense that we live in dark times.

Pinter then cuts to Andy's two sons: the bed-bound Fred and the slightly older Jake. Clearly estranged from their father, they are also totally obsessed by him. They pass their days playing fantasy-games about him or parodying his former Whitehall world. And if there are echoes in their dialogue, it is of the bantering one-upmanship of *The Dwarfs*. It is no accident that Pinter's oldest friends, such as Michael Goldstein and Morris Wernick, were tickled pink by the play, constantly finding in it memories of the sly backchat of Clapton Road in the 1940s:

JAKE: It's very important to keep your pecker up.

30 Harold Pinter in his Holland Park studio, 2002.

31 Harold Pinter and his step-granddaughter, Eliza Fraser, 2000.

32 Harold Pinter and Antonia Fraser, Turin, 1996. 'Il Ritorno a Casa.'

33 Antonia Fraser, with Harold Pinter, outside Buckingham Palace celebrating the award of her CBE, 1999.

34 Corin Redgrave (Hirst) and Andy de la Tour (Briggs) in *No Man's Land*, National Theatre, London, 2001.

35 Keith Allen, Lia Williams, Lindsay Duncan, Andy de la Tour, Susan Wooldridge and Steven Pacey as the diners in *Celebration* at the Almeida Theatre, London, 2000.

36 Gina McKee (Kate), Jeremy Northam (Deeley), Helen McCrory (Anna) in *Old Times*, Donmar Warehouse, London, 2004.

37 Michael Gambon and Harold Pinter at the Gate Theatre, Dublin, 2005, on the occasion of Pinter's 75th birthday celebrations.

38 Harold Pinter in *Krapp's Last Tape*, Royal Court Theatre, London, 2006.

39 Harold Pinter on the steps of his house after the announcement of the award for the Nobel Prize for Literature, 2005.

40 Harold Pinter, with his Italian translator Alessandra Serra, receiving the Europe Theatre prize, 2006.

41 Harold Pinter, 2005.

FRED: How far up?
JAKE: Well . . . for example . . . how high is a Chinaman?
FRED: Quite.
JAKE: Exactly.

This has the East End vigour of early Pinter. But the verbal games-playing also centres on a dream-dad who left his fortune to his newborn son Jake and then blew it all on a gambling spree. Jake goes on to suggest that his father's speech all those years ago to the trustees 'was the speech either of a mountebank – a child – a shyster – a fool – a villain'. 'Or', chips in Fred, 'a saint.' The boys are not speaking of the real Andy; simply of the capacity of fathers to be shifting, contradictory figures and of all of us to contain multiple personalities. The idea is reinforced with the introduction of Maria, an old family friend and quondam lover, it would seem, of both Andy and Bel. '*Maria to them*' say the stage directions, implying she is conjured up in the boys' imagination. But Maria's memories of the young Andy are totally at odds with the querulous bully whom we have seen earlier and strike that note of aching nostalgia that is pure Pinter: 'And how he danced', she muses. 'How he danced. One of the great waltzers. An elegance and grace long gone. A firmness and authority so seldom encountered.' Her flushed, excitable memory of the youthful Andy – and indeed of the sexually arousing Bel – stands in ironic contrast to their present state of fractious solitude.

What we were; what we become. It's a contrast that runs right through Pinter, and never more sharply than here. But it's not a matter of woozy nostalgia. It is used to heighten the pathos and absurdity of Andy's descent into bedridden biliousness. Fending off thoughts of death, he wonders if he'll ever see another spring and 'all the paraphernalia of flowers'. Bel seizes on the phrase and its contrast to Andy's customary foul-mouthed tone:

> Yes, its quite true that all your life in all your personal and social attachments the language you employed was mainly coarse, crude, vacuous, puerile, obscene and brutal to a degree. Most people were ready to vomit after no more than ten minutes in your company. But this is not to say that beneath this vicious some would say demented exterior there did not exist a delicate, even poetic sensibility, the sensibility of a young horse in the golden age, in the golden past of our forefathers.
> (*Silence.*)

Bel's speech is funny, touching, endlessly suggestive. It implies that there was in Andy – as in all of us, perhaps – some finer nature that has been coarsened by worldly experience. It could also mean that Bel, in order to protect herself from Andy's bedridden bollockings, has invented a totally romantic persona. At the same time, it suggests that in any marriage the present is constantly shadowed by the past. 'One of the pitfalls we identified early on in *Moonlight*,' says David Leveaux, 'is that because this is a play about dying, it could somehow become cadent from beginning to end. That would have been wrong because it's not a memory-play of that kind: Harold's introduction of the past often has instant and cataclysmic effects on his characters. This speech of Bel's about Andy's latent delicate sensibility is a good example. It's followed by a silence. In that moment an infinite sense of the memory of the past should flood in and modify the way we understand this relationship. Wittgenstein said that "What may not be said in words we must pass over in silence" and that is one of those moments. You mustn't complicate it: simply suggest the imprint of the past on the present.'

It's a difficult play to get right: full of recurring themes, but also sudden jolting mood changes. Repeatedly, Pinter comes back to Bridget who is not a static wraith but a restless, pacing figure who at mid-point cries 'I am walking slowly in a dense jungle'. And as Leveaux says, a lot of the play's meaning resides in the title: 'It's a punning title. The thing about moonlight is that it's the last light you see before total darkness. It's after the sun. It's a very brief, black, intense light which fades too. That tells us about the territory the play occupies which is that we're between one stage and another, which is very similar to the territory of *No Man's Land*. There's a sense of passage which is crucial to the work. With Bridget, I said to Claire Skinner who played her that she should be in motion during that central speech when she talks about being in a jungle. Harold endorsed that, saying that the problem is that she is always on a journey.'

Pinter, in fact, constantly varies the texture to keep the play moving. He cuts back to Jake and Fred playing their name-dropping games; gives Ralph – Maria's husband and a soccer referee *manqué* – a richly funny speech charting his progress from seafaring to the arts; and shows Jake, Fred and Bridget (two years before her death) in their teens when they still had the joshing, querulous intimacy of a real family. Intriguingly, it's a scene that owes its existence to Antonia Fraser. 'What was unusual about *Moonlight*,' she says, 'is that we were sitting in the same room as he wrote it and Harold was reading bits out as he went along. I did just say that I'd like to know more about Bridget and her brothers so he wrote that scene in. I don't really have any creative input. What I do is provide a sounding-board. Once Harold has finished a play, you'd better believe it. It's just that when the egg yolk is forming I happen to be there . . . You see Bridget, for instance, grows all the time. In the first draft, she didn't exist. Then she became a voice and finally a person. I wrote in my diary about *Moonlight* that I was the midwife because I was saying to Harold, "Push, shove, because it's going to be a long one – eighty minutes." But the point about being a midwife is that the birth would have happened anyway.'

Pinter doesn't just vary the texture. He ups the emotional ante as the play goes on. The key point comes with Andy's rage against the dying of the light. If, as he asserts in a tangibly Websterian phrase, 'the past is a mist', then the future also offers an endless dark horizon. It is a prospect Andy finds almost too terrible to contemplate. 'But personally', he says, 'I don't believe it's going to be pitch black for ever because if it's pitch black for ever what would have been the point of going through all these enervating charades in the first place? There must be a loophole. The only trouble is, I can't find it.' Ian Holm delivered these lines at the Almeida with scorching fury; a fury born out of a sense that, in a world without reason or religion, life is as meaningless as death and our whole existence without point or purpose. It is always a mistake to assume that a character speaks for an author. Pinter himself has a great relish for life. As he once told me, family, friends, cricket, poetry all give him joy. But in mining his subconscious to create Andy, he also expresses his own darkest fears.

From here on, the play crests a series of emotional waves. In one astonishing scene, Andy, stumbling about in search of a whisky, enters Bridget's territory and senses her presence in the moonlit background. His cry of 'Ah darling. Ah my darling' poignantly and achingly captures the hunger of the living for the dead. The following scene, between Jake and Fred, also echoes that desire to eliminate the barriers that separate us. Jake, in defending his father against Fred's derisive scorn, claims: 'He loved me. And one day I shall love him. I shall love him and be happy to pay the full price of that love.' 'Which is', says Fred, 'the price of death.' Only through and beyond death are we able, one infers, to express our buried feelings about those closest to us. As John Lahr astutely says: 'The play rests on this awful paradox: in the war of independence between father and son, death is both a gift and goal.'

Pinter sustains this emotional intensity right to the end. First he underscores Andy's isolation by a visit, possibly imagined, from Maria and Ralph. Their delight in the glowing success of their three offspring is counterpointed by Andy's pathetic dreams of his own fantasy-grandchildren. His essential solitude is emphasised by the following scene – the most heartbreaking in all Pinter – in which Bel phones Jake and Fred, who pretend that they are a Chinese laundry. As played by Anna Massey, Douglas Hodge and Michael Sheen in the original, it tore at the heart. Partly because of Bel's genuine desperation. Partly because of the emotional cost to the two sons of the rejection of their father. Pinter also paces the scene perfectly. When the phone rings, it is Jake who instantly answers 'Chinese laundry?' as if this were a prepared defence-mechanism against a call he obviously expects. His inability to cope is shown by the way he quickly passes the phone over to Fred. Their apparently armour-plated stonewall tactic is thrown slightly when Bel enters into their game and asks 'Do you do dry cleaning?' Fred shifts the responsibility – and the phone – back to Jake, who is left shaken and stirred. And when Bel finally puts the phone down, Jake's remorse is expressed through anger: 'Of course we do dry cleaning. Of course we do dry cleaning. What kind of fucking laundry are you if you don't do dry cleaning?' Stated simply, it is a scene of denial: two sons reject their father, their past, their filial bond. Yet at the end you feel that the two young men have paid an overwhelming spiritual price.

That scene is the emotional climax to the play, but Pinter follows it with three variations on the theme of death. We see Andy edging towards extinction, still believing that Bridget and his grandchildren are outside the door. Jake and Fred fantasise about a memorial service for the exotically named d'Orangerie, with Fred concluding 'I loved him like a father'. And finally the ghostly Bridget has a cryptic soliloquy describing a family invitation to a party and her own solitary arrival at a dark, deserted house bathed in moonlight. 'That speech,' says David Leveaux, 'is partly about Bridget's total separation from the parents, her sense of exile. I also think it describes the moment of her death. When I first read it, I felt, "I've had that dream." It's an incredible description of a sixteen-year-old child going to a party on their own, dressed in something old and going down a path to a house that is dark inside and empty. I think it's a speech about dying alone; and that's certainly what I suggested to Claire. I think Harold's trying to put on stage something that is almost unspeakable which is the experience of death.' Indeed, as Bacon says in one of his essays, 'Men fear death as children fear to go into the dark'.

Moonlight is a fine and moving play about dying, disconnection, loss and yearning for communion. But it is also a play about fathers and sons and, consciously or not, it seems to derive from deep inside Pinter's own psyche. Antonia Fraser reveals that Pinter started writing the play after he'd been down to Brighton to have lunch with his father and it is not hard to detect in the play some of the ambivalence which Freud saw as characteristic of the father–son relationship: a mixture of rivalry and tenderness. By all accounts, Pinter's father Jack was always a very authoritarian figure, a man of strong opinions and decisive action. Donald Freed recalls a story Pinter told him about his childhood which seemed to have great significance. As a boy of fourteen, Pinter had taken his father lunch at the tailor's shop in the East End where he worked. An officious manager intervened and shouted at the father, 'All right, Pinter, let's get back to work.' The young Harold was appalled, made a rude gesture towards the manager and told his father that he shouldn't be spoken to like that. At which point Jack Pinter slapped the young Harold hard across the face saying, 'I have to work here.'

It's a story that reveals the young Pinter's innate insubordination, social conscience and deep filial regard. And all the evidence is that, throughout his adult life, Pinter and his father got on terribly well, although their mutual affection was punctuated by fierce and vehement rows about Israeli politics. Jack Pinter was always a convinced Zionist, while his son has been openly critical of Israel's attitude towards the Palestinian refugees and the Vanunu case. Pictures in the *Jewish Chronicle* of Pinter protesting outside the gates of the Israeli Embassy did not always go down too well. In fact, at one point when the debate between father and son got really heated during a family get-together, Antonia Fraser turned to Frances, Pinter's mother, and said, 'They're so alike, aren't they?' Pinter clearly inherits much of his father's strength and will-power, and something of that seeps into the portrait of Andy in *Moonlight*, who, whatever his mortal fears, is a figure of enormous domestic dominance.

Moonlight deals partly with the ambivalence of sons towards fathers, but it is also about a father's fear of estrangement from his sons. To what extent is it inspired by the relationship between Harold Pinter and Daniel? Pinter himself is understandably reluctant to see the play as autobiographical. Nevertheless, you can't help feeling that it is constantly informed by a sense of private pain. Daniel himself, as Pinter told me, had 'a precocious brilliance' and at the age of eleven had his poetry published in *Transatlantic Review*. As a student at St Paul's School he also had his work printed in an anthology of school poetry edited by Gavin Ewart. 'His poems,' says Pinter, 'were quite remarkable. They have an ease on the page.' Daniel was clever, talented, good-looking. He got a scholarship to Magdalen College, Oxford, and seemed set for great things. But he had a nervous breakdown while at Oxford, never found a real outlet for his talents and now lives as a recluse in the Fens where for many years he has been working on an ambitious musical collage. However, he and his father mutually decided in 1993 that they were better off not seeing each other.

When Pinter talks about his relationship with Daniel, it is with evident pain but also genuine love. 'He's a man of total integrity,' he says. 'He's also very brilliant. He has a brilliant mind, a fertile mind. His critical powers are refined to the nth degree. He explores them to look at himself. He's been working for the last six or seven years on a modern opera for which he has written the words and music. It's a hard look at life and it shows his remarkably creative imagination. I know it's a truism, but the children of writers, if they're writers themselves, are up against a series of psychological brick walls. Daniel's determination to free himself from me has been the source of his alienation. But there's something in the middle of all this that just has to be said. We were very close when he was a child and in his teens. I would say that he would understand the fact that, although we haven't seen each for two years, we are still very close. But in terms of regular contact, I think you have to acknowledge your own impotence. I don't know what I have to do. I've nothing to propose that isn't going to land us in the cart once more. He's a true man who has always found life very difficult.'

For Pinter, who loves children and who would have liked a large family of his own, the progressive separation from Daniel is obviously a source of anguish. It also seems to be reflected in *Moonlight* – not only in Andy's cry of 'Where are the boys?' but in his final sad enquiries after his imagined grandchildren. Yet when I ask Pinter if he had Daniel in mind when writing the play, his reply is surprisingly emphatic. 'No. I can definitely say that he was not consciously in my mind. Looking back, I can see that there are certain parallels. But at the time of writing the play, there wasn't a total sense of alienation between us; more a spasmodic state of alienation. I'm not in any doubt that the two boys are the two boys. I've also no doubt that my understanding of alienation was influenced by my own experience and my own observation. But I'm not the only person who is alienated from his own child. A lot of the play is also about facing up to death; but I'm not, I hope, at the moment at death's door.'

I see Pinter's point. He did not sit down deliberately to write a play about his own predicament, neither are the characters in it to be identified with actual people. Pinter himself is not Andy, and Daniel is neither Jake nor Fred. Yet even though the play is not precisely and literally autobiographical, I would still argue that its power to move us derives from the fact that it is rooted in an overwhelming sense of personal guilt and loss. It has an authenticity that comes from experience. Pinter's achievement is to objectify his private doubts and torments so that they become universally comprehensible. That is why the play spoke as clearly as it did to audiences and critics. Pinter's plays are frequently greeted with puzzled incomprehension on their first appearance. Not so here. Jack Tinker in the *Daily Mail* wrote: 'There is about his [Pinter's] new play a brilliance, a profundity and a passion I had not thought to see again. It takes you by the throat, the mind and – very oddly for him – the heart, in a fashion not found in his middle work.' Benedict Nightingale in *The Times*, acknowledging the work's debt to *The*

Homecoming, claimed that 'Pinter has written few more fascinating plays' and John Peter in the *Sunday Times* wrote: 'This dark, elegiac play, studded with brutally and swaggeringly funny jokes, is one of Pinter's most haunting minor works.' The first night at the Almeida was an extraordinary affair: an ultra-fashionable event filled, before and after, with the noisy chat of London's literati, much of which was duly reported in the papers the morning after. Yet *Moonlight* was much more than a transient news event. It showed Pinter confronting his own grief and demonstrating, with unflinching candour, that in an age shorn of value-systems and beliefs, we face 'death's dateless night' in a state of mortal terror.

Nineteen Festival Time

One of the ideas coursing through *Moonlight* is that reason itself is dead; that it has no answers in an illogical, irrational world devoid of apparent meaning. That idea also lies at the heart of Pinter's screen adaptation of Kafka's *The Trial* which had its cinematic release in June 1993, just four months before the première of *Moonlight*. It would be idle to suggest that one work directly influenced the other. Kafka's novel had been cooking away in Pinter's mind since he first read it at the age of seventeen. What it does prove is the crucial oneness of Pinter's imaginative world; that his vision of man's essential solitude in a baffling and hostile universe permeates his being and carries over from one project to the next.

In a sense, Pinter had been preparing himself to adapt *The Trial* since his late teens. The chance to turn dream into reality finally seemed to have arrived in the summer of 1989 when he was commissioned to write a screenplay for the Hungarian director Istvan Szabo. Their ideas about screening Kafka, however, were irreconcilably opposed. Pinter wanted the film to be as faithful and realistic as possible, setting the story in its precise historical context; Szabo, on the other hand, wanted Josef K to be seen as the archetypal Jewish victim and wanted to outdo Orson Welles in cinematic Expressionism. It was something of a relief, therefore, that the Szabo film was never made and that in 1992 the project passed into the hands of BBC Films with Louis Marks, an old colleague of Pinter's, as producer and eventually David Jones as director. At least all three were speaking the same language and shared a common vision of Kafka.

The Trial is open to endless interpretations. It can be seen as a satire on bureaucracy, as a prophetic account of the workings of Communism, as a religious allegory, as a study of an innately Jewish guilt-complex. It has also acted as a constant magnet for adapters. Jean-Louis Barrault and André Gide in the 1940s, Jan Grossman in the 1960s, and Steven Berkoff in every decade since have turned it into a heightened theatrical spectacle. It was also transformed by Orson Welles in 1962 into a famously nightmarish film shot in the disused Gare d'Orsay in Paris and starring Anthony Perkins as a sweating, anxious Josef K dwarfed by giant sets, including an office filled with hundreds of desks. All these versions used Expressionist techniques, ignoring the fact that Kafka's novel allows the story's allegorical meaning to grow out of a cumulative naturalism. They also invested the story with a posthumous irony: because we have experienced the growth of a politicised bureaucracy and the mechanisation of society in which the individual is reduced to helpless impotence, it was assumed that Kafka was simply prophesying the horrors of the twentieth century.

Pinter's intention was both more radical and realistic: to strip away the layers of interpretation and go back to first base. He explained his method quite clearly in the publicity material for the BBC film:

> Kafka didn't write a prophetic book. He wrote a book that was based in the Austro-Hungarian Empire, before the First World War. So what you have is an apparently solid structure in every way – the buildings, the furniture, the money, the attitudes, and so on – within which there is a worm eating away. And it certainly eats through Josef K. With Kafka the nightmare takes place in the day. It's certainly not abstract or fantastic; it is very plain and proceeds in a quite logical way. Although it ceases to be logical when you try to examine it, you don't know where the natural flow of events slips into something which is totally inexplicable . . . I felt it to be a very simple narrative. K is arrested and everything follows quite clearly from that. He resists the whole endeavour, the growing oppression. But while he's resisting and in a sense dictating the terms – he's very strong and by far the most intelligent person in the story – he's nevertheless drowning in quicksand. He neither is, nor sees himself to be, a victim. He refuses to accept that role. Kafka obviously employs the whole idea of how a bureaucratic system works but he's also looking at something quite different. And that is – I have to use the term – religious identity. One of the captions I would put on *The Trial* is simply: 'What kind of game is God playing?' That's what Josef K is really asking. And the only answer he gets is a pretty brutal one.

Pinter's screenplay is a model of scrupulous intelligence reminding one of the very real affinity between himself and Kafka: both non-practising Jews, both balancing an awareness of the horrors of existence with a comic and ironic tone, both confronting the aspirations of the self with an implacably hostile universe. Which may explain why Pinter's version of *The Trial* is so faithful to the original, treating it not as a visionary nightmare but as a story emanating from the particularities of pre-1914 Prague. Pinter's Josef K, like Kafka's, is not visibly foredoomed but a young man who believes in logic, progress and the solubility of his problems. He is also equipped, as in the book, with a mixture of intellectual arrogance and sensual weakness. Pinter does not pin his own private meaning on the story, but allows the reader or viewer to tease out their own interpretation. For me, the turning point comes in the climactic encounter with the Priest in the cathedral where Josef K argues that everyone is prejudiced against him, to which the Priest responds: 'You don't seem to understand the essential facts. The verdict does not come all at once. The proceedings gradually merge into the verdict.' This is an almost direct transcription of Kafka and implies that the trial is unending, constant and circumambient: a metaphor for life itself. Like the peasant in the parable told by the Priest who waits all his life outside the door seeking admission to the Law, Josef K puts his trust in some form of external salvation. In the end, he learns that there are no answers. As Francis Gillen says in his masterly analysis of Pinter's screenplay: 'K's tools for dealing with his arrest are those of logic, reason, the inheritance of the Western tradition.' What he finally learns is that those weapons are useless in a world devoid of reason and that man is totally alone: an idea that spills over into *Moonlight*.

This makes the film sound abstract, whereas the virtue of Pinter's screenplay is that it relies on solid backgrounds: a world of claustrophobic bedrooms, of mahogany-and teak-furnitured banks, of dingy wooden tenement staircases leading to the noisy populous courtroom itself. David Jones, who came into the project long after the script was written, also came to share Pinter's vision. 'I wasn't,' he says, 'convinced by the pure period approach initially. Once I'd gone to Prague itself – Szabo, incidentally, wanted to shoot the film in Budapest – I was persuaded, since the city's own reality is so extreme. Also when I went back to the novel I realised it was written in this prosaic, deadpan style with a very sharp, intense vision. Insofar as I had a guiding light during the shooting, it was Buñuel because he can make the most bizarre things happen and yet pretend that nothing strange is happening. It seemed to me that was the way to go; there is another way which Welles and Berkoff took. We also cast Kyle MacLachlan as K: he was open, feisty, marginally too good-looking, but one of the points we wanted to make is that there is something narcissistic about K.'

The finished film is honest, intelligent, faithful to its source. If it doesn't wholly succeed, it is not because of the realistic historical approach adopted by Pinter and Jones; it is because, as Harold Bloom argues, Kafka's longer narratives are better in parts than as complete works. The film also failed to cause a stampede at the box office. In America, as Jones says, the general attitude seemed to be 'Why doesn't the guy get a good lawyer?' In Britain, the critics – with the striking exception of Iain Johnstone in the *Sunday Times* –

yearned for the familiar Expressionist approach. It also didn't help the film's commercial prospects that the very week it opened in London cinemas, the BBC (who had co-produced the film) decided to screen the Orson Welles version on television. *The Times* ran a factitious story about an angry Pinter accompanied by a picture, plucked from the archives, of the man himself looking moodily incandescent. Pinter wrote to the Editor: '*The Times* described me as "irate" about the screening by the BBC of Welles's *The Trial*. The truth is that I have said absolutely nothing to anyone about the matter. Will *The Times* accept my description of its headline as "recklessly irresponsible"?' Pinter, as usual, was in a no-win situation. He was marked down as 'Angry', and if he protested about misrepresentation, that only perpetuated the myth.

The Trial was released in June 1993. Oddly enough there was more than a touch of Kafka about the work Pinter was directing at the Royal Court in the same month: David Mamet's *Oleanna*, in which an American college student and her male professor both pin their faith in legalistic processes which fail to resolve human dilemmas. Carol, the student, has recourse to her feminist 'group' and ultimately to the college's judicial system when she claims to have been harassed and even 'raped' by her tactile professor; equally John, who is patronising and overbearing, talks on the phone of going to law when a proposed house-purchase is threatened. Mamet's play touches on many issues; but at its heart is a despair over a society that seems to deny intellectual freedom and resorts instead to ideological jargon and the force of law.

If one wanted proof of Pinter's power and skill as a director, *Oleanna* certainly provided it. In New York, Mamet's own production – played, when I saw it, by Mary McCann and Treat Williams – was an intellectually loaded affair about a dowdy no-hoper getting her sadistic revenge on a perfectly pleasant prof. No wonder, you felt, it had inspired retaliatory violence and cries of 'Hit the bitch' from members of the audience. Pinter's production, however, evened up the score so that you saw the strengths and weaknesses of both parties. David Suchet's professor mixed paternalist concern with intellectual condescension in his airy dismissal of higher education as ' a fashionable necessity'. Lia Williams's Carol was not some feminist caricature but a muddled, tremulous student subtly aware of her physical attraction. Pinter invested the play with sexual tension and a genuine territorial dynamic. The moment when Carol sat astride the professor's desk was a perfect demonstration of her new-found authority.

The supreme irony was that Pinter's devout respect for the author's text brought him into head-on conflict with Mamet. For the New York production, Mamet changed the ending at the point where the professor, goaded beyond endurance by the student's line 'Don't call your wife baby', raised a chair as if to strike her. After threatening violence, in Mamet's production, he lowered the chair and the evening ended with the two characters staring at each other in a state of exhausted complicity. Pinter reverted to Mamet's original ending in which the professor kicks and hits the student and she, almost oblivious to her physical punishment, forces him to read a statement confessing 'that I have failed in my responsibilities to the young'. Mamet's first ending makes it a drama of recantation in the line of *Galileo* and *The Crucible*; the version he staged in New York left you feeling you had witnessed a human tragedy. You can argue the case for either; on balance, I prefer the latter. But Pinter's insistence on playing the original text led to some pretty vehement faxes whizzing across the Atlantic before a compromise was reached and a slip was inserted in the programme announcing that 'the original ending is performed with the agreement of the author'. Given Mamet's acknowledged reverence for Pinter, it was a sad fracas. The relationship was only fully repaired when the two men found, a couple of years later, that they had both been dropped from a peculiarly challenging film project. Nothing unites like a shared humiliation.

However, 1993 was a cracking year for Pinter. True, *The Trial* wasn't much liked, but his production of *Oleanna* was praised to the skies and transferred to the Duke of York's in September. *Moonlight* followed it to the Comedy – rapidly becoming Pinter's West End base – in November. In September, Pinter also donated sixty boxes of manuscripts to the British Library (still housed in the British Museum), having rejected offers from America where the Archive could easily have fetched $1 million. Pinter's gesture was dictated by a mixture of genuine emotion and practical necessity. He needed to clear some space in his crowded study; but Sally Brown, the Library's curator of modern literary manuscripts, feels the key moment came when Pinter paid a visit to discuss the possibility of donating the boxes. She was finding – as people on first acquaintance with Pinter sometimes do – conversation a little awkward, so to fill in the pauses she showed him Wilfrid Owen's notebook containing the War Poems including 'Anthem for Doomed Youth'. She left Pinter to study it on his own and, his voice filled with emotion, he handed it back saying, 'This is one of the most moving things I've ever seen.' That, she felt, was when Pinter made the decision to entrust his manuscripts to the Library. At a private lunch at the British Museum to celebrate the donation, Sir Anthony Kenny, on behalf of the British Library, said it was the first time he could recall a living writer making such a generous gift (Rattigan's papers came in after his death). Pinter, in his reply, had a swipe at a profile in the *Observer* the previous day which yet again harped on his anger and his writer's block. He reckoned to have written some twenty-six plays and twenty film scripts: 'Some case,' he said, 'of writer's block.' But you felt that what moved him was the symbolic nature of the occasion and the feeling that his papers were now safely in the preserve of a great national institution. As he said, 'The British Library stands for dignity and value in a Britain in decline.'

Two weeks after that donation Pinter and I engaged in a rare public discussion at the Shelbourne Hotel in Dublin as part of the city's International Writers' Festival. I suspect we were both a bit apprehensive. In the event, Pinter talked about his work and his politics with a mixture of ebullience and passion; though it was an object-lesson to me in how irony is constantly misreported. Pinter talked freely about the way his early work was concerned with the shifts and ambiguities of power, but of how his 1980s plays were unambiguously about power and powerlessness. He also attacked President Clinton's recent decision to bomb Baghdad in retaliation for an alleged assassination plot against ex-President Bush. He went on to point out that a friend of a friend – a woman who was a celebrated artist in Iraq and director of an art museum – had been killed in the bombing along with her husband. Pinter noted that Clinton, on his way into church after the raid, was asked whether he thought the missile-action had been successful. He said, 'Well, I think it was successful and I feel good about it. And I think the American people are going to feel good about it.' As Pinter wryly commented, 'It's nice to know that. But the person who didn't feel good about it was the best friend of this friend of mine who is now dead. Nobody gives a shit about her really. Or the art museum. Or about anything. Whether the American people really do feel good about it, I haven't the faintest idea. But I think they are seduced into some kind of machismo that is disastrous.'

As always, Pinter focuses on the reality behind the rhetoric, but also at the way language is constantly perverted. That morning's papers were full of stories about the way President Yeltsin had suspended the Russian parliament while still being applauded, in diplomatic circles, as a true democrat. As Pinter said, 'That, I believe, is turning language upside down. Whatever Yeltsin did, it's not exactly a democratic action, is it? To dissolve your parliament. What everyone's talking about, I suggest, is that it's good for business.' Pinter's hatred of hypocrisy and double-think extends, however, just as much to art as to politics. Answering a question from the floor, he rejected the idea of state censorship but said one had to be on one's guard against works that pretend to show violence or rape for what it is, while having a high old time doing it. He revealed that he had been asked by Sam Peckinpah to write the script for his 1971 movie *Straw Dogs*. He read a draft treatment and replied that he wouldn't touch it with a bargepole. Peckinpah replied that he would write it himself and send him the finished script to prove what a noble and dignified work it was. Pinter replied on the first day of shooting with a telegram that read: 'Good luck for the biggest load of self-indulgent crap I've ever read in my life', which Peckinpah pinned to the notice-board for the whole unit to see. Posterity, however, proved Pinter's point.

I began to see why Pinter gets pissed off with the way he is reported. A few days after our Dublin colloquy, the *Evening Standard* ran a piece dubbed 'Who's Afraid of Harold Pinter?' The conclusion seemed to be: almost everybody. It dwelt on the fear he is supposed to inspire in fellow-artists. It also recounted an anecdote Pinter told during our interview about his first meeting with Samuel Beckett when the famed recluse rushed round Paris at five in the morning to find Pinter some bicarbonate of soda to overcome the consequences of a heavy drinking-bout. Pinter capped this anecdote about his own fallibility and Beckett's kindness by saying, with an obvious twinkle, 'Now I hope you find that a very moving story,' at which the audience roared. I said that it certainly showed Beckett's compassion for other people. 'Or,' chipped in Pinter, 'for people with indigestion.' More laughter. Such palpable irony was obviously lost on the *Standard* who reported that the audience laughed because they assumed Beckett would do anything to escape Pinter droning on.

While he was in Dublin, Pinter also finalised details with Michael Colgan, the go-ahead director of the Gate Theatre, for an ambitious project to be mounted in May 1994: the first-ever Pinter Festival in which six plays would be staged over a three-week period. It was a sequel to a Beckett retrospective which the Gate had staged, to international acclaim, in 1991. Mostly it is dead writers who get to be celebrated in seasons of their work, but Colgan's bold idea was to acknowledge a living writer, to introduce Dublin audiences to some of the less familiar plays, and to put long and short pieces together in illuminating juxtaposition. The whole event – with a large white banner spread across Grafton Street proclaiming 'Pinter Festival' – caught Dublin's imagination and was a real artistic eye-opener.

The weekly pairings were as follows: *The Dumb Waiter* was teamed with *Betrayal*, *One for the Road* with *Old Times*, *Landscape* (directed by Pinter himself) with *Moonlight* (restaged by Karel Reisz). Given Pinter's obvious affection for Ireland – and the frequent references to it in his work – local critics naturally saw the Festival as a kind of homecoming. They also seemed less hung up about Pinter's politics than their British counterparts. And the mixture of British and Irish actors yielded fascinating dividends. In *One for the Road*, the casting of Michael Pennington as Nicolas and of Irish actors as the imprisoned family had a chilling local resonance without obliterating the larger point that ruling élites the world over cloak themselves in God and country. And in *Old Times*, the fact of Pennington's Englishness as Deeley, as against the palpable Irishness of Catherine Byrne's Kate and Olwen Fouéré's Anna, reinforced the character's increasing marginalisation.

What really struck home, however, was the unified nature of Pinter's sensibility. We all knew that *The Dumb Waiter*, for instance, was a political thriller. What hit one this time was that Ben and Gus are like a married couple, bickering, raking over old times and, in the end, falling into the roles of betrayer and betrayed. And while *Betrayal* seems instantly classifiable as a personal play, it also deals with the power-politics of adultery and the sense that wherever two people are gathered in a room, there is always a third, unseen presence. Casting also heightened the ironic overlap. In one day you could see Ian McElhinney as the testy Ben in *The Dumb Waiter*, steeling himself for the ultimate betrayal, and then as the cuckolded Robert in *Betrayal*, vainly seeking to hide his pain in the Venetian scene under a camouflage of lewd innuendo. As the Festival proceeded, the internal connections became ever more apparent. In *Landscape*, a damn-near-definitive production, we saw Ian Holm and Penelope Wilton as the married middle-aged domestics apparently doomed to eternal non-communication. And in the restaged version of *Moonlight*, the same pair (married in real life) played Andy and Bel, reinforcing the point that this is also very much a play about deadlocked wedlock. Much more than at the Almeida, Holm's dying hero seemed propelled by savage mockery as if trying to needle a wife who had retreated into irony and embroidery.

The essential unity of Pinter's imagination was quickly seized on by the critics. Fintan O'Toole wrote in the *Observer*: 'In a sense the whole debate since the sixties about whether Pinter is a political playwright or a playwright of personal life misses the point which the Festival has tended to bring home so powerfully: that his distinctive theatre comes from applying the categories in which thriller-writers and left-wingers see repressive political states to sex, marriage and domesticity.' John Peter in the *Sunday Times* echoed the point: 'To me, Pinter's plays have always been political in the sense that Ibsen's plays are political: they explore the private roots of power, the need to dominate and mislead, the terror of being excluded or enclosed, the compromising contagion of past actions, the compulsion to re-imagine the past.' And Alastair Macaulay in the *Financial Times* remarked, refreshingly, on Pinter's humanity: his respect, and even love, for his characters in their constant fear of isolation; their search for security and contact; their awareness of desertion and loss. The whole Festival was both a revelation and a tonic. It heightened the ironies, echoes and complexities that bind together Pinter's work and encouraged Colgan to undertake another Pinter Festival in the spring of 1997.

Pinter was feted in Dublin in 1994. In the same year, many of his major plays enjoyed revivals elsewhere. At New York's Roundabout Theatre in January, David Jones directed a hot-ticket revival of *No Man's Land* starring Jason Robards as a ritually alcoholic Hirst and Christopher Plummer as an affectedly Bohemian, la-di-da Spooner: 'it is funnier', wrote Irving Wardle, 'than any English performance I have seen.' In March, Sam Mendes, one of the bright young hopes of the British theatre, came up with a stunning revival of *The Birthday Party* at the National's Lyttelton Theatre. Tom Piper's seaside-boarding-house set loomed forward from the dark recesses of the Lyttelton stage – ironically accompanied by the jaunty signature tune from *Housewives' Choice* – and finally receded into a world of terraced streets under scudding clouds, exactly catching the play's mix of the real and the symbolic. Casting also redefined character. Anton Lesser's Stanley was a prickly, snarling, unshaven outsider who got a malignant pleasure out of making Meg's skin crawl. Bob Peck's Goldberg was less a stereotypical Jewish-uncle figure than a stultified, cuff-shooting Organisation Man. But the most significant reinterpretation was Trevor Peacock's Petey, who seemed at the end to pose a genuine threat to Goldberg and McCann. This was a point that particularly thrilled Pinter: 'When Petey says he's going to look after his peas and not go back to the beach, you can feel the hysteria on the part of Goldberg and McCann. For a moment, Petey is the strongest man on stage. Finally he can't resist the invaders, but they are vulnerable, worried, anxious men.'

At the same time, *Le Retour* (*The Homecoming*) was enjoying a huge success in Paris at the historic Théâtre de l'Athénée. When I saw it, a young audience roared its head off at the scatological humour while still drawing in its breath at the play's reversal of conventional values. Jean-Pierre Marielle – who later won a Molière, the top French acting prize – was also a superb Max: both a ferocious, stick-wielding bully and a closet sentimentalist. Yet the production also demonstrated – despite an excellent translation by Pinter's friend and long-time collaborator Eric Kahane – the author's essential Englishness and the difficulty of capturing the play's nuances in another culture. For a start, the director Bernard Murat seemed to assume that the play was taking place near London docks: ships' foghorns and seagull cries punctuated the black-outs as if the play should be called *A View from London Bridge*. That peculiar English quality of the piss-take also seemed lost on some of the French actors. Patrick Chesnais played Lenny with a rasping, sulphurous anger, totally missing the irony in his attack on Teddy for taking his cheese roll or his mocking send-up of his brother's American lifestyle. And the relationship between Lenny and Ruth seemed to be based on mutual attraction rather than wary, cock-and-vixen suspicion.

That was a straightforward misinterpretation, but translating Pinter into another tongue is itself a notoriously difficult exercise. Martin Esslin wrote a famous article in *Encounter* in March 1968 itemising some of the howlers in existing German translations, particularly of *The Birthday Party*. Cricketing metaphors eluded the Germans so that 'Who watered the wicket in Melbourne?' became '*Wer hat an das Stadttor vom Melbourne gepinkelt?*' Literally, and somewhat surreally, 'Who peed against the city-gate in Melbourne?' Likewise, McCann's 'What about Drogheda?', with its historical echoes of Cromwellian oppression of Ireland, became in German '*Was ist mit Staerkungsmitteln?*' Which literally means 'What about fortifying tablets or drugs?' on the assumption of some affinity between 'Drogheda' and '*Droge*', meaning 'drug'.

Kahane, who has translated almost all of Pinter's plays into French and who is an experienced writer himself, is far too wily and experienced to fall into those kind of traps, but he is aware of others that exist. 'Pinter is very spare,' he says, 'but in French, unless you're very careful, a text might end up about 10 to 25 per cent longer. In *Betrayal*, for instance, there is this long conversation about the womb and the baby boy. Now there's no such word as "womb" in French. The only equivalent is "*entraille maternelle*", so you have to use two words instead of one. When I first mentioned that to Harold, he was half-shocked, half-amused. Place names are also very difficult. "Bolsover Street", for instance, sounds very different in French because the emphasis there is on the second syllable and carries echoes of "*overs*" which is French for "ovaries". So you get a very different joke instead of "Balls-over" in English.

'But I try to translate Harold's plays through exact photography while making them sound as if written in French. When Max says he'll be "chuffed to the bollocks to see his son" that becomes "*réchauffé les couilles de voir son fils*" which literally means "warmed his balls off". Similarly, "wet wick" in French becomes "*une couille morte*" or "a dead ball". There'll be an equivalent of just about every word and expression and you just have to find it. "Taking the piss" occurs in *The Hothouse* and it was "*payer sa fiole*" which is argot in a way, though not quite as strong. It's not the humour or the words that are the problem. The main difficulty is the way French directors see Pinter. His work terrifies a lot of them so that, when there's a pause, they'll have an overlong pause. But Harold and I have known each other for a quarter of a century now, ever since I first did *The Lover* and *The Collection*, and I really love and admire him. I love doing his plays, though creatively he nearly killed me at one point because when you translate Harold's plays, it's very hard to write plays of your own. It's happened to me with novels, too. I once translated *Lolita* which took two years of my life, but Nabokov is such a brilliant writer it became impossible to do books of my own.'

Pinter might sympathise with Kahane on that point, for – with hit productions running concurrently in London, New York and Paris – Pinter spent much of his time in 1994 trying to crack the problem of translating *Lolita* to the screen. It's a sad saga that reveals a lot about the treacherous politics of the movie business. Nabokov's novel had been filmed before in 1962 by Stanley Kubrick, who tiptoed circumspectly around its central erotic obsession by casting the mature-looking Sue Lyon as the eponymous nymphet. But Adrian Lyne, a young British director whose Hollywood box-office successes included *Fatal Attraction* and *9½ Weeks*, approached Pinter early in 1994 with the idea of doing a new version. Lyne had worked as Pinter's first assistant when Pinter was shooting a scene from *The Homecoming* in 1967 for a documentary about British art and culture. The two men got on well and Pinter was fascinated by the idea of remaking *Lolita*. As he told me in April 1994, 'I haven't seen the Kubrick film for years, but I remember the girl there was at least four years too old, which goes against the point of the story. She should be about twelve, which in itself constitutes a problem. I just have to write it, not cast it, but I'm very aware of the sexual problem inherent in the story. I'm fascinated by the task ahead of me because of the tone of voice. I think it's the most difficult thing I've had to do since Proust. It's partly a question of how far you use first-person narration which, in principle, I'm against, but which in Nabokov is so brilliant.'

Nabokov's novel started life as a thirty-page short story set in France and written in Russian. In the mid-1950s he rewrote it in English, only to find it being turned down by four American publishers. It was first published by Olympia Press in France, but in Britain did not see the light of day until 1959. It comes prefaced with a fictive foreword by John Ray Jr, Ph.D., claiming it to be a document written by Humbert Humbert in legal captivity shortly before his death. It then launches into the first-person confessions of Humbert, a European-educated scholar, whose sexual tastes were fixed at the age of thirteen when his girlfriend Annabel died of typhus. Going to America, he becomes erotically obsessed by Lolita, the twelve-year-old nymphet daughter of the widow Charlotte Haze, with whom he lodges. In order to be near the daughter, Humbert marries Charlotte, but just as he is planning to murder her, she is run over by a car. Humbert takes Lolita away from summer camp and the two of them set off on a car journey across

America. In the second part of the novel we witness his progressive degradation. Lolita matures into a college girl increasingly bored with her demanding 'Dad', and in the course of another car trip takes off with the mysterious writer Clare Quilty who has shadowed her and Humbert's movements. Eventually Humbert discovers that Lolita, now married and pregnant, was abandoned by Quilty when she refused to take part in a pornographic film. He tracks Quilty down, shoots him and dies in prison while Lolita herself dies in childbirth on Christmas Day.

Nabokov himself disclaimed any moral intention. He was motivated more by a state of 'aesthetic bliss' and indeed the central relationship can be read as a paradigm of his love affair with the English language. The book *is* erotic, but also scholarly, playful, linguistically exuberant. It is, in addition, as the American critic Leslie Fiedler discerningly noted, part of a movement in modern fiction (of which William March's *The Bad Seed* and William Golding's *The Lord of the Flies* are other examples) to provide counter-stereotypes to the myth of the innocent child. As Fiedler says, its subject is the seduction of a middle-aged man by a twelve-year-old child:

> The subject involves multiple ironies; for it is the naïve child, the female, the American who corrupts the sophisticated adult, the male, the European. In a single work, Richardson, Dickens and Henry James are controverted, all customary symbols for the encounter of innocence and experience stood on their heads. Nowhere are the myths of sentimentality more amusingly and convincingly parodied and it is surely for this reason that the book was, for a time, banned.

Since Fiedler wrote that in 1958, films like Martin Scorsese's *Taxi Driver* (1975) and Louis Malle's *Pretty Baby* (1978) have dented even further the myth of childhood innocence by openly representing teenage prostitution. At the same time, society itself, both in Britain and America, has become increasingly alert to the problems of paedophilia and child pornography. The climate in which Pinter sat down to write the script was thus a delicate one in which gains in expressive freedom had been offset by a growth in moral censoriousness. That said, he does a remarkable job in turning Nabokov's novel into a screenplay, shirking none of the sexual issues and solving the technical difficulties.

Pinter frames the story by beginning with Humbert's arrival at Coalmont, Illinois, in 1952 in search of the now-married Lolita. With nice irony, he also expands on some judgemental lines from John Ray Jr's fictive foreword and puts them into the hero's own mouth. 'My name is Humbert', he announces in a voice-over as he drives down the Coalmont street. 'You won't like me. I suffer from moral leprosy. I am not a nice man. I am abnormal. Don't come any further with me if you believe in moral values. I am a criminal. I am diseased. I am a monster. I am beyond redemption.' This not only intrigues us; it allows us to view the rest of the story through the prism of Humbert's self-hatred and also establishes him as the tragic victim of his own obsessive nature. But Pinter also establishes the source of Humbert's obsession by flashing back in Shot 6 to the Côte d'Azur in 1924 when the fourteen-year-old boy fell in love with the thirteen-year-old Annabel only to lose her through death: a crucial explanatory sequence omitted in the Kubrick version.

Pinter's screenplay, which follows the basic line of Nabokov's story, highlights Humbert's vulnerability and self-destructiveness, Lolita's brattishness and sophistication. But while following the tragic arc of the narrative, it is also erotic and funny. In one sequence, Lolita extends her legs teasingly over Humbert's lap while he is lying on a sofa and talking breathlessly and nonsensically of art as a vast river 'in which you'll find gushing out Michaelangelo and Piero della Francesca and Bob Hope and Pablo Picasso and Jack Benny and Schnozzle Durante and Leonardo da Vinci'. The male libido confronts childhood knowingness as Lolita bites into an apple, licks her glistening lips, and wriggles and squirms on the hapless Humbert's lap.

Any adaptor faces two key problems: the book's first-person narration and the high-octane exuberance of Nabokov's prose. Pinter solves the difficulties by objectifying the story, so that Lolita's consciousness of her power exposes Humbert's helpless adoration, and by weaving Nabokov's fanciful language, where possible, into the dialogue. What Pinter emphasises, however, is Humbert's state of enthralled erotic subservience. At one point when they are careering from motel to motel, Humbert tells Lolita how he wants to be a dream dad protecting a dream daughter. In the book this goes: 'My *chère* Dolores, I want to protect you, dear, from all the horrors that happen to little girls in coal sheds and alleyways and alas, *comme vous le savez trop bien, ma gentille*, in the blueberry woods during the bluest of summers.' In the film, Pinter transposes this to a scene on a motel patio where Humbert has given Lolita a chocolate sundae, only to be met by a hard-edged intransigence:

LOLITA: You know what it said in the sign by the café as we drove in here? Ice-cold drinks. I want an ice-cold drink.
HUMBERT: You have your chocolate sundae.
LOLITA: Yes, but I want an ice-cold drink after the sundae. Give me the money and I'll go to get it.
HUMBERT: You're not going anywhere.

LOLITA: But I want an ice-cold drink.
HUMBERT: Now darling I simply want to protect you from all the horrors
    that can happen to little girls in coal sheds and alleyways.
LOLITA: Oh yeah?
HUMBERT: And in blueberry woods too.
LOLITA: I just wanted a drink.

You may lose the rhythmical cadence of Nabokov's prose and Humbert's patronising use of French phrases. What Pinter registers, however, is Lolita's blackmailing canniness as against Humbert's self-deceiving fatherliness. Lolita's 'Oh yeah?' cruelly suggests she has him sussed out and can wind him round her little finger. Avoiding both prurience and pornography, Pinter's screenplay is a masterly study of a man who is doomed by an ungovernable sexual obsession and who is, in a sense, manipulated by a teasing nymphet. For all its early playfulness, the overall impression is of the pathos and sadness of misdirected human desire.

You would have thought any director would have jumped at using such a script, but when I spoke to Pinter in January 1995 he had just learned that his screenplay was not being used. He was not best pleased. 'It's a helluva thing,' he said. 'It's Hollywood. I came back from my last meeting with Adrian Lyne in Los Angeles and wrote the version you have read. That was my final screenplay and I sent it to Adrian and he was very pleased. Then I heard that the company behind it, Caralco, was going bust. There was a certain amount of annoyance from me because if they were going bankrupt, I wasn't going to be paid. Finally I was paid and I never heard another word. Not a word. Then my agent Judy Daish phoned and said that Adrian had put another writer on to the script. I've only recently learned that the writer is – believe it or not – David Mamet. I'd be astonished if Mamet wasn't working from my script, partly because there's a lot of Adrian Lyne in it and he's not going to throw six months' work away just like that.'

The sequel to all this, in the autumn of 1995, was that Pinter learned from Mamet that *his* version of *Lolita* owed nothing to Pinter's and that Mamet himself had been suddenly and inexplicably dropped from the project. The latest news from Hollywood was that Stephen Schiff, a magazine-writer who once did a rather bilious profile of Pinter in *Vanity Fair* and then dropped him a card assuring him of his love and affection, was writing a new script. By now, Pinter was detached about the whole thing; his one abiding fear was that they would make the film as pornographic as possible. One can only wonder at the crazy ways of Hollywood that buys the rights to one of the greatest post-war novels, hires the best British and then the best American playwright to do separate screen versions of it, and, in the end, junks both of them to hand it over to a journalist and profile-writer. It all goes to prove the truth of William Goldman's adage in *Adventures in the Screen Trade*: the single most important fact of the entire movie industry is that 'Nobody Knows Anything'.

Twenty Onwards and Upwards

Every writer has setbacks; but of all the dramatists who emerged in the late 1950s to redefine the landscape of British theatre, Pinter is easily the most durable. John Osborne, who sadly died at the end of 1994, bequeathed us one genuinely mythical work (*Look Back in Anger*), some fine early plays and two magnificently wounded volumes of autobiography. He was a giant writer who deserves comparison with Pinter. The key difference is that by the end of his career, Osborne seemed a stranded romantic, railing intemperately at a theatre with which he felt little sympathy. Arnold Wesker, who shares Pinter's East End Jewish background, goes on valiantly turning out plays, prose-pieces and a recent volume of autobiography; but his theatrical reputation rests largely on his admirable early plays and he is more honoured abroad than at home. John Arden, who wrote a handful of flinty, morally ambiguous, linguistically exuberant plays at the start of his career (of which *The Workhouse Donkey* is the best), seems even more cut off from modern British theatre. He lives in Galway and has increasingly turned his attention to historical fiction.

Pinter, however, has dug in, stayed the course, lived to see all his major plays frequently revived and for over three decades been an all-round man of the theatre capable of earning his living as actor, director or writer: a kind of radical, more intellectually adventurous Noël Coward. Unlike Coward, who stayed stuck, like a wedged gramophone needle, in the Empire-loving attitudes of his youth, Pinter has moved with the times. Even when not writing plays, his fingers also still itch. One evening in January 1995, sitting in the same room where our conversations had first begun, he suddenly read out to me a poem he had just written:

Don't look.
The world's about to break.

Don't look.
The world's about to chuck out all its light
And stuff us in the chokepit of its dark,

That black and fat and suffocated place
Where we will kill or die or dance or weep
Or scream or whine or squeak like mice
To renegotiate our starting price.

Pinter wasn't soliciting comment or approbation, but listening to him read the poem I was struck by its visceral quality. It seemed full of impacted physical rage at the darkness sweeping our world, at our impotence in the face of cataclysm, at the petty compromises we make to keep the system going. 'Chokepit' has extraordinary force suggesting subterranean asphyxiation, and the peremptory starkness of the opening lines leads to a conclusion implying that instead of recognising evil, we seek to appease it or adopt a *sauve-qui-peut* attitude.

In subsequent months, another poem and two short stories popped through my letter box. One of the stories, 'Girls', is a wickedly funny piece that refutes the notion of Pinter as a bit of a gloomy bugger. It starts enticingly:

> I read this short story in a magazine where a girl student goes into her professor's office and sits at his desk and passes him a note which he opens and which reads 'Girls like to be spanked.' But I've lost it. I've lost the magazine. I can't find it. And I can't remember what happened next. I don't even know whether the story was fiction or fact.

The speaker goes on to tease out, in pseudo-forensic style, the various possibilities lurking behind the girl's note. From whose point of view was the story told? Was the girl speaking for herself or was she offering an all-embracing proposition? And what of the professor? What did he make of it all? 'What kind of professor was he anyway?' asks the speaker. 'What was his discipline?' It is a light, funny piece that nags away at the implications of the central proposition. But behind it there is a perfectly serious point about the ambiguity of language and the way words shift their meaning depending on whether they are spoken from a subjective or objective viewpoint. Even a story alters its colour and purpose depending on who is telling it. Pinter's own fable is itself a neat linguistic joke: by Wittgenstein out of *Oleanna*.

In his mid-sixties, at a time when he might well be forgiven for easing off, Pinter also remains perennially active in the British theatre: a comment on both his physical stamina and his relish for being at the centre of the action. In the summer of 1995 he pitched camp at the Chichester Festival Theatre – rescued from its normal somnolent placidity by Duncan Weldon and Derek Jacobi – first to direct Ronald Harwood's *Taking Sides* and then to play the lead in a revival of *The Hothouse*. Both productions subsequently moved into the West End.

It's not hard to see why Pinter was so keen to direct Harwood's play. The two men had first met in 1953 when both were members of Donald Wolfit's company, had joined forces in many a PEN protest on behalf of imprisoned writers, and socially had remained good friends. They dined regularly and played squash and tennis together for many years, though always with a strong competitive edge. As Harwood says of their tennis matches, 'It's a dour game. Harold doesn't believe in talking when you cross at the net.' But beyond the claims of friendship, you can see why Pinter was so drawn to Harwood's play. It is about an issue of central concern to him: the role of the artist in a totalitarian society and the question of whether art can ever transcend politics. It is a theme that haunts the twentieth century. It is explored in Klaus Mann's *Mephisto*, Günther Grass's *The Plebeians Rehearse the Uprising*, Truffaut's film *The Last Metro* and, most memorably of all, in Hindemith's opera *Mathis der Mahler*, where the sixteenth-century painter Mathias Grünewald symbolises the composer's own predicament in Nazi Germany. Harwood's play, like all these, is based on a specific case. The conductor Wilhelm Furtwängler remained in Germany throughout the Hitler regime and in 1946 went under investigation, in the American occupied zone of Berlin, as to whether he should be brought before a de-Nazification tribunal. Harwood asks all the right questions. Can art be kept separate from politics? Can it help to counter the effects of an evil ideology? Is the artist a privileged person exempt from the normal rules of society? Some critics thought that Harwood loaded the dice on Furtwängler's behalf by making the American Major carrying out the investigation a boorish philistine. As Paul Taylor wrote in the *Independent*: 'a man incapable of responding to the sublimity of music is the weak antithesis, rather than best antagonist, of someone who has been culpably deaf to everything but musical sublimity.' But Pinter's riposte is that the American Major's philistinism is a calculated pose designed to force Furtwängler, and those who believe in the sanctity of art, to prove their case.

For Harwood, the experience of working with Pinter for the first time since they had appeared together in Wolfit's *Lear* was an unalloyed pleasure. 'As a director,' he says, 'Harold is the best I've ever worked with. Unequivocally. No one creates a pleasanter, more agreeable atmosphere in which the work can take place which is one of the keys to a good director. His care and precision, his affection for the actors was marvellous. The way he works is also very interesting. He doesn't give a talk about the play. He says, "Let's just find out what it's about." He also makes sure the moves are always justified. There's a slightly static, almost stylised, quality to his work. He will say to an actor, "Do you feel that move is absolutely necessary?" or, "Don't feel you have to move just because you've been there a long time." He's also a great respecter of the text. He asked me for just four changes. Two were very minor, one I rejected and one was absolutely crucial. There's a moment in the second act when one of the characters, who's an ex-Nazi, originally said to the American Major: "Ask him about von Karajan. That'll be useful. Ask him about Herbert von Karajan." Harold said that you want to put that before and end the scene on: "Ask him about his private life." He was absolutely right. It made a much better end to the scene and showed that Harold has a very traditional theatrical instinct.'

That instinct for what works was also very evident in Pinter's own play *The Hothouse* which turned up in a lethally funny production directed by David Jones at the Minerva in August 1995. What made it even more arresting was that Pinter himself, in cryptically menacing moustache and a tweed suit once owned by Peter Willes, played the ex-Colonel Roote in charge of a state-run 'rest home'. Critics made some fascinating comparisons. For Robert Hanks in the *Independent on Sunday*, the play was 'in the tradition of staff-room comedies, St Trinian's or *Whack-O*, where teachers blunder desperately in their efforts to contain the uncontainable'. For Benedict Nightingale in *The Times*, this sinister setting, where patients have numbers, are permanently locked up and can be raped or murdered without anyone outside being the wiser, 'is like the secret police headquarters of *One for the Road* or the military prison in *Mountain Language*'. Both statements are true: the play works as institutional comedy and political prophesy. What this revival proved, however, was its ability to switch mood and tone at lightning speed. One minute it's high absurdity as Roote, having provided a lasciviously detailed description of patient 6459, denies all knowledge of her. But a moment later you feel a chill in the spine as Roote, asked what should be done with the newborn baby, brusquely replies 'Get rid of it'.

What this memory-jogging production also proved was how many details in the play were an extrapolation from, or even a record of, Pinter's own experience. One of the key scenes is the grilling of Lamb, who has electrodes attached to his wrists and earphones to his head through which terrifyingly piercing sounds are transmitted. Out of the blue I got a letter from a Sussex theatregoer Mrs Joan Cox, who had seen *The Hothouse* and who had worked as a secretary in the Department of Psychology at the Maudsley Hospital which was run in the 1950s by Professor Hans Eysenck:

My job was to recruit volunteers for physiological testing. These tests were physical measures to try and identify introvert or extrovert personalities other than by Eysenck's original questionnaire. At this time unemployment was low and it was quite difficult to get hold of people who were free during the day. I managed to get hold of housewives, postal workers and actors, one of whom was Barry Foster, looking very elegant and attractive but resting at the time and apparently quite glad of the thirty shillings a day we paid him. He rang up one day and said he couldn't come again as he'd got some work but could he send along an actor friend by the name of Harold Pinter. He came along and, after he had undergone several tests, one of the psychologists who was running a test of vision came out and said, 'Joan, don't send me any more actors, they're far too imaginative.' I can't help wondering whether Pinter's actor's imagination had based his play on his experiences at the Maudsley.

To which the answer is, 'Yes.' But what is also interesting is the extent to which the play incorporates Eysenck's techniques, which jettisoned Freudian theories in favour of controlled experiments to eliminate behaviour the patient regards as undesirable. The difference is that in *The Hothouse*, Eysenck's behavioural therapy is appropriated by the state.

Barry Foster not only recommended Pinter to the Maudsley. He also remembers reading *The Hothouse* when it was first written and being stunned by it. At that stage he recalls it was actually going to be called *The Grave's a Fine and Private Place* and that Pinter was thinking of sending it to his old employer Donald Wolfit. Oddly enough, Wolfit's biographer and Pinter's colleague Ronald Harwood also worked as a guinea-pig at the Maudsley in the 1950s. He too, quite independently, arrived at the conclusion that *The Hothouse* is a very autobiographical play. 'It struck me,' he says, 'when I first saw it at Hampstead in 1980, and again at Chichester, that nearly all the characters represent some aspect of Harold's personality. The authoritarian director who runs the place embodies his more demonic side. But he's also there in Lamb who is all innocence: Harold still has that same quality of innocence in that something quite ordinary can fill him with wonder. Even his sensuality is there in the female character. They're all aspects of Harold in the same way that Ibsen's characters are fragments of the author.' Harwood's point is confirmed by the way Pinter weaves into the action an incident that actually occurred during his touring years with the great actor-manager Anew McMaster. At one point in the play, Roote is drinking with an insolent subordinate Lush, who cheekily suggests that at last his boss is beginning to get results with the patients. 'What was the number?' he enquires. '6459, I think.' At this point, Roote throws his whisky in Lush's face. Lush coolly wipes his face, refills the glass and hands it back to Roote. Lush makes another needling remark and Roote again throws the whisky directly in his face. It is about to happen a third time when Lush grabs Roote's glass from his hand and holds it above his head crying 'Cheers'. As played by Pinter and a subversively nonchalant Tony Haygarth, it became a classic piece of comic business.

It is, however, an almost exact replica of a less-than-comic incident from Pinter's past. 'I was in Ireland in 1950,' he recalls, 'touring with Mac. We were in a place called Roscrea and one night I was drinking in a pub with Pat Magee and Joe Nolan who was both the business manager and an acting member of the company. We were all pretty pissed and Joe Nolan raised his glass to me and said, "Cheers, you filthy Yid." I threw my whisky straight in his face and he took off his glasses and wiped his eyes. He then said, "Another whisky for the gentleman," handed me the glass and repeated his remark: "Cheers, you filthy Yid." Again, I threw my whisky in his face. This happened a third time and then he wiped his eyes and said, "I can't afford any more whiskies." Joe Nolan was pretty stupid, so it was hard to take his anti-Semitism too seriously, but I never forgot the incident and worked it into the play.'

Pinter was highly, and rightly, praised for his performance in *The Hothouse*. Particularly striking was his revelation of the character's thuggish brutality and spiritual coarseness under the clipped military façade. And while one of his earliest plays was being rediscovered in Chichester and London, his latest, *Moonlight*, was starting to enter the international repertory. Peter Zadek staged a production at the Berliner Ensemble – in conjunction with Hamburg's Thalia Theater – in May 1995 that gave one a totally new vision of the play. In Berlin, Andy seemed less a suburban Lear than a comic figure out of Molière raging ineffectually against nature. But the real focus was on Bel, superbly played by Angela Winkler as a woman full of sensuous affection and extrasensory awareness: she soothed and caressed her dying husband, seemed alert to the ethereal presence of Bridget, registered anguish at the suffering of the estranged Fred and smiled secretly to herself whenever the ex-referee appeared. The production had its oddities, such as Eva Mattes's louche appearance as Maria in a bowler hat and a monocle, but Winkler perfectly embodied Pinter's point that the dead and the unseen take permanent root in our memory. Karel Reisz also re-directed the play in October at the Roundabout's Laura Pels Theatre on Broadway. Like Zadek, Reisz emphasised the vaudevillian jokiness of the Jake-and-Fred scenes, but he countered that by highlighting the all-pervasive sense of loss and solitude. In her final soliloquy, Bridget moved towards Bel, who was standing over her dead husband, and then backed away to centre stage and spun round, palms open, in the emptiness. 'The spinning', wrote John Lahr in the *New Yorker*, 'is Reisz's touch; but it seems right for the play's chilling, unmoored sense of disconnection.' Like all first-rate plays, *Moonlight* is capable of infinite variation.

Even on his home territory, there seemed to be a decisive shift in attitudes to Pinter in the mid-1990s. For a start, he achieved a Coward-like all-rounder's theatrical ubiquity. For one brief moment in 1995 he was starring in *The Hothouse* at the Comedy, had his production of *Taking Sides* running at the Criterion, and a revival of *Old Times*, featuring a beautifully enigmatic Julie Christie, playing at Wyndham's. In March of that year, he also won the David Cohen British Literature Prize, at £30,000 the most lucrative literary prize in the UK and one awarded every two years in honour of a lifetime's achievement (V. S. Naipaul was the previous winner in 1993). Pinter was both surprised and thrilled to get the award. In his acceptance speech he talked about his own unliterary origins, about the influence of Joe Brearley on his thinking, about his discovery of Beckett and about the early humiliation of *The Birthday Party*. He also took a swipe at his critics:

> I'm well aware that I have been described as 'enigmatic, taciturn, terse, prickly, explosive and forbidding'. Well, I do have my moods like anyone else, I won't deny it. But my writing life, which has gone on for roughly 45 years and isn't over yet, has been informed by a quite different set of characteristics which have nothing whatsoever to do with those descriptions. Quite simply, my writing life has been one of relish, challenge, excitement. Those words are almost, perhaps, truisms. But in fact they are true. Whether it be a poem, a play or a screenplay – if the relish, challenge and excitement in the language and through that language to character isn't there then nothing's there and nothing can exist.

The David Cohen Prize certainly gave Pinter a boost. It also seemed to go down well with that voice of middle England, the *Daily Telegraph*. It not only published a sympathetic interview by David Sexton, but also a highly flattering column by John Casey, a Fellow of Gonville and Caius College, Cambridge, which argued that Pinter had written 'three or four unquestionable masterworks' and that he was 'one of the best English playwrights of all time'. Casey suggested that 'The French equivalent of Pinter would now be one of the immortals of the Académie Française and would as a matter of course be addressed as *cher maître*.' Heady stuff. But Pinter was rather more exercised by Casey's quotation of an article by Frank Johnson which had attacked Pinter for suggesting that *Mountain Language* was 'very close to home'. Johnson's point was that bourgeois capitalist societies have led the world in abolishing torture in the last three centuries. This incensed Pinter. 'That word "torture",' he said to me. 'There is no torture as such in *Mountain Language*. There is simply brutality. It is true that a man is seen briefly with a hood. But we hooded the IRA. There's plenty of brutality in British prisons and in relation to Ireland. They say that we have led the world in doing away with torture. But (a) there is no torture in *Mountain Language* and (b) they can't even read the fucking plays properly.'

Any fear, in fact, that Pinter's political anger might be smothered by the warm embrace of the Establishment was quickly dispelled by his public activities and by a conversation we had in 1995. Pinter's opposition to post-war American foreign policy, and in particular to the smokescreen of double-think that surrounds it, remains unyielding. And he expressed it as potently as he ever has in a bitterly ironic letter to the *New York Review of Books* in June 1994. His letter was triggered by an article by Jason Epstein about the film *Schindler's List*. Epstein's main point was that the film's focus on its hero's salvation of hundreds of Jews was misplaced in a century that had lived through the mass-murder inspired by Hitler, Stalin and Mao. Pinter's letter claimed there was a signal omission in Epstein's account of moral and political turpitude: the United States of America. He pointed to the US's contempt for international law; to the bombings of Laos, Cambodia and Iraq; to intervention in the Dominican Republic, Grenada and Panama; to the deaths of hundreds of thousands of people in Indonesia, Guatemala, Nicaragua, Chile, El Salvador, Angola, the Philippines, Turkey, Haiti, East Timor:

> The dirty work is normally done by the locals, of course, but the money, the resources, the equipment (all kinds), the advice, the information, the *moral support*, as it were, has come from successive US Administrations. Of course, there is a difference. Hitler, Stalin and Mao, in one way or another, *intended* the death of millions. The US has, I suggest, accepted that the death of millions is inevitable if its 'national interests' are to be protected – in other words, if its power is to be maintained . . . The great difference between the ruthless foreign policy of the United States and other equally ruthless policies is that US propaganda is infinitely cleverer and the Western media wonderfully compliant. The responsibility for the countless atrocities committed in the name of 'democracy' is something which perhaps Mr Epstein might also consider.

Henry Woolf told Pinter that on the campus where he teaches in Saskatchewan people 'suffocated with rage' at the equation between the crimes committed by Fascist and Communist dictators and those committed in America's name, but Pinter remains convinced that the failure of the *New York Review of Books* to print any letter in reply was a brilliant piece of editorship. 'I'll go to my grave,' he says, 'believing that there must have been some response but that they simply refused to publish it.'

Pinter doesn't mince words. Indeed, he has an Orwellian preoccupation with their exact use. Neither does he concern himself with the niceties of diplomacy. In April 1995 he was invited to receive an honorary doctorate from Sofia University at a time when six of his plays were in production in the Bulgarian capital. It would have been easy to make a soft-soap acceptance speech full of pious platitudes. Instead, Pinter offered a tough, uncompromising talk, to an audience which had just emerged from the stranglehold of Communism, pointing up the fallibilities of Western democracies. He seized, unsurprisingly, on America, citing the fact that between 40 and 50 million people live below the poverty line, that Dan Quayle withdrew from the Republican Presidential nomination because he couldn't afford the requisite $20 million and that, in the vast majority of states, you can be executed even if you are under eighteen or mentally retarded, 'thus bringing the US into line with Pakistan, Yemen and Saudi Arabia'. In a country believing that its economic problems could be solved by a US-led world, the speech received a mixed reaction.

Yet in many ways the most significant part of the speech was its introduction in which Pinter forged an unmistakable link between his artistic and political concerns. He began:

> It probably won't surprise you to hear that words have dominated my life. In my own work, I've always been aware that my characters tend to use words not to express what they think or feel but to disguise what they think or feel, to mask their actual intentions, so that words are acting as a masquerade, a veil, a web, or used as weapons to undermine or to terrorise. But these modes of operation are hardly confined to characters in plays. In the world in which we live, words are as often employed to distort or to deceive or to manipulate as they are to convey actual and direct meaning. So that a substantial body of our language is essentially corrupt. It has become a language of lies. These lies in themselves can become so far-reaching, so pervasive, so consuming that even the liar thinks he is telling the truth. As has also been demonstrated many times, when words are used with a fearless and rigorous respect for their real meaning, the users tend to be rewarded with persecution, torture and death.

That seems to me the definitive answer to those who argue that Pinter's overtly political plays represent a regrettable deviation from his stock-in-trade as a purveyor of domestic menace, or that his public activism, particularly in the 1980s, was designed to camouflage writer's block. Pinter, as in his acceptance of the David Cohen Award, makes it plainer than any pikestaff that his central, ungovernable concern is with language; and that there is an umbilical connection between its creative potential and its political misuse. Poets may or may not be the unacknowledged legislators of the world, but they should undoubtedly be more alert than anyone to the violation of language.

What is commendable about Pinter is that his political anger gets more, not less, intense with the years. In his mid-sixties, by which time most people have long retreated into private life, he seems to feel the pain of the world more acutely than ever. And if he is exercised by the way his attitudes are reported, it is partly because he feels it is a diversion from the real issue. As he once said to me, 'People never ask what I'm angry *about*.' But his sensitivity on the issue became clear when, in a wide-ranging discussion about politics in January 1995, I asked him if he felt an 'ungovernable' concern about the state of the world. He took my epithet as pejorative and told me the following story.

'A few months ago Antonia and I went to a dinner at Oxford for Nadine Gordimer. At my table were Nadine, John Bayley and the Principal of the College. I was sitting next to the Principal and, in the course of the evening, the subject of Israel came up. The Principal said to me, "I cannot hear a word against Israel." She was Jewish. I said, "I'm Jewish too and I have a lot to say about Israel. There is a lot to say about Israel." She said, "I refuse to hear a word." I simply said, "I think this is unreasonable." I was very clear. I didn't raise my voice. I was quite clinical. I mentioned Vanunu and the West Bank and I said that these are facts you have to recognise, particularly if you are Jewish. She said, "No – there is a larger truth." I said, "We obviously disagree," and the matter was dropped. We went on to talk about something else. Anyway, John Bayley was writing a column at that time in the *Evening Standard* and said that the Principal and I had a blazing row and that I – "crimson with fury" – attacked her on the subject of Israel. I said to Antonia, "What do I do?" She said, "Forget it. If you write a letter, John Bayley will simply do another column saying he looked pretty crimson to me." I saw John Bayley at some other do and said, "You shouldn't have written what you did. You're entering into that world of junk newspapers where people say things like 'Harold Pinter was crimson with fury' not because it's true, but simply because it reads well."'

Pinter may be sensitive about stereotyping, but when I ask him whether a writer should ban the performance of his plays in countries he disapproves of, he is both open and self-mocking. 'I'll reply to that,' he says, 'in several ways. There are a number of countries whose policies I violently disapprove of. Turkey, for example. But I was very happy about *Mountain Language* being done in that country, particularly as it was against the law. South Korea is a lousy dump, but there are performances of my work there. I was also very pleased when *Betrayal* was done in China, and when Poland or Hungary or Czechoslovakia in the days of Communism did my stuff. It would have been idiotic of me to say that I don't approve of your government because the people doing the plays didn't approve of the bloody government either. The only exception to this was South Africa under apartheid when the majority of British writers withdrew their work. But I guess that what we're really talking about is the United States. I have, in fact, contemplated the withdrawal of my plays from there. But firstly, there are people there who want to do the plays. And secondly, for me to act like that would be to shoot myself in the foot. People would say, "Who gives a fuck anyway?" I could write the reactions myself: "What a relief! We need never sit through another damned Pinter play!" If I withdrew my plays, I don't exactly think it would change American foreign policy.'

How much protest can achieve is always a moot point. On a positive note, Pinter cites the example of a PEN delegation which visited the Malawian Embassy to protest about the imprisonment of the poet Jack Mapanje, who was eventually released and who paid tribute to the effectiveness of international demonstrations. Pinter also told me – this was in January 1995 – that he and a PEN group were going to the Nigerian Embassy to protest about the treatment of the Ogoni writer Ken Saro-Wiwa. In November, Saro-Wiwa and eight other activists were brutally hanged, but this in no way invalidates the need for vigilant protest. Indeed, rather more activity in advance from Commonwealth leaders might have changed the situation. Pinter's comment on the Nigerian hangings, reproduced on the front page of the *Guardian* on 11 November, was also succinct and unanswerable: 'Murder is the most brutal form of censorship.'

Pinter does not rent his conscience out for hire. He tries to focus his protest on areas where he feels Britain, and the West, have a direct responsibility. 'Which is certainly true,' he says, 'in East Timor, Central America, Latin America, Turkey, in that we give them money, arms, weapons of all kinds.' What depresses him is the level of ignorance and inactivity in Britain, among the press and politicians, about the abuses in the world. He cites as an example the bombing and suppression of Turkish and Kurdish newspapers with the loss of several journalists' lives. 'Are the press, individuals, organisations, political parties going to keep silent or do something about it? . . . I just can't stop with all these things. One of the images that will never go away is of Argentina and those beautiful young men and women who "disappeared" and of everything that happened to them. I feel such a profound disgust that they're forgotten and that our governments are in all cases complicit. In this country, I'm also appalled at the way the Left is regarded as old fashioned and out of date. What nauseates me is the propaganda success of this kind of terminology because the actual facts remain. The facts remain that in Central America at least three out of four people are poverty-stricken. Treated like shit. It's not a static situation. Capitalism only finally succeeds when the majority of the people are considered as dead: cannot speak, move, answer, are told they're living in a benevolent society. Take what you get and you're fucking lucky to get it. The older I get, the more I feel the offence of it.'

That sense of engagement with the world – with the open wound of politics – is intense. Indeed, it often bears fruit at the most unexpected moments. Pinter had a busy year in 1995 directing *Taking Sides* and acting, from August to November, in *The Hothouse*. He planned a relatively quiet year in 1996. His only firm commitment was to direct a West End revival of Reginald Rose's *Twelve Angry Men*, though he was taking a paternal interest in a plan by Christopher Morahan to make a film for BBC TV of *The Dwarfs* scripted by Kerry Crabbe (indeed, he went scouting for locations in Hackney with the director). Before rehearsals for the stage play got under way, however, Pinter and Antonia went off for a winter holiday in Barbados. They returned on 22 January. Two days later, Pinter was having an early evening meeting with the costume-designer for *Twelve Angry Men* in the small housecum-workroom at the back of the family residence in Holland Park when suddenly the need to set pen to paper descended. 'It was a perfectly amiable meeting,' says Pinter, 'but at that moment I couldn't wait to end it. As soon as the chap had gone, I started to write. And I continued to write over the next few days in a kind of fever.' Within ten days the resulting play *Ashes to Ashes* had gone through four drafts, was finished, typed up and sent on its way in the world. Once Pinter gets an idea, he creates in a kind of white heat.

The process of writing was fierce and intense, but one of the central images of the play came from Pinter's choice of holiday reading in Barbados: Gitta Sereny's biography of Albert Speer who was Hitler's favourite architect, Minister for Armaments and Munitions from 1942, and virtually the Führer's second-in-command. 'It's a staggering book,' says Pinter, 'and I was very struck by the fact that Speer organised and was responsible for the slave-labour factories in Nazi Germany. Yet he was also, in some ways, a very civilised man and was horrified by what he saw when he visited the factories. That image stayed with me. Also, the fact that these factories had no proper lavatories and that there were these primitive privies on the factory floor that were, literally, full of shit. Reading the book also triggered lots of other associations. I've always been haunted by the image of the Nazis picking up babies on bayonet-spikes and throwing them out of windows. I wasn't actually sitting on holiday thinking I must write a play about all this, but when I got back home something instantly happened. I started writing, as usual, on a yellow pad with two characters called A (a man) and B (a woman) and the first line originally was him asking her 'What kind of things?' I simply took it from there. I had to find out more about who these characters were.'

Ashes to Ashes is an extraordinarily powerful work: elusive, mesmeric, disturbing. Undeniably there are echoes of previous Pinter plays: the male desire to excavate and possess a woman's past and the snatches of popular song recall *Old Times*; the equivocal relationship between interrogator and victim reminds one of *One for the Road*; the background of barbarism and cruelty suggests *Mountain Language* and *Party Time*. Yet the play also has its own utterly distinctive, haunting tone in which the real and the dreamlike, the concrete and the phantasmagoric, effortlessly merge. The play also conclusively proves that for Pinter the 'personal' and the 'political' are not separate, vacuum-sealed categories: it operates both as a twisted, perverted love story and as an evocation of the arbitrariness and cruelty of state power.

The setting is a room in a country house with a garden beyond. The time is early evening, but as the light outside fades, the lamplight in the room unnervingly intensifies. The occupants of the room are Devlin and Rebecca, both in their forties and apparently intimately connected. Lovers? Husband and wife? Interrogator and victim? At first we are not sure. Devlin stands, Rebecca sits: a sign that the power is vested in him. And initially Rebecca, in response to Devlin's questions, is explaining the habitual action of a man she once passionately knew:

REBECCA: Well . . . for example . . . he would stand over me and clench his fist. And then he'd put his other hand on my neck and grip it and bring my head towards him. His fist . . . grazed my mouth. And he'd say, 'Kiss my fist.'

DEVLIN: And did you?

REBECCA: Oh, yes. I kissed his fist. The knuckles. And then he'd open his hand and give me the palm of his hand . . . to kiss . . . which I kissed.
(*Pause.*)
And then I would speak.

DEVLIN: What did you say? You said what? What did you say?

(*Pause.*)

REBECCA: I said, 'Put your hand round my throat.' I murmured it through his hand, as I was kissing it, but he heard my voice, he heard it through his hand, he felt my voice in his hand, he felt my voice in his hand, he heard it there.

(*Silence.*)

DEVLIN: And did he? Did he put his hand round your throat?

REBECCA: Oh, yes. He did. He did. And he held it there, very gently, very gently, so gently. He adored me, you see.

DEVLIN: He adored you?

(*Pause.*)

What do you mean, he adored you? What do you mean?

(*Pause.*)

Are you saying he put no pressure on your throat? Is that what you're saying?

REBECCA: No

DEVLIN: What then? What are you saying?

REBECCA: He put a little ... pressure ... on my throat, yes. So that my head started to go back, gently but truly.

DEVLIN: And your body? Where did your body go?

REBECCA: My body went back, slowly but truly.

DEVLIN: So your legs were opening?

REBECCA: Yes

(*Pause.*)

DEVLIN: Your legs were opening?

REBECCA: Yes.

(*Silence.*)

It is a shocking opening image which has its reverberant echo later on and defines much of the play's territory: a world of brutality, power and domination, but also one of anxiety, insecurity and reckless curiosity. It is also a play in which nothing is ever quite what it seems. Even this graphic opening sequence implies a mixture of sexual enforcement and willing submission and throughout Devlin and Rebecca shift disquietingly between different roles. And although it is a play of minimal physical movement, by the end there has been a decisive and important change in the balance of power.

In the first movement of the play, Devlin plies Rebecca with endless obsessive questions about this other man she has intimately known – his height, his breadth, his depth – before suddenly addressing her as 'my darling'. 'No one', she responds, 'has ever called me darling. Apart from my lover.' We seem to be in an English country house witnessing a jealous middle-aged man's fevered enquiries about his live-in partner's erotic past. That past acquires a more sinister edge when Rebecca describes how her former lover took her to 'a kind of factory'. Devlin presses her for more details. 'They were all wearing caps . . . the workpeople . . . soft caps . . . and they took them off when he came in, leading me, when he led me down the alleys between the rows of workpeople.' The image, inspired by the Speer book, is of a cowed workforce and an autocratic controller. 'They had total faith in him', explains Rebecca. 'They respected his . . . purity, his . . . conviction. They would follow him over a cliff and into the sea, if he asked them, he said. And sing in a chorus as long as he led them. They were in fact very musical, he said.' The locale is not particularised: we could be in any oppressive state. But Pinter clearly draws on his memory of the book about Speer when Rebecca says: 'I wanted to go to the bathroom. But I simply couldn't find it. I looked everywhere. I'm sure they had one. But I never found out where it was.' Pinter is not writing specifically about the Nazis, but about the umbilical connection between the kind of sexual Fascism so graphically described in the opening scene and its political counterpart; about a world of brute masculine power and naked submission. The point becomes startlingly and dramatically clear when Rebecca, having told Devlin earlier that her lover worked for a travel agency, suddenly reveals: 'He was a guide. He used to go to the local railway station and walk down the platform and tear all the babies from the arms of their screaming mothers.' This elegant country drawing-room opens up into European history.

Much of the play's mesmeric quality derives, in fact, from the way Pinter interweaves an obsessive personal inquisition with an insidious revelation of a world of systematised cruelty. The two things interact and cross-fertilise; they are not contained in separate compartments. Rebecca, for instance, attempts to sidetrack Devlin's nagging enquiries by talking about the echoing sound of a police siren: as it fades away in her ears, so it becomes louder in someone else's. She loses possession of what she naïvely calls this 'beautiful sound'. Devlin responds, 'Don't worry, there'll always be another one. There's one on its way to you now. Believe me. You'll hear it again soon. Any minute.' One is reminded of the threat contained in the last line of *The New World Order* where Des tells his fellow-interrogator that their victim will be able to shake him by the hand ' . . . in about thirty-five minutes'. And when Rebecca describes the way a 'perfectly innocent' pen rolled off the coffee table while she was writing a laundry list, Devlin warns her that, whether or not she lives in this house, she can't say things like that. 'Like what?' enquires

Rebecca. 'That that pen was innocent', replies Devlin. 'You think it was guilty?' responds Rebecca. Devlin is not simply engaging in semantic nit-picking. He reminds one strongly of Lenny in *The Homecoming*, reconstructing reality through language and determining that a whore was diseased because 'I decided she was'. But where Lenny seeks to control language purely for purposes of domestic power, Devlin's linguistic manipulation also carries with it the chill echoes of officialdom.

Rebecca's diversionary tactics, however, make Devlin realise he is losing the initiative in this psychological cat-and-mouse game. He feels he is in a quicksand. 'Like God', Rebecca replies sharply. Devlin seizes on this in an attempt to regain lost ground, to attack Rebecca's 'truly disgusting perception', and to invoke the vacancy and horror of a world without God: 'It'll be like England playing Brazil at Wembley and not a soul in the stadium. Can you imagine? Playing both halves to an absolutely empty house.' The speech is both funny and chilling. There is something wildly inappropriate about Devlin's comparison of a godless universe to an empty soccer stadium. At the same time, the word 'stadium' evokes memories of those South American detention centres for the 'disappeared'; the mind also harks back to Nicolas in *One for the Road* self-righteously claiming that 'God speaks through me'. And when Devlin invokes the, to him, horrifying picture of absence, stalemate, paralysis and 'a world without a winner', it is a reminder of a society polarised, like the capitalist world, between triumphalist victors and hopeless losers. In this classic Pinter power-play, Devlin not only seeks to possess Rebecca's body and soul. He also appropriates her perceptions as well as her past experience. She has talked of babies, mothers and platforms. He asks: 'What authority do you think you yourself possess which would give you the right to discuss such an atrocity?' Her response is literally self-denying: 'I have no such authority. Nothing has ever happened to me. Nothing has ever happened to any of my friends. I have never suffered. Nor have my friends.'

All the power seems to reside in Devlin. Yet, as always in Pinter, authority breeds insecurity, and bullying assertiveness is a sign of weakness rather than strength. In a deeply revealing, very funny and contradiction-riddled speech, Devlin harps on about Rebecca's assumed lover, wishes that she had confided in him (Devlin) about the affair, assumes an other-worldly superiority ('When you lead a life of scholarship you can't be bothered with humorous realities, you know, tits, that kind of thing'), talks longingly of a wife and ends with an extraordinary *cri de cœur*:

When you have a wife you let thought, ideas and reflection take their course. Which means you never let the best man win. Fuck the best man, that's always been my motto. It's the man who ducks his head and moves on through no matter what wind or weather who gets there in the end. A man with guts and application.

(*Pause*.)

A man who doesn't give a shit.

A man with a rigid sense of duty.

(*Pause*.)

There's no contradiction between these last two statements.

Believe me.

(*Pause*.)

Do you follow the drift of my argument?

This speech, coming halfway through, marks a decisive turning point in the action: almost an Aristotelian peripeteia. From now on the emotional initiative passes from the prying, inquisitive Devlin to the apparently submissive Rebecca. Ignoring his riddling contradictions – his worship of winners combined with a belief in strategic survival – she describes a vision of looking out of the window of a house in Dorset and of seeing guides ushering a crowd of people into the sea: 'The tide covered them slowly. Their bags bobbed about in the waves.' Obviously this is a deliberate echo of the oppressed workers in her lover's factory who, he assured her, 'would follow him over a cliff and into the sea'. It also subliminally reminds us that England has its potential for submission to despotic authority. Rebecca goes on to describe a condition of mental elephantiasis in which if you spill an ounce of gravy which becomes a vast sea of gravy, you are the *cause* rather than the *victim* of the accident. And in a phrase which makes sense only retrospectively, she guiltily and cryptically observes: 'It was you who handed over the bundle.' Invoking the strange half-world between dream and reality, she also outlines an image of a frozen city in which she arrived at a railway station. 'And my best friend', she continues, 'the man I had given my heart to, the man I knew was the man for me the moment we met, my dear, my most precious companion, I watched him walk down the platform and tear all the babies from the arms of their screaming mothers.'

The whole play, it gradually becomes clear, is built round echoes, dreams, memories; and exactly as in *Old Times*, the act of describing one's memories lends them a living actuality. Yet what makes the play so genuinely dislocating is the swiftness of the transitions from diurnal reality to prophetic dream. Devlin tries to shift the discussion back to the hard world of fact where he can exert some control: to Rebecca's visit to her sister Kim and the kids, and to the kids' early attempts to talk. But even as she recalls going to tea with her

sister or a subsequent visit to a cinema, Rebecca's world acquires the linea-
ments of a dream. The film she describes sounds like a peculiarly surreal
comedy, switching one moment from a New York restaurant to an expedition
to the desert, and the man sitting in front of her in the cinema never laughed
once but 'just sat like a corpse'. Devlin, it is clear, is floundering and tries to
drag her back to concrete reality. 'Now look', he cries, 'let's start again. We
live here. You don't live in Dorset . . . or *anywhere else*. You live here with me.
This is our house. You have a very nice sister. She lives close to you. She has
two lovely kids. You're their aunt. You like that.' But the more Devlin tries to
pin Rebecca down, the more slippery and elusive she becomes. 'We can't start
again', she insists. 'We can end again.' Devlin doggedly maintains that it's a
misuse of language: you can only end something once. 'No', she replies. 'You
can end once and then you can end again.' Not only is Rebecca asserting that
in any relationship there is no fixed terminal point. It is she who is claiming
control of the situation through language. The power-roles have been subtly
reversed.

The play now enters its final movement. Devlin is still naggingly questioning Rebecca about her former lover; she has moved on to a different plane of
recollection. She describes being in a room at the top of a tall building. In the
street below she saw an old man and a little boy walking together dragging
suitcases. 'Anyway, I was about to close the curtains but then I suddenly saw a
woman following them, carrying a baby in her arms.' The woman follows the
man and boy until they turn a corner and are gone. She kisses the baby girl.
She listens to its heartbeat. But Rebecca's objective description turns into
subjective identification as she *becomes*, in her imagination, that woman carrying a baby. 'I held her to me', Rebecca says of the child. 'She was breathing.
Her heart was beating.'

Just as Rebecca, by an imaginative transference, becomes that woman
evocative of refugees the world over, so at precisely this point Devlin also
becomes the sadistic lover who has haunted him throughout the play. With the
circularity of a dream, he repeats exactly the gestures Rebecca has described
earlier, gripping her neck with his left hand, clenching his fist and urging her
to kiss it. She neither speaks nor moves, rejecting both his bunched fist and
the palm of his hand. Where she had formerly asked her lover to put his hand
round her throat, her mute resistance now obliges Devlin to use force.
Devlin, who throughout has questioned, cajoled, pleaded with and even bul-
lied his female partner, has finally turned into the Fascistic lover whose
identity he secretly craved. In turn, Rebecca, at first sexually compliant and
politically submissive, has learned both the need for resistance and imaginative empathy with the bereft and the persecuted. That much is clear from the

final incredibly moving moments in which, to an accompanying verbal echo, she describes being taken to a station, wrapping her baby in a shawled bundle so that it would escape detection, being called back when the baby cried out, being separated from the child and placed on a train. On her arrival at 'this place', she met a woman she knew:

REBECCA: And she said what happened to your baby
ECHO: your baby
REBECCA: Where is your baby
ECHO: your baby
REBECCA: And I said what baby
ECHO: what baby
REBECCA: I don't have a baby
ECHO: a baby
REBECCA: I don't know of any baby
ECHO: of any baby
   (*Pause.*)
REBECCA: I don't know of any baby
   (*Long silence.*
   Blackout.)

Like much of Pinter's work, *Ashes to Ashes* demands and yet at the same time tantalisingly resists total explication. It appeals to one instinctually and emotionally, rather than purely cerebrally. Much of its power, for instance, stems from its command of theatrical atmosphere. The two figures. The spacious room. The garden beyond. The light outside darkening while that inside brightens. Even as you read it, you can see it clearly in front of you. But it also stirs memories of previous Pinter plays, while remaining hauntingly particular.

What finally is it about? While it operates on a multiplicity of levels, I think one can pin down certain specific themes. Power, obviously, and the notion that in any given situation 'strong' and 'weak' are relative terms, and that the balance can quickly shift from one to the other. It also deals with language and the attempt, on the part of both characters, to reconstruct reality through words. Devlin, at first, seeks to control Rebecca partly through semantic definition only to find the tables being turned. And like much of Pinter's work, it shows that women have a flexibility, a freedom, an imaginative sympathy frequently denied to men who are locked into unyielding power-structures. Just as the lover is admired by his workers for his 'purity' and 'conviction', so Devlin aspires to 'a rigid sense of duty'. But what is most remarkable about this play is its effortless ability to unite the domestic and the political, the English and the global. It is as if the world of *Landscape* and *Old Times* has merged with that of *One for the Road* and *Mountain Language*. On the domestic level, it is not just about the terminal stages of a fractured relationship, but is haunted by images of babies, children, childlessness. Devlin invokes a song title 'I'm nobody's baby now' which Rebecca punctiliously corrects to '*You're* nobody's baby now'. Devlin is fascinated by Kim's children and their imitative baby-talk. Kim's husband, who has deserted her for another woman, desperately wants to come back because 'he misses the kids'. Rebecca sees a woman in the street who follows a man and boy until they turn the corner and are gone. And the abiding, recurrent image is of babies snatched from their mother's arms leading finally to the detection of Rebecca's bundle. Through the use of an echo – a technique that Webster deployed to similar effect in *The Duchess of Malfi* – the word 'baby' chimes through the final section like a poetic refrain. It is as if babies and children are *both* the symbol of innocence and hope *and* an emblem of the capacity for cruelty of the authoritarian state.

While, for Pinter, the personal and the political have always been closely allied, in this play they are more deeply enmeshed than ever. The unseen lover's sexual power-games provide a microcosmic image of his own Fascist and capitalist instincts. What makes him even more dangerous is that, initially, he is 'adored' by Rebecca and 'respected' by the cowed workers. Devlin, by his envious identification with the lover and his relentless interrogation of Rebecca, becomes complicit in society's cruelty. Again, what makes him so dramatically disturbing is his recognisable jealousy and lack of demonic otherness. And Rebecca, by her imaginative transformation into a dispossessed mother, is translated from her own affectless innocence into a world of universal suffering. The play gets under one's skin precisely because it is not dealing with some alien or distant world: it acknowledges the potential for oppression and resistance that lies within all of us.

Even physically, the play seems to exist in several dimensions at once. The characters' names, Devlin and Rebecca, are neutral, but the immediate reference points are English: Wembley and Dorset specifically, but even the country house with its garden beyond implies we could be in England. But beyond that exists a world of frozen, mud-caked cities, of derelict station platforms, of cross-border checkpoints, of children arbitrarily snatched from their mother's arms. We seem to be in the English shires and yet in Auschwitz, Bosnia or any one of a score of places where atrocities became, or indeed still are, part of the landscape. That is the larger point made by this poetic, intensely felt, imagination-haunting play which, for Pinter, seemed to be compelled rather than chosen: that, as he often says, there is no 'them' and 'us', and that the Fascist instinct is universal and compatible with a regard for the external forms of civilisation. It is a play which forces men to examine their own sexual coerciveness and women their own guilty compliance. But beyond that it implies that we all have within us the capacity for resistance and for imaginative identification with the sufferings of others. Therein, implies Pinter, lies the only hope for change. It is, at one and the same time, one of his most profoundly personal plays and one of his most deeply political.

In performance, the play seemed even richer than it had on the page. New levels of meaning began to appear. The piece, played in a small, intimate space, also acquired an extraordinary emotional intensity. What happened was that in the autumn of 1996 the Royal Court, during a two-year renovation of its Chelsea base, took over two theatres in the West End: the Duke of York's and the Ambassadors. The latter was itself ingeniously divided into two separate spaces. One of them was a steep 140-seat theatre created by William Dudley out of the Ambasssadors circle: almost a miniaturised Epidaurus. Stephen Daldry, the Court's director, asked Pinter to christen the space with his own production of *Ashes to Ashes*. It opened on 19 September 1996, with Lindsay Duncan playing Rebecca and Stephen Rea Devlin; and, despite receiving the usual batch of mixed reviews ranging from the hostile and the bewildered to the ecstatic, it proceeded to pack the theatre for six weeks.

Seeing the play after reading it, several things became clear. One was how well it worked on a purely atmospheric, theatrical level. Eileen Diss's setting was discreetly anonymous: two huge beige armchairs dominated a living-room that gave on to an imagined garden and that was gradually enveloped by gathering dusk. Pinter also directed the actors so that every movement and gesture was freighted with meaning. At first the actors talked as if in the midst of an on-going domestic conversation: by the end, they had retreated into the depth of the armchairs, seemingly locked – like the characters in *Landscape* – into their separate worlds. Rea's Devlin, much gentler than the character one had imagined from the printed page, had the dogged, persistent quality of a man for whom truth lay in semantic definition; Duncan, clad in a simple print dress, exuded both an English-rose innocence and a strange solipsistic solitude that opened up to admit universal suffering. The tone was cool, quiet, controlled, which gave seismic force to the occasional changes of register: when Rebecca suddenly said, of her ex-lover, 'He used to go to the local railway station and walk down the platform and tear all the babies from the arms of their screaming mothers', it was as if a thunderbolt had been unleashed.

On stage, the play both made literal sense and acquired endless meta-phorical possibilities. Pinter had mentioned to me in advance the impact of Gitta Sereny's book on Albert Speer. What I had not realised, until reading it, was that Speer in his seventies had fallen in love with a German woman half his age who was married to an Englishman by whom she had two children: she had, in fact, written to Speer an admiring letter after reading his book, *The Secret Diaries*, and the two of them had fallen in love while he was working on his final, unfinished project on the SS. This is not to say Pinter's play is directly about that relationship, but the questions it raises inform his work. Is there, he seems to ask, some peculiar sexual magnetism about men associated with appalling acts of cruelty? It is the paradox explored by Sylvia Plath when, in a poem addressed to an imagined father, she wrote 'Every woman adores a Fascist, / The boot in the face, the brute / Brute heart of a brute like you.' But equally Pinter's play asks how men with fascist tendencies can function simultaneously as adoring lovers. It echoes the question tackled by the South African poet Breyten Breytenbach in 1972 in 'Letter from Abroad to Butcher', dedicated to 'Balthazar', i.e., Prime Minister John Vorster, which seeks to relate the state torturer to the happily married man: 'Does your heart also stiffen in your throat', enquires the poem, 'when you touch the extinguished limbs with the same hands that will fondle your wife's mysteries?'

Ashes to Ashes, on stage, made realistic sense. But it also posed large questions about the unresolvable contradictions of human nature, about the gulf between male and female attitudes, about our ungovernable responsibility for the societies in which we live. Alastair Macaulay was absolutely right when he wrote in *The Financial Times* that, while we search for meaning, 'it may be more important to say that *not* understanding Pinter is a very great pleasure. To feel the elusiveness of his meaning is, in fact, to come very close to its essence. People, he keeps saying, are inexplicable. And the poetic beauty of his art lies, of course, in the way he says this and shows it.' But it is also significant that when Macaulay, in a private letter to Pinter, suggested that the play was implying that 'No man is an island', Pinter leapt enthusiastically on the phrase and endorsed it.

It was precisely this point about the invisible chain of suffering and our connection one to another that seemed to baffle or annoy many literal-minded critics: in particular, the use of specific English place-names in a work that embraced European tragedy. Using the Holocaust as a reference-point, Charles Spencer asked in the *Daily Telegraph*, 'Does he [Pinter] really believe that such horrors are likely to happen in Britiain? Does he think they are happening already?' Paul Taylor made much the same point in the

Independent: 'As for the suggestion that all of this could easily happen in Britain – Rebecca tells of the vision she had while looking out of a window in Dorset and of guides shepherding crowds of people to their deaths in the sea – I found myself worrying how these mooted comparabilities might strike someone actually living in a totalitarian regime or, indeed, a Holocaust survivor.'

One should point out that, in the immediate dramatic context, Rebecca's vision is instantly denied by Devlin: 'When was that? When did you live in Dorset? I've never lived in Dorset.' And, of course, Pinter is not equating modern Britain with Nazi Germany or saying that we live in a totalitarian society. What he is saying, if I interpret him aright, is those who live in societies that proclaim themselves free and democratic should be alert to any attempt to curb or deny that freedom. In a much misquoted speech, John Philpot Curran said in 1790: 'The condition upon which God hath given liberty to man is eternal vigilance.' Pinter's play simply asks us to be eternally vigilant.

He himself expanded on that idea in a public interview he gave in Barcelona in December 1996, just after his production of *Ashes to Ashes* had played there as part of a Pinter Festival. He was asked by Mireia Aragay if the play was about Nazism. He replied: 'No, I don't think so at all. It *is* about the images of Nazi Germany; I don't think anyone can ever get that out of their mind. The Holocaust is probably the worst thing that ever happened because it was so calculated, deliberate and precise and so fully documented by the people who actually did it. Their view of it is very significant. They counted how many people they were murdering every day and they looked upon it, I take it, like a car delivery service. How many cars can you make in one day, how many people can you kill in one day? And there's the whole question of how many people knew what. In the recently published *Hitler's Willing Executioners*, Daniel Goldhagen claims that the majority of the German public was well aware of what was happening . . . But it's not simply the Nazis that I'm talking about in *Ashes to Ashes* because it would be a dereliction on my part simply to concentrate on the Nazis and leave it at that.'

Pinter goes on to emphasise that countries calling themselves democracies, including the United States, Great Britain, France, Germany and Spain, subscribe to 'repressive, cynical and indifferent acts of murder' by selling arms to brutal regimes; that in the United States the death penalty is retained in 38 states out of 50; and that in Britain, citing the treatment of unmarried mothers and single parents, the current political philosophy is 'to punish and to attribute blame and guilt to the innocent victim'. He ends by saying: 'I don't call that particularly democratic. The word democracy begins to stink.

These things, as you can see, are on my mind. So in *Ashes to Ashes* I'm not simply talking about the Nazis. I'm talking about us and our conception of our past and our history and what it does to us in the present.'

That could hardly be more explicit. Pinter is not drawing a direct parallel between the modern Western democracies and Nazi Germany. He is simply saying that the power of the state constantly encroaches on individual liberties and that the word 'democracy' loses all meaning when you help foreign governments to murder their own citizens. But, if *Ashes to Ashes* ultimately asks us to recognise we cannot detach ourselves from the world's cruelties, Pinter himself lives out his own maxim about the need for eternal vigilance. On 8 January 1997 he wrote a letter to *The Times* about the Police Bill, then passing through Parliament 'with no discernible opposition from Her Majesty's Opposition', that would legalise the 'bugging' of private property by the police: he envisaged a scenario in which a private citizen who discovered his or her home was being bugged could be placed under arrest for obstructing a police officer in the course of his duty. He asked the Home Secretary to confirm or deny this scenario.

Michael Howard promptly replied in *The Times* the next day, justifying the need for 'intrusive surveillance' whilst waffling on about the provision of 'effective safeguards' for ordinary citizens. But there were also letters supporting Pinter's arguments from the Liberal Democrat peer Lord Rodgers and from members of the London Criminal Courts Solicitors' Association. They pointed out that the situation was even worse than Pinter suggested and that 'fundamental rights' were being sacrificed with barely a whimper from the Labour Party: the right to silence had been lost under the Criminal Justice and Public Order Act 1994, the burden of proof had shifted to the defendant under the Criminal Procedure and Investigations Act 1996, and the Police Bill would enable the authorities to bug the solicitor's office or barrister's chambers of the defendant. Pinter undeniably helped to open up the debate on the Police Bill; and it is no accident that two weeks later the House of Lords threw the Bill into chaos by rejecting its provision for the bugging of telephones and adopting amendments from the Liberal Democrats and the newly aroused Labour Party. Pinter had stepped in where many Labour MPs, even followers of Engels, feared to tread.

Pinter remains, to his credit, a permanent public nuisance: a questioner of accepted truths both in life and art. In fact, the two persistently inter-act. In December 1996 he wrote a fierce, polemical piece in the *Guardian* attacking not just American foreign policy and its disastrous consequences but the sanctimonious self-righteousness in which it was cloaked through fervent appeals to the American People and to the Creator. As Pinter succinctly wrote: 'God belongs to every American. Successive American Presidents have made this quite clear.' He tackled the same theme, in a comic-ironic manner, in a monologue he wrote shortly after which was staged as part of an intimate revue, *Then Again* . . ., at the Lyric, Hammersmith, in March 1997. Entitled 'God's District', the sketch also bears out Saul Bellow's rueful observation that 'We take foreigners to be incomplete Americans – convinced that we must hasten and help their evolution.' Pinter presents us with an impassioned American female salvationist on a recruiting mission to London. As she baldly announces 'I'm here in Putney to save souls', the air is heavy with the sound of Bibles being punched. Pinter's familiar knowledge of London topography – 'I haven't met one soul in Putney', cries the speaker, 'that doesn't need saving, that isn't crying out to be saved. And that goes for Shepherd's Bush and also for that vast ruined hinterland of nothingness to the left of Wandsworth Bridge, facing south' – is combined with a suave assault on America's proprietorial attitude not just to religion but to the world at large. The speaker has clearly traversed the globe wrapped up in her inherited colonial attitudes: in Brazil she was appalled by the native Indians with their 'savage rituals', perpetual pipe-blowing and traditional nudity. Having announced that Brazil was bad but that London is going to be easy – no pipe-blowing in Putney or Hammersmith – this globe-trotting Elmer Gantry comes to her lung-busting climax: 'But I want to make one thing very clear. Nothing I've said should lead you to believe that God was (or is) American. He wasn't (and isn't). He was (and is) some kind of Greek or something. But Jesus was definitely born in North Carolina.' At the end the speaker solicits our love and invites the audience, in no uncertain terms, to 'give it to me'. Pinter certainly gives it to her right between the eyes, scoring two palpable hits: against both American religious salvationism and reflex imperialism. It's nice to know that Pinter, much of whose best early work lay in his revue-sketches, hasn't lost his lightness of touch; and that his active political conscience doesn't preclude a wickedly sardonic humour.

Twenty-One Memory Man

I began this book by saying I hoped to unlock the mysteries surrounding Pinter's life and work, but in a sense the more you learn, the more those mysteries deepen. Pinter is a man of infinite complexity and abundant contradiction, but the first thing to say is that whatever the areas of sadness in his private life such as the failure of his first marriage and his recent estrangement from his son, and whatever his political discontent, the bedrock of his existence since 1975 has been his totally reciprocated love for Antonia Fraser. His work may dwell upon an Edenic memory of past happiness, but in the present Pinter has clearly found contentment, security and passion in his second marriage. Anyone who doubts that has only to look at a poem he wrote in 1990 titled 'It is Here' and subtitled 'for A'. It is that rare thing in English verse: a poem celebrating requited married love. It reads:

What sound was that?

I turn away, into the shaking room.

What was that sound that came in on the dark?
What is this maze of light it leaves us in?
What is this stance we take,
To turn away and then turn back?
What did we hear?

It was the breath we took when we first met.

Listen. It is here.

If Pinter enjoys married life and the bonus of an inherited family, he also takes pleasure in many other things: poetry, cricket, the company of friends. He has been heavily involved with the Greville Press now for twenty years helping, with Anthony Astbury and Geoffrey Godbert, to select work for publication, editing two anthologies and, incidentally, putting some of his own money into the imprint. He is also chairman and match manager of the Gaieties Cricket Club, supervising the twenty-two summer fixtures they play each year, including, ironically, one against Sidcup. For Pinter, this is no idle occupation. The Gaieties play to win. Indeed, one side, expecting a casual game of cricket, cancelled the fixture against them because of their quasi-professional seriousness. The side often contains a number of theatre folk, such as director Sam Mendes and actors Harry Burton and Jonathan Cake, as well as an outstanding Oxonian batsman and Eliot-scholar, Ian Smith. And to watch Pinter as I did at Hampstead Cricket Club patrolling the boundary, chivvying and encouraging the players, and urging them on to greater achievements, is to realise that he makes Raymond Illingworth look like a poor motivator of men. I sometimes think Pinter takes more pride in the Gaieties than he does in the ubiquity of his own plays.

What clearly binds people to Pinter – both professional colleagues and friends from Hackney days – is his loyalty and sense of fun. As Peter Hall says, 'Throughout those difficult years at the National Theatre he was a tower of support. I would just add what good company he is. You see in the way he tells stories and anecdotes his strong sense of the ridiculous.' Countless others testify to his almost sacred belief in friendship; and even if he sometimes falls out with his intimates, he is also quick to forgive. He was, understandably, somewhat miffed by Simon Gray's lightly disguised portrayal of him as Hector Duff – 'the world's most famous playwright' – in the TV film of *Unnatural Pursuits*. Gray's own version of events is that no slight was intended. His original aim was for Pinter to play himself but, when Pinter read the script, he declined. The name was changed and, through what Gray now concedes was an error in casting, the character emerged as a waspish Scot. In the end, what irked Pinter was that the playwright was mocked for his sense of political engagement, but the momentary coolness between the two writers was soon settled by a cordial lunch.

Alongside the gift for companionship, there is obviously another, darker side to Pinter which has been heavily publicised in recent years. There is undeniably a combative element to his nature which relishes, when the drink has started to flow, an intellectual barney. I noticed how in Dublin, at dinner after our interview at the Writers' Festival, his eyes sparked when a local literary figure implied that he thought Dr Johnson was a more important figure than Swift: Pinter, finding one of his own idols challenged, went sailing into battle with all guns blazing. There is also running through him some deep vein of discontent which is inseparable from his creative spark. Totally placid men rarely make good writers, but with Pinter in particular there is a detestation of cant, of sloppy thinking, of unprincipled assertion that is a direct reflection of his theatrical concern with language. It would be a gross slur on Pinter to suggest that he expects everyone to share his own point of view. Indeed, it is conspicuous that many of his best friends in theatre, such as Simon Gray and Ronald Harwood, are not precisely on his political wavelength. But what he really dislikes, I suspect, is people who don't stick to their principles or who use words casually or thoughtlessly. What others classify as rudeness or ferocity is really an aspect of Pinter's impassioned integrity – not always a comfortable quality. Sincerity in society, said Somerset Maugham, is like an iron girder in a house of cards. And Pinter, in his insistence on speaking the truth at whatever social cost, has some of the qualities of Molière's Alceste in *Le Misanthrope*. Alceste flouts custom by acting on his beliefs and speaking precisely as he thinks; and although Pinter has not, like Alceste, ended up in self-imposed exile, he has something of the character's fierce attachment to principle and uncompromising political stance. As Tynan shrewdly noted: 'The road from Alceste's stand to the doctrine of civil disobedience is long and tortuous, but not impassable.'

Pinter, as I have suggested, seems to have inherited the artistic instinct of his paternal forbears and the religious scepticism of the Moskowitz side of the family. And if one were to play the amateur psychiatrist, one might argue that Pinter, loving both his parents with equally intense devotion, also combines his father's dominating strong-mindedness with his mother's instinctive warmth and generosity. That there is a complex duality in Pinter's nature those closest to him readily acknowledge. Antonia Fraser admits that he can be socially explosive, but adds that if he hurts someone's feelings he will always write the next day and apologise. 'Believe it or not,' she says, 'in everyday domestic life, Harold is completely unexplosive. There's never any rage or anger of the "Where's my shirt?" variety. On the other hand, if someone at a dinner party said, "We've just had the most wonderful holiday in Turkey," I'd get up and go and hunt for the corkscrew.'

Pinter's integrity ('In all the years I've known him,' says Antonia, 'I've never known him tell a fib') may be socially unnerving, but it also pervades his work. He never writes if he has nothing to say. He never accepts commissions purely for the money: easy enough, you might say, when you are well-off, but true almost without exception of the young Pinter. And what he writes is as pared down and economical as possible, which is partly what people mean when they call him, as they frequently do, a poet. In the theatre, 'poetry' is a loaded term and one that we tend to associate with rhetoric, ornateness and lofty grandeur. But Chekhov showed that prose, by implying as much as it stated, could achieve the effect of poetry. And Eliot, in that tantalising fragment *Sweeney Agonistes*, showed that poetry could incorporate the staccato rhythms of everyday speech. Pinter owes a debt to both of them, but he has taken the process infinitely further by deploying the slang, the ironic undercutting and the occasional baroque formality of native East End speech which is what Noël Coward presumably meant when he called him 'a Cockney Ivy Compton-Burnett'. Even in his overtly middle-class plays such as *Old Times*, *No Man's Land* and *Betrayal*, he constantly blasts through the decorous surface to reveal an undertow of brutality and savagery. Language in Pinter's plays operates on many levels – as a mask, a weapon, a source of evasion – but it is always used with distilled accuracy to reveal character. Pinter's faithful reproduction of the repetitions, hesitations and lacunae of everyday speech, alongside the exuberance of street argot, is his single most important contribution to British drama. Post-Pinter we learned to hear plays differently and became impatient with verbal excess. As Peter Hall says, 'He made us realise that poetic drama could be mined out of real demotic speech. The theatre is a place of poetry and ambiguity, but it's not like sequins stuck on to an existing surface: it's organic. I think Harold is a masterly poet. And that's why he finally towers above everybody else, whatever their merits. "Pinteresque" is simply the label of his style. He has created an entire world out of Cockney speech.'

Belief in the omnipresent power of memory is another of his hallmarks. Even more than territorial domination or the quest for personal supremacy, it is, I believe, the defining theme of his plays. Pinter's characters live as much in the past as in the present, and are haunted by a recollection, however fallible, manipulative or imaginary, of some lost and vanished world in which everything was secure, certain, fixed. As I've suggested, this theme has its roots in Pinter's own life: specifically in the intellectual excitement and perfect camaraderie of his Hackney teens. It is also connected with Pinter's own literary sensibility and his gift for measuring out his life, not through dates or facts, but through images, phrases, smells and sense-impressions. 'Memory', wrote Baudelaire 'is the great criterion of art.' He was referring specifically to the visual artist's attempted recollection of a Platonic ideal of beauty, but he went on to quote some words of E. T. A. Hoffmann's *The Last Adventures of the Dog Berganza* that seem to me applicable, phrase by phrase, to Pinter:

True memory, considered from a philosophic angle, consists, I suppose, only in a very lively imagination, easy to stimulate and, in consequence, able to evoke in support of every sensation the scenes of the past, endowing them, as if by magic, with life and character appropriate to each; at least I have heard the thesis developed by one of my former teachers, who had a prodigious memory, although he could not remember a single date or a single proper name.

Pinter is not *that* bad over dates and names; but he has exactly that same 'lively imagination' which can conjure up past scenes and emotions, whether it be walking over Hackney Downs with Joe Brearley quoting Webster, conversations in distant pubs in Roscrea or painful emotional partings in Kilburn flats. Memory is what gives his work its strong emotional undertow. It also, in an age of historical amnesia, motivates a lot of his political thinking.

The mystery of creativity can never finally be solved, but what strikes me, through talking to Pinter and his contemporaries as well as through constant exposure to the plays, is the extent to which he is a highly personal and even autobiographical writer. His work, to many people, seems objective, detached, ironic, even slightly cold; the exact antithesis of his contemporary, John Osborne, who was romantic, impassioned, and who left his emotional scars exposed for all to see. And it is perfectly true that there is no author's spokesman in Pinter's plays, no obligatory 'nut' of message and that he leaves his audience free to form its own moral conclusions about the behaviour of his characters. But Pinter, in all his major plays, works from life as well as his own subconscious and discovers archetypal patterns in his own and his friends' experiences. Obviously there is no golden rule that covers all the plays and no fixed quota of personal recollection, but *The Birthday Party* was triggered by a specific encounter in grotty seaside digs, *The Caretaker* by a particular set of relationships in a Chiswick house, *The Homecoming* by Morris Wernick's action in concealing his marriage from his Jewish parents, *Old Times* by memories of Bohemian London life and triangular tensions in a Chelsea flat, *Betrayal* by Pinter's experience of infidelity and *Moonlight* by a first-hand knowledge of separation and loss. None of the plays is finally *about* the particularities of Pinter's own life and it would be fatally limiting if they were seen simply as essays in personal revelation. Like all good drama, they transcend the immediate circumstance of their creation and will go on being reinterpreted from one generation to the next. Yet if they are strong and tenacious plays, it is because they are rooted in the world of private experience and because Pinter is able to perceive, in Joan Bakewell's haunting phrase, 'the significance of his own life'.

The plays continue to be produced all over the world. But Pinter in his sixties remains unremittingly active, though also highly selective in what he undertakes. He was invited, for instance, by the Glyndebourne Opera House to direct a revival of Britten's pacifist work *Owen Wingrave*, which was originally conceived for television; he declined simply because he felt that, in the opera house, the director was restricted by the implacable demands of the music (one would still love to see Pinter applying his brand of supercharged minimalism to a medium often characterised by excess busyness). But his own production of *Ashes to Ashes*, after its London première in September 1996, is scheduled to travel to Barcelona as part of the city's own Pinter Festival. The Gate Theatre Dublin is also planning another celebration of his work in 1997 with productions of *Ashes to Ashes*, *No Man's Land*, *A Kind of Alaska* and *The Collection*, in which Pinter himself will appear. And there is talk of another movie based on a recent novel about the First World War. Far from slowing up or lapsing into mellow contentment, he remains creatively energetic and politically committed.

But you cannot possibly sum up Harold Pinter in a nutshell: he is too complex, too elusive, too contradictory. Outgoing with friends, yet guarded with strangers. Extremely funny, yet sensitive to slight. Inordinately generous, yet intensely competitive. Loyal and trusting, yet fiercely protective of his privacy. As Ronald Harwood, who has known him for over forty years, says, 'He can be very aggressive; at the same time, if I was really in trouble, financially or emotionally, I would turn to Harold because I know he would be rock solid in support.' One might apply to him a phrase of Voltaire's: 'No one has found or will ever find.' What one can say is that there is a unity and wholeness about his imaginative world that makes him, in my view, one of the great dramatists not just of our day but of the century. Maybe of all time. Pinter's life has undergone extraordinary and rapid transitions: he has made the journey from Hackney to Holland Park, he has exchanged a world of scruffy theatrical digs for one of considerable style, and he has swapped obscurity for the manifold attractions and multiple inconveniences of fame. In the course of that journey there have been inevitable shifts of tone and emphasis. The milieu of his plays has changed, with occasional digressions, from one of shabby squalor to desolate comfort. He has pared his work down to the bone, gradually eliminating the paraphernalia of realism. He has also read more widely, travelled to Central America, and become ever more sensitive to the open wound of politics. And he has become more impatient with the easy denigration of any form of activism. But the fascinating paradox of Pinter is that, while moving with the times, he has also, as an artist, stayed faithful to his vision, his instincts and to his own internally consistent world. He has forged a direct connection between the private and public faces of power. He has shown that the lies and evasions we deploy in our domestic lives are mirrored by the even more monstrous corruption of language in public life. He has stayed true to his initial sense of life's precariousness and insecurity. And he has continued to draw from his experience and to mine his subconscious to discover universal patterns of behaviour. Like all first-rate artists – Proust, Kafka, Beckett at one end of the scale; Waugh, Greene and Wodehouse at the other – he has mapped out his own country with its distinctive topography; one of whose existence we were always dimly aware, but which never took precise shape until he charted it for us. Yet the quality that most sharply defines Pinter's dramatic world is its attempt to alleviate the fears and anxieties of the present through the memory of a past and now-unattainable happiness. It is that which, finally, gives his work its universal resonance and ensures it a fretful immortality.

Afterword 'Let's Keep Fighting'

'I'm not sure what I've been doing for the last ten years,' Harold Pinter remarked over lunch one day in the summer of 2006. In fact, in the decade since this book first appeared, he has had what Lady Bracknell would call 'a life crowded with incident'. He has written a new play, three filmscripts, sheaves of poems, several sketches, and has created, with composer James Clarke, a pioneering work for radio, *Voices*. He has acted on stage, screen and radio and directed plays by himself and Simon Gray. He has appeared on countless political platforms, made speeches, given interviews and used the broadcast media to attack American foreign policy. His work has been extensively celebrated in festivals at Dublin's Gate Theatre and New York's Lincoln Center. His theatrical achievements and capacity for protest were recognised with the award of the Nobel Prize for Literature in 2005; and his Nobel Lecture, *Art, Truth & Politics*, although studiously ignored by the BBC and much of the British press, has been circulated around the globe in print and video form. In the spring of 2006 Pinter also went to Turin to accept the Europe Theatre Prize which prompted a demonstration of public affection that surprised even him. As if this were not enough, Pinter has in the last five years twice come close to death: first through cancer of the oesophagus and then through a rare skin disease called pemphigus. Having twice conquered death, he is now in constant pain from a form of septicaemia which afflicts his feet and makes movement slow and laborious. But he has faced hospitalisation and illness with stoic resilience and his spirit remains as combative as ever. As he wrote in 2005 to Professor Avraham Oz, one of Israel's leading internal opponents of authoritarianism: 'Let's keep fighting.'

Given all this, it seemed only right to add a new chapter to my existing biography. But looking back over what has been for Pinter a tumultuous, and even traumatic, decade, I am struck by the way his awareness of death is accompanied by a comparable rage for life. Philip Roth in his sombrely impressive novel, *Everyman*, says of his septuagenarian hero that 'eluding death seemed to have become the central business of his life and bodily decay his entire story'. But Pinter, although twice staring death in the face, has never allowed himself to be, like Roth's hero, defined by illness and pain. Over lunch he talks animatedly about future projects including playing Beckett's Krapp at the Royal Court and his own Max in *The Homecoming* on Radio Three. And it occurs to me that it is the intensity of Pinter's response to life that links his art and politics. I suspect that Pinter's political anger is driven by something more than moral disgust with the rhetoric of power. Behind the anger lies a belief in the validity of every single human life and a detestation of a philosophy that treats death as a numerical abstraction: as 'collateral damage' or a necessary by-product of the 'war on terror' or the battle to impose 'freedom' and 'democracy'. But what is significant about the last decade is the way the public percep-tion of Pinter has changed. He has moved from being a frequently mocked voice in the wilderness to a spokesman for vast numbers around the world who share his anger at a debased political culture. There are several reasons for that shift in opinion: the palpable lies over Iraq's 'weapons of mass destruction', the disastrous aftermath of the war itself, the sabre-rattling over Iran's uranium-enrichment by the world's nuclear club. Reading the deluge of mail that followed Pinter's Nobel Prize and Lecture, you realise that the former outsider has turned into an iconic figure: one who is recognised not just as a transformative playwright but as a champion of truth.

For obvious reasons, both personal and political, an awareness of mortality haunts much of Pinter's work over the past decade. In 1997 his father Jack, a working-class Hackney tailor who had supported his son's literary aspir-ations from the outset, died in a Hove nursing home at the age of ninety-five. Pinter remained close to his father even though they had sharply differing opinions over Israeli government policy. But everyone who has had to cope with the death of a parent knows that grief is often delayed by the bureau-cratic rituals that accompany it. And, following his father's demise, Pinter wrote a poem called simply 'Death' and sub-titled 'Births and Registration Act 1953'. Since it occupies a central place in Pinter's thinking, has palpable political resonance and was indeed the climax of his Nobel Lecture, it is worth quoting in full:

> Where was the dead body found?
> Who found the dead body?
> Was the dead body dead when found?
> How was the dead body found?
>
> Who was the dead body?

Who was the father or daughter or brother
Or uncle or sister or mother or son
Of the dead and abandoned body?

Was the body dead when abandoned?
Was the body abandoned?
By whom had it been abandoned?

Was the dead body naked or dressed for a journey?

What made you declare the dead body dead?
Did you declare the dead body dead?
How well did you know the dead body?
How did you know the dead body was dead?

Did you wash the dead body
Did you close both its eyes
Did you bury the body
Did you leave it abandoned
Did you kiss the dead body

What instantly hits one about the poem is its factual tone and its use of interrogation and repetition: its fourteen direct questions and seventeen reiterations of the word 'death' in twenty-one lines suggest that officialdom inexorably drains language of meaning. 'Only in the last stanza,' as Pinter's playwright friend Donald Freed pointed out, 'does the sense of love and loss break through the sterile public nomenclature and it happens with tremendous force because it's postponed until the very last moment.' But, while the poem strikes a chord with anyone who has had to cope with the rituals that follow the death of a relative or friend, it also has a clear political meaning. The ceaseless questions bring to mind *Mountain Language*. The repetition of the word 'abandoned' also implies an unknown or unidentified corpse that is a casualty of conflict or war. What the poem suggests is that the unnamed body is not a numerical cipher but exists in a network of human relationships and demands reverence and love. Pinter had always had a concrete awareness of death dating back to his adolescent passion for Webster. But he goes further in this poem by implying that we seek to minimise death either by shrouding it in the stultifying language of bureaucracy or by abstracting it from a world of feeling and thought. When the poem was published in the first 1998 edition of a collection of prose, poetry and politics, *Various Voices*, Alastair Macaulay elaborated in his *Financial Times* review on an idea he had already expressed in a private letter to the author referred to earlier:

'While Pinter observes the distances between people, he also observes – with disconcerting force – the connections between them. "No man is an island" might be one of his mottoes.' But it is worth recalling how the Donne quotation, from *Devotions Upon Emergent Occasions*, goes on: 'Any man's death diminishes me because I am involved in Mankind.' That idea is central to Pinter's poem and his political credo. In a world where the consequences of political actions are camouflaged by meaningless statistics and Orwellian Newspeak, Pinter is haunted, to an unusual degree, by the significance of each individual death.

Pinter's keen awareness of mortality and compensating hunger for life are also apparent in a remarkable screenplay he wrote in 1997: *The Dreaming Child*, adapted from a short story by the Danish author Karen Blixen, published in her 1942 collection, *Winter's Tales*. The project came to Pinter through the actress Julia Ormond, who had bought the rights to Blixen's fable and was determined to see it filmed. 'I had enormous respect for both Julia and her vision,' says Pinter. 'But she was intent on directing, as well as producing, the film and in the end it was this that brought the project to its knees. The money-men simply wouldn't give her the chance.' Which is sad because Pinter's screenplay is on a level with his work for Joseph Losey. It is also a perfect riposte to the sceptics who argue that Pinter's political engagement has diluted his aesthetic sensibility. Without destroying the fabric of Blixen's story, Pinter turns it from an essentially aristocratic endorsement of the power of imagination into a riveting study of a divided Victorian England: a place where, as Disraeli wrote in *Sybil*, 'the Privileged and the People formed Two Nations'.

Blixen's story concerns a slum child, Jens, who is endowed with an extra-sensory imaginative power. Adopted by the wealthy but childless Jakob and Emilie, Jens embodies a totality of vision: he is both instinctively at home in the grand house and yet retains vivid memories of his slum origins. But it is only through Jens's death that Emilie, who before her marriage had rejected an impassioned lover, is regenerated: it is as if the spirit of the dreaming child has passed into her and she is able to become a poetic fabulist like him. It is an intriguing story and you can see why Ormond and Pinter were attracted to it. But Blixen, who married her baronial cousin and later lived on a Kenyan coffee plantation, clings to a conservative belief in fate. Pinter, however, retains the source's narrative structure while investing it with new meaning: a point seized on by Francis Gillen in a masterly analysis of the screenplay published in *The Pinter Review: 1997–8*. 'What Pinter accomplishes,' says Gillen, 'is both a faithful rendering and an enlargement of political consciousness.' Exactly so. Pinter enriches the story by heightening its social context; and, in so doing, he demolishes the convenient myth that his political fervour has somehow diluted his art.

Transposing Blixen's story to Victorian England, Pinter keeps affluence and poverty in permanent opposition. As in all his screenplays, he begins with a rapid opening montage that establishes the main narrative strands and motifs. The opening cuts swiftly between Emily's rejection of her lover, Charley, in 1861, the simultaneous birth of a bastard boy in the Bristol slums and Emily's country-house life in 1868 as wife to Tom Carter, heir to a shipping business. Two time-periods are contrasted. So also are two worlds: moonlit gardens, grand balls, summer hammocks are offset by images of a Dickensian slum-house where a woman dies in labour. Only gradually does the meaning of those initial images become clear: Emily's ingrained physical inhibition, her passionless marriage, the birth of the dreaming child, Jack. But Pinter constantly counterpoints the Two Nations. Even when they inter-sect, there is only baffled incomprehension. Tom, Emily's husband, is seen retreating in horror from a Bristol brothel. Emily, charitably visiting the poor, withdraws her beneficence when she spies a beer bottle on a windowsill. And in the very next scene Emily, sitting in her boudoir, dresses down her cook for a recent meal: 'Overdone pigeon is uneatable. Last Thursday was most unfortunate.'

But the ultimate intersection of the two worlds comes with Jack's transi-tion from the slums to the big house where he is both at home and not at home: eerily familiar with his surroundings yet more at ease with the servants than with his adoptive parents. It's a story with odd echoes: of Truffaut's *L'Enfant Sauvage* in Jack's preternatural awareness, of *The Go-Between* in the portrait of two polarised class-systems. But the supreme virtue of Pinter's film is that it avoids the mystical sentimentality inherent in Blixen's original. In Blixen, Jack's death is a convenient device leading all too easily to Emily's spiritual regeneration: in Pinter's version not only does Jack's death have its own tragic weight but, as Gillen points out, 'Emily's own journey is really just beginning.' There's a brilliant final scene between Emily and Tom in a sunlit wood where she shows glimmers of understanding. She claims that Jack was her and Charley's son: a palpable untruth but a symbol of her potential emergence from her circumscribed existence. Emily also questions Victorian patriarchal repression by harking back to her rejection of Charley's passion and asking Tom, 'Why do you make us – encourage us – to think in that way?' Echoing Blixen, Emily later claims to have found 'a grace in the world' which Tom claims to understand. But the final shot of Emily and Tom sitting on a tree stump in the receding distance leaves several questions open. What sacrifice is Tom prepared to make? Is a marriage of true equals possible in Victorian society? And will Emily's awakening lead to any real change in a world still governed by class, property, wealth and social circumstance? Pinter leaves this unresolved. But his achievement is to have taken a story about the magical power of art and turned it into a critique of Victorian values. Pinter politicises Blixen without destroying her poetic spirit.

This ability to reconcile seeming opposites, evident throughout *The Dreaming Child* where death and life are held in precarious balance, is a key to Pinter's continuing vitality over the past decade. In particular, he sees politics and art as inseparable rather than antithetical. Writing, acting and directing seem to fuel his political energy. At the same time, his engagement with public issues nourishes and sustains his creative work. In the year immediately following Labour's election victory in May 1997, for instance, Pinter was phenomenally busy. He directed a new Simon Gray play, *Life Support*, in the West End. He played a peroxided homosexual gangster in Jez Butterworth's film of his stage hit, *Mojo*. He also played another homosexual, the suavely dressing-gowned Harry, in his own play, *The Collection*, first at Dublin's Gate Theatre as part of Michael Colgan's second Pinter Festival (April 1997) and then at London's Donmar Theatre (May 1998). Pinter lent the dominating Harry his own form of sophisticated menace. As Susannah Clapp noted in the *Observer*, 'It's impossible to hear Pinter whisper the word "kitty" without assuming that catricide is on the cards.' Pinter also delicately implied, rather than extravagantly signalled, Harry's sexual orientation by such casual gestures as a practised massage of his partner's neck. Only Nicholas de Jongh dissented, arguing, in the *Evening Standard*, that Pinter's Harry was 'about as gay or camp as a night in Knightsbridge Barracks': not, given some of the allegations one has heard about Her Majesty's mounted cavalry, the most felicitous of put-downs.

But Pinter's busyness as actor and director was no obstacle to political action. Rather the reverse in that, over the same period, he constantly articulated his opposition to New Labour policy, specifically its unwavering support for a threatened US air-strike against Saddam Hussein for non-compliance with weapons inspectors. It is important to see Pinter's protests in context. After Labour's electoral triumph in May 1997, Tony Blair enjoyed a prolonged honeymoon with the British press. Also, at that stage, there was remarkably little public opposition to President Clinton's policy towards Iraq. This continued even when, in February 1998, Washington drew up plans, with British support, for a barrage of air-raids against Iraq. But Pinter was one of a handful of people in Britain alert to the coming dangers. On 11 February 1998 he attended an Emergency Committee on Iraq at the House of Commons in which he attacked existing sanctions on Iraq and expressed his 'nausea' and 'humiliation' at the British government's 'lapdog support of Clinton'. He went on Channel 4 News that night to make the same points. And a few days letter he sent 'An Open Letter to the Prime Minister' that was published in the *Guardian* and which is important because it forms a vital matrix for ideas developed in his Nobel lecture.

With America ratcheting up the rhetoric on Iraq, Pinter launched his own pre-emptive strike on US foreign policy. He acknowledges in the Open Letter that Saddam's record in the field of human rights is 'indeed appalling: brutal, pathological'. But Pinter goes on to remind Blair that the US has 'supported, subsidised and, in a number of cases, engendered every right-wing military dictatorship in the world since 1945'. Pinter also lists the lasting damage wreaked by American weaponry on Vietnam, Laos, Cambodia. He pins down the sophistry by which the US 'describes the Kurdish resistance forces in Turkey as "terrorists" whereas it referred to its own vicious Contra forces in Nicaragua as "freedom fighters"'. And Pinter nails the hypocrisy by which the US refuses the right to inspection of its own nuclear capability and supply of chemical arsenals on grounds of national security while demanding unlimited access to Saddam's weapons. Having applauded George Kennan for his rare truthfulness in declaring in 1948, when head of the US State Department, that America must ruthlessly pursue its 'immediate national objectives', Pinter ends with an ironic sally to Blair himself: 'Oh, by the way, meant to mention, forgot to tell you, we were all chuffed to the bollocks when Labour won the election.'

I've no idea whether Pinter's letter was ever read by Tony Blair or whether Alastair Campbell judiciously removed it from the daily news clippings. Either way, it had no effect on government policy and, as far as one can tell, precious little on public opinion. It is true that questions were being asked in the press about the 'special relationship', but they were more about Blair's support for an American President badly damaged by the Monica Lewinsky scandal than for his endorsement of Clinton's foreign policy. Over four nights in December 1998 the air-strikes against Iraq duly took place with American fighters and British Tornadoes carrying out 650 sorties on 250 targets. With America and Britain taking unauthorised military action, in opposition to other world leaders, this was a dry run for the larger conflict to come in 2003 but there was little public outcry. As Anthony Seldon recalls in his biography of Blair, 'There were no marches or demonstrations and precious few angry outbursts.' What protests there were came from individuals like Pinter and a handful of left-wing MPs alert to the dangers of American adventurism and disregard for international law.

Pinter was equally intransigent the following year in his opposition to

NATO air-strikes against Serbia in an attempt to end President Slobodan Milosevic's policy of ethnic cleansing of Kosovan Albanians. And, whatever the moral legitimacy of NATO's military intervention, there is little doubt as to its consequences: television stations, schools and hospitals were bombed, the Chinese Embassy in Belgrade was hit, sixty civilians were killed by an Allied bomb in the market city of Nis. And if Serbia finally agreed in June to the withdrawal of its troops from Kosovo, it was as much because of Russian pressure as because of three months of aerial bombardment. Many people questioned NATO's tactics: Pinter, however, was one of the few who publicly attacked its intentions. He did so in a thirty-minute BBC2 programme called *Counterblast* in May 1999. And he reiterated his arguments, in forensic detail, in a speech to the Confederation of Analytic Psychologists in London in June. He began by saying, 'I shall argue here this evening that the NATO action in Serbia had nothing to do with the fate of the Kosovan Albanians but was yet another blatant and brutal assertion of US power.' And he went on to make several key points: that the negotiation process between Serbs and Kosovars at Rambouillet in February 1999 was never fully exhausted; that the military attack gave Milosevic the excuse to escalate his atrocities; that the bombing of civilians was no accident but part of an attempt to terrorise the population; that, in addition to the lives lost, priceless Byzantine treasures had been destroyed; and that NATO was America's missile and its expansion to embrace much of Eastern Europe was dictated by American economic imperialism.

Not everyone, even on the liberal left, shared Pinter's point of view. His friend Vaclav Havel, in a speech to the Canadian Senate and House of Commons on 29 April, said: 'There is one thing no reasonable person can deny: this is probably the first war that has not been waged in the name of "national interests" but rather in the name of principles and values. If one can say of any war that it is ethical, or that it is being waged for ethical reasons, then it is true of this war.' Robin Cook, whose stance over the Iraq war Pinter came to admire, strongly believed as Foreign Secretary that military force was necessary to prevent the horror of ethnic cleansing. And Stanley Hoffmann, a Harvard history professor, in the *New York Review of Books* for 20 May weighed up the consequences of action versus inaction: while acknowledging the dangers of the former, he began from the premise that it was not NATO that had 'violated' Yugoslav sovereignty but Milosevic who had violated, by abolishing it, Kosovo's autonomy. Even Pinter's intellectual opponents, however, would be forced to concede the moral consistency of his argument: that the defence of 'civilisation against barbarism' – the favourite phrase of western politicians – is undermined by the spectacle of cluster bombs going off in Serbian marketplaces cutting children to pieces. I am among those who believe that, in the face of Milosevic's monstrous policy of ethnic cleansing, the use of ground forces would have been legitimate. But Pinter takes a more clear-cut and morally absolute line: for him all death diminishes mankind, not least when cloaked in grandiloquent rhetoric.

But even as Pinter became more involved in public protest, he continued to direct and act. In the spring of 1999 he directed at the Palace Theatre, Watford, his eighth Simon Gray play, *The Late Middle Classes*: a fine, semi-autobiographical piece about the repressiveness of English family life in the 1950s. Pinter's direction was not just socially precise. It also caught the period's pervasive sense of guilt and, with a cast headed by Harriet Walter and Nicholas Woodeson, the production seemed destined for the West End; but to the anger of Pinter and Gray (eloquently recorded in the latter's book, *Enter a Fox*), it never reached its intended home, the Gielgud Theatre, where, in a particularly grubby piece of theatrical politics, its place was usurped by a rubbishy, short-lived musical, *Boyband*. That same year also saw the release of Patricia Rozema's radical screen version of *Mansfield Park* in which Pinter played a darkly glowering, slave-owning Sir Thomas Bertram; Pinter's 'searing power' (in the words of Claudia Johnson in the *TLS*) added real weight to Rozema's explicit connection between the institution of slavery abroad and the confinement of women at home. Pinter loved working on a piece of politicised Austen that was as far removed as could be from the usual plodding literalism and Laura Ashley prettiness. But even given Pinter's formidable energy, I wondered if he ever felt any tension between his artistic and political lives. 'I don't see it like that,' he said. 'You can pursue two things at the same time. I don't think my political activities have blunted my artistic life or damaged it in any way. I've written a number of poems that are essentially political and I've made a number of speeches that combine both aspects of my life. I don't see my creative life and my political work as separate or opposed to each other at all.'

But despite this range of activities, the world was hungry for a new Pinter text. And there was a sense of anticipation when it was announced that the Almeida would be staging in March 2000 a double bill comprising Pinter's very first play, *The Room*, and a brand new one, *Celebration*. The pairing of Pinter's latest play with his first was actually the brainchild of his wife, Antonia Fraser, which suggests she has untapped potential as a theatrical producer. Not only that: it was through Antonia's encouragement that Pinter persevered with turning a few embryonic scenes into a play. 'For once,' says Pinter,

'the starting point wasn't a specific word or image. *Celebration* was simply drawn from accumulated memories and experiences . . . I do go to restaurants. So one day I just started to write *Celebration*. I do remember I was . . . we were on holiday in Dorset at the time . . . I started to write it and I wasn't at all sure about it . . . I wrote one or two scenes and I wasn't sure about what I was doing. One of Antonia's sons, Benji, and his wife were staying with us. Antonia, who hadn't seen the script, just said one evening after dinner, "Why don't you just read us what you've done?" I said, "I don't know about that." She said, "Oh, come on." So, with some reluctance, I did. Before I knew where I was, they were all collapsing with laughter and that triggered me. I went back to the study I had down there and wrote the whole damn thing in a few days. And it was at that point the Waiter started to emerge as a character.'

It's interesting that it was the family's laughter that spurred Pinter on, for one's first reaction to *Celebration* is that this is one of Pinter's funniest plays. This is Pinter the Cockney humorist having a high old time recording, satirising and even secretly relishing the coarseness, crudity and vulgar materialism of the nouveau riche. We are in a swank London restaurant and the focus is on two sets of diners. At Table One are two couples: Lambert and Julie, Matt and Prue. The men are brothers who have married two sisters and all four are celebrating Lambert and Julie's wedding anniversary with raucous abandon. At Table Two are Russell and Suki, a young banker and his sexy wife, whom he has cheated on with a secretary and whom he treats with insulting derision. And at first we laugh easily at this comedy of bad manners in which the diners exhibit their privileged loutishness and in which memory has dwindled into a form of sexual twitch. 'Sometimes,' says Suki recalling her past as a plump young secretary, 'I could hardly walk from one cabinet to another I was so excited.' Lambert meanwhile boorishly remembers how on his wedding day he was all ready to have sex at the altar until stopped by Matt, his fraternal best man; though quite whether he was on heat for his intended wife or future sister-in-law is left open. The two sets of diners also noisily converge when Lambert realises he knows Suki, whom he proudly claims to have fucked when she was eighteen.

To those who think Pinter exaggerates the vulgarity of the super-rich, I would simply cite two anecdotes. Penelope Wilton – who appeared in a later Dublin and London reading of *Celebration* – told me of dining in one of London's most fashionable theatrical restaurants where Chris Smith, the then Labour Arts Minister, was greeted with derisive shouts of 'Poof' from a group of drunken diners. I also recall travelling back from Paris by Eurostar one Sunday evening in a first-class compartment. At one table a visibly wealthy woman regaled her companions with stories of how she and her husband had been asked to tone down their orgasmic cries by a hotel manager. Not only did the whole compartment hear her story, but so too did her teenage daughter who, squirming with embarrassment, was one of the party.

That memory came to mind while I was watching *Celebration* because Pinter suggests these diners, for all their braying laughter and recollected lusts, are a strangely rootless bunch with a depleted sense of family. Although it is a wedding anniversary, they rarely talk of children; and, when they do, it is either as pawns in a marital power game or as total strangers with whom they have lost contact:

PRUE: They always loved me much more than they loved him.
JULIE: Me too. They loved me to distraction. I was their mother.
PRUE: Yes, I was too. I was my children's mother.
MATT: They have no memory.
LAMBERT: Who?
MATT: Children. They have no memory. They remember nothing. They don't remember who their father was or who their mother was. It's all a hole in the wall for them. They don't remember their own life.

There is sadness and bitterness behind these remarks recalling the estranged sons, Fred and Jake, in *Moonlight*. But there is also acute irony. Children are rebuked for having no memory. Yet the adult diners themselves have a single-track memory almost entirely concerned with their sexual exploits. It is, Pinter suggests, the restaurant staff who are endowed with long-term recollection. At times this is comically sentimental as when Richard, the smooth owner, ludicrously suggests his chic eaterie is based on an oak-beamed village pub he once knew: 'Old men smoking pipes, no music of course, cheese rolls, gherkins, happiness. I think this restaurant – which you so kindly patronise – was inspired by that pub in my childhood. I do hope you notice you have complimentary gherkins as soon as you take your seat.' Meanwhile Sonia, the maitresse d'hotel, is not slow to share her memories of life as a hapless mistress. Asked about a past Moroccan lover, she announces: 'He's dead. He died in another woman's arms. He was on the job. Can you see how tragic my life has been?' The staff, in fact, seem to have far more interesting and resonant lives than the people they obsequiously serve.

Pinter carries this joke to its limits through an intrusive young Waiter who regales the diners with stories of his grandfather, an idea totally transformed by the climax when Pinter invokes a world of poetic mystery that contrasts with the prosaic fixity of the restaurant culture. The idea of the buttonholing Waiter is, of course, not a new one: Shaw used it to great effect in *You Never*

Can Tell. Pinter himself has also in his time been a bit of a space invader. As recalled earlier in the book, as a young man he had worked as a waiter at the National Liberal Club, a post from which he was abruptly sacked after interrupting a conversation between two guests to set them right on the publication date of the first English edition of Kafka's *The Trial.*

Pinter's Waiter, however, is more than a comic device. Even his Mittyesque riffs about his mythic grandfather are not quite as dotty as they first seem. They are a symbol of his capacity to live in a memory-filled world long lost to the diners. They also link the Waiter, who refers to the restaurant as 'my womb', to a long line of refuge-seeking Pinter figures, going back to Rose in *The Room*, Len in *The Dwarfs* and Stanley in *The Birthday Party*. You can see this, in psychological terms, as a reflection of what Freud called 'the phantasy of intra-uterine existence'. You can also see it in more political terms. Intriguingly Pinter's old mate, Henry Woolf, at a New York conference in 2001 related 'this concentration on interiors' to Pinter's Jewishness and suggested the focus on rooms was a projection of the post-Holocaust Jewish urge to live inside one's head. Either way, the Waiter's comic arias are more pointed than initially appears. The first, addressed to Russell and Suki, is virtually a litany of modernist icons from Eliot to Joyce. But the real point is that the list of the grandfather's supposed chums coincides exactly with the young Pinter's own literary heroes. The Waiter's second memory trip, linking movie stars and the Mafia, is directed towards Lambert and Matt, who talk like flash hoodlums; in reality, they are 'strategy consultants' whose job is 'enforcing peace' and who seem close kin to the shadowy agents of state power Pinter depicted in political sketches such as *Precisely* and *The New World Order*. And the Waiter's third speech, depicting his grandfather as an altruistic saint, is addressed to both sets of diners for whom, you deduce, Christian charity is not a major priority.

After the diners have left, Pinter also gives the Waiter a soliloquy that radically shifts the tone. For a start the grandfather suddenly becomes a real person: 'When I was a boy my grandfather used to take me to the edge of the cliffs and we'd look out to sea. He bought me a telescope. I don't think they have telescopes any more. I used to look through this telescope and sometimes I'd see a boat. The boat would grow bigger through the telescopic lens. Sometimes I'd see people on the boat. A man, sometimes, and a woman or sometimes two men. The sea glistened.' One is reminded of the way Pinter, in *A Slight Ache*, *Landscape*, *Old Times*, *Moonlight* and *Ashes to Ashes*, uses a memory of sea and cliffs as an emotional touchstone: something, I suspect, that stems from his own recollections of the Cornish coastline where he'd go for long solitary walks as a wartime evacuee. The telescope also evokes a vanished world, long before video games and home computers, where children were delighted with simple, imagination-stimulating gifts. And the telescope's capacity to bring shimmering, long-range objects into focus seems in stark contrast to the brutishly foreshortened recollections we have encountered amongst the diners.

But the Waiter goes on: 'My grandfather introduced me to the mystery of life and I'm still in the middle of it. I can't find the door to get out. My grandfather got out of it. He got right out. He left it behind him and he didn't look back . . . He got that absolutely right . . . And I'd like to make one further interjection.' What does this suggest? The grandfather's proffered introduction to 'the mystery of life' recalls the aged Lear's offer to Cordelia to 'take upon 's the mystery of things': a not improbable connection since, at the time he was writing *Celebration*, Pinter was working on a projected screenplay of *King Lear*. Lear's death, of course, prevents his fulfilling his dream of exploring the mystery of the universe with his daughter. And when the Waiter says his grandfather 'got right out', he could mean that he died or that he chose to escape the restrictions of daily routine and social conformity by which the Waiter himself feels trapped. But beyond the words lies an invocation of a world of familial connection and long-range memories at odds with the emotional bankruptcy of the diners. In that sense, the speech offers as decisive a tonal shift as that of the captive Jimmy's soliloquy at the end of *Party Time*. The point was reinforced in Pinter's Almeida production, where Danny Dyer was left speaking the lines in a slowly fading spotlight. And in a fine, non-naturalistic production I saw in Reykjavik in 2006, the Waiter was suddenly thrust into silhouetted darkness against the background of a white-ribbed, circular set that simultaneously suggested both womb and cage. But what is striking is the journey on which this short play has taken us. It starts with the Waiter's simple enquiry, 'Who's having the duck?' It ends with him alone on stage saying, 'And I'd like to make one further interjection.' But to whom is he speaking? To us? To the imaginary diners? To himself? What matters, however, is his unquenchable urge to communicate. There is also a Shavian echo, in that one thinks of John Tanner still unabashedly talking at the end of *Man and Superman*. And if these should turn out to be Pinter's last lines of original dialogue written for a public stage, they seem strangely appropriate. Towards the end of his life, no less than at its beginning, Pinter himself hasn't lost the urge to make one further interjection.

Not that critics in 2000 saw *Celebration* in such poetic, elegiac terms: what everyone seized on was the crackling theatrical vitality of the piece as played by Keith Allen, Andy de la Tour, Lindsay Duncan and Lia Williams. Oliver Reynolds in the *TLS* even saw it as 'a satyr play commenting on some of the themes and procedures of Pinter's work as a whole'. Critics also highlighted both the evident dissimilarities and hidden connections between the two plays in the double bill. Alastair Macaulay stressed the former, saying that 'Together *The Room* and *Celebration* add up to a split-focus view of London such as Dickens shows in *Our Mutual Friend*: dregs and froth, deliberation and rush, pathos and apathy, past and present, mystery and satire.' But Robert Butler in the *Independent on Sunday* chose to emphasise the thematic links: 'These plays are about the same thing. To call it a "theme" is too finickety. Both plays steep themselves in territory and proprietorship, power struggles between men and women, the sudden picking on words and – most clearly of all – the indeterminacy of experience. Nearly every statement is countered by another that undermines it.' I too was hit by the continuity of Pinter's imagination. Between 1957 and 2000 the milieu of his plays had radically changed, reflecting the outward changes in his own life from struggling actor to affluent member of the talentocracy. Yet, seen in tandem, the two plays hauntingly proved that Pinter's artistic identity remained as constant as his personal character. He was still obsessed by the pervasive power of memory and time.

If *Celebration* and *The Room* were full of personal echoes, *King Lear*, the screenplay of which Pinter completed in March 2000, also summoned up vivid memories. In the early 1950s Pinter had, at different times, played Edgar and Edmund in Anew McMaster's touring company and later watched Donald Wolfit's titanic performance at close quarters as one of his attendant knights. These facts may help to explain Pinter's decision to eliminate much of the notoriously unplayable Edgar's part while heightening the role of Lear's retinue. 'I hardly cut a line of Lear himself,' says Pinter, 'but I was pretty ruthless about the subplot. You know Edgar's long speech when he decides to become Poor Tom? I cut that and just had him looking into a stagnant pond, dirtying himself and saying, "Edgar, I nothing am." I also wrote in non-dialogue scenes such as Lear riding out into the storm and abandoning his knights, who remain outside the castle freezing. But otherwise it was very much Shakespeare's Lear.' Too much so, I'd say. After a characteristic opening montage of twenty shots – showing a group of knights galloping across a frozen plain while inside a Norman castle the key players are ritually dressed – the screenplay faithfully adheres to Shakespeare's structure and language. But Pinter's fidelity, while admirable in theory, means that Lear's momentous journey is never reimagined in cinematic terms. Filmed Shakespeare presents an eternal problem: how to avoid doubling the verbal with the pictorial image. But the best screen Shakespeare – Welles's *Chimes at Midnight*, Olivier's *Henry V*, Kozintsev's *Hamlet* – shows an imaginative freedom that allows the camera to do much of the work of the original text. Pinter's screenplay, emphasising the wintry rigour of Lear's landscape, also never really acknowledges another problem: that Peter Brook in 1969 had made a film of *King Lear*, based on his own famous Stratford production, which was, in Michael Kustow's words, 'a grave, muted film, black and white, without music, pared down, scrubbed'. Shot in the treeless, snow-covered plains of Jutland, it created precisely the sense of conflict with hostile nature that Pinter was seeking in his version. Although starring Paul Scofield, Brook's film had virtually sunk without trace; Pinter's loyally Shakespearean screenplay, commissioned by Tim Roth, never made it past the money-men at Film Four, which may be sad but is hardly surprising.

But if *King Lear* failed to reach the screen, one of Pinter's most cherished film projects, his adaptation of Proust's *Remembrance of Things Past*, was successfully translated to the stage in November 2000. This project owed much to the ebullient chutzpah of director Di Trevis. Without telling Pinter in advance, Trevis had cheekily adapted his existing *Proust Screenplay* in 1996 for a private performance by twenty-seven second-year drama students at LAMDA. Simply staged, with twelve chairs and a piano, it worked well; and, having nervously told Pinter what she had done, Trevis was invited to re-create the event at the National Theatre Studio in 1999 before a small invited audience including Pinter himself, Joseph Losey's widow and the NT's new director, Trevor Nunn. Pinter was highly impressed and worked further with Trevis on the script, refining, reordering, cutting and condensing; and to his credit, Nunn agreed that the new joint version should be presented at the Cottesloe in 2000 to mark Pinter's seventieth birthday.

There were conflicting views about the finished result. Purists argued that one was watching a double distillation: first Pinter's own filmic version of Proust's oceanic novel and then the Pinter-Trevis adaptation of the screenplay. And obviously there was no way the stage could match Pinter's astonishing opening sequence in the screenplay of thirty-five shots implanting the sights and sounds that form the matrix of Marcel's memory. But if there were inevitable sacrifices in the staging, there were also tangible gains. One was the sense that Proust's narrator, Marcel, was both a participant in and observer of his own life: in Trevis's production Sebastian Harcombe's Marcel was continually present so that everything led to the final moment where time that was lost was found and fixed forever in art. Trevis's vivid production also brought out Proust's gift for Balzacian social comedy. Trevis had herself played Odette in a Glasgow Citizens version of Proust – called *A Waste of Time* – two decades previously and had clearly absorbed something of director Philip Prowse's fascination with glittering social decadence. The opening party at the Guermantes's house in 1921 established, for instance, both the mercilessness of time and the vindictive triumph of the moneyed middle classes: aristocrats gossiped wanly on gilt-framed chairs about death and decay, a haggard vicomtesse staggered past high on cocaine, the hostess meanwhile engaged avant-garde dancers to provide a chic cabaret. There were also excellent individual performances in the Balzacian mould: David Rintoul's Charlus was, in Paul Taylor's words, 'a lofty, magnificent old queen with a glare that both spoils for a snooty fight with his inferiors and burns to be beaten up and abused by them'. Trevis's production proved, as had an earlier Radio Three version of the *Proust Screenplay*, that Pinter's adaptation was supremely actable. It also manifested something we had long suspected: the profound affinities between Pinter and Proust. As John Peter wrote in the *Sunday Times* of Trevis's production: 'You are in a no-man's-land of reminiscence and recall, in flight from the past but with a gnawing need to reconstruct it. Time as a sequence keeps stopping, suspended in an interchange between past and present, just as it does in Pinter's *The Homecoming*, *Old Times* and *No Man's Land*.' I too felt that Pinter's total immersion in Proust back in 1972 had both enriched his own work and confirmed his masonic fellowship with an artist haunted by what Beckett called 'that double-headed monster of damnation and salvation – Time'.

Pinter, who was seventy in October 2000, could hardly have been indifferent to the passage of time. But the old appetite for life was still there. At a four-day June conference at London's Russell Hotel, organised by the Harold Pinter Society, I recall him doing a one-man reading of *Celebration* in which he characterised all nine speakers, especially the sexy Suki, with Dickensian gusto. He was also on good form at a seventieth birthday party organised by his publishers and used to launch a selection of essays from friends and colleagues called, inevitably, *Celebration*. What is striking about the volume is the way personal tributes become a form of self-revelation. For David Hare, Pinter is a poet who has 'cleaned the gutters of the English language'. John Pilger meanwhile sees Pinter as a shining exception to the complicity of the Anglo-American intelligentsia with government: 'The other day I sat down to compile a list of other writers remotely like him, those "with a voice", and an understanding of their wider responsibilities as writers. The page was blank save for Pinter.' Robert Winder observes how even Pinter's passion for cricket is far removed from a jocular, country-house pursuit: 'Harold stands for a different tradition, a more urban and exacting idea of cricket as a bold theatre of aggression.'

A year filled with activity – parties, celebrations, radio appearances in *Moonlight* and *A Slight Ache*, Patrick Marber's revival of *The Caretaker* with

Michael Gambon as a mountainously repulsive, accent-slithering Davies – also yielded its own fascinating coda: a new prose piece called *Tess* which first appeared in *Tatler* in November and which was gaudily advertised on its front cover as 'Harold Pinter on Sex among the Upper Classes'. In fact, that's a not inaccurate description of a short, sharp, blisteringly funny piece in which the eponymous heroine offers a wild account of her family's farouche sexual history: this is Pinter letting his prose off the leash, having a high old time at the expense of the bed-hopping upper crust yet also offering a hint of the surrealism that pervades *Celebration*. There are also disturbing undertones. The piece starts with Tess buttonholing a man at a party claiming: 'Hello. I think you knew my mother once. You knew her when I was a child. It was before my time actually.' Given the mother's gamey past, the suspicion occurs that Tess may be addressing her real father. There's certainly a whiff of incest in Tess's description of her adored brother: 'Never interested in love or anything of that sort. Oh, I mean apart from me. He calls me Sis. Takes me to dances.' As Tess rattles on, it also becomes clear that her mother was a *grande horizontale*: 'She got a medal for it once. She would wear it on special occasions – oh, banquets at the Royal Academy – with a sash across her breasts.' Propelled into high-class whoredom by her husband's sudden poverty, Tess's mother took to her role with voracious enthusiasm; and the implication is that Tess herself has inherited her mother's appetites and possibly even her chosen profession. The piece is a heady *jeu d'esprit* which I've seen Penelope Wilton perform on various festive occasions in Dublin and Turin with a sexy aplomb. But as in *Celebration*, Pinter uses lists – in this case of all the places to which Tess has travelled, ranging from Honolulu to Wormwood Scrubs – to create a sense not just of the diversity but also the unfathomable strangeness of our existence. Even in the process of raising laughs Pinter creates a sense of mystery.

Tess put the comic cap on what had been a remarkable year: at an age when many of his contemporaries had either abandoned theatre for fiction or autobiography or found themselves the victim of casual neglect, Pinter was constantly revived and ceaselessly busy. He even found time to appear in two more films: as the white-suited Uncle Benny in *The Tailor of Panama* and as the hectoring director, slowly stripping John Gielgud's silent Protagonist of his dignity and identity, in David Mamet's version of Beckett's *Catastrophe*. And Pinter's iconic status was confirmed when in July 2001 New York's Lincoln Center staged a comprehensive, two-week festival devoted to his work. If the event was the brainchild of the Lincoln Center's Nigel Redden, it was Michael Colgan of Dublin's Gate Theatre who supplied the bulk of the material: the Almeida's double bill of *The Room* and *Celebration* were complemented by new Dublin productions by Robin Lefevre of *One for the Road*, starring Pinter himself, and of *The Homecoming*, with Ian Holm as a Lear-like Max, alongside Karel Reisz's versions of *Landscape* and *A Kind of Alaska*. Henry Woolf also appeared in the little-known *Monologue* and there were talks, panels, debates and a wide selection of films. I flew over to give an Introduction to Pinter in a surprisingly packed tenth-floor Kaplan Penthouse on a sweltering afternoon. Arthur Miller, Edward Albee and John Guare took part in a Playwrights' Panel. And Mel Gussow did a public interview with Pinter that was so over-subscribed it had to be switched, at the last minute, from the scheduled 285-seat venue to the Juilliard School Auditorium. What was striking was that Pinter's animadversions on American foreign policy in no way dented his popularity in New York: in fact, they seemed to be echoed by his appreciative audience, as the following extract from the Gussow interview indicates: 'I realise,' said Pinter, 'I am in New York and I am sometimes accused of being anti-American. All I can say is that I am not anti the Lincoln Center for a start. (*Some audience laughter and applause.*) And I am not anti the two million people you have in prison over here, and I'm not anti the forty million people who live under the poverty line. (*More audience applause.*) What I am anti – or rather what I am subjecting to my critical scrutiny – are the actions of successive United States administrations, which I think are really open to question and cannot masquerade any longer, as they have been doing for many, many years, under moral stances because the moral stances no longer work. (*Audience applause.*) So. (*Audience laughter.*)'

The gulf between moral postures and brutal reality is, in fact, the subject of *One for the Road*, which was a big hit both in New York and at a previous week-long run at the New Ambassadors in London. What both Lefevre's production and Pinter's performance brought out, quite brilliantly, was the masked cruelty and underlying insecurity of the torture-sanctioning state-agent, Nicolas. The production began with a long, silent prelude in which Pinter's Nicolas knocked back several whiskies before confronting his victims, thus suggesting, in Paul Taylor's words, 'a lonely, troubled figure who has found a home by subsuming himself entirely in the bogus family of the state'. But what was truly shocking was the contrast between Nicolas's playful irony towards his victims and his residual brutality. Pinter flashed his dentist's smile at Lloyd Hutchinson's Victor and rolled the word 'insouciant' round his tongue as if it were a fine wine, suggestively caressed Indira Varma's tattered, serially raped Gila and dandled their son on his knee with creepy parodic paternalism. Yet when Pinter evoked the 'common heritage' from which Victor was excluded he instinctively bunched his left fist, and when he described Gila's late father as 'iron and gold' it was in tones of awestruck admiration. This was the smiler with the knife under the cloak, and for me it evoked memories of Olivier's Richard III in its malevolent irony.

Pinter's own revival of *No Man's Land* at the National Theatre in December 2000 also came as a revelation. This was all the more surprising in that the play arrived freighted with memories: of Richardson and Gielgud in Peter Hall's original production, of Pinter himself and Paul Eddington in David Leveaux's Almeida revival. We felt we had known this before: this mysterious meditation on age, death, memory, time and art. But Pinter's revival, partly through the chemistry of the casting of Corin Redgrave and John Wood as Hirst and Spooner, reminded us that the play offers a confrontation between two contrasting forms of desperation: between one man plagued by inconsolable memories of the past and another who exists only in a hectically self-created present. Under Redgrave's cultivated, upper-class, clubman exterior there seemed to be an almost demonic, guilt-haunted figure trying to lay the ghosts of his fierce remembrance: when he urged Spooner to 'tender the dead as you yourself would be tendered' it was with the urgency of a man who might literally have known a Passchendaele no-man's-land. Wood's amazing Spooner, on the other hand, was a figure of dizzying self-invention. Claiming to know his champagnes, he hilariously drained a glass in a single gulp as if it were a pint of bitter. His jaw-dropping astonishment on learning that Hirst was a famous poet also made me realise, for the first time, that Spooner can be seen as a total fraud: a man who has picked up all the Eliotesque rhythms of the minor versifier but who knows sod all about poetry itself. But what made the production so moving was Wood's quixotically chivalric attempt to rescue Hirst from his doomed stasis. Redgrave and Wood are both actors of exceptional intelligence; and, while the former has inherited his father's gift for suggesting the panic and insecurity within Establishment figures, the latter has a quicksilver, manic inventiveness and capacity to live in the moment. Alastair Macaulay in the *Financial Times*, who was not one of the production's admirers, claimed 'there is a great deal of acting going on'. But I felt that Pinter's production illuminated the desperation in his own play and that Redgrave and Wood, stylistically different but indissolubly linked, eclipsed memories of Gielgud and Richardson.

Pinter relished working on *No Man's Land*. Yet sadly, the period of rehearsal late in 2002 was to be the last time that Pinter experienced something many of us take for granted: a state of pure, uncomplicated good health. No sooner was the play up and running at the Lyttelton than the blow fell. In Pinter's own words:

After *No Man's Land* had started in December, I was suffering from what appeared to be very bad indigestion so I went to see a specialist who was very jolly as many doctors are. He arranged to do an endoscopy in which a long tube is thrust down your gullet. He was smiling away and saying, 'I'm sure it's just indigestion and we'll soon get to the bottom of it.' So I had an anaesthetic for the endoscopy, went to sleep in my cubicle and woke up an hour later. The doctor came in looking very grave and said, 'You appear to have cancer.' And truly my first thought was, 'At least that's wiped the smile off your face.' Admittedly I had one or two other thoughts later but that was my first thought. Anyway, it turned out to be cancer of the oesophagus, which affects the canal from the mouth to the stomach. I went into the Royal Marsden and had the operation: the odds apparently were 95 per cent against coming through it and I can't pay high enough tribute to the surgeon, Jeremy Thompson, who saved my life.

Obviously the chemotherapy left me feeling pretty weak but I carried on. Then in 2005 I found I had developed a rare skin disease called pemphigus: nothing to do with the cancer but it leaves terrible blisters and ulcers in the mouth. I was in and out of hospital where I was treated by a wonderful dermatologist called Chris Bunker. It was in the midst of all this, in October 2005, that the news of the Nobel Prize came through. I'd also just had a bad fall whilst I was in Dublin for my seventy-fifth birthday that left me with several stitches in my head. I was seriously ill but I had to sit down and write the Nobel Lecture which had to be delivered in December. As I was finishing writing the speech, the doctor phoned and said, 'Your blood tests are very bad and I want you to come into hospital immediately.' I said, 'What do you mean, "immediately"?' He said, 'I mean now, this very minute.' I said to Anne, my secretary, 'I'm going to finish this fucking speech because I may never get another chance,' and so I did. And then I went into hospital and, before I knew where I was, I was fighting for every last breath and felt I was dying. But I knew I had to make the damn speech so I came out of hospital one Sunday and recorded it during the day. Undoubtedly Chris Bunker, who treated me for the skin disease, saved my bacon. But part of the treatment consisted of a heavy dose of steroids which led to my legs getting unbelievably swollen. Now my legs are all right but I have this ulcer in my foot – a form of septicaemia – which requires constant attention and which means I'm in and out of hospital every other day. I suppose I must have had a period of reasonable health between the cancer and the skin disease but it's all become a kind of blur. It reminds me of a line in Beckett's *Watt*: 'To think when one is no longer young and yet not old that one is not yet old and one is no longer young. That is perhaps something.' So I suppose there was a time between the two illnesses when I had a Beckettian moment of consolation. But I find it hard to remember. I have to say that the most important thing of all which has kept me going – apart from two brilliant surgeons – is my wife, Antonia.

Even to a layman, it is clear that Pinter's physical and mental toughness has sustained him through prolonged bouts of illness and two close encounters with death. 'If I hadn't anything to do,' he says, 'it would be easy to sink into a mess of self-pity and lethargy.' No danger of that with Pinter: it's almost as if his unyielding opposition to American global dominance has been a fortifying factor. Astonishingly, even while he was undergoing chemotherapy for his cancer, he wrote and appeared in *Press Conference*: a new addition to a 45-minute collection of his revue sketches that were given early evening performances at the National's Lyttelton Theatre in February 2002. Despite his shaven head and slightly shrunken frame, Pinter performed *Press Conference* with all his old relish; and, as in *One for the Road*, I was struck by his ability to endow a brutal apparatchik with a lethal irony. In the sketch Pinter played an ex-head of Secret Police, in an unnamed country, who now found himself Minister of Culture and who saw no essential contradiction between those two roles: 'We believe in a healthy, muscular and tender understanding of our cultural heritage and our cultural obligations. These obligations naturally include loyalty to the free market.' Flashing blood-freezing smiles of complicity at the neutered hacks, Pinter went on to announce: 'Critical dissent is acceptable – if it is left at home. My advice is – leave it at home. Keep it under the bed. With the piss pot.' And, having expressed a moral obligation to protect the ordinary Jack and Jill from corruption and subversion, Pinter's Minister added a vital coda: 'Under our philosophy . . . he that is lost is found' – a direct quotation from St Luke's Gospel and a reminder that even the devil can quote Scripture for his purpose. In one sense, the sketch was a reiteration of Pinter's well-known views. What was original was the form it took, reminding us of a point often made by John Pilger about the media's collusion with the state and the erosion of liberty and vital freedoms.

By performing *Press Conference* during his chemotherapy, Pinter was both defying the gravity of his own illness and protesting against the cancer within the body politic. And, although Pinter scrupulously refused to treat his own disease as some kind of universal metaphor, over the next few years he produced a remarkable sequence of poems that explored both the personal and the political. 'Cancer Cells', written in March 2002, was prompted by a remark by a nurse at the Royal Marsden: 'Cancer cells are those which have forgotten how to die.' That image is pursued in a startling 18-line poem which sees cancer as a duel-to-the-death between the patient and his murderous tumour, one in which the odds are heavily stacked in favour of the latter: 'The black cells will dry up and die / Or sing with joy and have their way. / They breed so quietly night and day, / You never know, they never say.' Countless English poems confront death: very few deal with the process of dying or the insidious nature of cancer in which the cells become an active, even jubilant, force. Three years later, when suffering the onset of pemphigus, Pinter wrote a poem called 'Death May Be Ageing', one that stresses death's capacity to disarm and ambush you, to take you by surprise even 'as you dress to kill'. But, as always, Pinter's concrete apprehension of death was accompanied by an equal rage for life: something beautifully expressed in an intervening poem written in 2004, 'To My Wife', which expresses Pinter's gratitude to Antonia for his continuing existence: 'You were my life / When I was dead / You are my life / And so I live.' You have to go back to Herrick or Suckling to find such a limpid expression of undying love.

Poetry also became a way of responding to the invasion of Iraq in March 2003: Pinter wrote a number of poems before and during the event that were published in a slim volume called *War*. The caricature view of Pinter's anti-war poems is that they are scatological propaganda. Don Paterson virtually said as much in the annual T. S. Eliot Lecture in 2004: 'To take a risk in a poem is not to write a big sweary outburst about how crap the war in Iraq is, even if you are the world's greatest living playwright. Because anyone can do that.' But that is to underestimate the variety of tones and techniques Pinter uses in his war poetry. 'Meeting', written in August 2002, is a sombre, elegiac, Owenesque poem about the union of the generations of the dead. My own favourite, 'After Lunch', dating from September 2002, offers a satiric, almost Jacobean vision of the well-dressed living picnicking amongst the mountainous dead and even using their remains as culinary instruments: Gotham's playgrounds seem to merge with Golgotha in the quasi-Websterian image of the living lounging about 'decanting claret in convenient skulls'. Even 'God Bless America' (January 2003), which seems to be the kind of poem Paterson has in mind, is imbued with a mordant melancholy as it contrasts America's missionary zeal with the mortal consequences of its actions ('And all the dead air is alive / With the smell of America's God'). And in 'Weather Forecast', written in the month the invasion began, Pinter uses the spare, simple language of meteorological predictions to envisage a bleak, post-nuclear, wintry nothingness. The idea that Pinter simply shoots from the lip in his war poems, uttering a foul-mouthed anti-American tirade, is a travesty of the truth. You can, if you wish, classify the poems as propaganda; but since they are propaganda on behalf of the living and against a self-righteous militarism, that places them in an honourable tradition.

Poetry for Pinter increasingly became a political instrument, a means of registering his protest at the drift of public events. As such, it was no less effective – and conceivably more so – than making speeches or participating in rallies, of which Pinter did his fair share. In November 2002, in Turin to accept an honorary degree, he put his own sufferings into perspective. 'Earlier this year,' he said,

> I had a major operation for cancer. The operation and its after-effects were something of a nightmare. I felt I was a man unable to swim, bobbing about under water in a deep, dark, endless ocean. But I did not drown and I am very glad to be alive. However, I found that to emerge from a personal nightmare was to enter an infinitely more pervasive public nightmare – the nightmare of American hysteria, ignorance, arrogance, stupidity and belligerence.

In January 2003 Pinter spoke to 150 peace campaigners at the Houses of Parliament, describing Britain as 'a whipped dog because of our government's contemptible subservience to the US'. On 15 February he addressed the famous anti-war demonstration in Hyde Park attended by more than a million people. A week later he was reading his poems at City Hall for a 'Not in Our Name' rally hosted by Ken Livingstone. On 11 June he read the poems from *War* to a packed throng at the National's Olivier Theatre and again attacked America's declared aim of 'full spectrum domination'. Having chaired the event, I can testify to the audience's heartfelt response; I also sensed that Pinter, for all his occasional frailty, was nourished by his oppositional anger and the feeling that he was now speaking for the many rather than a beleaguered few.

Pinter also found time to work on a number of other projects. In the spring of 2003 he took a benign interest in a new stage version by Kerry Crabbe of his 1950s novel *The Dwarfs*, which played at London's Tricycle Theatre. Crabbe's version, which started out as a film treatment, suffered from its fragmented structure and twenty-nine different scenes. Where it gained over Pinter's own adaptation was in its restoration of the character of Virginia, who becomes the catalyst for a savage rupture between the brooding rep actor, Mark, and the restless City worker, Pete – characters closely based on Pinter himself and Ron Percival. Christopher Morahan's production also nicely caught the strange sexual tension of the early 1950s: a world of tingling suspense and suspenders, where lovers played out their furtive rituals in front of quietly hissing gas fires. A year later Pinter also directed his ninth Simon Gray play, *The Old Masters*, which found its way into his old stamping ground, the Comedy Theatre. It seemed bitterly ironic that *The Late Middle Classes*, a much better play, had died on the road. But, although Gray's new piece took its time, it had one big scene between the scholarly Bernard Berenson and the wheeler-dealing Joseph Duveen revolving around the authentication of *The Adoration of the Magi* (is it a Giorgione or a Titian?). And in the clash between Edward Fox's lordly Berenson and Peter Bowles's Mephistophelian Duveen, Pinter showed that he had lost none of his skill in handling actors. I once asked a leading actress what made him such a good director. She said, very simply: 'When Harold gives you a note in rehearsal, he allows you time to digest it rather than expecting you to act upon it at once. But that's because, unlike most Oxbridge-trained directors, he understands how actors work.'

No sooner had he put the finishing touches to *The Old Masters* than Pinter turned to an unlikely but richly rewarding project: a new screen version of Anthony Shaffer's *Sleuth* intended for Michael Caine and Jude Law as starring partners and to be directed by Kenneth Branagh. In 1970 Shaffer's West End play had totally rewritten the rules of the theatrical thriller: instead of a whodunnit we were confronted by an ingenious whodunwhat in which the fun lay in guessing not so much the identity of the criminal as the nature of the crime. But *Sleuth* was so clever that it virtually killed off, in the theatre at least, the kind of country-house thriller in which cardboard characters heave great lumps of expository dialogue at each other. A big hit in its day, Shaffer's play was turned in 1973 into a faintly ponderous Joseph L. Mankiewicz movie in which Olivier starred as Andrew Wyke, a famous writer of detective novels who plays humiliating games with his wife's lover, Milo Tindle, played by Michael Caine, that act as a convoluted cover for murder; though who is the victim and who is the aggressor is left in suspense until the very end.

Since Pinter had spent much of his young life playing dodgy Agatha Christie thrillers in weekly rep, it is nice to think of him paying homage to her nemesis by undertaking a new version of *Sleuth*. But Pinter's script is less an act of homage than a radical makeover. Where Shaffer's screenplay depends heavily on wiggery-pokery – giving Olivier licence to appear variously as Fu Manchu, a Western sheriff and a Cockney charlady – Pinter's version exploits the continuing power-play between the two men. While preserving the essential plot points, Pinter also makes the dialogue entirely, and often hilariously, his own. When Andrew boasts of his fame as a crime writer, which extends even to Holland, Milo asks, 'You speak Dutch yourself, do you?' To which Andrew replies, 'Yes, how did you know? I have a

Dutch uncle.' Old Pinter trademarks also appear. Andrew tries to persuade Milo of the injustice of the legal system, telling him 'It's like farting Annie Laurie down a keyhole': an old Pinter favourite which appears in *Moonlight* and which the Hackney gang pinched from Joyce Cary's rumbustious wartime novel, *The Horse's Mouth*. And although driven by the dictates of character, Pinter's dialogue expresses his own innate scepticism. At one point Andrew, visited by a curious police inspector, engages him on the topic of religion:

> ANDREW: Shall I tell you what God's trouble is?
> INSPECTOR BLACK: What?
> ANDREW: He has no father. No family roots. Rootless. Nowhere to hang his hat. Poor bugger. I pity him.

Pinter's *Sleuth* is a classic demonstration of the virtues of creative infidelity in the art of screenwriting. Without vandalising Shaffer's original, Pinter makes it his own; and what you notice is the way he uses the story to pursue his familiar preoccupations. Class and status, central to Pinter's oeuvre, echo through the film from the first moment in which Milo turns up at Andrew's house in a little car which the host unfavourably compares to his much larger one. *Sleuth* also explores a theme present in *The Dwarfs*, *The Servant*, *The Collection* and *Betrayal*: the peculiar nature of 'triangular desire' in which two men are capriciously bound by the desire to possess the same woman. In the early stages this erupts in the form of rancid sexual jealousy:

> ANDREW: I understand you're fucking my wife.
> MILO: That's right.
> ANDREW: Right. Yes. Right. So we've cleared that up.
> MILO: We have.
> ANDREW: I thought you might have denied it.
> MILO: Why should I deny it?
> ANDREW: Well she is my wife.
> MILO: Yes, but she's fucking me.
> ANDREW: Oh, she's fucking you too? Well, I'll be buggered – sorry!

The idea of Milo as a passive sexual figure, who excites Andrew's envious admiration, acquires extra resonance towards the film's end when the story's homoerotic implications become apparent. But, without divulging all the script's secrets, it is fair to say that Pinter both relished his task and worked extremely hard at it, producing a seventh and final draft in May 2005. And when you read it you can see why Pinter had such a good time on *Sleuth*. He inherited a proven structure while inventing new dialogue that explores male insecurity, vindictive gamesmanship, the unreliability of narrative and the politics of domestic power, all classic Pinter themes.

If *Sleuth* is a fine piece of traditional craftsmanship, *Voices* – which appeared on Radio Three on 10 October in celebration of Pinter's seventy-fifth birthday – demonstrated Pinter's continuing adventurousness. This was an extraordinary, nerve-jangling, radiophonic experiment in which a collage of Pinter texts about our pervasive inhumanity was combined with an audacious musical score by James Clarke. The initial idea came from Clarke himself who, having studied Pinter for A level and been much impressed by *Ashes to Ashes*, wrote to Pinter suggesting a collaboration. 'We had lots of meetings,' says Clarke, 'in which Harold talked about the way violence can be evoked with a few economical strokes.' Pinter eventually came up with a text combining extracts from *One for the Road*, *Mountain Language*, *Party Time*, *Ashes to Ashes* and *The New World Order* that exposed human cruelty while implicitly expressing a yearning for tolerance. Clarke then composed a score which doesn't so much illustrate as embody and extend Pinter's meaning. A potent example occurs when a phrase from *Mountain Language* – 'Tell her to speak the language of the capital' – is followed by the reverberating sound of an Azeri singer that echoes the culture actively being suppressed. Beckett in *Words and Music* had shown how radio could combine two different art forms as a metaphor for the creative act. *Voices* was something more: a compressed opera in which, as in Webern and Stockhausen, silence itself became part of the musical texture. With a cast of Pinter regulars – including Gawn Grainger, Roger Lloyd Pack, Anastasia Hille and Indira Varma – and a technically dazzling radio production masterminded by Ned Chaillet, *Voices* was a bold venture into new territory. Introducing it at a special preview, Pinter described the creative process between himself and Clarke as one of 'Walking together into hell. Not just my hell or his hell but the hell that we all share here and now.'

Aside from *Voices* on Radio Three, Pinter's seventy-fifth birthday went conspicuously unmarked in his native land. It was once again the Gate Theatre, Dublin, that staged a weekend hooley for the Hackney hero that was to herald, though no one realised it at the time, seven of the most momentous days in Pinter's life. Having organised three previous Pinter Festivals, Michael Colgan was a dab hand at assembling an array of talent in honour of a writer he passionately admired. 'If I stage Pinter,' says Colgan, 'it is because I believe he has totally redefined the nature of drama and because, like Beckett, he appeals to my taste.' And Colgan certainly pulled out all the stops. In the course of a weekend, there were new productions of *Old Times* and *Betrayal*, readings of *Family Voices* and *Celebration* and a brand new anthology, largely put together by Colgan, Alan Stanford and Pinter himself, drawn from the plays, poetry and prose. The whole weekend was a star-encrusted affair featuring Michael Gambon and Jeremy Irons, who had both flown in specially from foreign movie locations, as well as Derek Jacobi, Sinead Cusack, Janie Dee and Stephen Rea. At a Sunday-evening performance of the anthology, the house rose to Pinter as, walking shakily and supported by a stick, he read a climactic poem in tribute to Antonia. At a celebratory dinner afterwards, foaming with the cream of the acting community and a bevy of playwrights including Tom Stoppard, Frank McGuinness and Conor McPherson, the great moment came when Janie Dee, in a figure-hugging black dress, sang 'Happy Birthday, Mr Pinter' in huskily seductive, Monroesque tones.

The following day – Pinter's actual birthday – Colgan also hosted an intimate lunch for himself, Penelope Wilton and Harold and Antonia before the guests departed for London. Around five o'clock the Pinters drove to the airport to catch a private plane. And then, on a grey, rainy Dublin evening, disaster struck. As Pinter recalls: 'I was getting out of the car at the airport and, as I did so, my stick slipped and I went down with it and hit my head on a very hard piece of pavement. There was blood all over the place and a huge trench in my forehead. I was rushed back to the main hospital in Dublin where I stayed for the next four hours and had nine stitches in my head. One moment I was enjoying life greatly after the most wonderful weekend that left me very moved. The next moment I was flat out in hospital thinking that, with all my other illnesses, I was going to die.' Although he was allowed to travel home late on the Monday evening it was a Pinter who, having been emotionally stirred, was now very badly shaken.

Two days of anxious recuperation followed. Then, on the morning of Thursday, 13 October, Pinter was sitting quietly in his study in Aubrey Road when, at around 11.40, the phone rang. It was a preliminary call to ascertain that he was at home and to advise him that he was shortly to receive a call from the chairman of the Nobel Committee. A few minutes later the phone rang again and Pinter was told that he had won the Nobel Prize for Literature. As Pinter told me later that day, 'I was speechless and remained so for another couple of minutes. But I was very moved by this even though I hadn't really taken it in.' Pinter wasn't the only one who hadn't fully taken it in. At one minute past twelve, at the time of the official announcement, a presenter on Sky News blurted out the information that Harold Pinter was dead. After a pause worthy of his subject, he corrected himself to state, 'In fact, Harold Pinter has won the Nobel Prize for Literature.' But it was that kind of day, when everything happened at dizzying speed. Pinter's phone line was quickly jammed. E-mails poured in. And the Pinters' home in Holland Park was besieged by camera crews, reporters and photographers. Eventually Pinter appeared on his doorstep to say a few words. With cuts and bruises still visible around his left eye and a bandaged forehead only partly covered by a jaunty cap, Pinter cut a raffish figure like some veteran sailor who had precariously survived a particularly gruelling round-the-world yacht race.

I was one of the few journalists who managed to get through to him that day and at 5.30 p.m I turned up at his study to interview him. He relived the extraordinary events of the week with a stunned amazement. But I recalled Suzanne Beckett's reaction, when news that her husband had won the Nobel became public, that it was a 'catastrophe' in that it meant a ceaseless invasion of their privacy. Without sharing Suzanne Beckett's dismay, Pinter understood what prompted it. 'The invasion,' he told me, 'has already started. All my friends have been communicating all day long. On the other hand some journalists have behaved appallingly. They've been ringing the door insisting on entrance. They don't like it if you don't respond like a chimpanzee. But I'm not a chimpanzee and I don't intend ever to be a fucking chimpanzee. Not that I've anything against chimpanzees. But when I think back to past winners of the Nobel Prize, I feel I'm in remarkable company. I never thought this would happen to me – in fact, this morning when I picked up my *Guardian* I wondered idly whether the Turkish writer, Orhan Pamuk, had won the prize. He's a remarkable writer and I scanned the pages to see if he had won, not realising they hadn't announced it yet. I don't know what the criteria are and I'm very curious to find out when I go to Stockholm.' After the interview, Pinter kindly lent me his desk in his first-floor study so that I could urgently transcribe it. He himself, meanwhile, went downstairs to be interviewed by Kirsty Wark for *Newsnight*. After we'd both finished, we swapped places so that I could use his downstairs phone to transmit copy to my paper. Finally around 7 p.m. Pinter came downstairs to be driven to the Ivy for a seventy-fifth birthday dinner long arranged by his publisher, Faber and Faber. As he descended the stairs he was shakily holding onto the banister with one hand and clutching a glass of wine in the other. Instinctively, I offered to take his glass. 'If you take the glass, I'll take you,' said Pinter, echoing Ruth in *The Homecoming*. And so, beaming broadly, he was driven off to the Ivy to conclude a tumultuous day.

But in a sense, the drama had only just begun. Pinter spent the next few weeks working on his Nobel Lecture eventually entitled *Art, Truth & Politics*; and even now I am not sure that the radical nature of that Lecture has been fully grasped. What Pinter is saying is that art and politics are linked but proceed from different premises: that art is driven by the search for a truth which remains elusive while politics, as currently practised, is driven by the creation of palpable fictions even though there is a bedrock truth. Pinter is not putting the artist on a pedestal or claiming moral superiority. But as a dramatist, he argues that 'the search for the truth' can never stop; and he is ultimately claiming that the same rigour should be applied to the rhetoric, evasions and downright lies used by politicians. That is what makes Pinter unusual: his belief that truth is indivisible. And, although Pinter goes on to claim that over the years the public has been 'hypnotised' into accepting the fabrications of politicians, there is abundant evidence to show they have woken from their dream. Iraq, Abu Ghraib, Guantanamo have all bred a public scepticism about the verbal camouflage of politics; and Pinter's Lecture played its part in nourishing that climate of suspicion.

The Lecture is also ingeniously structured. It starts with a candid look at Pinter's own creative process. 'Most of the plays,' he tells us, 'are engendered by a line, a word or an image'; and it is interesting that the word 'engendered' later recurs in a more sinister context. Pinter records how *The Homecoming* and *Old Times* were triggered by a single line or image. He also explains that overtly political theatre presents different problems and requires different artistic solutions: *Mountain Language* is 'brutal, short and ugly' while *Ashes to Ashes* shows 'a lost figure in a drowning landscape, a woman unable to escape the doom that seemed to belong only to others'. But, even if the final truth of art remains unknowable, the exploration of it requires linguistic precision; and it is that precision which Pinter finds missing in politics, which is about the maintenance of power. 'To maintain that power,' says Pinter, 'it is essential that people remain in ignorance of the truth, even the truth of their own lives. What surrounds us therefore is a vast tapestry of lies, upon which we feed.' Pinter then goes on to furnish examples: the lies, for instance, told about Nicaragua which, after the Sandinista revolution, was described by President Reagan as a 'totalitarian dungeon'. Proceeding from the particular to the general, and echoing his Open Letter to Tony Blair, Pinter claims that 'the United States supported and in many cases engendered every right-wing military dictatorship in the world after the end of the Second World War.' But condemnation is balanced by irony as Pinter acknowledges the brilliance of the United States in exercising a clinical manipulation of power while masquerading as a force for good. He even volunteers to become President Bush's speechwriter offering a parody of the Manichean simplicities of Bush's pulpit politics. And the speech ends with Pinter's own poem, 'Death', as if to remind us of the reality that lies behind political rhetoric.

Written with clinical care, Pinter's speech was delivered with masterly theatrical effect. Having been rushed back into hospital in late November,

Pinter emerged on Sunday, 4 December, to record the speech for Channel 4's supplementary channel, More4. The image of Pinter sitting in a wheelchair, with a rug over his knees and framed by an image of his younger self, was oddly Beckettian: memories of Hamm in *Endgame* leapt to mind. The voice, with a husky rasp caused by pemphigus, also seemed to gain in resonance as Pinter warmed to his theme: it was as if he had been physically recharged by the moral duty to express his innermost feelings. Watching the speech live, as it were, on television on 7 December, I was also struck by Pinter's reliance on his actor's instinct for knowing how to reinforce a line or heighten suspense. And arriving in Stockholm three days later for the Nobel Prizegiving – which Pinter was forbidden by his doctors to attend – I learned that Sweden's young actors had been impressed by the speech's technique as well as its content. Although Faber's CEO, Stephen Page, nobly stood in for him, it was sad that Pinter himself couldn't be there for the ceremony. I would love to have seen Pinter summoning up his old rep training for the prize-giving where each recipient, formally attired in white tie and tails, is required to bow to the Swedish king, the bust of Alfred Nobel and the assembled audience. After the ultra-formal proceedings in the Concert Hall, everyone then repairs to a prodigious banquet in the Italianate City Hall. It is an astonishing event. Between each Lucullan course, the guests are serenaded by flower-bearing singers from Uppsala and betasselled students process down a giant staircase bearing the standards of their unions. After the pomp and circumstance of the prize-giving, it is as if we had suddenly landed in the world of Busby Berkeley.

But what was fascinating were the reactions to Pinter's Nobel Prize and Lecture. And since they were overwhelmingly positive, it is worth picking out the few negative ones. The most startling fact was that Pinter's Nobel Lecture on 7 December was totally ignored by the BBC. You would have thought that a living British dramatist's views on his art and global politics might have been of passing interest to a public service broadcaster. There was, however, no reference to the speech on any of BBC TV's news bulletins that night or indeed on its current affairs programme, *Newsnight*. Instead, as Pinter points out, *Newsnight* carried an item on how much President Bush loves dogs and how much dogs love him (lapdogs, presumably). And, although I received urgent messages to ring *Newsnight*, it was not, I learned, to discuss Pinter's Nobel Lecture but David Cameron's debut at Prime Minister's Question Time. In the press, there was also a handful of attacks on both the award and the Lecture. In the *Independent* the normally sensible Johan Hari dismissed the Lecture in advance as a 'rant' and falsely claimed that Pinter would have refused to resist Hitler; in fact, he has repeatedly said that, had he been of age, he would have accepted conscription in World War II. More predictably, Christopher Hitchens was wheeled out to dismiss Pinter as 'a bigmouth who has strutted and fretted his hour upon the stage for far too long'. And in the *Daily Telegraph* historian Niall Ferguson attacked the Lecture, arguing: 'Nobody pretends that the US came through the Cold War with clean hands. But to pretend that its crimes were equivalent to those of its Communist opponents – and that they have been wilfully hushed up – is fatally to blur the distinction between truth and falsehood.' But Pinter denies that he ever made any comparison in his speech between atrocities committed by the Soviet Union and China and those of America. 'All I ever said,' he retorts, 'is that Soviet atrocities were comprehensively documented but that American actions weren't. I didn't go into comparisons as to who killed more people as if it were a contest. Ferguson distorted the whole bloody thing.'

Explore the Pinter Archive, however, and you find two large boxes containing the thousands of letters Pinter received from friends, colleagues, public eminences and total strangers applauding both the prize and his political stance. Sometimes the tone is quite light. Mike Nichols succinctly asks, 'What took them so long?' Arnold Wesker says, 'Congratulations. Glad they chose one of the Hackney Jewboys.' Jeffrey Archer, sounding a note struck by many, says, 'I thought nothing could surpass winning the Ashes. I was wrong.' But what is impressive is the support shown by literary and political heavyweights. Ohan Pamuk recalls that, when Pinter and Arthur Miller visited Turkey twenty years previously, he was their guide to Istanbul. In congratulating Pinter on a prize for which he himself was a serious contender, Pamuk also recalls Pinter's support over the years and movingly hopes that he might be able to attend the writer's forthcoming Istanbul trial. Carlos Fuentes calls Pinter's prize 'the most deserved ever' and, after the Lecture, thanks Pinter for endorsing 'the truth of the lie of art with a searing clarity that damns for ever the lies we are served as truth in politics'. And Kofi Annan, the UN Secretary General, writes: 'Throughout your career you have had the courage to be honest and outspoken on some of the most important and difficult issues facing humanity, from the personal and the domestic to the global.' This was one of the letters to which Pinter replied: 'There are,' he responded, 'difficult issues facing humanity and your clarity and dignity in the position you hold means a great deal to many people including me.'

But perhaps the most surprising letter arrived on 27 January 2006 from the man whom Pinter had repeatedly said should be arraigned before the International Criminal Court of Justice at the Hague: Tony Blair. It is worth quoting his letter in full:

Dear Harold,

I am writing to congratulate you on your recent award of the Nobel prize for Literature. I apologise for the delay in doing so.

It is a great honour for you personally and, by extension, a great boon to this country that we should have produced another Nobel Laureate in writing, one of the trades at which we have always excelled.

British theatre benefited greatly from the shot in the arm that you and others provided and your drama has already stood the scrutiny of time, the toughest judge of all.

We, of course, differ fundamentally on the war in Iraq, on the nature of the terrorist threat we face and on the relationship this country has with the United States.

You rehearsed the disagreement in your acceptance speech. But that does not mean that I would not like to extend to you my admiration for your considerable achievement which honours a lifetime's work.

Yours ever,

Tony

Pinter replied on 6 February:

Dear Prime Minister,

Thank you very much for your letter to me about the Nobel prize for Literature.

I was glad that you acknowledged that we have profound differences of opinion about various political issues but this did not affect my appreciation of your kind and generous words.

Yours sincerely,

Harold Pinter

One is immediately struck by the contrast between the first-name informality of Blair's letter and the cryptic formality of Pinter's response. Blair's generosity also in no way softens Pinter's attitude towards him. 'I find his subservience to the US,' Pinter says, 'disgusting, deplorable, detestable and his invasion of Iraq with the US totally illegitimate and immoral. And, as you know, I consider him to be a war criminal. Having said that, although he knows I consider him to be a war criminal, I am nevertheless not in prison. If I'd said this in many countries, such as Turkey, I'd be in gaol. If I said this in America, I'd be in big trouble. Here that is not the case. So there is still a shred of free speech. The other side of the coin, of course, is the woman who went to Trafalgar Square and read out the names of the war dead and who, in consequence, has a criminal record.'

But of all the responses to Pinter's Nobel Lecture, perhaps the most moving and insightful came from his old Hackney friend, Moishe Wernick, now living in Canada. Wernick wrote: 'I felt that, as you composed that speech, there was more going on, more besides US foreign policy. I felt this particularly when you included your poem, Death, at the end of the speech. I felt, and this is hard to articulate, that it was a "sign off". I felt that many emotions travelled along with the construction of the political content of the speech, emotions that covered the whole range of your life. Perhaps this is utter nonsense. I was very moved by Death when you first sent it to me – it rang bells. I felt that the poem did not actually belong to the speech, it belonged to you. Well, make of that what you can. I wish I had seen you in action on that day. Love, Moishe.' What Moishe Wernick spotted, which few others did, was the sense of mortality that pervaded the speech. Written at a time when Pinter himself seemed close to death, it feels like a defiant last testament from a writer who is determined not to go quietly into the dark.

While the Nobel was obviously a landmark in Pinter's life, a sequence of other awards also fell into his lap in his seventies. In 2002 he was made a Companion of Honour at Buckingham Palace. In 2004 he was awarded the Wilfred Owen prize for poetry opposing the Iraq conflict. In 2005 he won Prague's annual Franz Kafka Prize. And in March 2006 he went to Turin to receive the Europe Theatre Prize. Created in the early 1990s and originally based in Taormina, this was a coveted award that had long been dominated by the big bow-wow European directors: Ariane Mnouchkine, Peter Brook, Giorgio Strehler, Lev Dodin and Luca Ronconi were among the previous recipients, with Heiner Muller almost the only writer to be honoured. As the sole British member of the jury, I had long argued for recognition of dramatists and five years previously had advocated Harold Pinter. Despite the reservations of a French juror who argued that Edward Bond was Britain's leading playwright, the nomination of Pinter met with rapturous approval and he was duly informed he had won. However, because of murky local politics and Taormina's financial problems, the Prize was put on ice until a suitable host-city could be found. Then, by a miraculous coincidence, on the very day that Pinter's Nobel Prize was announced, it was agreed that Turin, flush with money as the site for the Winter Olympics, would host the event in March 2006; and it is fair to say that it did so with munificent generosity.

For me the events of the Turin weekend are a blur of hyperactivity. I found myself hosting a two-day conference on 'Pinter: Passion, Poetry and Politics' at which critics and scholars from England, France, Germany, Greece, Italy and North and South America all delivered excellent papers. I also did a Saturday-morning interview with Pinter in Turin's lavishly baroque main theatre. But what was striking was the electrifying effect that the presence of Pinter himself had on all concerned. Everyone wanted to talk to him; and, returning to the hotel one evening to find a vast throng outside its doors, I assumed, for one heady moment, it was for the celebrated author rather than, as it turned out, for the visiting Inter-Milan football team. But, although constantly besieged, in the public interview Pinter was at his most communicative. He spoke openly about his recent encounters with death, his political views and the conflict, in writing, between free-flowing instinct and the conscious, organising self:

> I'm not aware of my consciousness working in that way at an early stage of writing. After it's got to a certain point, I then work very hard on the text, quite consciously. In other words, I just don't live in my unconscious the whole damn time. I keep an eye on it. But one of the most exciting things about being a writer is finding the life in different characters whom you don't know at all. To a certain extent, you've got to let them live their own life. But there's also a conflict constantly going on between you as the writer and them as the characters. Who's in charge? There's no easy answer to that. I suppose finally the author is in charge. Because, whether the character likes it or not, all I've got to do is take out my pen and do that (*a gesture of swift erasure*) and he's lost a line. It may be one of his favourite lines of dialogue (*laughter*). But I've got the pen in my hand.

This was Pinter talking, candidly, about the working process; and I had the sensation, as he spoke, that he was both responding to the warmth of his Turin audience and aware that he was possibly doing one of his last major public interviews. But the bond, both political and artistic, between Pinter and his audience became even more evident at the Sunday-night prize-giving ceremony. As he received his prize, Pinter made a short, impromptu speech in which he said he was very moved to receive the award. 'I've had,' he said, 'a long and happy relationship with Turin and indeed with Europe as a whole. But I'd like to see the day come when Europe gets its act together and stands up against American power. In fact, I'd like to see Europe echo the example of Latin America in withstanding the economic and political intimidation of the United States. This is a serious responsibility for Europe and all of its citizens.' His words went down a storm. And it was significant that in the presentation of the Dublin anthology that followed – for which Jeremy Irons, Charles Dance and Penelope Wilton had all flown in – it was Michael Gambon's explosive rendering of 'American Football' that threatened to blow the roof off the theatre.

Just before the Turin event, Pinter told me that he intended to take things quietly in future: to read, spend time with his family (he has six step-children and sixteen grandchildren), play a bit of bridge, supervise the Gaieties Cricket Club. Since he had twice confronted death, I also wondered if he ever, even as a lifelong secularist, envied those who had the consolation of faith. 'It's too big a subject for the lunch table,' he said. 'But all I can really say about religion is that I don't understand it. I feel that religious belief is at one and the same time extremely profound and totally childish. I'll say this, though. I do enjoy the silence and peace of an English country church. What does Philip Larkin say in "Church Going"? "A serious house on serious earth it is." I can really appreciate that.'

It would be misleading, however, to end with an elegiac image of Pinter: an old man with a stick quietly reading, playing Saturday-night bridge or pottering about English country-churches. The reality could hardly be more different. For, whatever his current physical restrictions, Pinter has an unassuageable hunger for life. In May 2006 he wrote a very funny short sketch, *Apart From That*, which he and Antonia performed at an evening in aid of the Longford Trust: as two people trade banalities over their mobile phones there is a hint of something ominous and unspoken behind the clichéd chat. Early in June, Pinter also attended a celebration of his work in cinema organised by the British branch of the Academy of Motion Pictures. 'To jump back into the world of Pinter's movies,' said David Hare who organised a brilliant selection of film clips, 'is to remind yourself of a literate mainstream cinema, focused as much as Bergman's is on the human face, in which tension is maintained by a carefully crafted mix of image and dialogue.' Later that month Pinter also performed in an evening for Human Rights Watch at the Royal Court. And he was back at the Court in October to do 10 performances in the Theatre Upstairs of Beckett's *Krapp's Last Tape*. All tickets for the performances were snapped up within sixteen minutes of the box-office opening. I'm not sure what people expected: possibly the sight of a desperately fragile Pinter struggling heroically against the physical odds. What they got was something totally and startlingly different: the most rigorous, unsentimental and overpowering interpretation of Beckett's terminal drama imaginable. It is true that Pinter's Krapp, hunched over a tape-recorder listening to his recollections of 30 years ago, was confined to a motorised wheelchair. But there was little pathos or lyricism in Pinter's reading. This was a man in a room – superbly evoked in Hildegard Bechtler's set by a spartan grate that looked as if it had never been lit – surveying his past life with angry exasperation and sardonic bitterness. At two precise moments Pinter also looked anxiously over his left shoulder into the crepuscular darkness as if he felt he was being stalked by death. But it was the final image that was unforgettable. As Krapp announced that he wouldn't want his earlier years back – 'not with the fire in me now' – Pinter sat staring into the slowly fading light in aghast, agonised silence as a death-bell distantly tolled. The reviews were ecstatic: probably the best Pinter has received in his entire life. But some reviews assumed a symbiotic connection between Beckett's character and Pinter himself. What this overlooked was that we were actually watching a masterly piece of acting: one lovingly prepared over several months with the play's consummate director, Ian Rickson. Maybe Pinter's performance was shadowed by his own recent brushes with mortality. But the gap between the character and the actor was highlighted by a remark Pinter made a few months earlier in an interview with Kirsty Wark for BBC's *Newsnight*. 'Shall I tell you what I really think?' Pinter said at one point. 'I think that life is beautiful but the world is hell.' Inside that seeming paraodox lies much of the essence of Pinter. As you trace the arc of his career, since his earliest days in Hackney, you find a very un-Krapp-like delight in the bounty of existence and everything it brings from love, friendship and sex to poetry, theatre and cricket. Yet Pinter is also endowed with a raw sensitivity to the cruelty and injustice that pervade our planet, which is why he has spent so much of his energy in protest. These two things – a passionate humanist fervour and a despair at society's failings – coexist in Pinter and explain what makes him both such exhilarating company in private and a public figure of fierce moral intensity. And my guess is that as long as there are injustices to be corrected and lies to be checked, he will never dwindle into benign passivity. In the remaining years of a rich life he will, I suspect, continue to play a few shots and follow his own injunction to Avrahim Oz: 'Let's keep fighting'.

Appendix Art, Truth & Politics

The Nobel Lecture

In 1958 I wrote the following:

> 'There are no hard distinctions between what is real and what is unreal, nor between what is true and what is false. A thing is not necessarily either true or false; it can be both true and false.'

I believe that these assertions still make sense and do still apply to the exploration of reality through art. So as a writer I stand by them but as a citizen I cannot. As a citizen I must ask: What is true? What is false?

Truth in drama is forever elusive. You never quite find it but the search for it is compulsive. The search is clearly what drives the endeavour. The search is your task. More often than not you stumble upon the truth in the dark, colliding with it or just glimpsing an image or a shape which seems to correspond to the truth, often without realising that you have done so. But the real truth is that there never is any such thing as one truth to be found in dramatic art. There are many. These truths challenge each other, recoil from each other, reflect each other, ignore each other, tease each other, are blind to each other. Sometimes you feel you have the truth of a moment in your hand, then it slips through your fingers and is lost.

I have often been asked how my plays come about. I cannot say. Nor can I ever sum up my plays, except to say that this is what happened. That is what they said. That is what they did.

Most of the plays are engendered by a line, a word or an image. The given word is often shortly followed by the image. I shall give two examples of two lines which came right out of the blue into my head, followed by an image, followed by me.

The plays are *The Homecoming* and *Old Times*. The first line of *The Homecoming* is 'What have you done with the scissors?' The first line of *Old Times* is 'Dark.'

In each case I had no further information.

In the first case someone was obviously looking for a pair of scissors and was demanding their whereabouts of someone else he suspected had probably stolen them. But I somehow knew that the person addressed didn't give a damn about the scissors or about the questioner either, for that matter.

'Dark' I took to be a description of someone's hair, the hair of a woman, and was the answer to a question. In each case I found myself compelled to pursue the matter. This happened visually, a very slow fade, through shadow into light.

I always start a play by calling the characters A, B and C.

In the play that became *The Homecoming* I saw a man enter a stark room and ask his question of a younger man sitting on an ugly sofa reading a racing paper. I somehow suspected that A was a father and that B was his son, but I had no proof. This was however confirmed a short time later when B (later to become Lenny) says to A (later to become Max), 'Dad, do you mind if I change the subject? I want to ask you something. The dinner we had before, what was the name of it? What do you call it? Why don't you buy a dog? You're a dog cook. Honest. You think you're cooking for a lot of dogs.' So since B calls A 'Dad' it seemed to me reasonable to assume that they were father and son. A was also clearly the cook and his cooking did not seem to be held in high regard. Did this mean that there was no mother? I didn't know. But, as I told myself at the time, our beginnings never know our ends.

'Dark.' A large window. Evening sky. A man, A (later to become Deeley), and a woman, B (later to become Kate), sitting with drinks. 'Fat or thin?' the man asks. Who are they talking about? But I then see, standing at the window, a woman, C (later to become Anna), in another condition of light, her back to them, her hair dark.

It's a strange moment, the moment of creating characters who up to that moment have had no existence. What follows is fitful, uncertain, even hallucinatory, although sometimes it can be an unstoppable avalanche. The author's position is an odd one. In a sense he is not welcomed by the characters. The characters resist him, they are not easy to live with, they are impossible to define. You certainly can't dictate to them. To a certain extent you play a never-ending game with them, cat and mouse, blind man's buff, hide and seek. But finally you find that you have people of flesh and blood on your hands, people with will and an individual sensibility of their own, made out of component parts you are unable to change, manipulate or distort.

So language in art remains a highly ambiguous transaction, a quicksand, a trampoline, a frozen pool which might give way under you, the author, at any time.

But as I have said, the search for the truth can never stop. It cannot be adjourned, it cannot be postponed. It has to be faced, right there, on the spot.

Political theatre presents an entirely different set of problems. Sermonising has to be avoided at all cost. Objectivity is essential. The characters must be allowed to breathe their own air. The author cannot confine and constrict them to satisfy his own taste or disposition or prejudice. He must be prepared to approach them from a variety of angles, from a full and uninhibited range of perspectives, take them by surprise, perhaps, occasionally, but nevertheless give them the freedom to go which way they will. This does not always work. And political satire, of course, adheres to none of these precepts, in fact does precisely the opposite, which is its proper function.

In my play *The Birthday Party* I think I allow a whole range of options to operate in a dense forest of possibility before finally focussing on an act of subjugation.

Mountain Language pretends to no such range of operation. It remains brutal, short and ugly. But the soldiers in the play do get some fun out of it. One sometimes forgets that torturers become easily bored. They need a bit of a laugh to keep their spirits up. This has been confirmed of course by the events at Abu Ghraib in Baghdad. *Mountain Language* lasts only 20 minutes, but it could go on for hour after hour, on and on and on, the same pattern repeated over and over again, on and on, hour after hour.

Ashes to Ashes, on the other hand, seems to me to be taking place under water. A drowning woman, her hand reaching up through the waves, dropping down out of sight, reaching for others, but finding nobody there, either above or under the water, finding only shadows, reflections, floating; the woman a lost figure in a drowning landscape, a woman unable to escape the doom that seemed to belong only to others.

But as they died, she must die too.

Political language, as used by politicians, does not venture into any of this territory since the majority of politicians, on the evidence available to us, are interested not in truth but in power and in the maintenance of that power. To maintain that power it is essential that people remain in ignorance, that they live in ignorance of the truth, even the truth of their own lives. What surrounds us therefore is a vast tapestry of lies, upon which we feed.

As every single person here knows, the justification for the invasion of Iraq was that Saddam Hussein possessed a highly dangerous body of weapons of mass destruction, some of which could be fired in 45 minutes, bringing about appalling devastation. We were assured that was true. It was not true. We were told that Iraq had a relationship with Al Quaeda and shared responsibility for the atrocity in New York of September 11th 2001. We were assured that this was true. It was not true. We were told that Iraq threatened the security of the world. We were assured it was true. It was not true.

The truth is something entirely different. The truth is to do with how the United States understands its role in the world and how it chooses to embody it.

But before I come back to the present I would like to look at the recent past, by which I mean United States foreign policy since the end of the Second World War. I believe it is obligatory upon us to subject this period to at least some kind of even limited scrutiny, which is all that time will allow here.

Everyone knows what happened in the Soviet Union and throughout Eastern Europe during the post-war period: the systematic brutality, the widespread atrocities, the ruthless suppression of independent thought. All this has been fully documented and verified.

But my contention here is that the US crimes in the same period have only been superficially recorded, let alone documented, let alone acknowledged, let alone recognised as crimes at all. I believe this must be addressed and that the truth has considerable bearing on where the world stands now. Although constrained, to a certain extent, by the existence of the Soviet Union, the United States' actions throughout the world made it clear that it had concluded it had carte blanche to do what it liked.

Direct invasion of a sovereign state has never in fact been America's favoured method. In the main, it has preferred what it has described as 'low intensity conflict'. Low intensity conflict means that thousands of people die but slower than if you dropped a bomb on them in one fell swoop. It means that you infect the heart of the country, that you establish a malignant growth and watch the gangrene bloom. When the populace has been subdued – or beaten to death – the same thing – and your own friends, the military and the great corporations, sit comfortably in power, you go before the camera and say that democracy has prevailed. This was a commonplace in US foreign policy in the years to which I refer.

The tragedy of Nicaragua was a highly significant case. I choose to offer it here as a potent example of America's view of its role in the world, both then and now.

I was present at a meeting at the US embassy in London in the late 1980s.

The United States Congress was about to decide whether to give more money to the Contras in their campaign against the state of Nicaragua. I was a member of a delegation speaking on behalf of Nicaragua but the most important member of this delegation was a Father John Metcalf. The leader of the US body was Raymond Seitz (then number two to the ambassador, later ambassador himself). Father Metcalf said: 'Sir, I am in charge of a parish in the north of Nicaragua. My parishioners built a school, a health centre, a cultural centre. We have lived in peace. A few months ago a Contra force attacked the parish. They destroyed everything: the school, the health centre, the cultural centre. They raped nurses and teachers, slaughtered doctors, in the most brutal manner. They behaved like savages. Please demand that the US government withdraw its support from this shocking terrorist activity.'

Raymond Seitz had a very good reputation as a rational, responsible and highly sophisticated man. He was greatly respected in diplomatic circles. He listened, paused and then spoke with some gravity. 'Father,' he said, 'let me tell you something. In war, innocent people always suffer.' There was a frozen silence. We stared at him. He did not flinch.

Innocent people, indeed, always suffer.

Finally somebody said: 'But in this case "innocent people" were the victims of a gruesome atrocity subsidised by your government, one among many. If Congress allows the Contras more money further atrocities of this kind will take place. Is this not the case? Is your government not therefore guilty of supporting acts of murder and destruction upon the citizens of a sovereign state?'

Seitz was imperturbable. 'I don't agree that the facts as presented support your assertions,' he said.

As we were leaving the Embassy a US aide told me that he enjoyed my plays. I did not reply.

I should remind you that at the time President Reagan made the following statement: 'The Contras are the moral equivalent of our Founding Fathers.'

The United States supported the brutal Somoza dictatorship in Nicaragua for over forty years. The Nicaraguan people, led by the Sandinistas, overthrew this regime in 1979, a breathtaking popular revolution.

The Sandinistas weren't perfect. They possessed their fair share of arrogance and their political philosophy contained a number of contradictory elements. But they were intelligent, rational and civilised. They set out to establish a stable, decent, pluralistic society. The death penalty was abolished. Hundreds of thousands of poverty-stricken peasants were brought back from the dead. Over 100,000 families were given title to land. Two thousand schools were built. A quite remarkable literacy campaign reduced illiteracy in the country to less than one seventh. Free education was established and a free health service. Infant mortality was reduced by a third. Polio was eradicated.

The United States denounced these achievements as Marxist/Leninist subversion. In the view of the US government, a dangerous example was being set. If Nicaragua was allowed to establish basic norms of social and economic justice, if it was allowed to raise the standards of health care and education and achieve social unity and national self respect, neighbouring countries would ask the same questions and do the same things. There was of course at the time fierce resistance to the status quo in El Salvador.

I spoke earlier about 'a tapestry of lies' which surrounds us. President Reagan commonly described Nicaragua as a 'totalitarian dungeon'. This was taken generally by the media, and certainly by the British government, as accurate and fair comment. But there was in fact no record of death squads under the Sandinista government. There was no record of torture. There was no record of systematic or official military brutality. No priests were ever murdered in Nicaragua. There were in fact three priests in the government, two Jesuits and a Maryknoll missionary. The totalitarian dungeons were actually next door, in El Salvador and Guatemala. The United States had brought down the democratically elected government of Guatemala in 1954 and it is estimated that over 200,000 people had been victims of successive military dictatorships.

Six of the most distinguished Jesuits in the world were viciously murdered at the Central American University in San Salvador in 1989 by a battalion of the Alcatl regiment trained at Fort Benning, Georgia, USA. That extremely brave man Archbishop Romero was assassinated while saying mass. It is estimated that 75,000 people died. Why were they killed? They were killed because they believed a better life was possible and should be achieved. That belief immediately qualified them as communists. They died because they dared to question the status quo, the endless plateau of poverty, disease, degradation and oppression which had been their birthright.

The United States finally brought down the Sandinista government. It took some years and considerable resistance but relentless economic persecution and 30,000 dead finally undermined the spirit of the Nicaraguan people. They were exhausted and poverty stricken once again. The casinos moved back into the country. Free health and free education were over. Big business returned with a vengeance. 'Democracy' had prevailed.

But this 'policy' was by no means restricted to Central America. It was conducted throughout the world. It was never-ending. And it is as if it never happened.

The United States supported and in many cases engendered every right-wing military dictatorship in the world after the end of the Second World War. I refer to Indonesia, Greece, Uruguay, Brazil, Paraguay, Haiti, Turkey, the Philippines, Guatemala, El Salvador and, of course, Chile. The horror the United States inflicted upon Chile in 1973 can never be purged and can never be forgiven.

Hundreds of thousands of deaths took place throughout these countries. Did they take place? And are they in all cases attributable to US foreign policy? The answer is yes they did take place and they are attributable to American foreign policy. But you wouldn't know it.

It never happened. Nothing ever happened. Even while it was happening it wasn't happening. It didn't matter. It was of no interest. The crimes of the United States have been systematic, constant, vicious, remorseless, but very few people have actually talked about them. You have to hand it to America. It has exercised a quite clinical manipulation of power worldwide while masquerading as a force for universal good. It's a brilliant, even witty, highly successful act of hypnosis.

I put to you that the United States is without doubt the greatest show on the road. Brutal, indifferent, scornful and ruthless it may be but it is also very clever. As a salesman it is out on its own and its most saleable commodity is self-love. It's a winner. Listen to all American presidents on television say the words, 'the American people', as in the sentence, 'I say to the American people it is time to pray and to defend the rights of the American people and I ask the American people to trust their president in the action he is about to take on behalf of the American people.'

It's a scintillating stratagem. Language is actually em-ployed to keep thought at bay. The words 'the American people' provide a truly voluptuous cushion of reassurance. You don't need to think. Just lie back on the cushion. The cushion may be suffocating your intelligence and your critical faculties but it's very comfortable. This does not apply of course to the 40 million people living below the poverty line and the 2 million men and women imprisoned in the vast gulag of prisons which extends across the US.

The United States no longer bothers about low intensity conflict. It no longer sees any point in being reticent or even devious. It puts its cards on the table without fear or favour. It quite simply doesn't give a damn about the United Nations, international law or critical dissent, which it regards as impotent and irrelevant. It also has its own bleating little lamb tagging behind it on a lead, the pathetic and supine Great Britain.

What has happened to our moral sensibility? Did we ever have any? What do these words mean? Do they refer to a term very rarely employed these days – conscience? A conscience to do not only with our own acts but to do with our shared responsibility in the acts of others? Is all this dead? Look at Guantanamo Bay. Hundreds of people detained without charge for over three years, with no legal representation or due process, technically detained forever. This totally illegitimate structure is maintained in defiance of the Geneva Convention. It is not only tolerated but hardly thought about by what's called the 'international community'. This criminal outrage is being committed by a country which declares itself to be 'the leader of the free world'. Do we think about the inhabitants of Guantanamo Bay? What does the media say about them? They pop up occasionally – a small item on page six. They have been consigned to a no man's land from which indeed they may never return. At present many are on hunger strike, being force-fed, including British residents. No niceties in these force-feeding procedures. No sedative or anaesthetic. Just a tube stuck up your nose and into your throat. You vomit blood. This is torture. What has the British Foreign Secretary said about this? Nothing. What has the British Prime Minister said about this? Nothing. Why not? Because the United States has said: to criticise our conduct in Guantanamo Bay constitutes an unfriendly act. You're either with us or against us. So Blair shuts up.

The invasion of Iraq was a bandit act, an act of blatant state terrorism, demonstrating absolute contempt for the concept of international law. The invasion was an arbitrary military action inspired by a series of lies upon lies and gross manipulation of the media and therefore of the public; an act intended to consolidate American military and economic control of the Middle East masquerading – as a last resort – all other justifications having failed to justify themselves – as liberation. A formidable assertion of military force responsible for the death and mutilation of thousands and thousands of innocent people.

We have brought torture, cluster bombs, depleted uranium, innumerable acts of random murder, misery, degradation and death to the Iraqi people and call it 'bringing freedom and democracy to the Middle East'.

How many people do you have to kill before you qual-ify to be described as a mass murderer and a war criminal? One hundred thousand? More than enough, I would have thought. Therefore it is just that Bush and Blair be arraigned before the International Criminal Court of Justice. But Bush has been clever. He has not ratified the International Criminal Court of Justice. Therefore if any American soldier or for that matter politician finds himself in the dock Bush has warned that he will send in the marines. But Tony Blair has ratified the Court and is therefore available for prosecution. We can let the Court have his address if they're interested. It is Number 10, Downing Street, London.

Death in this context is irrelevant. Both Bush and Blair place death well away on the back burner. At least 100,000 Iraqis were killed by American bombs and missiles before the Iraq insurgency began. These people are of no moment. Their deaths don't exist. They are blank. They are not even recorded as being dead. 'We don't do body counts,' said the American general Tommy Franks.

Early in the invasion there was a photograph published on the front page of British newspapers of Tony Blair kissing the cheek of a little Iraqi boy. 'A grateful child,' said the caption. A few days later there was a story and photograph, on an inside page, of another four-year-old boy with no arms. His family had been blown up by a missile. He was the only survivor. 'When do I get my arms back?' he asked. The story was dropped. Well, Tony Blair wasn't holding him in his arms, nor the body of any other mutilated child, nor the body of any bloody corpse. Blood is dirty. It dirties your shirt and tie when you're making a sincere speech on television.

The 2,000 American dead are an embarrassment. They are transported to their graves in the dark. Funerals are unobtrusive, out of harm's way. The mutilated rot in their beds, some for the rest of their lives. So the dead and the mutilated both rot, in different kinds of graves.

Here is an extract from a poem by Pablo Neruda, 'I'm Explaining a Few Things':

And one morning all that was burning,
one morning the bonfires
leapt out of the earth
devouring human beings
and from then on fire,
gunpowder from then on,
and from then on blood.
Bandits with planes and Moors,
bandits with finger-rings and duchesses,
bandits with black friars spattering blessings
came through the sky to kill children
and the blood of children ran through the streets
without fuss, like children's blood.

Jackals that the jackals would despise
stones that the dry thistle would bite on and spit out,
vipers that the vipers would abominate.

Face to face with you I have seen the blood
of Spain tower like a tide
to drown you in one wave
of pride and knives.

Treacherous
generals:
see my dead house,
look at broken Spain:
from every house burning metal flows
instead of flowers
from every socket of Spain
Spain emerges
and from every dead child a rifle with eyes
and from every crime bullets are born
which will one day find
the bull's eye of your hearts.

And you will ask: why doesn't his poetry
speak of dreams and leaves
and the great volcanoes of his native land.

Come and see the blood in the streets.
Come and see
the blood in the streets.
Come and see the blood
in the streets!

Let me make it quite clear that in quoting from Neruda's poem I am in no way comparing Republican Spain to Saddam Hussein's Iraq. I quote Neruda because nowhere in contemporary poetry have I read such a powerful visceral description of the bombing of civilians.

I have said earlier that the United States is now totally frank about putting its cards on the table. That is the case. Its official declared policy is now defined as 'full spectrum dominance'. That is not my term, it is theirs. 'Full spectrum dominance' means control of land, sea, air and space and all attendant resources.

The United States now occupies 702 military installations throughout the world in 132 countries, with the honourable exception of Sweden, of course. We don't quite know how they got there but they are there all right.

The United States possesses 8,000 active and operational nuclear warheads. Two thousand are on hair trigger alert, ready to be launched with 15 minute's warning. It is developing new systems of nuclear force, known as bunker busters. The British, ever cooperative, are intending to replace their own nuclear missile, Trident. Who, I wonder, are they aiming at? Osama bin Laden? You? Me? Joe Dokes? China? Paris? Who knows? What we do know is that this infantile insanity – the possession and threatened use of nuclear weapons – is at the heart of present American political philosophy. We must remind ourselves that the United States is on a permanent military footing and shows no sign of relaxing it.

Many thousands, if not millions, of people in the United States itself are demonstrably sickened, shamed and angered by their government's actions, but as things stand they are not a coherent political force – yet. But the anxiety, uncertainty and fear which we can see growing daily in the United States is unlikely to diminish.

I know that President Bush has many extremely competent speech writers but I would like to volunteer for the job myself. I propose the following short address which he can make on television to the nation. I see him grave, hair carefully combed, serious, winning, sincere, often beguiling, sometimes employing a wry smile, curiously attractive, a man's man.

'God is good. God is great. God is good. My God is good. Bin Laden's God is bad. His is a bad God. Saddam's God was bad, except he didn't have one. He was a bar-barian. We are not barbarians. We don't chop people's heads off. We believe in freedom. So does God. I am not a barbarian. I am the democratically elected leader of a freedom-loving democracy. We are a compassionate society. We give compassionate electrocution and compassionate lethal injection. We are a great nation. I am not a dictator. He is. I am not a barbarian. He is. And he is. They all are. I possess moral authority. You see this fist? This is my moral authority. And don't you forget it.'

A writer's life is a highly vulnerable, almost naked activity. We don't have to weep about that. The writer makes his choice and is stuck with it. But it is true to say that you are open to all the winds, some of them icy indeed. You are out on your own, out on a limb. You find no shelter, no protection – unless you lie – in which case of course you have constructed your own protection and, it could be argued, become a politician.

I have referred to death quite a few times this evening. I shall now quote a poem of my own called 'Death'.

> Where was the dead body found?
> Who found the dead body?
> Was the dead body dead when found?
> How was the dead body found?
>
> Who was the dead body?
>
> Who was the father or daughter or brother
> Or uncle or sister or mother or son
> Of the dead and abandoned body?

Was the body dead when abandoned?
Was the body abandoned?
By whom had it been abandoned?

Was the dead body naked or dressed for a journey?

What made you declare the dead body dead?
Did you declare the dead body dead?
How well did you know the dead body?
How did you know the dead body was dead?

Did you wash the dead body
Did you close both its eyes
Did you bury the body
Did you leave it abandoned
Did you kiss the dead body

When we look into a mirror we think the image that confronts us is accurate. But move a millimetre and the image changes. We are actually looking at a never-ending range of reflections. But sometimes a writer has to smash the mirror – for it is on the other side of that mirror that the truth stares at us.

I believe that despite the enormous odds which exist, unflinching, unswerving, fierce intellectual determination, as citizens, to define the *real* truth of our lives and our societies is a crucial obligation which devolves upon us all. It is in fact mandatory.

If such a determination is not embodied in our political vision we have no hope of restoring what is so nearly lost to us – the dignity of man.

Select Bibliography

PRIMARY SOURCES

All Pinter's stage plays are published by Faber and Faber, both in single editions and as Faber Contemporary Classics entitled *Plays One*, *Two*, *Three* and *Four*. *Plays One* contains Pinter's speech at the National Student Drama Festival in 1962; *Plays Two* a conversation with Richard Findlater on 'Writing for Myself' from 1961; *Plays Three* his speech on being awarded the German Shakespeare Prize in Hamburg in 1970; *Plays Four* his speech on receiving the David Cohen British Literature prize in 1995. (Up to 1981, Methuen published the plays singly and in four collected editions.) *One for the Road* was published in a single edition by Methuen with a fascinating conversation between Pinter and Nick Hern about the play and its politics. All the screenplays so far filmed are published by Faber and Faber either in collected editions or – in the case of *The Proust Screenplay*, *The Heat of the Day* and *The Trial* – as single volumes.

Other work by Pinter:
Collected Poems and Prose (Faber and Faber, 1991)
The Dwarfs (Faber and Faber, 1990)
Jimmy (Jonathan Wax for Pendragon Press, 1984; contains Pinter's essay on Jimmy Wax)
A Speech of Thanks (privately printed by Faber and Faber, 1995; contains Pinter's speech on receiving the David Cohen British Literature Prize)
Ten Early Poems (Greville Press Pamphlets, 1992)
100 Poems by 100 Poets, edited by Harold Pinter, Geoffrey Godbert and Anthony Astbury (Methuen and Greville Press, 1986; paperback edition, Faber and Faber, 1991)
99 Poems in Translation, edited by Harold Pinter, Geoffrey Godbert and Anthony Astbury (Faber and Faber, 1994; paperback edition, 1996)

There is, given his alleged reclusivity, a wealth of interview material with Pinter. Most of it, up to 1993, is listed in *File on Pinter*, compiled by Malcolm Page (Methuen, 1993). The most consistently valuable source-book, on which I drew frequently and gratefully, is *Conversations with Pinter* by Mel Gussow (Nick Hern Books, 1994). Of the articles written by Pinter, I recommend two in particular: 'The US Elephant Must Be Stopped', *Guardian*, 5 December 1987, and 'Nicaragua', BBC *World* magazine, March 1992, published by World Publications Ltd. Interviews I found particularly helpful include:
Joan Bakewell, 'In an Empty Bandstand', *Listener*, 6 November 1989
Lawrence M. Bensky, an interview first published in *Paris Review*, Fall 1966, and

reprinted in *Theatre at Work*, edited by Charles Marowitz and Simon Trussler (Methuen, 1967)

Patricia Bosworth, 'Why He Doesn't Write More', *New York Times*, 27 October 1968

Barry Davis, 'The 22 From Hackney to Chelsea', *Jewish Quarterly*, Winter 1991–2

Anna Ford, 'Radical Departures', *Listener*, 27 October 1988

Miriam Gross, 'Pinter on Pinter', *Observer*, 5 October 1980

Philip Purser, 'A Pint with Pinter Helps to Dispel the Mystery', *News Chronicle*, 28 July 1960

Kathleen Tynan, 'In Search of Harold Pinter', *Evening Standard*, 25–6 April 1968

SECONDARY SOURCES

Critical commentary on Pinter overflows the shelves. For the academic specialist, a guide through the forest is supplied by *Harold Pinter: An Annotated Bibliography* by Steven H. Gale (G. K. Hall, 1978). For the Pinter scholar, and the general reader who wishes to keep abreast of the latest Pinter productions and of current thinking on his work, the annual edition of *The Pinter Review* edited by Francis Gillen and Steven H. Gale (University of Tampa Press, Tampa, Florida) is an indispensable vade-mecum. My debt to it is enormous and I list below some of the articles from it consulted and quoted:

Mark Auburn, 'Pinter, Trevor and Quiller "in the Gap"',1994

Katherine H. Burkman, 'Harold Pinter's Death in Venice: *The Comfort of Strangers*', 1992–3

Robert Conklin, '*Old Times* and *Betrayal* as Rorschach Test', 1992–3

Carlos Fuentes, 'Pinter: A Culture of Absence', 1990

Francis Gillen, 'Between Fluidity and Fixity: Harold Pinter's novel *The Dwarfs*', 1990

–'From Chapter Ten of *The Dwarfs* to *Mountain Language*: The Continuity of Harold Pinter', 1988

–'Introduction to Harold Pinter's unpublished novel, *The Dwarfs*', 1987

Ronald Knowles, 'Harold Pinter, Citizen', 1989

Susan Hollis Merritt, 'The Pinter Archive', 1994

Harold Pinter, 'Evacuees', 1994

–'The New World Order' and 'American Football', 1991

Judith Roof, 'Staging the Ideology Behind the Power: Pinter's *One for the Road* and Beckett's *Catastrophe*', 1988

Debra A. Sarbin, '"I Decided She Was": Representation of Women in *The Homecoming*', 1989

David Vilmure, 'Harold Pinter: *Ten Early Poems*', 1992–3

Critical studies of Pinter most frequently consulted were:

William Baker and Stephen Ely Tabachnick, *Harold Pinter* (Oliver and Boyd, 1973)

Katherine H. Burkmann and John L. Kundert Gibbs (eds.), *Pinter at Sixty* (Indiana University Press, 1993; particularly essays by Carey Perloff, Martin Esslin, Jeanne Colleran, Judith Roof, Alice Rayner, Hersh Zeifman and Francis Gillen)

Bernard F. Dukore, *Harold Pinter* (Macmillan, 1982; revised edition, 1988)

Martin Esslin, *Pinter the Playwright* (Methuen, 1982; revised edition of book originally published as *The Peopled Wound*, 1970)

Steven H. Gale (ed.), *Critical Essays on Harold Pinter* (G. K. Hall, 1990; includes valuable essays by Christopher C. Hudgins, Vera M. Jiji, Beverley Houston and Marsha Kinder, Katharine Worth)

Lois Gordon (ed.), *Harold Pinter: A Casebook* (Garland Publishing, 1990; includes crucial essays by Ruby Cohn, Austin E. Quigley, David Lodge, Linda Ben-Zvi, Katherine Burkman and Susan Hollis Merritt, as well as Pauline Flanagan's memories of Ireland and London)

Ronald Knowles, *Understanding Harold Pinter* (University of South Carolina Press, 1995)

John and Anthea Lahr (eds.), *A Casebook on Harold Pinter's The Homecoming* (Davis-Poynter, 1974)

David T. Thompson, *Pinter – The Player's Playwright* (Macmillan, 1985; contains a list of all Pinter's performances in rep)

Simon Trussler, *The Plays of Harold Pinter: an Assessment* (Gollancz, 1973)

Michael Scott (ed.) *Harold Pinter: The Birthday Party, The Caretaker and The Homecoming: a Casebook* (Macmillan, 1986)

Other books consulted and referred to:

Margaret Atwood, *The Handmaid's Tale* (Virago, 1987)
Deirdre Bair, *Samuel Beckett* (Jonathan Cape, 1978)
Charles Baudelaire, *Selected Writings on Art and Literature* (Penguin Books, 1992)
Samuel Beckett, *Murphy* (John Calder, 1958)
Morris Beckman, *The 43 Group* (Centreprise, 1992)
Thomas Bernhard, *Gathering Evidence* (Vintage, 1994)
Jorge Luis Borges, *Labyrinths* (Penguin Books, 1970)
Neville Cardus, *Autobiography* (Collins, 1947)
Humphrey Carpenter, *W. H. Auden* (Oxford University Press, 1981)
David Caute, *Joseph Losey* (Faber and Faber, 1994)
Joseph Conrad, *Victory* (Penguin Books, 1989)
T. S. Eliot, *Four Quartets* (Faber and Faber, 1944)
–*The Waste Land and Other Poems* (Faber and Faber, 1940)
John Elsom (ed.), *Post-War British Theatre Criticism* (Routledge & Kegan Paul, 1981)
Stephen Fay, *Power Play* (Hodder & Stoughton, 1995)
F. Scott Fitzgerald, *The Last Tycoon* (Penguin Books, 1960)
Christopher Fitz-Simon, *The Boys* (Nick Hern Books, 1994)
John Fowles, *The French Lieutenant's Woman* (Jonathan Cape,1969)
Sigmund Freud: Art and Literature (Penguin Books, 1990)
Helen Gardner, *The Art of T. S. Eliot* (Faber and Faber, 1968)
William Goldman, *The Season* (Bantam Books, 1970)
Adam Hall, *The Berlin Memorandum* (Collins, 1965)
Peter Hall's Diaries, ed. John Goodwin (Hamish Hamilton, 1983)
Peter Hall, *Making an Exhibition of Myself* (Sinclair-Stevenson, 1993)
L. P. Hartley, *The Go-Between* (Hamish Hamilton, 1953)
Peter Hennessy, *Never Again* (Jonathan Cape, 1992)
Eric Hobsbawm, *The Age of Extremes* (Michael Joseph, 1994)
Ruth Inglis, *The Children's War* (Collins, 1989)
Kazuo Ishiguro, *The Remains of the Day* (Faber and Faber, 1989)
Bernard Kops, *The World is a Wedding* (MacGibbon and Kee, 1973)

Charles Marowitz, Tom Milne and Owen Hale (eds.), *The Encore Reader* (Methuen, 1965)

Robin Maugham, *The Servant* (Falcon Press, 1948)

Kenneth O. Morgan, *The People's Peace: British History 1945–1990* (Oxford University Press, 1990)

Penelope Mortimer, *The Pumpkin Eater* (Hutchinson, 1962; Penguin Books, 1970)

Nicholas Mosley, *Accident* (Hodder & Stoughton, 1955)

Vladimir Nabokov, *Lolita* (Putnam's, 1955)

Peter Parker (ed.), *The Reader's Companion to the Twentieth-Century Novel* (Fourth Estate and Helicon Publishing, 1994)

Marcel Proust, *Remembrance of Things Past*, translated by C. K. Scott Moncrieff and Terence Kilmartin (Chatto & Windus, 1981–2)

Christopher Ricks, *T. S. Eliot and Prejudice* (Faber and Faber, 1988)

Oliver Sacks, *Awakenings* (revised edition, Picador, 1991)

François Truffaut, *The Films in My Life* (Penguin Books, 1982)

Martin Turnell, *The Novel in France* (Hamish Hamilton, 1950)

Kenneth Tynan, *Tynan Right and Left* (Longman, 1967)

Edmund Wilson, *The Shores of Light* (Farrar, Straus & Giroux, 1952)

Index

100 Poems by 100 Poets (HP co-editor) 270
À la recherche du temps perdu (Proust) 222–33
Abbey Theatre, Dublin 209
Abbott and Costello 90
ABC TV 111
About Time Too (Mortimer) 157
Absence of War, The (Hare) 307
Abu Ghraib 423, 433
Academy of Motion Pictures 429
Accident (Mosley) 184, 185, 187
Adventures in the Screen Trade (Goldman) 362
Afore Night Come (Rudkin) 157
Agate, James 46
Age d'or, L' (Buñuel) 40
Al Quaeda 433
Albee, Edward 276, 412
Alcatl (regiment) 436
Aldwych Theatre, London 140, 142, 156, 157, 162, 171, 175, 176, 179, 196, 197, 198, 200, 201, 203, 209, 219
Alexander, Bill 217, 220
Alexandra Theatre, Birmingham 49, 75
Alexandra Theatre Rep Company 74
All Over (Albee) 276
Allen, Keith 407
Allende, Salvador 234
Almeida Theatre, Islington 245, 325, 330, 336, 338, 343, 347, 355, 403, 407, 411, 413
Ambrose Place, Worthing (No. 14) 131, 148, 155–6
American Embassy, London 305
American Film Theater series 240
American Place Theatre 195
Amis, Martin 327
Amnesty International 298, 335
Amour de Swann, Un (film) 231
Amsterdam 129, 179
Anderson, Michael 150, 184
Angola 370
Annan, Kofi 425
Anouilh, Jean 35

anti-Semitism 17, 18, 19, 81, 368
Antonioni, Michelangelo 240, 314
Any Other Business 88
Apollo Theatre, London 107
Apollo Victoria Theatre, London 291
Archer, Jeffrey 425
Arden, John 128, 203, 333, 363
Ardrey, Robert 168
Argentina 374
Aristophanes 289
Arlott, John 30, 31
Armchair Theatre (ABC TV) 111
Art of Hunger, The (Auster) 95
Artaud, Antonin 203
Arts for Nicaragua Fund 305
Arts Theatre, Cambridge 83
Arts Theatre, London 51, 74, 114, 126, 145, 149
As You Like It (Shakespeare) 46
Ashcroft, Dame Peggy 181, 196, 201, 234, 253, 255, 271, 287, 294
Associated Rediffusion 110, 135, 142
Astbury, Anthony 270, 388
Astoria dance hall, Charing Cross Road, London 48
Atalante, L' (Vigo) 12
Atkins, Eileen 312
Attlee, Clement 152
Atwood, Margaret 304
Aubrey, James 207
Auburn, Mark 184
Auden, W. H. 153, 251, 257, 299
Aurelius, Marcus 34
Auster, Paul 95
Autobiography (Cardus) 245
Avventura, L' (Antonioni) 240
Awakenings (Sacks) 278, 280, 281, 284–5
Ayckbourn, Alan 32, 106, 141, 146, 203

Bacall, Lauren 301
Bach, Johann Sebastian 63, 323

Bacon, Francis 344
Bad Seed, The (March) 359
Baghdad 353
Bailey, Paul 308
Baker, Terence 209
Bakewell, Joan 60, 135, 204, 257, 264–5, 266, 287, 388
Bakewell, Michael 96, 156, 231, 264, 266–7
Balzac, Honoré de 409–10
Bancroft, Anne 158
Barbados 374
Barbican Centre, London 305
Bardach, Emilie 178
Barker, George 12, 270
Barker, Howard 258
Barnes, Kenneth 20
'Baron, David' *see under* Pinter, Harold
Barrault, Jean-Louis 348
Barrie, Sir James M. 151
Barry, Michael 111
Barry O'Brien Company 49
Bart, Lionel 8
Barton, John 83, 175
Bate, Anthony 199
Bates, Alan 127, 129, 222, 297
Battersea Reserve Library, London 43
Baudelaire, Charles 18, 387
Baxter Somerville, J. 85
Bayldon, Geoffrey 156
Bayley, John 372
BBC- *see* British Broadcasting Corporation
BBC2 Play of the Week 267
BBC Audience Research 111
BBC Enterprises 334
BBC Films 348
BBC Radio 30, 73, 101, 111, 124, 131, 142, 323
BBC Radio 3 231, 298, 323, 327, 396, 420
BBC Television 111, 158, 191, 201, 235, 333, 374
BBC Third Programme 96, 100, 111, 115, 156, 159, 196
BBC World Service 89
Beale 55
Beaumarchais, Pierre de 240
Bechtler, Hildegard 429
Beck, Reginald 207
Beckett, Samuel 13, 15, 34, 44, 56, 69–70, 86, 96, 141, 297, 393; attends Jung lecture 68; contribution booed at New York Film Festival 191; HP broadcast reading 323; HP compared to 128, 201; HP discovers 43, 50, 369; HP first meets 354; HP in

plays by 255, 396, 429–30; influences HP 64, 65, 84, 197, 251; and paring down the dramatic situation 180; and *The Proust Screenplay* 223–4; radio and 420
Beckett, Suzanne 422
Beckman, Morris 17
Becque, Henri 149
Bedales 181
Beerbohm, Max 251
Beethoven, Ludwig van 12, 52
Belgrade 402
Bell, Mary Hayley 50
Bell, Tom 111
Belli, Gioconda 336
Bellow, Saul 387
Ben-Zvi, Linda 235–6
Benjamin, Walter 228
Bennett, Arnold 10
Benny, Jack 52
Benthall, Michael 13
Bentley, Eric 89, 138
Berger, John 335
Berger, Senta 182
Bergman, Ingmar 225, 429
Berkeley, Busby 424
Berkoff, Steven 11, 348, 350
Berlin 179, 368
Berlin airlift 21–2
Berlin Film Festival 150
Berlin Memorandum, The (Hall) 181
Berliner Ensemble 50, 368
Bernhard, Thomas 7
Bernhardt, Sarah 251
Berry, Cicely 31
Betrayal (Jones) 267
Bevan, Aneurin 22
Beyond the Fringe 8, 107, 292
Bielefeld 129
Big One, The (anti-nuclear show) 291
Billington, Kevin 92, 220, 252
Biographia Literaria (Coleridge) 205
Birmingham 49, 74, 106
Birmingham Rep 36, 151, 217, 220
Black Comedy (Shaffer) 162
Black and White Milk Bar, Fleet Street, London 31
Blair, Tony 400, 423, 425–6, 438–9
Blakeley, Colin 220
Blakemore, Michael 239
Blasted (Kane) 132
Blithe Spirit (Coward) 255
Blitz! 8
Blitz, the 7, 8, 18
Blixen, Karen 398–400

Bloom, Harold 350
Blow Up (Antonioni) 314
Board of Conscientious Objectors 24
Bogarde, Dirk 152, 153, 185, 188, 208
Bond, Edward 132, 162, 333, 427
Bond, Philip 147
Bono, Laura del 237
Booth Theater, New York 194
Borges, Jorge Luis 106
Boston, Massachusetts 179
Boulting, Ingrid 241
Bournemouth 49, 50, 53, 76
Bowen, Elizabeth 8, 313
Bowles, Peter 418
Box, Sidney 184
Boyer, Charles 231
Boys, The (Fitz-Simon) 37
Bradley, A. C. 107
Bradnum, Frederick 47
Bragg, Melvyn 307
Branagh, Kenneth 418
Brand, Daniel (HP's son): birth (1958) 75;
    changes name from Pinter 255; early
    childhood 92, 93, 131, 265, 277; estranged
    from father 93, 345, 346, 388; gifts as a
    poet 93, 345; in Hanover Terrace 180;
    and his grandparents 339; at Oxford
    University 93, 345; as a recluse 93, 345;
    school education 181, 345; Vivien unable
    to bring up alone 253
Brasseur, Pierre 179
Brawne, Fanny 134
Bray, Barbara 73, 95, 96, 100, 101, 223–4,
    231, 267
Brearley, Joe 11, 13, 20, 22, 155, 156, 163,
    369, 392
Brecht, Bertolt 77, 95, 175, 289
Bremerhaven 179
Brenton, Howard 20, 132, 203
Breton, André 236
Breytenbach, Breyten 384
Bridson, D. G. 100
Brien, Alan 48, 109
Briggs, Johnny 246
Brighton 176, 339, 344
Bristol 64, 71
Bristol Evening Post 72
Bristol Hippodrome 72
Bristol Old Vic 72–3
Bristol Old Vic Theatre School 73
Bristol University Drama Department 66,
    67, 73
British Broadcasting Corporation (BBC)–
    see also under BBC 26, 31, 73, 87, 92, 100,
    101, 251, 252, 266, 307, 309, 323–4, 349,
    351, 424
British Library 320, 352, 353
British Museum 352
British Union of Fascists 17, 33
Brook, Peter 175, 285, 409, 427
Brothers Karamazov, The (Dostoevsky) 15,
    179
Brown, Sally 352
Bryant, Michael 325
Buchan, Rita 75
Bukovsky, Vladimir 234
Bunker, Chris 414
Buñuel, Luis 12, 35, 40, 44, 65, 350
'Burnt Norton' (Eliot) 217
Burra, Edward 29
Burton, Harry 385
Burton, Richard 142
Bury, John 199, 200, 239, 324
Bush, George (Sr) 335, 353
Bush, George W. 423, 438–9, 441
Butler, Robert 408
Butley (Gray; film) 240–41
Butley (Gray; play) 211, 221–2, 240
Butterworth, Jez 400
Byam Shaw, Glen 36
Byrne, Catherine 220, 355

Cabourg, France 231
Caerhays, Cornwall 6, 7
Caine, Michael 109, 418
Cake, Jonathan 385
Cambodia 370
Cambridge 83
Cambridge Daily News 83–4
Cambridge University 20, 94
Cambridge University Magazine 94, 132
Cameron, David 424
Campaign for Nuclear Disarmament 291
Campbell, Archie 100
Campbell, Cheryl 326
Campden Hill Square, London 271
Campton, David 106
Canada 402
Cannes Film Festival 208, 222
Cape Town 129
Caralco 361
Cardenal, Ernesto 336
Cardiff 176
Cardus, Neville 245–6
Cargill 55
Carné, Marcel 222
Carroll, John 252
Carron, Leslie 142

Carry On movies 55
Cary, Joyce 12, 419
Casey, John 369
Casson, Christopher 37
Casson, Sir Hugh 126
Catastrophe (Beckett) 411
Cator Manor, Blackheath 276
Cauté, David 186, 190, 207, 208, 211
Celine, Louis-Ferdinand 236
Central America 329, 373, 374, 393
Central American University, San Salvador 436
Central School of Speech and Drama 31, 36, 38
Chaillet, Ned 323
Channel Four 310, 322, 333
Chaplin, Charlie 300
Chapman, Gerald 219
Cheblak, Abbas 327
Chekhov, Anton 122, 149, 187, 268, 390
Cherry Lane Theatre, New York 142
Cherry Orchard, The (Chekhov) 105
Chesnais, Patrick 356–7
Chesterfield rep 29, 37
Chesterton, G. K. 26
Chevalier, Maurice 197
Chichester Festival Theatre 364, 367, 368
Chien Andalou, Un (Buñuel) 12, 35, 40
Children's War, The (Inglis) 6
Chile 305, 335–6, 370, 436–7
Chimes at Midnight (Welles) 408
China 288, 310, 373, 402, 425
Chiswick High Road, London (No. 373) 75, 92, 114–15, 116, 121, 130, 131, 155
Christie, Agatha 39, 43, 50, 52, 55
Christie, Julie 208, 215, 220, 369
'Church Going' (Larkin) 429
Churchill, Sir Winston 22
Circe and Bravo (Freed) 302–3
Clapp, Susannah 400
Clapton Pond 2, 4, 5, 11, 58
Clark, Alan 335
Clarke, James 395, 420
Clause 28 307, 310, 319
Clayton, Jack 157
Clément, René 222
Cleverdon, Douglas 30
Clinton, Bill 353, 400
Close of Play (Gray) 270, 271
Clough, Arthur Hugh 259
Clurman, Harold 179, 302
Cobbold, Lord 196
Cocktail Party, The (Eliot) 84
Cocteau, Jean 232

Codron, Michael 106; asks HP to direct *Butley* 211; and *The Birthday Party* 74, 75, 83, 85; and *The Caretaker* 126–7; and *The Lover* 145; and *Pieces of Eight* 107; and *Quartermaine's Terms* 271; revues 88; West End début 55, 74; working relationship with HP declines 148–9
Cohen, Alexander 179
Cohn, Ruby 261
Colchester Rep 49, 50, 51, 55
Cold War 21
Coleman, Uncle 29–30
Coleridge, Samuel Taylor 205
Colgan, Michael 354, 356, 411, 420–1
Collected Shakespeare 10, 64
Colleran, Jeanne 311, 312
Columbia Pictures 155, 324
Columbus, Christopher 327
Comedy Theatre, London 197, 324, 326, 338, 352, 369
Common Pursuit (Gray) 297
Commonwealth immigrants 70
Company (Sondheim musical) 195
Compton-Burnett, Ivy 387
Confederation of Analytic Psychologists 402
Congress, US 434–5
Conklin, Robert 214
Connaught Theatre, Worthing 49, 148, 155
Conrad, Joseph 289, 290
Contras (in Nicaragua) 304–5, 435
Conway Hall, Red Lion Square, London 12
Cook, Peter 8, 19, 107
Cook, Robin 402
Copenhagen 179
Cornell, John 219
Cornwall 6, 7, 23, 55
Cortese, Valentina 238
Cottesloe Theatre, South Bank, London 259, 278, 409– *see also* National Theatre
Counterblast (BBC) 402
Courtenay, Tom 20
Coveney, Michael 284, 297, 325
Coward, Noël 53, 95, 276; calls HP 'a Cockney Ivy Compton-Burnett' 387; and *The Caretaker* 128–9, 142; HP compared with 363, 369; HP directs *Blithe Spirit* 255; McMaster and 37; and *No Man's Land* 249; and *Old Times* 214, 219; and *Party Time* 332
Cox, Mrs Joan 366–7
Crabbe, Kerry 374, 417
Craig, Michael 325
Craig, Wendy 153
Cranham, Kenneth 116, 121, 124

Crécy, Odette de 223, 227
Crisp, Quentin 66, 67
Criterion Theatre, London 51, 209, 222, 369
Critic at Large (radio programme) 131
Cronin, A. J. 10
Crosbie, Annette 268
Crowley, John 295
Crucible, The (Miller) 77, 352
CSC Rep 310
Cuba 288
Cuka, Frances 199
Cukor, George 303
Curtis, Alan 88
Cusack, Sinead 421
Cushman, Robert 100, 284, 329–30
Czechoslovakia 373

Daily Express 127, 254
Daily Herald 110, 127
Daily Mail 253, 346
Daily Mirror 110
Daily Telegraph 84, 330, 369, 384
Daily Worker 161
Daish, Judy 73, 361
Daldry, Stephen 383
Daley, Mayor Richard 195
Dance, Charles 428
D'Arcy, Margaretta 203
Darkness at Noon (Koestler) 297
Darlington, W. A. 84, 110
Dateline London (radio programme) 131
Daumier, Honoré 33
David Cohen British Literature Prize 11, 369, 372
Davies, Lindy 215, 220
Day-Lewis, Sean 84
de Jongh, Nicholas 400
de la Tour, Andy 407
De Niro, Robert 241
Death and the Maiden (Dorfman) 328
Death in Venice (Mann) 317
Death in Venice (Visconti) 208
Death of a Salesman (Miller) 252
Death of the Heart, The (Bowen) 314
Dee, Janie 421
Deeds 258
Deep Blue Sea, The (Rattigan) 262
Deighton, Len 181
Delderfield, R. F. 74
Delon, Alain 231
Democratic Convention (Chicago, 1968) 195, 196
Dench, Dame Judi 268, 284–5
Denham, Maurice 100

Dennis, Nigel 106, 128, 212–13
Dent, Alan 13–14
Desmonde, Jerry 91
Devine, George 36
Devotions Upon Emergent Occasions (Donne) 398
Dexter, John 239
Dick Whittington 37
Dickens, Charles 55, 56, 297, 359, 408
Dickins, Anthony 29
Disraeli, Benjamin 398
Diss, Eileen 383
Doctor in the House (Gordon) 74
Dodin, Lev 427
Doll's House, A (Ibsen) 95, 170, 173, 289
Dominican Republic 370
Donmar Theatre, London 400
Donne, John 219, 398
Don't Look Now (du Maurier) 317
Doré, Gustave 336
Dorfman, Ariel 328
Dos Passos, John Roderigo 236
Dostoevsky, Fyodor Mikhailovich 10, 18
Douglas, Lew 22
Douglass, Stuart 161
Drabble, Margaret 307
Dreaming Child, The (Blixen) 398–400
Dromgoole, Patrick 73
Drummond, John 84
du Garde Peach, L. 49, 75
du Maurier, Daphne 317
Dublin 37, 132, 271, 356
Dublin International Writers' Festival 92, 353, 385
Dubliners (Joyce) 209
Duchess of Malfi, The (Webster) 13, 30, 382
Duchess Theatre, Catherine Street, London 13, 114, 128, 209
Duino Elegies (Rilke) 281
Duke of York's Theatre, London 37, 352
Dukore, Bernard 168
Dunaway, Faye 302
Duncan, Lindsay 383, 407
Düsseldorf 129
Dworkin, Ronald 306
Dyer, Danny 407

'East Coker' (Eliot) 248
East, Robert 270
East End, London 8, 9, 17, 19, 162, 344
East Timor 335, 370, 373
Eastbourne 49, 75, 76, 131
Eddington, Paul 336–8, 413
Ede, Chuter 17

Edgar, David 50, 203, 327
Edinburgh Film Festival 150
Edwards, Hilton 37
El Salvador 335, 370, 436
Eliot, T. S. 10, 173, 248, 406, 413; HP reads
  aloud to Pauline Flanagan 40; HP tours
  London churches with choruses from *The
  Rock* 21; influences HP 64, 194, 242, 251,
  390; 'objective correlative' 63
Elstree Studios 207
Embassy Theatre, Swiss Cottage 47
EMI 207
Empson, William 270
Encore (theatre magazine) 88, 106, 128
Encounter 128, 357
Endgame (Beckett) 242, 246, 424
Enfant, Sauvage L', (Truffaut) 399
Enfants du Paradis, Les (Carné) 222
Engel, Susan 72–3, 88, 113
English Stage Company 74
Enter a Fox (Gray) 403
Entertainer, The (Osborne) 77
Entertaining Mr Sloane (Orton) 177
Epitaph for George Dillon (Osborne) 75
Epstein, Jason 370
Essen 129
Esslin, Martin 69, 122, 136, 168, 175, 357
Ettlinger, Max 39
Europe 428
European Broadcasting Union 158
Europe Theatre Prize 427
Evening Standard 84, 180, 288, 313, 321, 354,
  372
Evening Standard Award for Best Play (*The
  Caretaker*, 1960) 130
Everett, Rupert 317
Everyman (Roth) 395
Ewart, Gavin 345
Exiles (Joyce) 205–6, 209–11
Eyre, Richard 258
Eysenck, Professor Hans 366, 367

Faber and Faber 422
Fairbanks, Douglas, Snr 300
Fairmead Court, Kew 131, 155
Falklands War 290–91
Farmer, Sir George 196
Fascism 33, 204; *Ashes to Ashes* and 377, 380,
  383; in Hackney 17–18, 19, 27; *The Heat
  of the Day* and 313, 314; *Party Time* and
  333–4; Pirandello and 94; *The Remains of
  the Day* and 324; *Reunion* and 315; and a
  self-preoccupied wealthy élite 331;
  Tennessee Williams and 302

Father, The (Strindberg) 276
Fay, Stephen 291
Feast, Michael 251
Ferguson, Niall 425
Ferris, Paul 111
Fiedler, Leslie 359
Field, Sid 91
Figaro, Le 130
Film (Beckett) 191
Film Four 409
Financial Times 84, 128, 153, 284, 297, 330,
  355, 384
Finney, Albert 20, 300
Firth, Colin 326
Fitz-Simon, Christopher 37
Fitzgerald, Scott 241
Flanagan, Pauline 39–41, 53, 79, 218, 255
Fleming, Ian 181
Flint (Mercer) 209
Follett, Ken 305
Ford, Ford Madox 259
Forrest, Michael 147
Fort Benning, Georgia 436
43 Group 17, 19
43 Group, The (Beckman) 17
Foster, Barry 43, 45; dreams with HP of
  being famous classical actors 45; on HP at
  Central School of Speech and Drama
  31–2; on HP's artistic sensibility 44; and
  McMaster's company 38–9; as a Maudsley
  'guinea-pig' 367; in *Mountain Language*
  313; in *A Night Out* 111; in *Party Time*
  331; in *The Rear Column* 271; in *A Slight
  Ache* 97; in *The Trojan War Will Not Take
  Place* 291
Foster, Frank 246
Fouéré, Olwen 220, 355
Four Quartets, The (Eliot) 242
Fowles, John 272, 274, 275
Fox, Edward 418
Fox, James 153, 324
Foxwell, Ivan 181
Frankfurt 89
Franklin family 5
Franklin, Rose *see* Moskowitz
Franks, Tommy 439
Franz Kafka Prize 427
Fraser, Lady Antonia (HP's second wife) 12,
  252, 253, 277, 278, 291, 345, 372, 374; at
  Caerhays 7; contrast with Vivien over
  politics 287–8; goes into hiding with HP
  254; HP's affair with 234, 252, 253; and
  HP's family history 2; on HP's home in
  Hanover Terrace 180, 245; on HP's

integrity 390; on HP's memory 1;
influence on HP's writing 235, 255, 261,
403–4; and June 20 Society 307, 308;
marries HP 271–2; on *Moonlight* 339,
342–3, 344; in protest over Nicaragua 305
Fraser, Hugh 253
Frazer, Sir James 168
Fred and Julia Neilson Terry company 36–7
Freed, Donald 302, 303, 344, 397
French Lieutenant's Woman, The (Fowles)
272, 274
Freud, Sigmund 112, 326, 344
Friedkin, William 209
Friends, The (Wesker) 203
Friends of Turkey 298
From Russia with Love (Fleming) 181
Fuentes, Carlos 321–2, 425
Funeral in Berlin (Deighton) 181
Furtwängler, Wilhelm 365

Gabin, Jean 12
Gaieties Cricket Club 388–9, 429
Gale, John 142
Gale, Steven H. 215, 216
Galileo (Brecht) 77, 352
Galloway, George, MP 305
Gambon, Michael 214, 302, 313, 314, 411,
421, 428
Garbo, Greta 231
Gardner, Helen 242
Garel-Jones, Tristan 336
Gascoigne, Bamber 84, 149, 156
Gascoyne, David 270
Gate Theatre, Dublin 42–3, 201, 220, 295,
354, 393, 395, 400, 411, 420
Gathering Evidence (Bernhard) 7
Gee, Mr (schoolteacher) 19
Geneva 179
Georgia Story 51
German Shakespeare Prize 204
Giacometti, Alberto 236
Gide, André 348
Gielgud, Sir John 251, 252, 285, 337, 411,
413
Gielgud, Lewis 251
Gielgud, Val 95, 96, 267
Gielgud Theatre, London 403
Gilbert, James 126
Gill, Peter 209
Gillen, Francis 62, 64, 350, 398, 399
Gilliatt, Penelope 125, 153, 171–2, 175,
176–7, 190
Gilman, Richard 179
Gingold, Hermione 197

Girard, René 138
Giraudoux, Jean 290, 291
Girls of Slender Means, The (Spark) 12
Giscard d'Estaing, Valéry 231
Glanville, Brian 110
Glasgow Citizens Theatre 409
Glass Menagerie, The (Williams) 257
Glasshouse Productions 193
Globe Theatre, London 270
Glyndebourne Opera House 392
Go-Between, The (Hartley) 206, 209, 399
Goalen, Barbara 113
Godbert, Geoffrey 270, 388
Goethe, Johann Wolfgang von 117
Golden Bough, The (Frazer) 168
Golden Touch, The (musical by More and
Gilbert) 126
Goldhagen, Daniel 385
Golding, William 359
Goldman, William 194–5, 362
Goldsmith, Oliver 145
Goldstein, Michael (Mick): on an encounter
with a Fascist gang 17–18; and
Beethoven's use of silence 52; and *The
Dwarfs* 58, 69; friendship important to
HP 11; and *The Homecoming* 164; and
HP's relationship with Pauline Flanagan
40; lives in Australia 11; and male
friendship 138; as a member of the
Hackney gang 11, 12; and *Moonlight* 340;
and music 51–2, 58; and private space 27;
watches cricket at Lord's with HP 14
Gordimer, Nadine 372
Gordon, Giles 297
Gordon, Lois 98
Gothenburg 179
Government Communications Headquarters
(GCHQ) 310
Graham, W. S. 270
Grainger, Gawn 333, 337–8, 420
Granada 313
Grand Prix (Palme D'Or) (Cannes Film
Festival) 208
Grand Prix Spécial du Jury (Cannes Film
Festival) 190
Granger, Derek 84, 86
Granta 149
Grass, Günther 365
Gray, Simon 178, 211, 240, 253, 270, 271;
first memory of HP 221; and HP's
directing 222, 395, 400, 403, 418; and
media's pursuit of HP 254; and off-stage
dramas 297; on *Unnatural Pursuits* 389
Greene, Graham 329, 393

Greenwich Theatre 276
Greer, Dr Germaine 307
Grenada 370
Greville Press 29, 270, 336
Griffith, D. W. 300
Griffiths, Trevor 203
Grocers' Company 11
Gross, John 117
Grossman, Jan 348
Groucho Club, Soho 308
Grout, James 21, 302
Grove Press 191
Grünewald, Mathias 365
Guantanamo Bay 423, 437–8
Guardian 129, 149, 176, 238, 278, 298, 305, 329, 337, 373, 386– *see also Manchester Guardian*
Guardsman, The (Molnár) 149
Guare, John 412
Guatemala 305, 335, 370, 436
Guild of British Television Producers and Directors 149
Guinness, Sir Alec 183
Gulf War 327, 329–30
Gussow, Mel 79, 206, 211, 212, 216, 222, 257, 267, 286, 303, 309, 412

H-Blocks (Maze Prison) 105
Hackney 26, 396; *The Caretaker* shot on location in 142; Fascism in 17–18, 19, 27; *The Homecoming* rooted in 162; HP born in 1; HP evokes 2; as HP's retreat 21; as a Pinter Eden 5, 34, 58, 83; racism in 70
Hackney Boys' Club 11, 12, 19, 59, 235
Hackney Downs 11, 392
Hackney Downs Grammar School 8, 10–13, 15, 19
Hackney Empire 90
Hackney Gazette 17
Hackney Public Library 10, 21
Haigh, Kenneth 39
Hailsham, Lord 70
Haiti 370
Hall, Adam 181–4
Hall, David 74, 85
Hall, John 72–3
Hall, Sir Peter 51, 142, 240; and *Betrayal* 259, 260, 261; and *The Homecoming* 162–3, 164, 168, 169, 175–6, 179, 324, 325; and HP as associate director at the National Theatre 234; on HP as a 'masterly poet' 387; HP's loyalty to 156–7, 239, 389; and *A Kind of Alaska* 284; and *Landscape* 196, 199, 201, 203; and *Macbeth* 194; and *No*

Man's Land 245, 246, 250–51, 252, 253, 413; and *Old Times* 216, 217, 219–20, 238; and *Other Places* 278; and a playwright's way of talking 16; and *The Trojan War Will Not Take Place* 290; working relationship with HP 141–2, 149, 150, 203, 291, 324
Hall, Willis 128
Halliwell, Kenneth 326
Haltrecht, Montague 177
Hamburg 64, 204, 205, 209, 224, 250, 368
Hamilton, Michael 52
Hamilton, Patrick 43, 44
Hamlet (Kozintsev) 408
Hamlet (Shakespeare) 34, 39, 59, 63, 295–6
Hamlett, Dilys 34–6, 218–19, 219
Hammerstein, James 209
Hampstead Cricket Club 389
Hampstead Theatre 270, 302, 367
Hampstead Theatre Club 109
Hampstead Town Hall 219
Hancock, Sheila 107
Handmaid's Tale, The (Atwood) 304
Hang of the Gaol, The (Barker) 258
Hanks, Robert 366
Hanover 129
Hanover Terrace, London 160, 180, 181, 211, 245, 253, 276, 277
Hanson, Harry 53
Harcombe, Sebastian 409
Hard-Boiled Egg, The (Ionesco) 191
Hare, David 20, 203, 258, 307, 410, 429
Hari, Johan 424
Harold Pinter Society 410
Harris, Roberta 276
Hartley, L. P. 206, 208, 209, 222
Harwood, Ronald 45–7, 53, 199–200, 364–7, 390, 393
Hauser, Frank 30, 31
Havel, Vaclav 255, 402
Hawthorne, Nigel 129
Haygarth, Tony 312, 368
Heat of the Day, The (Bowen) 313
Heath-Stubbs, John 270
Hebbel, Friedrich 130
Helpmann, Robert 13
Helsinki 179
Hemingway, Ernest 10, 77, 84, 90, 193
Henry IV Part One (Shakespeare) 213
Henry IV Part Two (Shakespeare) 109
Henry V (Olivier) 408
Henry VIII (Shakespeare) 31
Hepburn, Katharine 317
Herbert Read Memorial Lecture 322

Here We Come Gathering (King) 48
Herrick, Robert 416
Hewes, Henry 169, 174
Heyman, John 207
Hickey, William 254
Hicks, Greg 325
Higgins, Aidan 222, 267
Hille, Anastasia 420
Hindemith, Paul (*Mathis der Mahler*) 365
Hiroshima Mon Amour (Resnais) 225
Hirst, George 245, 246
His Majesty's Theatre, London 37
Hitchcock, Alfred 28, 48
Hitchcock, Jane Stanton 322
Hitchens, Christopher 425
Hitler, Adolf 81, 184, 315, 316, 365, 370,
   374, 424
Hizmet, Nazim 327
Hoban, Russell 299
Hobsbawm, Eric 234, 291, 327
Hobson, Harold 74, 85, 86, 176, 240, 249,
   264
Hochwalder, Fritz 158
Hodge, Douglas 337, 343
Hodge, Patricia 267, 314
Hoffmann, E. T. A. 391
Hoffmann, Stanley 402
Hoggart, Richard 140
Hollow, The (Christie) 50
Holm, Ian 201, 343, 355, 412
Holroyd, Michael 209–10, 307
Homme Qui, L' 285
Honduras 335
Hong Kong Festival 252
Hope-Wallace, Philip 149, 176
Hopkins, John 240
Hordern, Sir Michael 141, 209
A Horse! A Horse! (du Garde Peach) 49, 75
Horse's Mouth, The (Cary) 12, 419
Howard, Anthony 306
Howard, Michael 386
Howitt, Peter 313, 326
Huddersfield Rep 49, 58
Hudgins, Christopher C. 192
Hughes, Alan 214
Human Rights Watch 335, 429
Hungary 373
Hunter, N. C. 86
Hurry on Down (Wain) 56
Hurt, John 147, 148, 300
Hussein, Saddam 327, 400, 433, 440
Hutchinson, Lloyd 412
Hutton, Len 14
Huxley, Aldous 222

Hyde Park 417
Hyland, Frances 21

I am a Camera (Isherwood) 53
Ibsen, Henrik 95, 100, 122, 124, 177–8, 210,
   213, 257, 325, 355, 367
ICA (Institute of Contemporary Arts) 322
Iceman Cometh, The (O'Neill) 122
Illiers, France 231
Illingworth, Raymond 385
'I'm Explaining a Few Things' (Neruda)
   439–40
Imperial College Film Society 12
Importance of Being Earnest, The (Wilde) 39,
   213, 239–40, 257
In Town Tonight (radio programme) 131
Inadmissible Evidence (Osborne) 221
Incident at Tulse Hill (East) 270
Independent 313, 329, 330, 337, 365, 385
Independent on Sunday 322, 328, 331, 366
Index on Censorship 306
Indonesia 370
Inglis, Ruth 6
Innocents, The 41, 255, 337
Inspector Calls, An (Priestley) 43
International Court of Justice, The Hague
   305, 327, 425, 438
Intimate Theatre, Palmer's Green 49, 74, 75
involuntary memory 225
Ionesco, Eugène 74, 84, 94, 100, 127, 191
IRA 271, 307, 370
Iraq 370, 400, 421, 426, 427, 433, 438–40
Irons, Jeremy 231, 267, 268, 271, 421, 428
Ishiguro, Kazuo 324
Israel 327, 345, 372
Israeli Embassy, London 345
Istanbul Journalists' Association 297
ITV 110
Ivory, James 324
Izzard, Bryan 100

Jackson, Glenda 300
Jacobi, Derek 364, 421
James, Henry 74, 359
Janácek, Leoš 51–2
Jane Eyre (Brontë) 53
Jarrott, Charles 161
Jarvis, Martin 291
Jay, Margaret 307
Jayston, Michael 325
Jellicoe, Ann 86
Jenkins, Peter 306–7, 308
Jesuits 436
Jewel, Jimmy 77

Jewel and Warriss 77, 90, 91
Jewish Chronicle 109, 163, 177, 345
Jews: Ashkenazic 2; marriage to a non-Jew
  40–41, 53–4, 163–4, 177; Sephardic 2
Jhabvala, Ruth Prawer 324
Jiji, Vera M. 168
Johnson, Claudia 403
Johnson, Frank 308, 369–70
Johnson, Jill 50, 51
Johnson, Richard 300
Johnson, Dr Samuel 389
Johnstone, Iain 350
Jones, David: and *Betrayal* 267; and *The
  Birthday Party* 106–7, 146; and *The
  Homecoming* 175–6; and *The Hothouse*
  366; and *Landscape* 199; and *Langrishe Go
  Down* 222, 267, 268, 269–70; and *No
  Man's Land* 356; and *Old Times* 214, 217,
  220, 302; and *The Trial* 348, 350
Jones, John Bush 246
Joseph, Stephen 31, 32, 106
Jour s'élève, Le (Carné) 12
Joyce, James 35, 282, 406; and *Family Voices*
  279; HP directs *Exiles* 205–6, 209–11; HP
  writes on Joyce in school magazine 15;
  HP's parents and *Ulysses* 10; influence on
  HP 64; and the interior monologue 191
Judaism: Passover 4; Yom Kippur 54
Juilliard School 412
June 20 Society 307–9, 321
Jung, Carl Gustav 68

Kael, Pauline 182, 208, 274
Kafka, Franz 23, 49, 393; and Dickens 297;
  HP adapts *The Trial* 348–51; HP's
  childhood reading of 15, 18; influence on
  HP 64, 84, 127–8; Kahane, Eric 356,
  357–8
Kaleidoscope (Radio 4) 59–60
Kane, Sarah 132
Kaplan Penthouse 412
Karajan, Herbert von 366
Kazan, Elia 241
Keaton, Buster 191
Keats, John 134, 202
Kemal, Yasher 299
Kemp-Welch, Joan 110, 142
Kennan, George 335
Kennedy, John Fitzgerald 288
Kenny, Sir Anthony 352
Kent, Jonathan 336
Kerr, Walter 179
Killers, The (Hemingway) 77, 84, 90, 193
Killers, The (Siegel) 77

King, Philip 48
King Lear (Brook) 409
King Lear (Shakespeare) 297, 365, 407
King's Theatre, Hammersmith 45, 53
Kingsley, Ben 267, 300
Knowles, Ronald 77, 314
Koestler, Arthur 297
Kohl, Margie 282
Kohler, Estelle 220
Konapinski, Julie 19
Kops, Bernard 8
Kosovo 402
Kozintsev, Grigori 408
Krapp's Last Tape (Beckett) 396, 429–30
Kroll, Jack 194
Kubrick, Stanley 358, 360
Kundera, Milan 313
Kurdish language 309, 310
Kurds 298, 299, 373; and London
  production of *Mountain Language* 313
Kustow, Michael 409
Kuwait 327

Labour Party 400
Lahr, John 176, 339, 343, 369
Laing, R. D. 192
LAMDA 409
Lane, John Francis 238
Langrishe Go Down (Higgins) 222
Laos 370
Larkin, Philip 143, 429
Last Adventures of the Dog Berganza, The
  (Hoffmann) 391
Last Metro, The (Truffaut) 365
Last Tycoon, The (Fitzgerald) 241
Late Middle Classes (Gray) 403, 418
Late Night Line-Up (television programme)
  204
Late Show, The (BBC TV programme) 333
Latin America 373
Launceston Place, South Kensington 255
Laura Pels Theatre, Broadway 368
Law, B. J. (Jimmy) 40, 60, 191; comments on
  The Birthday Party and *The Dumb Waiter*
  90; and Dilys Hamlett 34–5; and Fascist
  gang incident 18; on HP 15; and HP in
  academia 20; and music 12
Law, Jude 418
Lawrence, D. H. 10, 12
Lawson, Leigh 215
Lawson, Mark 330
Le Carré, John 181
Lea Bridge Road *shul*, east London 9
Lean, David 317

Lefeaux, Charles 100
Lefevre, Robin 412
Lehmann, Beatrix 83
Leicester 106
Leigh, Vivien 53, 134
Leighton, Margaret 208
Lerner, Alan 197
Lesser, Anton 356
Lester, Richard 289
Letelier, Orlando 303, 335
Leveaux, David 63, 325, 326, 336, 340, 342, 344, 413
Levin, Bernard 127–8
Life Support (Gray) 400
Limerick 38
Lincoln Center, New York 209, 395, 411–12
Lipman, V. D. 2
Lipstein, Isidor (HP's uncle) 3
Lipstein, Sophie (née Pinter; HP's aunt) 3, 4
Lipstein, Steve (son of Sophie and Isidor Lipstein) 3
Lipstein, Sue (HP's cousin) 3
Listener 1, 100
Living Theatre 195, 203
Livingstone, Ken 417
Lodge, David 108
Loewe, Frederick 197
Lolita (Nabokov) 358–9, 360
London County Council 11, 17, 20
London Echo: An Interview with John Wain (radio programme) 131
London Independent Productions 184, 190
London Palladium 52
London Review of Books 329
Long Day's Journey into Night (O'Neill) 257
Longford, Lord 255
Longford family 280
Longford Trust 429
Look Back in Anger (Osborne) 74, 75, 84, 86, 363
Lord Malquist and Mr Moon (Stoppard) 58
Lord of the Flies, The (Golding) 359
Lord's Cricket Ground 14, 21
Los Angeles 214, 302
Losey, Joseph: and *Accident* 184, 185, 186, 189; and *The French Lieutenant's Woman* 274; and *The Go-Between* 206, 207, 208; and HP's political awareness 287; and involuntary memory 225; Pinter and Losey as 'the perfect team' 208, 398; and *The Proust Screenplay* 222, 223, 231, 277; and *The Servant* 142, 150, 152, 153
Love from a Stranger (Christie) 39, 50
Lovibond, Andrew 276, 277

Lunghi, Cherie 325
Lyne, Adrian 358, 361
Lyon, Sue 358
Lyric Theatre, Hammersmith 35, 74, 83, 84, 85, 107, 110, 293, 297
Lyric Theatre, Shaftesbury Avenue 322
Lyttelton Theatre, South Bank, London 258, 259, 270, 290, 309, 325, 356, 415- *see also* National Theatre

Macaulay, Alastair 355, 384, 397, 408, 413
Macbeth (Shakespeare) 13–14, 38–9, 194, 201
McCann, Mary 351
McCormick, F. J. 216
McDiarmid, Ian 336
Macdonald, Richard 153
McElhinney, Ian 355
McEwan, Ian 308, 317–20, 327
McGill, Donald 76
McGrath, John 20, 333
McGuinness, Frank 421
McLachlan, Kyle 350
McLean, Fiona 323
MacLiammoir, Micheal 37
McMaster, Anew 26, 36–9, 43–7, 51, 52, 64, 83, 367, 368, 408
McPherson, Conor 421
McWhinnie, Donald 30, 87, 95, 96, 111, 126, 127, 267
Magee, Patrick 39, 43, 156, 211, 278, 368
Mailer, Norman 196
Malawian Embassy, London 373
Malinowski, Bronislaw 108
Malle, Louis 359
Mamet, David 351–2, 361, 411
Man and Superman (Shaw) 407
Man in the Glass Booth, The 193, 194, 195
Man who Mistook his Wife for a Hat, The (Sacks) 285
Manchester Guardian 84- *see also Guardian*
Mankiewicz, Joseph L. 418
Mann, Joe *see* Moskowitz, Judah
Mann, Klaus 365
Mann, Richard *see* Moskowitz, Harry
Mann, Thomas 317
Mansfield Park (Rozema) 403
Manzi, Carlo 110
Mao Tse-tung 184, 370
Marat/Sade (Weiss) 157
Marber, Patrick 410
March, William 359
Marcos, Imelda 322
Marcus, David 43

Marielle, Jean-Pierre 356
Marks, Louis 348
Marlowe, Christopher 118
Marowitz, Charles 18
Marriage of Figaro, The (Beaumarchais) 240
Marriott, R. D. A. 96
Marx Brothers 40
Maryknoll 436
Maschwitz, Eric 215
Massey, Anna 284, 343
Master Builder, The (Ibsen) 178
Mattes, Eva 368
Maudsley Hospital, London 102, 366–7
Maugham, Robin 150, 153, 184
Maugham, W. Somerset 95, 390
Mauritius 338
Meiselas, Susan 334
Melville, Herman 100, 196
Mendes, Sam 80, 356, 389
Mephisto (Mann) 365
Mercer, David 204, 209, 287
Merchant, Ismail 324
Merchant, Vivien (HP's first wife) 74, 84, 93, 131, 160; in *Accident* 188; birth of Daniel 75; career 53, 54, 72, 135, 148, 194, 201, 252, 276, 277; and *The Caretaker* 114, 116, 133; in *The Collection* 133; contrast with Antonia over politics 287–8; death 276, 278; dichotomy within 134–5; and divorce 271–2, 276; in *The Homecoming* 133, 171; honeymoon in Mevagissey 7, 55; HP's women 'illuminated' by 134, 278; and *Landscape* 201–2; life after her divorce 276–7, 278; in *The Lover* 133, 145–9; marriage disintegrates *see under* Pinter, Harold; marries HP 53–4; and National Gallery recital 252, 253; in *Night* 197; in *A Night Out* 111, 113, 133; in *Night School* 133; in *Old Times* 216, 220; personality 112–13, 133–5, 173, 277; in *A Slight Ache* 100, 133; in *Sweet Bird of Youth* 301; in *Tea Party* 133; in *The Room* 109, 133; threatens to cite Antonia in a divorce 253, 254; use of stage-name 52–3
Mermaid Theatre, London 205
Messagero, Il 238
Metcalf, Father John 434
Mevagissey 6, 7, 23
MGM 207
MI5 307
Midsummer Night's Dream, A (Shakespeare) 32, 289

Miles, Michael 77
Mill, John Stuart 306
Millar, Ronald 50
Miller, Arthur 77, 297–8, 412
Miller, Jonathan 239
Milne, Tom 232
Milosevic, Slobodan 402–3
Milton, John 306
Minerva Theatre 366
Minetti, Bernhard 179
Mirren, Helen 317
Misanthrope, Le (Molière) 390
Miss Julie (Strindberg) 268
Mitchell, Denis 31
Mitchell, Warren 325
Mnouchkine, Ariane 427
Modern Drama (Jones) 246
Mojo (Jez Butterworth) 400
Molière 117, 368, 390
Molina, Alfred 326
Molnár, Ferenc 149
Moon is Blue, The 51
Morahan, Christopher 8, 209, 235, 237, 314, 374, 417
More, Julian 126
Morgan, Kenneth O. 70
Morley, Sheridan 302–3
Mortimer, Jennifer 16, 58, 59, 61, 65, 71, 99, 218
Mortimer, John 99, 307
Mortimer, Penelope 157, 307, 308
Moskowitz, Ben (HP's uncle) 3
Moskowitz, Fay (HP's aunt) 3
Moskowitz, Harry (HP's maternal grandfather) 3
Moskowitz, Judah (HP's uncle) 3–4, 164
Moskowitz, Lou (HP's uncle) 4
Moskowitz, Rose (née Franklin; HP's maternal grandmother) 3, 4, 9
Moskowitz family 4, 5, 9, 390
Mosley, Nicholas 184, 185, 186–7, 189
Mosley, Sir Oswald 17, 70
Mother, The (play) 47
Mother Courage (Brecht) 95
Mountbatten, Louis, 1st Earl Mountbatten of Burma 271
Mozart, Wolfgang Amadeus 149, 261
Muller, Heiner 427
Munich 179
Murat, Bernard 356
Murder at the Vicarage (Christie) 48
Murphy (Beckett) 43, 50, 69–70
Murry, John Middleton 222

Nabokov, Vladimir 358–61
Naipaul, V. S. 369
Naked Civil Servant, The 66
Nash, John 6
Nation, the 179
National Film Finance Corporation 184
National Gallery, London 252, 253
National Liberal Club 48, 406
National Service 21, 24
National Student Drama Festival 73, 132
National Theatre of Craiova, Romania 114
National Theatre, London 80, 114, 201, 234, 239, 240, 250, 251, 255, 258, 259, 271, 278, 284, 290, 291, 306, 312, 313, 389, 409, 413
NATO 402
Nazism 315, 316, 385–6
Nelson, Mr (teacher) 6
Neruda, Pablo 439–40
New Ambassadors Theatre, London 412
New Shorter Oxford English Dictionary, The 1
New Statesman 307
New Tenant, The (Ionesco) 94
New Theatre, London 37
New Theatre Magazine 128, 132
New York 179, 222, 433
New York Film Festival 191
New York Review of Books 184, 212–13, 306, 329, 370, 371, 402
New York Times 179, 195, 206
New Yorker 274, 330, 339, 369
Newman, Cardinal 13, 249
Newman, Sydney 158
News Chronicle 13, 127
Newsnight (BBC) 422, 424, 430
Newsweek 179, 194
Newton, Robert 216
Next of Kin (Hopkins) 240
Nicaragua 303–6, 322, 327, 334, 370, 423, 434–6
Nicaragua Solidarity Campaign 327
Nicaragua Water Fire pamphlet 336
Nichols, Mike 324, 425
Nichols, Peter 307
Nichols, Thelma 307
Nigerian Embassy, London 373
Nightingale, Benedict 176, 244, 252, 324, 326, 337, 346–7, 366
99 Poems in Translation (HP co-editor) 270
Nis 402
Nixon, Richard 303
Nobel, Alfred 424
Nobel Prize for Literature 395, 396, 421–7
Nolan, Joe 83, 368
Notting Hill, London 70

Notting Hill Gate 74, 75
Nottingham 53
Nottingham Playhouse 258
Nunn, Trevor 175, 239, 409

O'Brien, Barry 52
O'Brien, Edna 134, 136, 278, 311, 324
Observer 111, 121, 142, 156, 171, 176, 284, 325, 329, 352–3, 355
O'Casey, Sean 95
Odd Man Out (Reed) 215, 216, 237
Odeon Kensington 190
Odessa 2, 3
Oedipus at Colonus (Sophocles) 47
Of Mice and Men (Steinbeck) 66
Official Secrets Act 306, 310
Ohio Impromptu (Beckett) 199
Old Masters (Gray) 418
Old Vic 45, 239, 240, 244
Old Vic School 34, 36
Oldman, Gary 326
Oleanna (Mamet) 351–2, 364
Olivier, Sir Laurence 37, 75, 127, 231, 239, 408, 418
Olivier Theatre, South Bank, London 417– see also National Theatre
Olvidados, Los (Buñuel) 40
Olympia Press 358
O'Neill, Eugene 122, 123, 167, 257
Open Theatre 195
Opera House, Cork 37
Operation Desert Storm 330
Ormond, Julia 398
Orphée (Cocteau) 232
Orton, Joe 103, 110, 177, 326
Osborne, John 77, 84, 125, 134, 221; as a romantic 88, 363, 392; scandalises the Lord Chamberlain 162; and the state of Western civilisation 203; *Under Plain Cover* compared with *The Lover* 143; and weekly rep 45
Othello (Shakespeare) 36, 39, 239
Otherwise Engaged (Gray) 253, 255
O'Toole, Fintan 355
O'Toole, Peter 20
Our Mutual Friend (Dickens) 408
Owen, Alun 53
Owen, Wilfred 352
Oxford 83, 84
Oxford Mail 84
Oxford Times 84
Oxford University 20
Oz, Professor Avraham 395, 430

Pack, Roger Lloyd 297, 333, 420
Page, Stephen 424
Pagett, Nicola 302
Painter, George 232
Pakistan 371
Palace Court, Bournemouth 49, 52
Palace Theatre, Watford 301, 403
Palmer's Green, north London 49, 53
Pamuk, Orhan 422, 425
Panama 370
Paris 130, 179, 231
Paris Review 57
Parisienne, La (Becque) 149
Paterson, Don 416
Patriot for Me, A (Osborne) 162
Pavilion Theatre, Torquay 49, 67
Paz, Octavia 219
Peacock, Trevor 356
Pearson, Richard 83
Peck, Bob 356
Peckinpah, Sam 353–4
Peer Gynt (Ibsen) 213
PEN 255, 297, 365, 373
Pennington, Michael 149, 220, 295, 354, 355
Pentecost (Edgar) 50
People Today (radio programme) 131
People's Palace, Mile End Road, London 12, 13
Percival, Ron: appearance 12, 14, 33, 316;
    and *The Dwarfs* 12, 58, 59, 417; in the
    Hackney gang 12, 15; HP's portrait of
    33–4; HP's sexual rivalry with 16, 316; in
    later life 316; personality 12, 14, 28, 33
Peril at End House (Christie) 50
Perkins, Anthony 348–9
Perloff, Carey 310, 311
Peter, John 245, 326, 347, 355, 410
Peter Hall's Diaries (Hall) 140, 239, 246, 251,
    253, 291
Peter Pan (Barrie) 37
Peterborough 53
Peters, Ant 276
Philippines 370
Phipps, Diana 254
Piccadilly Theatre, London 126
Pickford, Mary 300
Pigott-Smith, Tim 217, 220
Pilger, John 335, 410
Pinochet Ugarte, Augusto 287
Pinter – The Player's Playwright (Thompson)
    49
Pinter, Daniel *see* Brand
Pinter, Dolly (HP's aunt) 3
Pinter, Fanny (née Baron; HP's paternal
    grandmother) 3, 4, 5

Pinter, Frances (née Moskowitz; HP's
    mother) 2, 15, 112, 345, 390; birth 3;
    death 336, 338, 339; and HP's evacuation
    6; and HP's marriage to Vivien Merchant
    53, 54; marries Jack 4; and Pauline
    Flanagan 40; reaction to HP's
    conscientious objection 22;
    religious scepticism 5; in the Second
    World War 6, 7
Pinter, Harold: aesthetic convictions 62–3,
    211; affair with Antonia Fraser 234, 252,
    253; affair with Dilys Hamlett 26, 27,
    34–6, 218–19; Antonia's influence on his
    writing 235, 255, 261, 403–4; appearance
    31, 46, 88, 142, 221; the art and the
    politics 403, 422–3; attacks New York
    avant-garde theatre 195–6; attends
    Central School of Speech and Drama 31,
    36; awards 129–30, 131, 149–50, 190, 194,
    204, 208, 288, 301, 335–6, 369, 371, 372,
    395, 421–5, 427–9; awareness of death
    395–8; BBC ignore 424; becomes an
    associate director of the National Theatre
    234, 239; belief in validity of every
    individual 396; birth (10 October 1930) 1;
    and birth of son Daniel 75; changing
    public perception of 396; childhood
    solitude 5, 6, 18, 24; compared with Joyce
    209, 211; compared with Kafka 349;
    compared with Losey 208; complains of
    the drudgery of acting 45; as a
    conscientious objector 21–4, 92, 286;
    contented second marriage 388; creative
    process 116, 423, 428, 431–2; credo 94,
    323, 430; cricket 410; critics of 424–5;
    critique of Jewish tradition 80, 81; 'David
    Baron' stage-name 3, 47–8, 49, 51, 54, 55,
    69, 88, 96, 148; début as a writer on
    Broadway 131, 142; directorial methods
    145–8, 149, 365–6; discovers joys of acting
    13–14; and divorce from Vivien 270,
    271–2; during Second World War 4, 5–10,
    18, 24; early childhood 4, 5; early reading
    10, 15, 18; early theatre-going 13;
    education 5, 7, 8–15, 19–20; family 1–5;
    father's death 396; feminism 137, 143,
    157, 175, 273; and fidelity to the writer
    239, 240, 270–71, 303, 349; first
    recognition in print 13–14; first work for
    the BBC 31; goes back to drama school
    26; and a golden age in radio drama 95–7;
    growing preoccupation with solitude and
    separation 180; as a guinea-pig (Maudsley
    Hospital) 102, 367; and the Hackney gang

11–13, 16–18, 19, 24, 58, 59–60, 65, 69, 82, 115, 181, 235, 236, 286; handling actors 418; Harold Pinter Society 410; on the hazards and rewards of a dramatist's life 204; on his first marriage 277; health 395, 413–15, 421–2, 424; his most emotional play 338; on his son 345–6; identifies with Jewish suffering 81; increasing involvement in film and television 190–91; influenced by Beckett 43; and Jonathan Miller 239, 240; and June 20 Society 307, 308–9; and language used to camouflage truth 322–3; letters of support for 425; with McMaster's touring company in Ireland 26, 36–46, 51, 83, 367, 368; marriage to Vivien disintegrates 133, 145, 147, 148, 181, 193–4, 197, 201, 202, 234–5, 252–6, 277, 388; marries Antonia 271–2, 280; marries Vivien Merchant (1956) 53–4, 69; and the media 321; and memory 1, 15, 16, 52, 72, 75, 82, 93, 102, 116, 160, 178, 193, 197, 205, 216, 220, 224, 233, 256, 265, 281–2, 391, 392; and mother's death 336, 338, 339; as a much-loved only son 5, 6, 9, 15; Nobel Prize 421–7; odd-jobbing 48, 65, 115; and Pauline Flanagan 39–41, 53, 79; plays become smaller in scale (after 1965) 180; political awareness 286–305, 400–3, 412, 416–17, 423, 433–41; promotion of poetry 270; public perception of changes 396; at RADA 19–20, 25, 115; receives David Cohen British Literature Prize 11; relationship with parents 5, 6, 336, 390; religious scepticism 9, 79, 80, 92, 286, 390, 429; resigns from the National 291; resurgence of creative energy 324; and the role of the audience 95, 109; row with Visconti 234, 237–9; seventy fifth birthday 420–2; and Shield Productions 209; and silence 47, 52, 60, 132, 180; sixtieth year and the media 321, 323–4; starts to direct own work 131; starts to voice his political opinions 234; and success of *The Caretaker* 114, 131; sustained period in weekly rep (1955–7) 49–55; three-year creative crisis 278, 286, 293; translating into another language 357–8; value of the rep years 49–51; views on American foreign policy 370, 387, 434–41; views on Europe 428; views on Iraq 438–40; views on Sandinistas 435–6; views on war 416–17; and Vivien's early death 278; voice 31, 46, 337; on the vulgarity of the

super rich 404–5; Wax becomes his agent 73; in Wolfit's company 45–7, 365

AS ACTOR: Catastrophe 411; *The Collection* 400; *Krapp's Last Tape* (Beckett) 396, 429–30; *Mansfield Park* (Rozema) 403; *Mojo* (Butterworth) 400; *The Tailor of Panama* 411

AS DIRECTOR: *Blithe Spirit* (Coward) 255; *Butley* (Gray; film) 240–41; *Butley* (Gray; play) 211, 221–2, 240; *Circe and Bravo* (Freed) 302–3; *Close of Play* (Gray) 270, 271; *Common Pursuit* (Gray) 297; *Exiles* (Joyce) 205–6, 209–11; *Incident at Tulse Hill* (East) 270; *The Innocents* 41, 255, 337; *The Late Middle Classes* (Gray) 403, 418; *Life Support* (Gray) 400; *Next of Kin* (Hopkins) 240; *The Old Masters* (Gray) 418; *Oleanna* (Mamet) 351–2, 364; *Otherwise Engaged* (Gray) 253–4, 255; *Quartermaine's Terms* (Gray) 270, 271; *The Rear Column* (Gray) 270, 271; *Sweet Bird of Youth* (Williams) 301–2; *Taking Sides* (Harwood) 364–6, 369, 374; *The Trojan War Will Not Take Place* (Giraudoux) 290, 291; *Twelve Angry Men* (Rose) 374; *Vanilla* 322

INTERVIEWS: with Mireia Aragay (1996) 385; BBC World Service (1960) 89; Dublin International Writers' Festival (1993) 92–3; with Hewes (1967) 169, 174; with Mel Gussow (New York, 1988) 303; with Tynan on BBC Radio (1960) 124; with Kathleen Tynan (1968) 180–81

PERSONALITY: 392; anger, political 396; connection, belief in 398; cynicism about politicians 19, 34; as a drinker 31, 32, 53, 221, 354, 389; duality in his character 32, 390; generosity 32, 45, 141, 321, 390, 392; as good company 389; as a good listener 71, 122; good taste 44; hunger for life 429; integrity 390; intensity 396; love of London 40, 218; love of sport 7–8, 9, 12, 14–15, 19, 21, 135, 221, 277, 301, 323, 343, 365, 388–9; love of women 11, 16–17, 59, 99; nonconformity 24, 33, 46–7; reclusiveness 5; refusal to accept handed–down truths 12, 19, 88; sides with the underdog 48; stoicism against life's cruelties 34, 44; suspicion of bureaucracy 21, 22, 24, 48, 203; toughness 415

SPEECHES/TALKS: *Art Truth & Politics* 395, 422–4; German Shakespeare Prize (Hamburg, 1970) 64; International Writers' Festival (Dublin, 1993) 353;

National Student Drama Festival (Bristol, 1962) 64, 132, 133, 178, 224, 304; Nobel Lecture 395, 422–5, 427; Sofia University honorary doctorate speech (1995) 371–2

THEMES IN WRITINGS: betrayal 17, 58, 59–60, 65, 90, 92, 313, 315, 326; class 419; confrontation of a recluse with demands of outside world 67, 77, 78–9; corrupt bureaucracy 103, 104, 105; desolation and emptiness 13; dominance and subservience 56, 57, 65, 77, 118–20, 180; duality of the female psyche 133–6, 143; friendship jeopardised by sexuality 27; guilt 59; Ireland 42–3, 215, 268, 313, 354; language as a weapon of domination 107, 117, 124; male bonding/homoeroticism 133, 138–9, 210, 263; male friendship 12, 58, 59, 60–61, 256, 260, 263, 264; political theatre 433; private Edens 5, 12, 28, 34, 58, 61, 82, 236, 260, 290, 316, 388; resistance 78–9, 82, 180, 181–2; a room 26, 27, 61, 155, 406; shielding against reality with protective illusions 122–3; sightlessness 7, 68, 159; silence as a weapon of control 56, 57; a space 26, 27, 65; status 419; territorial battles 26–8, 44, 180

WRITING STYLE: 16; ability to invest a theatrical moment with weight and resonance 172–3; allowing the characters their own momentum 132–3; change in poetic style 41, 428, 432; cinema oeuvre 429; 'comedy of menace' 106; continuity of imagination 408; dialogue 18, 62, 71, 84, 90–91, 104–5, 108–9, 124–5, 153, 178, 183, 187–8, 189, 213–14, 242–3, 261, 262, 269, 283, 332–3, 340–41; East End slang 390, 391; economical style 180, 390, 391; influence of Webster 13; language operating on many levels 391; montage 399; musical sense of form in Betrayal 261; the Pinter pause 1, 52, 106, 108–9, 141–2, 145, 156, 176, 183, 222, 236, 357; precision 29, 141–2, 208; and rep drama 55, 76; use of dramatic flashbacks/flashforwards 10, 207; truth in drama 431, 432, 433–4; use of gesture 47

WRITINGS: The Dwarfs (novel) 3, 5, 11, 12, 13, 16, 34, 51, 58–65, 69, 91, 135, 136, 138, 147, 323, 417; Mac 39; 'The Black and White' 51, 107; The Queen of all the Fairies 2, 20–21, 26, 32–3, 44, 62, 115; Tess 411

PLAYS: Ashes to Ashes 374–86, 393, 406, 423, 433; The Basement (previously The Compartment) 28, 191–4, 209, 235; Betrayal 41, 42, 133, 136, 138, 191, 211, 257–67, 275, 314, 317, 323, 325–6, 336, 354, 355, 357, 391, 392, 419, 420; The Birthday Party 15, 32, 42, 48, 49, 50, 60, 74, 75–90, 92, 94, 95, 97, 100, 101, 102, 106–7, 109–10, 112, 113, 114, 118, 126, 127, 141, 155, 156, 157, 177, 192, 194, 205, 209, 211, 252, 266, 287, 290, 292, 295, 296, 323, 356, 357, 369, 392, 406, 433; The Caretaker 88, 108, 114–33, 141, 142, 153, 155, 177, 180, 193, 238, 244, 249, 257, 277, 297, 326, 392, 410; Celebration 403–8, 410, 411, 420; The Collection 133, 134, 137–42, 141, 143, 150, 154, 155, 168, 171, 210, 357, 400, 419; The Dumb Waiter 75, 88–92, 102, 109, 111, 287, 354, 355; The Dwarfs 12, 61, 145, 146, 147, 149, 257, 316, 340, 374, 406, 419; Family Voices 69, 278–80, 323, 420; The Homecoming 34, 48, 49, 54, 62, 64, 126, 129, 131, 133, 134, 136, 140, 142, 155, 156, 162–81, 191, 194, 235, 240, 243, 258, 289, 297, 311, 324–5, 331, 340, 346–7, 356, 358, 378, 392, 396, 410, 412, 422, 423, 431, 432; The Hothouse 83, 88, 100–106, 110, 113, 114, 128, 155, 177, 270, 286–7, 292, 357, 365–9, 374; A Kind of Alaska 278, 280–85, 290, 412; Landscape 7, 41, 180, 181, 191, 194–203, 209, 277, 354, 355, 382, 383, 406, 412; The Lover 133, 134, 142–9, 154, 155, 168, 171, 210, 288, 357; Mixed Doubles 197; Monologue 235–7, 412; Moonlight 7, 13, 49–50, 69, 93, 278, 338–48, 350, 352, 354, 355, 368–9, 392, 405, 406, 419; Mountain Language 62, 104, 289, 298, 299, 309–13, 323, 330, 333, 336, 366, 369–70, 373, 375, 382, 397, 410, 420, 423, 433; Night 197; A Night Out 101, 110–13, 133, 150; Night School 133, 135–7, 143, 154, 168; No Man's Land 26, 161, 180, 191, 234, 235, 238, 241–53, 255, 258, 275, 278, 336–9, 342, 356, 391, 410, 413; Old Times 7, 36, 61, 126, 135, 136, 191, 206, 208, 211–20, 222, 229, 234, 237–40, 244, 302, 331, 336, 354, 355, 369, 375, 379, 382, 391, 392, 406, 420, 423, 431; One for the Road 236, 289, 293–7, 299, 314, 317, 323, 328, 333, 354–5, 366, 375, 378, 382, 410, 412, 415, 420; Other Places triple bill 278–85, 286; Party Time 289, 330–34, 375, 407, 420; Precisely 323; The Room 66–73, 75, 77, 89, 97, 109, 113, 118, 132,

133, 159, 280, 403, 406, 408, 411; *Silence* 180, 191, 196, 197, 198–9, 203, 209; *A Slight Ache* 7, 8, 92, 93, 96–100, 113, 115, 133, 153, 155, 168, 171, 205, 233, 266–7, 406, 410; *Something in Common* 95–6; *Tea Party* 133, 134, 156, 158–62, 209; *Victoria Station* 278, 280, 293; *Voices* 395, 420
POEMS: 'After Lunch 416; 'American Football – A Reflection on the Gulf War' 329–30; 'Cancer Cells' 415–16 'Chandeliers and Shadows' 30; 'Chokepit' 363–4; 'Daylight' 54; 'Death' 396, 423, 441–2; *'Death May be Ageing'* 416; 'Episode' 41–2, 44; 'The Error of Alarm' 54–5; 'God Bless America' 416; 'I shall tear off my Terrible Cap' 32; 'The Islands of Aran seen from the Moher Cliffs' 41; 'It is Here' 388; *Kullus* 26–9, 30, 44, 56, 57, 135, 191, 235, 267; 'Meeting' 416; 'New Year in the Midlands' 29–30; 'Poem' 42; 'The Task' 56, 57; *Ten Early Poems* 29, 41; 'To My Wife' 416; *War* 416–17; 'Weather Forecast' 416
SCREENPLAYS: 348–51; *Accident* 184–91, 194, 208, 274; *The Caretaker* 125, 142, 149–50; *The Comfort of Strangers* 316–20; *The Dreaming Child* 398–400; The *French Lieutenant's Woman* 272–5; *The Go-Between* 205–9, 211, 222, 274, 399; *The Handmaid's Tale* 304; *The Heat of the Day* 8, 313–14, 316, 317; *King Lear* 408–9; *Langrishe, Go Down* 222, 267–70; *The Last Tycoon* 241–2, 275; *Lolita* 358–61; *The Proust Screenplay* 205, 222–33, 235, 267, 274, 275, 409–10; *The Pumpkin Eater* 155, 156, 157–8; *The Quiller Memorandum* 181–4, 268, 295; *The Remains of the Day* 324; *Reunion* 268, 315–17; *The Servant* 57, 133, 139, 142, 150–55, 157, 184, 208, 274, 288, 320, 419; *Sleuth* 418–20; *The Trial* 348–51; *Turtle Diary* 299–301; *Victory* 289–90
SHORT STORIES: 'The Examination' 51, 52, 56–7, 191; 'Girls' 364; 'Tea Party' 159
SKETCHES: *Apart From* That 429; The *Black and White* (transformed from a monologue) 31, 107–8; 'God's District' 387; *Last to Go* 108–9, 156; *The New World Order* 328–9, 377, 406, 420; *One to Another* 107; *Pieces of Eight* 107, 108; *Precisely* 291–3, 406; *Press Conference* 415; *Request Stop* 108
Pinter, Jack (HP's father): birth 3; death 396; encourages HP's writing 15; HP

inherits strong-mindedness 345, 390; and HP's education 7, 19; and HP's marriage to Vivien Merchant 53, 54; marries Frances 4; reaction to HP's conscientious objection 22; relationship with HP 344–5; in the Second World War 6; as a tailor 1–2, 344–5; and *Ulysses* 10; as a Zionist 81, 345
Pinter, Mary (HP's aunt) 3
Pinter, Nathan (HP's paternal grandfather) 2–3, 4, 9
Pinter, Rachel (HP's aunt) 3
Pinter, Sophie *see* Lipstein
Pinter Archive, British Museum 159, 162, 164, 242, 320, 352–3
Pinter family: as cultivated 2, 3, 5; and HP's marriage to Vivien Merchant 53, 54, 69; as Orthodox Jewish 5
Pinter Festivals 354–6, 400, 420
'Pinter: Passion, Poetry and Politics' (conference) 427–8
Pinter Review 184, 321, 398
'Pinteresque' 1, 135, 184, 192, 250, 391
Piper, Tom 356
Pirandello, Luigi 94, 122, 138
Planchon, Roger 238
Plath, Sylvia 384
Play (Beckett) 197
Playing with Fire (Strindberg) 142
Plays and Players 238
Pleasence, Donald 45, 116, 127, 129, 131, 160, 181, 241, 253, 326
Plebeians Rehearse the Uprising, The (Grass) 365
Plenty (Hare) 258
Plummer, Christopher 356
Poe, Edgar Allan 309
Poetry Ireland 43
Poetry London 29, 30
Point of Departure (Anouilh) 35
Poland 2, 3, 373
Port Stewart, Co. Londonderry 51
Portcullis Theatre, Monck Street, London 146
Porter, Cole 215
Porter, Eric 196
Portrait of the Artist as a Young Man, A (Joyce) 209, 279
Potterton, Gerald 203
Pound, Ezra 12
Powell, Dilys 191
Prague 349, 350, 427
Pretty Baby (film) 359
Prick Up Your Ears (film) 326

Priestley, J. B. 43
Private Lives (Coward) 165
Prix Italia (*The Lover*, 1963) 149
Proust, Marcel 10, 58, 73, 92, 116, 209, 215, 221–34, 268, 272, 277, 303, 358, 393, 409–10
Prowse, Philip 409
Pumpkin Eater, The (Mortimer) 157
Punch 142, 303
Purcell Room, South Bank 270

Quartermaine's Terms (Gray) 270, 271
Quayle, Dan 371
Quayle, Jenny 271, 297
Queen's Elm pub, Fulham Road, London 218
Queen's Theatre, London 253, 270, 271
Questors, Ealing 113
Quigley, Austin E. 250, 261
Quiller KGB (Hall) 184
Quiller Memorandum, The (Hall) 181, 182

Race Relations Act (1965) 71
Radio Times 96
Ragan, Ronald 335
Raine's Foundation School, east London 12
Rake's Progress, The (Auden libretto) 153
Rambouillet 402
Ramsay, Peggy 85
Rattigan, Terence 55, 67, 86, 122, 128, 129, 158, 241, 261, 262, 352
Rawlings, Margaret 13
Rayner, Alice 274–5
Rea, Stephen 383, 421
Reading Football Club 7–8
Reagan, Ronald 423, 435, 436
Rear Column, The (Gray) 270, 271
Recherche du temps perdu (Proust) 100, 409
Redden, Nigel 411
Redgrave, Corin 413
Redgrave, Michael 208, 271
Reed, Carol 215, 216
Regent Theatre, London 209
Reid, Beryl 107
Reisz, Karel 272–3, 274, 304, 354, 368, 369, 412
Remains of the Day, The 324
Resnais, Alain 225
Reykjavik 407
Reynolds, Oliver 407
Rhinoceros (Ionesco) 127
Rhode, Eric 225
Rhys, Keidric 29
Richardson, Maurice 111, 142–3

Richardson, Natasha 317
Richardson, Samuel 359
Richardson, Sir Ralph 251, 252, 336, 413
Richmond Theatre 88
Rickson, Ian 430
Rigby, Terence 251
Rigg, Diana 300
Right You Are (if you think so!) (Pirandello) 138
Rilke, Rainer Maria 281
Rimbaud, Arthur 10, 35
Ring for Catty (Cargill and Beale) 55, 74
Rintoul, David 410
River Café, Hammersmith 308, 309
Robards, Jason 356
Robbe-Grillet, Alain 272
Roberts, Rachel 21
Robinson, David 153
Robinson, Robert 189
Rock, The (Eliot) 21
Rockefeller, Governor Nelson 231
Rodger, Ian 100
Rodway, Norman 199
Roeg, Nicolas 317
Rogers, Paul 163, 167, 176, 284
Rome 237, 238
Romero, Archbishop Oscar 436
Ronconi, Luca 427
Roof, Judith 294–5
Roose-Evans, James 109
Roots (Wesker) 88
Rope (Hamilton) 43
Rope (Hitchcock) 28
Roscrea 82, 83, 368, 392
Rose, Reginald 374
Ross, Ducan 73
Rossetti, Dante Gabriel 272
Roth, Philip 395–6
Roth, Tim 409
Rothschild family 231
Roud, Richard 238
Roundabout Theatre, New York 356, 368
Royal Academy of Dramatic Art (RADA) 19–20, 31, 115
Royal Court Theatre, London 74, 75, 77, 86, 109, 127, 143, 305, 328, 351, 396, 429
Royal Institute of International Affairs 305
Royal Marsden Hospital 414, 415
Royal Shakespeare Company (RSC) 31, 126, 140, 141, 142, 155, 156–7, 175, 176, 177, 209, 211, 239, 277
Royle, Carol 220
Rozema, Patricia 403
RSC *see* Royal Shakespeare Company

Rushdie, Salman 307–8, 309, 316, 322, 337
Russell, Leonard 129
Russell Hotel, London 410
Russian pogroms 2
Rutherford, Malcolm 330
Rutherford and Son (Sowerby) 168–9
Rylands, Dadie 83

Sacks, Oliver 278, 280, 281, 282, 284–5
St Denis, Michel 36, 175
St Ives 23
St Joan (Shaw) 77
St Louis 214, 302
St Martin's Theatre, London 194
St Paul's School for Boys, London 181
Saison en enfer, Un (Rimbaud) 35
Salberg, Derek 74
Sandinistas (in Nicaragua) 335, 423, 435–6
Sarbin, Deborah 174
Saro-Wiwa, Ken 373
Sarraute, Nathalie 272
Saskatchewan 370
Sassard, Jacqueline 190
Saudi Arabia 310, 371
Saved (Bond) 162
Scales, Prunella 271
Scarborough 31, 32
Scarborough Studio Theatre 106
Schatzberg, Jerry 315
Schiff, Stephen 361
Schindler's List (Spielberg) 370
Schlesinger, John 239
Schlondorff, Volker 231, 304
Schnabel, Artur 3, 4
Schubert, Franz 13
Schwarzkopf, General Norman 330
Scofield, Paul 409
Scorsese, Martin 359
Scotsman 177
Scott, Hutchinson 86
Scott-Moncrieff, C.K. 223
Scruton, Roger 308
Seagulls over Sorrento 51
Seale, Douglas 36
Searle, Ronald 142
Season, The (Goldman) 194–5
Sebastyen, Amanda 311, 313
Second World War, HP evacuated 5–8, 9, 18, 24, 55, 97
Secret Honour (Freed) 303
Secret Society (television series) 310
Segal, George 182
Seitz, Raymond 434–5
Sellers, Peter 142

Separate Tables (Rattigan) 55, 67
Serbia 402–3
Sereny, Gitta 374, 384
Servant, The (Maugham) 150–51, 152, 153
Sexton, David 369
Shaffer, Anthony 418, 419
Shaffer, Peter 162
Shakespeare, William 13, 14, 43, 44, 59, 62–5, 107, 177, 216, 239, 408–9
Shaw, George Bernard 77, 203, 209–10, 289, 405, 407
Shaw, Robert 45, 181, 193, 194
She Stoops to Conquer (Goldsmith) 145
Sheen, Michael 343
Shelbourne Hotel, Dublin 353
Shepard, Sam 195
Sherman Theatre, Cardiff 114, 238
Shield Productions 209
Shubert Theatre, New York 301
Shulman, Milton 84, 110, 130, 313
Sidcup 122, 389
Sight and Sound 232
Silvester, Christopher 321
Simpson, N. F. 75, 96, 106
Sinn Fein 307
Siodmak, Robert 77
Skinner, Claire 342, 344
Slater, John 83, 84
Smith, Auriol 66, 72, 113
Smith, Chris 404
Smith, Ian 385
Smith, John, QC 308
Smith, Maggie 158, 300
Smith, Perry 330
Smith, R. D. 20, 30, 31, 36, 47–8, 73
Snowdon, Roger 35
Society of Film and Television Arts 208
Sofia University 371
Somoza Debayle, Anastasio 334
Somoza family (Nicaragua) 304, 435
Sondheim, Stephen 195
Sophocles 43
South Africa 129, 373
South Korea 373
South Sea Bubble (Coward) 53
Soviet mental hospitals 105
Sowerby, Githa 168–9
Spark, Muriel 12
Spectator 109, 297, 307
Speer, Albert 374–5, 377, 384
Spencer, Charles 330, 384
Spider's Web (Christie) 55
Spiegel, Sam 184, 241, 252, 253
Spooner, R. H. 245–6

Sport of My Mad Mother, The (Jellicoe) 86
Spread It Abroad (revue) 215
Springfield Park, east London 9, 11
Spy Who Came in from the Cold, The (Le Carré) 181
Spycatcher (Wright) 307
Stage Society 209, 210
Stage, The 36
Stalin, Joseph 184, 370
Stanford, Alan 421
Stanislavsky, Konstantin 337
Stein, Peter 178
Steinbeck, John 66
Stephane, Nicole 222, 223, 231
Stepney 2, 3
Stevens, Roger L. 126
Stock, Nigel 197
Stockhausen, Karlheinz 420
Stockholm 179
Stoke Newington 1–2
Stoke-on-Trent 31
Stoppard, Tom 54, 58, 288, 421
Stratford-upon-Avon 37, 45, 46, 141, 194, 201
Straw Dogs (Peckinpah) 353–4
Streep, Meryl 274
Streetcar Named Desire, A (Williams) 302
Strehler, Giorgio 427
Strindberg, August 142, 210, 262, 268, 276
structuralist criticism 95
Suchet, David 351
Suckling, Sir John 416
Summer Madness 317
Sunday Correspondent 321
Sunday Night at the London Palladium 111
Sunday Telegraph 189
Sunday Times 73, 74, 85, 129, 176, 191, 240, 245, 326, 347, 350, 355
Supple, Barry 14–15, 177
Sutton, David 106
Sweden 440
Sweeney Agonistes (Eliot) 194, 390
Sweet Bird of Youth (Williams) 301–2
Swift, Dean Jonathan 389
Sybil (Disraeli) 398
Sydney 179
Sydow, Max von 182
Synge, John Millington 42, 83
Szabo, Istvan 348, 350

T. S. Eliot Lectures 416
Taking Sides (Harwood) 364–6, 369, 374
Talking of Theatre (radio programme) 131
Tambimuttu 29

Tamburlaine the Great (Marlowe) 118
Taming of the Shrew, The (Shakespeare) 47
Taormina 427
Tartuffe (Molière) 117
Tatler 411
Tavistock Clinic 68
Taxi Driver (Scorsese) 359
Taylor, Elizabeth 142
Taylor, John Russell 153, 189
Taylor, Paul 313, 337, 365, 384–5, 410, 412
Tearle, Godfrey 38
Teatro di Roma 237
Temps, Le 233
Ten Little Indians (Christie) 39
Territorial Imperative, The (Ardrey) 168
Thalberg, Irving 241
Thalia Theater, Hamburg 368
Thatcher, Margaret, later Baroness 306, 318
Thatcherism 307, 319
Theatr Clwyd 220
Théâtre de l'Atelier, Paris 162, 175
Théâtre de l'Athénée, Paris 356
Theatre Royal, Brighton 85
Theatre Royal, Haymarket 301
Theatre Royal, Waterford 37
Theatre Upstairs, Royal Court 328, 429
Theatres Act (1968) 196
Theatres in the Round 31
Thistlethwaite Road, Hackney (No. 19) 2, 4, 5, 48, 69
Thomas, Dylan 12, 29, 30, 35, 41, 189
Thompson, David T. 49, 50
Thompson, Jeremy 414
Thompson, Mark 325–6
Three Sisters (Chekhov) 269
Tiller, Terence 30
Time Out 33
Time Present (Osborne) 134
Times Literary Supplement [TLS] 232
Times, The 86, 107, 153, 176, 189, 211, 234, 251, 324, 337, 346, 351, 366, 386
Tinker, Jack 346
Today (radio programme) 131
Tony Award for Best Play (1967) 194
Torquay 49, 53, 55, 67, 76
Tourneur, Cyril 236
Tower Theatre, Islington 106
Trafalgar Square 426
Transatlantic Review 345
Translations (Friel) 313
Travesties (Stoppard) 54
Tree, Beerbohm 37, 38
Trevis, Di 409–10
Trevor, Elleston 181

Trial, The (Kafka) 15, 348, 349, 406
Tribune 311
Tricycle Theatre, London 417
Trident missiles 291
Tripp, Fred 74
Troilus and Cressida (Shakespeare) 27
Trojan War Will Not Take Place, The (Giraudoux) 290, 291
Truffaut, François 40, 222, 223, 365, 399
Turin 395, 411, 417, 427, 428
Turista, La (Shepard) 195
Turkey 288, 293, 297–9, 306, 309, 313, 329, 370, 373, 426
Turnell, Martin 223
Turtle Diary (Hoban) 299
Tutin, Dorothy 220
Twelfth Night (Shakespeare) 15
Twelve Angry Men (Rose) 374
Tydeman, John 84
Tynan, Kathleen 180
Tynan, Kenneth 13, 47, 110, 121–2, 125, 204, 390
Tzara, Tristan 236

Uhlman, Fred 315
Ullmann, Liv 220, 302
Ulysses (Joyce) 10, 15, 209
Under Plain Cover (Osborne) 143
Uninvited Guest, The (Bell) 50
United Artists 300
United British Artists (UBA) 300
United States 417, 423, 426, 428, 434–41
Unity Theatre, Goldington Crescent, north London 35, 36
Universal Studios 289, 290
University of East Anglia 104, 261
Unnameable, The (Beckett) 50
Unnatural Pursuit and Other Pieces, An (Gray) 221, 385
Uppsala 424

Vaesen, Guy 52, 53, 54, 64, 116, 134–5, 145–6, 147, 148, 149, 167, 196, 253
Vanilla (Hitchcock) 322
Vanity Fair 361
Vanunu, Mordechai 327, 345, 372
Various Voices 397
Varma, Indira 412, 420
Venice 317
Vermeer, Jan 227
Victoria Park, London 60
Victory (Conrad) 289–90

Vietnam 303
Vilmure, David 29
Visconti, Luchino 208, 222, 225, 234, 237–40, 317
Volonakis, Minos 126
Voltaire 389
Vortex, The (Coward) 95, 276
Vosper 50

Wain, John 56, 270
Waiting for Gillian (Millar) 50
Waiting for Godot (Beckett) 51, 74, 89, 128
Walken, Christopher 317
Waller, David 201
Walter, Harriet 215, 403
Warchus, Matthew 260
Wardle, Irving 86, 106, 128, 168, 176, 194, 211, 251, 325, 331, 356
Wark, Kirsty 422, 430
Warriss, Ben 77
Wars of the Roses, The 294
Warwick Gallery 270
Waste of Time, A 409
Waste Land, The (Eliot) 40, 242
Watford 180
Watt (Beckett) 50, 414
Waugh, Evelyn 393
Wax, Jimmy 74, 111; becomes HP's agent 73; deal with Roger L. Stevens 126; and Shield Productions 209
Webern, Anton von 420
Webster, John 11, 30, 236, 343, 382, 392, 397
Webster, Noah 30
Wednesday Play (BBC TV) 158
Weidenfeld, Lord 321
Weldon, Duncan 364
Well of Loneliness, The (Hall) 239
Welles, Orson 127, 161, 348, 350, 351, 408
Wernick, Morris (Moishe) 7, 11, 12, 16, 17, 18, 21, 23, 24, 40, 122, 162–4, 340, 392, 427
Wesker, Arnold 88, 109, 110, 203, 204, 363, 425
West Bank 372
West of Suez (Osborne) 203
West Yorkshire Playhouse 260
Westbrook, John 252
Westcliff-on-Sea 53
Westminster Library, London 43
What the Butler Saw (Orton) 103
Whelan, Peter 113
Whitby Spa Rep Company 48–9
White Devil, The (Webster) 13

White, Professor Harry 42–3
Who's Who in the Theatre 36
Wilde, Oscar 39, 43, 239–40, 257
Wilfred Owen Prize 427
Willes, Peter 110, 366
Williams, Clifford 175
Williams, Emlyn 86, 122
Williams, Kenneth 148
Williams, Lia 351, 407
Williams, Major 6
Williams, Tennessee 257, 301, 302
Williams, Treat 351
Willis, Ted 128
Willmore, Alfred *see* MacLiammoir, Micheal
Willmore, Marjorie 37
Wilson, Edmund 227, 232
Wilton, Penelope 201, 355, 404, 411, 421, 428
Winder, Robert 410
Winkler, Angela 368
Winter's Tales (Blixen) 398
Witness for the Prosecution (Christie) 50
Wittgenstein, Ludwig 342, 364
Wodehouse, P. G. 393
Wolfit, Donald 13, 35, 38, 45, 46, 47, 52, 53, 64, 172–3, 365, 367, 408
Wolverhampton 83, 84
Wood, Grant 198
Wood, John 210, 211, 231, 413
Wood, Peter 74, 77, 79, 83, 86, 156
Woodeson, Nicholas 403
Woodthorpe, Peter 127

Woolf, Henry 11, 12, 13, 16, 18, 21, 22, 24, 28, 34, 44, 45, 58, 60, 61, 66–9, 72, 73, 75, 163, 235, 370–71, 406, 412
Woolf, Virginia 10, 191
Words and Music (Beckett) 420
Wordsworth, William 198
Workhouse Donkey, The (Arden) 363
World is a Wedding, The (Kops) 8
World magazine 334
Worm's Eye View (Delderfield) 74
Worsley, T. C. 128
Worsthorne, Peregrine 308
Worthing 155
Wrede, Caspar 36
Wright, Peter 307
Writers' Guild Ball 288
Wyndham-Davies, June 313
Wyndham's Theatre, London 220, 252, 302, 369

Yeats, William Butler 35, 39–44, 209, 258, 259, 263
Yeltsin, Boris 353
Yemen 371
York Rep 219
Yorkshire Cricket Club 8
You Never Can Tell (Shaw) 405–6
Young Vic 97

Zadek, Peter 49–50, 368
Zeifman, Hersh 279
Zuleika Dobson (Beerbohm) 189